LEONARDO DA VINCI
AND THE BOOK OF DOOM

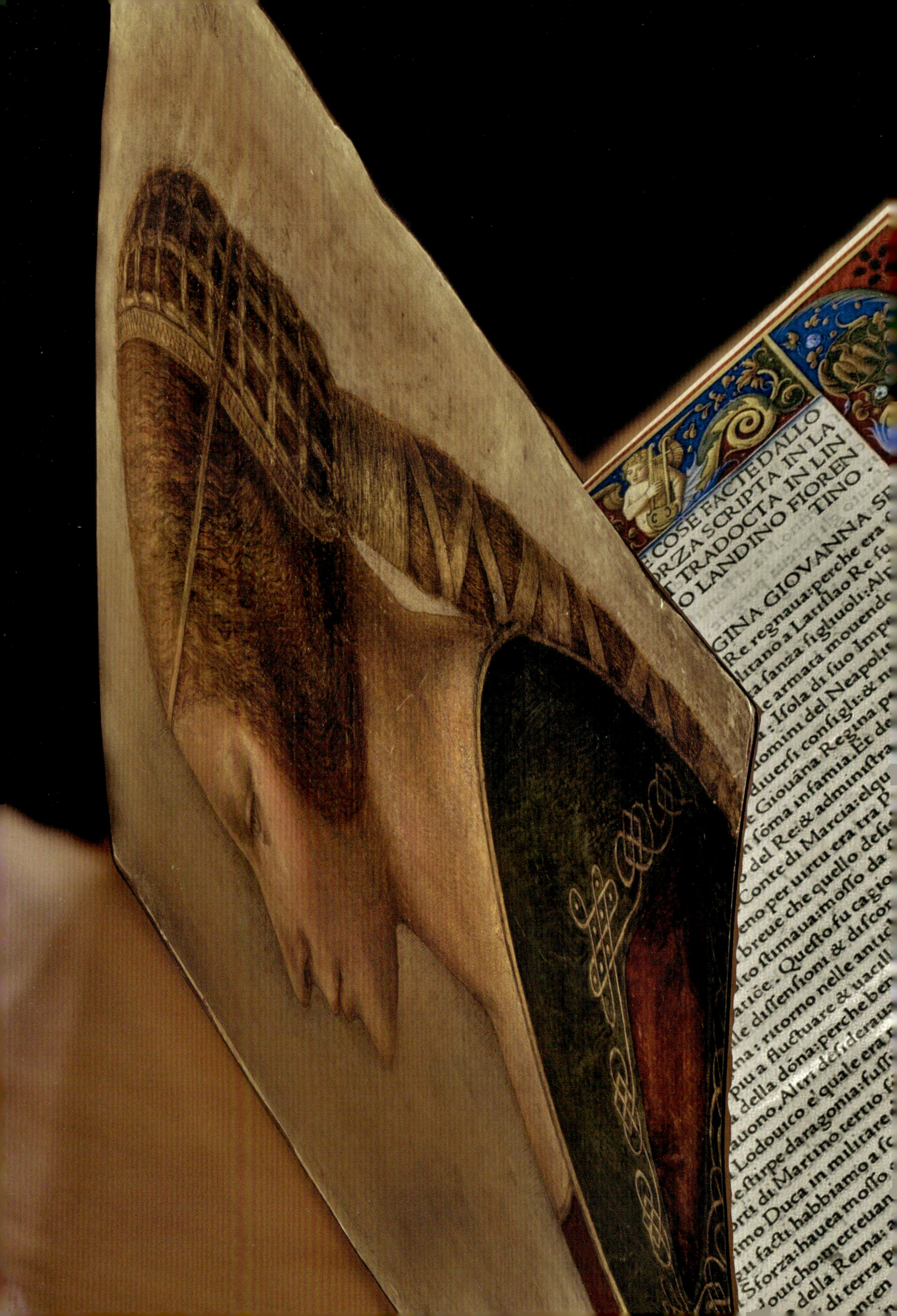
E COSE FACTE DALLO
RZA SCRIPTA IN LA
T TRADOCTA IN LIN
O LANDINO FIOREN
TINO.
GINA GIOVANNA S
Re regnaua: perche era
litano a Lanflao Re fu
a fanza figluoli: Al
e armata mouend
Ifola di fuo Impr
domini del Neapoli
diuerfi confgli: &
e Giouãna Regina
n fõma infamia. Et d
del Re & adminiftra
Conte di Marcia: el qu
eno per uirtu era tra p
breue che quello da
ftimaua: moffo da
& difcor

LEONARDO DA VINCI AND THE BOOK OF DOOM

BIANCA SFORZA, THE *SFORZIADA* & ARTFUL PROPAGANDA IN RENAISSANCE MILAN

SIMON HEWITT

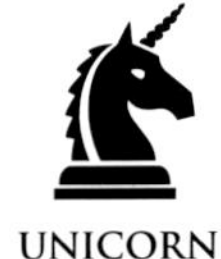

UNICORN

Published in 2019 by
Unicorn, an imprint of Unicorn Publishing Group LLP
5 Newburgh Street
London
W1F 7RG
www.unicornpublishing.org

ISBN 978 1 912690 57 2

Design by Nick Newton Design

Printed and bound in Turkey

Front Cover Leonardo da Vinci: *Portrait of Bianca Sforza* (1496) / miniatures by Gianpietro Birago from the *Sforziada* (National Library of Poland)
Back Cover *Allegory of Justice* (c.1495, unknown illuminator) from the manuscript *Paolo e Daria* (Kupferstichkabinett, Berlin)
Frontispiece *Sforziada* simulation – Pascal Cotte/Lumière Technology
Dedication *Spirits Having Flown – A Bell Tolls In Vigevano* (photo: Simon Hewitt)

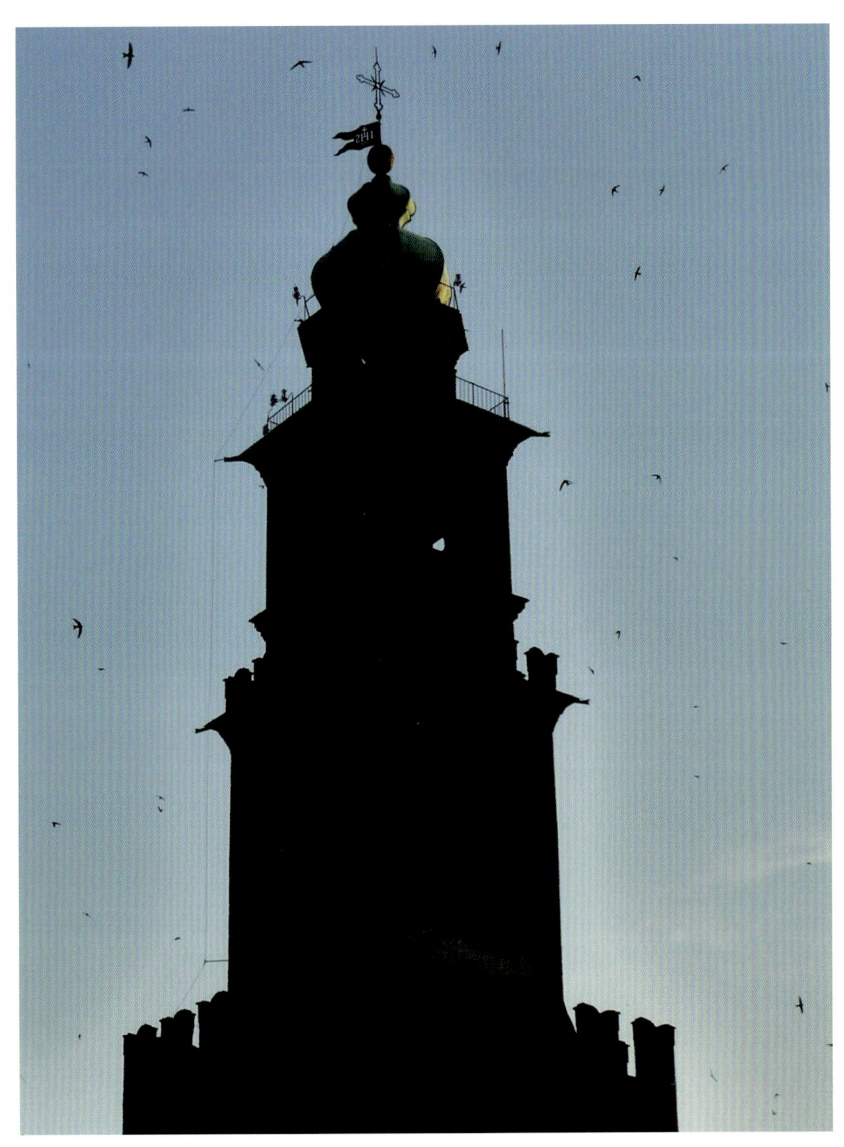

IN TRIBUTE
TO MY MOTHER
JEAN HEWITT
1934–2010

CONTENTS

ACKNOWLEDGEMENTS

Elisabetta Gnignera, whose knowledge of the Renaissance extends far beyond her specialist field of costume and fashion, kindly read my manuscript and made incisive suggestions. I am particularly grateful for her astonishing art-sleuthery as regards the history of the leather folder Giannino Marchig may have used to protect the *Portrait of Bianca Sforza.*

With their ultra-powerful multispectral imaging technique, **Lumière Technology** revolutionized the approach to analysing works of art and rewrote our knowledge of Leonardo da Vinci. The firm's chief technical expert **Pascal Cotte** is a fund of disinterested scholarship; his books on *The Lady with an Ermine* and the *Mona Lisa* are among the few to justify the term 'ground-breaking.' He and Lumière's CEO **Jean Penicaut** offered ready and often stimulating support throughout the writing of this book.

I would like to thank **Martin Kemp** for his prompt and precise replies to e-mails; **Cristina Geddo** for her forthright suggestions, for kindly sending me a copy of Luisa Cogliati Arano's pioneering 1995 study of Ambrogio de Predis and Milanese illuminators, and for alerting me to the date and details of the *Sforziada* printing in 1490; **Mina Gregori** for our two-hour discussion of Longhi, Zeri, Berenson and Marchig in her palatial Florence apartment; **Nadia Covini** for sharing her knowledge of Bianca Sforza's little-chronicled mother; and **Cristina Acidini** for her help in tracking down information on the Polish presence in Florence during the 19th century.

Mark Evans, the pre-eminent British authority on Gianpietro Birago, gave generously of his time and knowledge when we met at the Victoria & Albert Museum in London. I am grateful to the unfailingly helpful staff at the Ambrosiana Library (Milan), Fondazione Cini (Venice), Biblioteca Riccardiana (Florence), Biblioteca Reale (Turin) and the Bibliothèque de Genève, and especially to **Marzia Pontone** at the Trivulziana Library in Milan, not least for offering me magnificent facsimiles of the *Donatus Grammatica* and *Liber Iesus*; to **Laura Marazzi**, Director of the Museo Baroffio in Sacro Monte sopra Varese; and to **Hanka Gerhold** at the Kupferstichkabinett in Berlin, for cheerfully sacrificing her morning to serve as my obligatory 'minder' as I white-gloved my way through the priceless 1490s manuscript of Gaspare Visconti's *Paolo e Daria.*

My thanks to Warsaw's **Konrad Ajewski** for generously sharing his research into Zamoyski history and for translating into English, at my request, the full Polish text of Bogdan Horodyski's landmark *Sforziada* study of 1954. **Piotr Kondraciuk**, Deputy Director of the Zamoyski Museum in Zamość, was my erudite guide to the Zamoyski stronghold in southeast Poland where the *Sforziada* spent around 200 years – and kindly introduced me to Mayor **Marcin**

Zamoyski, who was happy to chat about family history and how his father, Count Jan Zamoyski, had saved the *Sforziada* from the Nazis during World War II.

Peter Silverman and **Kathleen Onorato** were unfailingly helpful throughout my research, without ever seeking to influence it. The late **Jeanne Marchig** was an hospitable and loquacious hostess during our many discussions at her home near Geneva. Her unflappably courteous partner, the late **Bryan Deschamp**, was an informative and entertaining lunch (and dinner) companion in Geneva and Rome. I would also like to thank Jeanne Marchig's American lawyer **Richard Altman**, and the distinguished art consultant **Giammarco Cappuzzo**, for their invaluable help.

I greatly appreciate the comments and encouragement proffered by **John Falding**, formerly of the *Financial Times*, and Louvre drawings curator **Françoise Joulie**, after they read the manuscript. I am grateful to **Kym Staiff** for his stylized analytic reproduction of the knot-patterned embroidery in Bianca Sforza's portrait, and to **Dima Goryachkin** for his innovative rendering of *Vitruvian Man*.

I would also like to salute two giants of the past: **Francis Haskell**, my professor at Oxford, whose lateral-thinking approach to art history remains an inspiration; and **Ivor Turnbull**, Founder-Editor of *Antiques Trade Gazette*, who gave me the chance to make writing about art my profession. Special thanks to my wife **Victoria**, and to my father **Ian** for his support and pertinent suggestions.

INTRODUCTION

'Is this the greatest art discovery of the century?'

That was the front-page headline in *Antiques Trade Gazette* on 17 October 2009, placed above my story about the portrait of a profiled young woman on vellum tentatively identified as *Bianca Sforza* (*c*.1483–96) – illegitimate daughter of Duke Ludovico Sforza, known as Il Moro, the ruler of Milan from 1480–1500.[1] The artist, it was claimed, was Leonardo da Vinci.

It was one of the biggest stories of my career and, in terms of internet hits, the biggest story ever covered by the respected, if slightly fusty, art-market weekly I had served as Paris correspondent since 1985.

Before filing my story I went to see the work in Paris. Not in the flesh – it was securely locked up in the Zurich Freeport – but on a giant computer screen at Lumière Technology, photographed by their pioneering, 240 million-pixel Multispectral Camera, which achieves images 150 times more powerful than those of an everyday digital camera.

The portrait's technical sophistication, psychological subtlety and minute rendering of detail bore the stamp of genius. But it was not my task to pronounce on the veracity of the new attribution to Leonardo da Vinci – merely to report on the reasons for making it. It was clearly by a left-handed artist, which pointed in Leonardo's direction, as did the fiendishly complicated knot pattern on the sitter's shoulder. Doubts, however, centred on the work's unusual support: vellum. Those doubts were dispelled when the volume for which the portrait was drawn was discovered in Warsaw: the fourth and final illuminated copy of the *Sforziada*, a glorified biography of dynasty patriarch Francesco Sforza (1401–66).

Why might Leonardo have illustrated such a volume? Did he have any contacts with *Sforziada* illuminator Gianpietro Birago? Did this discovery fit into the flow of Leonardo's Milanese career or was it, as some critics claimed, such a complete one-off as to be implausible?

My research into these questions led ultimately to this book. Initially I had no intention of writing one, merely to rustle up enough material for an article in the French monthly magazine *Beaux-Arts*, whose publisher Claude Pommereau was fascinated by the story. But the more I dug the more I unearthed. I was tugged into every corner of late 15th century

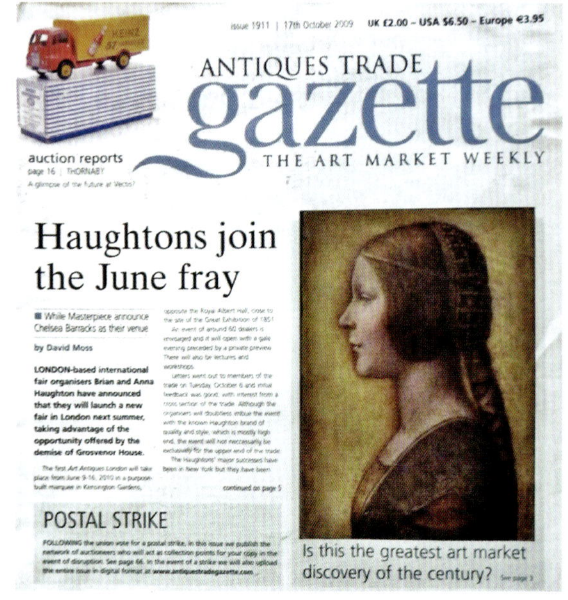

Lombardy – from Pavia to Vigevano and from Sacro Monte sopra Varese, up near Lake Maggiore, down to the ancient manuscript centre of Bobbio in Hemingway's beloved Trebbia Valley.

Regular rail journeys to Milan were supplemented by visits to Florence and a dozen other North Italian towns, then a flight southwest to Naples and a train southeast to Bari. There were trips to London, Tyrol, Gothenburg and Vilnius, to Visegrad and Esztergom on the Hungarian Danube, and to the bonded warehouse on the outskirts of Zurich where the portrait was securely locked away.

I drove up and down French country lanes in search of a ruined château in Mehun-sur-Yèvre (population 6,825), a frescoed prison cell in Loches (population 6,478), and a moated castle in Lys-St-Georges (population 234). I spent a day in Pskov[2] near the Russia/Estonia border and a weekend in a Polish *citta ideale* halfway between Lublin and Lvov. The tale led ultimately, like some fantastic adventure scripted by C.S. Lewis, to the banks of the Caspian.

What had begun as a desire to flesh out journalistic background turned into a full-blown research project that entailed visits to four of Italy's most venerable art libraries,[3] whose absence of red-tape delighted me: within minutes of arrival, I found myself handling (with requisite white gloves) illuminated manuscripts over half a millennium old.

The evidence explaining Leonardo's involvement in the final *Sforziada* soon piled up, and is presented in the following pages.

The Bianca portrait was far more than a one-off commission resulting from her new husband – Galeazzo Sanseverino – being a longstanding associate of Leonardo's. It was a by-product of the courtly cultural scene in Il Moro's Milan – a scene which reflected Il Moro's virtually every wish. This Duke was an enlightened yet unscrupulous despot whose hands-on approach to culture kept reminding me of Stalin. Leonardo da Vinci may have been the greatest artist who ever lived – but most of his creative output in Milan had to conform to Il Moro's idea of Art: as the ultimate vehicle for Propaganda.

Stalin's iron grip was focused on brainwashing the masses, creating the illusion of a Socialist paradise with himself as its airbrushed God. Il Moro – using a similar cocktail of blasphemy, perversion, terror and attention to coiffure – strove to manipulate an erudite élite and play mind games with members of his own family.

Il Moro's idea of art did not just concern paintings and pageantry, but every aspect of creative activity, from history books, manuscript illumination and poetry to clothing, altar-cloths, altarpieces, heraldry and architecture – culminating in Leonardo da Vinci's transformation of a palace hall into a glade of mulberry trees, where the good and the great assembled beneath the all-protecting branches of their illustrious lord (*moro* being a pun on the Italian for mulberry).

Making sense of Il Moro's cultural propaganda requires a multidisciplinary approach that exceeds the bounds of most art historical studies. The only major work to present a broad-sweeping survey of cultural activity in Il Moro's

Milan is Francesco Malaguzzi Valeri's *La Corte di Lodovico Il Moro*, published in four volumes between 1913–23. But Malaguzzi Valeri's approach was more encyclopedic than synthetic and, while impressive in scope, is now inevitably out of date (as well as print). Its abundant illustrations are nearly all in black-and-white and, by modern standards, woeful.

The *Sforziadas* were an integral part of a wide-ranging cultural programme that raged from the marriage of Il Moro's nephew in 1488 – which threatened the cosy authority Il Moro had enjoyed as Regent since 1480 – until 1499, when Il Moro was chased out by the French (he returned, briefly, in 1500). This turbulent decade can be split into two periods: until 1494, when Il Moro remained Regent, and needed to convince others of his credentials to become Duke; and after 1494 when, with that title secured, he could sit back and boast. The first three illuminated *Sforziadas* date from the earlier period. The fourth, originally containing Leonardo da Vinci's portrait of Il Moro's daughter Bianca, from the latter. This portrait, and the four de luxe editions of the *Sforziada*, are the chief focus of this book.

Bianca Sforza, the teenage heroine of Leonardo's portrait, was married on 20 June 1496. The *Sforziada* volume commissioned for her wedding became her memorial: she died just five months later – probably murdered, as this book reveals. Three years later the *Sforziada*'s commissioner, her all-powerful father Duke Ludovico Sforza, was overthrown. He spent the last eight years of his life in captivity – dying in a French prison cell. The volume accompanied his great-niece Bona to Poland, where she became Queen in 1518. She died in exile in 1557 – poisoned. Fifteen years later the male line of the Sforzas became extinct. The *Sforziada* passed into the hands of the Polish Chancellor, Jan Zamoyski. His first three wives died in childbirth, along with their infants. His only grandson died childless in 1665. This family line, too, became extinct.

Leonardo's portrait escaped from this Book of Doom into the mists of time. Its next known owner would be shot by the Nazis.

NOTES

1 Ludovico is known to history as Il Moro (The Moor), as he was to his contemporaries – although his nickname within the family was *Hozi*, based on Zio (Uncle).

2 Pskov was besieged throughout the winter of 1581/2 by Jan Zamoyski, Polish Chancellor and Commander-in-Chief, and probable onetime owner of the de luxe *Sforziada* that originally contained Bianca's portrait. Although a large, picturesque town of 200,000, with a magnificent hilltop kremlin, Pskov does not encourage visitors by rail. I had to arrive at 04:17 and took the next train out – at 17:00.

3 Trivulziana and Ambrosiana Libraries in Milan; Biblioteca Riccardiana in Florence; Biblioteca Reale in Turin.

HISTORICAL CAST

MILAN

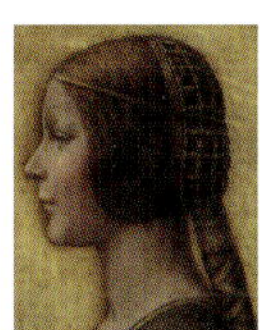

GIOVANNA BIANCA SFORZA (*c.*1483–96). Known simply as *Bianca*, the subject of Leonardo's full-page portrait in the final illuminated copy of the *Sforziada*. Il Moro's daughter by his mistress Bernardina Corradi; legitimized by ducal decree on 8 September 1489 before being made Lady of Bobbio & Voghera and betrothed to Galeazzo Sanseverino, whom she married on 20 June 1496. Died suddenly in Milan on 23 November 1496, apparently while pregnant, and was buried in Santa Maria delle Grazie.

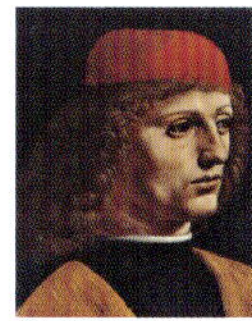

MARRIED (1496) Galeazzo Sanseverino (*c.*1458–1525). Son of famed *condottiero* Roberto Sanseverino. Appointed Il Moro's Army Captain and Ducal Equerry in 1488, becoming the régime's effective Number Two. Probable subject of Leonardo's portrait 'The Musician.' His brothers Gianfrancesco, Gaspare ('Fracassa') and Antonio Maria formed Il Moro's inner guard, with his half-brother Federigo an influential Cardinal. Last 20 years of his life spent in French service; killed at Battle of Pavia, and thought buried in the nearby Certosa.

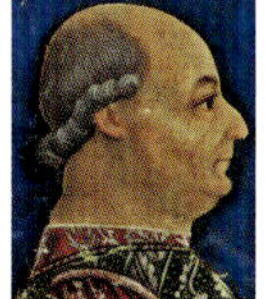

DUKE FRANCESCO SFORZA (1400–66). Bianca's grandfather and hero of the *Sforziada*. Reigned as 4th Duke of Milan from 1450–66 – the first Sforza Duke. Shrewd military strategist and wily political operator who used his 1441 marriage to Bianca Maria Visconti, illegitimate daughter of Duke Filippo Maria, as a springboard to taking over the duchy after the extinction of the Visconti line in 1447, reigning soundly for sixteen years.

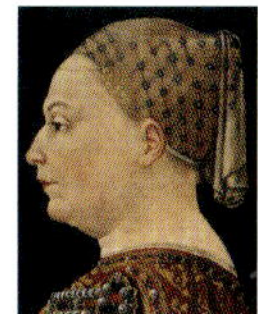

MARRIED (1441) Bianca Maria Visconti (1425–68). Daughter of the last Visconti Duke; revered family matriarch who died suddenly after a dispute with her eldest son Galeazzo Maria (rumoured poisoned at his behest).

CHILDREN: **Galeazzo Maria** (1444–76), 5th Duke of Milan; **Ippolita** (1445–88), mother of Isabel of Aragon and wife to Alfonso, son of King Ferrante of Naples; **Filippo Maria** (1448–92), mentally unstable; **Sforza Maria** (1451–79), Duke of Bari from 1464, died in suspicious circumstances while plotting a coup d'état in 1479; **Ludivoco 'Il Moro'** (1452–1508), 7th Duke of Milan; **Ascanio** (1455–1505), a scheming Cardinal and the Sforzas' Man in the Vatican; **Elisabetta** (1456–72); **Ottaviano** (1458–77). Francesco also sired many illegitimate children – notably **Giovanni Maria**, Archbishop of Genoa from 1498–1520.

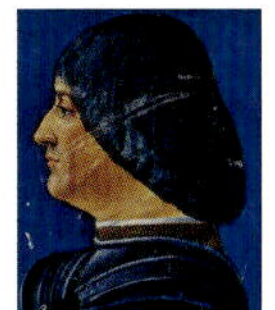

DUKE LUDOVICO SFORZA, 'IL MORO' (1452–1508). Duke of Bari from 1479, Regent of Milan 1480–94, then 7th Duke 1494–1500. Fourth son of Francesco Sforza, patron of Leonardo da Vinci and father of Bianca Sforza. Chronically superstitious and in thrall to astrology, but oversaw Milan's most glamorous decade, employing the finest available talent in all walks of cultural life. His mistresses Cecilia and Lucrezia were portrayed by Leonardo da Vinci – unlike his wife Beatrice d'Este, who gave him two sons, both future Dukes of Milan. A political wheeler-dealer who shifted alliance between Naples, Hungary, France and Austria before drowning in his own cunning and ending his days in a French prison cell.

MARRIED (1491) **Beatrice d'Este (1475–97)**. 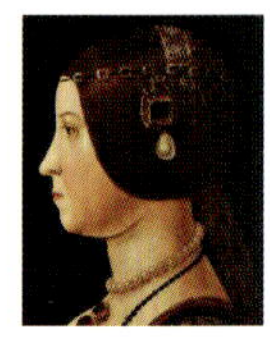
Diminutive *fashionista* born in Ferrara but brought up in Naples. Died when pregnant with her third child; Francesca dal Verme said to have confessed to her murder.

CHILDREN: **Ercole Massimiliano** (1493–1530), Duke of Milan 1512–15; **Francesco** (1495–1535), Duke of Milan 1521–35. Il Moro's illegitimate children included **Bianca** (*c.*1483–96) and **Leone** (1476–96); **Cesare** (1491–1512), by Cecilia Gallerani; and **Gianpaolo** (1497–1535), by Lucrezia Crivelli.

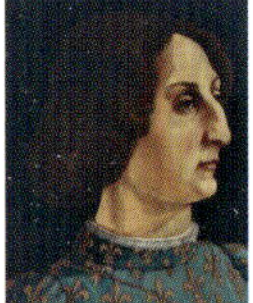
DUKE GALEAZZO MARIA SFORZA (1444–76). Reigned as 5th Duke 1466–76. Eldest son of Francesco Sforza. High-living culture-vulture with an obsessive love of music – but tyrannical, lecherous and sadistic; assassinated in church during Boxing Day mass.

MARRIED (1468) **Bona di Savoia (1449–1503)**. 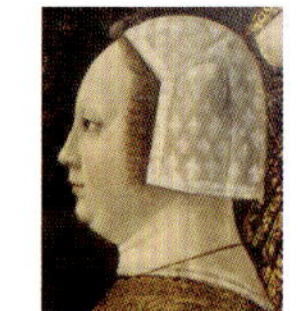
Sister-in-law of King Louis XI of France; ruled as Regent after her husband's death until elbowed aside by Il Moro in 1480 and temporarily exiled to France; back in Milan from 1483 until 1495, ending her life at Fossano in Piedmont. Erstwhile patron of Gianpietro Birago.

CHILDREN: **Gian Galeazzo** (1469–94), 6th Duke; **Ermes** (1470–1503), a later supporter of Il Moro, died in exile in Innsbruck; **Bianca Maria** (1472–1510), future Holy Roman Empress; **Anna** (1476–97), probable subject of the famous Ambrogio de Predis profiled portrait in the Ambrosiana, married Alfonso d'Este and died in childbirth. Galeazzo Maria's illegitimate children included the warlike **Caterina Sforza** (1463–1509), Countess of Forlì.

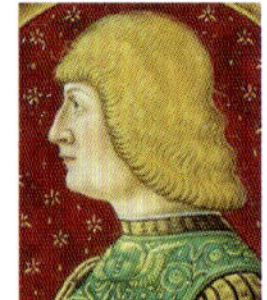
DUKE GIAN GALEAZZO SFORZA (1469–94). Nominal 6th Duke 1476–94 and, remarkably, the longest-serving of all Sforza Dukes – despite being effectively powerless under the assertive regency of his uncle, Il Moro, who is widely believed to have had him poisoned shortly after his 25th birthday.

MARRIED (1488) **Isabel of Aragon (1470–1524)**. 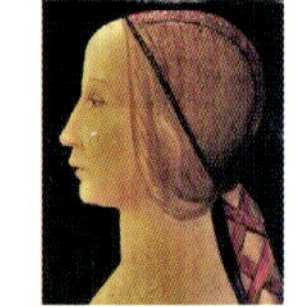
Daughter of King Alfonso II of Naples; fled Milan for Naples in 1500, settling in Bari with her daughter Bona in 1501.

CHILDREN: **Francesco 'Il Duchetto'** (1491–1511), popular 'heir apparent' kidnapped by Louis XII in 1499, spent rest of his life in France; **Ippolita** (1493–1501); **Bona** (1494–1557), future Queen of Poland; **Bianca Maria** (1495–6).

FERRARA

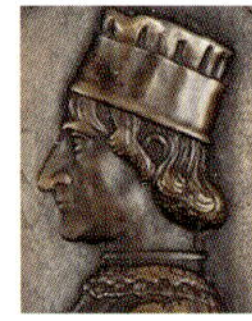
DUKE ERCOLE D'ESTE (1431–1505). Reigned 1471–1505. Theatre-loving, bet-hedging politico hemmed in by Milan and Venice; left elegant architectural mark on Ferrara city centre.

MARRIED (1473) **Eleonora of Aragon (1450–93)**. 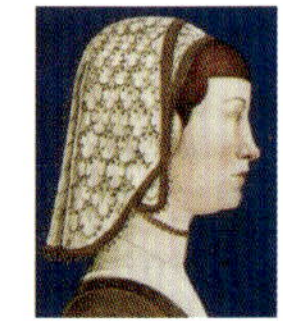
Younger daughter of King Ferrante of Naples.

CHILDREN: **Isabella** (1474–1539), Marchioness of Mantua and noted arts patron; **Beatrice** (1475–97), raised in Naples by her grandfather Ferrante, wife to Il Moro and Duchess of Bari & Milan; **Alfonso** (1476–1534), Duke of Ferrara from 1505, married Anna Sforza (1491) then Lucrezia Borgia (1502); **Ferrante** (1477–1540); **Ippolito** (1479–1520), an influential Cardinal who divided his time between Italy and Hungary; **Sigismondo** (1480–1524).

MANTUA

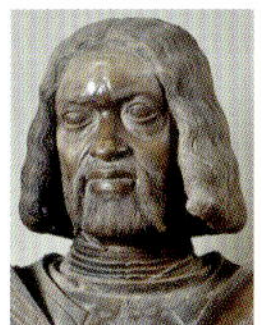

MARQUESS FRANCESCO II GONZAGA (1466–1519). Reigned 1484–1519. One of the leading *condottieri* of northern Italy for many years; long-term lover of Lucrezia Borgia.

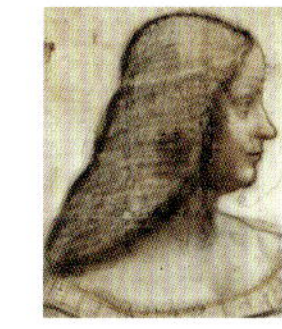

MARRIED: **Isabella d'Este (1474–1539).** Elder sister of Il Moro's wife Beatrice d'Este; famed as the leading female arts patron of the Renaissance. Sat for Leonardo when he visited her court; the resulting chalk and pencil portrait is now in the Louvre, but her requests for a painted version went unheeded. After the fall of Il Moro she welcomed his mistresses Cecilia Gallerani and Lucrezia Crivelli to Mantua. Eight children by Francesco Gonzaga, six of whom reached adulthood.

AUSTRIA

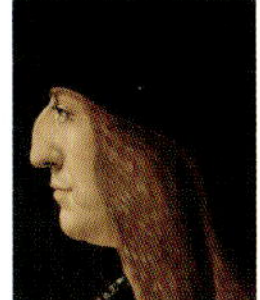

EMPEROR MAXIMILIAN I (1459–1519). Reigned 1493–1519, King of the Romans from 1486. Permanently impecunious potentate who reversed the anti-Sforza stance of his father **Friedrich III** (1415–93, Emperor 1452–93) in return for hefty bribes – granting Il Moro the Imperial investiture in 1495, and proving a reasonably loyal but militarily ineffectual ally.

MARRIED (1477) **Marie de Bourgogne (1457–82)**; only child of Charles the Bold, Duchess of Burgundy from 1477.

CHILDREN: **Philip 'the Handsome'** (1478–1506), briefly King of Castile after marrying Joanna of Castile (elder sister of English Queen Catherine of Aragon); **Margaret of Austria** (1480–1530), betrothed to Charles VIII in 1483 and brought up in France, but marriage called off in 1491; she then married first (1497) Juan of Aragon, Prince of Asturias (1478–97), then (1501) Duke Philibert II of Savoy (1480–1504). Regent of the Habsburg Netherlands from 1507 until her death.

MARRIED (1490) **Anne of Brittany (1472–1510)** by proxy; Maximilian never met her and the marriage was swiftly dissolved.

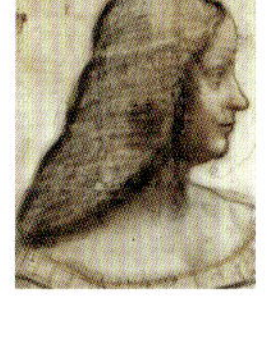

MARRIED (1493) **Bianca Maria Sforza (1472–1510).** Wedded for political and above all financial reasons; no *rapport*, no children.

HUNGARY

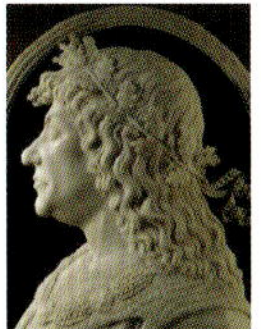

KING MATTHIAS CORVINUS (1443–90). Reigned 1458–90. The most successful monarch of mid-15th century Central Europe, conquering Bohemia and eastern Austria before his sudden death in 1490. An enthusiastic patron of Italian artists, craftsmen and illuminators; his extensive, rapidly assembled library remains his chief claim to posthumous fame.

MARRIED (1461) **Katarina of Poděbrady (1449–64)** from Bohemia; marriage was childless.

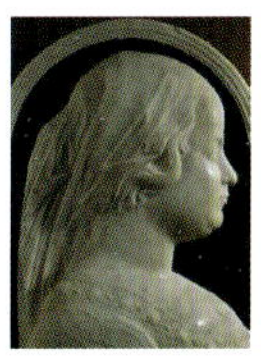

MARRIED (1476) **Beatrix of Aragon (1457–1508).** Elder daughter of King Ferrante of Naples; marriage also childless.

CHILDREN: **János** (1473–1504), born to Matthias's mistress Barbara Edelpock; betrothed, as Matthias's designated heir, to Bianca Maria Sforza in 1487, but the wedding was called off when Matthias's sudden death in 1490 consigned János to political oblivion.

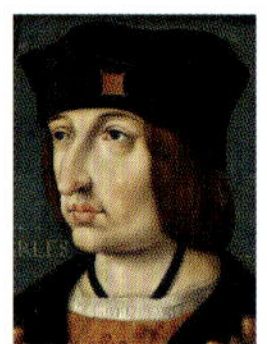

KING CHARLES VIII (1470–98). Reigned 1483–98, initially under the regency of his elder sister Anne de Beaujeu. Betrothed to the infant Margaret of Austria in 1483 but ultimately married Anne of Brittany. Invaded Italy with Il Moro's backing in 1494, conquering Naples, but was forced into humiliating retreat in 1495 by a pan-Italian League that included his supposed Milanese allies. Died in Amboise, officially of an accidental head wound but more probably of syphilis, aged 27.

MARRIED (1491) **Anne of Brittany (1477–1514)** after the annulment of her 1490 proxy marriage to Maximilian Habsburg.

CHILDREN: **Charles-Orland** (1492–95); **Charles** (1496); **François** (1497); **Anne** (1498).

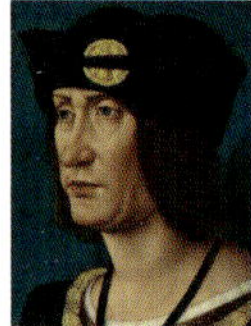

KING LOUIS XII (1462–1515). King of France 1498–1515, Duke of Orleans from 1465. As great-grandson of Gian Galeazzo Visconti exerted considerable nuisance value to Milan by voicing claims to the Duchy from his Asti powerbase just 80 miles away; conquered Milan a year after unexpectedly acceding to the French throne.

MARRIED (1476) **Jeanne de France (1464–1505)**, reportedly sterile and physically handicapped; their marriage was annulled by Pope Alexander VI in 1498.

MARRIED (1499) **Anne of Brittany (1477–1514)**, as per her marriage contract to Charles VIII – which stipulated that she marry Charles's successor if he died without a male heir; she gave King Louis two daughters but no son.

MARRIED (1514) **Mary Tudor (1496–1533)**, younger sister of King Henry VIII of England. No issue.

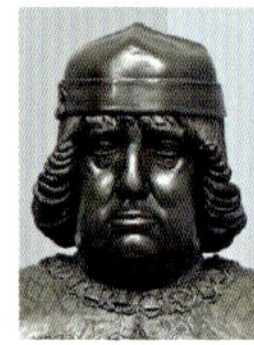

KING FERRANTE (1431–94). Reigned 1458–94. Hard-headed *Realpolitiker* who survived Barons' Plot of 1485 and was excommunicated by Innocent VIII in 1489; displayed ambivalent attitude towards Il Moro.

MARRIED (1445): **Isabella of Taranto (*c*.1424–65)**.

CHILDREN: **Alfonso** (1448–95), Duke of Calabria and briefly King of Naples; **Eleanora** (1450–93), Duchess of Ferrara, mother of Isabella and Beatrice d'Este; **Federico** (1452–1504), King of Naples 1496–1501; **Giovanni** (1456–85); **Beatrix** (1457–1508), **Francesco** (1461–86).

MARRIED (1476) **Giovanna of Aragon (1454–1517)**, Barcelona-born daughter of King Juan II of Aragon.

CHILDREN: **Giovanna** (1478–1518), briefly Queen of Naples (1495/6) as wife of her nephew [*sic*] Ferrandino; **Carlo** (1480–86).

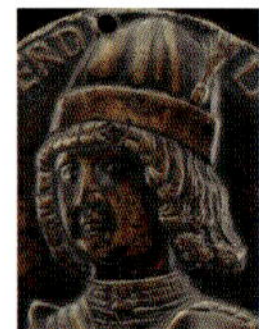

KING ALFONSO II (1448–95). Reigned 1494–95. As father of Isabel of Aragon, a ferocious opponent of Il Moro but, as the French advanced on Naples, abdicated in favour of his son Ferrandino and fled to Sicily, where he died a few months later.

MARRIED: **Ippolita Sforza (1445–88)**, Il Moro's elder sister.

CHILDREN: **Ferrandino** (1469–96), King of Naples 1495–96; **Isabel of Aragon** (1470–1524), Duchess of Milan (1488–94) and later of Bari (1500–24); **Pietro** (1472–91).

SIX GENERATIONS OF SFORZA-VISCONTIS

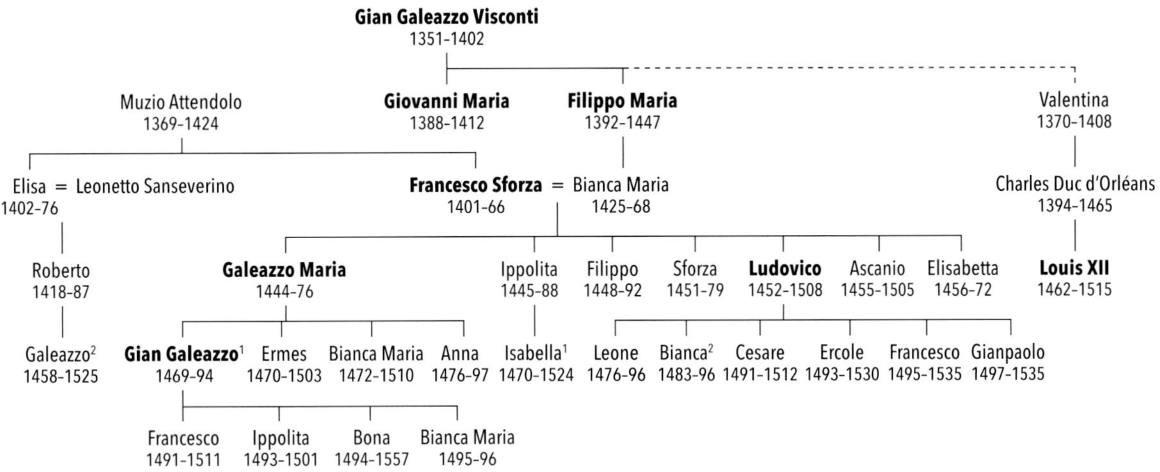

¹ Gian Galeazzo Sforza & Isabel of Aragon married in 1489
² Galeazzo Sanseverino & Bianca Sforza married in 1496

NOTES ON NAMES

* Leonardo's portrait of a teenage girl, initially dubbed *La Bella Principessa* before her identity had been firmly established, is here referred to as the *Portrait of Bianca Sforza*.

* The Bianca Sforza of Leonardo's portrait is not to be confused with either:
  – Bianca Maria Visconti, her grandmother, wife of Francesco Sforza and mother of Il Moro, or
  – Bianca Maria Sforza, her cousin, daughter of Il Moro's brother Galeazzo Maria and wife to Emperor Maximilian

* The four illuminated *Sforziadas* are referred to according to their current locations, *viz.* the *London Sforziada* (British Library); *Paris Sforziada* (Bibliothèque Nationale); *Uffizi Sforziada* (the Florence museum is home to the surviving cuttings from the mutilated volume, whose whereabouts are unknown); and the *Polish Sforziada* (now in the National Library in Warsaw, after spending many years in Zamość in southeast Poland).

* The equine monument in honour of Francesco Sforza, designed by Leonardo but never cast, is referred to as the *Sforza Horse*.

* English name equivalents have been used for **Isabel of Aragon** and her aunt **Beatrix of Aragon**, to help lessen the confusion with their namesake relatives, the sisters Isabella and Beatrice d'Este.

* Bianca Sforza's mother is here named as **Bernardina Corradi** (rather than *Bernardina de Conradis*, as hitherto favoured by most historians) in line with Nadia Covini's compelling article *Zanette e Cecilia* in the May 2011 edition of *Viglevanum* (the review of the Vigevano Historical Society), which cites a letter dated 20 January 1483 referring to *Bernardina Corradi* as Il Moro's mistress; this letter was sent from Milan by Ambassador Zaccaria Saggi to Federico Gonzaga, Marquess of Mantua from 1478–84. Neither *Conradis* nor *De Conradis* exist in Italy today, whereas *Corradi* is relatively common.

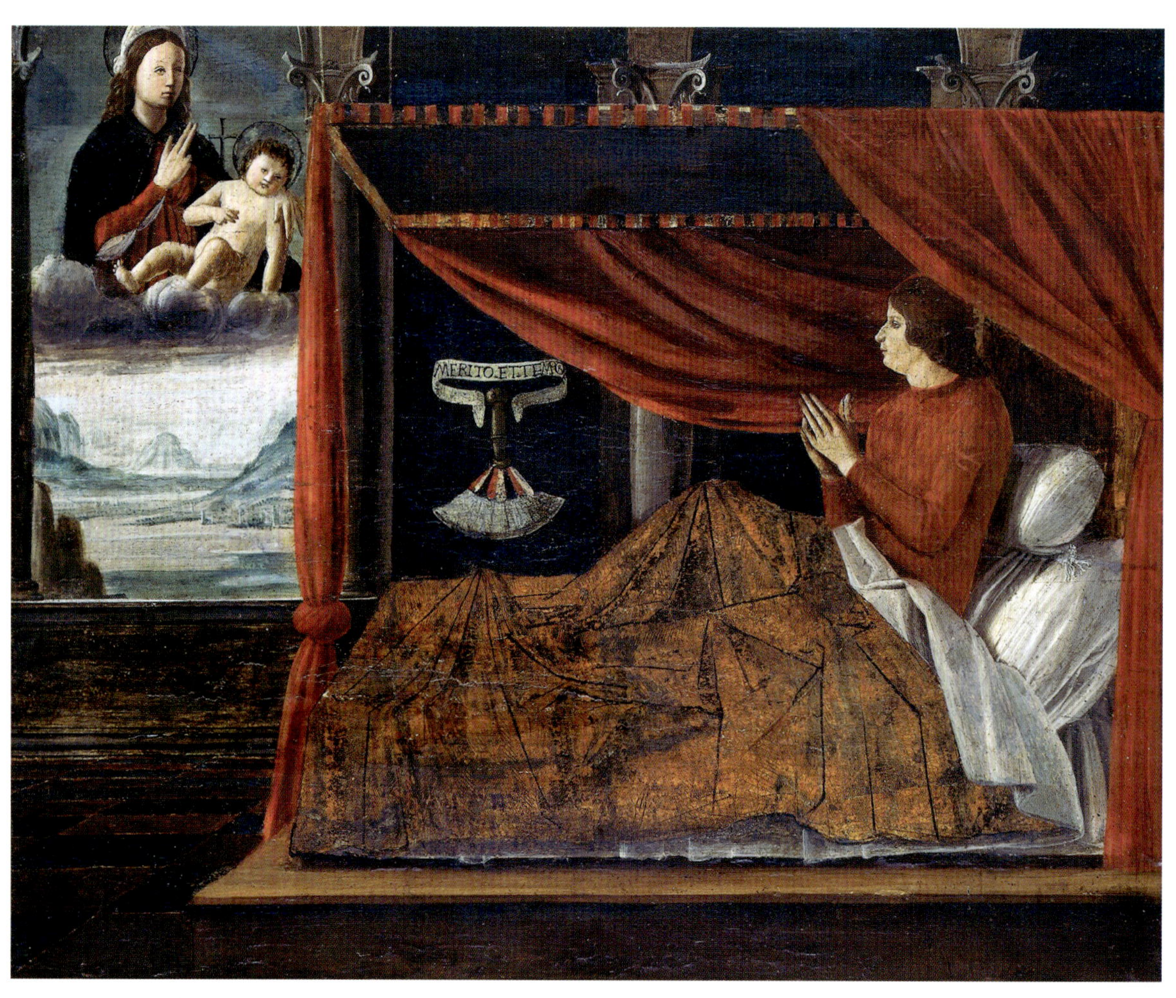

IL MORO PRAYING TO THE VIRGIN (c.1488) – TEMPERA ON PANEL 50 × 56 cm – MUSEO POLDI PEZZOLI

I

A DARK PRINCE RISES

LEONARDO ARRIVES AT THE COURT OF IL MORO

A SMALL, NAIVE PAINTING in Milan's Museo Poldi Pezzoli[1] shows **Ludovico Maria Sforza on what, shortly before, had been considered his death-bed. Now he is sitting up and giving thanks to the Virgin Mary to whom, like all his brothers and sisters, he owed his middle name. He is thanking His Lady for his recovery from the life-threatening illness that struck him down in Autumn 1487.**

For several months, reported diplomatic envoys,[2] he was feverish, in acute pain and semi-paralysed. When a Genoese delegation arrived in Milan to discuss a diplomatic agreement, Il Moro was described as *molestato da gravissima infermita ... si ridusse in estremo* ('suffering from a very serious illness ... at death's door'). On November 25 he was too ill to welcome the Bishop of Oradea, dispatched by King Matthias Corvinus of Hungary to celebrate the betrothal of Il Moro's niece Bianca Maria to King Matthias's son and heir János.[3]

Il Moro had been ruling Milan as Regent since 1480 on behalf of his young nephew Gian Galeazzo, born 1468. But the nominal Duke, now aged nineteen, proved incapable of assuming governmental responsibility during his uncle's illness. There was no shortage of contenders to replace him: Cardinal Ascanio Sforza,[4] Il Moro's younger brother; Gian Giacomo Trivulzio, Milan's leading general; and Count Giovanni Borromeo, head of the Ghibelline faction.[5] As rumours spread of Il Moro's impending death, Milan seemed on the brink of civil war.

But Il Moro pulled through. The Poldi Pezzoli painting celebrates his recovery, in the first months of 1488. It shows the bed-ridden Ludovico pale-skinned and brown-haired. In fact, the semi-spitting image of his elder brother, Galeazzo Maria, who had been overthrown – literally, inside a church, then slashed to bits – a dozen years before.

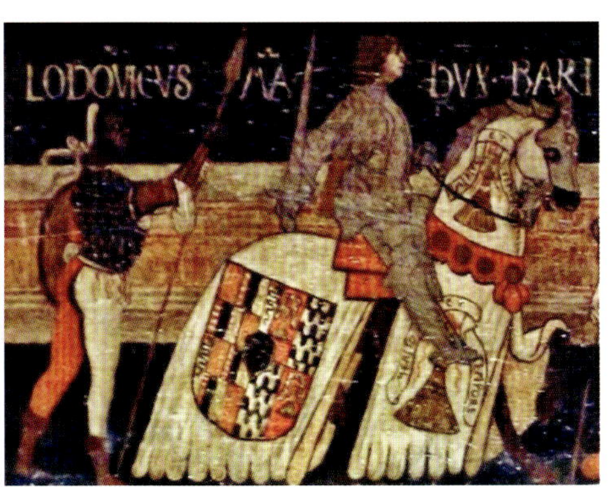

Ludovico still has brown hair a year or so later, in the three-knight procession along a chest known as the *Cassone dei Tri Duchi* – probably a wedding gift for his nephew Gian Galeazzo upon his marriage to Isabel of Aragon in January 1489. The chest (*left*) shows Gian Galeazzo and Ludovico following Galeazzo Maria on horseback like three wise, fairly equal men. Each has his emblem(s): fire-buckets for Galeazzo Maria; an axe-and-log and sifting-cloth for newly-wed Gian Galeazzo; and a clothes brush, or *scopetta*,[6] for Ludovico – like the one hanging on his convalescent bedroom wall.

One suspects that Ludovico was less hung up on the brush itself than on its attendant motto: *Merito et Tempore* (With Merit and Time). Ludovico felt he merited the Duchy of Milan more than his sickly, effete nephew – who may have suffered from the hereditary propensity to in-bred simple-mindedness that also affected Ludovico's elder brother Filippo Maria.

Time? Ludovico bided it. He was content to act as Regent until his time was ripe – i.e. once he had secured the official investiture as Duke from the Holy Roman Emperor.

Il Moro's rise to supreme power in Milan was, from a legal and genealogical point, improbable.[7] For a start, he had three elder brothers: Galeazzo Maria (born 1444), who reigned as Duke for a decade before being assassinated in 1476; Filippo Maria (born 1448), who displayed no political ambition before dying in October 1492; and Sforza Maria (born 1451), Ludovico's predecessor as Duke of Bari,[8] who was poisoned – possibly at Ludovico's behest – when the pair were in the town of Varese Ligure with their *condottiero* henchman Roberto Sanseverino, waiting for Neapolitan reinforcements from the nearby port of La Spezia as they plotted a tortuous incognito route, via Bobbio and Tortona, to their Milanese *coup d'état* of 1479.

That *coup* brought Ludovico to power, initially in a joint regency with his brother's widow, Bona di Savoia. After executing her chief advisor, Cicco Simonetta, Ludovico soon elbowed her aside. By 1481, with the acrimonious departure of Roberto Sanseverino for the rival state of Venice, his strongman rule over Milan had been established.

Il Moro's father Francesco Sforza had ruled as fourth Duke of Milan from 1450–66. Francesco was born a commoner: his rise to power derived from his success as a *condottiero* (mercenary general), which led to his wedding to Bianca Maria Visconti in 1441. The Visconti family had ruled Milan since 1277, initially with the title of *Signore* (Lord). In 1395 Gian Galeazzo Visconti obtained the title of *Duca* (Duke) from the Holy Roman Emperor, Wenceslas of Bohemia. He was succeeded in 1402 by his teenage son Giovanni Maria then, in 1412, by his second son Filippo Maria, who died without male issue in 1447. The fractious interregnum that ensued saw Milan briefly administered by the so-called Ambrosian Republic (named after the city's patron saint, *Ambrogio* or Ambrose, a 4th century Bishop of Milan).

The Sforzas were widely treated as upstarts. The Holy Roman Emperor, Friedrich III, refused them the Imperial investiture. Long-established Milanese families regarded the Sforzas – originally from Cotignola near the Adriatic coast, 170 miles southeast of Milan – as socially inferior. Sforza rule was also perceived by some as illegitimate: Gian Galeazzo Visconti's will had stipulated that, if his two sons died without male heirs (as proved the case), the Duchy should pass to the descendants of his eldest daughter, Valentina. Since 1465 the 'Legitimist' claimant had been Duke Louis of Orléans, Valentina's grandson.

Il Moro had initially promised to step down as Regent once his nephew Gian Galeazzo reached adulthood but, by the late 1480s, he was casting doubt on his nephew's physical and psychological fitness to rule. It was clear that Il Moro had no intention of handing him the reins of power.

His life-threatening illness of 1487 offered Bona di Savoia an unexpected chance to establish her son Gian Galeazzo upon the ducal throne. She therefore became a prime target in the purge that followed Il Moro's recovery. Her income and retinue were slashed, and she was effectively banished to her country seat of Abbiategrasso, 25 miles west of Milan.

Other high-profile victims were Aloisio da Terzago, Ducal Secretary and Master Of The Horse, and his brother-in-law Filippo degli Eustachi, State Treasurer and Castellan of Milan. In 1489 both were convicted of treason after a lengthy trial reported across Italy. Eustachi was jailed, Terzago condemned to death – reportedly left to starve in the dungeons of the Castle of Pavia.

Terzago was replaced as Master Of The Horse by Galeazzo Sanseverino, Ludovico's Captain-of-Arms and prospective son-in-law. Terzago's Milanese residence – the former Medici Bank, acquired in 1485 – was confiscated, and assigned to Sanseverino's fiancée: Ludovico's daughter, Bianca.

The brown-haired Ludovico is accompanied on the *Cassone dei Tri Duchi* by a Moor with a white head-band as groom. Ludovico began to use the Moor image in the mid-1480s, before adopting the ultimate means to Moorishness: black hair dye.[9] His new-found raven-hued locks (and, sometimes, attendant five o'clock shadow) may have reflected a desire to emulate the 'Raven King' – Hungary's powerful warlord Matthias *Corvinus*, with whom Il Moro was in regular contact during the second half of the 1480s.

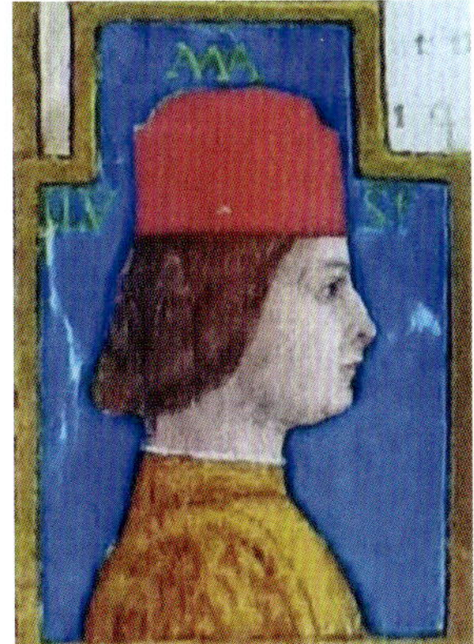

Despite extravagant rumours that Il Moro's father was an African cleric,[10] Ludovico Sforza actually had a 'white, pallid complexion, as I saw close-up' recalled the historian and famed portrait collector Paolo Giovio (1483–1552), who met him in person.[11] This description is in line with the pale-faced, brown-haired portrait of the fifteen-year-old Ludovico in his teenage history-book known as the *Codice Sforza*, now in Turin's Biblioteca Reale (*see left*).[12]

Two years after appearing with chestnut locks on a chest in 1489, Il Moro would be depicted in two different volumes, produced at pretty much the same time under his direct authority, with different-coloured hair. Brown in neither.

In a luxury manuscript biography of his grandfather, Il Moro has grey hair. In a de luxe printed biography of his father, Il Moro has black hair. What is going on?

In the aftermath of his life-threatening illness, Il Moro turned prematurely grey. Relatives and courtiers saw him with grey hair on a day-to-day basis, and this is how, throughout the 1490s, he was portrayed in books whose circulation was limited to his inner circle. But, if the target audience were a foreign or broader domestic public, unfamiliar with Ludovico's everyday appearance, he was depicted with hair that was very dark brown or raven-haired black. This is how he appears in two painted portraits of the mid-1490s, and in a book *not* intended for a domestic audience. As *Il Moro*: The Moor.

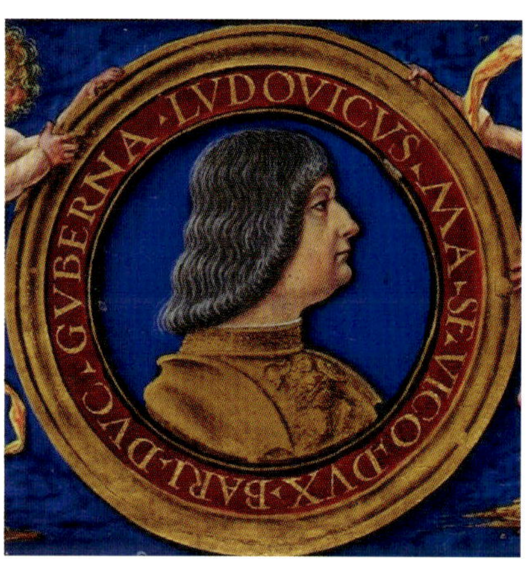

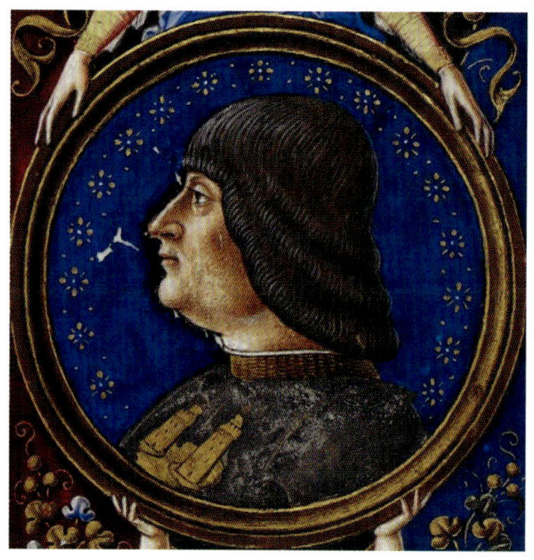

It was Bernardo Bellincioni (1452–92) who promoted the nickname of *Il Moro* – not just for its dusky overtones, but as a pun on the Italian for mulberry tree (*moro*), whose silkworms had been a major source of Milan's wealth since silk production had been introduced to Lombardy by Duke Filippo Maria Visconti in 1442. The late-fruiting mulberry[13] was also a symbol of wisdom and patience, which chimed in with Il Moro's *merito et tempore* motto.

Bellincioni was Il Moro's court poet. Before moving from Florence to Milan, in 1485, he had dubbed Lorenzo de' Medici *Il Lauro* – a pun on the laurel tree. He lost no time giving Ludovico the same verbal treatment. It would provide the base for an astute propaganda makeover and a most successful nickname, finding its ultimate visual form in a book illustration portraying Ludovico as a hardy mulberry tree and his nephew as a puny laurel.

Ludovico's rivalry with Lorenzo de' Medici[14] stemmed from their competing desire to be viewed as foremost Prince of the Renaissance. The rivalry lay behind Ludovico's obsession with all things Florentine[15] – manifest in his recruitment of Bellincioni and his choice of *lingua fiorentina* for the vernacular translation of the epic biography of his father Francesco, the *Sforziada*, assigned to the famous Florentine humanist Cristoforo Landino.

The biggest star to quit Tuscany for Lombardy, however, arrived unnoticed. **Leonardo da Vinci**.

ENTER LEONARDO

Leonardo da Vinci is first chronicled in Milan, as *magister Leonardus de Vinciis florentinus*,[16] in a contract dated 25 April 1483 for an altarpiece in San Francesco Grande, the city's second-biggest church.[17] Four days later Bianca Sforza is first chronicled, in a will drawn up in the name of her father, Il Moro.

The precise date of Bianca's birth is unknown, although there are grounds for supposing it was no earlier than 23 November 1482 and that she may have been born at much the same time as Leonardo arrived in Milan. She was named *Bianca* after Il Moro's mother, Bianca Maria, Duchess of Milan from 1450–66. Her own mother was Bernardina Corradi, about whom little is known.[18]

In the absence of other evidence, it is logical to assume that Leonardo da Vinci came to Milan in April 1483 to work on an altarpiece with the brothers Ambrogio and Evangelista de Predis. As the altarpiece contract listed all three at the same address, near the church of San Vincenzo in Prato to the southwest of the city, it appears Leonardo was lodging with them.

The last written mention of Leonardo in Florence dates from 28 September 1481. It is stated in a manuscript ascribed to the *Anonimo Gaddiano* (*c.*1540) that Leonardo was thirty when he came to Milan.[19] Even if this were an exact rather than rounded figure, Leonardo – born 15 April 1452 – could just as easily have come to Milan in early 1483; Sabba da Castiglione wrote in 1554 that, when he left Milan at the end of 1499, Leonardo had been working on an equestrian monument to Francesco Sforza for sixteen years (*et oltra cio si occupa nella forma del cavallo di Milano, oue sedecianni continui consomo*).[20]

Legend has it that Leonardo arrived in Milan strumming a silver *lira* (lyre) shaped like a horse's head – *fabricato d'argento gran parte in forma d'un teschio di cavallo* in the words of the celebrated 16th century art historian Giorgio Vasari.[21] Relying on secondary sources is asking for trouble. Vasari's brief biographies of Renaissance artists are so famous, and written so long ago, that they tend to be taken at face rather than fable value.

Leonardo doubtless came to Milan to further his career. He was not in the Florentine employ of Lorenzo de' Medici – who was, in any case, strapped for cash. Yet there is surely a grain of truth in what Vasari writes. There was indeed a horse involved when Leonardo moved from Florence to Milan: a horse not of silver, but of bronze – for an equestrian memorial to Francesco Sforza.

THE *VIRGIN OF THE ROCKS*

First, though, Leonardo teamed up with Ambrogio and Evangelista de Predis to work on a huge commission from the Confraternita della Concezione (Confraternity of the Immaculate Conception).

The brothers were well-connected. Their elder half-brother, Cristoforo, had been a court artist to Duke Galeazzo Maria (reigned 1466–76); Ambrogio worked at the ducal mint and was court artist to Il Moro. The altarpiece involved much work (gilding and side-panels as well as a vast main painting) and a tight deadline (inside the year). Ambrogio de Predis specialized in miniatures and portraits rather than large-scale religious works. If he and Evangelista, who served essentially as his assistant, were to secure the commission, they needed help.

They probably did not want to be overshadowed by some established local artist. But an up-and-coming talent, with a lick of Florentine prestige, was a different matter.

The contract – which respectfully dubbed Leonardo *magister* – called for a Madonna and Child with two prophets surrounded by angels. But Leonardo's painting, now in the Louvre, ignored this stipulation. It has no prophets, only one angel, and an added John the Baptist.

There has been speculation that Leonardo was inspired by the *Apocalypse Nova*, a 'semi-heretical text' by the Blessed Amadeus, a Franciscan friar who had died in Milan in 1482 and whose 'Gnostic interpretation of the dogma of the Immaculate Conception' viewed the Virgin and John the Baptist as 'the protagonists of the New Testament' rather than Jesus.[22]

Leonardo's imagery defied religious convention. The Virgin's protective hand would normally envelop her son Jesus, not John the Baptist. One would expect to find John the Baptist, not Jesus, down by the waterside. Angels tend to point at Jesus, not John the Baptist. In Leonardo's painting everything seemed the wrong way round. Or was it? Throughout his career he would embrace ambiguity almost as a creed.

A second version of the *Virgin of the Rocks* a decade later would remove the ambiguity – and replace it with a different message altogether. In the meantime, Leonardo had transformed a routine religious commission into a major talking-point: effectively, a PR stunt.

A similar eye for self-promotion surely underpins the list of professional capabilities he drafted for the attention of Il Moro – declaring he could 'carry out sculpture in marble, bronze and clay, likewise in painting, as well as anyone' (*conducerò in scultura di marmore, di bronzo et di terra, similiter in pictura, ciò che si possa fare ad paragone de omni altro*).

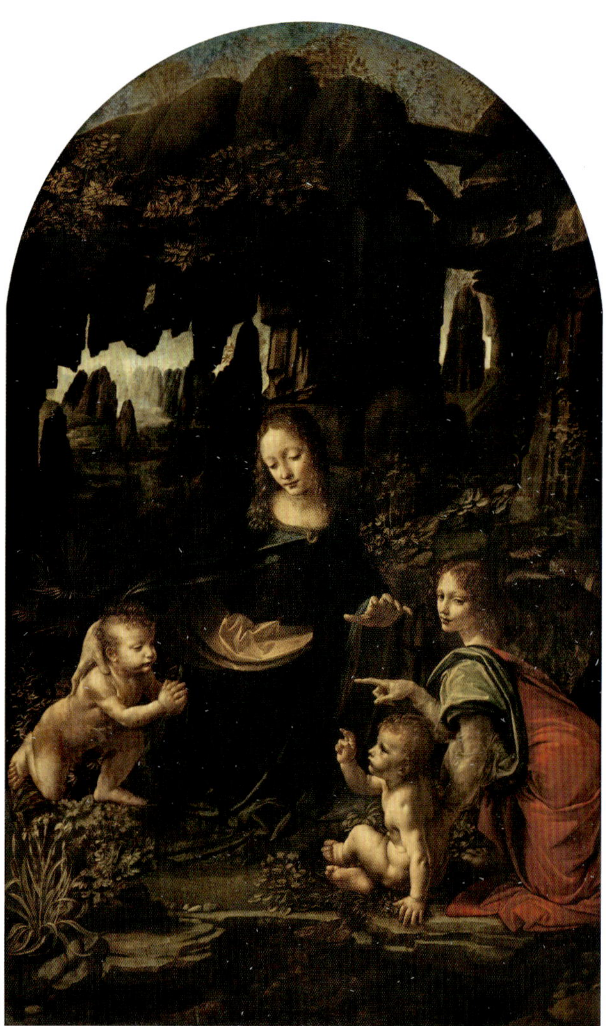

Leonardo added this immodest self-appraisal as a footnote to a string of boasts about his skill as an engineer. He need hardly have bothered. Il Moro soon knew he could paint. His *Virgin of the Rocks* caused a sensation.

LEONARDO'S 'MUSICIAN'

On 23 April 1485 Il Moro informed his Ambassador to Hungary, Maffeo da Treviglio, that he had commissioned Leonardo to paint a Madonna for King Matthias Corvinus, 'as devout as he knows how.'[23]

The painting has not survived. But the diplomatic missive suggests Leonardo had swiftly caught Il Moro's eye and patronage – and that his ability as an artist was the cause.

Six weeks later, on 3 June 1485, Ferrara Ambassador Giacomo Trotti reported to his master, Duke Ercole d'Este, that Il Moro and court favourite Galeazzo Sanseverino had been wearing identical costumes studded with pearls, rubies and diamonds, and embroidered with *un burato d'oro cum doe mani che l ten da ogni canto ... et le lettere dicono 'tale ad ti quale ad mi'* ('a gold *buratto* held by two hands from either side ... and letters saying *tale ad ti quale ad mi*').[24]

The *buratto* – a sifting-cloth used to separate flour from bran – was one of the Sforzas' favourite iconographic devices.

Its accompanying motto *tal a ti qual a mi* ('To You As To Me') was coined by Bona di Savoia as a mocking threat of retaliation against her philandering ducal husband Galeazzo Maria. The *buratto* and its motto rapidly became associated with matrimonial equality – quoted, for instance, in the 1494 deed transferring land from Il Moro to his wife Beatrice d'Este (British Library *Add. MS 21413*) and (twice) in Birago's 1496 frontispiece for the *Sforziada* commemorating the marriage between Galeazzo Sanseverino and Il Moro's daughter Bianca.

So to read of the *buratto* being used on garments sported by two men is distinctly odd. Were they lovers?

They were second cousins. Galeazzo Sanseverino was born in Milan in 1458. His grandmother was Il Moro's aunt: Francesco Sforza's half-sister Elisa. Galeazzo was the fourth son of Roberto Sanseverino, the legendary *condottiero* who engineered Il Moro's *coup d'état* in 1479.

When Roberto split from Il Moro in 1481, and entered Venetian service, he took his four eldest sons with him. But Galeazzo defected from Venice to Milan in 1483: a major propaganda coup for Il Moro – as well as psychological revenge on Roberto. What was the bait? The future hand of Il Moro's new-born daughter, Bianca?

Galeazzo was renowned for his effete finery. He was a man with whom the ladies felt at ease – he regularly squired Beatrice d'Este in the early years of her marriage to Il Moro – but is not recorded with any mistress before or after the death of Bianca in 1496, five months into their marriage. He did not remarry for another 21 years.

What light does this suggestive track record shed on Galeazzo's close friendship with Leonardo da Vinci? And on his relationship with Il Moro, whose infatuation with Galeazzo led him to ignore all criticism of him, with ultimately catastrophic consequences?

Galeazzo's rise was spectacular. By 1488 he had leapfrogged over Gian Giacomo Trivulzio, a career soldier and scion of one of Milan's leading families, to become Il Moro's *Capitano Generale*. In July 1488 the Ferrara ambassador reported on the lavish jewellery Il Moro had ordered for himself and Galeazzo Sanseverino.[25] Galeazzo was betrothed to Bianca on 10 January 1490 – shortly after she had been naturalized by ducal decree on 8 September 1489, at the age of six.[26]

Galeazzo Sanseverino occupied the same post under Il Moro as Francesco Sforza had under the Visconti. Once betrothed to Bianca, Galeazzo stopped signing himself *Sanseverino* and adopted the formula *Sforza Vicecomes* (Sforza Visconti). In contemporary documents he was unfailingly referred to as *Messer Galeaz*. He became, to all intents and purposes, as much a Sforza as his *fiancée*.

Galeazzo Sanseverino would stalk the wings and stages of Renaissance power for the next thirty-five years, seated at the right hand of the Duke of Milan, the Holy Roman Emperor and the King of France in one of the most extraordinary international careers the world has ever seen.

And that's not all. As a celebrity jouster, Galeazzo Sanseverino proved virtually invincible. He was a patron of Leonardo da Vinci and the famous mathematician, Luca Pacioli. He was friends with the great German humanist Willibald Pirckheimer and the even greater Albrecht Dürer.

Yet, to history, he remains a shadowy figure, and it is widely believed that no portrait of him has survived.

*

The 'Portrait of a Musician' is first recorded in the Ambrosiana in Milan (where it remains) in 1672 when, in *De Origine et Statu Bibliothecae Ambroisianae Hemidecas*, Librarian Pietro Bosca identified the sitter as a 'Duke of Milan' and remarked on his elegance and lifelike quality (*vultum Mediolanensis Ducis tanta elegantiam quantam fortassem cum viveret sibi illa Dux exoptaverat*).[27] That the earliest known reference to the portrait should assume the sitter to be of elevated social status has been ignored by the many modern commentators who view the snatch of musical score bottom right – painted over and rediscovered only when the painting was cleaned in 1905[28] – as proof that the blond-haired gentleman was a professional musician.

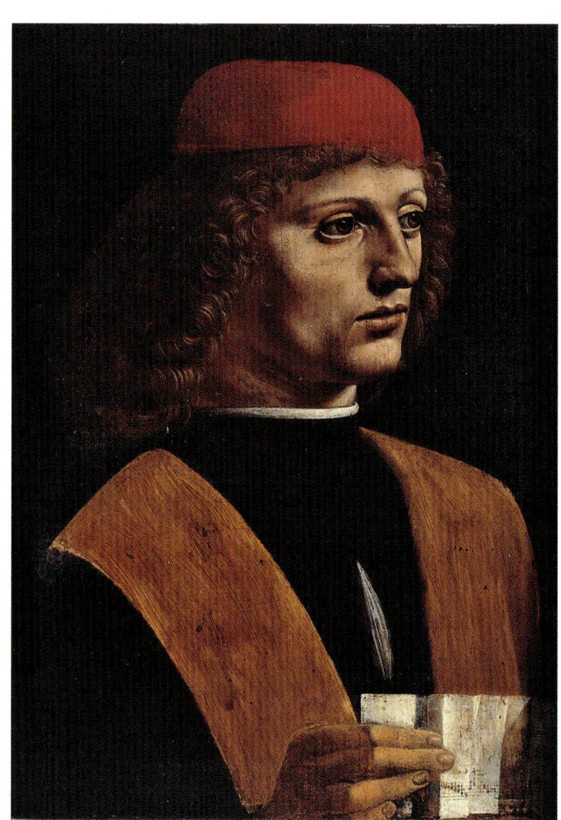

Potential candidates include Franchino Gaffurio (Choirmaster at the Milan Duomo); composer Josquin Desprez (intermittently in Milan during the 1480s);[29] and instrument-maker Atalante Migliorotti (briefly in Milan during the 1480s before returning to his native Florence). But Gaffurio and Desprez were born in the early 1450s: too old to be considered Leonardo's sitter, painted in the mid-to-late 1480s and clearly aged around thirty. Migliorotti is thought to have been born in 1466 – too young.

The idea that Leonardo, at a time when he was striving to consolidate his ducal patronage, would devote his first major Milanese portrait to a musician is implausible.[30] His subsequent portraits of Il

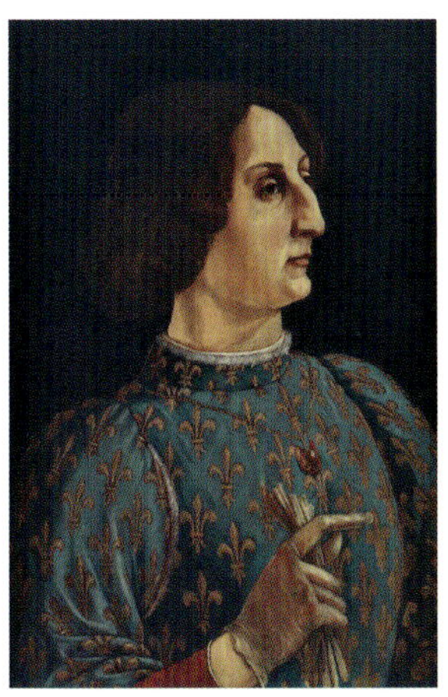

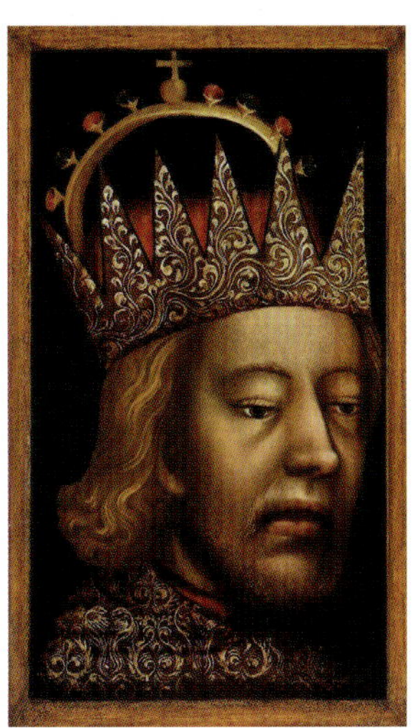

Moro's mistresses Cecilia Gallerani and Lucrezia Crivelli, and of his illegitimate daughter Bianca Sforza, suggest Leonardo was the man Il Moro turned to immortalize his nearest and dearest. That this ducal talisman should be assigned the portrait of a mere court employee requires a leap of several octaves of faith.

And to suppose that Leonardo would underline the sitter's profession, by granting him a snatch of score, implies that his subject was so obscure that the viewer needed a visual aid to identify him. Such a supposition implies Leonardo was glib. How can such a mundane approach be squared with Leonardo's penchant for subtle allusion? And, if a portrait of a court *musician* were indeed commissioned, why did nobody ever commission a portrait of the court's superstar *artist*, the great Leonardo himself?

Even supposing that the sheet of music is connected to the sitter's profession: why, given that it is being brandished at the viewer, is it a tiny, rumpled scrap of paper rather than a handsome score? There was plenty of room in the portrait for a score as big as, say, the ermine in Leonardo's next portrait. The sitter's sketchy costume almost cries out to be covered by something more substantial.

'The Musician' has been the subject of persistent misapprehension for over 300 years. It was once ascribed to Bernardino de' Conti. Based on the misguided assumption that the Ambrosiana's alluring *Portrait of a Lady* – today hung in the same room – was its companion piece, and on the equally misguided assumption that this companion piece portrayed Beatrice d'Este, Duchess of Milan, the 'Duke' was identified as Il Moro – in bewildering ignorance of the scores of images dotted around Milan that show Il Moro and 'The Musician' to have looked about as similar as Barack Obama and Donald Trump.

It makes no sense historically or psychologically for Leonardo to have painted the portrait of a musician. The sitter's elevated social status is further reinforced by the precedents for the sitter's distinctive pose.

An immediate precedent was the Piero Pollaiolo portrait of Il Moro's elder brother, Duke Galeazzo Maria, painted during his State visit to Florence in 1471. The portrait has remained in Florence, hanging initially in the Medici Palace, now in the Uffizi. By adopting this pose for his debut Milanese portrait, Leonardo was importing a dash of that Florentine sophistication by which Il Moro set such store.

But there was another, even more illustrious origin of the pose: the early 1360s portrait of Habsburg Duke Rudolf IV (1339–65), known as *Der Stifter* (The Founder). The portrait – like Leonardo's 'Musician' – shows a youngish man with blond, shoulder-length hair. It is to be found in Vienna[31] but, as it is considered the first-ever European portrait with a three-quarter pose, its reputation must have reached Milan, where Rudolf died after attending the wedding of his younger brother, future Duke Leopold III (1351–86), to Viridis Visconti (1352–1414) – cousin of Gian Galeazzo Visconti, the first Duke of Milan and grandfather of Sforza dynasty matriarch Bianca Maria Visconti.

In other words, the Leopold–Viridis marriage heralded the first dynastic alliance between the Sforzas' Visconti ancestors and the Habsburgs upon whom the Imperial investiture to Milan would depend.

But why is the scrap of paper so small, and why on earth is it folded into nine, like a miniature Cubist curtain? Is Leonardo trying to show off his mastery of shadow and perspective? If this is a score composed by a musician, why is he not holding it up proudly? Why isn't he singing?

The sheet's paintwork has clearly suffered over time. Some of the music has been erased, doubtless as a result of over-painting and restoration. What remains shows three rows of staves (some of six lines, some just five) peopled by crotchets spangled with the odd minim and semibreve. It does indeed look like a *bona fide* score. But of what?

According to Jean-Michel Renard, a leading authority on Medieval and Renaissance music and President of France's *Chambre Nationale des Experts Spécialisés* (National Experts Association), the composition is 'not Gregorian but very probably religious' and 'strongly recalls' a passage in the *Veni Sancte Spiritus* by the English composer John Dunstaple (*c.*1390–1453) – known to have been familiar to Milanese music-lovers, as it is cited by Franchino Gaffurio in his *Practica Musicae Utriusque Cantus* written around 1480.[32] Renard finds the snatch of score 'realistic' and 'fully compatible with the late 15th century.' He suggests that 'the barred (?) C at the top of the stave might be a key-signature, as choral chant was often written in this key.'

There are various reasons why Leonardo might have wished to quote the *Veni Sancte Spiritus* (sung at mass during Pentecost). It is said to encapsulate the Golden Sequence, sometimes known as the 'Fingerprint of God' – the musical equivalent of the *Golden Section* or *Golden Ratio*[33] illustrated by Leonardo's *Vitruvian Man* (and later explored by his friend Luca Pacioli in *De Divina Proportione*).

Veni Sancte Spiritus starts with the words *Veni, Sancte Spiritus, et emitte caelitus lucis tuae radium*: imploring the Holy Spirit to 'emit rays of heavenly light' brings to mind Leonardo's previous painting, the *Virgin of the Rocks*, and the presence of the obscure, androgynous-looking Archangel Uriel, whose name means 'God is my Light.'[34]

Finally, the notion of summoning the Holy Spirit presages Leonardo's *Lady with an Ermine*, and ties in with Il Moro's messianic ambition for his most immediate circle to be blessed with divine grace.

Il Moro's will, drawn up at the end of 1498, advises that 'wise management of the Ducal Stables and Chapel Choir is especially recommended; good horses and good singers are always to be kept for the Duke's pleasure and the honour of his name.' This emphasis on, and association between, music and horses was epitomized and embodied by Galeazzo Sanseverino – Il Moro's Master of the Horse, and a renowned and enthusiastic singer.

We know of that enthusiasm from Galeazzo's own letters. He regularly boasted about his vocal prowess to Isabella d'Este, Il Moro's sister-in-law.

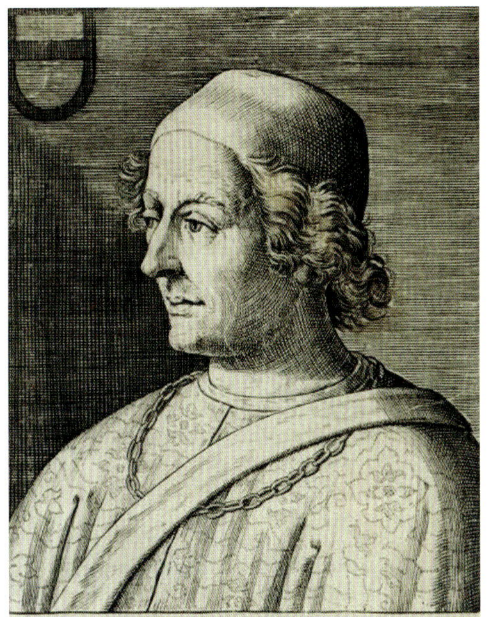

ROBERTO SANSEVERINO

There is one final piece of evidence that underscores the identification of 'The Musician' as Galeazzo Sanseverino. As remarked by Italian historian Pierangelo Laurora, the painting served Pompilio Totti (*c*.1590–1639) as the basis for his engraved portrait (*left*) of Galeazzo's father, Roberto Sanseverino, in his *Ritratti et Elogi di Capitani Illustri* published in Rome in 1635.[35]

Laurora claims the two images share 'strikingly coincidental' facial details whose 'anthropometric measurements' suggest they are one and the same person – albeit with Roberto's portrait clearly that of an older man.

The portraits share the same big eyes, large nose, thick eyelids and prominent chin. In terms of pose, Totti's Roberto is virtually a mirror-image of Leonardo's 'Musician.'[36]

Totti's book is a handsome, early example of what might be termed Popular History, and features 129 biographies (mostly two or three pages long) of 'Illustrious Captains' – many completed by a single-phrase physical description (Roberto Sanseverino had brown eyes and hair, we are told.)

Each biography is accompanied by an engraving of the 'captain' concerned, from the 12th (Barbarossa) to the 17th century (Cardinal Richelieu) via Christopher Colombus, Cesare Borgia and the Albanian warlord Skanderbeg. We also find Matthias Corvinus, Ercole d'Este, Maximilian I, Prospero Colonna, Stefan Batory and *Giovanni Zamoyski de Zamośći*:[37] perhaps the only time this disparate, decade-spanning array have ever been cited alongside leading Sforzas in the same volume until now.

Each portrait features the subject's coat of arms in the top corner. Curiously, we find a lion rampant, rather than the Sforza viper, accompanying Francesco Sforza and Il Moro. Whereas Muzio's profile echoes his portrait in the *Giovio* series, and Francesco's is close to his image in the *Sforziada*, the depiction of Il Moro bears no resemblance to his unmistakable profile mounted on walls and buildings throughout Milan.

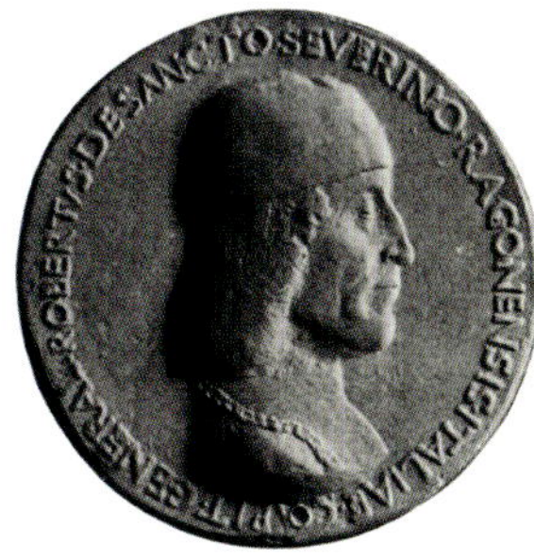

Il Moro's claims to have been an 'Illustrious Captain' are, in any case, dubious – about on a par with those of his *Capitano Generale* Galeazzo Sanseverino, who is conspicuously absent from Totti's tome. Galeazzo's father Roberto is, like Il Moro, illustrated by a portrait that bears no similarity to his appearance.

We have two records of what Roberto Sanseverino looked like: a medal struck in the 1480s (*left*), honouring him as Italy's grandest *condottiero*; and his tombstone effigy in Trent Cathedral where he was initially buried (*see p.138*).

Both show an elderly, lantern-jawed character with a large forehead and gaunt cheeks – a man who bears scant resemblance to the soft-featured visage Totti chose for Roberto in his book of Illustrious Generals. Although Totti mentions Roberto's burial in Trent Cathedral, it is clear he never clapped eyes on his medal – or set foot in Trent Cathedral (which was then, admittedly, on foreign soil – remaining Austrian until 1919).

Further evidence is provided by the coat of arms Totti quotes in the top left of his Roberto engraving. This simple shield with its single horizontal bar belonged to the House of Sanseverino all right – but not to Roberto's branch. Roberto had his own arms, incorporating his honorary admission to the House of Aragon by the King of Naples in 1461. His shield was halved between the blood-and-gold stripes of Aragon and the red-on-white band of the Sanseverinos (embellished with a red border and various stars).

This is the shield that appears on Roberto's tombstone in Trent; in various choral manuscripts commissioned for his son, Cardinal Federigo, in the early 1490s; and in the Birago frontispiece to the *Sforziada* marking his son Galeazzo's marriage to Bianca Sforza in 1496.

In other words, Totti had no certified image of Robert Sanseverino to use as his template for his engraved portrait. He was improvising.

What did he fall back on?

Leonardo da Vinci's 'Musician.'

In the late 1480s Roberto Sanseverino was nearly seventy. 'The Musician' is clearly the portrait of a much younger man. Why would Totti have used it, unless seeking a family resemblance? Unless he believed 'The Musician' to be a portrait of Roberto's son Galeazzo?

Roberto Sanseverino was born in 1418 in Caiazzo, 25 miles north of Naples, son of Leonetto Sanseverino and Elisa Sforza – the younger sister of future dynasty patriarch Francesco Sforza, with whom Roberto was brought up in Milan after his father Leonetto died in 1420. Roberto supported Uncle Francesco throughout his life, and was rewarded with the fiefdoms of Colorno (just north of Parma) and Pontecurone (between Tortona and Voghera). In 1458 Roberto made an epic voyage to Palestine before trundling across the Sinai Desert to Cairo on a donkey, recording his adventures in a diary of immeasurable historic (and navigational) significance.[38]

Such was Roberto's prestige that, when Francesco died in 1466, he took temporary charge of the Duchy of Milan pending the return from France of Francesco's son Galeazzo Maria who, in 1474, granted him another fiefdom – that of Castelnuovo Tortonese (now Castelnuovo Scrivia), later inherited by his son Galeazzo. Roberto was the military brains behind Il Moro's return to Milan as Regent in 1479, and rewarded with the fiefdom of Lugano. But the two men fell out irrevocably in 1481 and Roberto quit the duchy.

Soon after he was hired at great cost as *Capitano Generale* by the Venetians, who in 1483 created him Lord of both Montorio Veronese (just outside Verona) and of the magnificent walled town of Cittadella (25 miles northeast of Vicenza on the road from Venice to Trent). He led the Venetian conquest of Ferrara in 1484, with the subsequent Peace of Bagnolo marking the apogee of his career:

Padua historian Giandomenico Spazzarini (1429–1515) likened him to the Emperor of Italy (*Robertus totius Italiae imperator*).[39]

In 1487 Roberto Sanseverino was back in action, leading Venetian troops during a border war in the Adige Valley, south of Trent, against Archduke Sigmund of Austria (1427–96), Lord of Tyrol. It ended with a Venetian defeat near Castel Beseno on 10 August 1487. Sanseverino was killed. His body was recovered by the Tyroleans and transported to Trent, where it was buried with great pomp by Bishop Ulrich von Frundsberg in the church of San Francesco Saverio.

Sanseverino's bloodstained armour was removed and mounted on a wooden horse in the nearby Duomo to celebrate the Tyrolean victory. This suit of armour, made by Antonio Missaglia of Milan, was then removed to Innsbruck, later entering the collection of Archduke Ferdinand II (1529–95) at Schloss Ambras before being moved to Vienna in 1806 – initially to Schloss Belvedere then, in 1886, to the Kunsthistorisches Museum. It remains on display today in the Neue Burg on nearby Heldenplatz.

The day of the battle – the Feast of St Lawrence – was declared a public holiday in Trent and remained so until the city was transferred from Austria to Italy in 1919.

BRAMANTE'S 'HERACLITUS'

There is another, famous unidentified portrait from 1480s Milan. Or rather double-portrait, known as *Heraclitus & Democritus* and frescoed by Donato Bramante in the home of Gaspare Visconti in 1487/8.

Gaspare Visconti (1461–99) hailed from a distinguished branch of Milan's former ruling family. His great-grandfather (also Gaspare) had been ambassador to the Council of Constance in 1415 and to Emperor Sigismund in 1431; his grandfather Pietro placed the ducal cap upon Francesco Sforza in 1450; his father (yet another Gaspare) was made a *cavaliere* by Francesco Sforza and took part in the Sforza embassy to Ferrara in 1452 in honour of Emperor Friedrich III, later serving as Siniscalco under Galeazzo Maria Sforza. He died in 1470.

In April 1472 the young, fatherless Gaspare Visconti was betrothed to Cecilia, the daughter of ducal chancellor Cicco Simonetta and his wife Elisabetta Visconti. In 1478, aged seventeen, he was created *Consigliere Ducale* (Ducal Councillor). In October 1486, shortly after Ludovico Sforza had started identifying himself with a Moor, Gaspare acquired a four-year-old 'Ethiopian' slave, Dionisio, brought to Italy from Tunis. He also acquired a palatial new house in Milan on what is now Via Lanzone, near the church of Sant'Ambrogio.[40] Soon afterwards he commissioned his illustrious lodger, Bramante, to fresco the hall on the *piano nobile* with a series of *Uomini d'Arme* or Men at Arms, transferred to canvas and moved to the city's Brera art museum in 1901/2.

Visconti extolled Bramante as a man whose strands of knowledge were *piu numerose delle stelle, dei granelli di sabbia, dei santi in paradiso* (more

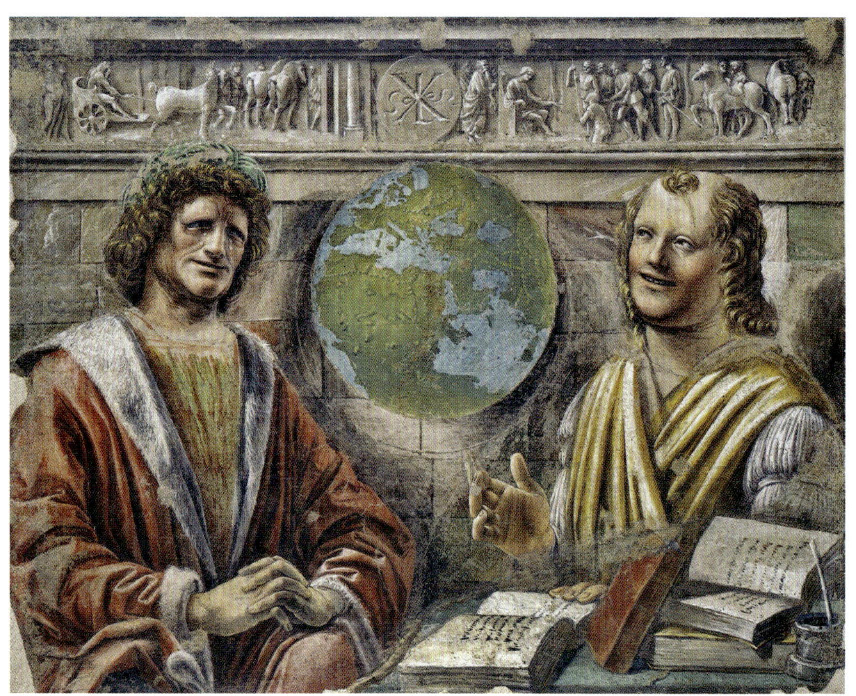

numerous than the stars, the grains of sand, and the saints in paradise). Although primarily remembered as an architect, Bramante was also an outstanding artist – as his *Christ at the Column*, now also in the Brera, reveals.

Bramante's *Men at Arms* are portrayed within domed niches that bring to mind his apse in the church of Santa Maria presso San Satiro (designed around the same time), and share its uncanny mastery of perspective. The idea behind them derives from Petrarch's *De Viris Illustribus* (*c.*1330–50), with its biographies of Roman generals and statesmen from Romulus to Titus, and from Boccaccio's slightly later *De Casibus Virorum Illustrium* (*c.*1360). A classical influence on both works was Suetonius with his *De Vita Caesarum* and *De Viris Illustribus*. Bramante may also have had in mind the *Sala dei Giganti* frescos commissioned for the Palazzo Carraresi in Padua around 1370 by Francesco il Vecchio da Carrara, or the intarsia panels in Federico da Montefeltro's Urbino *studiolo*.

Amidst all his Men at Arms, Bramante included a panel portraying the ancient philosophers *Heraclitus & Democritus* sitting either side of a globe – almost certainly a *réplique* of a painting owned by Marsilio Ficino in Florence, known to have featured 'a sphere of the world; on one side Democritus laughing, and on the other Heraclitus weeping ... because the mass of mankind is a monstrous, mad and miserable animal.'[41] A background frieze – divided in two by an unidentified *LX* monogram – depicts two scenes: the Triumph of Saturn (*left*) and the Judgment of Jupiter (*right*). Saturn's chariot is drawn by a horse whose trotting gait is similar to equine sketches made by Leonardo when designing his monument to Francesco Sforza. Saturn's steed is positioned directly above the head of Heraclitus.

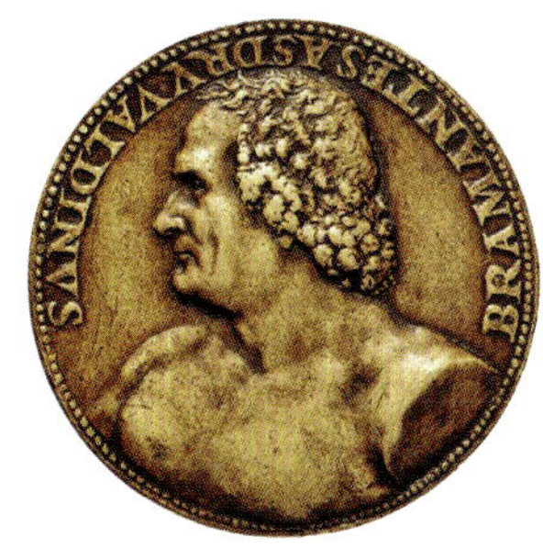

Carlo Pedretti suggests that Bramante would have learned about the Ficino fresco from Leonardo, who must have seen it in Florence as a young man.[42] Gaspare Visconti took a keen interest in Ficino as well. In the mid-1490s he composed a fragmentary treatise on love by paraphrasing and rearranging parts of Ficino's *De Amore*.[43]

Pedretti has suggested that Bramante's *Heraclitus & Democritus* were portraits of Leonardo and Bramante – an idea persuasively developed by Charles Nicholl in his richly researched biography of Leonardo,[44] and indirectly supported by the contention of artist and art historian Gian Paolo Lomazzo (1538–92) that the *Uomini d'Arme* were portraits of contemporary soldiers (he cited Beltramo, Pietro Suola il Vecchio and Giorgio Moro da Ficino).

The idea was lent subliminal support by the catalogue to the *Bramante a Milano* exhibition at the Brera in 2014/5 which, although it stopped short of formally identifying *Heraclitus & Democritus* as Leonardo and Bramante, plastered the head of *Democritus* on the front cover, over the name *Bramante* in giant letters.

An image of middle-aged Bramante – heavy jowls, receding hairline – appears on a medal struck in his honour by Caradosso (*above left*). Its likeness with the Brera fresco is plain to see. We have no similar image of Leonardo in the late 1480s, but evidence that he is the Heraclitus to Bramante's Democritus comes from an undated, unsigned painting first reproduced by Malaguzzi Valeri in 1915. 'According to Milanese tradition' it portrays *Luini e Leonardo*.[45] Both figures are shown with their left hand emerging from their cloaks – an apparent reference to Leonardo's left-handedness.

Luini e Leonardo dates from the second half of the 16th century, presumably based on a Luini original. It was shown under the title *Eraclito e Democrito* at the 2015 *Leonardo* exhibition in Milan's Palazzo Reale, dated as *c.1570* and attributed to Giovan Ambrogio Figino (1553–1608) – who apprenticed with Lomazzo.

It was published shortly afterwards, again entitled *Eraclito e Democrito*, in *Illuminating Leonardo: A Festschrift for Carlo Pedretti Celebrating His 70 Years of Scholarship*[46] – but this time with the artist confidently given as Giralomo Figino (dates unknown), who trained with Leonardo's protégé, Francesco Melzi.

The work's ownership was listed as the Benvenuti Martinez Collection – just as it had been by Malaguzzi Valeri a century before.

The authorship of the red chalk drawing in the Venice Accademia (*see p.34*), showing a mirror-image of the Leonardesque old man, is equally uncertain.

To confuse matters further, a work in identical style, entitled *Three Men with a Woman Holding a Cat* and featuring exactly the same hand-peeping-out-of-a-cloak idea, was attributed to Lomazzo when offered by Sotheby's New York in 2012.[47]

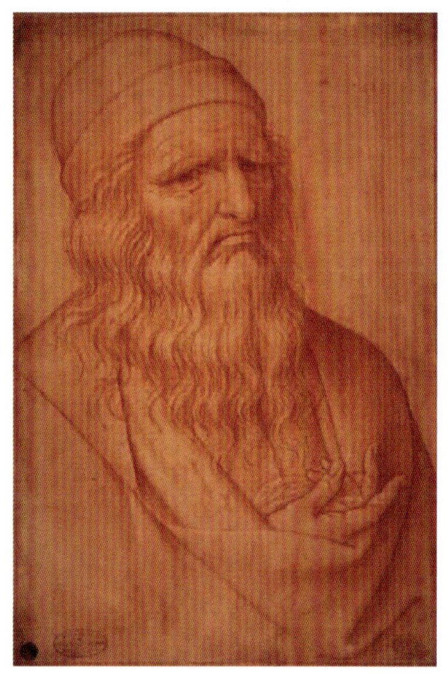
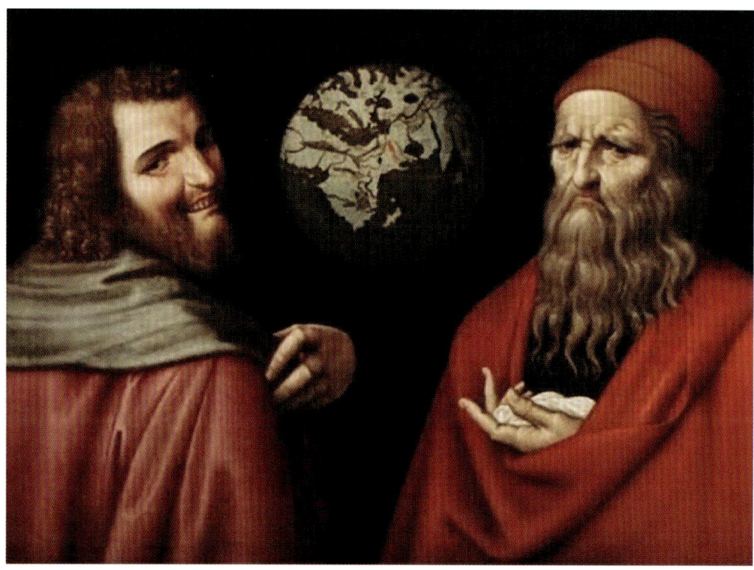

Lomazzo's interest in Leonardo was fostered by Melzi. He was also friends with Luini's son Aurelio (1530–93), who owned Leonardo's magnificent *St Anne* cartoon now in London's National Gallery.

What emerges from this complex web of attribution is a clear 'line of descent' from Leonardo to Lomazzo and the Figinos, via Melzi and Luini – and the probability that the painting in the Benvenuti Martinez Collection is by Giralomo or Giovan Ambrogio Figino, based on an original by Bernardino Luini whose dating is facilitated by geographical considerations.

The globe in the Bramante fresco appears to be based on Ptolemy's world map from the second century AD. Given that Africa merges into the Antarctic, it clearly pre-dates the discovery of the Cape of Good Hope by Portuguese navigator Bartolomeu Dias in 1488.

The globe in the later work, with Africa much as we know it today, appears based on the *Waldseemüller Map* published in 1507. Leonardo returned to Milan in 1506 and stayed until 1513. If the Martinez picture is indeed based on a Luini original, the original must date from between 1507 and 1513.

In other words, we may well be seeing here two depictions of Leonardo: clean-shaven in his mid-thirties, and with his famous beard, aged about sixty.

'SAINTS AND DEVOTEES'

Another painting from the period retains similar mystery to Bramante's *Heraclitus & Democritus* – partly because it is squirrelled away in the bowels of London's National Gallery, which has owned it since 1929.

It is clunkingly entitled *The Virgin and Child with Four Saints and Twelve Devotees* and routinely ascribed to the same unknown artist who painted the

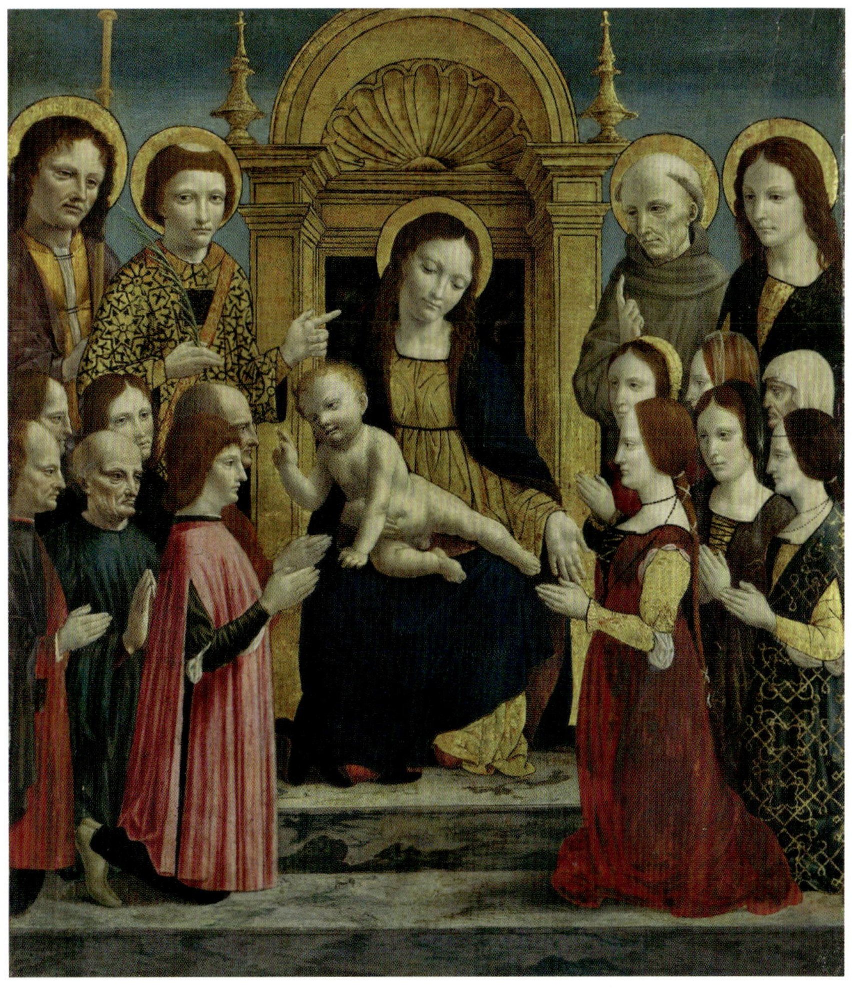

compositionally similar *Pala Sforzesca*, starring Il Moro and Beatrice d'Este, in 1494/5 (*see p.124*).

Both works celebrate a married couple. The young man kneeling on the left of the National Gallery picture has an unmistakable resemblance to Il Moro's short-lived ducal predecessor, Gian Galeazzo. The lady facing him can only be his wife Isabel of Aragon. She is clad in Aragonese colours of blood-and-gold, and sports a *coazzone* (ponytail). One of her ladies-in-waiting is wearing a gown with the knot-patterning that would become popular in 1490s Milan, not least with Leonardo da Vinci.

The marriage between Il Moro's young nephew Gian Galeazzo (born 1469) and his cousin Isabel of Aragon (born 1470) was planned when both were infants – reflecting the importance of a stable Milan/Naples relationship to the balance of Italian power. As alliances go, it was double-edged: until Gian Galeazzo reached his majority in 1489, and Isabel sailed up the Tyrrhenian Sea to join him, Naples would be a firm supporter of Milan and its Regent; Il Moro faced a much tougher struggle to cling to power once a Neapolitan princess had been dispatched to Milan expecting to be acclaimed its rightful Duchess.

On 24 November 1488 a modest sixteen-man Milanese embassy left Genoa for Naples to fetch Isabel.[48] She returned with a hefty dowry and a battalion of 400 people transported by a mini-armada of eleven ships, landing at Genoa on 18 January 1489 after a stormy three-week voyage (necessitating a four-day stop in Leghorn). She brought with her an elaborately braided ponytail of Spanish origin, the *coazzone*, that would remain the official female hairstyle of the Sforza court for the next ten years.

Isabel was officially welcomed to Milanese territory by Leonardo da Vinci's giant Moor-on-Horseback automaton[49] at Tortona a week later, ahead of the marriage ceremony in Milan.[50] Yet the main wedding festivities – the *Festa del Paradiso* orchestrated by Leonardo – were postponed for one whole year, until 13 January 1490.

The delay was ostensibly to respect a period of mourning for Isabel's late mother (and Il Moro's elder sister) Ippolita, who had died in August 1488. In the event, the *Festa* was staged just days after the *promessa di matrimonio* (betrothal) between Il Moro's daughter Bianca and Galeazzo Sanseverino.

BERGOGNONE AT THE CERTOSA DI PAVIA

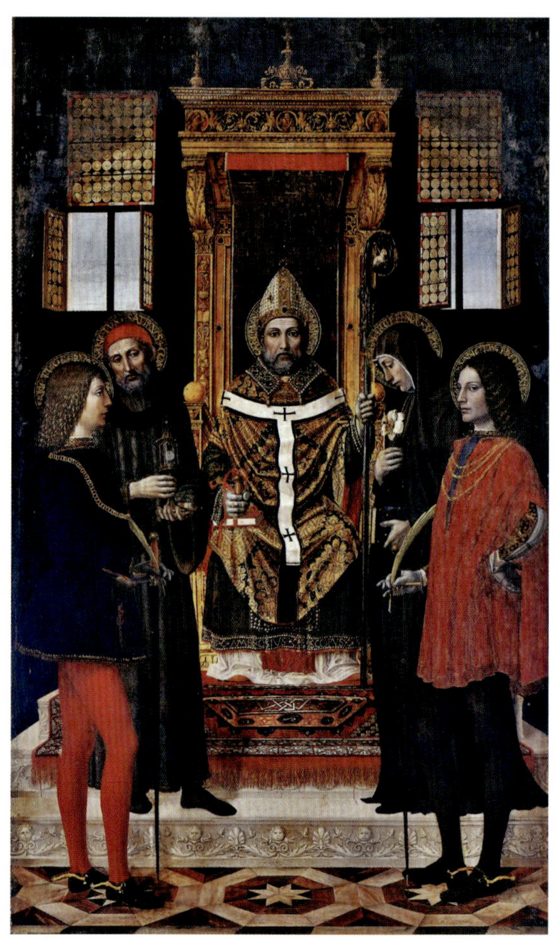

More figures from the Sforza court lurk unidentified in the Certosa di Pavia, the Carthusian monastery fifteen miles south of Milan whose giant church was conceived as a Visconti mausoleum. From 1488 until well into the 1490s, Ambrogio da Fossano (*c.*1450–*c.*1524) – known to art history as 'Bergognone'[51] – was Artist-in-Chief at the Certosa, in charge of implementing a programme of political propaganda masquerading as devotional imagery that is unique in the annals of purportedly Christian art.

His altarpiece *St Ambrose Enthroned with Saints Satirus & Marcellina and Gervasius & Protasius* (1490) in the Cappella di Sant'Ambrogio – compositionally based on Piero della Francesca's *Virgin and Child Enthroned with Four Angels* (Frick Collection) – features St Ambrose, Milan's patron saint, on a canopied throne. To the left are the standing figures of SS Satirus and Gervasius; to the right, the figures of SS Marcellina and Protasius. The figure of SS Gervasius is a portrait of Galeazzo Maria Sforza (*see above right*). This has implications for interpreting all Bergognone's work at the Certosa – starting with the identity of his martyred twin, St Protasius.

Both figures are holding a sword and palm-sprig and wearing gold spurs, but there are also significant differences. The fair-haired Gervasius is clad in funereal black and wearing a gold chain (evoking the Ducal chain of office) around his neck; the dark-haired Protasius is clad in scarlet and wearing three narrower gold chains sometimes associated with the ducal heir apparent. Gervasius is in strict, ducal profile, looking admiringly at his twin; Protasius is in three-quarter profile (with part of his right-eye visible), averting his gaze. He is surely intended to evoke Galeazzo Maria's younger brother, Il Moro, portrayed as the teenager he was when Galeazzo Maria succeeded their father Francesco in 1466.

The work's symbolism, and the identity of Protasius, may have become lost down the centuries, but will not have been lost on the Sforza court. Gervasius/Galeazzo Maria has a vacuous, slightly doltish expression; Protasius/Il Moro looks more alert and knowing, exuding quiet confidence, as if gazing into the future; he is clad in assertive, optimistic scarlet. The message: Il Moro, not Galeazzo Maria's son Gian Galeazzo, is the coming man.[52]

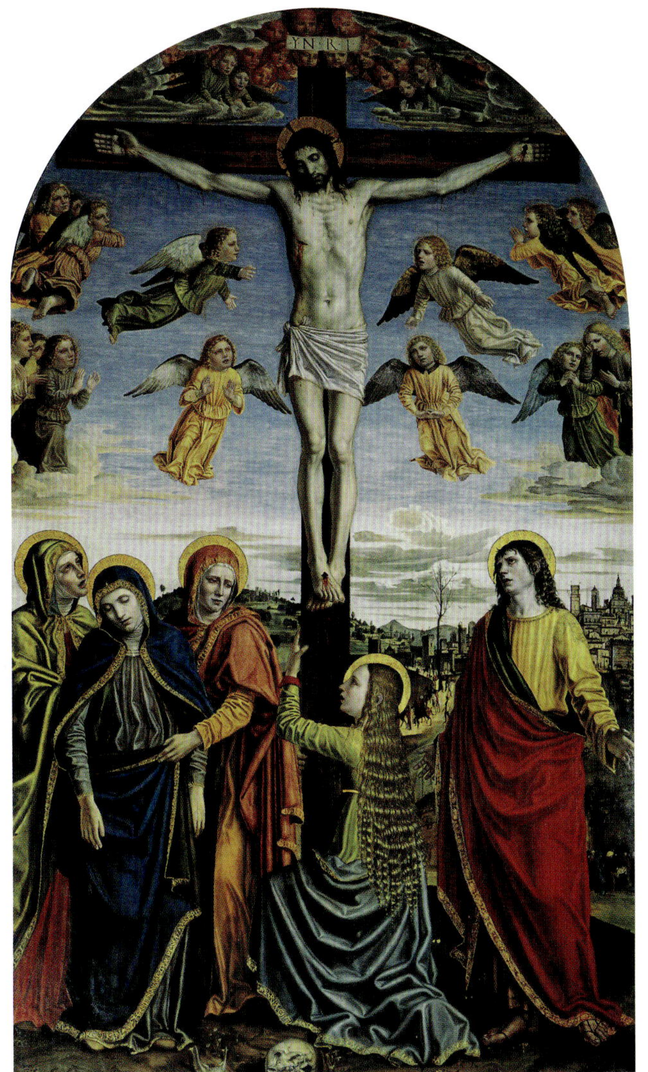

Bianca Sforza's 1490 betrothal to Galeazzo Sanseverino was celebrated through verse, on paper and in paint. Court poet Bernardo Bellincioni declared that the couple had everything (*nulla cosa a questa coppia manca*). A sumptuously illuminated manuscript extolled their common ancestor, Muzio Attendoli. Within five months of the betrothal, Bergognone completed a magnificent *Crucifixion* for the Certosa di Pavia, signed and dated *Ambrosius Fosanus pinxit 1490 Maii 14.*

Its Mary Magdalene is no seasoned harlot or repentant sinner, but a pre-pubescent girl who bears an unmistakable resemblance to the full-page portrait of *Bianca Sforza* drawn by Leonardo six years later: same domed forehead, firm jaw-line, hint of double-chin, long straw-coloured hair – and the same green-and-red clothing. Her left ear – merely outlined with the utmost subtlety in her *Sforziada* portrait[53] – emerges from beneath her hair in awkward, pixie-like fashion.

St John has the same square jaw, broad cheeks, fleshy nose, thick neck and wavy, shoulder-length, blondish hair as Leonardo's 'Musician,' and is clad in the blood-and-gold colours of the House of Aragon to which the Sanseverinos honorarily belonged.

The cross is topped by a cluster of angels clad in green, with a further fourteen angels (the same number as the putti in Birago's *bas-de-page* in the London *Sforziada* – see p.78) in green, gold and white fluttering to either side of the stricken Christ. These angels are not mere ciphers but express individual psychological reactions, ranging from awe and disbelief to shouts of dismay and tear-stained anguish. They find an echo in Birago's pioneering ability to invest putti with their own personalities.[54]

A hilly town looms in the background – a symbolic Jerusalem identifiable as Pavia by its domed cathedral then under construction. Birago's *bas-de-page* in the Polish *Sforziada*, celebrating the union of Bianca and Galeazzo, also features Pavia in the background (*see p.152*).

The composition of Bergognone's *Crucifixion* appears based on a slightly smaller fresco in the Certosa by an unknown 15th century artist. Although this features three figures (Virgin, Mary Magdalene and St John), not five, the pose of St John is almost identical – but he is clad in orange and pink rather than scarlet and gold. Scarlet is reserved for Mary Magdalene, along with pale blue; Bergognone changes the colours of both protagonists entirely.

More significantly, he alters Mary Magdalene's pose and position. In the fresco she is to the left of the cross, next to the Virgin; in Bergognone's work she is to the right, next to St John (reflecting the Bianca/Galeazzo association), and the green of her bodice is echoed by the green lining of his red toga. Bergognone also alters the angle of her head so as to portray her (somewhat awkwardly) in the profiled position obligatory for portraits of Sforza family members.

The same profile as her portrait by Leonardo in the Polish *Sforziada*.

NOTES

1 The Poldi Pezzoli Museum catalogue entry reads: '*Pittore Lombardo del XV Secolo:* Ludovico il Moro a letto invoca la Madonna con il Bambino *(c.1490), tempera on panel 40 × 50cm, entered museum 1883 (inv. 1636)*' and notes that the bedroom window looks out over a landscape that '*has a feel of Leonardo.*'

2 Diplomatic reports addressed from Milan to Francesco Gonzaga, Duke of Mantua, as cited in *Carteggio degli Oratori Mantovani, vol. XIV (1485–94), ed. Marzia de Luca.*

3 Bernardino Corio, *Patria Historia* (1503).

4 Il Moro's uneasy relationship with his ambitious younger brother Ascanio had seen the latter banished to Ferrara shortly after Il Moro's return to Milan in 1479. In Autumn 1487, with Il Moro rumoured to be on his deathbed, Ascanio galloped back from Rome with an eye on his succession: small wonder Il Moro refused to help him become Archbishop of Milan in 1488. Their brotherly rift was later glossed over, given the importance to Il Moro of having his brother Cardinal as his eyes and ears in the Vatican, but Il Moro remained wary – refusing to entrust the Castello Sforzesco to Ascanio's custody when he fled to Austria in 1499.

5 Broadly speaking, Guelphs favoured the Pope, Ghibellines the Holy Roman Emperor.

6 The *scopetta* (sometimes translated as *whisk-broom*) is thought to have been devised by Francesco Sforza, and is also occasionally referred to as a *scovino.*

7 All told, eight candidates with a stronger claim to the Duchy conveniently died, were murdered, or found themselves elbowed aside before Ludovico attained full power. It was a sequence worthy of *Kind Hearts And Coronets.*

8 Sforza Maria was made Duke of Bari by King Ferrante of Naples in 1464.

9 In Summer 1496 Isabella d'Este would write to Barone, the court jester in Milan, asking him to find out how 'Messer Galeazzo and others who, like him, are the glass of fashion, manage to dye their hair black on certain occasions, and afterwards resume the natural colour of their locks.' One suspects they were just imitating Il Moro, Dyemaster-in-Chief. The Sforzas were a family of blonds. They veered no darker than chestnut.

10 Massimo Elli, in *Leonardo da Vinci, Orene e Il Libro dell'Amadio* (Lion's Club of Vimercate, undated), claims that Il Moro was conceived while Francesco Sforza was away from Milan campaigning against the Venetians – and speculates that his likely father was a 'Franciscan friar, Amadeus Menez de Silva' (known as the 'Blessed Amadeo'), who 'made his appearance in Milan around the end of 1451.' Elli is led to this outlandish conclusion because 'it can only be assumed that Amadeus's complexion was dark since he was born in Morocco of a Moroccan father.' To some sources, Amadeus was born in Ceuta on the North African coast, then owned by Portugal; to others, in Camp Maior, Portugal. His 'African' father – admits Elli elsewhere – was actually 'a very rich prince of the Royal House of Castille.'

11 'Egli fu piu tosto d'una carnagione bianca e pallida che nero, come abbiamo veduto d'appresso' – Paolo Giovio (1483–1552), *Dialogo dell'Imprese Militari et Amorose.*

12 *Codice Sforza* – Biblioteca Reale, Turin (*Varia 75*).

13 Constance J. Moffat (*Heraldic Imagery at the Sforza Court in the 1490s*, University of California 1986) claims that the mulberry tree was originally the emblem of Il Moro's elder brother Sforza Maria (1451–79), but provides no evidence for this intriguing assertion.

14 This rivalry took a bookish turn with the Florentine *editio princeps* of the *Complete Works* of Homer in 1489 – complete with a full-page portrait of Lorenzo de' Medici's eldest son and heir Piero by Gherardo di Giovanni del Fora, who also worked for Matthias Corvinus ... to whom Il Moro was about to ally himself by marriage.

15 Il Moro was aping his father Francesco, who had hired the Florentine Filarete (*c.*1400–69) as his main architect in the 1450s; apart from remodelling the Castello Sforzesco and designing the Ospedale Maggiore (the new city hospital), Filarete devoted a *Trattato di Architettura* to an ideal city called *Sforzinda* (whose megalomaniac name and concept anticipated Peter the Great's *St Petersburg* by 250 years); give or take a letter not two, Filarete's architectural *Sforzinda* served as titular inspiration for the literary *Sforziada*. Francesco Sforza's attitude to Florence was coloured by the fact that Cosimo de' Medici underwrote his campaign to seize the Duchy in 1450, and continued to support his early years as Duke via the Medici Bank – hence the sumptuous new premises Francesco provided for the Bank in Via dei Bossi.

16 L. Beltrami, *Documenti e Memorie riguardanti la vita e le opere di Leonardo da Vinci* (Milan, 1919).

17 San Francesco Grande suffered a partial collapse in 1688 and was demolished in the late 18th century.

18 Nadia Covini, *Zanette e Cicilia: Potere, Sangue e Passioni nella Milano di Ludovico Il Moro* (*Vigevanum* – Società Storica Vigevanese, May 2011).

19 Anonimo Gaddiano (Biblioteca Nazionale Centrale di Firenze, Cod. Magliab. XVII).

20 Sabba da Castiglione, Ricordi (Venice, 1554).

21 Giorgio Vasari, *Le Vite dei Più Eccellenti Pittori, Scultori e Architetti*.

22 Pietro C. Marani, *Leonardo da Vinci – The Complete Paintings* (Harry N. Abrams, Inc., New York 2003).

23 Cited by Martin Kemp in *Leonardo* (Oxford University Press, 2004).

24 Quoted in Malaguzzi Valeri, *La Corte di Lodovico Il Moro* (Milan, 1913–23).

25 Despatches of Ambassador Trotti preserved in the Archivio di Stato di Modena.

26 Alessandro Giulini, *Bianca Sanseverino Sforza figlia di Lodovico il Moro* (Giornale della Società Storica Lombarda, 1912).

27 *Pietro Bosca*, De Origine et Statu Bibliothecae Ambroisanae Hemidecas.

28 The likeliest reason for the music-sheet's obliteration is that it identified the sitter to its contemporary audience, and that the portrait came into the possession of someone who did not want that identification acknowledged or perpetuated. The portrait may have been acquired and mutilated by the French mercenary general Gian Giacomo Trivulzio when he took possession of Galeazzo

Sanseverino's palazzo in Vigevano in 1499. Similar mutilations, also attributable to Trivulzio, affected the Uffizi *Sforziada* and the Sala della Asse in Milan's Castello Sforzesco.

29 And also in Hungary – yet more evidence of the Milan-Hungary cultural axis (*cf* the London *Sforziada*).

30 This did not prevent the idea being propounded by Luke Syson in the catalogue of the *Leonardo* exhibition at the National Gallery in London in 2011.

31 The portrait was originally displayed above Rudolf's tomb in the Stephansdom and is now in the Vienna Dommuseum.

32 The Dunstaple passage to which Renard refers reads [A / G/ A] dotted B – F – E – D long – G – A.

33 The Golden Ratio is attained when a line is divided into two parts, with the figure obtained by dividing the length of longer section by the length of the smaller section corresponding to the total length divided by the length of the longer section. Its value is 1.618033989, approximately.

34 Archangel Uriel is known as 'Regent of the Sun' in Milton's *Paradise Lost*.

35 Pierangelo Laurora, *Il Musico di Leonardo: Una Identità Svelata* (2004). Laurora claims that contemporary documents refer to the existence of a portrait of Galeazzo Sanseverino – in a red hat *dal portamento signorile, dall'aspetto affascinante* (of lordly demeanour and charming appearance) with *capelli ricci* (curly hair) – in his palazzo in Vigevano.

36 Totti's image of Roberto was reproduced with the same identity by Claudio Rendina in *I Capitani di Ventura* (Newton Compton, Rome 1985).

37 Totti cites Andrea Baiano's *Panegirico del Zamośći* among the 80 works in his bibliography (along with the *Sforziade del Simonetta*).

38 According to Roberto's diary, he left Milan on 30 April 1458, travelling by horse to Pavia then by boat down the Ticino and Adige to Choggia, crossing the lagoon to Venice on May 7 and remaining there for nine days, attending the Feast of Ascension (May 11) celebrations. The voyage to Jaffa included stops at Dubrovnik, Durazzo (June 2/3 at St Dominic monastery, where he learnt that Alfonso I of Naples was dead; that the people of Trani and Barletta in Apulia had revolted; and that the Turks were mustering a big army to attack Skanderbeg at Kruje), Methoni, Iraklion, Rhodes and Cyprus. He travelled by donkey to Jerusalem, then by foot/camel to Cairo via Mount Sinai, by donkey back to Jerusalem and then Acre, where he boarded a ship on October 12, stopping on the islands of Milos and Sapienza before landing back in Italy, at Ancona, on December 25 and making a pilgrimage to nearby Loretto.

39 Padua historian Giandomenico Spazzarini (1429–1515) even likened Roberto to the Emperor of Italy (*Robertus totius Italiae imperator*).

40 Visconti's palazzo was later owned by the Panigarola family responsible for donating the Leonardesco *paliotto* to Santa Maria sopra Varese.

41 Ficino, *Divini Platonis Omnia Opera* (Basel, 1561).

42 C. Pedretti, *Leonardo da Vinci on Painting – A Lost Book* (1964), pp.252–59.

43 Marsilio Ficino, *Commentarium in Convivium Platonis de Amore* (1469).

44 Charles Nicholl, *Leonardo da Vinci* (Penguin Books, London 2007).

45 Malaguzzi Valeri, *op. cit.* Bernardino Luini (*c.*1480–1532) was born in Dumenza near Luino on Lake Maggiore and trained with Leonardo in Milan during Leonardo's second stay in the city (1506–13).

46 Constance Moffat & Sara Taglialagamba (eds), *Illuminating Leonardo: A Festschrift for Carlo Pedretti Celebrating His 70 Years of Scholarship* (Brill, Leiden/Boston 2016).

47 *Three Men with a Woman Holding a Cat*, oil on panel 43 × 61cm, offered at Sotheby's New York on 26 January 2012 (lot 17) as *Property of the Lise Haas Trust*, but unsold against an estimate of $150,000–200,000.

48 Isabel of Aragon brought with her a dowry of 80,000 gold ducats, although Il Moro accused the Neapolitans of sending fake coins.

49 This automaton, placed on Tortona's main square, was described in contemporary accounts as *una gigantesca statua equestre con la testa di un moro armata di scudo e scimitarra che, al passaggio della sposa, si scopre e saluta con un inchino.*

50 Isabel of Aragon was spurned on her wedding night (28 January 1489), and she and her husband Gian Galeazzo ridiculed by Il Moro; their marriage was not consummated for another fifteen months.

51 Bergognone's earliest known works date from around 1480. After a period of near-monopoly at the Certosa of Pavia, he moved to nearby Milan in the mid-1490s. From 1500 he appears to have worked in Lodi and Bergamo as well. In 1514 he returned briefly to the Certosa di Pavia, producing a frescoed *Madonna del Latte* for the refectory, and lunettes with half-length figures of Apostles. His last documented work (now in the Brera) is an *Assumption* from 1522, featuring Lake Maggiore and the Visconti/Sforza Castle of Angera.

52 An earlier instance of Il Moro using art to figuratively (if not physically) obliterate the memory of Galeazzo Maria was the decoration he commissioned for the Castello Sforzesca's hall of ceremonies, just prior to his wedding to Beatrice d'Este in January 1491 – when frescoes painted for Galeazzo Maria in the 1470s, extolling his rôle in Sforza/Milanese history, were replaced by paintings of victories and memorable deeds of Francesco Sforza, beneath a ceiling spangled with gold stars on a blue background. The image of Francesco Sforza on horseback, under a triumphal arch, greeted visitors as they entered the hall.

53 As pointed out by Martin Kemp in *La Bella Principessa – The Story of the New Masterpiece by Leonardo da Vinci* (with Pascal Cotte; Hodder & Stoughton, London 2010).

54 Mark Evans, *New Light on the Sforziada Frontispieces of Gianpietro Birago* (British Library Journal Vol. 13 n°2, Autumn 1987).

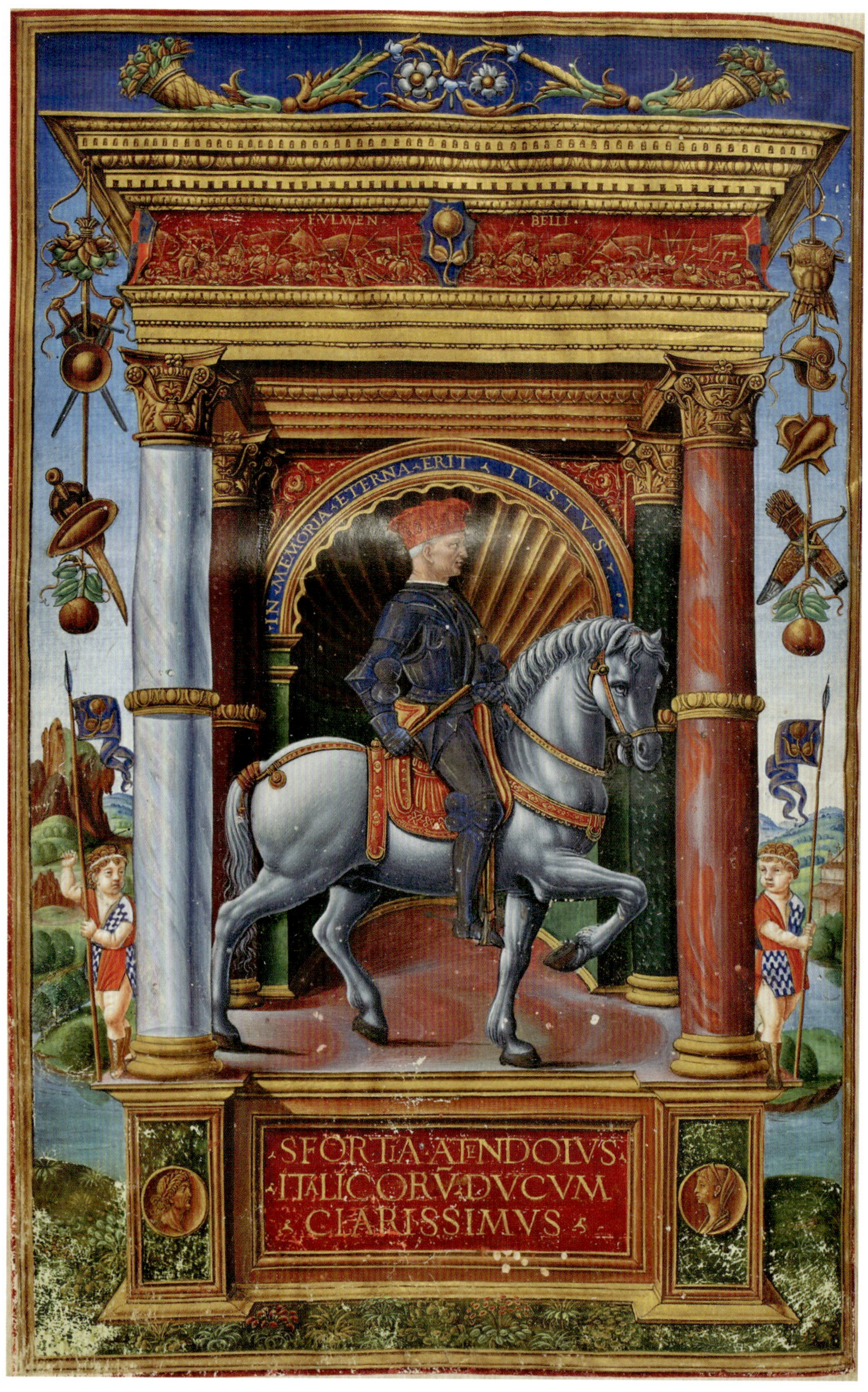

VITA DI MUZIO DEGLI ATTENDOLI (FOL. 4v) – BIBLIOTHEQUE NATIONALE DE FRANCE (MS ITAL. 372)

II

GREAT GRANDFATHER

MUZIO ATTENDOLO: COMMON ANCESTOR

HARD ON THE HEELS of Bianca's betrothal came the production of a de luxe manuscript biography of Francesco Sforza's father Muzio Attendolo, entitled *Compendio dei Gesti del Magnanimo et Gloriosissimo Signore Sforza* and drafted back in the 1450s by Milanese court official Antonio de' Minuti. What prompted its sudden re-emergence over thirty years later?

PROVENANCE

1491 Ducal Library, Pavia
1499 Bibliothèque du Roi, Blois (later Fontainebleau, Paris)
1792 Bibliothèque Nationale, Paris

MUZIO ATTENDOLO

Muzio Attendolo Sforza (1369–1424), the *condottiero* founder of the Sforza dynasty, was born in Cotignola – fifteen miles from the Adriatic, between Imola and Ravenna in northeast Italy – into a family of rural nobility. He was christened Giacomo, prompting the nickname *Giacomuzzo* – shortened to *Muzio*. Tradition has it that he left home to join a band of mercenaries led by Boldrino da Panicale, and later teamed up with Alberico da Barbian, who nicknamed him *Sforza* (The Strong) for his physical prowess.

Muzio fought for and against Gian Galeazzo Visconti, Duke of Milan, before being hired by Niccolo III d'Este. In 1409 he was made *Gran Conestabile* to King Ladislao of Naples and would remain in Neapolitan service for the rest of his life, latterly under Ladislao's sister, Giovanna II – who, in 1417, sent him (and his sixteen-year-old son Francesco) to help the Pope fight the Central Italian warlord Braccio da Montone.

In 1424 Muzio was dispatched to quell a rebellion at L'Aquila, 75 miles inland from Rome, and is said to have drowned in the River Pescara trying to rescue one of his men.

Muzio married three times and had seventeen children, the first nine out of wedlock – including Francesco (1401–66), the future Duke of Milan, and his sister Elisa (1402–76), who married Leonetto Sanseverino in 1412. Both Muzio's son and grandson paid tribute to their Cotignola roots upon becoming Dukes of Milan – and not just by punningly adopting the quince (*cotogna*) as one of their heraldic emblems. In 1451 Francesco Sforza launched a Lent festival in Cotignola, known as the *Segavecchia* (climaxing in a masked parade commemorating the beheading of a local witch) and staged to this day. In 1494 Il Moro elevated Cotignola – never more than a small town (current population 7,500) – to the illustrious status of *città* (city) after the defeat of Neapolitan troops at neighbouring Mordano, in a battle of watershed significance to Italian history.

Cotignola's late-14th century Palazzo Sforza (*right*) was destroyed in World War II. It has since been rebuilt and hosts the town museum.

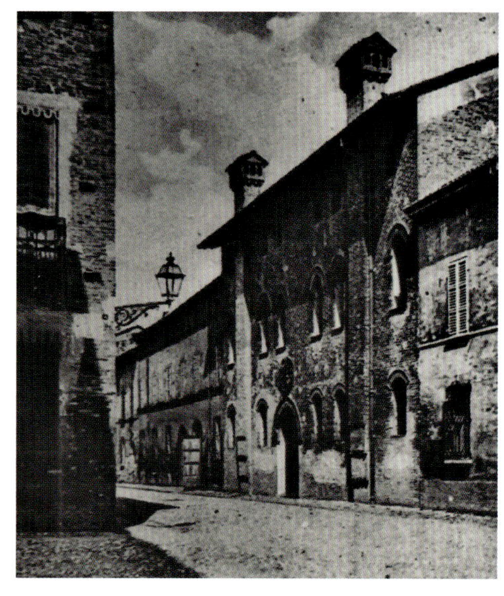

ANTONIO DE' MINUTI

Antonio de' Minuti (*c.*1400–70), also known as Antonio Placentino (*of Piacenza*), served under Muzio Attendolo, then wrote about him while a senior official in the chancellery of his son Francesco. The Muzio biography De' Minuti wrote in the 1450s was never published – but three manuscript versions were produced between 1490–92.

The first (*right*), completed on 10 June 1490 by the scribe Elia del Pozzo, is now in Milan (Biblioteca Trivulziana *142*). The second, richly illuminated, was completed on 20 September 1491 by scribe Bartolomeo Gambagnola of Cremona, and is now in Paris (Bibliothèque Nationale *ital. 372*). The third, completed on 24 July 1492 by scribe Julia Sforza, is now in Wrocław (Biblioteka Uniwersytecka, *Rehdigeranus 299*).[1]

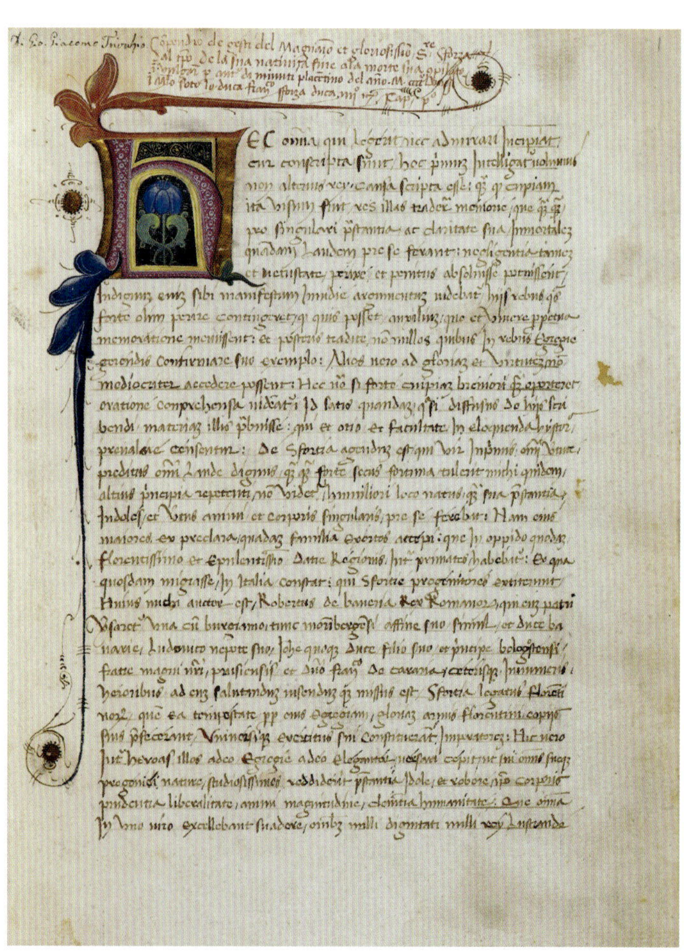

Why did Il Moro suddenly resurrect De' Minuti's forgotten manuscript about his grandfather?

Surely because Muzio's daughter, like Il Moro's, married a Sanseverino. And Muzio was the great-grandfather of both Bianca Sforza and Galeazzo Sanseverino.

THE PARIS MANUSCRIPT

The manuscript now in Paris, completed in September 1491, is exceptionally luxurious, with *three* illuminated pages: a full-page miniature of Muzio on horseback beneath a triumphal arch; and two frontispieces with text and borders with a similar layout to the four *Sforziada* frontispieces illuminated by Birago.

This 114*ff*, 33 × 22cm vellum manuscript was commissioned by Ducal Secretary Marchesino Stanga. Its colophon dates completion as *Die vigesimo septebris MCCCCLXXXX primo*[2] and its lavish illuminations will have been many months in the making.

FULL-PAGE MINIATURE

The full-page miniature of Muzio, with no body of text, has no parallel in any of the four *Sforziadas* – and is echoed only by the illuminated Latin *Sforziada* intended for Emperor Maximilian (*see p.194*).

The anonymous miniature features a white-haired Muzio in a red cap, wearing black armour similar to that worn by Il Moro in his portrait by Ambrogio de Predis for the *Donatus Grammatica* (*see p.217*).

Muzio rides a splendidly rendered grey charger with a red and gold saddle, evoking the giant horse being designed by Leonardo da Vinci as a monument to Muzio's son Francesco Sforza.

Muzio's charger also recalls the equine statue of Marcus Aurelius in Rome 'upon which Leonardo finally settled' around 1490 as the model for his Sforza monument, according to Martin Kemp, who calls the horse's pose 'ceremonial' and likens it to a 'high-stepping walk.'[3]

This image of Muzio – of whom no contemporary portrait is known (his 'Giovio' portrait in the Uffizi is posthumous) – also evokes Paulo Uccello's fresco of English mercenary Sir John Hawkwood (*c.*1323–94) in the Florentine church of Santa Maria del Fiore (*below*). Hawkwood – known in Italy as Giovanni Acuto – was made Lord of Cotignola by Pope Gregory XI in 1372, and left his mark on the town with a mighty tower, the *Torre Acuto*, rebuilt after World War II (*see right*).

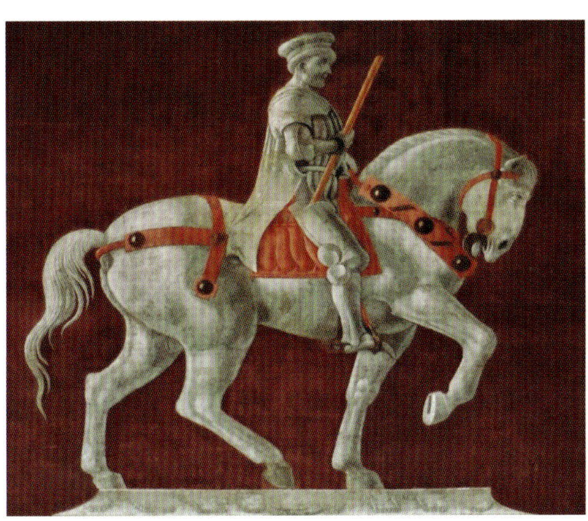

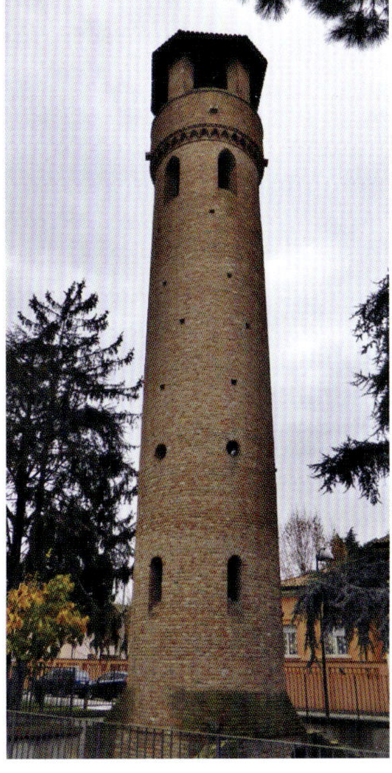

Muzio appears in the frontispiece within a grandiose triumphal arch with Ionic corner columns in different-coloured marble (speckled brown and black behind, veined white and porphyry-red to the front), each with a gadrooned gold band halfway up. The columns support a heavy cornice with gold-on-red battle scenes around a central gold quince and the motto **FULMEN BELLI** (roughly, *Blitzkrieg*), with a quartered Milanese shield in each corner. The cornice is topped by a massive architrave, itself topped by two horns of plenty ending in floral scrolls.

The back of the archway features a recess or alcove in the form of a large scallop, of the type common in the Renaissance in a religious context – most famously, perhaps, in Piero della Francesca's *Montefeltro Altarpiece* (1472–74), and used repeatedly by Bramante in the late 1480s at San Satiro Milan. The alcove is ringed by a semi-circular inscription reading **IN MEMORIA ETERNA ERIT IUSTUS** (*The Righteous Shall be Remembered Forever*).

The plinth at the foot of the monument bears another inscription, in gold letters on a red ground, reading **SFORTIA ATENDOLUS ITALICORU DUCUM CLARISSIMUS** (*Attendolo Sforza – Most Illustrious of Italian Dukes*). The inscription is flanked by a profiled, laurel-wreathed male medallion to the left, and a profiled female medallion to the right.

Two bare-legged infant standard-bearers stand to either side of the arch, sporting white headbands, boots, and jackets with Milanese livery of quartered red and blue/white wave-pattern; the one on the left wears toe-less boots, the one on the right has normal ones. They are set against a verdant background of river, fields, trees and mountains, with part of a church visible bottom right. The infants' banners (gold quinces on a blue ground) point up towards a series of golden military trophies (shields, swords, breastplate, helmet, bow and arrows) that dangle from the cornice and end in a leafy-topped quince. The same trophies would be re-quoted in the Polish *Sforziada* (*see p.152*).

Muzio's profile recalls the style of Ambrogio de Predis. The foreground is of dark green grass, not unlike that of the *bas-de-page* in the first illuminated (London) *Sforziada*, but additionally studded with wild flowers – some strikingly similar to those in the first (Louvre) version of the *Virgin of the Rocks*, upon which Ambrogio worked with Leonardo da Vinci.

FIRST FRONTISPIECE

The first of the frontispieces (*folio 1r*) contains the start of the text, citing the year 1397 in connection with Ruprecht III of Bavaria (1352–1410), King of the Romans:

> *Inicium et origo generationis magnanimi et prestantissismi viri domini Sfortie de Attendolis de Cotognola repertum per serenissimum principem dom. Robertus de Bavaria, Romanorum Regem in Padua ano domini MCCCLXXXXVII.*

> ('At the start and origin of the dynasty was Lord Attendolus Sforza of Cotognola, a great and accomplished man remarked upon by the Most Serene Prince Ruprecht of Bavaria, King of the Romans, in Padua in 1397.')

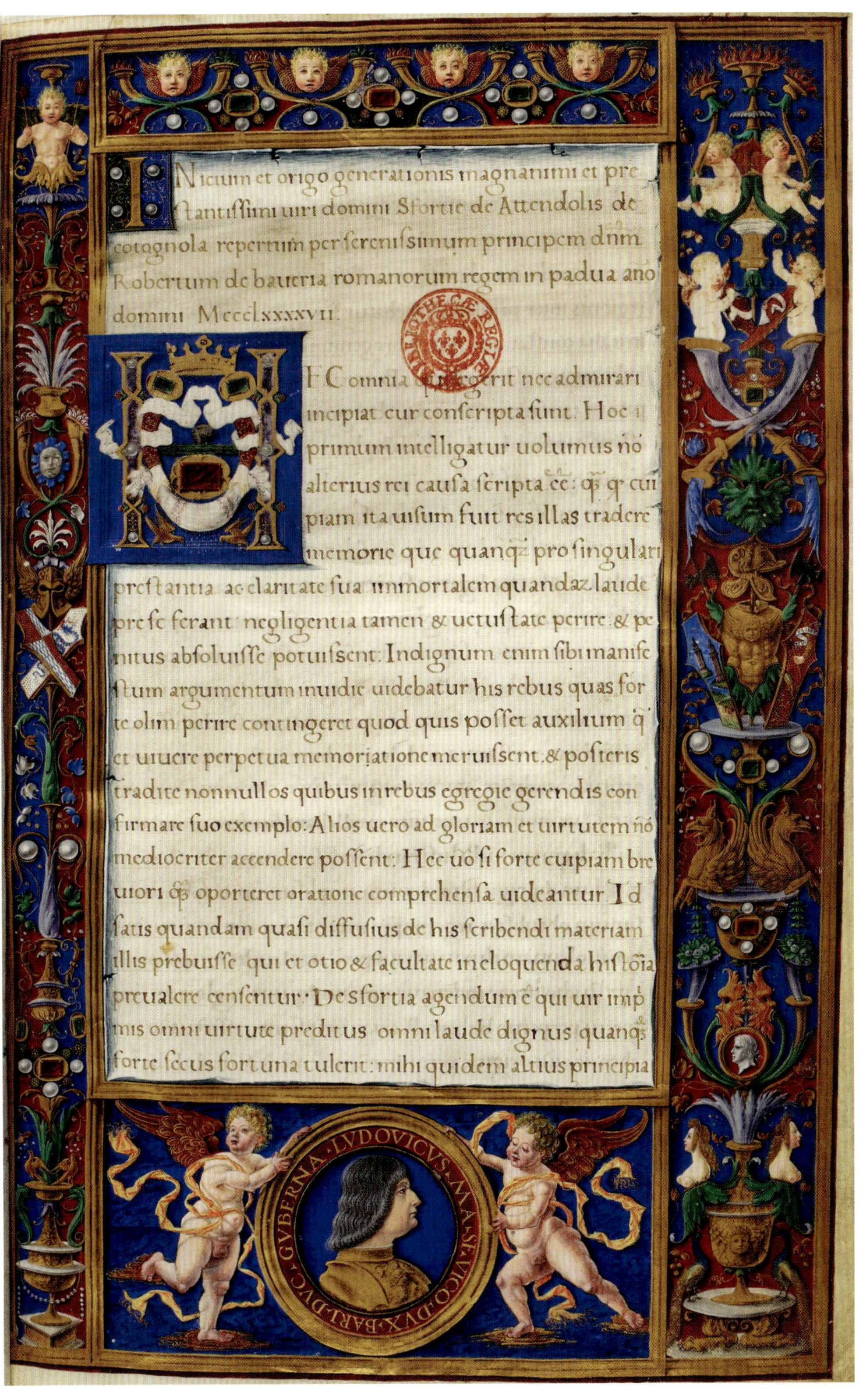

VITA DI MUZIO DEGLI ATTENDOLI (FOL. 1r) – BIBLIOTHEQUE NATIONALE DE FRANCE (MS ITAL. 372)

The place occupied by a square profile medallion in the other frontispiece (and illuminated *Sforziadas*) is occupied by an elaborate, crown-topped illuminated initial incorporating the sifting-cloth device associated with matrimonial alliance, with sifted grain falling through it and being pecked at by two birds (*see right*).

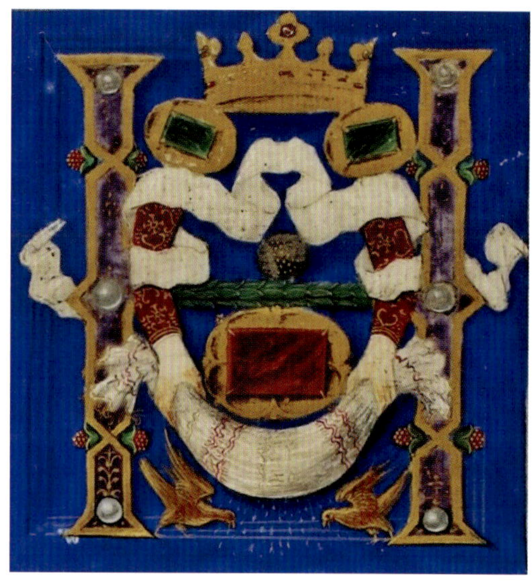

HAUT-DE-PAGE

The preface features four winged cherub-heads framed by crossed, curved, flaming torches, separated by precious stones (emerald–ruby–emerald) surrounded by four white pearls on alternating red/blue/green grounds. This cherub-head arrangement is common in Renaissance iconography, but it may be significant that the arrangement here recalls the cornice in Ghirlandaio's *Birth of Mary* fresco in the Tornabuoni Chapel (Santa Maria Novella, Florence) – although the latter (dating from 1486–90) has swags between the heads instead of torches.

BAS-DE-PAGE

A large roundel, of the type to feature in the right-hand border of three of the four illuminated *Sforziadas*, is flanked by two naked winged angels festooned with ribbons, set against a ground of an identical blue to that used inside the roundel. This portrays a grey-haired Il Moro in a prestigious gold breastplate, facing right as he does on Milanese coinage (his roundel portraits in the *Sforziadas* show him facing left). This skilful portrait looks like the work of Ambrogio de Predis. Unlike the roundels in the first two illuminated *Sforziadas*, which have no inscription, the one here is inscribed around the rim, in coin-like fashion, ***LUDOVICO MA VICO DUX BARI DUC GUBERNA***. This image is, in fact, an exact copy – with identical inscription (specifying Il Moro's status as Milan's *Governor* or Regent) – of a medal minted to commemorate Il Moro's recapture of Genoa in 1488. Genoa's twin-lighthouse emblem appears in a shield in the right-hand border of this page, and Genoa was one of the principal subjects of Birago's frontispiece in the London *Sforziada*. The image on Il Moro's breastplate has yet to be definitively identified; it appears to portray a classically attired figure of indeterminate gender – possibly Minerva, the Roman Goddess of Wisdom.

RIGHT BORDER

Divided into ten horizontal red and blue bands. Showing, from the bottom up: a gold urn on a low, circular table with clawed feet, flanked by two peacocks (*red ground*); two profiled, topless females with long blond hair (*blue ground*); gold leaves (*red ground*); two golden leaf-masks above a small red medallion with white male antique profile, flanked by gold and lilac horns of plenty whence foliage emerges to either side of a ruby/pearl cluster (*blue ground*); two gold gryphons (*red ground*); emerald/pearl cluster flanked by gold ribbons (*blue ground*); gold breastplate and helmet, flanked by two axes and two shields, the one on the left with the towers of Genoa, that on the right with the axe and log emblem (*red ground*); green leaf-mask (*blue ground*); two gilt-rimmed lilac horns (*red ground*), each bearing a winged cherub holding a shield (one with the sifter emblem, the other with a scopetta) beneath a flaming gold torch, with winged cherubs either side each holding another flaming torch (*blue ground*).

LEFT BORDER

The unusually complicated ground is divided into five sections: *blue/red* at the bottom, with dove-topped fountain; *red/blue* with emeralds, ruby and pearls, and tiered urn; *blue/red* with leaves, two pearls and slender stem with green and unusual lilac-coloured foliage, topped by a gold winged helmet above crossed shields (a combination that will recur in the Polish *Sforziada*), one shield with a viper, the other with red/wave-pattern quarters. Given that *galea* is Latin for helmet, the presence of a gold helmet in both borders may be a reference to the name *Galeazzo*[4] – and therefore to Il Moro's new son-in-law, Galeazzo San-severino. Finally, reading upwards, comes a *plain red* ground with blue-framed flower mask beneath an urn with lilac foliage; then a *plain blue* ground with naked cherub cut off at the waist, which dissolves into a leafy skirt.

SECOND FRONTISPIECE

The second illuminated frontispiece (*folio 5r*) faces Muzio's full-page miniature and contains two wadges of text. The upper section, in capital letters, specifies that the book is a *compendium* of the doings of the *Magnanimo et Gloriosissimo* Lord Sforza from cradle to grave, and was written [i.e. completed] in the vulgate by Antonio Placentino in Milan in 1458, under the reign of its fourth duke, *Francesco Sforzia* [*sic*]. The lower section sees the start of Placentino's text.

HAUT-DE-PAGE

A central, circular medallion with a profiled young Moor (facing left), wearing a white bandeau and red shirt with green collar, is flanked (to the left) by two hands holding another sifting-cloth and the bannered inscription *TAL A TI QUAL A MI* (*To You As To Me*); and (to the right) by a hand wielding an axe at a log, and the bannered inscription *TUTO EL TORTO VA IN* (roughly, *All Wrongs Will Be Righted*). The axe-and-log emblem is often associated with Muzio Attendoli – evoking his supposed origins as a woodcutter (legend has it that, when invited to join a band of travelling mercenaries, he hurled his axe at a nearby oak-tree, exclaiming 'If it stays in, off I go!').[5]

BAS-DE-PAGE

A coat of arms is shown on a grassy riverbank with trees and stones, flanked by gold-winged putti wearing no chains. Distant blue mountains rise against a pale blue sky. Two of the putti are positioned either side of the shield and are hoisting it on to a wooden support. The other two, at either end of the image,

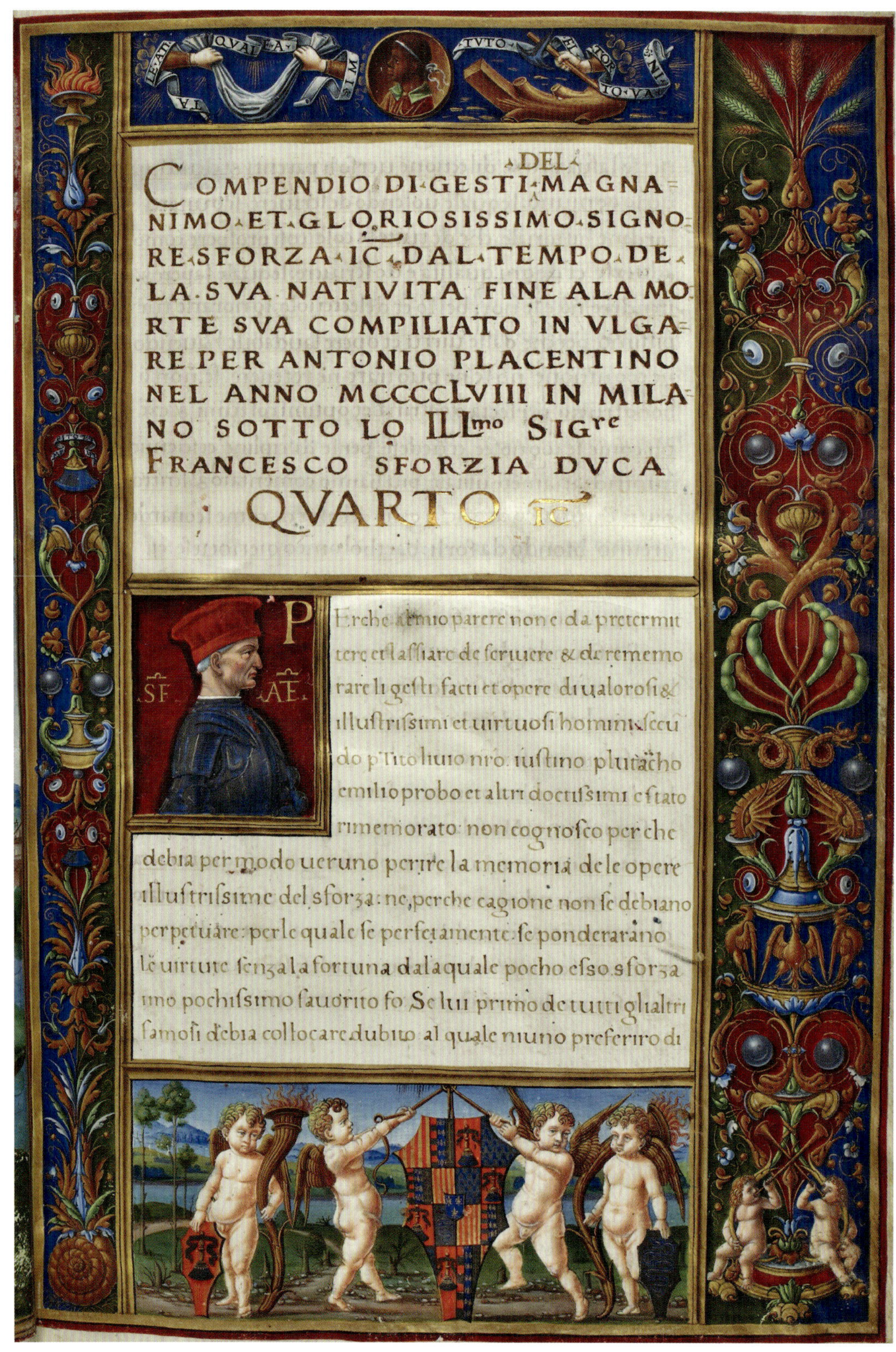

VITA DI MUZIO DEGLI ATTENDOLI (FOL. 5r) – BIBLIOTHEQUE NATIONALE DE FRANCE (MS ITAL. 372)

support blazing horns of plenty over their shoulders and are propping up two smaller shields: one with Il Moro's *scopetta* device (to the left), the other with the Visconti/Sforza viper (to the right).

The main coat of arms here warrants close consideration, as it appears not to have been used anywhere else. It strongly resembles the shield used by Il Moro as Duke of Bari (complete with escutcheoned *fleurs-de-lys*) – as found in the London and Uffizi *Sforziada* frontispieces, on the *Cassone dei Tre Duchi*, and sculpted as a marble roundel now in the Castello Sforzesco. Yet it is not quite the same. Il Moro's usual Bari arms are divided into eight, with two segments devoted to each of the *scopetta*, wave-pattern, viper, and arms of Naples; in other words, the Naples:Milan ratio is 25:75. Here, however, the proportion is 50:50, as the shield is effectively quartered between the arms of Naples (top left/bottom right) and the Milanese wave pattern/*scopetta*.

RIGHT BORDER

Green/blue halved, again with red ground for central motifs. Topped by nine ears of alternating ripe and unripe barley. The main decoration takes the form of a tiered fountain with two trumpeting cherubs at the base beneath two large black pearls; a frieze of three birds (phoenixes?) with outstretched wings; and two winged dragons.

LEFT BORDER

Blue/green halved, with red ground for central motifs. Left column topped by a flaming torch; twice features the *scopetta* (little broom) emblem – once separately, ringed by a banner with the motto *MERITO ET TEMPORE*; once in a smaller version further down. There is a spiralling shell at the foot of the column. Black pearls, scrolls and foliage complete the decoration.

INITIAL MEDALLIONS

Muzio's bust from his equine portrait is reprised inside a square medallion wearing black armour and red hat on a red ground, with the gold letters *SF ATE* and an initial *P* top right introducing the first word of text (*Perche*). The awkward combination of red hat on red ground has prompted heavy shading around the profile (shading around a profiled face was a tenet of Leonardo da Vinci's artistic philosophy, reinforcing the suggestion that the profile here is the work of his associate Ambrogio de Predis). Muzio is shown here with the stereotypic features of the silver-haired patriarch, albeit one with short, straight hair, as if to distinguish him from his son Francesco – who was invariably portrayed, by Ambrogio and others, with unruly curls at the nape of his neck.

DATE

1491. The manuscript was finished by scribe Bartolomeo Gambagnola on 20 September 1491. It is probable, though not certain, that the illuminations were completed at around the same time.

INTERPRETATION

Each of the three illuminated pages appears to be by a different artist, none of them Gianpietro Birago. If Ambrogio de Predis were responsible for the three profiled medallions, that could make four artists working on one book – indicative of its prestige and importance.

The illumination shows close similarities with that of the London *Sforziada* (*see Chapter V*). It is likely that the two were done within a few months of one another, with ideas going to and fro between the artists involved and Il Moro himself – although the London *Sforziada* appears to have had the last aesthetic word, as one would expect given that it was the work of the celebrated Birago: it is compositionally more assured, artistically more vibrant, and oozes greater grandeur (*cf* the *bas-de-page*, where fourteen putti flank Il Moro's coat of arms rather than just four).

The London *Sforziada* did not, however, receive a full-page miniature – even though it contained a page near the front that would remain blank and could logically have hosted an illuminated image of the book's hero, Francesco Sforza, on horseback.

The Muzio illuminations have little of the humour that would become a hallmark of Birago's *Sforziada* work. Nor do they indulge Il Moro's taste for self-aggrandizement to anything like the same extent as the *Sforziadas* – or contain any of the domestic and international political allusions that would pepper the *Sforziada* frontispieces.

Il Moro is shown here with grey hair, in the London *Sforziada* with black – a sign that this Muzio manuscript was destined for an inner circle of ducal acquaintances aware that Il Moro's hair had turned grey in the late 1480s. In the Muzio manuscript, the Moor's head in the *haut-de-page* roundels is a profiled young boy, exuding cheerful innocence; in the London *Sforziada*, he is a hairy-chested he-man shown front-on.

It is curious that (only) the first page of this manuscript should be in Latin – presumably there is a connection here with the mention of the King of the Romans, who had the power of investiture over the Duchy of Milan.

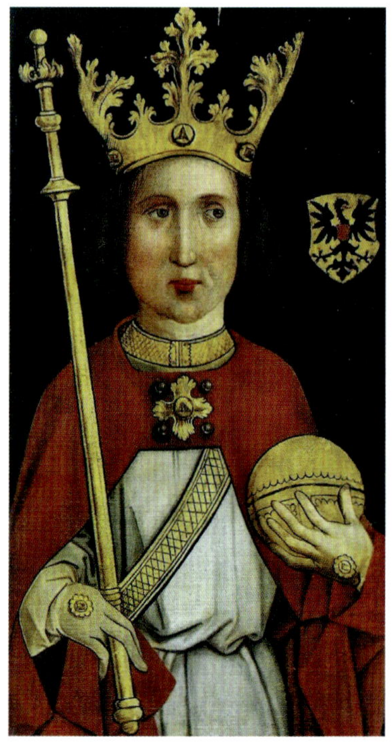

Even more intriguing is the opening mention of Ruprecht III of Bavaria (*right*), who succeeded Wenceslas of Bohemia as King of the Romans in 1400 (not by 1397, as implied in the frontispiece). It was no peaceful transition: Wenceslas was deposed (and would, in fact, outlive Ruprecht by nine years, dying in 1419). Ruprecht is mentioned here in Padua; there is evidence (an edict issued in his name) of his presence in the town on 5 April 1402, during an unsuccessful campaign to defeat Gian Galeazzo Visconti – the only Duke of Milan (prior to Il Moro in 1495) to obtain the Imperial investiture … from Wenceslas of Bohemia, in 1395. In other words, citing the rather obscure Ruprecht could be construed as something of a snub towards the Sforzas' dynastic Visconti predecessors.

Like Muzio, Galeazzo Sanseverino had no blood ties to the Viscontis. His betrothal to Il Moro's daughter Bianca propelled him into the Sforza inner circle and was surely the underlying reason for the commissioning of this manuscript – which shares several iconographic similarities with the illuminated *Sforziada* produced in 1496 to mark their marriage (*see Chapter IX*).

It may well have been deemed appropriate for Galeazzo to be associated with the Bari arms of his father-in-law: supporting this idea is the increased prominence, in this one-off 'Muzio' coat of arms, of the blood-and-gold stripes of Aragon – 50 per cent of the Sanseverino arms since 1461. The Aragon stripes are now twice as prominent as on Il Moro's regular Bari shield: here they occupy one-quarter of the shield rather than one-eighth.

HISTORY

This sumptuous volume of Sforza family history was almost certainly lodged in the Ducal Library in Pavia after its completion in 1491. The handwritten mention *de Pavye au Roy Loys XII* at the end of the book (fol. *111v*, the same page as the colophon) indicates that it was among the volumes looted by the French in 1499 and dispatched to the royal library then in Blois.

It is now in Paris, in the Bibliothèque Nationale (*MS ital. 372*), and remains the property of the French state.

NOTES

1 Gary Ianziti, *Humanistic Historiography under the Sforzas* (Oxford University Press 1988).

2 The full inscription reads *Bartholomeus Gabagnola Cremonensis scripsit: mandato Magfici domini Marchisini Stanghe: ducalis: Secretarii: Die vigesimo septebris MCCCCLXXXX primo.*

3 Martin Kemp, *Leonardo da Vinci – The Marvellous Works of Nature and Man* (Oxford University Press, 2006).

4 *cf* D.R. Edward Wright, *Ludovico Il Moro, Duke of Milan, and the Sforziada by Giovanni Simonetta in Warsaw* (2011).

5 Julia Cartwright (Mrs Henry Ady), *A History of Milan under the Sforza* (Methuen & Co, London 1907).

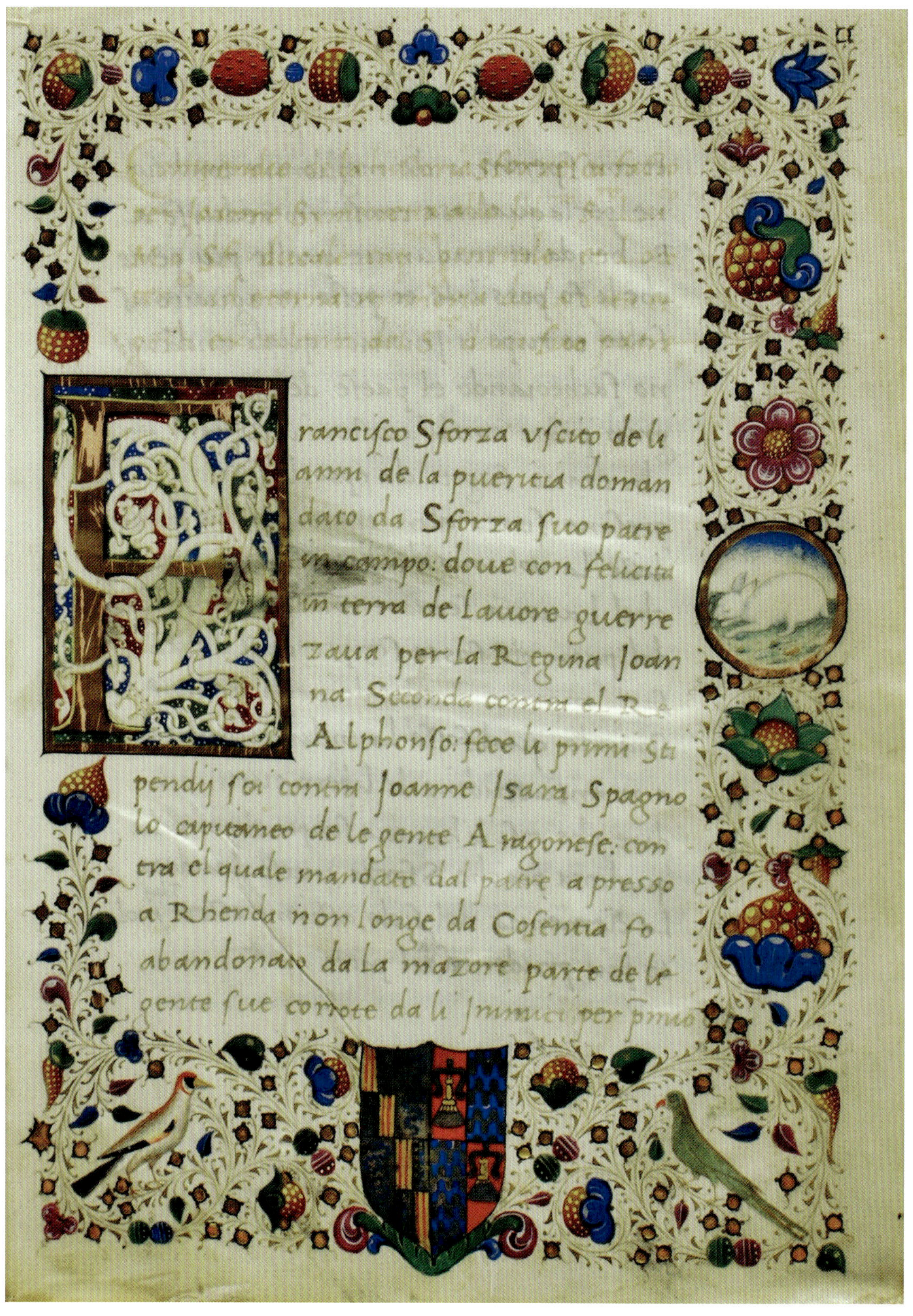

rancisco Sforza vscito de li
anni de la pueritia doman
dato da Sforza suo patre
in campo: doue con felicita
in terra de lauore guerre
zaua per la Regina Joan
na Seconda contra el R.
Alphonso: fece li primi sti
pendij soi contra Joanne Isara Spagno
lo capitaneo de le gente Aragonese: con
tra el quale mandato dal patre a presso
a Rhenda non longe da Cosentia fo
abandonato da la mazore parte de le
gente sue corrote da li Inimici per pmo

III

SHAPING THE SFORZIADA
LANGUAGE AND LAYOUT

AT THE SAME TIME as the lavish manuscript in honour of his grandfather, Il Moro's greatest literary project was nearing conclusion: the printed biography of his father Francesco, the first Sforza Duke of Milan. After two Latin editions, in 1483 and 1486, the printing of an Italian translation was set in motion in March 1490, three months after the Bianca–Sanseverino betrothal. It was to be one of the most ambitious publishing projects of the Quattrocento – including four presentation copies printed on vellum and adorned by artists of the highest renown.

FRANCESCO SFORZA

Francesco Sforza was born on 23 July 1401 in San Miniato (between Florence and Pisa), the illegitimate son of Muzio Attendolo and Lucia da Torsano. His

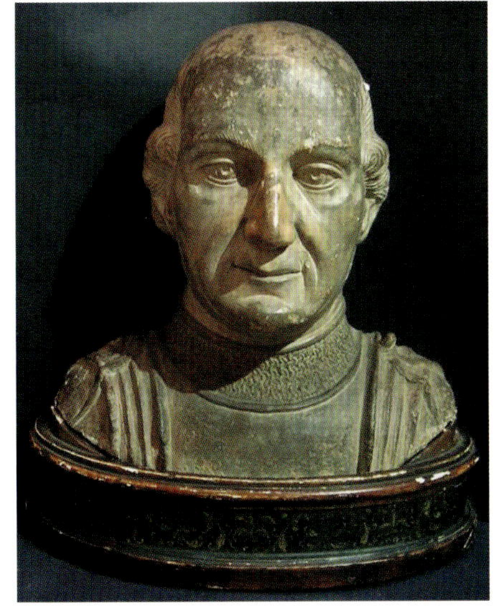

childhood was divided between the Este court in Ferarra and Tricarico, 100 miles east of Naples, of which he was made Count in 1412 by King Ladislao of Naples. In 1418 he married Polissena Ruffo (1400–20), whose mother Ceccarella was a Sanseverino, and from 1419 fought alongside his father Muzio until his death in 1424.

Subsequently – as a *condottiero* in the service of Naples, the Pope and Milan – Francesco established a precocious reputation as a cool-headed tactician and skilled commander. In 1433 he was betrothed to Bianca Maria Visconti, illegitimate daughter (and only child) of Filippo Maria, Duke of Milan. The marriage took place in Cremona, her dower town, on 25 October 1441, and produced eight children: Galeazzo Maria (1444–76), Ippolita (1446–88), Filippo Maria (1448–92), Sforza Maria (1451–79), Ludovico (1452–1508), Ascanio (1455–1505), Elisabetta (1456–72) and Ottaviano (1458–77).

Relations with his tetchy father-in-law, however, were erratic; Francesco Sforza flitted between Milan, Venice and Florence, with whose forces he helped crush Milanese troops at Anghiari on 29 June 1440 (a battle later commemorated by Leonardo da Vinci). In February 1447 Francesco was appointed *Capitano Generale* (commander-in-chief) of the Anti-Venice League (Milan, Naples and the Pope). After Filippo Maria's death, six months later, he was retained as

Captain General of Milan's new 'Ambrosian Republic' but when, in 1449, the Republic concluded a peace treaty with Venice behind his back, Francesco blockaded Milan and starved it into submission – entering the city in triumph on 26 February 1450 to be acclaimed Duke.

He proved a canny, pragmatic ruler whose most enduring legacy to Milan remains the Ospedale Maggiore, the colossal city hospital he founded in 1456; he also oversaw the rebuilding of the Castello Sforzesco. In 1464 he gained control of Genoa, a vital maritime outlet for his landlocked duchy, but failed to obtain the ducal investiture from the Holy Roman Emperor and died in Milan on 8 March 1466, aged sixty-five.

He was succeeded by his eldest son Galeazzo Maria, whose initial priority was stamping his own personality on the ducal throne by escaping his parents' shadow – especially after the sudden death of his mother Bianca Maria in 1468, for which many held him responsible. Things changed when Charles the Bold, Duke of Burgundy, met Holy Roman Emperor Friedrich III at Trier on 29 September 1473 – fuelling rumours that Charles was keen to add Milan to his possessions. Galeazzo Maria reacted by instigating negotiations with Friedrich III over the Imperial investiture. The aura and valour of his father Francesco were, along with his mother's Visconti heritage, his key arguments. Plans for an imposing monument and epic written tribute to Francesco promptly took shape.

THE SFORZA HORSE

The monument was to take the form of a giant equestrian statue. On 26 November 1473 Galeazzo Maria bade his head of public works, Bartolomeo Gadio, find a sculptor capable of producing one.[1]

Gadio proved unable to do so, but Il Moro took up the project soon after seizing power in 1480 – perhaps spurred into action by news that Venice was planning to erect a bronze equestrian statue in honour of their late Army Captain (and longtime Milanese foe) Bartolomeo Colleoni (1400–75).

The *Sforza Horse* was intended to be on the triple-lifesize scale that Antiquity reserved for the Gods,[2] and potentially the grandest and most prestigious commission to which any sculptor could aspire. Leonardo's last Florentine work, his unfinished *Adoration of the Magi*, was dotted with such a preposterous array of steeds in multifarious poses that it almost looks like a CV application.[3] Perhaps his interest in horses was also fired by his former master, Andrea del Verrocchio, who had recently applied to make the Colleoni memorial – securing the commission after a competition in 1483. Another Florentine, Antonio Pollaiolo, submitted two designs for the Sforza memorial, possibly at the bidding of Lorenzo de' Medici.[4] Both show Francesco on horseback: leaping over a city and a fallen soldier. But Pollaiolo moved to Rome in 1484 to work for the Pope, and there is no evidence that he was available for, or seriously interested in, the Milanese commission.[5]

Leonardo initially appears to have targeted military engineering as the most likely route to Milanese long-term court employment. Nine of the ten points in his undated draft 'testimonial' (or letter of self-recommendation) to Il Moro[6] concern his ability to design weapons, bridges and tunnels. It is surely no coincidence that Leonardo arrived in Milan when the Duchy was squaring up to the Republic of Venice during the War of Ferrara (1482–84).

The existence of this 'testimonial' is proof that Leonardo was not dispatched to Milan with a glowing recommendation to Il Moro from Lorenzo the Magnificent.

The testimonial *does* mention the *Sforza Horse* – but only briefly at the end, when Leonardo notes ingratiatingly that he could execute the bronze horse to 'celebrate for eternity the memory of your father and the noble house of Sforza' (*in eterno celebrerà la memoria di Vostro padre e della nobile casata degli Sforza*).

Leonardo was duly hired for the job. But the first mention of him in this capacity does not occur until 22 July 1489, in a letter to Lorenzo de' Medici from his Milanese ambassador. The *Sforza Horse* had remained on the drawing-board for most of the 1480s – until Il Moro's nephew Gian Galeazzo attained his majority and acquired a wife and, with his status as Regent no longer secure, Il Moro surged into PR overdrive.

THE *SFORZIADA*

The written tribute was to be in the form of a Francesco Sforza biography, authored – in Latin – by Giovanni Simonetta (1420–90), a senior official at the Sforza court and younger brother of the long-serving Sforza Chancellor, Francesco 'Cicco' Simonetta (1410–80). It would become known as the *Sforziada*.

Giovanni Simonetta began writing his Francesco Sforza biography – which he titled *Commentaries* to evoke Julius Caesar's famous precedent – in 1473, as part of his duties in the Ducal Chancellery. Galeazzo Maria was only appraised of the project in 1475, when it was nearing completion. According to *Sforziada* historian Gary Ianziti,[7] Simonetta drafted the text in three phases, beginning with the period he knew first hand: Francesco Sforza's rise to power and his reign as Duke (1446–66). Simonetta then attacked Francesco's early career (1420–33); and finally the years 1433–46. The two latter phases, involving archive research rather than personal recollections, appear to have taken longer to write.

The original idea of a Francesco Sforza biography, however, can be ascribed to the classical scholar Francesco Filelfo (1398–1481). After a career that took him to Venice, Constantinople, Hungary, Bologna, Florence and Siena, Filelfo settled in Milan in 1440 at the invitation of Duke Filippo Maria Visconti, later transferring allegiance to his successor Francesco Sforza. He would instill a lifelong passion for history into Francesco's teenage son Ludovico: the illuminated volume of extracts from Greek and Roman history used by the adolescent Ludovico, known as the *Codice Sforza*, survives in Turin's Biblioteca Reale (*MS*

Varia 75, page shown right). The future Il Moro is said never to have let a day go by without having passages from Ancient or Modern History read out to him.[8]

In the early 1450s Filelfo penned an epic poem about how Francesco Sforza became Duke of Milan, inspired by the *Iliad*, divided into 24 books and dubbed *La Sforziade*; only the first eight books were ever published (in 1461). Filelfo also began assembling material for a more general history *de vita et rebus gestis Francisci Sphortiæ*, which ultimately came to nothing. He clearly took a paternal interest in Simonetta's Francesco Sforza biography, congratulating him in 1476 upon the completion of his *elegantissimi commentarii*.[9] His letter would be reproduced in the printed editions of Simonetta's *Sforziada*, albeit dated 10 June 1479 – perhaps to imply that the *Sforziada* was completed just before Il Moro returned to Milan, rather than written under Duke Galeazzo Maria.

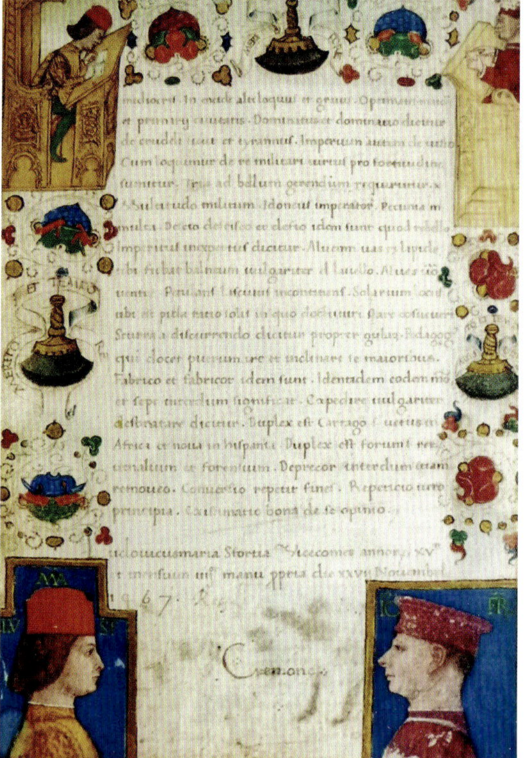

Although the *Sforziada* would owe its published existence to Il Moro, it owed him nothing in terms of its conception. Nonetheless, Il Moro lost no time in appreciating its propaganda potential after returning to Milan as Regent, poring over Simonetta's manuscript less than three weeks after ending his political exile – as we learn from a dispatch from the Mantuan Ambassador, Zaccaria Saggi, dated 29 September 1479:

> *Today I read in the room of this most illustrious Lord Ludovico ...* the Commentaries of Duke Francesco *written by Giovanni Simonetta, about which Lord Ludovico is so enthusiastic that he now wants to read a passage every day, and he began four days ago. So far [it is] the only copy of the work available, but I hope it will be printed.*[10]

Il Moro's interest may well have helped author Giovanni Simonetta escape the headless fate of his brother Cicco: Giovanni got off with temporary banishment to Vercelli on the western fringes of the Duchy. But, however much he enjoyed Simonetta's *Sforziada*, Il Moro did not rush the manuscript into print. First he passed it on to court poet Il Puteolano (*c.*1430–90) to have its narrative tweaked to suit Il Moro's political interests.

Il Puteolano, born Francesco dal Pozzo, hailed from Parma and forged his academic reputation as reader in Rhetoric & Poetry in Bologna, where he founded a printing press and produced an *editio princeps* of Ovid. In 1476 he composed the funeral ode to Galeazzo Maria Sforza and next year, at the invitation of Cicco Simonetta, moved to Milan to teach. After Simonetta's 1480 execution he gradually ingratiated himself with Il Moro, who sent him as his ambassador to Pope Innocent VIII and made him a Milanese citizen. In his preface to the first edition of the *Sforziada*, Il Puteolano gratefully extolled Il Moro's leadership qualities, noting how, 'since you have assumed such great responsibilities, you spend your days holding audiences, investigating, administering justice, moderating, setting in order, adorning the kingdom of our little king your nephew [Gian Galeazzo]'.[11]

THE TWO LATIN EDITIONS OF THE *SFORZIADA*

On 6 July 1481 Antonio Zarotto of Milan was granted a six-year ducal privilege to print 400 copies of the *Sforziada* – the first work of history, suggests Ianziti, written expressly for the printing press.[12]

It was just a decade since the first book had been printed in Milan (*De Verborum Significatione* by Festus). The first book printed in Italy was Cicero's *De Oratore*, which rolled off the press that Konrad Sweynheym and Arnold Pannartz had set up in the Benedictine monastery at Subiaco (30 miles east of Rome) in 1465.[13]

The first edition of the *Sforziada* ran to 584 pages in *quarto* format (approx. 30.5 × 22.5cm). By contemporary standards, such a page-count and print-run represented a publishing venture of Babylonian proportions.[14] The colophon indicates that printing was completed on *decimo kalendas Februarias* (January 23); Ianziti argues convincingly that the year must have been 1483. Printing must have lasted around eighteen months. The book left the presses just three months before Leonardo da Vinci is first recorded in Milan.[15]

Most quires in the first edition comprised eight folios, but three quires have 6*ff* and one just 2*ff* (a-z⁸, A-E4, F-G⁶, H-K⁸, L4, M-N⁸, O4). The book began with Il Puteolano's three-page *Oratio* to Ludovico Sforza, followed by Simonetta's two-page *Praefatio* dedicated to Duke Gian Galeazzo; Filelfo's letter was placed at the end of the volume.

The book was promptly circulated by Sforza functionaries among diplomats, civil servants and decision-makers in Italy and abroad, including the King of France. Florentine Chancellor Bartolomeo Scala (1430–97) received a copy from Carlo Barbavaro, a senior civil servant in the Milanese chancellery, and waxed ecstatic in his letter of thanks – assuring Barbavaro that 'such was the similarity in the events, the commanders and the style that I felt I was reading the books of Caesar.'

Printing of the second edition was completed on 23 September 1486. This was not a straightforward reprint: although again of *quarto* format, the number of lines of text per page was increased from 42 to 54, and the number of pages reduced from 584 to 376 – presumably to reduce costs.

Most quires comprised eight folios, but three quires have 6*ff* and one just 4*ff* (a-h⁸, i⁶, k-m⁸, n4, o-r4, s4, t-z4, &4, A⁴).

TRANSLATING THE *SFORZIADA*

A translation of the *Sforziada* into the vernacular was set in motion shortly after the first edition. As well as spreading the book's impact among people unable to read Latin, the translation into *lingua fiorentina* (as the forerunner of modern Italian was then termed) reflected Il Moro's fascination with all things Florentine. A Florentine literary celebrity was hired as translator: Cristoforo Landino (1424–98).

Landino was one of the most renowned scholars of the Renaissance: tutor to Lorenzo de' Medici, lecturer on Petrarch, translator of Pliny and member of the Platonic Academy in Florence headed by Marsilio Ficino. The Duke of Urbino was among his illustrious patrons.

Landino was also a prolific author in his own right. He penned commentaries on the *Aeneid* (1478) and *Divine Comedy* (1481), and wrote poems – one extolling Ginevra de' Benci, the sitter for Leonardo da Vinci's earliest surviving portrait. In the rarefied circles of Florentine's cultural elite, Leonardo may well have known Landino, whose *Sforziada* translation – forwarded by Lorenzo the Magnificent – arrived in Milan on 4 August 1485.[16]

Ianziti contends that Landino's translation lacks the power of Simonetta's original text, commenting: 'Those who are accustomed to applaud the triumph of the vernacular over the *artifice* of Latin would do well to compare Simonetta's hard-hitting original with the vagaries of Landino's rendering.'

A full-length, 252*ff* vellum manuscript version of Landino's translation is housed in Milan's Biblioteca Ambrosiana (*A 271 inf.*). Its listed provenance includes the Ducal Library in Pavia and Giovanni Antonio Secco, Conte di Borello & Vimercate (tutor to Il Moro's son Massimiliano in the 1490s).

This manuscript measures 36 × 24cm and runs to 34 lines per page on smooth, slightly shiny vellum. It was submitted to Simonetta for his observations. His caustic remarks are elegantly penned in the margin, on average every two pages or so, but at times (e.g. *fol.* 94) he scythes through a whole paragraph and demands major revision. In one passage he inveighs about a 'falsehood' added by Landino and sarcastically dubs him *El Poetono* ('little poet').

The manuscript is illuminated with beautifully gilded initials, some featuring devices beloved of Il Moro – such as the horse's bit and the *scopetta* with *Merito et Tempore* motto (*below left*) – although the cherub-flanked coat of arms at the foot of the frontispiece (*below right*) takes the form of a shield quartered with the Visconti viper and Sforza *vair* (wave) pattern,[17] rather than Il Moro's arms as Duke of Bari.

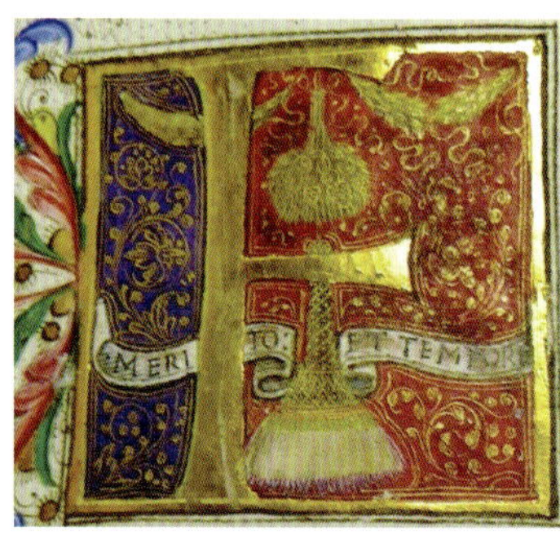

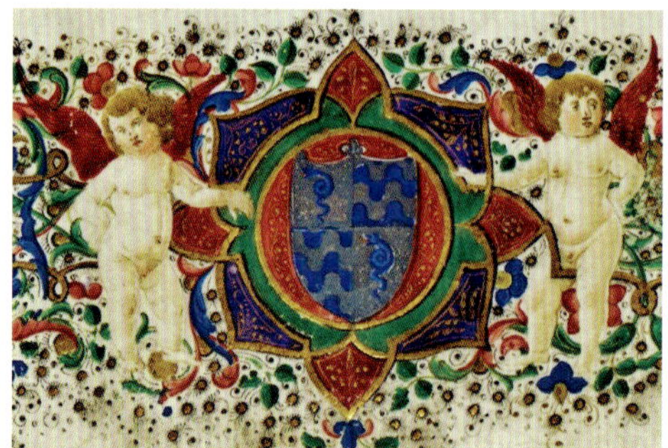

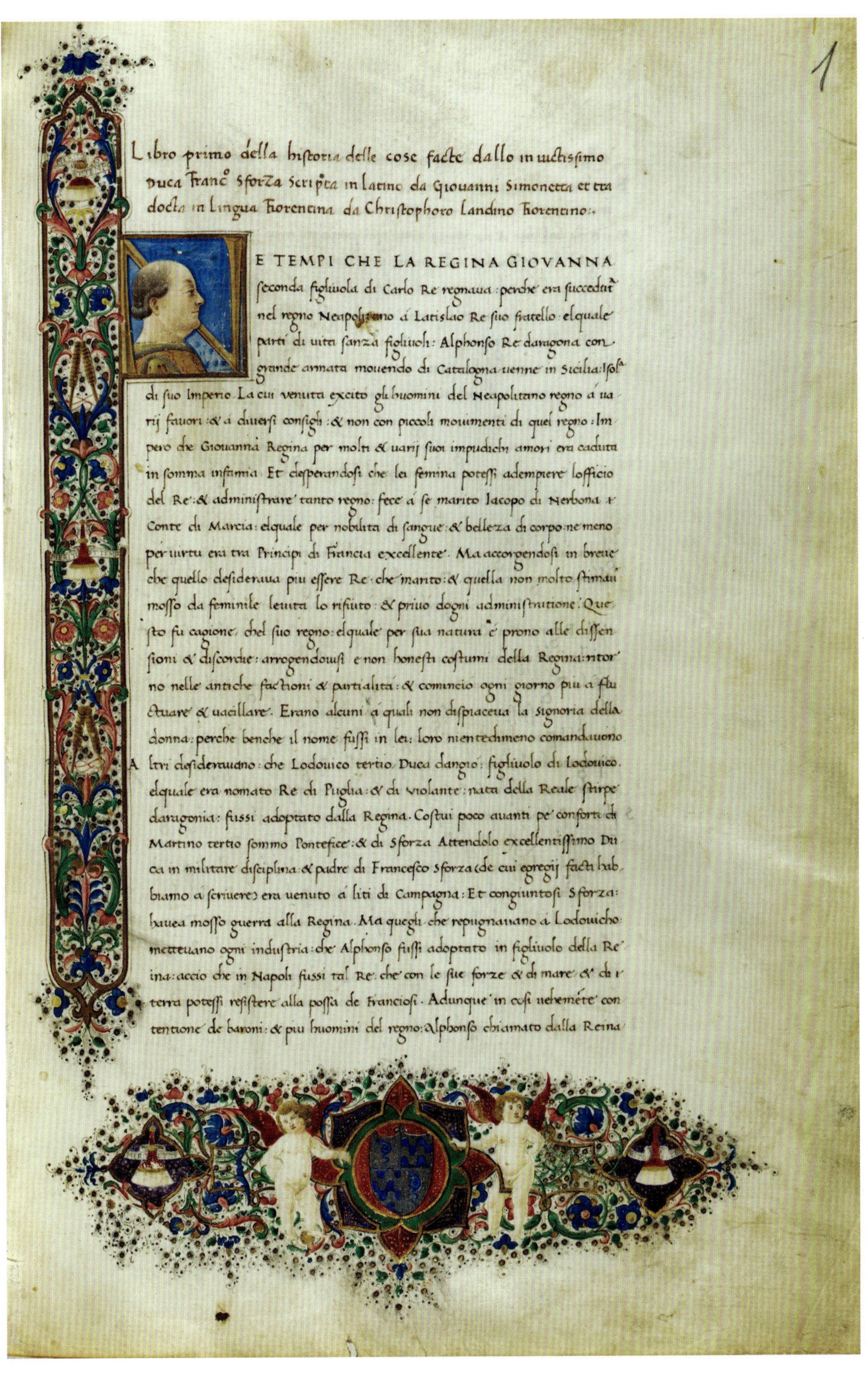

Libro primo della historia delle cose facte dallo inuictissimo
Duca Franc̄ Sforza scripta in latino da Giouanni Simonetta et tra
docta in Lingua Fiorentina da Christophoro Landino Fiorentino:

E TEMPI CHE LA REGINA GIOVANNA
seconda figliuola di Carlo Re regnaua: perche era succeduta
nel regno Neapolitano á Latislao Re suo fratello: elquale
parti di uita sanza figliuoli: Alphonso Re daragona con
grande armata mouendo di Catalogna uenne in Sicilia: Isola
di suo Imperio. La cui uenuta excito gli huomini del Neapolitano regno á ua
rij fauori: & á diuersi consigli: & non con piccoli mouimenti di quel regno: Im
pero che Giouanna Regina per molti & uarij suoi impudichi amori era caduta
in somma infamia. Et desperandosi che la femina potessi adempiere lofficio
del Re: & administrare tanto regno: fece á se marito Iacopo di Nerbona et
Conte di Marcia: elquale per nobilita di sangue: & belleza di corpo: ne meno
per uirtu era tra Principi di Francia excellente. Ma accorgendosi in breue
che quello desideraua piu essere Re: che marito: & quella non molto stimaui
mosso da feminile leuita lo rifiuto: & priuo dogni administratione: Que
sto fu cagione, chel suo regno: elquale per sua natura è prono alle dissen
sioni & discorche: arrogendouisi e non honesti costumi della Regina: ntor
no nelle antiche fachioni & partialita: & comincio ogni giorno piu á flu
ctuare & uacillare. Erano alcuni á quali non dispiaceua la signoria della
donna: perche benche il nome fussi in lei: loro nientedimeno comandauono
Altri desiderauano: che Lodouico tertio Duca dangio: figliuolo di Lodouico.
elquale era nomato Re di Puglia: & di Violante: nata della Reale stirpe
daragonia: fussi adoptato dalla Regina. Costui poco auanti pe' conforti di
Martino tertio sommo Pontefice: & di Sforza Attendolo excellentissimo Du
ca in militare disciplina & padre di Francesco Sforza (de cui egregij facti hab
biamo á scriuere) era uenuto á liti di Campagna: Et congiuntosi Sforza:
hauea mosso guerra alla Regina. Ma quegli che repugnauano a Lodouicho
metteuano ogni industria: che Alphonso fussi adoptato in figliuolo della Re
ina: accio che in Napoli fussi tal Re: che con le sue forze: & di mare: & di r
terra potessi resistere alla possa de Franciosi. Adunque in cosi nehemēte con
tentione de baroni: & piu huomini del regno: Alphonso chiamato dalla Reina

Alternating red-handled *scopetti* and horse's bits (two of each) appear in the left border of the first page of the main text – equivalent to the frontispiece in the illuminated *Sforziadas*. This page has an uncertain, old-fashioned look, yet introduces a feature that would become a staple of the illuminated *Sforziadas*: a profiled portrait of Francesco Sforza (*see right*). He is shown on a pale blue ground, wearing a gold breastplate and epaulettes with red highlights. The portrait is smaller and less assured than its subsequent *Sforziada* equivalents.

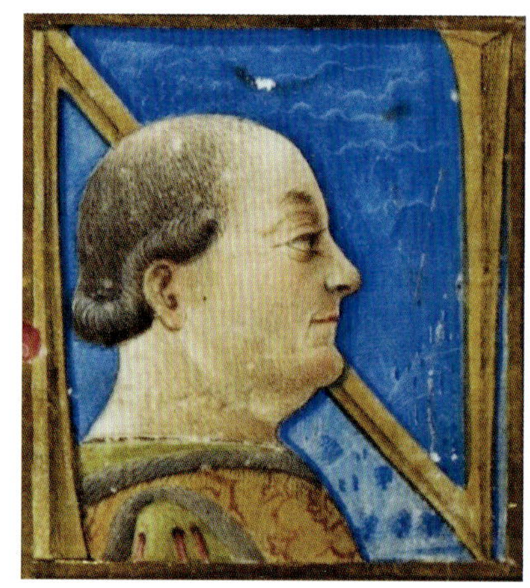

The manuscript probably dates from around 1486, and shows the format of the 1490 printed edition taking shape. The first quire, consisting of six folios rather than the more usual eight, features three prefatory texts introducing the book: Landino's *Proemio* (*page 1 – folio a1r*), starting with an initial *B* with much delicate gold and the *Merito et Tempore* device (the *scopetta* with its habitual red handle); Il Puteolano's *Orazione* (*page 5 – a3r*); and Simonetta's *Proemio*, which begins halfway down page 8 (*a4v*) and continues to page 10 (*a5v*). Pages 11 and 12 (*a6*) are blank. The main text begins on page 13: the first folio in the second quire.

A small-format, 197 × 144mm, 56*ff* handwritten summary of Landino's translation was also produced (*see p.52*). It is not dated but was probably produced around 1487. It is now in Milan's Biblioteca Trivulziana (*Cod. 1327*) and is known as the *Compendio de la Historia Sforzesca*.

Compared to the future illumination of the printed *Sforziadas*, its plant-motif frontispiece also looks old-fashioned. This time, however, the shield at the foot of the page (*see right*) features Il Moro's coat of arms as Duke of Bari. The presence and position of this coat of arms presages the frontispiece of the London *Sforziada*, albeit with a significant difference: the *fleurs-de-lys*, later to be impaled on Il Moro's Bari shield, is absent.

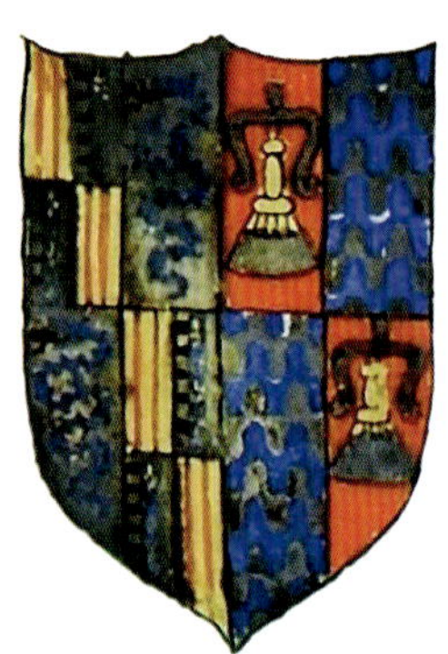

PREFACING THE 'FLORENTINE' *SFORZIADA*

The edition begins with four short texts (riddled with spelling mistakes and inconsistencies) that occupy nine pages in all.

FILELFO'S *EPISTOLA*
1 page, 17 lines
Epistola de Francesco Philelfo ad Gioanne Simoneta Ducale Secretario

A short, punning message to author Simonetta, dated 1479, praising his ability to render *la memoria deli homini perpetuamente ... con tanto ordine & tanto ornato*.

LANDINO'S *PROHEMIO*
3 pages, 128 lines (*a1r-a1v-a2r*)
Prohemio di Christophoro Landino Fiorentino nella Traductione di Latino in Lingua Fiorentina della Sforziada di Giovanni Simoneta ad lo Illustrissimo Lodovico Sforza Visconte

Landino's unctuous address to Il Moro extols Lorenzo de' Medici for promoting the spread of the Florentine language throughout Italy, and even to France and Spain; cites [Julius] Caesar and Alexander [the Great] in the same breath; and also mentions Fabius Maximus, Cato the Elder, Cato the Younger, Themistocles and Philopoemen (among others) as Classical figures with whom Francesco Sforza stands worthy comparison.

IL PUTEOLANO'S *ORATIONE*
3 pages, 118 lines (*a2v-a3r-a3v*)
Oratione di Francesco Puteolano Poeta Parmigia no all Illu. et Moderatissimo Principe Lodovico Sforza Visconte Duca di Bari Traducta di Lingua Latina in Fiorentina per Christophoro Landino Fiorentino

After expressing his *non mediocre admiratione* for Il Moro, *Principe candidisimo*, Il Puteolano stresses the superiority of literature over art, claiming that the memory of great rulers and generals of the past – led by Julius Caesar, but his list also includes Pyrrhus, Hannibal, Cyrus, Alexander the Great, Fabius, Papirius, Marcellus, Scipio, Trajan and Mark Antony – has been preserved thanks to writers and historians such as Pliny, Suetonius and Tacitus rather than monumental works of art. Even the Seven Wonders Of The World, and buildings created from the most expensive materials, fail to stand the test of time; pictures and statues are no good either, as they deteriorate or are destroyed.

However clichéd and appropriate in a volume of hagiography, Il Puteolano's remarks appear wantonly tactless and polemical – reflecting the fiery rivalry between artists and writers at the Sforza court. Leonardo would address the Puteolanos of his world in his *Trattato della Pittura* (*c.*1492), lambasting poets and writers as *beasts*, and calling for painting to be upgraded to one of the higher arts. This *Paragone* discussion would remain a leitmotif of intellectual debate in 1490s Milan, encouraged by Il Moro himself – and evoked in the Uffizi *Sforziada* (*see Chapter VII*) before culminating in the 'Academia Leonardi Vici' and the decorative scheme for the Sala delle Asse (*see Chapter XIII*).

SIMONETTA'S *PROEMIO*
2 pages, 80 lines (*a4r-a4v*)
Proemio di Giovanni Simonetta ne Commentarii della Cosse Facte da Francesco Sforza Duca de Melanesi Tradocto di Latina in Fiorentina Lingua da Christophoro Landino Fiorentino

Simonetta evokes Francesco Sforza as a worthy heir to Filippo Maria Visconti, and – implicitly referring to the superior merits of Il Moro when compared to his nephew Gian Galeazzo – stresses the importance of *virtu* as well as *heredita*. This represents a significantly different approach from Simonetta's original *Praefatio* for the first Latin edition of 1483, dedicated to Gian Galeazzo as Duke of Milan. In 1483 Gian Galeazzo was barely a teenager: Il Moro could afford to indulge in magnanimous diplomatic niceties, safe in the knowledge that his status as Regent was beyond dispute. By 1490, with Gian Galeazzo a recently married adult, that status was highly debatable – so the new, Florentine

Sforziada lauded Il Moro exclusively, implying that he merited to retain his power over a Duchy once ruled by his illustrious father.

START OF TEXT

> *: NE TEMPI CHE LA REGINA Giovanna Seconda figliuola di Carlo Re regnava: perche era succeduta nel regno Neapolitano a Latislao Re suo fratello: el quale parti di vita sanza figlioli: Alphonso Re daragona con grande armata movendo di Catalogna venne in Sicilia: Isola di suo Imperio.*

The Florentine text of the *Sforziada* begins with a tour of the Mediterranean in the company of Queen Giovanna II of Naples (1373–1435) – daughter of Carlo III and Margherita of Durazzo. Carlo III died in Visegrád on the Danube Bend in 1386 (future home to Matthias Corvinus's country palace) and was buried downriver in Belgrade; Margherita died in Salerno in 1412. Margherita's family hailed originally from what is now Albania, and – interesting footnote – her mother was born Margherita da Sanseverino.

Giovanna was born in Zadar on the Dalmatian coast; her parents were briefly King and Queen of Hungary. She became Queen of Naples in 1414 after the death of her brother Ladislao. In 1420, twice-married but childless, she appointed Alfonso of Aragon (1386–1458) – after a brief betrothal to his brother Juan – as her heir; what the *Sforziada* omits to mention is that she repudiated him in 1424 and, when she died in 1435, was succeeded by René d'Anjou of France. In 1438 Alfonso left Aragon for Catalonia, then set sail for Sicily with a *grande armata* – but it took him until 1441, and a six-month siege, to finally oust René before ruling Naples as Alfonso I from 1442–58.

Fighting for Naples. Italians in Hungary. French and Spanish in Italy. And a Sanseverino to boot: the first few lines of the *Sforziada* offer an unintended résumé of the key issues spanning Il Moro's time in power.

PRINTING THE 'FLORENTINE' *SFORZIADA*

The printing of the 'Florentine' edition was commissioned on 29 March 1490 in the name of Pietro Giustino Filelfo, nephew of Il Moro's former history teacher. No fewer than 700 copies were ordered, on paper watermarked with Sforza fire-buckets to be provided by Gian Antonio Calusco. Each page was to be of large, folio format (around 35 × 24.5cm) with 44 lines per page and 208 pages in all. Pietro Filelfo also ordered four extra copies to be printed entirely on parchment, which he promised to supply himself.[18]

These four de luxe copies were hybrid landmarks at a watershed in the history of books, art and scholarship – when the vernacular was supplanting Latin; the printed volume was starting to render illuminated manuscripts redundant; and engravings were in the process of supplanting illuminations as the usual method of book illustration.

The printing of the Florentine edition presumably began in April 1490, shortly after Filelfo placed his order. We do not know when it was completed. Ianziti

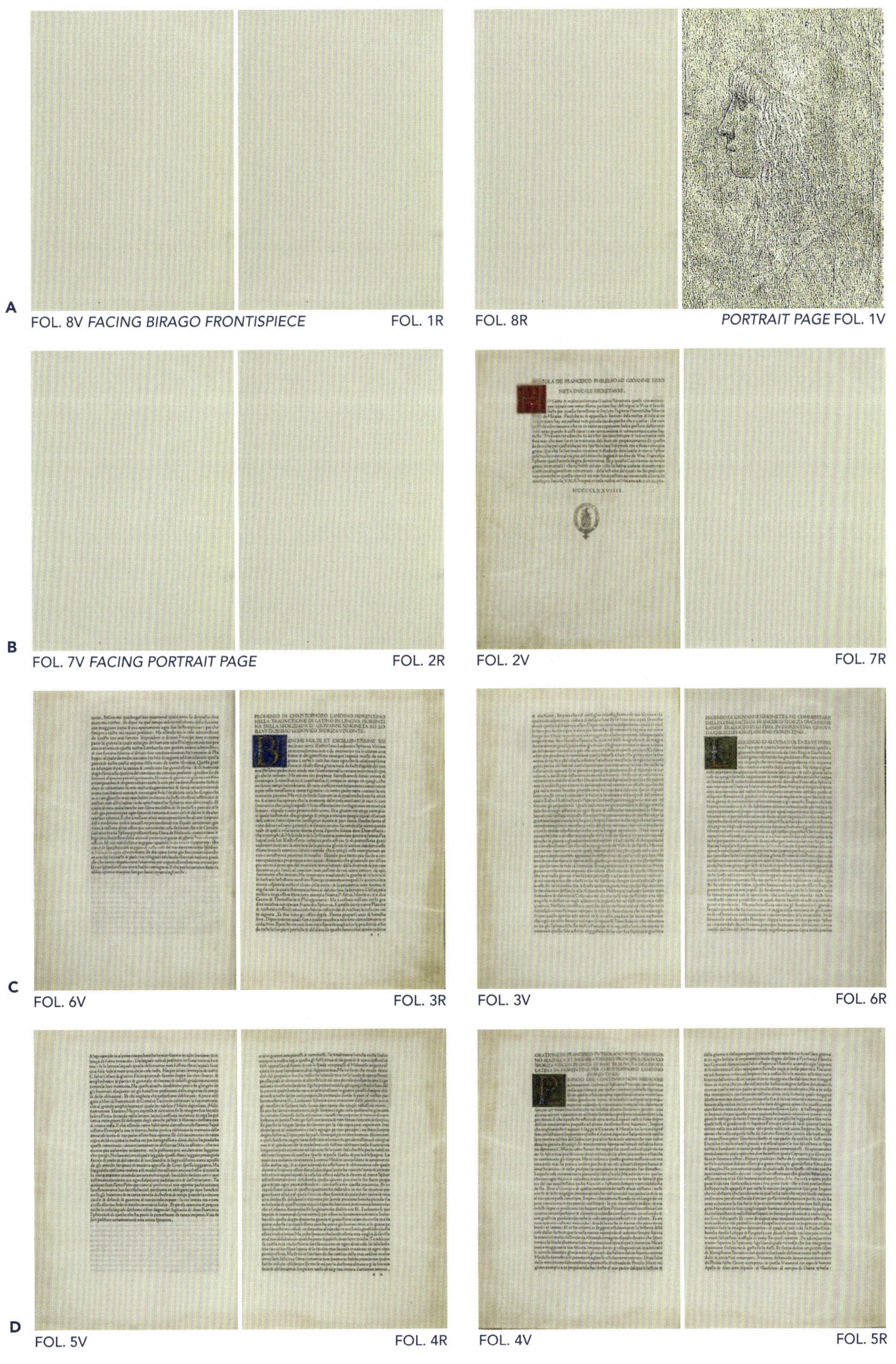

A   FOL. 8V *FACING BIRAGO FRONTISPIECE*   FOL. 1R   FOL. 8R   *PORTRAIT PAGE* FOL. 1V

B   FOL. 7V *FACING PORTRAIT PAGE*   FOL. 2R   FOL. 2V   FOL. 7R

C   FOL. 6V   FOL. 3R   FOL. 3V   FOL. 6R

D   FOL. 5V   FOL. 4R   FOL. 4V   FOL. 5R

has shown that it took around eighteen months to print the First Edition of 400 copies. Although the Florentine Edition contained fewer pages, it had a larger print-run: 700 copies. Printing cannot have been completed much before the end of 1490 – probably not until the first few months of 1491. The colophon is intriguingly vague. Instead of recording the day on which printing was finished, it only mentions a year: *MCCCCLXXXX.*

LAYOUT OF THE 'FLORENTINE' *SFORZIADA*

The book's first 25 quires comprised eight folios, the 26th and final quire just 4*ff* (a-z⁸, &⁸, ç⁸, R⁴).

Individual page layout was standard for Italian incunabula. The body of text is slightly left of centre, and nearer to the top of the page than the bottom. Four sections of the page are therefore available for illumination: a narrow left margin; a wider right margin; a horizontal bar at the top of the page; and a larger, rectangular box at the bottom of the page. The two margins were a natural haunt for trophies, musical angels and small portrait medallions. The largest section, the *bas-de-page*, offered room for a more elaborate composition, commonly featuring coats of arms. Space was also set aside for each of the 31 chapters to begin with a large illuminated initial.

The layout of the first quire, however, was anything but standard, and differed significantly from the handwritten draft of Landino's translation, where the prefatory texts had occupied **ten of the quire's twelve pages.** In the printed version the first quire was extended to **sixteen pages,** even though **only nine pages contained text** with seven pages left blank: *ff 1r, 1v, 2r, 7r, 7v, 8r, 8v.* The whole of the quire's outer sheet (*folios 1 & 8*) was left blank – which appears, at first glance, unseemly, costly and unnecessary, and could easily have been avoided by having each prefatory text start on a right-hand (recto) page: both Filelfo's *Epistola* (*2v*) and Il Puteolano's *Orazione* (*4v*) start on a left-hand page.

What can have justified such a contorted layout?

Surely the fact that the first quire of the 1490 edition of the *Sforziada* was designed to accommodate a full-page illustration on its eighth folio: page 15 (*a8r*).

As a result, the *verso* of the previous folio (page 14) had to remain blank, to avoid the risk of the illustration being smudged by print. The *verso* of the illustrated page (page 16) also had to remain blank, because it was positioned opposite the first page of the second quire (page 17) containing the first page of the volume's main text, destined for illumination in the four presentation copies printed on vellum.

With the whole of the first sheet of the initial quire left blank, it could be worked on by the artist independently, with no concern for the printing process, and only added to the rest of the quire – and to the volume's 51 other sheets – at the moment of binding.

But what sort of full-page illustration can have been envisaged?

1 Patrick Boucheron, in *La Statue Equestre de Francesco Sforza: Enquête sur un Mémorial Politique* (*Journal des Savants*, 1997), pp.421–99, deems it 'significant' that Duke Galeazzo Maria's interest in erecting an equine monument to his father came shortly after the refusal of powerful Milanese nobleman Giovanni Borromeo to let his son Giberto serve as a *camerio* at court. The furious Duke threatened to confiscate Borromeo's Angera fiefdom in retaliation.

2 In *De Sculptura*, one of the earliest treatises on sculpture, published in Florence in 1504, Pomponius Gauricus records that the Classical world assigned lifesize statues to Sages and Virtuous Men (e.g. Plato or Homer); a 150 per cent scale to Sovereigns (e.g. Alexander the Great); and double-lifesize for Heroes (e.g. Hercules or Theseus).

3 A 'traité du cheval' is how André Chastel (in *Art et Humanisme à Florence au Temps de Laurent le Magnifique*) describes Leonardo's *Adoration of the Magi*.

4 Boucheron, *op. cit.*

5 Antonio Pollaiolo's designs are now in the Robert Lehman Collection (Metropolitan Museum, New York) and the Staatliche Graphische Sammlung, Munich. Pollaiolo was also a hapless contender to design Bartolomeo Colleoni's equestrian monument in Venice.

6 *Codex Atlanticus* 1082/391r-a.

7 Ianziti, *op. cit.*

8 Il Moro also cast his historian's eye over his Visconti heritage. In 1481 he invited Filelfo's former pupil Giorgio Merula (1430–94) to come from Venice and write a *History of the Visconti*. Merula arrived in 1482 but failed to complete the task before his death.

9 Ianziti (*op. cit.*) affirms that this letter, dated 29 August 1476, is contained in the definitive collection of Filelfo's Letters.

10 Ianziti (*op. cit.*), p.212.

11 Simonetta, *Commentarii Rerum Gestarum Francisici Sfortiae* (Antonio Zarotto, Milan 1483).

12 Ianziti, *op. cit.*

13 P. Veneziani, *Panfilo Castaldi*, in *Dizionario Biografico degli Italiani*, Vol. 21, Milan/Rome 1978. I am indebted to Cristina Geddo for this information.

14 Ianziti, *op. cit.*

15 G. Ianziti, *The First Edition of Giovanni Simonetta's De Rebus Gestis Francisci Sfortiae Commentarii – Questions of Chronology and Interpretation* in *Bibliothèque d'Humanisme et Renaissance*, Vol. 44 (1982), pp.137–47. A copy of the 1490 edition sold for £1,035 at Christie's London on 3 April 1996. Another copy was sold on eBay on 5 April 2011; its first leaf was described as missing and replaced with a facsimile printed on ancient paper (*cf* Uffizi *Sforziada* below).

16 Simone Foà, *Landino, Cristoforo* in *Dizionario Biografico degli Italiani*, Vol. 63 (2004); see also R.M. Comanducci, *Nota sulla versione landiniana della Sforziade di Giovanni Simonetta* in *Interpres XII* (1992), pp.309–16.

17 This wave-pattern, known heraldically as *vair*, is said to originate from the lining of cloaks with the fur of *pteromys volans* – commonly known as the Siberian Flying Squirrel, although found as far west as the Baltic – whose blue/black skins and white undersides were cut and sewn together to produce an alternating pattern.

18 A. Ganda, *Pietro Giustino Filelfo Editore della Sforziade di Giovanni Simonetta* in *Studi in Memoria di Paola Medioli Masotti, a cura di Franca Magnani* (Loffredo Editore, Naples 1995), pp.73–86. I am indebted to Cristina Geddo for referring me to this article.

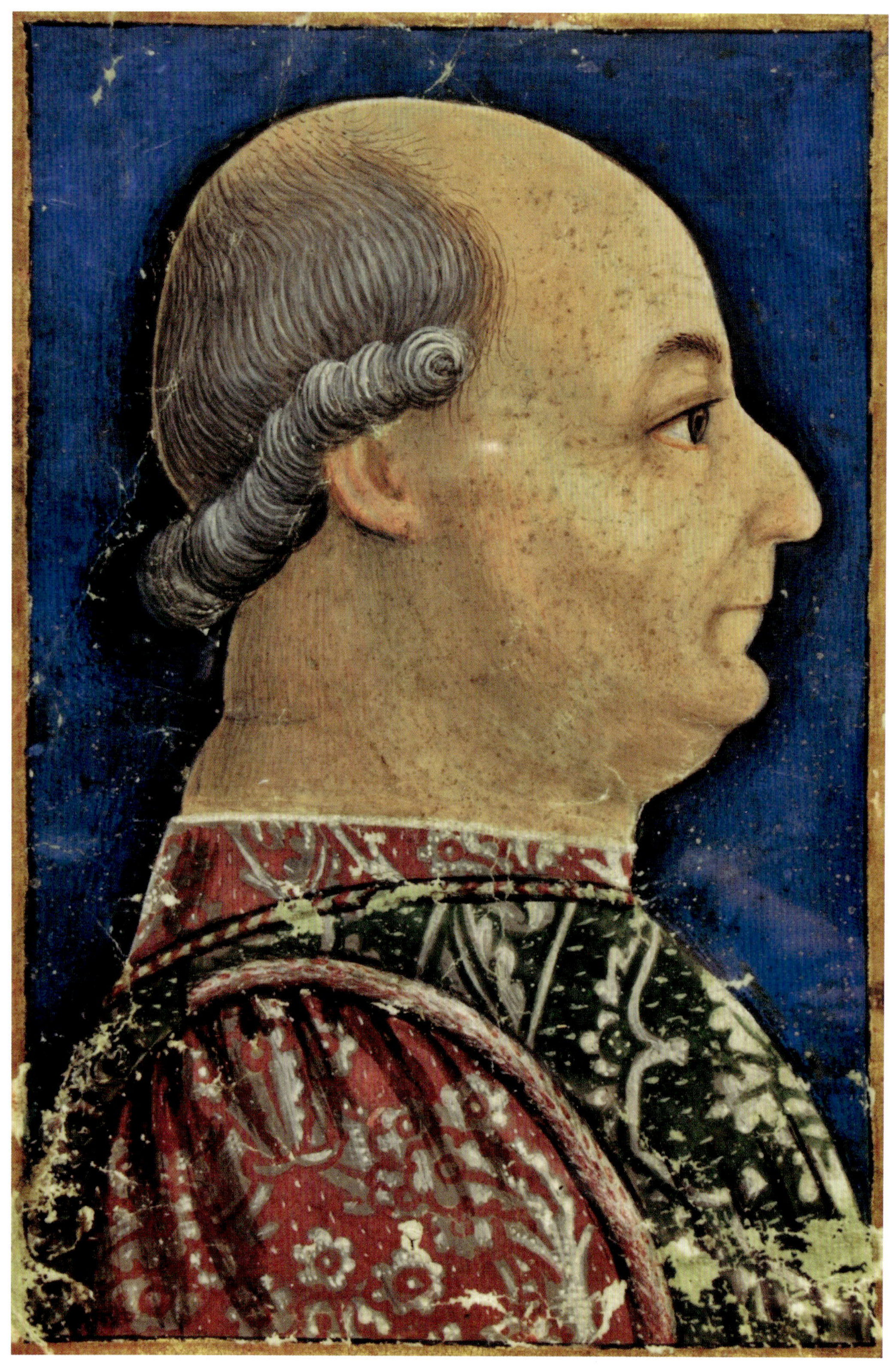

FRANCESCO SFORZA (c.1460) – TEMPERA ON VELLUM 19 × 14 cm – BIBLIOTECA TRIVULZIANA (CODEX 786)

IV

ILLUMINATION
AMBROGIO DE PREDIS & GIANPIETRO BIRAGO

THE FULL-PAGE ILLUSTRATION envisaged for the first illuminated Sforziada was almost certainly a wedding portrait – inspired by Florentine precedent.

In May 1488 Piero de' Medici, Lorenzo the Magnificent's son and heir, married Alfonsina Orsini in Florence. Early in 1489, to mark the occasion, Piero was presented with a luxurious *editio princeps* of the *Works of Homer* in Greek, printed on vellum and containing a full-page portrait (*left*) of the sixteen-year-

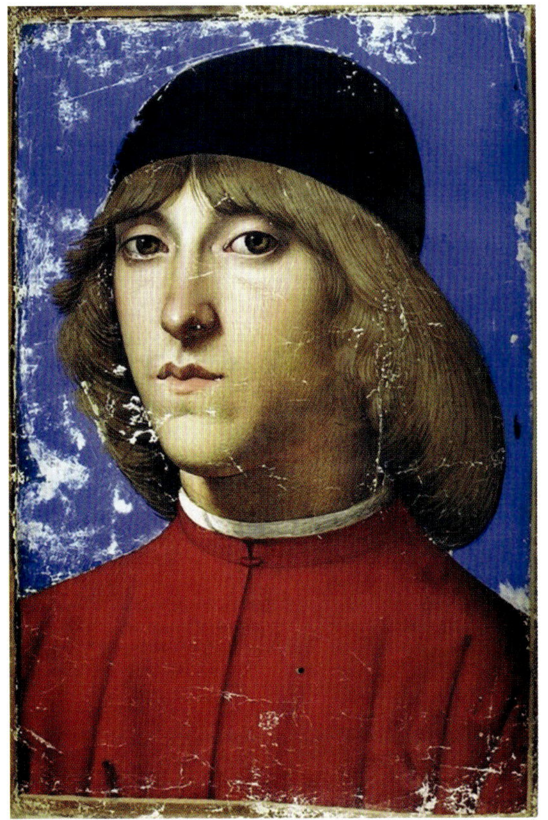

old Piero, in tempera, by the celebrated Florentine illuminator Gherardo di Giovanni del Fora.

The volume is now in the Biblioteca Vittorio Emanuele III in Naples (*Segn. SQ XXIII, K 22*). Its colophon indicates that printing was completed by Bartolomeo de' Libri on 9 December 1488. Its dedication, by the Florentine nobleman Bernardo de' Nerli, is dated 13 January 1489.[1] Its dimensions are a spectacular 33 × 22.5cm.

At 35 × 24.5cm, the four vellum copies of the *Sforziada* were even bigger. Three have survived virtually intact, and are now to be found in the British Library (London), Bibliothèque Nationale (Paris) and Biblioteka Narodowa (Warsaw). Illuminated fragments from the fourth copy are owned by the Uffizi Gallery in Florence.

None currently contain a full-page illustration – although there is conclusive evidence that the copy now in Warsaw originally contained a full-page portrait by Leonardo da Vinci.

The novel Florentine idea of a de luxe volume printed on vellum and containing a full-page portrait surely served as a model. But the illumination of this 'Warsaw' *Sforziada* can be dated with certainty to 1496 – six years after the four vellum presentation copies were printed. It is therefore likely that one of the three earlier copies was originally destined to receive a full-page illustration – doubtless the first vellum copy to be illuminated after printing was completed.

The art of portraiture requires different skills from that of frontispiece illumination. The *Sforziadas*, from the outset, therefore required decorative input from two different specialists. An accomplished portraitist was required to furnish the four vellum copies with a medallion image of the book's hero, Francesco Sforza, at the start of the text.

Each of these miniature portraits is subtly different, both in mood – ranging from solemn to cheerful – and physical appearance: the wrinkles on Francesco's forehead are hardly visible in the first frontispiece, yet his brow is deeply furrowed by the fourth. These miniatures are of such precision and psychological refinement that they can only be the work of a master portraitist.

The four Francesco miniatures are based on the standard image of the family patriarch from the final years of his rule – declined on coins, in stone and on vellum.

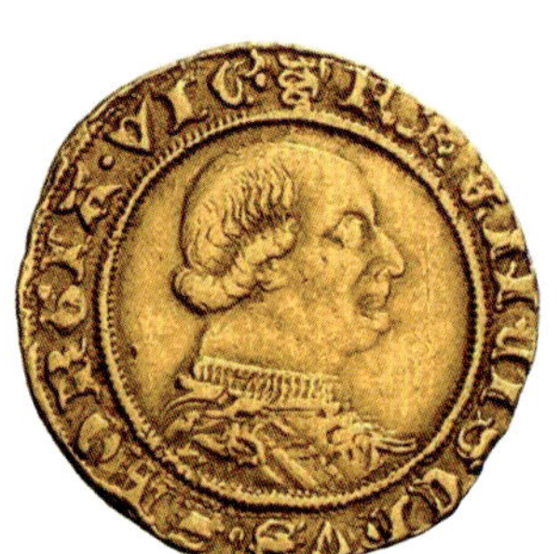

The 1462 Milan gold ducat showed Francesco in a breastplate (*right*) – as he would appear in the *Sforziadas*. It was considered the first coin of the Renaissance to ape Classical precedent by featuring the ruler's profile.[2]

Cristoforo Romano's high-relief plaque, now in the Bargello Museum in Florence, shows Francesco in a tabard with his favourite greyhound emblem high up his chest.[3]

A work on vellum (*see p.66*) shows a freckled Francesco in a floral-patterned, dark green tabard with mulberry-coloured collar and sleeves. It measures 19.2 × 14.5cm and is to be found in a manuscript written between 1454 and 1460 for Francesco's eldest daughter Ippolita,[4] now in the Trivulziana (*Cod. 786*).[5]

Il Moro would later add his own portrait – also on a deep blue ground within a gold frame – to the grammar book he commissioned for his son Massimiliano in the late 1490s, which also includes a full-page, profiled portrait of his son. Both portraits (*see p.217*) are acknowledged as the work of Ambrogio de Predis.

AMBROGIO DE PREDIS

Ambrogio's family is first documented in Lombardy in 1467. Although the name probably originated from the village of Preda near St-Moritz, close to the Swiss/Italian border, the family are thought to have settled in Milan by 1450, living near the Porta Ticinese in the south of the city. Ambrogio's father Leonardo, a nobleman,[6] married three times and had six sons, four of whom were artists. His first wife, Margherita Giussani, bore Cristoforo, Aloisio and Evangelista. His second wife, Margherita de Millio, bore Giovan Francesco. His third wife, Caterina Corio, bore Bernardino and Ambrogio, the youngest.

The eldest brother, Cristoforo de Predis, was an illuminator of significant talent and reputation. He is first mentioned in September 1467, in a legal document concerning the division of his paternal estate. Although he is described as deaf and dumb (*mutulus, qui licet ad nutum intellegat, ut omnibus notum est, tamen loqui non potest*), the new Duke of Milan, Galeazzo Maria Sforza, intervened personally to override the law (which deemed deaf-mutes incapable of managing their own financial affairs). Favoured status among the Sforzas would be retained by this artistic family until the end of the century.

Cristoforo's securely attributed works all date from the 1470s. They include the *Libro d'Ore Borromeo* (Ambrosiana *MS SP42*), commemorating the wedding of Giovanni III Borromeo (1439–95) to Cleofe Pio di Carpi; the *Antifonario Ambrosiano* in the Museo Baroffio at Sacro Monte sopra Varese, signed *OPUS–XPOFORI–DE PREDIS–MUTI 1476*; and a sheet in the Wallace Collection signed and dated *147 ...* , showing a profiled Galeazzo Maria Sforza kneeling in prayer against a background battle-scene.[7]

Cristoforo's most remarkable achievement is *Le Storie di San Gioacchino ed Anna e della Fine del Mondo* (History of SS Gioacchino & Anna and the End of the World), an illuminated epic replete with apocalyptic, proto-Surrealist visions that include flying fish and a lunar landscape. It was completed for Galeazzo Maria Sforza and Bona di Savoia in 1476 (Biblioteca Reale, Turin, *MS Varia 124*). Its narrative verve, humour, compositional drama and over 300 individual miniatures mark it down as one of the first comic-strip books.

The vellum portrait of Francesco Sforza in his daughter's book may also be the work of Cristoforo. The wide-eyed expression and sharply-defined eyelashes are typical of portraits by his younger half-brother Ambrogio, and also recall the profile of Galeazzo Maria in the Wallace Collection.

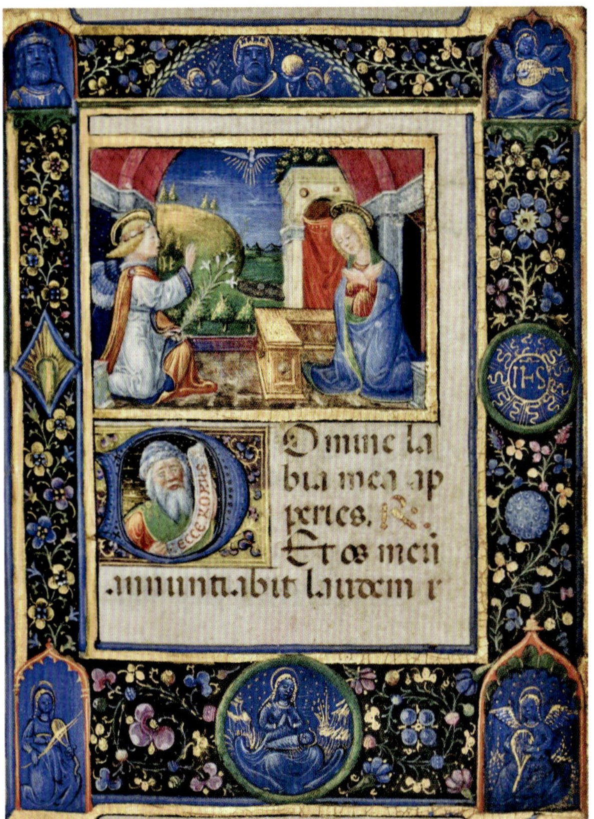

The middle brothers Bernardino and Evangelista (who died in 1491) both collaborated with Ambrogio without appearing to achieve independent artistic status. Evangelista is first mentioned in a document dated 1472, and was living with Ambrogio near the Porta Ticinese, close to the church of Sant' Eustorgio, when Leonardo da Vinci lodged with them in 1483.

Ambrogio de Predis is thought to have been born in Milan in the early 1450s. On 11 May 1474 he is recorded as receiving payment for fourteen miniatures in a Book of Hours commissioned for the adolescent Francesco Borromeo.[8] These are Ambrogio's first known works and reflect the stylistic influence of his half-brother Cristoforo – with whom Ambrogio is also believed to have collaborated on the *Libro d'Ore Borromeo* now in the Ambrosiana.[9] Folio 14 of Francesco Borromeo's *Book of Hours*, featuring the Annunciation, has notable borders of tiny flowers (*see left*).

Ambrogio was also employed by the Milanese Mint – possibly under Duke Galeazzo Maria, and definitely by 1479, the year Il Moro returned to

Milan. In 1482 Ambrogio is documented as working for Il Moro as a portraitist (*ritrattista ducale*), receiving a *pezza di raso* (length of satin) for an unspecified commission thought to have been a portrait (now lost) of Il Moro's future mother-in-law Eleonora d'Este.[10]

Ambrogio would remain a key cog in the court propaganda machine throughout Il Moro's twenty years of power – above all as his official portraitist. One of Ambrogio's finest portraits is also one of his smallest: that of Matthias Corvinus, King of Hungary. It appears in the frontispiece (*see right*) of a codex prepared for Matthias in 1488.[11]

The codex contains the 22-page *Epitalamion* or *Epitalamium in nuptiis Blancae Mariae Sfortiae et Johannis Corvini*, delivered on 25 November 1487 by Gian Francesco Marliano, *Gonfaloniere* (standard-bearer) of the Milan Senate, at the proxy wedding of Il Moro's niece Bianca Maria and János, the illegitimate son and designated heir of the Matthias Corvinus, 'King of Hungary, Bohemia & Dalmatia' as

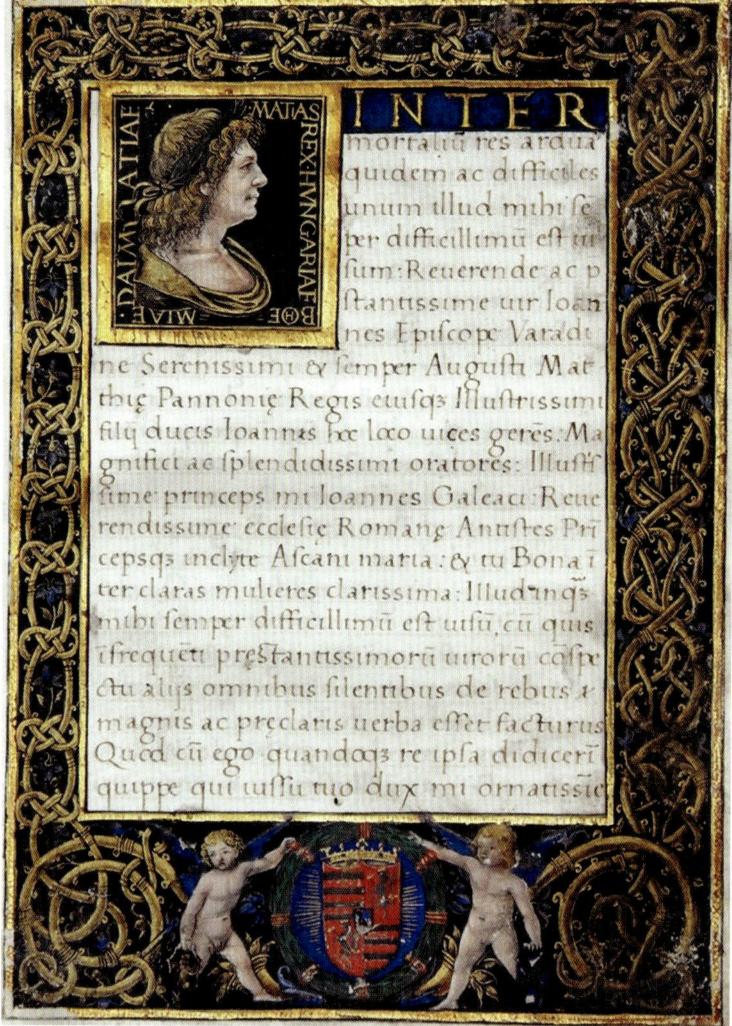

he is styled here (*MATIAS REX HVNGARIAE BOHEMIAE DALMATIAE*). Since 1592 the slim volume, 21 × 14.8cm, has been in the little town of Volterra, northwest of Siena, where it is housed in the Biblioteca Guarnacci (*Cod. Lat. 5518.IV*). It also contains the Hunyadi and Sforza coats of arms, and a dedicatory letter from Marliano to Matthias Corvinus dated 1 January 1488.

The borders contain the sort of interlacing *vinci* knot patterning for which Leonardo is famous, although it is even more similar to the patterns found on the garments of the angel of the *Virgin of the Rocks* and the Ambrosiana's *Portrait of a Lady* – both widely attributed to Ambrogio de Predis. Such 'ties that bind' were appropriate decoration for a codex celebrating a wedding. They are interspersed with violet flowers: columbine, a symbol of fertility associated with Aphrodite, the Goddess of Love. Their symbolism and meticulous detail recall the flowers in the first (Louvre) version of the *Virgin of the Rocks*, on which Leonardo and Ambrogio began work in 1483, and presage the spray of columbine held aloft in the painting of *Flora* by Leonardo's pupil and executor Francesco Melzi, now in the Hermitage (*Inv. GE 107*).

THE CORVINUS MEDALLION

Mario Salmi (1889–1980) was the first art historian to propose Ambrogio de Predis as the author of the medallion portrait.[12] The codex's battered original binding[13] adds weight to this attribution: it has almost exactly the same design as the binding of the *Donatus Grammatica* commissioned around a decade later by Il Moro for his son Massimiliano (Biblioteca Trivulziana, *cod. 2167*), containing the profiled portraits of father and son unanimously attributed to Ambrogio de Predis.

Although this seems to have escaped previous commentators, the portrait medallion of Matthias Corvinus must have been a slightly later addition to the codex. It appears to have been affixed to the frontispiece with glue, which has seeped slightly halfway along the bottom, and positioned with less than perfect precision – the left-hand edge of the medallion does not run altogether parallel to the adjacent frontispiece border.

If the medallion were not designed in Milan at the same time as the rest of the codex, it implies that the artist wished to make his portrait of Matthias Corvinus in person. His profile was clearly inspired by the oak-wreathed marble bust of Matthias (now in the Museum of Fine Arts in Budapest) sculpted by Giovanni Dalmata in the mid-1480s. De Predis, however, has Matthias face right rather than left, and replaces his oak leaves with laurels. Above all, he imbues his portrait with the twinkle-eyed spontaneity that was his hallmark.

Ambrogio was an inveterate traveller, who later visited Rome and enjoyed at least two lengthy stays in Innsbruck. He may have been part of the eighty-man delegation that, under Guidantonio Arcimboldo (future Archbishop of Milan), visited Hungary in February 1488 to discuss plans for Bianca Maria's bridal journey.

Ambrogio's profile of Matthias appears to have met with instant approval, and was promptly requoted by three volumes formerly in the Corvinus Library: Cortesius's *De Laudibus Bellicis* now in the Herzog August Bibliothek, Wolfenbüttel (*Cod. Guelf. 85.1.1*), where the profile appears top left, in a similar position at the start of the text; the Philostratus *Opera* now in the National Széchényi Library, Budapest (*Cod. Lat. 417*), where it appears in the left-hand margin; and the *Biblia Sacra* now in the Universitätsbibliothek, Erlangen (*MS UER 6*), where it appears in the middle of the front cover.

With its virtually square format, right-facing profile and descriptive lettering, the Matthias medallion also formed a template for the *Sforziada's* opening medallions of Francesco Sforza, which are almost exactly the same size.

Ambrogio de Predis will have been the first name Il Moro pencilled in for his de luxe *Sforziada* project – before seeking to employ a frontispiece illuminator of comparable genius, able to convey propaganda with unforgettable wit and humour.

GIANPIETRO BIRAGO

While the contract for printing 700 copies of the Florentine edition of the *Sforziada* (and four more on vellum) was being negotiated in March 1490, Gianpietro Birago was almost certainly in Rome, working for Bishop Vitéz, Hungary's Ambassador to the Vatican. There is no evidence he had set foot on Milanese soil for nearly twenty years.

Birago grew up in or near Milan and trained as an illuminator in the late 1460s under Cristoforo de Predis, presumably alongside Ambrogio. Cristoforo's influence can be seen in the wide-eyed figures of Birago's early works. Cristoforo's zany humour and gift for story-telling, apparent in his *Storie di San Gioacchino ed Anna*, would have a lasting impact on Birago's approach.

Birago was long known as *Pseudo Antonio da Monza* or *Master of the Sforza Hours*, only emerging from artistic anonymity in 1938 when his signature was discovered in a Brescia choir-book. He appears to have been a lay priest, signing himself *Presbyter*; his work reflects intimate knowledge of the Bible and religious texts. Like Ambrogio de Predis, he was probably born around 1450. There is no evidence that he was related to Pietro Birago, a courtier and army general under Il Moro, or Daniele Birago, apostolic protonotary and privy councillor.

We have no official record of Gianpietro Birago's appearance, but a tiny face recurs so frequently in the margins of his illuminated pages that one wonders if it is a self-portrait. It shows a chubby-faced man with tufty, slightly receding blond hair and a defiant grin.

The first works by Birago to be signed and dated (1471/4) are illuminations for *Corali* (choir books) for Brescia Cathedral, now to be found in the city's Pinacoteca Tosio Martinengo (*MM 22/23/25*). One shows a pulpit scene modelled on a late 1460s Vicenzo Foppa fresco in Milan's Portinari Chapel – early evidence of Birago's enduring propensity to derive creative inspiration from the works of

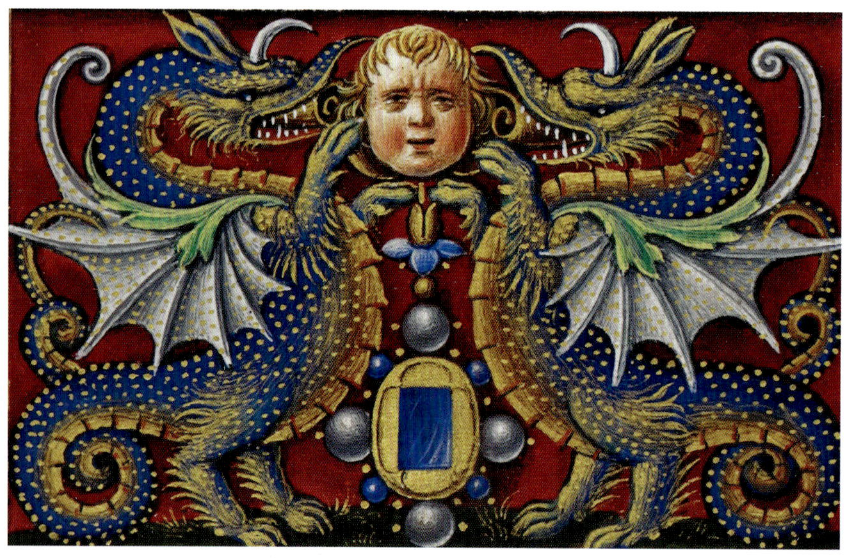

his contemporaries. Brescia was then a Venetian possession, and cosmopolitan Venice had a burgeoning printing industry, founded by the German Johannes de Spira (or Speyer) in 1469.

The nascent industry had urgent need of illuminators to embellish all its new books. The leading Venetian employer of illuminators was the Frenchman Nicolas Jenson (1420–81), who had arrived in Venice from Germany in the late 1460s and, in 1470, set up his own press. During the next decade he printed over 150 works, mostly in Latin. He remains famed for his elegant, pioneering and influential *Roman* typeface.

Jenson employed an artistic stable that also included Girolamo da Cremona (1451–83), with whose style Birago shares affinities; both seem to have been strongly influenced by Mantegna. There are also similarities between Birago's work and that of the older Ferrarese miniaturist Taddeo Crivelli (1425–79). Commentators agree that Birago worked in Venice from the mid-1470s, but no works from the period with the *Birago* signature are known. Could this be because he was using a different name?

An Italian translation of Pliny the Elder's *Historia Naturalis*, 41.5 × 28cm, printed by Jenson in 1476 and now in the University of California (Elmer Belt Library of Vinciana, *A1.P719hI*), contains a faintly discernible signature that reads *Petrus V.m.......* which, suggests Lilian Armstrong in *The Painted Page – Italian Renaissance Book Illumination 1450–1550*, stands for *Vimercate*, a town twelve miles northeast of Milan on the road to Bergamo, and just ten miles east of the village of Birago.

Several other Venetian volumes are ascribed to the same *Petrus V.* The stylistic, iconographic and historical evidence for Birago's authorship is compelling. We can only speculate as to why Birago might have chosen to be known in Venice by his second Christian name and the town he presumably came from. It may be significant that he took to signing the prints he made towards the end of his career not *Birago* but *D.MAR.V* ('in the name of the Virgin Mary') – a practice Louis XII outlawed in 1506.

Coincidentally, the Pliny was translated into Italian (or *Florentine*) by Cristoforo Landino, the future translator of the *Sforziada*. Its frontispiece appears to presage the *mise-en-page* of those in the *Sforziadas*, as well as sharing some of their imagery. As in three of the four illuminated *Sforziadas*, the right-hand border has a medallion profile just over halfway up: it depicts a helmeted warrior similar to one portrayed by Leonardo da Vinci in a silverpoint drawing from the late 1470s (British Museum *inv. 1895-9-15-474*).[14]

Beneath the profile is a covered font: an unusual item to find in an illuminated book, but one that recurs in exactly the same place in the final illuminated *Sforziada* now in Warsaw. The left margin of the Pliny frontispiece features gymnastic putti – one putto kneeling as another stands on its back. The London *Sforziada* features two kneeling putti receiving comparably unceremonious treatment. The Pliny's *bas-de-page* again resembles that of the London *Sforziada* in featuring a coat of arms flanked by putti – two of them again wearing waist-length jackets that leave their genitals exposed. Homoerotic putti pepper Birago's œuvre, with Armstrong suggesting Marco Zoppo (1433–78), active in Venice during the 1470s, as a likely influence.

The *haut-de-page* also presages the London *Sforziada* by having a gold-framed central medallion containing a male portrait gazing heavenwards.

An intriguing feature of the Pliny frontispiece is a luxuriant date palm near the top of the right-hand border, encircled mid-trunk by a gold crown and with its shallow roots gripping a gold sphere. The date palm is a Sforza heraldic device: a palm frond, studded with red dates, routinely emerges from the top of Sforza crests (originally accompanied by an olive branch, later by a spray of laurel leaves – which Il Moro would, in turn, replace with a mulberry branch in 1495).

Opposite the date palm, near the top of the left-hand border, is a blackened, lifeless tree of the sort often found in Birago's work, beneath the bannered motto *RENO/VERA* and a skull. A woman and child are shown beneath a ruined building behind the tree.

Armstrong believes this image could refer to the assassination of Galeazzo Maria Sforza in 1476 (the year the Pliny was printed). She believes the woman and child may represent his widow Bona and their young son Gian Galeazzo, and that the RENO/VERA motto refers either to the *true reign* of Galeazzo Maria's offspring, and/or the need for that reign to be *renovated* – the implication being that the line of succession has been waylaid.

This interpretation is reinforced by the presence not just of a helmeted warrior (the Latin for helmet, *galea*, offering a pun on Galeazzo), but of a weeping cupid atop the sealed font.

The original owner of the volume is not known, but the *404ff* **Breviarum Romanum**, 32.8 × 23.4cm, printed on vellum by Jenson in 1478 and now in Glasgow University Library (*Hunterian Bf.1.18*), was presented to Leonardo Botta, Milanese Ambassador to Venice from 1470–80 – i.e. a Galeazzo Maria appointee who did not long survive in his post once Il Moro had gained power. It appears to be illuminated by the same hand. If Birago were producing imagery for despondent supporters of Galeazzo Maria, this might be why he steered clear of Milan for years to come – and adopted a pseudonym.

Trademark Birago features to be found in the Breviary now in Glasgow include a foreground littered with rocks; stylized, angular mountains; a combination of leafless trees and trees in leaf; and hose in the Milanese colours of blue, white and red. The figure of a winged putto supporting a medallion, wearing only a jacket that ends just above his private parts, reappears in an almost identical context in the London *Sforziada*. There are also, on different folios, two scenes involving a gaggle of putti beneath bell-shaped leafy canopies: in one, eight putti standing and chattering; in the other, seven putti sitting around a large cooking-pot, all holding spoons. A group of fourteen playful putti festoon the London *Sforziada*.

Two undated Venetian manuscripts ascribed to Petrus V... also warrant attention: a **Breviary (Use of Rome)**, 29 × 20cm, now in the Houghton Library at

Harvard (*MS Typ 219*); and a Latin translation of the **Chronica by Eusebius of Caesarea**, 31 × 22cm, now in the Bibliothèque de Genève (*Ms Lat. 49*). Both are illuminated with rocky landscapes dominated by square arches topped by massive entablatures, with medallioned plinths supporting pilastered columns pawed by clambering putti. The Houghton Breviary can be dated to around 1480, the Eusebius *Chronica* to a couple of years later.

The Harvard Breviary frontispiece also features a kneeling figure praying to a heavenly God, in exactly the same manner as Duke Galeazzo Maria in the 1470s battle scene by Cristoforo de Predis; and an incongruous wire-haired terrier that bears a passing resemblance to the white dog in Verrocchio's *Tobias & the Angel* (National Gallery), thought to have been contributed by his pupil Leonardo.[15] An almost identical dog appears in the *Sforza Hours*.

As well as working in Venice, Birago may also have stayed in nearby Padua and in Bergamo, just 25 miles northeast of Milan, but part of the Venetian Republic from 1428–1797.

Birago produced a full-page miniature of the *condottiero* Bartolomeo Colleoni (1400–75) for Antonio Cornazano's *Commentatorium Liber de Vita et Gestis Bartholomei Colei* now in Bergamo (*Biblioteca Civica Angelo Mai, inv. Cassaforte 2.04*). Birago also based some of his playful cherubs in the London *Sforziada* on those sculpted by Amadeo for Colleoni's grandiose funeral chapel in Bergamo: a seditious choice in that Colleoni, as Captain-General of the Venetian Republic, was a fierce rival of the Sforzas.

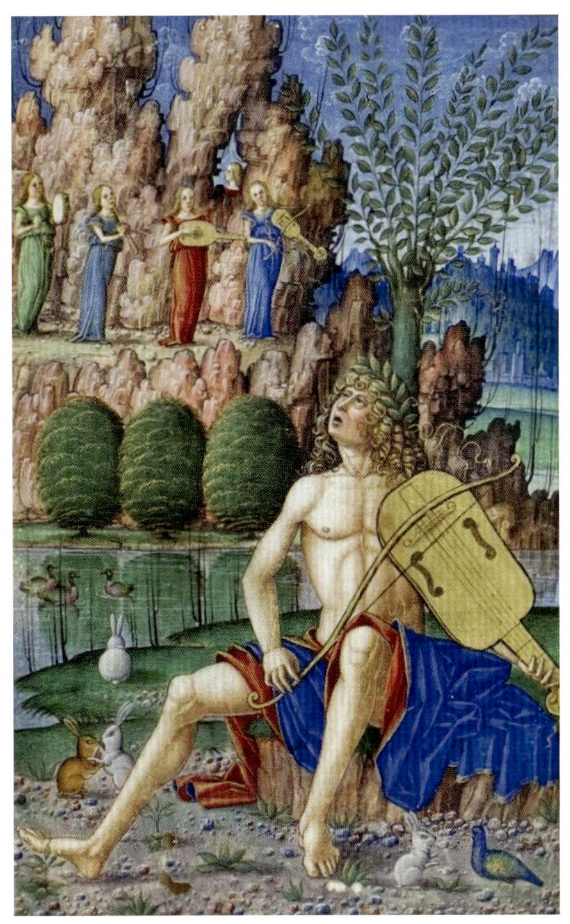

Birago appears to have remained on Venetian soil for much of the 1480s. He almost certainly illuminated the *Commissio of the Procurators of San Marco* now in Oxford's Bodleian Library (*MS Ashmole 811*), and Vittorio Cappello's *Oratio Panegyrica* in the British Library (*Add. MS 21463*), whose first folio features Doge Marco Barbarigo (reigned 1485–86).

Birago produced, probably in Venice or Padua, two spectacular full-page miniatures inspired by Ovid, illustrating *Apollo and The Muses* (*left*) and *Apollo and Daphne* (*see p.266*), for a swanky book of sonnets – penned in gold and silver ink on green and purple pages – acquired by the German humanist Willibald Pirckheimer, who studied in Padua from 1488–91. The book is now in Wolfenbüttel's Herzog August Bibliothek (*cod. 277A*). The *Apollo* miniatures show Birago adopting an increasingly confident, distinctive and spatially sophisticated style that would bear fullest fruit in the *Sforziadas* and *Sforza Hours*. Their style and palette are close to Birago's little-known illuminations for an undated manuscript version of Jacobus de Voragine's *Golden Legend* now in the Polish National Library (*BOZ 11*). An assured sense of composition, and a cartoonist-like ability to succinctly convey emotion, characterize Birago's *Golden Legend* imagery (*see right*) – as does a tendency to give his characters wavy/curly hair that would become obsessive during his time in 1490s Milan.

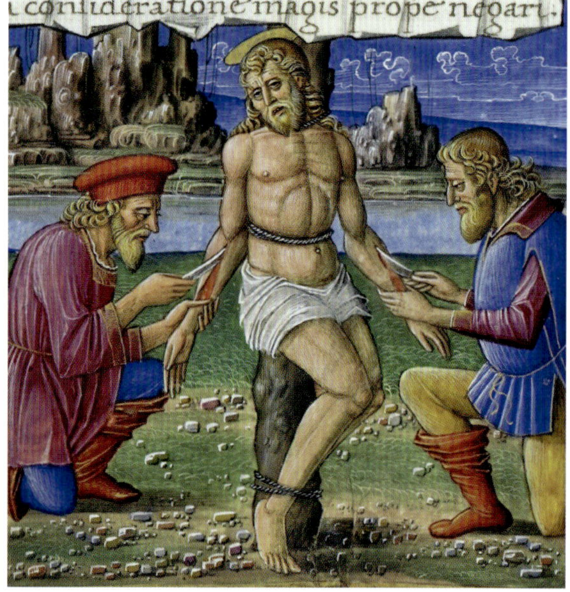

Europe's most spectacular library of the 1480s was assembled by King Matthias Corvinus. Although there is no evidence that Birago visited Hungary, Matthias was the intended recipient of two Birago commissions.

The first of these concerned the frontispiece of a manuscript presentation copy of *Parthenice* by Baptista Mantuanus (1447–1516), which the author sent to Matthias during the 1480s and is now in Budapest's National Széchényi Library (*Cod. Lat. 445*). The frontispiece is badly damaged, though hallmark Birago putti frisking around the columns remain apparent. The text is prefaced by a square medallion incorporating a Virgin & Child modelled on Bellini's *Madonna col Bambino* painted in 1460s Venice (now in Milan's Castello Sforzesca).

Mantuanus may have met Birago in Rome, where he was Vicar General of the Mantuan Congregation of Carmelites. Birago was in Rome by 1489 at the latest: his other Corvinus project was assigned by János Vitéz,[16] Bishop of Veszprém and King Matthias's Ambassador to the Pope. Vitéz commissioned Birago to illuminate a *Pontifical* he was planning to present to his sovereign. The project, however, was abandoned in the wake of Matthias's sudden death on 6 April 1490, with just 24 miniatures (nine large, fifteen small) completed. Bishop Vitéz returned to Hungary without the *Pontifical*, which has remained in Rome ever since and is now in the Biblioteca Apostolica Vaticana (*Ott. Lat. 501*). Birago's illuminations are of note for their pedimented frames which, suggests Laura Paola Gnaccolini, were modelled on those designed under Pinturicchio for the Sala de Misteri in the Vatican's Borgia Apartments.[17]

The departure of Bishop Vitéz left Birago in search of a new patron. As one of the most respected and experienced illuminators in Italy, he is unlikely to have been short of offers. Cardinal Ascanio Sforza, Il Moro's younger brother and Vatican insider, is the man most likely to have appraised Il Moro of Birago's availability. But Birago, whose relationship with Milan's ducal court seems to have been ambivalent, may well have baulked at a direct approach from Sforza top-brass – with a softly-softly approach to his recruitment adopted.

On 8 July 1491 Ambrogio de Predis was recorded in Rome as lodging with the Confraternita di Santo Spirito et Santa Maria in Sassia, where he signed in as an *illuminator ac civis Mediolanensis*. The reason for his visit is not chronicled.

De Predis is usually referred to in Sforza documents as a painter. Did he choose to style himself an *illuminator* on this occasion because his trip to Rome was on book-related business? Was that business to entice his former colleague Gianpietro Birago back to Milan after a two-decade absence?

NOTES

1 The dedication is followed by a short preface by Demetrio Calcondila (or Chalcondylas), a Crete-born scholar who moved to Italy after the fall of Constantinople in 1453, teaching Francesco Sforza's daughter Ippolita and publishing Italy's first book in Greek – the *Grammar* of Constantinus Lascaris – in Milan in 1476.

2 Luisa Cogliati Arano & Ermano Aslan, *Le Monnayage Milanais de Louis XII et ses Antécédents sous les Sforza in La Monnaie, Miroir des Rois – Hôtel de la Monnaie* (Paris 1978); Cogliati Arano: *La Monetazione di Luigi XII ed i Suoi Precedenti Sforzeschi – La Zecca di Milano* (Milan 1984).

3 Francesco Sforza's eldest son and successor Galeazzo Maria followed his example, in 1474 introducing the silver lira with his own portrait, promptly dubbed a *testone*. Before long, the ruler's profile on coinage became widespread across Europe; but Ambrogio de Predis (and later Leonardo) took painted profiled portraits to new psychological levels.

4 Ippolita married the Duke of Calabria (future Alfonso II of Naples) in 1465 [their daughter Isabel of Aragon, mother of Bona Sforza, married Francesco Sforza's grandson Gian Galeazzo in 1489].

5 Arguably the first full-page manuscript portrait of the Renaissance was produced in the early 1450s, for a modestly-sized 18.7 × 13cm volume devoted to the *Vita e Passione du San Maurizio* (Paris, Bibliothèque de l'Arsenal, MS 940, fol. 38v). The portrait – variously attributed to Jacopo Bellini or the youthful Andrea Mantegna (his son-in-law) – shows Jacopo Antonio Marcello (*c.*1399–1465), a Venetian Senator and Mitt Romney lookalike who compiled this life of St Maurice for René d'Anjou. Like Francesco Sforza, Marcello was a Knight of the Order of the Crescent founded by René in 1449, with St Maurice as Patron.

6 Caterina Gilli Pirina, *Dizionario Biografico degli Italiani*, Vol. 39 (1991).

7 Cogliati Arano (*op. cit.*) cites the Jacobsen Institute's stylistic comparison between this work and the *Corvinus Missal* in the Vatican Library (Urb Lat. 110), dating from around 1488/9, as 'an important finding for understanding the international impact of Cristoforo's art,' adding: 'We keep coming back to the date of 1488 already quoted for the *Epitalamio* illuminated by Ambrogio de Predis. It is clear that the King of Hungary was a good client for the De Predis family.'

8 This Book of Hours was shown at TEFAF Maastricht in 2017 by Dr Jörn Günther, a Basel dealer in manuscripts, miniatures and incunabula. According to Dr Günther, it belonged in the 18th century to Francesco Aloysio Filippi; was sold in 1921 by Georges Petit in Paris as part of the Engel-Gros Manuscript Collection; featured in the H.P. Kraus exhibition of *Fifty Medieval and Renaissance Manuscripts* in 1958; and was subsequently acquired by an American private collector.

9 Fernanda Wittgens, *Cristoforo de Predis* in *La Bibliofilia 36* (1934), cited by Dr Jörn Günther in his description of the Book of Hours made for Francesco Borromeo (2017).

10 Archivio di Stato, Modena (*Ricordi de la Salvaroba del Castello*, a.c. 65).

11 Cogliati Arano, in her 1995 article *Miniatori Lombardi al Tempo di Leonardo – I De Predis* published in *FIM Antiquari* (n°7), claims it was Matthias Corvinus himself who commissioned Ambrogio de Predis to illuminate the Marliano *Epitalamion* in 1488. She suggests other Lombard illuminators to work for Matthias included Butinone (for Antonio Bonfini's 1489 Latin translation of the *Trattato del Filarete*, now in the Biblioteca Marciana in Venice); Francesco da Castello (whose name appears in the Kalmancsehi Breviary now in the National Library in Budapest); and Matteo of Milan, whom she tentatively identifies as the Master of the *Messale Arcimboldi*.

12 It seems to have become fashionable to contest the authorship of Ambrogio de Predis: the miniature is skittishly attributed to Matteo da Milano by P.L. Mulas (*Arte Lombarda dai Visconti agli Sforza*, Milan 2015, pp.378/9), and was labelled 'Circle of Leonardo' at the exhibition *Mattia Corvino e Firenze: Art & Humanism at the Court of the King of Hungary* held at the Museo di San Marco in Florence in 2013. A reappraisal of the exceptional versatility and refined skills of Ambrogio de Predis is long overdue. As a portraitist able to present his subjects with gleaming-eyed good humour he stands comparison with Frans Hals.

13 Both covers of the epithalamion have been mutilated: their central feature (presumably a coat of arms) has been removed, and the small shields in each corner have been obliterated with red wax. The frontispiece of the Uffizi Sforziada was similarly vandalized (*see Chapter VII*), as was an inscribed shield on the ceiling of the Castello Sforzesco's Sala della Asse. In each case motivation appears to have been fanatical anti-Sforza hostility.

14 Elisabetta Gnignera (correspondence with the author 10.6.2013) believes the profile shows a warrior.

15 *cf* David Alan Brown, *Origins of a Genius* (Yale University Press, 1998); Birago's image of St Sebastian in the *Sforza Hours* (fol. 193v) features not only a curly-coated terrier, but also a figure (bottom left) wearing what resembles a jokey dog-hair wig.

16 János Vitéz (namesake nephew of Archbishop János Vitéz, famed for his library) studied in Paris and served Matthias Corvinus as Chancellor. He became Bishop of Sirmium in 1482 and Bishop of Veszprém in June 1489. He was later Bishop of Vienna under Emperor Maximilian, and Chairman of the Sodalitas Literaria Danubia founded by Konrad Celtis.

17 Laura Paola Gnaccolini's *Giovan Pietro Birago: Miniatore per Re Mattia Corvino* (Arte Lombarda, 2003) presents detailed insight into Birago's work for Bishop Vitéz.

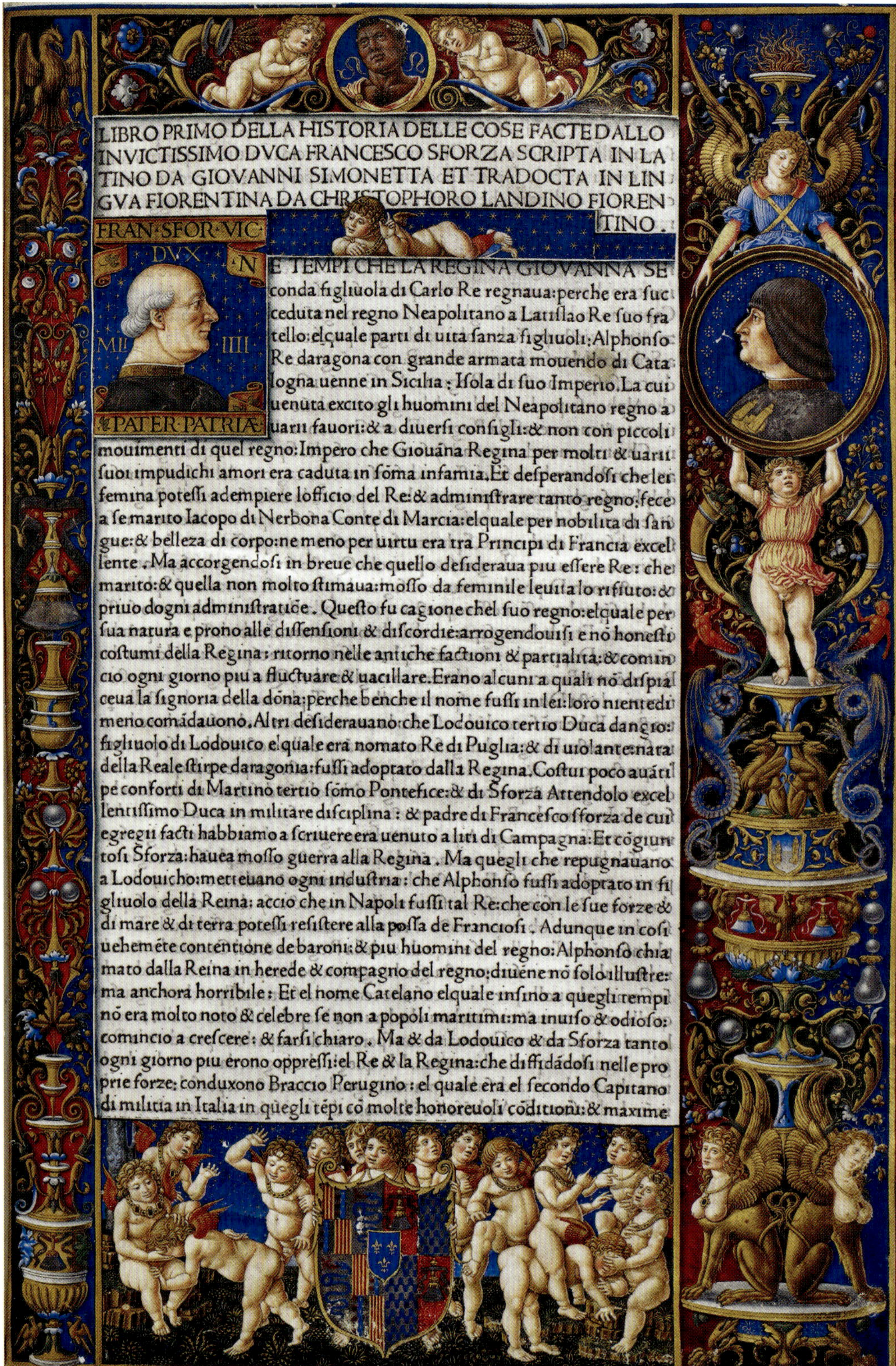

SFORZIADA (FRONTISPIECE) – BRITISH LIBRARY, LONDON (GRENVILLE 7251)

V

RIDDLE OF THE SPHINXES
THE DIPLOMATIC SFORZIADA

ON 29 MARCH 1490 an order was placed for 700 copies of the 'Floren-tine' *Sforziada*, plus four extra copies on parchment.[1] The first of these special copies to be illuminated glorified a new-look Il Moro with visual references to Hungary, Genoa and France. But this splendid volume was not put to the use originally intended – with the folio set aside for a full-page portrait left forever blank.

PROVENANCE

1491 King Charles VIII of France
1498 Bibliothèque du Roi, Blois (later Fontainebleau)
1600 (?) Jacques-Auguste de Thou (1553–1617)
1617 (?) Jacques-Auguste de Thou II (1609–77)
1680 (?) Jean-Jacques Charron, Marquis de Menars (1643–1718)
1706 (?) Cardinal Armand Gaston Maximilien de Rohan-Soubise (1674–1749)
1749 Charles de Rohan, Prince de Soubise (1715–87)
1789 Comte Justin MacCarthy-Reagh (1744–1811)
1815 George Hibbert (1757–1837)
1829 Philip Augustus Hanrott (1776–1856)
1833 Sir Thomas Grenville (1755–1846)
1847 British Library, London

FRANCESCO SFORZA MEDALLION

Francesco is shown on a blue ground spangled with stars (15 six-armed asterisks, 29 four-armed crosses, 46 dots). **FRAN SFOR VIC** (*FRANCISCUS SFORTIA VICECOMES*, i.e. Francesco Sforza Visconti) and **PATER PATRIÆ** (FATHER OF THE FATHERLAND) appear in black letters on gold banners (embellished with laurel leaves) above and below. The title PATER PATRIÆ was originally bestowed in Ancient Rome – first upon Marcus Furius Camillus by the Senate in 386 BC. Later recipients included Julius Caesar. It will have had more immediate resonance to Renaissance readers for being posthumously assigned to Francesco's old ally Cosimo de' Medici by the Signoria of Florence in 1465: the inscription on his tomb-slab reads *COSMVS MEDICES - HIC SITVS EST - DECRETO PVBLICO - PATER PATRIAE.*[2]

Francesco (like Muzio Attendoli in the manuscript discussed in *Chapter II*) is wearing black armour. In powerful close-up it can be seen that his breast-plate features the tree emblem with a hand and collar reaching down towards a large greyhound. His expression is cheerful and serene. Faint wisps of unruly hair emerge from the back of his head. This subtle portrait displays the skill of Ambrogio de Predis: no comparable gift for portraiture is apparent from Birago's known œuvre. The title **DVX MLI IIII** (DUX MEDIOLANI IV or *4th Duke of Milan*) appears in gold letters on the blue ground; *DVX* is centred, immediately beneath the top gold banner; *MLI* and *IIII* appear either side of Francesco's head, at chin level. The text's initial *N* in black, and the same size as the other lettering on the gold banner, is positioned on a downward slant, leading into the *Sforziada's* first sentence.

ROUNDEL

A gold-rimmed profile of Il Moro – similar to that used on coins struck during his reign,[3] albeit with his profile in reverse – is positioned in the right margin very slightly lower than the Francesco medallion, on a blue ground ringed with seventeen rosettes. The artistic quality of Il Moro's profile is slightly inferior to that of Francesco's, and doubtless by the hand of Birago – perhaps colouring over a portrait under-drawing by Ambrogio de Predis.

Like his father, Il Moro wears a gold collar and black breastplate, adorned in gold with the twin-tower emblem of Genoa.[4] The same towers (or rather lighthouses, guarding the entrance to the port of Genoa)[5] also appear on the central roundel on the front of this *Sforziada's* velvet binding.

Il Moro's hair, grey in the Muzio volume, is here black. This was not his natural colour, but sporadically used in portraits with the presumable intention of playing up a macho image. This appears to be the first time Il Moro is officially depicted with black hair – part of a 'new-look' campaign launched after his near-fatal illness of 1487/88.

HAUT-DE-PAGE

A smaller roundel on a blue ground features a hirsute, curly-haired, hairy-chested Moor gazing heavenwards, his neck surrounded by undulating ribbons. He is wearing a bandau and orange toga – evoking the ceremonial,

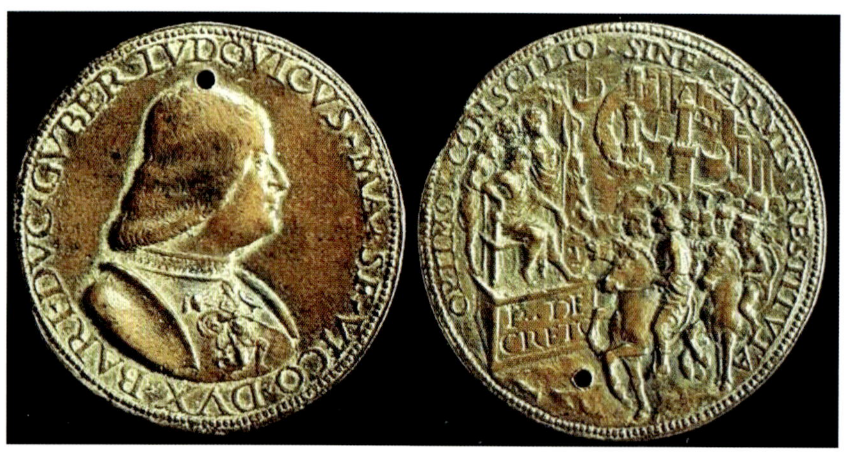

CARADOSSO: 1488 MEDAL COMMEMORATING RETURN OF GENOA TO MILANESE RULE – TWIN LIGHTHOUSES FEATURE ON REVERSE

gold-bordered *toga picta* worn by Roman emperors and generals borne in triumph. He is flanked by horns of plenty and cherubs kneeling in a pose that recalls Leonardo's *St Jerome* in the Vatican.

The roundel also recalls the one in the *haut-de-page* of the frontispiece to Pliny's *Natural History* printed in Venice in 1476, attributed to Birago in *Chapter IV*; and may be intended to recall the Moor descending from Heaven in a headband (flanked by four angels) in Leonardo da Vinci's theatricals celebrating the wedding of Giovanni Adorno and Eleonora Sanseverino, half-sister of Galeazzo, in December 1490.

BAS-DE-PAGE

The largest decorative emblem on the entire page is an intricate coat of arms whose importance is enhanced by being flanked by a virtual rugby team of putti – not just a couple, as in the Marliano *Epitalamion* and *Muzio* frontispieces. This virtuoso Birago showpiece fields fourteen playful putti with gold wings, split into two groups of seven on either side of Il Moro's coat of arms as Duke of Bari, impaled with the French *fleurs-de-lys*. They are in a grassy, slightly rocky field, whose vegetation evokes the *Virgin of the Rocks* (and Leonardo's earlier *Annunciation*) beneath a starry blue ground identical to that of the Francesco Sforza medallion. Twelve of the cherubs wear identical chains recalling the ceremonial chain-necklace worn by the Duke of Milan, although some of the chains appear thicker than the others. The two cherubs on the far left, at the foot of a tree, have different necklaces. One is standing, and wears a single precious stone (probably an emerald). The other is seated, and sports three stones (two rubies either side of an emerald).[6]

The scene has some similarities with a Birago engraving in the Kupferstichkabinett in Berlin (*below*). According to Warner, the games played are *Hot Cockles* (on the left) and *Buck, Buck, How Many Horns Do I Hold Up?* (on the right).[7] Portraying putti in this context may perhaps be a reference to the youth and infantile nature of Gian Galeazzo. Evans suggests the second game evokes the transience of tyrannical regimes, and also that the groups of putti derive from those in the terracotta reliefs in the sacristy of Santa Maria presso San Satiro in Milan, designed by Bramante in the 1480s and interspersed with

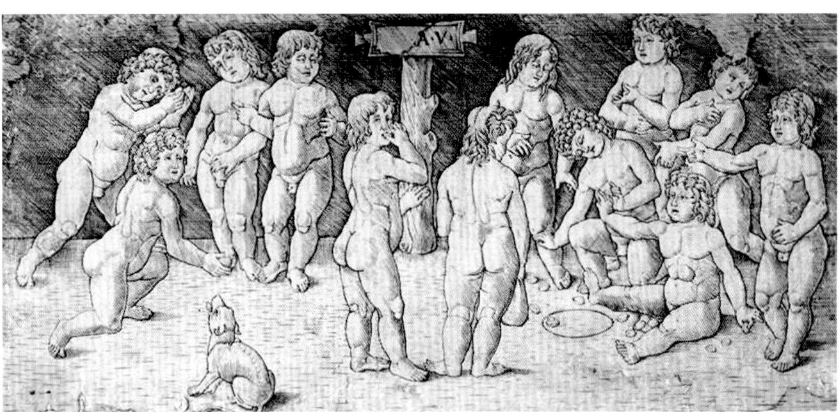

high-relief roundels – made by Agostino Fonduli in 1483 – that recall the *haut-de-page* Moro roundel here.[8] Fonduli was recommended for the San Satiro job by none other than Birago's associate Ambrogio de Predis, who lived close to Fonduli near the Porta Ticinese. The two were friends: Fonduli was a witness to the *Virgin of the Rocks* contract signed by Ambrogio, his brother Evangelista and Leonardo da Vinci in April 1483.[9]

There are a number of iconographical similarities between San Satiro and Birago's first *Sforziada* frontispiece, including winged sphynxes, putti brandishing horns of plenty, and gryphons in the right-hand column of the *Sforziada* frontispiece which echo those on a pilaster in the San Satiro sacristy.

Playful putti proliferated in Renaissance Italy, but those Birago appears to have drawn closest inspiration from are to be found gallivanting around the tomb of the *condottiero* Bartolomeo Colleoni in Bergamo, designed by Birago's contemporary Giovanni Antonio Amadeo.[10] Birago quotes directly from this tomb's marble frieze (*below left*) in the *bas-de-page* of the London *Sforziada*, but adds a fifth cherub to Amadeo's composition – who appears to be committing sodomy (*below right*). As the only cherub to have smooth rather than curly hair, and as one of the few figures with ginger hair in Birago's œuvre, it is tempting to see this as a mischievous reference to Leonardo da Vinci – whose youthful Florentine trial for homosexuality appears to have provoked ribald comment in Sforza Milan (*see Chapter XII*).

The political message of this *bas-de-page*, then, is playfully satirical. It centres on the heraldic shield and on the two cherubs to the left, who wear more elaborate chains than the others. The seated blond cherub with triple-jewel chain, taking part in the spanking games, symbolizes the effete Gian Galeazzo, the official but powerless Duke. The darker-haired cherub (in single-stone necklace) standing behind him, raising a disapproving hand and looking alarmed at all the infantile behaviour, represents Il Moro: the level-headed Regent needed to restore order.

Birago would later, in the Uffizi and Polish *Sforziadas*, daringly combine Moro/cherub imagery – to produce dark-skinned cherubs.

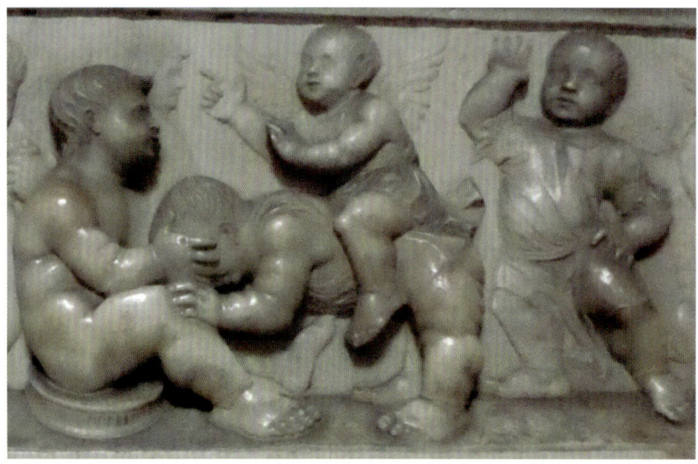

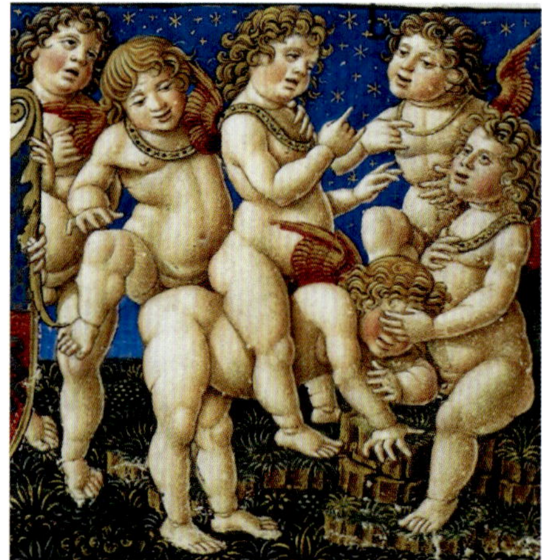

Red/blue halved, with a green ground for central motifs, and topped by a majestic angel in blue tunic with red collar and sleeves holding – and reverentially looking down upon – a roundel with a profile of Il Moro. It has been suggested that the design of this sheltering angel, with wings outspread, harks back to the iconography of Roman emperors.[11] The angel is topped by a flaming plinth flanked by scrolling foliage; a quince appears in the top corners of the border. The roundel is borne by a winged putto in a gold tunic raised as if by a gust of wind, saucily revealing its naked midriff – a descendant of the cherub supporting a laurel-rimmed coat of arms in Birago's frontispiece to a *Breviary* (*Use of Rome*) printed in Venice in 1478.

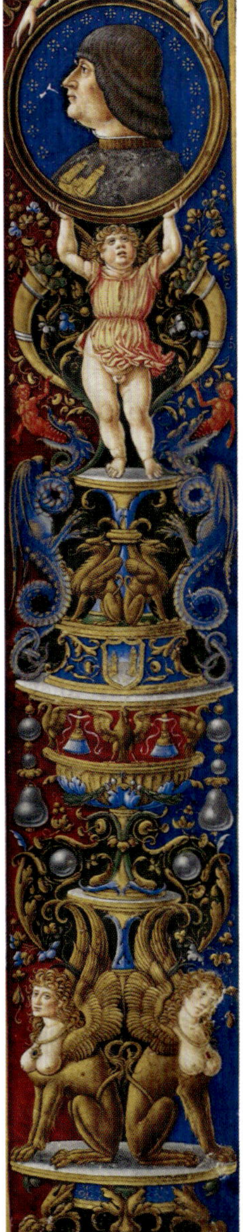

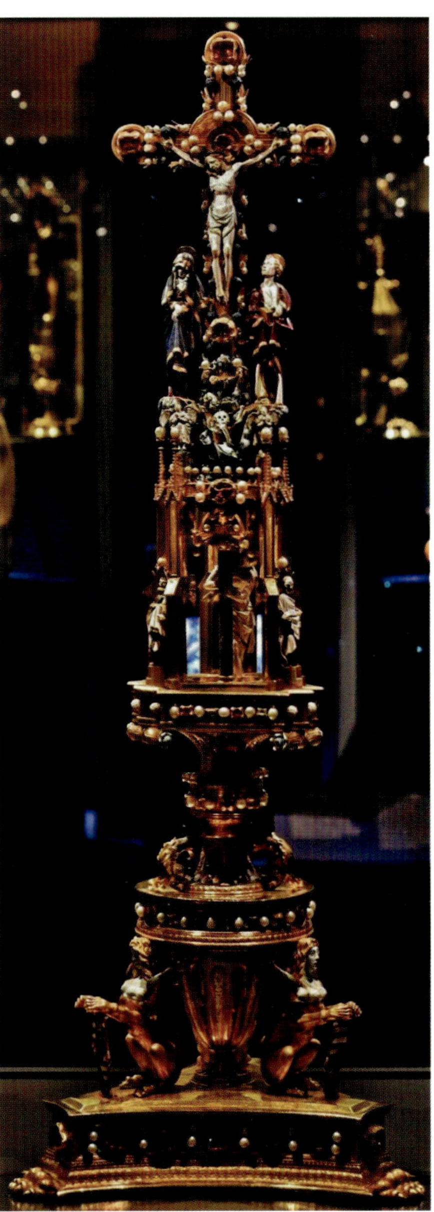

This putto is perched on top of a multi-tiered fountain flanked by Visconti vipers transformed into ferocious winged dragons, each regurgitating (or swallowing) a tiny red human figure. The fountain features a shield with the Genoa[12] twin-tower emblem between two gryphons and an alternating frieze of *scopetti* and phoenixes (*see far left*).

The base of the fountain is flanked by two bare-breasted sphinxes with lions' bodies and tails, large wings and long blond hair. Both sport a necklace: one set with an emerald, one with a ruby. These sphinxes are inspired by those at the base of the lower section of the *Corvinus Calvary* made by Lombard goldsmith Cristoforo Foppa– better known as Caradosso – for Matthias Corvinus in the late 1480s, now in Esztergom Cathedral (*left*).[13] By aping the tiered structure of this spectacular work, but topping it not with a crucifix but a portrait of his patron, Birago makes his first blasphemous association of Il Moro with Christ. It is tempting to see a parallel with the very dark-haired Christ in Bergognone's 1490 *Crucifixion* in the Certosa di Pavia (*see p.37*).

The elongated back paws and squatting posture of Caradosso's and Birago's sphinxes are identical; their head and breasts are flesh-coloured, their bodies golden; they have the same gold

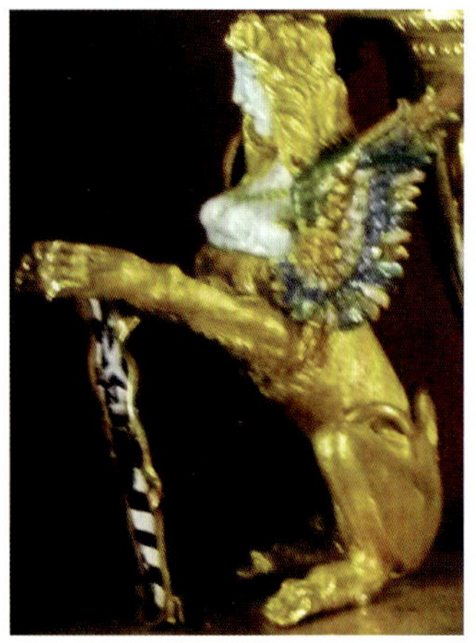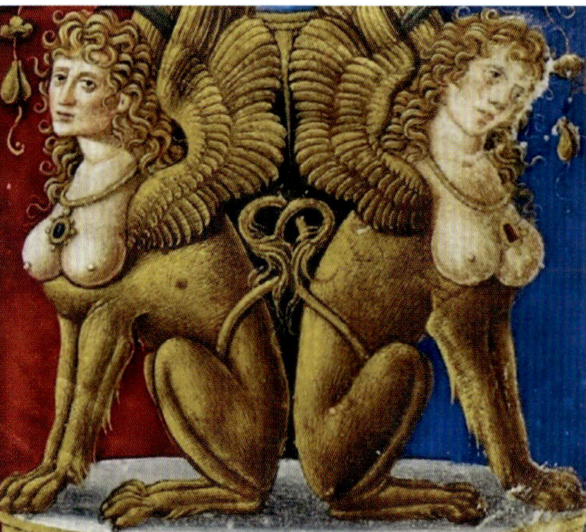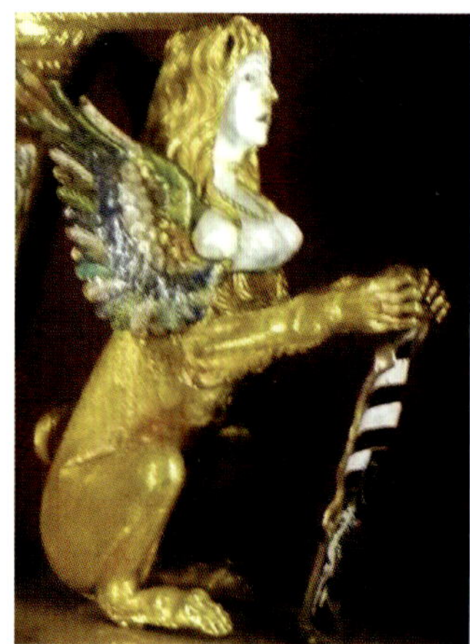

necklaces with gemstone pendant; their tails are whisked up behind them (albeit with a greater flourish by Birago); and the squat, lion-claw feet of the bases are the same.

Further proof of Birago's intimate knowledge of, and long-lasting enthusiasm for, Caradosso's design can be found in a print he made in Milan a decade or so later – with similar bare-breasted sphinxes, this time holding shields, as they do in the *Corvinus Calvary*.[14]

Priest or not, Birago was a man of the flesh: his voluptuous sphinxes are far more buxom than those in Esztergom. His interest in female anatomy would be a significant feature of his frontispiece for the Polish *Sforziada* (*see Chapter IX*).

LEFT BORDER

Green/blue halved, with a red ground for central motifs. The border is topped by a golden eagle and twice features Il Moro's *scopetta* emblem: once separately, ringed by a banner with its motto ***MERITO ET TEMPORE***; and, in a smaller version lower down, on the side of a gadrooned urn with leafy satyr masks on either side.

UNIQUE EXTRA FEATURE

Just above the profile of Francesco, on an identical star-spangled blue ground, is a reclining winged putto in a gold chain, wearing gold-topped red (right leg) and blue (left leg) stockings. This putto's pose and page position presage similar putti in the *Sforza Hours*. They derive from the Borromeo *Libre d'Oro* illustrated by Cristoforo de Predis.

This reclining putto gazes down at Francesco with a cheeky smile, and points up with his left hand towards the Roman Moor. His message seems to be along the lines of 'See what he has managed to achieve!'[15] This is the only instance in any *Sforziada* of the gap between the four lines of capital-lettered introductory preamble, and the start of the text proper, being filled by an illustration – which reinforces the impression that especial care was lavished on this frontispiece and that it was probably, therefore, the first of the four.

BINDING

This is the only *Sforziada* to retain its original binding (*see below*). This is of dark red velvet, with five nielloed metal bosses. Such cover designs were in constant use throughout the late 15th century.

The central roundel (*see p.90*) is decorated with the twin-tower Genoa motif and a semi-illegible inscription probably intended to convey the (Spanish) motto associated with the emblem: *TAL TRABALIO MES PLASES POR TAL THESAUROS NON PERDER* ('such labour pleases me if it means not losing such a treasure'); the four corner bosses are plain.

Just one of the three original silver clasps remains – decorated on one side with a Moor's head (*below*), and on the other with a *scopetta* and the motto *Merito et Tempore*.

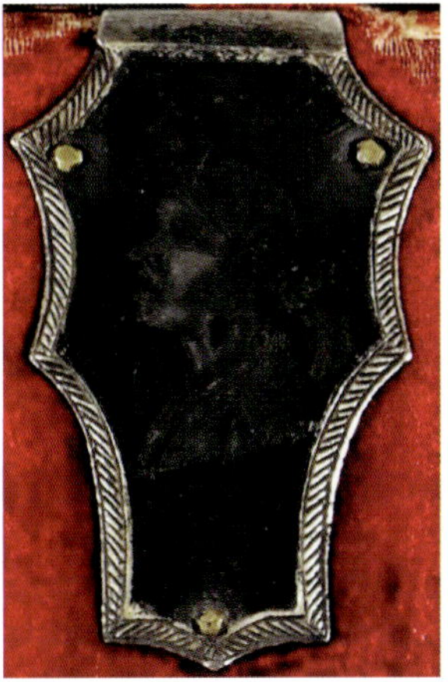

DATE

Between late 1490 and early 1492. This is commonly accepted as the first, and grandest, of the four copies of the Florentine *Sforziadas* illuminated by Birago. As printing was only commissioned in late March 1490, and must have taken several months, the earliest potential dating for this frontispiece is late 1490. A more probable dating is 1491.

HISTORICAL BACKGROUND

The (Florentine) Italian version of the *Sforziada* was prepared by Cristoforo Landino in 1484/5. An elegant manuscript copy of his translation was drafted, then submitted to *Sforziada* author Giovanni Simonetta whose comments were reflected, or more usually ignored, in the definitive Florentine text. The literary and design process was so painstaking that the translation was printed – in an exceptionally large and luxurious format – only six years after Landino was first contacted.

Most commentators assume that Il Moro commissioned the first of the four presentation copies printed on vellum for himself: Birago's frontispiece features his coat of arms, profiled portrait and repeated *scopetta* emblem. Yet the frontispiece makes no allusion to Il Moro's wedding to Beatrice d'Este on 17 January 1491 which, when printing was completed, must have been imminent – or extremely recent. The volume cannot, therefore, have been designed to celebrate this marriage, and it is barely conceivable that it was intended for Il Moro: how could he have explained to his new wife – or to the courtiers and diplomats shown the volume – that a book in his own honour ignored the most important personal event of his life? (One half-suspects that the colophon's vague *MCCCCLXXXX* was used to avoid indicating that printing ended on a date embarrassingly close to 17 January 1491).

Birago's portrayal of Il Moro with his hair dyed black, rather than its natural grey (as in the Paris and Uffizi *Sforziadas*), is further evidence that this first presentation copy was primarily intended for a foreign audience unfamiliar with Il Moro's everyday appearance.

The similarities between the frontispiece's square-format portrait medallion and that of Matthias Corvinus in the Marliano *Epitalamion*, and the quoting of the sphinxes from the Corvinus *Calvary* now in Esztergom, suggest this first *Sforziada* presentation copy was originally intended for Hungary.

King Matthias had assembled the most prestigious library in Europe, and the largest after the Vatican's. What better way for Il Moro to be associated with this library – predominantly stocked with books from Florence rather than Milan – than by presenting it with a book in *lingua fiorentina* that would leave its Florentine counterparts in the Danubian shade?

The links between Milan and Matthias Corvinus harked back to 1464 when, six years after his election as King of Hungary, Matthias had unsuccessfully sought the hand of Francesco Sforza's eldest daughter Ippolita. She wed instead Alfonso, eldest son of King Ferrante of Naples; Matthias later married Alfonso's sister Beatrix.

In 1474, the year after the birth of his illegitimate son János Corvinus, Matthias made a pilgrimage to Santiago de Compostela – visiting the great Visconti-Sforza Library in Pavia on his way back to Buda. His own library, christened the *Bibliotheca Corviniana*, would become the talk of Europe – with János named as co-owner.

In 1484 Il Moro recognized János as Matthias's heir. When Matthias assured Il Moro that his wife Beatrix – whom he had married in 1476 – could not have children, Il Moro agreed to the marriage between János and Il Moro's twelve-year-old niece Bianca Maria, elder daughter of Duke Galeazzo Maria. She had been betrothed as an infant (in January 1474) to her cousin Philibert I of Savoy, but he died in 1482. An exchange of gifts in early 1485 may, on Il Moro's behalf, have included a *Madonna* by Leonardo da Vinci.[16]

Hungary's importance to Il Moro's diplomatic scheme of things has been neglected in the wake of the spectacular efforts he subsequently made to woo first France, then Habsburg Austria – which disposed of the official investiture to the Duchy of Milan. But, in the 1480s, there was no purpose in Il Moro's seeking the support of Holy Roman Emperor Friedrich III – who had thrice spurned requests for the investiture from Il Moro's father Francesco, and made it abundantly clear he would not bestow a Habsburg kiss of approval on any member of the 'usurper' Sforza clan. In any case, Habsburg power seemed on the wane: Matthias Corvinus seized Vienna in 1485, consolidating his status as the foremost sovereign of central Europe.

The marriage *per procuram* between Bianca Maria and the absent János took place in Milan on 25 November 1487. Il Moro escorted his niece to the altar but was too ill to remain for the ceremony, conducted by Matthias's envoy János Filipec, Bishop of Oradea.[17] Bianca Maria's dowry was set at 100,000 gold coins and her departure for Hungary slated for November 1488.

In February 1488 Il Moro sent Guidantonio Arcimboldi (future Archbishop of Milan) to Hungary to plan the bridal journey – and deliver fresh gifts, including a precious manuscript for Matthias's library, the Marliano *Epitalamion* (*see p.70*). Arcimboldi informed Il Moro that Matthias – still only 45 – was ill with gout, and his wife Beatrix keen to scupper the János-Bianca Maria marriage. This was rescheduled for Spring 1489 – by when Matthias's gout was so severe he could hardly walk, and the marriage further postponed until September. Il Moro kept up the pressure, writing an avuncular letter to young János requesting a copy of a rare manuscript by Festus Pompeius, and dispatching the goldsmith Caradosso to Buda. When the wedding was again put off, to Spring 1490, Il Moro wrote cajolingly to János, assuring him that Bianca Maria was keen to rush into his arms.[18] In March 1490 the Milan ambassador reported rumours that the sickly Matthias was now thinking of marrying János to an Austrian princess to shore up his succession.[19]

This, then, was the situation when the Florentine edition of the *Sforziada* was sent to the printers on 29 March 1490. It would have been entirely logical for Il Moro to commission a magnificently illuminated copy of the *Sforziada* for the man whose backing was needed for the marriage to go ahead, and whose appetite for splendid books was legendary. His son János would have been the most likely subject of the full-page portrait which the layout of this 1490 edition was specifically designed to accommodate.

An 18 × 14cm silverpoint drawing believed to portray *János Corvinus* is to be found in the Musée Bonnat-Helleu in Bayonne.[20] It is attributed to the same Ambrogio de Predis who immortalized Matthias in the Marliano *Epitalamion* – the same Ambrogio de Predis to whom prospective bride Bianca Maria referred five years later as *el nostro pinctore*, with a casual familiarity borne of a longstanding collaboration whose roots can be traced back to her

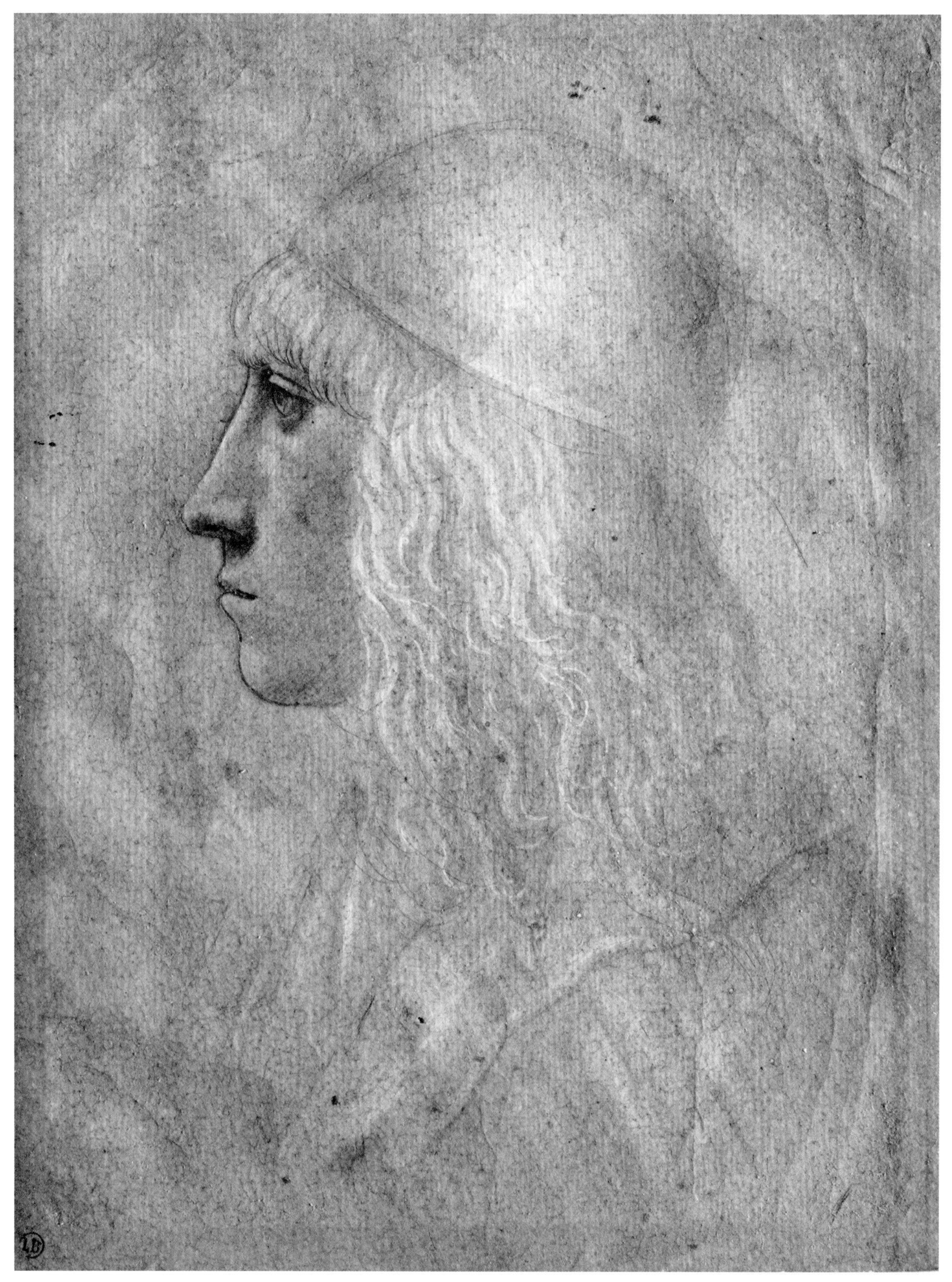

AMBROGIO DE PREDIS: *JÁNOS CORVINUS* – SILVERPOINT 34 × 25 cm – MUSEE BONNAT, BAYONNE

father's avuncular concern for the well-being of Ambrogio's elder half-brother and fellow court-artist, Cristoforo.[21]

The Bayonne portrait is on blued paper – rarely found in Milan but more common in Venice, where it was made using a dye produced from imported indigo. De Predis may have acquired a supply of blued paper in Venice *en route* to Hungary in 1488; it is worth noting that two of Leonardo da Vinci's infrequent drawings on blued paper include designs (now in Windsor Castle), usually dated to 1488/9, for the equestrian monument to Francesco Sforza.

Furthermore, the left-facing profile in the silverpoint drawing occupies the page in almost exactly the same proportions as Leonardo's portrait of Bianca Sforza for the Polish *Sforziada*. In each case the head occupies half the page.

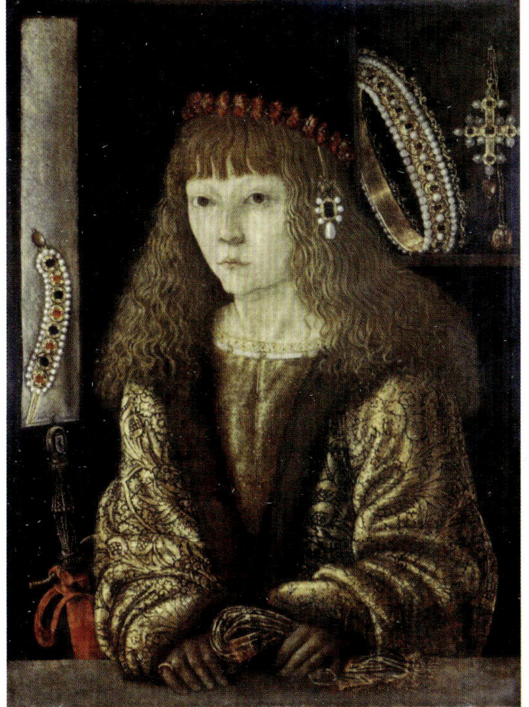

The profiled youth has the same lank hair, sullen expression and long, straight nose found in several portrayals of János – notably *János Corvinus als Hochzeiter* by Ferrara court artist Baldassare Estense (*left*), doubtless painted for Duchess Eleonora d'Este, the sister of János's stepmother Beatrix, following János's betrothal to Bianca Maria (Alte Pinakothek, Munich, *Inv. 12441*).

A stylized depiction of János, in coloured enamel, also appears on Caradosso's *Calvary* support – in a Chariot of the Moon drawn by two unicorns said to symbolize love or fidelity.

The blued-paper youth is portrayed in the strongly outlined profile mandatory in Sforza Milan for portraits of the aristocratic élite. He wears the same brimless cap as Piero de' Medici in Gherardo's full-page portrait for the Greek Homer, and is shown at around the same age (mid-teens).

Gherardo – a friend of Leonardo da Vinci from their Florence days – was also working as an illuminator for Matthias Corvinus in the late 1480s. One of his most famous miniatures, thought to have been produced jointly with his brother Monte, is the frontispiece for the Corvinus Bible now in Florence's Biblioteca Medicea Laurenziana (*Plut. 15. Cod. 17*).

This shows King David praying to God in an Italianate landscape with three kings in the middle distance – clearly identifiable as Charles VIII (King of France), Matthias Corvinus (King of Hungary) and Maximilian Habsburg (King of the Romans). Matthias is clad in gold, figuratively pointing the way to Bethlehem.

The absence of a Milanese representative amongst this noble gathering is sure to have irked Il Moro, especially in a work emanating from Florence, and to have provided further motivation for his new *Sforziada* to outshine Gherardo's *Homer* by including its own, slightly larger full-page portrait.

But no full-page *Sforziada* portrait of János was ever completed. Matthias died suddenly in Vienna on 6 April 1490 after eating an unripe fig. Il Moro heard the news on April 15, and immediately wrote to Beatrix asking her to back János as the new king.[22] On April 20 Il Moro wrote to János, urging him to seize the Hungarian throne. Il Moro's plans for a dynastic alliance to bolster his political authority were up in the air. It is unlikely to be coincidental that, on April 23, Leonardo da Vinci resumed work on one of Il Moro's pet propaganda projects, the *Sforza Horse*.

When Vladislas Jagiellon, King of Bohemia, emerged as a prime contender for the Hungarian throne, Il Moro offered Hungary's most influential cleric, Bishop Tamás Bakócz, a costly array of silver to engineer a wedding between Vladislas and Bianca Maria. Vladislas was elected king on July 15. But any lingering hopes of Bianca Maria becoming Queen of Hungary were dashed on October 4, with Vladislas's *Realpolitik* marriage to Dowager Queen Beatrix. Young János, still only seventeen, faded from the political scene.

Bianca Maria would continue to be used as a diplomatic pawn, ultimately marrying Habsburg Emperor Maximilian I in November 1493, six weeks after her marriage to János had been annulled by the Pope.

INTERPRETATION

Once the János/Bianca Maria wedding had fallen through, Il Moro found himself with a vellum *Sforziada* whose blank pages, designed to accommodate a full-page portrait, now made little sense. This luxurious book, conceived as a diplomatic tool, could no longer be sent as a wedding-gift to a Hungary – although one of the most striking iconographic features of its illuminated frontispiece, the *Calvinus Calvary*, appears to pay tribute to the volume's originally intended destination.[23]

Il Moro was compelled to seek alliance elsewhere. The *Sforziada's* repeated use of the twin-tower motif suggests he looked to France.

The twin towers of Genoa appear three times in this copy of the *Sforziada*: on Il Moro's breastplate; on a small shield halfway up the right-hand border; and engraved on the cover's central roundel (*right*).

Genoa was a French fiefdom, but of crucial importance to Milan as an outlet to the sea. It was first brought under Milanese sway by Francesco Sforza in 1463; lost by Bona di Savoia in 1477; then recovered by Il Moro in 1488, after he had sent troops to Genoa under Gianfrancesco Sanseverino (Galeazzo's eldest brother) and pressured Paolo Fregoso, Cardinal Archbishop of Genoa, into accepting a Milanese protectorate – ostensibly against Florentine aggression.[24]

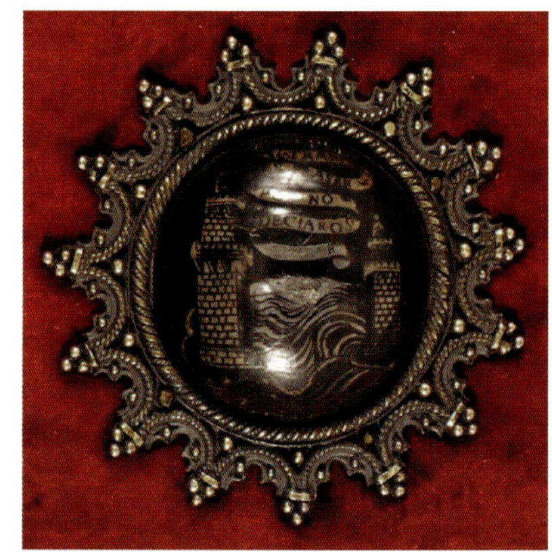

Il Moro appointed Agostino Adorno as the new Governor of Genoa. His brother Giovanni – the city's Military Commander – was promptly betrothed to Eleonora Sanseverino (Galeazzo's younger sister).

The most prominent feature of Birago's frontispiece is Il Moro's coats of arms as Duke of Bari, showcased in the *bas-de-page*. Except that they are not the coat of arms of the Duke of Bari. Il Moro's original arms as Duke of Bari, quoted in the Trivulziana's *Compendio de la Historia Sforzesca* (*see p.52*) produced around 1486/7, did *not* include a *fleur-de-lys* escutcheon.

The first surviving evidence of this added escutcheon appears on the *Cassone dei Tre Duchi* probably made as a wedding gift for Gian Galeazzo in early 1489. What does it mean?

Suggestions that the added *fleurs-de-lys* refer to the Este coat of arms, and therefore to Il Moro's marriage to Beatrice d'Este, are spurious. The impaling of a small shield on the centre of a larger one may indeed be a heraldic means of representing family alliance – but that is not the case here. Although *fleurs-de-lys* appear in the Este arms, they do so within red-and-white *édenté* (dog-tooth) borders; in other words, looking quite different from the simple blue shield with three gold lilies instantly recognizable as the French royal emblem since the early Middle Ages.[25]

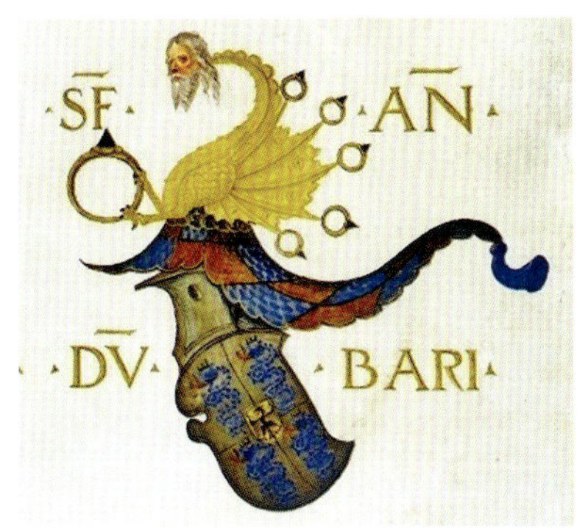

But an impaled shield can also represent dynastic allegiance. A telling example is the shield with the Habsburg eagle impaled on quartered Sforza vipers (*left*) that represents Il Moro's second son Francesco at the head of a 1498 legal document in Milan's Archivio Storico Civico, alongside the arms of Il Moro and his elder son Massimiliano.

The use of the *fleur-de-lys* escutcheon in the London *Sforziada* is, then, a sign of allegiance to France. It draws attention to the fact that Genoa was officially under French suzerainty.

Birago's frontispiece in the London *Sforziada* appears to convey the message that, having reconquered Genoa, Il Moro was keen to receive the French investiture – and be considered the worthy heir to his illustrious father.

In Summer 1490, with hopes of a Hungarian dynastic alliance fast fading, Il Moro sent an envoy to France to sound out Charles VIII about renewing the Genoese investiture. Charles VIII had become king in 1483 at the age of thirteen. Now he was twenty – and keen to emerge from the assertive regency of his elder sister Anne. Prompted by some Il Moro largesse, Charles responded favourably. In April 1491 he dispatched an embassy to Milan to conduct the investiture ceremony – officially in the name of Duke Gian Galeazzo, but effectively cementing France's *de facto* recognition of Il Moro as ruler of Milan.

The London *Sforziada* may have been presented to the French delegation on this occasion,[26] or sent to King Charles VIII shortly afterwards – perhaps as a gift upon his marriage to Anne of Brittany in Langeais on 6 December 1491. In 1494, when Charles VIII arrived in Italy at the head of a French army, Il Moro presented him with a tiny prayer-book, again illustrated by Birago (*see p.92*).

Supposing the London *Sforziada* to have been presented to Charles VIII by Il Moro would explain how it wound up in the French royal library without

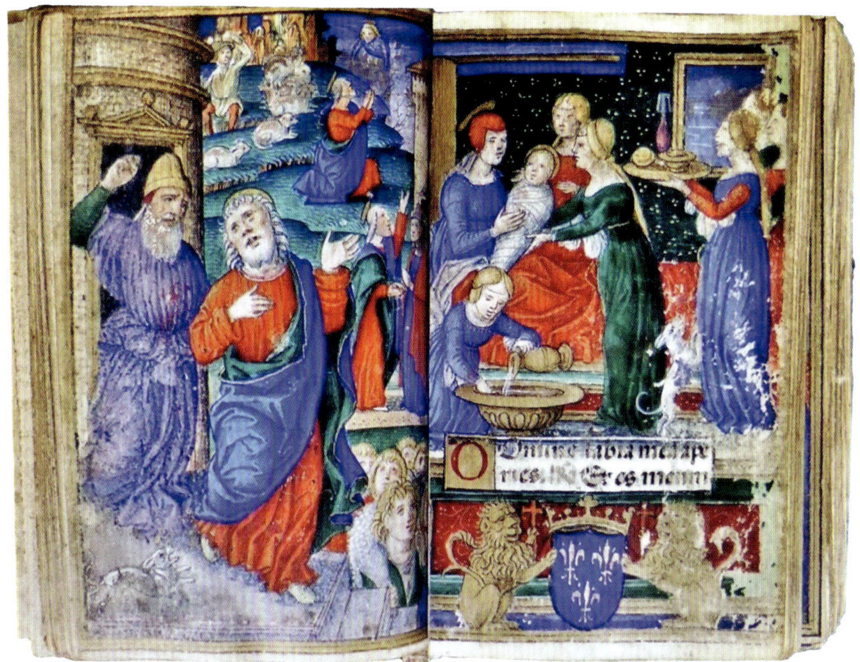

featuring the inscription *de Pavye au roy Louis XII* routinely added to the books (including the Paris *Sforziada* and *Muzio* biography) plundered from Pavia by the French in 1499/1500. It would also explain why this volume is the only one of the four illuminated *Sforziadas* to retain its original binding: it would be logical for a volume received as a gift to be kept unaltered – rather than, had it been a spoil of war, having the outward signs of its original owners removed.

Evidence of the volume's presence in the French Royal Library comes from the fact that its frontispiece medallion of Francesco Sforza appears to have served as the model for the restoration of the mutilated equivalent medallion from the Uffizi *Sforziada* (*see p.109*). The London *Sforziada* volume was sold at the estate sale of Charles de Rohan, Prince de Soubise, in 1789, entering his library through a line of sales and bequests that can be traced back to royal librarian Jacques-Auguste de Thou (1553–1617), Grand Master of the Bibliothèque du Roi from 1593.[27]

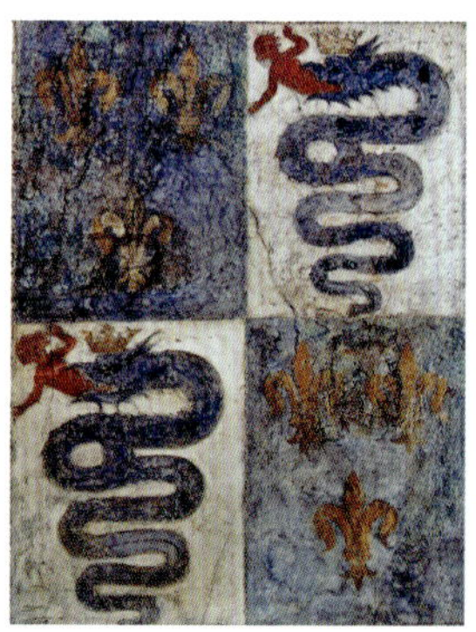

Il Moro had another reason to adopt the *fleurs-de-lys*: it had, briefly, become an heraldic part of the Sforza arms in 1468, after the marriage of his brother Galeazzo Maria to Bona di Savoia. Shields with viper/*fleurs-de-lys* quarters would be used in books and documents over the next decade – and remain painted on walls and carved atop pillars in Milan's Castello Sforzesco (*see right*). Galeazzo Maria famously entered Florence on his State visit of 1472 clad in a doublet embroidered throughout with *fleurs-de-lys* – and was shown wearing it by Piero Pollaiolo in his fastidious official portrait (*see p.27*).

Using the *fleurs-de-lys* was a way for Il Moro to reinforce his credentials as his brother's worthy successor. And the emphasis on Genoa provided an indirect reference to another Italian port under Sforza sway: Bari, of which Il Moro became Duke in 1479. Bari was under Neapolitan suzerainty. In the London *Sforziada*, Il Moro is sending out the message that France is more important to him than Naples – the duchy of his sister-in-law, Isabel of Aragon, official Duchess of Milan. French-Neapolitan rivalry would underpin Il Moro's diplomacy in the years to come.

While Birago's London *Sforziada* frontispiece makes references to France and Hungary, there is a notable absentee: their mutual enemy, Austria. Il Moro held out scant hope of obtaining the Imperial investiture in the short term: Holy Roman Emperor Friedrich III had vowed never to bestow the honour on any Sforza. As late as 1492 Il Moro was offering his niece Bianca Maria as a prospective bride for France's ally James IV of Scotland. Circumstances would only change in 1493, when it was announced that Friedrich was suffering from gangrene. His estranged son and heir, Maximilian, was determined to chart his own course – and accept Bianca Maria as his wife (along with a colossal dowry). Almost overnight the Holy Roman Empire became the lynchpin of Il Moro's diplomacy, as evoked by the Birago frontispiece in the Uffizi *Sforziada*.

In the meantime, a second illuminated *Sforziada* was required – for the Ducal Library in Pavia, to complement the majestically illuminated *Muzio* manuscript completed in Autumn 1491.

Domestic events, though, were not panning out to Il Moro's liking. His effeminate ducal nephew, after spurning his bride for over a year, now had a healthy son. Il Moro's young bride, meanwhile, was showing no signs of producing an heir.

Birago's contribution to the London *Sforziada* is largely bereft of the humour and irony that drip from his later frontispieces – another reason for supposing its target audience was foreign and its *raison-d'être* diplomatic. For his next *Sforziada* frontispiece he was briefed to ratchet up the satire to Gale Force Ten.

NOTES

1 A. Ganda, *Pietro Giustino Filelfo editore della Sforziade di Giovanni Simonetta in Studi in memoria di Paola Medioli Masotti, a cura di Franca Magnani* (Loffredo Editore, Naples 1995), pp.73–86. I am indebted to Cristina Geddo for pointing out this article to me.

2 Pope Innocent VIII (reigned 1484–92) was known as *Padre della Patriae*. The title was also used by Vittorio Emanuele II, the first king of a united Italy (reigned 1861–78).

3 According to Evans (1982), the profiles are based on medals struck in 1488 to commemorate the recent recapture of Genoa. There is an illegible emblem (clearly not the two towers) on Il Moro's breastplate on this coin; the inscription around the rim refers to him as *DUX BARI* and *DUC GUBER* (i.e. Duke of Bari and 'Governing Duke,' or Regent, of Milan). The towers do, however, appear on the reverse of this medal in the background to a busy scene designed by Cristoforo Caradosso, which portrays Il Moro on a throne in front of a gathering of knights, with the inscription on the base of his throne reading *P^X DECRETO* (Peace Decreed) and the inscription around the rim *OPTIMO CONSCILIO SINE ARMIS RESTITUTIA* (The Best Counsel is Restoration Without Arms): a reference to the relatively peaceful nature of his re-conquest of Genoa in 1487/8. A Francesco Sforza medal was also struck at the same time; it features his dog-and-pine emblem on the breastplate, as per his appearance in this *Sforziada*.

4 In September 1492, just before visiting Genoa, Isabella d'Este received from Il Moro a new dress made of gold and silver fabric embroidered with the two lighthouse towers in the port of Genoa, bearing a Spanish motto (*Tal trabalio mes plases par tal thesauros non perder*) stressing that the city was too good to lose.

5 The lighthouses make an appropriate emblem for the port-city given that the etymology of Genoa is *Janua* – Latin for gateway.

6 A ruby-emerald combination is also to be found in ceremonial necklaces worn by Beatrice d'Este and other Sforza princesses. A ruby-sapphire combination is worn by Beatrice in the *Pala Sforzesca*.

7 George F. Warner, *Miniatures & Borders from the Book of Hours of Bona Sforza, Duchess of Milan, in the British Museum* (1894).

8 Evans – who assigns the terracotta work in San Satiro to Agostino de' Fondutis (also known as Agostino Fonduli) – suggests that the wreath-framed male busts (heads of prophets) which alternate with the putti may have been a model for the Moor's head roundel in Birago's frontispiece.

9 Grazioso Sironi, *Nuovi Documenti Riguardanti la Vergine delle Rocce di Leonardo da Vinci* (Florence 1981).

10 Giovanni Antonio Amadeo (*c.*1447–1522) was born in Pavia and commissioned by Colleoni to complete his funerary chapel begun by Guiniforte and Francesco Solari. Amadeo was also hired by Duke Galeazzo Maria Sforza to work at the Certosa di Pavia, notably on the bas-reliefs on the façade. He also worked in Cremona, collaborated with his brother-in-law Pietro Antonio Solari at the Ospedale Maggiore in Milan, helped decorate the Milan Duomo, and worked for Bramante at Santa Maria presso San Satiro. In 1488 Amadeo was commissioned by Cardinal Ascanio Sforza to work with Bramante on Pavia Cathedral. He worked for Il Moro at Vigevano, and was in charge of works at the church of Santa Maria presso San Celso in Milan.

11 Suggestions made by D.R. Edward Wright (*op. cit.*) and Yvonne Hackenbroch in *Goldsmiths' Work from Milan* (1965).

12 Francesco Sforza was invested with the fief of Genoa (and Savona) by King Louis XI of France in December 1463. In Spring 1477 Genoa rose against Sforza rule. In Summer 1478 French envoy Philippe de Commines invested the new boy duke Gian Galeazzo with Genoa as a French fief; but another rebellion expelled Sforza rule. In 1487 Archbishop Paolo Fregoso persuaded Genoa to return to the Sforza Protectorate – partly to defend Genoa against the threat of Florence, which had just taken nearby Sarzana. Gianfrancesco Sanseverino was dispatched to seal the deal in Autumn 1488. In 1490 Il Moro petitioned Charles VIII for the renewal of the Genoese investiture – duly granted for 8,000 ducats. Charles VIII sent an embassy to Milan under his Scottish Chamberlain, Bernard Stuart d'Aubigny, for the official investiture ceremony in Spring 1491. A second French embassy was sent to Milan in January 1492, and a treaty of alliance drawn up whereby Charles VIII acknowledged the Duke of Bari, by name, as party to the alliance in his capacity as Regent. Helping achieve such recognition – of immense prestige and benefit to Il Moro given his tenuous right to continue ruling – may have been one of the principal aims of Birago's London *Sforziada* frontispiece.

13 The sphinxes were part of a stand made by Caradosso to support the Calvary attributed to Hermann Ruissel, made in Paris in 1402 for the ageing Philip the Bold, Duke of Burgundy, and now in the treasury of Esztergom Cathedral. It is not known how Ruissel's Calvary reached Hungary; it disappeared after the death of Philip the Bold in 1404, and is said to have been acquired by the widow of one of his creditors, Pierre Varopel. Caradosso is mentioned as being in Hungary in a letter from Il Moro dated 21 August 1489. In May 1494 János Corvinus sold the Calvary to Tamás Bakócz, Bishop of Eger.

14 Birago would also cite his distinctive sphinxes in the *Sforza Hours*.

15 Alternatively, the cheeky cherub may be suggesting that Il Moro feels he has at last lived up to the confidence his father showed him as a boy: in April 1464, when Ludovico was just twelve, Francesco gave him the keys of Milan and made him Captain of a Crusade against the Turks with the fighting banner of a Golden Lion (Constance J. Muffat, *Heraldic Imagery at the Sforza Court in the 1490s* – M.A. thesis in Art History, University of California, 1986).

16 On 23 April 1485 Il Moro – who would later send a Leonardo altarpiece (probably the Louvre version of the *Virgin of the Rocks*) to Emperor Maximilian – wrote to his Hungarian ambassador, Maffeo da Treviglio, that: 'Since we hear that His Majesty delights in pictures, and we have here a most excellent painter with whose genius we are well acquainted and who, we are sure, has no equal, we have ordered this master to paint a figure of Our Lady, as beautiful and perfect and holy as he can imagine, without sparing pains or expense. He has already set to work, and will undertake nothing else until this picture is finished, and we are able to send it as a gift to his said Majesty.' According to Franz-Joachim Verspuhl (*Michelangelo Buonarroti und Leonardo da Vinci* – Walfstein-Stämpfli, Göttingen 2007), Leonardo had even received a letter from Matthias on 13 April 1485 commissioning him to paint a Madonna for him. Nothing is known about such a work, but it suggests Leonardo's reputation as a painter was firmly established, both in Milan and internationally, by Spring 1485. Leonardo's links with Matthias may have dated back to the 1470s: Kenneth Clarke (*Leonardo da Vinci*, 1939) suggests that Leonardo helped produce the bronze reliefs in Verrocchio's workshop (now lost) 'which Lorenzo de' Medici sent to Matthias Corvinus.' It is hardly surprising that Leonardo was well-disposed towards the Hungarian king, quoting in his *Treatise on Painting* a story about Matthias comparing gifts he had received on his birthday (February 23): a poem in his honour and a painting of his beloved, with Matthias much preferring the painting as it served a 'nobler sense' than the poem 'which might be for the blind.' This passage offers notable insight into Leonardo's view on the *Paragone* debate comparing the relative merits of the arts.

17 Bishop Filipec had spent much of April in Milan before departing for France, where he engaged in ultimately futile negotiations throughout the summer for King Matthias to obtain custody of Prince Djem, younger son of Sultan Mehmed II. Djem had fled to Europe after his father's death in 1481, hoping to muster support against his brother Bayezid II. Instead, he was taken prisoner by the Knights Templar on Rhodes, then by Charles VIII, with Bayezid offering his jailers hefty bribes not to release him. Matthias was keen to help Djem gain the Ottoman throne as part of his quixotic designs for a crusade against the infidel Turks.

18 Il Moro may not have been altogether unhappy at the marriage's delay due to struggles in raising Bianca Maria's dowry. Evidence of this can be found in the written instructions (dated 12 April 1490) sent to Francesco Casati, the Sforza envoy to the Este Court in Ferrara, conveying Il Moro's readiness to flout tradition by allowing the marriage of Anna Sforza (to Alfonso d'Este) to take place before that of her elder sister Bianca Maria – providing the House of Este agreed that payment of Anna's dowry (by Il Moro) be delayed. I am indebted to Elisabetta Gnignera for bringing this document in the Milan State Archives to my attention.

19 Péter E. Kovács, *Mattia Corvino e la corte di Milano* (2003). Kovács refers to this prospective bride as *Anna, la principessa d'Austria*, but I have been unable to trace any eligible Austrian princess called Anna at this time.

20 Luisa Cogliati Arano was the first to identify the subject of this portrait as János Corvinus in her article *Miniatori Lombardi al Tempo di Leonardo – I De Predis*, published in issue n°7 of *FIMantiquari* (1995). I am indebted to Cristina Geddo for kindly bringing this article to my attention.

21 Bianca Maria referred to Ambrogio de Predis as 'el nostro pinctore' when he was part of the sizable retinue that accompanied her to Innsbruck after her proxy marriage to Emperor Maximilian in 1493 (F. Calvi, *Bianca Maria Sforza Visconti*, Milan 1888, p. 49).

22 Il Moro heard the news from Venice; much to his annoyance, the report from the Milanese Ambassador to Hungary only reached him three days later, on April 18.

23 It is a moot point as to whether citing the *Calvary* in the frontispiece was Birago's own idea or inherited from a provisional design for the frontispiece drawn up before his appointment, when a Hungarian marriage was still on the cards. As there is no evidence Birago ever visited Hungary, he presumably saw Caradosso's *Calvary* design in Milan, where it must have been talk of the court.

24 Fregoso's thinking on the matter was facilitated by the promise of the lordship of Savona and a 4,000-ducat stipend. Always one to keep politics in the family, Il Moro offered the hand of his (illegitimate) niece Chiara Sforza (widow of Pietro dal Verme – of whom more later) to the Archbishop's son Fregosino.

25 D.R. Edward Wright, *op. cit.* The Este *fleurs-de-lys* appear (to quote heraldic terminology) *within a bordure indented gules* or (alternative heraldic gobbledygook) *with sixteen tintures or gobbits, gyronwise.*

26 Cartwright reports that the (four) French ambassadors were miffed by the unglamorous diplomatic gifts bestowed upon them before they returned to France. If the most important gift they received was a Sforza history book, their disappointment is understandable.

27 De Thou's personal library was one of the most famous in France, running to 6,600 volumes by his death. Under his successors it swelled to 13,171 volumes by 1679 (*Catalogvs Bibliothecae Thvanae*), shortly before its sale to Jean-Jacques Charron, Marquis de Menars (1643–1718) – whose library was acquired in turn by Cardinal Armand de Rohan-Soubise, Bishop of Strasbourg, for 40,000 livres in 1706. This library was inherited by the Cardinal's great-nephew, Prince Charles de Soubise, in 1749, and auctioned in an epic four-month estate sale in early 1789. D.R. Edward Wright has speculated that the book was initially lodged in the Ducal Library at Pavia, then presented by Louis XII to Pierre de Rohan-Gié, Chef de Conseil du Roi, after the French conquest of Milan, remaining with his descendants until the death of Charles de Rohan, Prince de Soubise, in 1787. Wright does not explain why the book lacks the mention *de Pavye au roy* – or why Louis XII should have chosen to part with an illuminated *Sforziada* featuring the French *fleurs-de-lys* yet retain a *Sforziada* with exclusively domestic Milanese imagery (i.e. the copy now in the Bibliothèque Nationale).

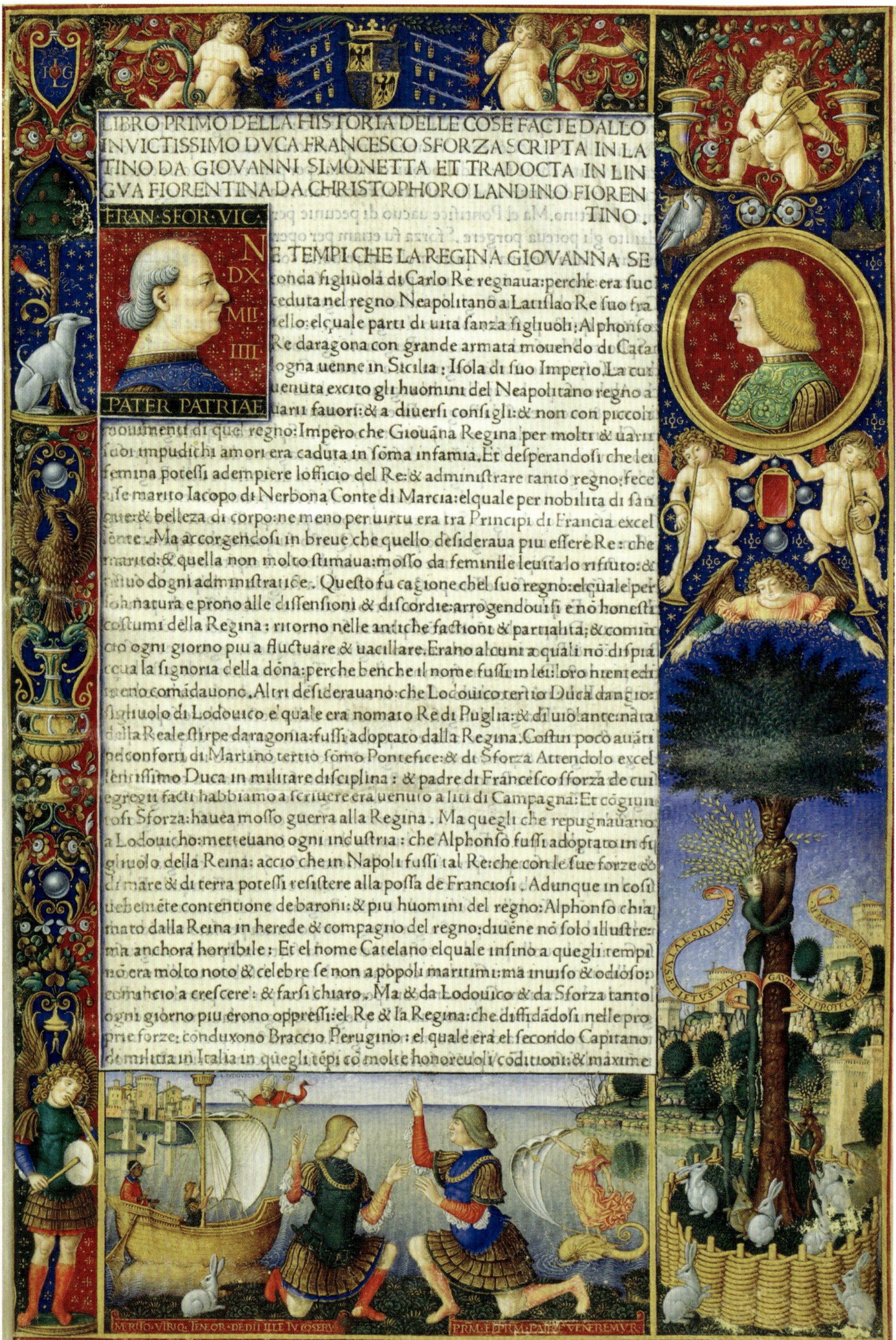

SFORZIADA (FRONTISPIECE) – BIBLIOTHEQUE NATIONALE DE FRANCE (RES. VEL. 724)

VI

A TREE AND A WEED
THE SURREALIST SFORZIADA

WITH HIS POLITICAL PROSPECTS at their lowest ebb since his return to Milan in 1479, Il Moro had Birago portray him as a fount of avuncular wisdom and the helmsman of the State – and his nephew as a puny nincompoop.

PROVENANCE

1492 Ducal Library, Pavia
1500 Bibliothèque du Roi, Blois (later Fontainebleau, Paris)
1792 Bibliothèque Nationale, Paris

FRANCESCO SFORZA MEDALLION

Francesco is shown on a red ground spangled with two dozen dotted sunbursts. **FRAN SFOR VIC** and **PATER PATRIAE** appear in gold letters on black backgrounds (not banners) above and below. In *FRAN*, the bottom right of the letter R slightly overlaps with the bottom left of the letter A. The AE in *PATRIAE* is not written as a diphthong. Francesco wears a flower-patterned blue breastplate with gold highlights and collar. His head is slightly larger than in the London *Sforziada*; as a result, the word DUX has been reduced to *DX* in order to fit in. His expression is also different: he is smiling and seems to exude avuncular bonhomie, although his brow is tightly furrowed. The initial *N* leading into the text appears in gold, positioned top-right of the red ground, above **DX MLI IIII**, also in gold letters, right-justified over three rows; *DX* at eyebrow-level, *MLI* at mouth-level and *IIII* at collar-level. A few more unruly wisps of hair emerge from the back and top of Francesco's head.

ROUNDEL

Positioned, as in the London volume, very slightly lower than the Francesco medallion, this time showing a profile of Gian Galeazzo (again similar to that used on Milanese coinage) within a gold frame, on a red ground spangled with 30 six-armed stars. He has a gold collar and matching sleeves, and a green breastplate with a winged angel-head amidst scrolls and flowers. The colours appear significant: both Il Moro (at the foot of the page) and Francesco (in his medallion) are wearing blue breastplates in this *Sforziada*. Gian Galeazzo is the odd man out.

HAUT-DE-PAGE

The crown-topped Sforza/Visconti arms appear on a star-spangled blue ground, with a palm-frond emerging to the left and a laurel-branch to the right. Flanking the shield are three rows of flaming ragged staffs with fire-buckets: a ducal device favoured by Galeazzo Maria, but also used by Il Moro – as on the cover of the *Donatus Grammatica* he would commission for his son a few years later (*see Chapter XII*). This coat of arms is sometimes interpreted as an allusion to Gian Galeazzo, ostensibly the main subject of the frontispiece, but probably refers to the office of Duke of Milan – implying that Il Moro has as much claim to the rôle as his nephew. The latter interpretation is supported by the fact that one of the naked putti flanking the coat of arms is holding a *scopetta* – Il Moro's favourite device.

BAS-DE-PAGE

The scene here is the most complex in the four *Sforziada* frontispieces, and the only one to extend across and upwards into the right-hand column. The composition is in three parts.

The main scene shows Gian Galeazzo (in green breastplate) and his far larger uncle Il Moro (in blue) both kneeling, facing each other on a grassy bank that again echoes the stylized greenery in Leonardo's *Annunciation* and *Virgin of the Rocks*; Gian Galeazzo's legs are positioned in absolutely identical fashion (*see below*) to those of the infant to the left in Leonardo's *Virgin of the Rocks*. Both have gold chains, golden epaulettes and skirts, red sleeves with white elbow frills, and red stockings (Birago frequently uses stockings as a means of identity – here to imply parity between Uncle Moro and his ducal nephew). Il Moro has blue epaulettes, Gian Galeazzo green. Gian Galeazzo is pointing towards Il Moro with his left hand, and towards St Louis of Toulouse (1274–97) on the horizon with his right; Il Moro is pointing heavenwards in the direction of Francesco Sforza. Il Moro has grey (not black) hair,[1] as if to emphasize

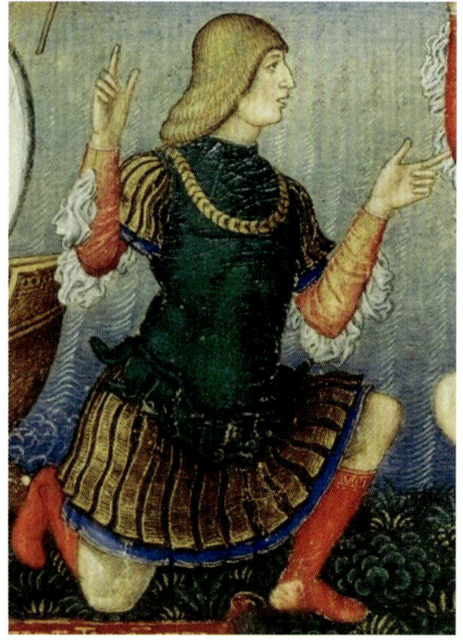

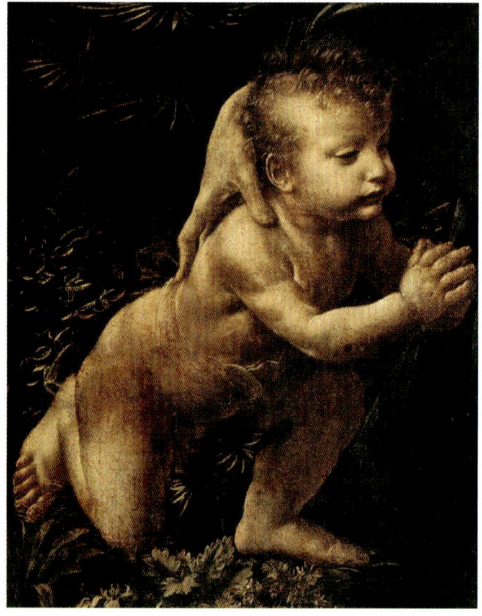

his avuncular concern for his nephew – this is Il Moro the family man, not Il Moro the warlord, politician or lover. The profiles of both figures, with their distinctive eyelashes, suggest Ambrogio de Predis may have provided the under-drawing.

Two red banners with gold lettering run along the foot of the image. The one to the left, beneath Gian Galeazzo, reads **MERITO VTRIQUE TENEOR - DEDIT ILLE TV COSERVA** (*there is merit on both sides: he gave, you will keep*). The banner to the right, beneath Il Moro, reads **PRM - ET PRM PATRIAE VENEREMUR**. Translating this is trickier: the abbreviation *PRM* is ambiguous, no doubt deliberately. It could stand for *PATREM* (father) or *PATRUUM* (uncle), and the phrase could be a call to *revere* the *Father* (Francesco) or *Uncle* (Il Moro) of the *Fatherland*. In either case, the intention is to associate Il Moro with his father as ruler of Milan – with the relentless use of the word *Father(land)* meant to stress that Francesco was Il Moro's father, not Gian Galeazzo's.

To the left is a ship (of state) with a single mast and white sail; a Moor (in red tunic with blue collar) is at the helm and Gian Galeazzo (again in green) is sole passenger.[2] The ship is being blessed by the figure of St Louis of Toulouse, Il Moro's patron saint, from way out at sea; his flailing cape is the same red as the Moor's tunic. The ship has just left a harbour with two lighthouses at the entrance – a reference to Genoa (*cf* Il Moro's emblems in the London *Sforziada*).

Facing Genoa across a broad expanse of smooth water (the Tyrrhenian Sea) is hilly Naples (*shown below in a contemporary painting*) with its waterfront castle (Castel Nuovo), beneath terraces lined with verdant trees and bushes (suggestive of a more luxuriant climate) and a hilltop fortress (Castel Sant'Elmo). Sailing from Naples towards Genoa on a dolphin with a white sail tied to its tail is a young, blond-haired woman in a pink dress with her right breast exposed: the symbolic figure of Fortune, physically embodied here by Gian Galeazzo's wife Isabel of Aragon, who sailed from Naples to Genoa to marry him at the end of 1488. Her exposed breast could be a reference to her recent motherhood or a snide reference to her sexual morals.

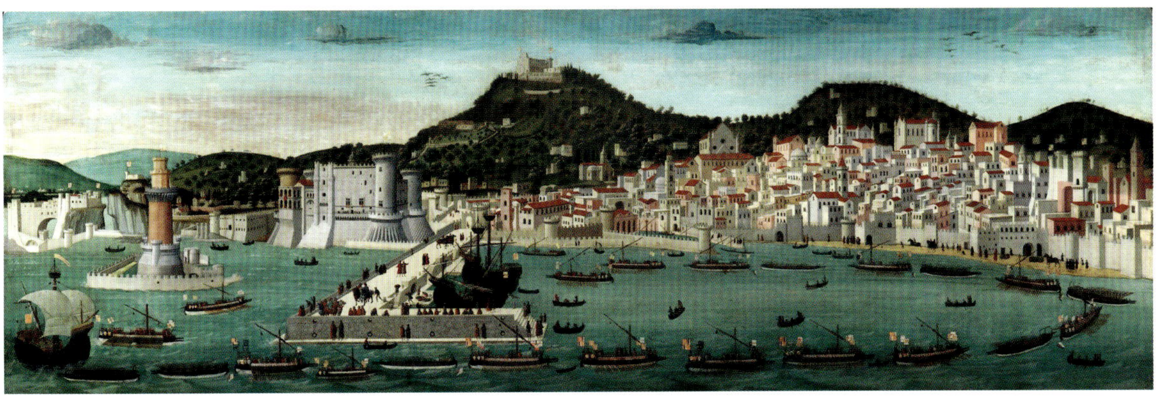

This is Birago's most ambitious *Sforziada* border, and the only one not divided into different-coloured grounds. To the right of the waterfront is one of the most extraordinary images of the Renaissance. It shows a towering mulberry tree with a vigorous panoply of leafy branches dotted with red fruit, and a dark male face worked into the top of the dark brown trunk. Mr Mulberry (Il Moro) is supporting a thin, sickly green sapling (Gian Galeazzo) whose pale face is topped by a 'crown' of sparse branches with unhealthy brown leaves. The sapling comes up to no more than the chest of the sturdy tree figure, and is clinging to it despairingly, as if dependent on it for survival. Leaning on the foot of the sapling is a similar, but much smaller, green sapling with a green face and the same sparse brown leaves springing from its head. At the foot of the brown tree-trunk is a brown sapling, smaller yet far more vigorous than its green counterpart. The leaves springing from its head blend artfully into a flourishing background bush, to form a crown; its legs and arms are dynamically bent; it is not leaning on the tree trunk for support, but standing freely, and gesticulating mockingly at its green-sapling counterpart.

The tree and saplings are growing in a circular grassy enclosure within a wicker fence (*below right*), perhaps intended to symbolize the Garden of Eden; six hares/rabbits are inside the fence (four white, two brown) with two more white ones just outside, apparently trying to get in. The circular fence is not a Birago creation, but appears in various 15th century manuscripts – notably in a large miniature dubbed *The Coronation of the Poet* in the Trivulziana (*MS 763*), and in a miniature in Raffaele Vimercati's *Oroscopo* (Trivulziana *MS 1329*), wherein Gian Galeazzo's father, Galeazzo Maria, kneels before his crowned father Francesco. The association of Il Moro with his father Francesco was the underlying theme of much of Il Moro's propaganda. His association with the figure of a 'poet' implies he is the author, or chooser, of the verses quoted on banners around the tree – and, by extension, of all the quotes on this and other frontispieces (an association echoed by his description, in the Uffizi *Sforziada*, as an *auctor*). These allusions to Il Moro's involvement in the *Sforziada* frontispieces mirror his hands-on approach to all cultural activity during his reign.

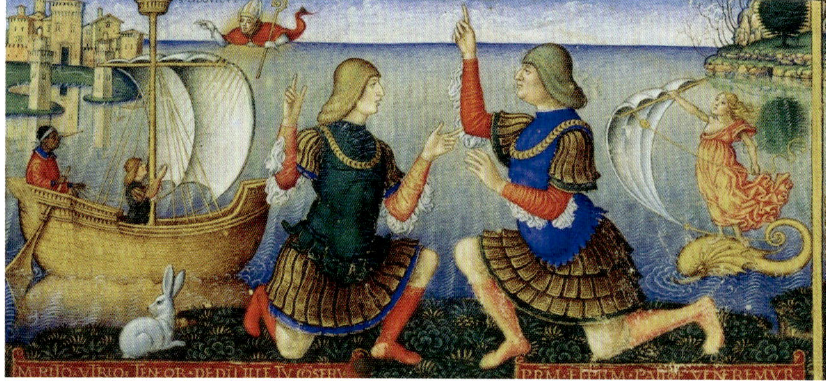

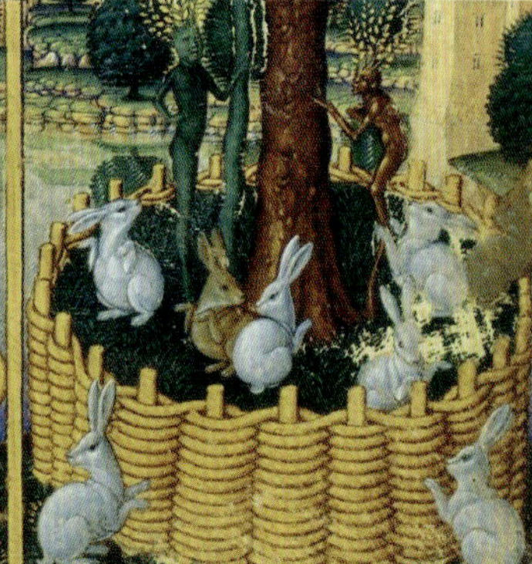

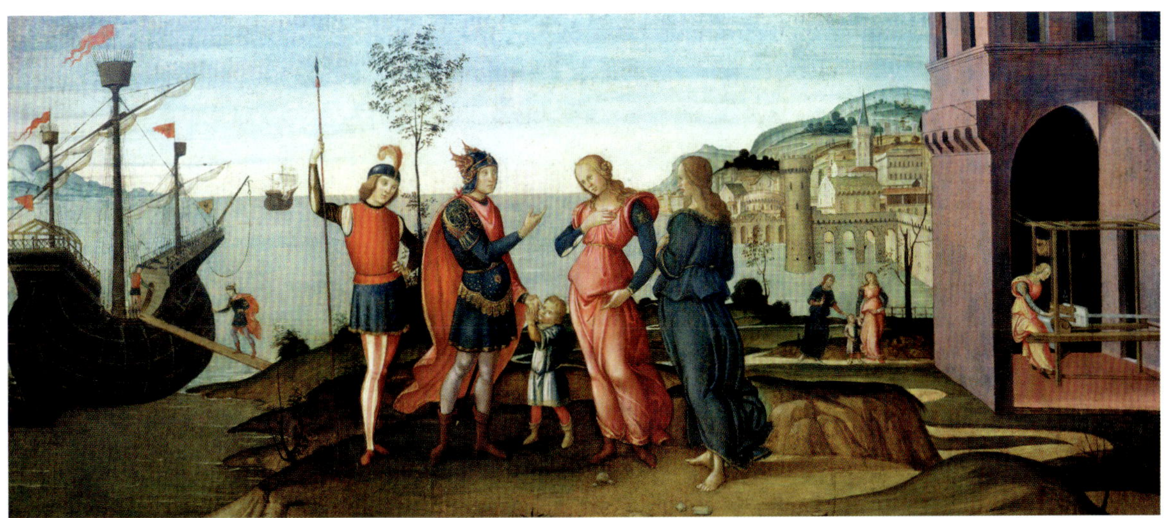

MASTER OF APOLLO & DAPHNE
ULYSSES LEAVING FOR TROY
91 × 198 cm
G. SARTI, PARIS

Two gold banners with black lettering are entwined around the mulberry-tree and taller green sapling. The one on the left, featuring words apparently spoken by the sapling (Gian Galeazzo), reads **DVM VIVIS - TVTVS - ET LETVS VIVO** (*While you are alive, I live safe and happy*). The one on the right reads **GAVDE FILI PROTECTOR TVVS ERO SEMPER** (*Rejoice, my son, I shall always be your protector*).

The foreground scene (*see p.100 bottom-left*), with figures on a shore, and a three-masted boat about to set sail, is strongly reminiscent of – and probably inspired by – *Ulysses Departing for Troy* (tempera on panel 91 × 198cm), a work ascribed to The Master of Daphne & Apollo active in Florence from 1480. The form of the boat,[3] with its tall central mast and crow's nest, is similar; a ship can be seen on the horizon in exactly the same spot as the figure of St Louis of Toulouse; and the figures of Ulysses/Gian Galeazzo (both clad in green-and-red military attire) and of Penelope/Isabel of Aragon (both with long blond hair and wearing ankle-length pink dresses) are so similar as to rule out coincidence. Both scenes feature a hilly town to the right: Naples/Ithaca.[4]

This Florentine Master, inspired by the *Aeneid*, displays a couple of stylistic traits after Birago's own heart: a rock-strewn foreground; and leafless, spiky-branched trees (even though abundant foliage elsewhere suggests the scene is set in spring or summer).

It may be no coincidence that this frontispiece quotes an artist associated with the story of *Daphne and Apollo*, which Birago himself illustrated in another context,[5] and whose Ovidian tale of a human metamorphosed into a tree is the inspiration behind the mulberry image here. If we search Birago's Milanese entourage for a source of knowledge about works of art from 1480s Florence – the example here is one of many – Leonardo da Vinci would be the first name to spring to mind.

The right border is topped by a naked putto playing a *lira da braccio*, on a red ground strewn with acorns, flanked by horns of plenty full of barley (*left*) and grapes (*right*). Below, to the left, is a dove on sunburst ringed by a scroll reading **A BON DROIT**. To the right is a triple-sempervivium with, as usual, the central plant higher than the other two, above the motto **MIT ZAIT** (*With Time*). Both were among the most popular Sforza devices, although inherited from the Viscontis (legend has it that the dove on sunburst was invented by Petrarch) – the implication being that Il Moro has time and right on his side, i.e. will one day be Duke.

The Gian Galeazzo medallion immediately below is supported by two putti with gold wings, blowing trombones, separated by a ruby pendant flanked by four pearls and eight tiny, raspberry-like stones. Beneath them we see the head, shoulder and protectively outstretched arms of a larger angel clad in pink and green, embracing the mulberry tree in his downward gaze: the same idea of Il Moro receiving divine protection as in the London *Sforziada*, where his medallion portrait is held by a sheltering angel.

The medallion is surrounded by a dark blue ground spangled with gold stars and a repeated cruciform logo reading *IOLG* – a combination of IOG (for *Iovannes Galeas*, i.e. **G**ian **G**aleazzo) impaled on a giant **L** (for **L**udovico). The design of this elaborate cross is similar to the patterned motif – again in gold on a blue ground – on the gown worn by Il Moro's niece Bianca Maria in a full-page miniature now in Vienna (Österreichisches Nationalbibliothek *MS Series Nova 2622*, fol. 5v).[6]

LEFT BORDER

This is topped by a gold-rimmed shield with a blue ground, featuring the *IOLG* monogram in gold letters beneath the outstretched arms of an angel with the same wide-armed pose as the much larger angel above the mulberry tree in the right-hand column. The central *O* is transformed here into a red heart, imbued with a pioneering kitsch that Jeff Koons might not have eschewed. Below (and adjacent to the Francesco medallion), on a gold-starred blue ground, is a white greyhound seated beneath a conical, four-tiered pine tree featuring three rows of pine cones (six in all). A hand with broad red cuff is emerging from the left, holding a gold collar. Below is a phoenix supporting a large pearl in its upstretched wings as it rises from a gadrooned fountain, above another pearl surrounded by stylized flowers and foliage. At the foot of the column is a winged-angel drummer-boy/flautist. He has a green breastplate, blue sleeves, and the same red socks as the adjacent kneeling figures of Gian Galeazzo and Il Moro. Beneath the greyhound the border is divided into green/red grounds, with a blue ground in between.

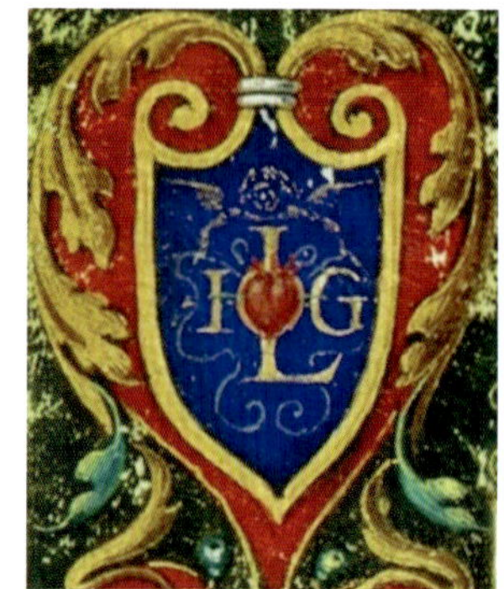

DATE

Probably first half of 1492. The volume was doubtless lodged in the Ducal Library in Pavia – it is the only *Sforziada* to contain the mention *De Pavye au roy Louis XII[e]*, signalling its removal by the French in 1500.

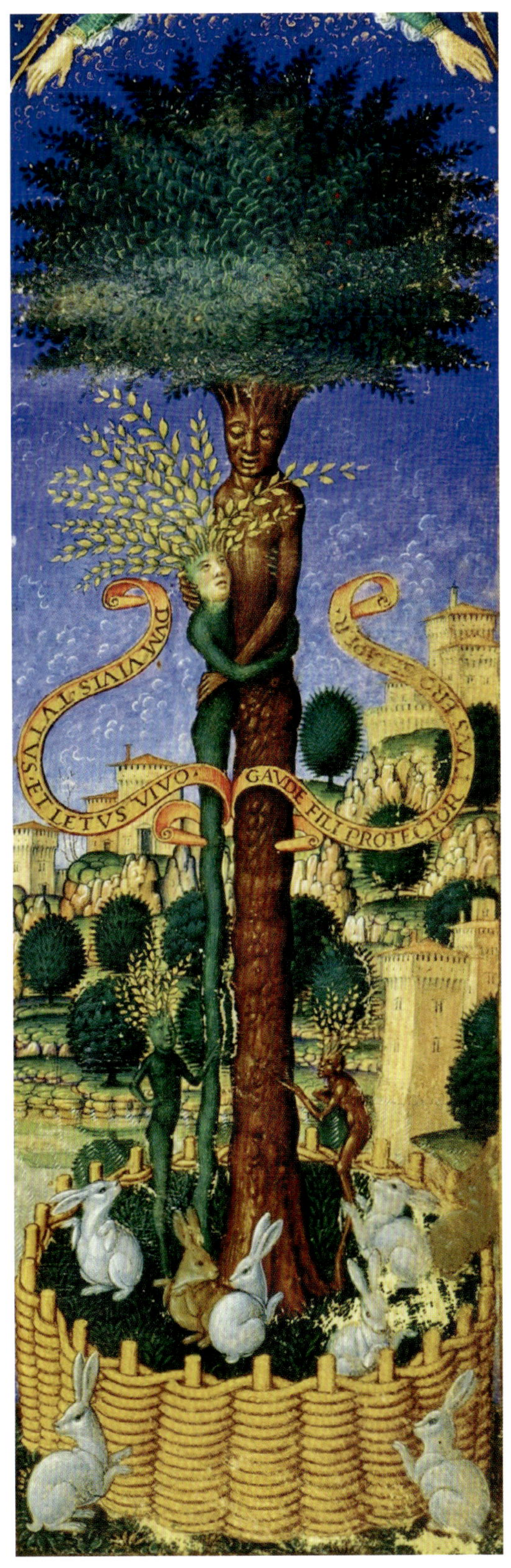

INTERPRETATION

The almost symmetrical contrasts with the London *Sforziada* – blue ground medallions of Francesco Sforza and Il Moro in one, red ground medallions of Francesco Sforza and Gian Galeazzo in the other – suggest the two frontispieces were conceived at broadly the same time.

Between the birth of Gian Galeazzo's son Francesco ('Il Duchetto') in January 1491, and the birth of his own first *legitimate* son, Ercole, in January 1493, Il Moro's grasp on power was precarious. His status as Regent was increasingly tenuous and he had even – in terms of physically ensuring the dynastic succession – been outperformed by his supposedly effeminate nephew.

This frontispiece therefore aims to undermine Gian Galeazzo psychologically and stress that he and his offspring are unfit to rule. It also throws down a naval gauntlet from Milan to Naples.

The two saplings at the foot of the mulberry tree doubtless represent Il Duchetto and Il Moro's *bastard* son Cesare, born three months later on 3 May 1491 – with their age difference reflected in their relative heights. The implication is that Gian Galeazzo's son was another weed, whereas Il Moro's infant son Cesare, although a bastard, was of stronger stock – a message similar to that propounded by Leonardo's *Lady with an Ermine*, where that stock is portrayed as divine (*see Chapter VIII*).

Birago's proto-Surrealist mulberry, confusing a human being with a tree, derives from Ovid's *Metamorphoses* tale of *Daphne and Apollo*, which Birago had illustrated for a book of poems – now in Wolfenbüttel – a few years before. Birago's mulberry is one of the nastiest and most cynical images in the history of art. By having his own nephew portrayed as a large weed, Il Moro sought to undermine Gian Galeazzo's confidence in his ability to rule and provoke his emotional disintegration. It is a telling and callous illustration of Il Moro's (ultimately successful) attempts to instil into his nephew a feeling of total submission to, and dependence on, his uncle – to the detriment of his wife and his right to exercise his prerogatives as Duke.

The frontispiece portrays Gian Galeazzo four times in all.

At the foot of the page he is being lectured to by Il Moro about the virtues of patriarch Francesco. Both figures are kneeling, with Gian Galeazzo in the distinctive pose adopted by John the Baptist in Leonardo da Vinci's *Virgin of the Rocks* – implying that Il Moro is imbued with Christ-like superiority.

The image featuring Gian Galeazzo in a ship (of state), being steered out of a port with a twin-towered entrance (Genoa) by a Moorish (we could almost say *Maorish*) helmsman, implies that Gian Galeazzo is destined for exile (an *internal* exile as it turned out – detained at Il Moro's pleasure in the Castle of Pavia). The ship is about to assert its mastery of the Tyrrhenian Sea over a Neapolitan fleet pathetically represented by a girl on a dolphin, whereas Ludovico Sforza can count on French support epitomized by his patron saint, St Louis of Toulouse. It is not impossible that the presence of St Louis, who died of fever at the age of 23, is a sickening reminder of Gian Galeazzo's lingering ill-health (he would die at the age of 25, probably poisoned).

The mildly erotic figure on a dolphin, arriving from Naples, represents Isabel of Aragon. The message to Gian Galeazzo: his wife is some sort of frivolous floozy, shown here free and rather too easy, flitting around with her right breast exposed while her husband occupies the ship of state – at a heavy cost to his domestic happiness. Gian Galeazzo is likened to the Ulysses who was parted from his wife as he sailed for Troy.

Il Moro was desperate to detach Gian Galeazzo from his less gullible wife, whose vociferous complaints about Il Moro's behaviour were a source of diplomatic embarrassment.

Detach him?

'There is no news here,' wrote the Dowager Marchioness of Montferrat from Milan on 2 May 1492, 'save that the Duke of Milan has beaten his wife.'

It is reported that, when Il Moro arrived in Pavia in Spring 1492, his nephew first refused to see him but, after sulking for a few days, was soon on affectionate terms with his uncle again.

Being portrayed as a giant weed[7] would make anyone sulk.

Another indication that this *Sforziada* may date from early 1492 is provided by the remodelling of the venerable Visconti Library, on the third floor of the West Tower in the Castello di Pavia (*right*). Il Moro spent the summer of 1492 in Pavia with his newly pregnant wife.

During that summer Pavia also witnessed festivities in honour of the christening of Il Duchetto (Count of Pavia). These festivities had originally been slated for Summer 1491, but postponed. Il Moro suavely informed Isabella d'Este this

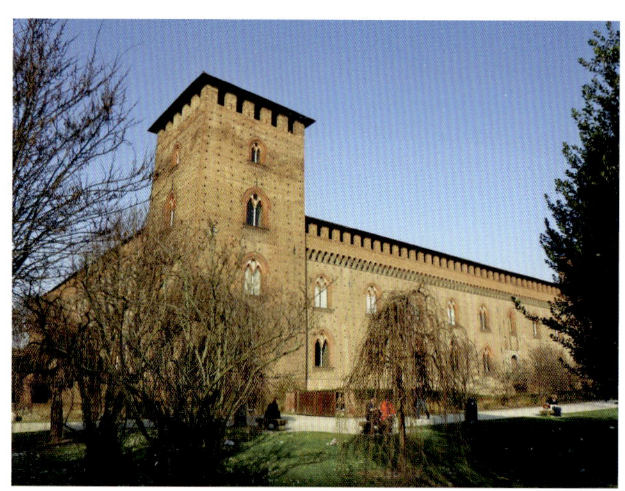

was because she was unable to attend. The more likely reason is that Il Moro delayed festivities until his wife Beatrice d'Este, Isabella's sister, herself became pregnant with Il Moro's son and heir (to be born in January 1493), thereby stealing Il Duchetto's thunder.

One final point. Gian Galeazzo is portrayed as a laurel tree (*lauro*). Another *Lauro*, Lorenzo de' Medici, died on 9 April 1492. The irony will not have been lost on Birago's readers. This frontispiece is not just about an uncle's superiority over his nephew. It evokes the superiority of *Il Moro* over *Il Lauro* – and of Sforza Milan over Medici Florence.

NOTES

1 Both the roundel portrait, and the kneeling figures of Il Moro and Gian Galeazzo at the foot of the page, have smooth hair (actually mistaken for wigs by the great French librarian Joseph Van Praet in 1822!), which flies in the face of Birago's ubiquitous Leonardesque predilection (psychological obsession would hardly be stretching it) for wavy/curly hair.

2 The image of Il Moro as a Moor manning the helm of the Ship of State appears to have first occurred in a sonnet by the Sforza court poet Bernardo Bellincioni: *Talché la nave enterera in porto/ Né com'altri credea ir per perduta/ Ché sempre la trarra dal camin torto/ Mentre al timone e l'Etiopo Italico*. Bellincioni died on 12 September 1492 – further suggesting the frontispiece was produced by Summer 1492.

3 There is a delightful coincidence here in that 1492 – a likely date for this voyage-of-departure frontispiece – was the year that a native of Genoa, Cristoforo Colombo (Il Moro's almost exact contemporary), set off on a voyage aiming to reach the East Indies but which led instead to the discovery of America. Columbus left Palos de la Frontera, near Seville, on August 3 and sighted land on October 12, arriving back in Europe in early March 1493.

4 It is said that Francesco Filelfo (1398–1481) looked to the *Aeneid* for inspiration when penning over 12,000 lines about Francesco Sforza for his prototype *Sforziada*.

5 Herzog August Bibliothek, Wolfenbüttel (*Cod. 277A Etr.*).

6 This anonymous, extremely deft miniature is part of a small Milanese prayer book or *Office di Santo Spirito* owned by Bianca Maria in Austria, and shows her receiving the blessing of God the Father and the heavenly host. She is standing on a tiled balcony with a red and gold frieze of playful putti, overlooking a rocky landscape with river, trees and distant stylized figures outlined in black. The style, notably of her silhouette, recalls Ambrogio de Predis. This prayer book may be the *officioletto* for which Bianca Maria expressed thanks to Il Moro in a letter dated 12 August 1499.

7 Leonardo also drew a disparaging allegorical comparison between uncle and nephew – in his drawing of a Cock (Gian Galeazzo) protected by Prudence (Il Moro), now in Christ Church, Oxford.

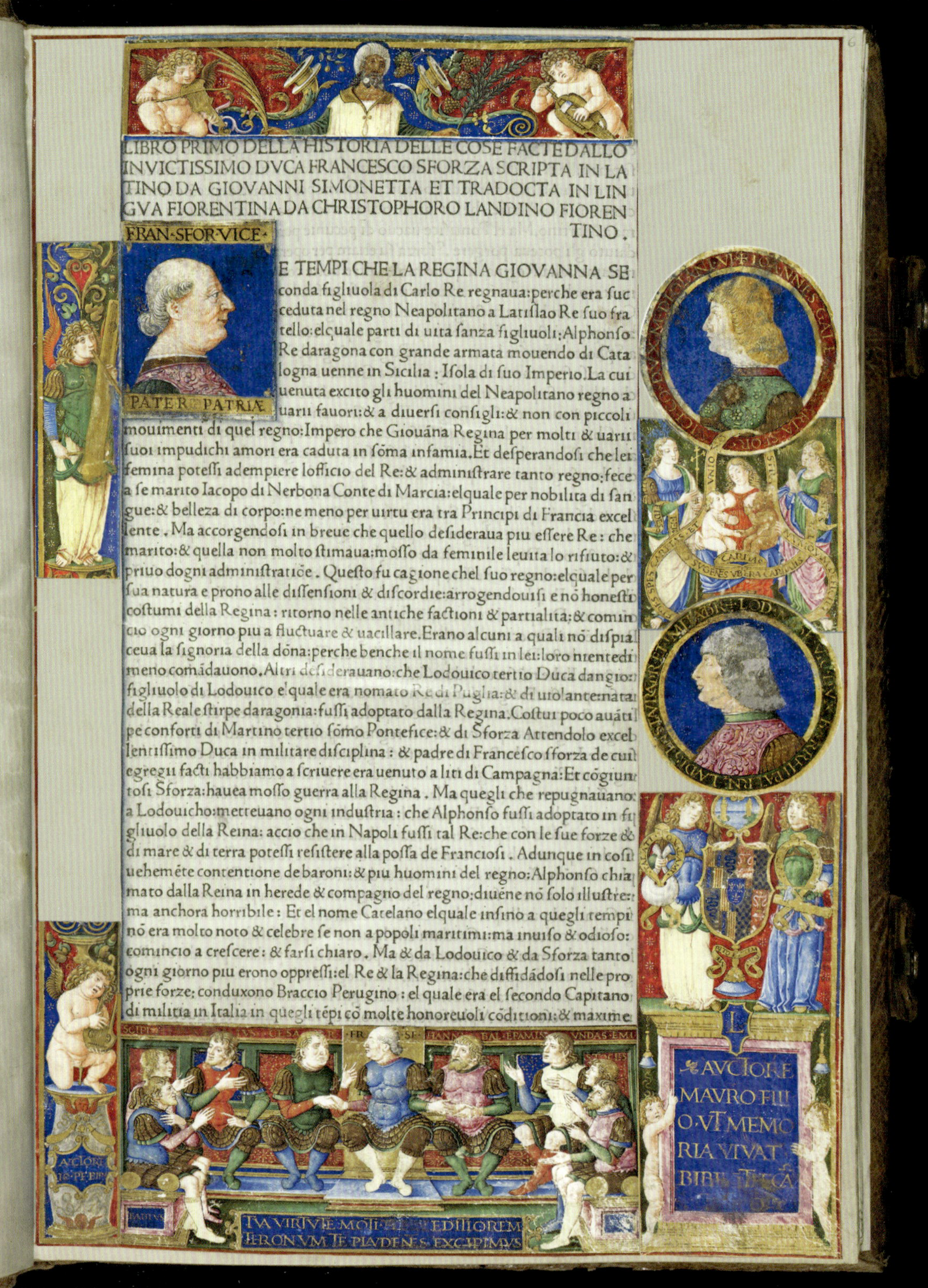

SFORZIADA (FRONTISPIECE RECONSTITUTION) – GALLERIA DEGLI UFFIZI, FLORENCE (INV. 1890)

VII
CUT UP AND DRIED?
THE DISMEMBERED SFORZIADA

BIRAGO'S THIRD *SFORZIADA* FRONTISPIECE was mutilated, with its illuminations removed and split up. Here re-assembled in correct order for the first time in colour,[1] they sizzle with sarcasm, stylistic inconsistencies and sexual innuendo.

PROVENANCE

1493 Library of Ludovico Sforza, Vigevano (?)
1500 Bibliothèque du Roi, Blois
1659 (?) Cardinal Luigi Capponi, Florence

VOLUME

– Capponi Library, Florence
– Vatican Library (1746)
– Hôtel Soubise, Paris (*c.*1810)
– Vatican Library (*c.*1815)
– Lost (stolen?) between 1860–1925

FRONTISPIECE

– Pitti Palace (Galleria Palatina), Florence (by 1664)
– Uffizi Gallery, Florence (by 1880)

The third illuminated *Sforziada* has had a hard life. It was mutilated in the wake of the French invasion of Milan in 1499, and later dismembered, possibly in the 17th century. Its Birago frontispiece was removed in or before 1664, and subsequently cut up into nine separate images, together accounting for about 80 per cent of its original illuminated material. Uffizi cataloguing data indicates that these images were recorded in the Pitti Palace (Galleria Palatina) by 1664, during the reign of Ferdinando II de' Medici; we do not know whether they were cut up before or after they entered the Medici collections – although, as they all appear to have arrived together, it is perhaps more likely that they were cut up in the Pitti Palace to facilitate individual display. They were inventoried in the Uffizi Gallery in 1880; first published by Malaguzzi Valeri in 1917; and featured in the catalogue of the exhibition *Mostra Storica Nazionale della Miniatura* (n°659) in Rome in 1954. The cuttings are individually mounted on card, and show signs of wear through handling, and of fading through exposure to light. They were restored by Sergio Bon in 1977 and reproduced – apparently based on old black-and-white photocopies – by Evans in 1987 and McGrath in 2002. They have since been digitalized and were reproduced in colour for the first time – although in incorrect sequence – in the catalogue to the exhibition *Arte Lombarda dai Visconti agli Sforza* held in Milan in 2015.

The mutilated volume, lacking its illuminated frontispiece (replaced by another page, with the missing text copied out by hand), was bequeathed to the Vatican by the unmarried and childless Marchese Alessandro Gregorio Capponi (1683–1746),[2] famed book collector from an illustrious Florentine family and Chamberlain to Pope Clement XII. It is tempting to surmise that he inherited the volume from Cardinal Luigi Capponi (1582/3–1659), Head of the Vatican Library from 1649–59.

Given that the frontispiece cuttings are first recorded in Medici hands in 1664, they may have been removed from the volume in the wake of the Cardinal's death just five years earlier. There is no evidence as to how or when the volume first reached Florence.

The volume was among the cultural goods looted from Rome by order of Napoleon, then returned by Louis XVIII.

Joseph Van Praet (1754–1837), who saw the volume when it was in Paris, wrote in Volume V (entry 103) of his *Catalogue des livres imprimés sur vélin de la Bibliothèque du Roi* (1822) that this *Sforziada* was 'repris en 1815 par le commissaire du pape … le premier feuillet du texte, qui sans doute étoit décoré d'une bordure peinte, a été enlevé, et s'y trouve rétabli par le secours d'une plume qui a assez bien imité l'impression' (*taken back by the Pope's commissioner in 1815 … the first page of the text, doubtless decorated with painted borders, has been removed and replaced by handwriting that imitates print fairly well*).[3]

According to Gustave Brunet's *Dictionnaire*, Napoleon ordered the Vatican Archives to be removed to Paris in December 1809 – shortly after he had arrested and imprisoned Pope Pius VII. Over the next three years 3,239 chests were transported to the Hôtel de Soubise in Paris, home to the Archives Nationales; the French inventory of the operation ran to 102,435 entries. In 1815 Louis XVIII ordered the return of the archives to Rome, a process that lasted until December 1817.

The mutilated *Sforziada* is next referred to in the 1860s by Zappelli, who noted that it also lacked many of its illuminated initials (it is not clear if these had also been cut out or never filled in).[4] It is not, however, cited in the catalogue of the Vatican Library compiled in by 1925 by Tommaso Accurti and Stanislas Le Grelle.

Between the 1860s and 1925, therefore, it appears to have disappeared; investigation carried out by cultural officials in the context of the present book has established that there is no longer any trace of it in the Vatican Library (whose current catalogue cites no fewer than six Sforziadas – none of them, alas, a de luxe 1490 edition printed on vellum).

FRANCESCO SFORZA MEDALLION

Francesco is wearing a dark pink breastplate with floral patterning picked out in gold (broadly similar in design to his blue breastplate in the Paris *Sforziada*), green epaulettes and a gold collar (*below left*). The combination of pink breastplate and green epaulettes is a direct reversal of his colours in his prototype *Sforziada* portrait from around 1460 (*see p.66*). He appears to be smiling broadly, perhaps even chortling. There are the same whimsical wisps emanating from the back of the head as in the Paris *Sforziada*. The profile does not have quite the same precision as the Francesco medallions in the other *Sforziadas*, but this may be due to wear and retouching.

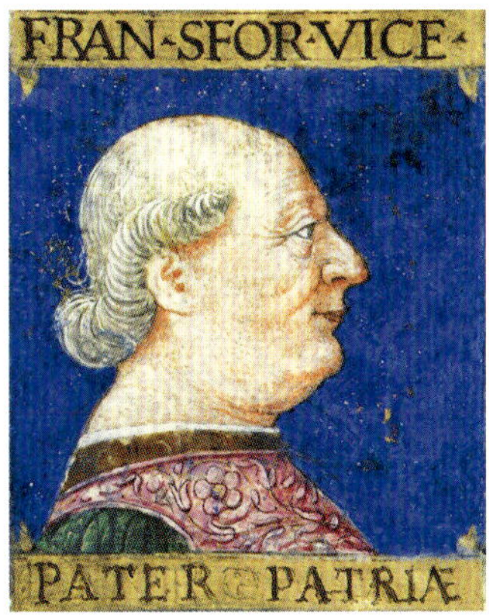
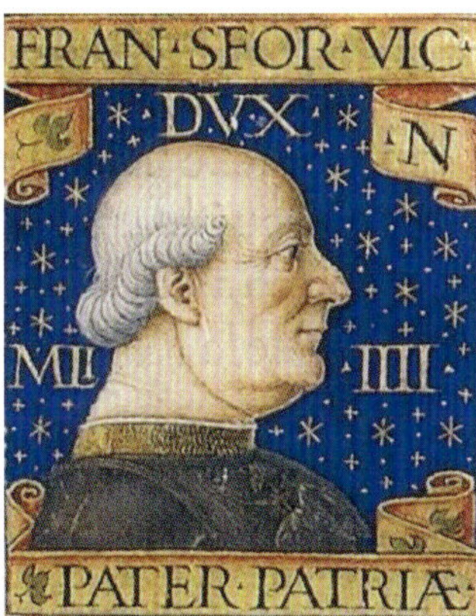

Francesco is shown on a plain, dark blue ground without stars. On magnified inspection the stars have been obliterated, with the background painted over in a blue slightly lighter than the original navy. This repainting has also obliterated the initial *N*, leading into the text, and the lettering *DUX MLI IIII* which appears in each of the other three *Sforziadas* (albeit with *DUX* abbreviated to *DX* in the Paris volume).

The lettering above and below the portrait is in dark letters on gold banners. The lettering is clearly not original: the *PATER PATRIÆ* lettering is particularly hesitant.

What appears in the three other *Sforziadas* as **FRAN SFOR VIC** is here written **FRAN SFOR VICE**, which suggests that whoever rewrote the lettering either made a mistake or thought that writing *VICE* not *VIC* might somehow enhance the medallion's appeal. In coins minted with Francesco's profile, *VICECOMES* (for VISCONTI) is usually abbreviated as *VIC*, sometimes as *VICECO*, but never as *VICE*.

As in the London frontispiece (*above right*), the **Æ** in **PATRIÆ** is written as a diphthong. This suggests the scribe used the London *Sforziada* as his model (even aping, albeit rather clumsily, its gold banners as the background for the lettering). If so, he must have been working in the French royal library, with the change of VIC to VICE perhaps a subconscious slip of the quill – representing the logical *French* abbreviation of *VICECOMES*. The medallion must have been restored in this way to make the frontispiece more presentable

– presumably before the volume was offered as a diplomatic gift (the most logical explanation of its subsequent presence in Florence).

ROUNDELS

This is the only *Sforziada* with two roundels, showing Gian Galeazzo above and Il Moro below; they are separated – and linked – by a square medallion with a biblical scene. Unusually, both roundels are framed by inscriptions identifying the sitters; no such identification was deemed necessary by Birago in any other *Sforziada*. Such inscriptions recall the coins on which these profiles were originally based; but here, in the verbose context of the page as a whole, they appear deliberately superfluous.

The inscription around Il Moro seems especially overblown: ***LOD M SF VIC DUX BARRHI PATERNE LAUDIS INSTAURATOR ET IMITATOR***. He is dubbed 'restorer' and 'imitator' of Francesco's glory – not the sort of reference normally found around the rim of a portrait or coin, implying that the subject of the other portrait roundel (Gian Galeazzo) has failed to live up to Francesco's high standards and neglected his memory. The rarer, longer version of *BARRHI* has been preferred to the more familiar spelling of *BARI*, which appears on Caradosso's medal of 1488 commemorating the reconquest of Genoa, and on the more concise, to-the-point inscription around the medallion portrait of Il Moro in the illuminated biography of Muzio Attendolo (*LUDOVICO MA VICO DUX BARI DUC GUBERNA*).

Il Moro has a green collar and gold epaulettes (the reverse colour combination to that of Francesco Sforza in his medallion) and, like Francesco, has an embossed dark pink breastplate with (faded) gold highlights. Il Moro's breastplate features the same angel-head design as Gian Galeazzo's in the Paris *Sforziada*. Il Moro's hair is again avuncular domestic grey, not macho official black.

Gian Galeazzo is wearing a red collar, gold sleeves and green breastplate with flower patterning, fronted by a golden sunburst. The inscription around the rim reads a conventional, if lengthy, ***IOANNES GALEAZ MARIA SFOR. VICECO DUX MEDIOLANI VI.***

The background of both roundels has been repainted, again obliterating the original background stars, in the same blue as the defaced medallion of Francesco Sforza -- a slightly lighter blue than that originally used by Birago.

HAUT-DE-PAGE

Occupying the same place on the page as the Moor's head in the London *Sforziada* is a dusky-skinned figure with majestic grey beard and white turban, wearing a white jacket with (faded) red stripes and green sleeves against a dark blue ground.

This figure seems deliberately ambiguous. He appears to be part Magus, bearing gifts to a new-born child. Not gold, frankincense or myrrh, but a palm-sprig and laurel-branch to anoint the new-born Sforza ruler: Il Moro's

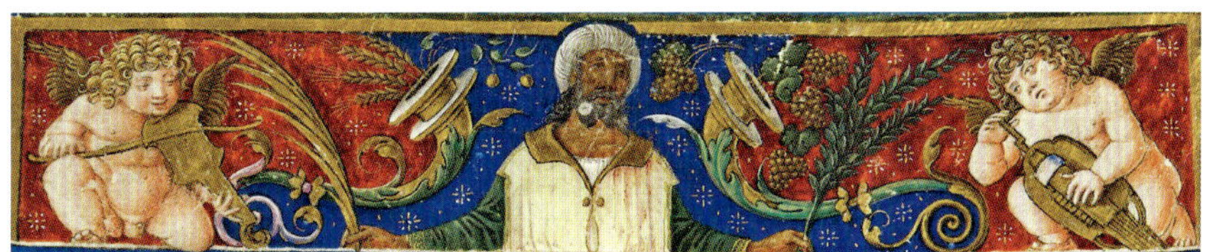

first-born legitimate son, Ercole (later Massimiliano) – the Moorish baby suckling at the breast of Charity in the right-hand border. And he is part Moor, in reference to Il Moro – or rather St Maurice, traditionally portrayed as dark-skinned and wearing, as here, a combination of red, green and white. He may also be intended to bring jokingly to mind Prince Djem, the Ottoman prince – half-brother of Sultan Bayezid II – incarcerated by the Pope.

He is flanked by scroll-ended, double-rimmed horns of plenty; ears of barley emerge from the horn on the left, bunches of grapes from the one on the right. At each end is a naked winged putto on a red ground – the one on the left is giggling as it plays a *lira da braccio*, the one on the right is holding a hurdy-gurdy. As with the three other *Sforziadas*, this page-top composition is within a self-contained, gold-framed border.

BAS-DE-PAGE

Francesco Sforza is portrayed as a top military man, chairing a council of eight generals from Antiquity,[5] identified in gold capitals on the red frieze running along the alternating red- and blue-panelled wall behind them – with the exception of the generals at either end, whose names appear on the side of the benches.

Four Roman generals are to Sforza's right: **FABIUS** [*c.280–203 BC*]; **SCIPIO** [*236–183 BC*]; **POMPEIUS** or *Pompey* [*106–48 BC*]; and **CESAR** or *Julius Caesar* [*100–44 BC*].

Four non-Roman generals are to his left: **HANNIBAL** *of Carthage* [*247–183 BC*, shown one-eyed – a reference to his loss of an eye when crossing the Appenines in 217 BC]; **EPAMINONDAS** *of Thebes* [*c.418–362 BC*]; **TEMISTOCLES** *of Athens* [*c.524–459 BC*]; and an end figure whose name is illegible, given that the bench-end, where it originally appeared, is badly worn – no doubt through constant handling (it is the natural place to hold the image between the thumb and index finger of the right hand).[6]

The identity of this final warlord has been the subject of speculation. Short-named non-Roman candidates include HECTOR, the Persian kings CYRUS, XERXES and DARIUS, and the Greek generals CIMON and PYRRHOS.

Both Cyrus (written *Cirus*) and Xerxes (written *Cerses*) are portrayed (bearded) in the *Codice Sforza*, Il Moro's lavishly illustrated history textbook from 1467, now in Turin's Biblioteca Reale (*MS Varia 75*). The shorter **CIRUS** must therefore be the most likely candidate, especially as his name recalls that of St Syrus (better known as San Siro of Milan soccer stadium fame), the first Bishop of Pavia.

The generals are all wearing the same uniform: breastplate, collar, high loose epaulettes, tight full-length sleeves, skirts and stockings. Francesco Sforza is the only figure portrayed with lion-head knee-guards, reminiscent of those worn by the standard-bearing Camillus in Ghirlandaio's 1480s Hall of Lilies fresco in Florence's Palazzo Vecchio. It is interesting to note that, in the silver beheading scene made in Verrocchio's workshop for the Baptistery in Florence in 1477/8, the helmeted soldier wears lion-head epaulettes, while the youth with salver – recently attributed to Leonardo da Vinci[7] – wears wolf-head knee-guards.

Only three generals are wearing knee-guards: Pompey and Caesar on the Roman side, and Hannibal from among the non-Romans. These four figures appear to be wearing clogs the same colour as their stockings; the other generals are in their stockinged feet. This curious imbalance may suggest Roman supremacy, in keeping with the overall context of a ducal investiture accorded by the Holy Roman Emperor.

Each general has an individual combination of blue, green, red, pink and white; skirt, epaulettes and knee-guards are in gold (that has tarnished to brown). Francesco Sforza sits on a plain white throne, slightly higher than the other generals, who are seated on continuous benching. Francesco and the four generals either side of him have their feet on a (red- and gold-trimmed) blue dais; the other four generals at the sides rest their feet on the (green-carpeted) floor.

Most of the figures are clean-shaven but Hannibal, Pompey and the right-end figure are bearded. Francesco Sforza is shaking hands with, and listening to, an ebullient Julius Caesar (after whom Il Moro's son Cesare, born to Cecilia Gallerani in 1491, was named). He is arm-in-arm with, and holding hands with (perhaps guiding), the 'one-eyed' Hannibal – even though he has his back turned to him. The scene echoes the handshake of the suckling infants in the medallion in the right-hand column.

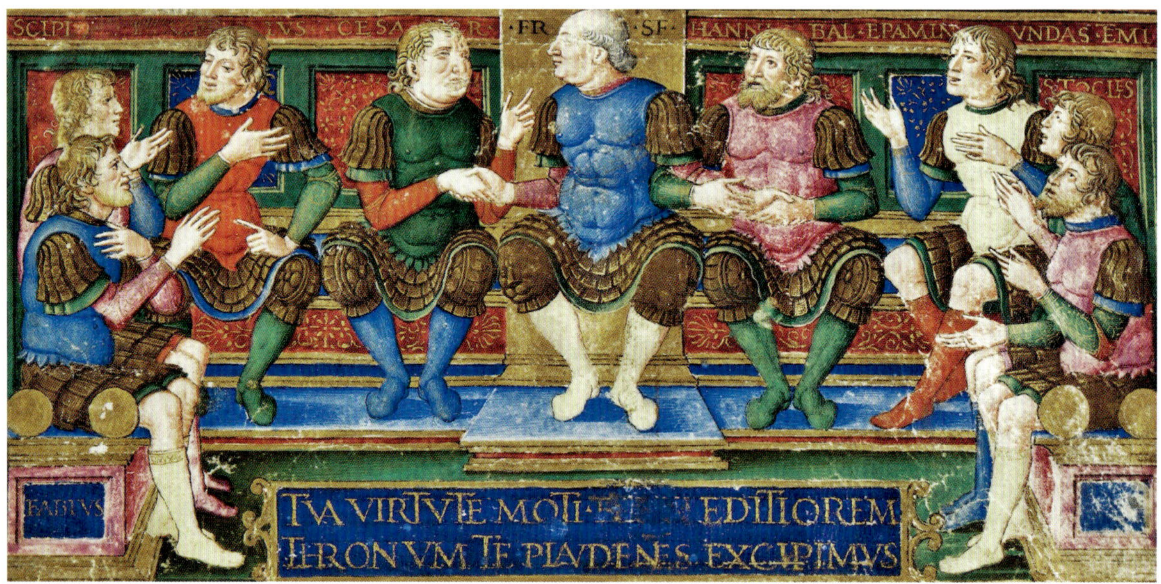

Alternating red and blue panels line the back wall. Unusually for a Birago frontispiece, this is an interior scene. A two-lined inscription beneath the dais, in gold letters on a dark blue ground within an elaborate gold frame, reads ***TUA VIRTUTE MOTI … EDITIOREM THRONUM TE PLAUDENES EXCIPIMUS***, which is untranslatable in this illegible form, but includes references to Francesco's virtue and actions, and his right to a higher throne. There may well be a pun involving *editus* (higher) and *editio* (edition or book).

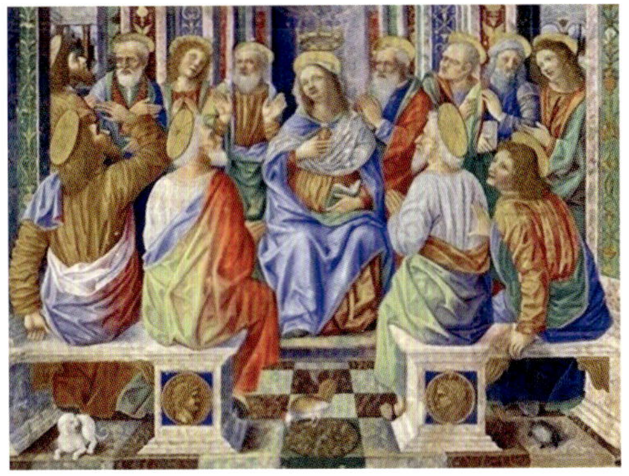

A possible iconographic source is the Pentecost scene attributed to Antonio da Monza (*left*), for a service-book produced in 1492/3 for the newly elected Pope Alexander VI, that shows the Apostles seated on very similar benches, receiving the Holy Spirit's gift of speaking in tongues (Albertina *inv. 1764*). The idea of a gathering of classical generals may also have been influenced by the eight *Uomini d'Arme* painted by Bramante in the Milan palazzo of court poet Gaspare Visconti in the late 1480s. Visconti is thought to have hosted 'academic' gatherings in his home, which would further tie in with the debating theme of Birago's *bas-de-page*.

RIGHT BORDER

The top corner is lacking. The two portrait roundels, and the square medallion between them, together take up roughly half the column. The medallion features a seated woman breastfeeding two naked babies (one blond, one a Moor) who (like Francesco Sforza and Julius Caesar at the foot of the page) are shaking hands. The left hand of the pale-skinned baby is placed over the heart, as if swearing obeisance to the dark baby, who has his right hand raised in apparent benediction in a gesture that recalls that of the infant Christ in the *Virgin of the Rocks*. The idea of unequal twins comes from Greek mythology and, as Elisabetta Gnignera has pointed out, doubtless influenced Leonardo da Vinci's *Lady with an Ermine*.[8]

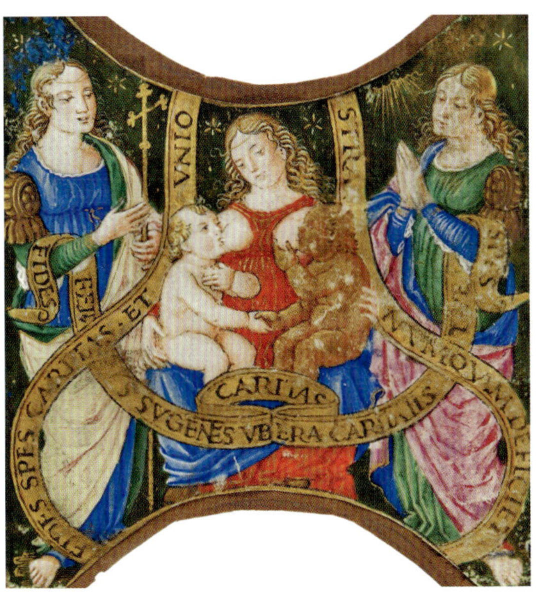

The mother-figure wears a Virginal red and blue gown. Two other, barefooted women stand on either side, both wearing incongruous gold epaulettes similar to those of the *bas-de-page* generals.

The one next to the white baby is in a (predominantly) blue and white gown with green sleeves and trim, holding a cross; she is gazing towards the black baby as if her cross is raised in blessing. The one next to the black baby is in a (predominantly) green and pink dress with blue sleeves and trim, and has her hands clasped in prayer; she is also gazing at the black baby, as if her prayers are directed to him. Each of the three women has a *lenza* (with *ferronnière*) around her forehead.

The composition appears to be closely based on two niello medallions (one currently displayed in the Castello Sforzesca in Milan) in honour of Beatrice d'Este, depicted kneeling alongside a Madonna & Child with two priestly male figures in attendance on either side. The breastfeeding Madonna is a common Renaissance image but, in this particular context, brings to mind the *Madonna Litta* (now in the Hermitage) attributed to Leonardo da Vinci and/or his pupil Giovanni Boltraffio; the *Madonna Litta* is also wearing a red chemise and blue cloak.

This is the second time that Birago uses infant offspring in allegorical fashion – after the saplings at the foot of the mulberry tree in the Paris *Sforziada*.

The medallion is swamped by two criss-cross lettered banners to ludicrous effect, with the top of one banner even protruding into the roundel above (something which was not respected when the page was cut up into separate pictures). **CARITAS** (Charity) is draped below the mother's lap; **FIDES** (Faith) over the arm of the woman to the left; and **SPES** (Hope) over the arm of the woman to the right.

One banner reads **FIDES SPES CARITA ET UNIO NOSTRA NUMQUAM DEFICIET** (*Faith, Hope, Charity and Our Union Will Never Fail*). 'Our' could refer to Beatrice and Il Moro, but is more likely to be an ironic reference to the union between Il Moro and Gian Galeazzo, here represented by their new-born children, with their own profiled portraits above and below.

The second banner reads **FELI…S SUGENTES UBERA CARITATIS TUE** (*Happy … Suck the Breasts of Your Charity*).

While it seems evident that the babes-in-arms refers to the two Sforza newly-borns – Il Moro's son and Gian Galeazzo's daughter – it is less clear (and perhaps, as so often with Birago, the ambiguity is intentional) whether the two respective mothers, Beatrice d'Este and Isabel of Aragon, are represented by the two flanking figures; or whether the seated mother-figure is actually intended to be Beatrice. Evidence in favour of the latter interpretation is provided by the colours of the robes worn by the female figures, as compared with correspondence (cited by Cartwright)[9] describing the costumes worn at the thanksgiving service for the two births held in Santa Maria delle Grazie on 25 February 1493. Teodora degli Angeli, maid-of-honour to Beatrice's mother Leonora, informed Isabella d'Este that her sister Beatrice was wearing 'red and blue silk with a blue silk mantle' – like the mother-figure in the medallion. Isabel was wearing 'green velvet and mantle of crimson velvet' – like the figure of HOPE standing next to her (green is also the colour Birago invariably assigns to her husband Gian Galeazzo).

To suggest that Isabel, the reigning duchess, needed *Hope* once a son had been born to the Milanese Regent smacks of the same snide irony encountered in the Paris *Sforziada*.[10]

The bottom right-hand corner of the frontispiece features a plinth topped by two winged angels flanking a shield with Il Moro's arms as Duke of Bari (with impaled *fleur-de-lys*), against a red background spangled with gold stars. The plinth and Bari shield look slightly askew, which may be due to Birago's awkward attempt at creating perspective by placing them at a slight angle. The Bari shield is topped by another, smaller shield featuring the two lighthouses of Genoa.

The angel on the left is clad in a blue breastplate with green sleeves over a white cassock with green waist-hangings. He is holding the sifting-cloth – with two hands rather than one, perhaps to imply that, whereas there had hitherto been two people involved in a union (Gian Galeazzo and Il Moro), there would henceforth be only one (Il Moro).

The angel on the right is clad in a green breastplate with blue sleeves over a blue cassock with pink waist-hangings. He has embedded an axe in a log – another traditional Sforza emblem, originally associated with Francesco Sforza's father Muzio Attendolo but regularly used by Il Moro. Again, its presentation here, by an angel, is just as incongruous as the sifting-cloth held by a single hand.

The angels' posture and attire, including their breastplates, epaulettes, cassocks and swag-like waist hangings, are identical to those in the image of *St Giles* in the *Sforza Hours* (*fol. 203v*), which may date from roughly the same time. But here both angels are awkwardly fronted by inscribed scrolls. The one around the sifter reads ***TAL A TI QUAL A MI***; the one above the axe and log is semi-illegible, but can be thought to read ***TUTO EL TORTO VA IN***.

No fewer than three *scopetti* can be seen: one beneath the shield, topped by a scroll inscribed ***MERITO ET TEMPORE***; the other two (smaller) dangling from the sides of the plinth.

A fatuous giant **L** (for *Ludovico*) on a shield is positioned at the top of the plinth; it recalls the contrived *IOGL* shield in the Paris *Sforziada*, but now the *IOG* (for Gian Galeazzo) is missing, repeating the sifting-cloth inference that a two-man union is giving way to individual rule.

The plinth's six-line inscription vaunts Il Moro's library: **AUCTORE MAURO FILIO - UT MEMORIA VIVAT BIBLIOTHECÃ ... .** The bottom line of lettering is so worn as to be illegible – the result of being gripped time and again between finger and thumb. It appears to start with a *D* and end in an *O*, and to be topped by at least one abbreviation sign; *DOMINO* ('to the Lord') seems a plausible possibility. The apparent importance of the word *Library* in the verbose context of the page as a whole adds weight to Mulas's suggestion that *bibliothecã* may refer here to Il Moro's personal library (presumably housed in Milan or Vigevano) rather than the official Ducal Library in Pavia, which already housed an illuminated *Sforziada* (the one now in Paris).[11]

Two unusually slender putti are playing hide-and-seek around the sides of the plinth. The one on the left is pointing towards the *L* shield with his right hand; the one on the right has his left hand positioned next to the word VIVAT. *Long Live Ludovico!* The sinister implication: Gian Galeazzo's time will soon be up.

Just over one-third of the border is missing and only two panels remain, trimmed to identical size.

Originally positioned at the foot of the left-hand column: a gold-winged putto strumming a lyre, kneeling on a stand in the form of a bulging white half-column. The background is red/green higher up, then blue/red from shoulder-height down. As the image is framed to the bottom and sides, its position in the page's bottom corner is indisputable.

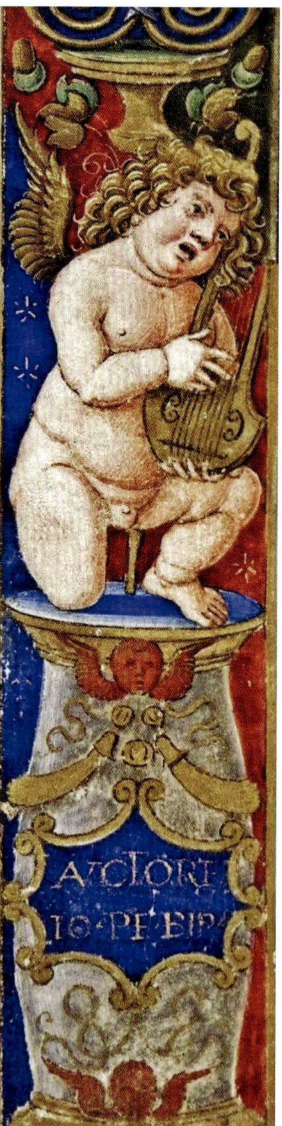

This kneeling putto is lit from the left, with his right leg casting a blue shadow across the top of the column. The stand has a narrow plinth and capital, both in gold, and both embellished by curious orange angel-heads whose precise nature is unclear: they appear superimposed on the stand in physically impossible fashion. Each angel-head is accompanied by trailing gold ribbons.

Occupying the middle of the column is a two-lined, gold-lettered inscription on a dark blue ground within a fussy gold frame, reading **AUCTORE IO PE BIR**. This is not merely an abbreviated signature: as with the corresponding plinth inscription in the right-hand column, the word *auctore* is unexpected – especially as Birago was an *illuminator* rather than an *auctor* (author). To find the word *auctor* cited twice on the same illuminated page may be linked to the *Paragone* debate as to the supremacy of the written word or visual image – a debate launched, in the context of the *Sforziada*, by Il Puteolano's oration at the front of the book.

There are some even more bizarre features to this apparently innocuous image of a musical cherub. Filling the gap between the top of the inscription and the top of the stand are two golden, proudly erect phalluses which, like the angel-heads, appear to have no physical link with the stand itself – artificially emerging from the coloured borders to the sides. Their impact in a family history book is quasi-pornographic.

Further evidence of Birago's ribald intentions are provided by the thin shaft that arbitrarily emerges from the top of the stand before seeming to disappear up the cherub's anus.

It is hard not to wonder if Leonardo da Vinci is the target of Birago's racy homophobic satire (and not for the first time, if the London *Sforziada* is anything to go on). Powering that supposition: the plinth's *ginger*-coloured angels; the fact that the cherub is strumming the instrument for which Leonardo was famous; and the cherub's peculiar kneeling posture in three-quarter profile, as propagated by Leonardo in the *Virgin of the Rocks*.

The figure may also refer to the famous quote by the Greek general Themistocles (portrayed in the *bas-de-page*) as cited in Plutarch's *Lives*: 'I never learned how to tune a harp or play the lute, but I know how to raise a small and inconsiderable city to glory and greatness.' Themistocles may even have been 'selected' to imply that these words applied to Francesco Sforza's achievements as regards Milan.

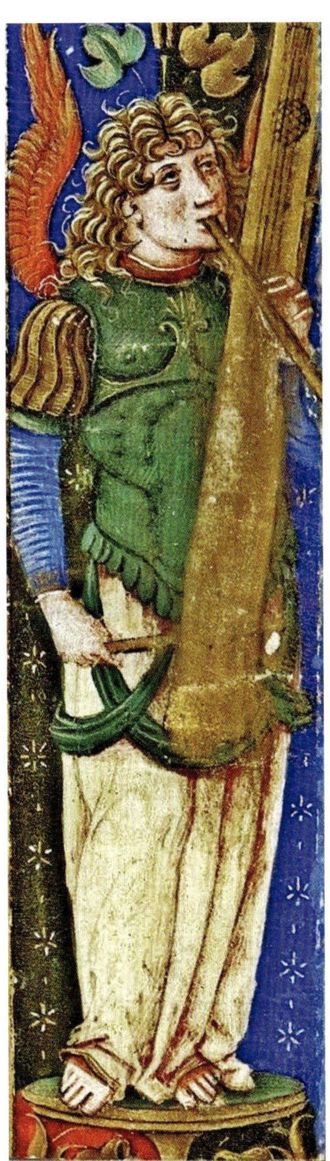

The second image in the left-hand column, originally positioned about halfway up the page, shows a barefooted angel, this time with orange wings, standing on a small circular plinth. He is wearing a green breastplate with blue sleeves and a baggy white robe or pantaloon, whose folds are outlined in red in a manner that recalls the billowing shirt of the *haut-de-page* Moor.

The background is blue/green higher up, then green/blue from waist down. The work has been cut off at the bottom and top.

This panel may have continued up more or less directly from the one below, as it is based on a similar concentric circle motif (albeit with a different-coloured background). Its upper border is not definitive, indicating that this panel was placed in an intermediary position in the left-hand border.

The standing angel is simultaneously playing a flute and drawing a bow over a psalterium (an elongated string drum, sometimes known as a *tambourin à cordes*). His enormous instrument protrudes from his midriff in most suggestive fashion, as Birago pursues his homosexual satire.

DATE

Between February 1493 and October 1494; most probably Summer 1493.

The frontispiece can be no earlier than February 1493 (Beatrice d'Este gave birth to her son Ercole on 25 January 1493, Isabel of Aragon to her daughter Ippolita a few days afterwards) and no later than Gian Galeazzo's death in October 1494. It may well date from late Summer 1493, its ebullient mood reflecting an Il Moro secure in the knowledge that he will shortly be receiving the ducal investiture from the future Emperor Maximilian. Il Moro received confirmation to this effect at the end of June 1493, a few weeks after the Treaty of Senlis had established a truce between France and Austria.

Il Moro and his wife Beatrice visited Ferrara in mid-May 1493,[12] attending a performance of *Menaechmi* by Plautus (a source for Shakespeare's *Comedy of Errors*), whose plot centres on twins and mistaken identity. On June 24 Maximilian wrote to Il Moro accepting his 400,000-ducat offer to marry Bianca Maria and grant Il Moro the Imperial investiture to Milan as soon as he had succeeded his 77 year-old father, Friedrich III, as Emperor. Il Moro could now indeed afford to offer 'Charity' to his hapless nephew and niece. Friedrich III was a sick man. His gangrened left leg had been amputated on 8 June 1493, and he would die eight weeks after Maximilian's missive, on August 19. Six days later, on St Louis's Day (August 25) – the feast day of Il Moro's patron saint – Il Moro's father-in-law Duke Ercole d'Este arrived in Milan from Ferrara with the Turkish costumes needed for a repeat performance of *Menaechmi*. One can imagine this Birago frontispiece being the source of much male merriment: its jocular nature suggests it pre-dated the court mourning which greeted the sudden death of Beatrice's 43-year-old mother, Duchess Eleonora d'Este, on October 11.

There are several signs that this frontispiece was produced under pressure. These range from sloppy workmanship (the wonky plinth) to a string of repeats from Birago's earlier work – whether from the first two *Sforziadas* (the two roundel portraits, the Bari arms, the *L* shield, the Genoa shield) or the *Sforza Hours* (the *St Giles* suffragan figures). Such haste would tie in with the possibility that the page were commissioned at the start of July 1493 (just after Il Moro had received news from Maximilian accepting the investiture deal) – with a deadline of August 25, and the visit of Ercole d'Este and family. Ercole being, of course, not just the grandfather of Il Moro's son – but also the man Il Moro's son was initially named after.

DISMEMBERMENT

D.R. Edward Wright has suggested that the frontispiece was dismembered to enhance the commercial value of the individual cuttings.[13] In support of this claim, Wright cites the strong market for individual illuminations in the early 19th century, and suggests the possible involvement of Luigi Celotti (1759–1843), a specialist Italian dealer in the field. Such an explanation can be discarded given that, according to the Uffizi archives, the cuttings were in the Pitti Palace (Florence) as early as 1664.

There is evidence to suggest that the frontispiece was mutilated much earlier, in an act of calculated vandalism. The medallion portrait of Francesco Sforza was defaced in a deliberate and revealing way: by painting over and obliterating his title of Duke of Milan, and by painting over the bannered inscriptions above and below his portrait. These banners and their lettering were clumsily replaced at a later date, with Francesco's name written in a format to be found nowhere else (*FRAN SFOR VICE*), and his honorific title (*PATER PATRIÆ*) inked in by an uncertain quill.

This defacement brings to mind another act of artistic vandalism that followed the arrival of French troops in Milan in September 1499: the painting-over of one of the four captioned shields on the ceiling of the Sala delle Asse (extolling Il Moro's close links with Emperor Maximilian), replaced by a new inscription mocking Il Moro after his defeat and flight. This change was probably ordered by Gian Giacomo Trivulzio (1440–1518), head of the French armed forces and interim Governor of Milan. Trivulzio – scion of a venerable Milanese family, and a leading Sforza general until the mid-1480s – held a titanic grudge against the Sforzas (and Sanseverinos). It is not hard to imagine him also venting his hatred on a book that extolled the Sforzas as the worthy heirs of Julius Caesar and the Roman Empire.

This raises the matter of Trivulzio's access to this third illuminated *Sforziada*. It cannot have been in Pavia, where the prestigious Ducal Library was raided under the direct authority of King Louis XII and removed to Blois. Trivulzio took possession of the Castello Sforzesco in Milan, and also of the Sforza *castello* in Vigevano. This third illuminated *Sforziada* could feasibly have been found in either venue. As Il Moro and his retainers had several days to hide or remove precious belongings from the Castello Sforzesco before the French reached Milan, but no such opportunity to safeguard belongings in Vigevano, which found itself in the military frontline, the latter venue seems more likely – especially as the castello in Vigevano was assigned to Trivulzio as a spoil of war.

The roundel portraits of Il Moro and Gian Galeazzo were defaced at the same time as the Francesco Sforza medallion – the same blue (slightly lighter than the original navy) was used in all three cases, clearly to ensure stylistic homogeneity, as the roundel backgrounds contained no lettering, only stars. This strongly suggests that these images were meant to be kept together, rather than cut up and sold individually.

It therefore seems likely that the damage to this third illuminated *Sforziada* took place in three phases: defacement in Italy in late 1499; partial restoration in France; and dismemberment in Florence, possibly during the reign of Ferdinando II de' Medici (1621–70), with the frontispiece removed and cut up, and the volume rendered presentable by receiving a handwritten copy of its newly missing page before entering the Capponi Library.

INTERPRETATION

Apart from being slightly rushed, this frontispiece also has a zany, jokey feel. It is festooned with banners and a surfeit of lettering, and there is the ungainly presence of two portrait roundels rather than one. This was a page destined for those in the know, intended purely for domestic consumption.

The central image of Francesco Sforza shaking hands with Julius Caesar, the most famous military (and political) leader of Ancient Rome, reflects Il Moro's successful campaign to obtain the investiture of the Holy Roman Empire from Maximilian Habsburg: the handshake appears to have sealed a deal.[14] Birago's message is that the Sforzas are worthy heirs to the heroes of Antiquity – but to present Francesco Sforza as their superior, placed higher than even Julius Caesar, is humorous nonsense.

Francesco Sforza, Il Moro and Gian Galeazzo are always shown in breastplates in their *Sforziada* medallion portraits – more to identify them as heirs of Antiquity than active generals, which Il Moro and Gian Galeazzo emphatically were not. Perhaps Birago's choice of the Classical world as the setting for this particular *bas-de-page* was fuelled by the 1493 publication of Herodian of Antioch's *History of the Roman Empire* in a Latin translation by Poliziano. The men of Antiquity in military attire are doubtless enjoying the barrack-room humour served up by the homosexual musicians in the left-hand column. After the cavorting ginger-haired cherub in the London *Sforziada*, indulging in the sort of behaviour for which Leonardo da Vinci was once denounced in Florence, Birago again teases the spotlight towards the most famous gay in the Milanese art world.

The suckling infant scene in the right-hand column surely refers to the quasi-simultaneous births of Il Moro's eldest son Ercole (later known as Massi-miliano) on 25 January 1493 and Gian Galeazzo's second child, Ippolita, a few days later. The scene is strikingly reminiscent of Leonardo's *Virgin of the Rocks*. Both feature a central mother, a cross on the left, and two babies – with the one on the left swearing allegiance to the one on the right. This impression is reinforced by the appearance elsewhere in the left-hand column of two angel musicians with stringed instruments who – as in the side panels commiss-ioned to accompany the second (London) version of the *Virgin of the Rocks* – offer a contrast of plucked instrument (lute in the painted version, lyre in the Birago frontispiece) and bow-played instrument (*lira da braccio* in London; psalterium *chez* Birago). To reinforce this impression of cross-reference, the bow-playing angel is clad in green in both versions.

The presence of paired figures throughout is obsessive: two musical cherubs in the *haut-de-page*; two portrait roundels; two female acolytes flanking the two infants; two winged angels holding Sforza insignia; two putti emerging to the sides of a plinth; two inscribed plinths; two 'authors' (Birago and Il Moro) mentioned on these plinths; two groups of Classical generals … .

Two other contemporary artworks from Sforza Milan have a similar two-person theme: Bergognone's *Sant'Ambrogio Altarpiece* in the Certosa di Pavia, featuring the twins SS Gervasio & Protasio, the 2nd century Milanese martyrs whose remains were unearthed by St Ambrose in 386; and the *Virgin of the Rocks*, with infant Christ and John the Baptist.

Birago makes one of the implications of the *Virgin of the Rocks* blasphemously clear: the black, breastfeeding baby – with a Cross, a Madonna and a Magus in attendance – is portrayed as the Son of Man. It is no surprise to find Birago quoting a work in which his *Sforziada* collaborator, Ambrogio de Predis, assisted the Florentine Maestro.

The *Hope-Faith-Charity* medallion, with its cross and Madonna figure, shows Il Moro positioning himself as a champion of Christianity – in a frontispiece that alludes to the Duchy of Milan's status as a fiefdom of the *Holy* Roman Empire.

The beturbanned *haut-de-page* Moor/St Maurice may well be a jokey refer-ence to the Turkish threat to Christendom. In 1480 the Turks briefly invaded Italy (Otranto) before pushing up the East Adriatic coast to modern Slovenia. As soon as he became Holy Roman Emperor, Maximilian announced special measures to push them back.[15] Pope Alexander VI so shared his concerns that he wrote to both Il Moro and Gian Galeazzo asking for help.[16]

The *haut-de-page* figure may also have been to designed to raise a smile and bring back family memories – of Beatrice's taste for practical jokes (she once turned up at the Certosa di Pavia disguised as a Turk),[17] and of her father's love of costume drama (to perform Plautus's *Menaechmi* in Milan, Duke Ercole borrowed Turkish costumes and turbans from the Marquis of Mantua, Fran-cesco Gonzaga – nicknamed *Il Turco*, possibly because he was the only north-ern Italian leader of the 1490s to sport a beard).

With three inscribed plinths, five wordy banners, two verbose, coin-like rim inscriptions – and both the frontispiece's destinatee (Il Moro) and illuminator (Birago) described as 'authors' – the emphasis on *words* on an *illuminated* page suggests that one goal of this frontispiece was to confront the relative merits of literature and the image. The joint mention implies Il Moro and Birago were joint authors of the page's complex iconography – and presumably of the other *Sforziada* frontispieces as well: hats off to one of history's earliest comedy double-acts. Incidentally, but not perhaps coincidentally, we read of Isabel of Aragon attending a party at the house of Gaspare di Pusterla on 27 February 1493 wearing a 'gown embroidered with books and letters.'[18]

The main scene, with its gesticulating generals, is also about Debate, and evokes two other contemporary works of art: the Antonio da Monza *Pentecost* scene destined for Pope Alexander VI – significant in that Pentecost is the moment when the Holy Spirit descends with the gift of the gab; and *The Last Supper*, which Leonardo is said to have begun painting in 1494 but may have begun planning somewhat earlier.

Gesticulation and animated discussion are common to all three images. Birago's *bas-de-page* also recalls the *Last Supper's* compositional division into groups of three.

What can have been the great debate at the Sforza court to which Birago is presumably alluding? Maybe the superiority of the Roman Empire – and, by implication, of its latterday counterpart, the Holy Roman Empire: a Guelph/Ghibelline debate *par excellence*.[19] Or maybe whether Il Moro's greater competence and experience made him a worthier ruler than the official Duke, his nephew Gian Galeazzo. Il Moro may well be embodied in Julius Caesar, whom Francesco treats as an equal; Gian Galeazzo, in contrast, is embodied by the one-eyed Hannibal, whom Francesco ostentatiously ignores, while condescendingly offering him his arm.

This frontispiece's unprecedented and omnipresent verbiage suggests that the *bas-de-page* also alludes to the *Paragone* debate as to whether the written word was a more effective and durable way to commemorate great men then the visual arts (painting/sculpture/architecture) – a view vigorously propounded by Il Puteolano in his *Sforziada* preface.

In his *Trattato della Pittura*, Leonardo da Vinci virulently defended the pre-eminent status of painting and dismissed some of his opponents as 'beasts,' claiming the artist surpasses the poet thanks to his ability to present his subject as a whole, rather than through the linear progression of words.[20] He would issue his own retort to Il Puteolano in the next illuminated *Sforziada* (*see Chapter IX*).

The frontispiece, as ever, strives first and foremost to glorify Il Moro – but also, by laying unusual stress on the glory of Francesco Sforza, to diminish Gian Galeazzo's importance as his mere grandson. Although Gian Galeazzo's portrait is featured above Il Moro's, this purported superiority is undermined by several factors: Gian Galeazzo's (white) baby pays obeisance to Il Moro's (black) baby; the presence of two shields (those of Bari and Genoa) representing Il Moro; by emblems associated with Il Moro – no fewer than three *scopetti* and a giant *L* on a shield in honour of Ludovico; and by a plinth extolling Il Moro for reviving his father's reputation.

The presence of a dark-skinned, Moorish figure top centre appears to be yet another reference to Il Moro, as does the page's use of pink – a colour not found in any of Birago's other frontispieces. Faded red? No: there is plenty of *un*faded red, often juxtaposing the pink. The pink – used for Il Moro's and his father's breastplates – is mulberry-colour, and a play on Il Moro's nickname … and further evidence that the sheet had partly the nature of a private in-joke.

But, as usual with Birago, the fun-and-games hide other allusions and levels of meaning which, on this page, are particularly numerous.

The plinth at the foot of the right-hand column supports, in turn, the *L* for *Ludovico*, as Il Moro was christened in 1452; the *scopetta* that became his personal emblem as a teenager in the 1460s; his shield as Duke of Bari, a title he acquired in 1479; the two towers of Genoa, the city he reconquered in 1488; his own portrait, as he appeared in the 1490s; and then his newborn son, evoking the Future. Not only, then, does this page evoke Il Moro's own steady rise (in keeping with his *Merito e Tempore* motto, shown here above the largest *scopetta*) towards the title of Duke of Milan – it also points to his future lineage.

Above the infant Image of the Future, however, remains the ducal profile of Gian Galeazzo: the last obstacle for Il Moro on his climb to the top. The sinister implication: this obstacle is to be removed.

Gian Galeazzo was doomed. Within eighteen months he was dead.

NOTES

1 The catalogue of the exhibition *Arte Lombarda dai Visconti agli Sforza* (Skira, Milan 2015) wrongly placed the portrait medallion of Il Moro above that of Gian Galeazzo.

2 The *Catalogo della Libreria Capponi*, drawn up by D. Giorgi and printed in Rome by Bernabo & Lazzarini in 1747, cites the *Sforziada* (p. 353) under *Simoneta Giovanni, Comentarj della cose fatte da Francesco Sforza …* , and is described as *in foglio, in membrana*. Alessandro Gregorio Capponi was Privy Chamberlain to the Pope and President for Life of the Vatican Museum. He devoted his life to book-collecting, also assembling a fine collection of antiquities and paintings. The library he left to the Vatican comprised about 5000 volumes, including 289 manuscripts.

3 J. Van Praet, *Catalogue des livres imprimés sur vélin de la Bibliothèque du Roi* (Paris 1822).

4 L. Zappelli, *Catalogus Codicum Sæculo XV Impressorum qui in Bibliotheca Vaticana Romæ Adservantur* (1853–68).

5 Pier Luigi Mulas has suggested the inspiration for this scene comes from the *Codice Sforza*. The mix of contemporary and classical figures was also a theme of the new Piazza in Vigevano, planned at about the same time as the Uffizi *Sforziada*, for which Il Moro commissioned several dozen roundel portraits (now heavily restored), mixing Sforza family members and such *uomini famosi* as Brutus, Scipio, Marius, Mithradates, Pompey, Caesar, Cato, Metellus, Vespasian, Trajan, Titus and Marcus Aurelius. The first time that members of the Sforza dynasty had been associated with ancient heroes was in Foppa's (now lost) portrayals of Francesco, Bianca Maria and their children alongside eight Roman emperors in the courtyard of the Medici Bank in Milan.

6 Evans speculates that the scene may be influenced by the iconography of the Nine Worthies or *Les Neuf Preux* (deriving from the *Golden Legend*), with the final soldier therefore likely to be Hector or Alexander the Great: these two figures, along with Julius Caesar, comprised the three pagan warriors who formed this worthy band of heroes. If this is true (and Birago illuminated a copy of the *Golden Legend* now in the Polish National Library in Warsaw), the very limited space available for the (illegible) name at the end of the bench – FABIUS only just squeezes on – suggests HECTOR as the likely candidate. The figure cannot be Alexander in any case, as the figure here is bearded, whereas Alexander was a noisy advocate of the shaven chin. Alexander's absence can be explained by Il Moro's nascent alliance with Maximilian Habsburg as Holy Roman Emperor: it was appropriate for Francesco Sforza to be shown on a par (here, shaking hands) with a previous Roman Emperor, of whom the most illustrious was Julius Caesar. To portray Alexander the Great as inferior to Julius Caesar would have been debatable to say the least.

7 Gary M. Radke, *Leonardo da Vinci and the Art of Sculpture* (Yale University Press, 2009).

8 Elisabetta Gnignera, *Cecilia o la Dama con l'Ermellino* in Pascal Cotte's *Lumière on the Lady with an Ermine – Unprecedented Discoveries* (LTMI Editions, Paris).

9 Julia Cartwright, *Beatrice d'Este, Duchess of Milan, 1475–1497* (J.M Dent & Co Ltd, London 1899).

10 The honours showered on Beatrice d'Este and her new-born son Ercole so infuriated Isabel of Aragon that she wrote to her father Alfonso calling on the Kingdom of Naples to intervene. She complained that it was Il Moro who administered the State, leaving her husband and herself powerless, without friends or money, with even their servants appointed by Il Moro. She also claimed their lives were at risk (and would later claim her husband was poisoned).

11 Pier Luigi Mulas, *Auctore Mauro Filio: Il Programma Iconigrafico dei Frontespizi Miniati dei Commentarii di Giovanni Simonetta* (1996).

12 On 17 May 1493 Il Moro, Beatrice and their infant son Ercole arrived in Ferrara accompanied by ten chariots and 50 mules laden with baggage. A week of festivities was staged by Duke Ercole, including a tournament on the Piazza in front of the Castello, with Galeazzo Sanseverino defeating Niccolò da Correggio, Ermes Sforza and his brothers Gianfrancesco and Gaspare. Performances of *Menaechmi*, Plautus's *Amphitryon* and *Cassina*, and other comedies were staged in the evenings in a theatre in the Gothic Palazzo della Ragione on the cathedral square. Beatrice then left for Venice with her mother, Alfonso d'Este and his wife Anna Sforza; Il Moro returned a few days later to Milan. On June 4 he was joined by Count Belgiojoso, who had galloped back from Senlis with news of the Franco-Habsburg alliance and Charles VIII's plans to invade Italy. With Charles VIII now officially on friendly terms with Maximilian, and even agreeing to support Il Moro's future investiture, Il Moro was happy to withdraw all opposition to the French expedition to Naples.

13 D.R. Edward Wright, *op.cit.*

14 On 25 April 1493 Il Moro instructed his ambassador Erasmo Brasca to make two proposals to Maximilian: the hand of Bianca Maria Sforza, with an enormous dowry of 300,000 ducats; and the secret request that Il Moro be granted the investiture of Milan (formerly granted to Gian Galeazzo Visconti but not obtained by the first three princes of the House of Sforza) for an extra 100,000 ducats [one source claims the wedding was agreed as early as 16 March 1493]. On 26 September 1493 Maximilian appointed Bishop Melchior of Brixen to represent him at his proxy wedding with Bianca Maria Sforza in Milan Cathedral on November 30.

15 According to dispatches in the Habsburg Archives, on 7 September 1493 (from Innsbruck) Maximilian informed Herzog Albrecht of Bavaria that he wanted to move against the Turks (who had recently reached Marburg and defeated the Hungarians in Croatia). To spearhead this fight, on September 17 (while still in Innsbruck), four weeks after his father's death, Maximilian announced plans for a secular Brotherhood of St George. A garrison town with a church was to be erected on the Turkish frontier – at Rann an der Sava in Carniola [now Brežice, Slovenia]. A year later, on 28 October 1494, Maximilian, his family and a gaggle of Imperial princes were inducted

as members of the St George Brotherhood in Antwerp Cathedral. Pope Alexander VI and numerous cardinals also became members. But the project fizzled out.

16 On 2 October 1494 Pope Alexander VI wrote to Gian Galeazzo and Ludovico Sforza, carefully styling them Duke of Milan and Duke of Bari, to the effect that 'for three months the Pope has been hearing about fresh Turkish attacks on Croatia. The Turkish Sultan wants to conquer the town of Segnia [Senj/Zengg] … the danger for Italy is pressing. The Pope begs and exhorts Dukes Gian Galeazzo and Ludovico, in this great danger, to give him help and advice, because the situation admits of no delay. Their Graces are begged to advise by October 15 of what help they can provide for the liberation of Christianity and Italy.'

17 Beatrice d'Este's wacky sense of humour finds an echo in this page (perhaps reflecting her status as mother to its black-baby hero). She once took her court ladies on an incognito shopping spree through the streets of Milan dressed in the simple linen *panicelli* head-dresses common in Naples, where she had grown up. Such headwear was unknown in Lombardy, and provoked slaps and cat-calls from local women (I am grateful to Elisabetta Gnignera for informing me about the *panicello*).

18 Cartwright, *op. cit.*

19 The Visconti and Sforza rulers of Milan were traditionally Ghibellines, i.e. supporters of the Holy Roman Emperor against the Pope, but the situation was not so simple during Il Moro's time, given Emperor Friedrich III's hostility to the Sforzas – and Pope Innocent VIII's hostility to Naples, which suited Il Moro. The deaths of Innocent VIII in 1492 and Friedrich III in 1493 saw a return to the status quo ante. (Il Moro's nemesis Trivulzio, as a Guelph, naturally welcomed the warmer relations between the Vatican and Naples that ensued under Pope Alexander VI.)

20 Leonardo also described music as the 'sister of painting' due to the harmonic proportions which allowed it to convey simultaneous effects – but a younger, slightly inferior sister, as sight was a superior sense to sound; and he contended that painting is an exercise of refinement, relying more on intellectual than physical capabilities, notably because of the need to take account of the rules of perspective. Leonardo also wrote:
'If you, historians, or poets, or mathematicians, had not seen things with your eyes, you could not report of them in writing … . Although you, O Poet, tell a story with your pen, the painter can tell it more easily with his brush, with simpler completeness and in a way less tedious to understand. You may call painting *dumb poetry*, but the painter may call poetry *blind painting*. Which is worse? To be blind or dumb? Although the poet is as free as the painter to invent his fictions, they are not as satisfactory to men as paintings; for, although poetry is able to describe forms, actions, and places in words, the painter deals with the actual similitude of the forms, in order to represent them.'

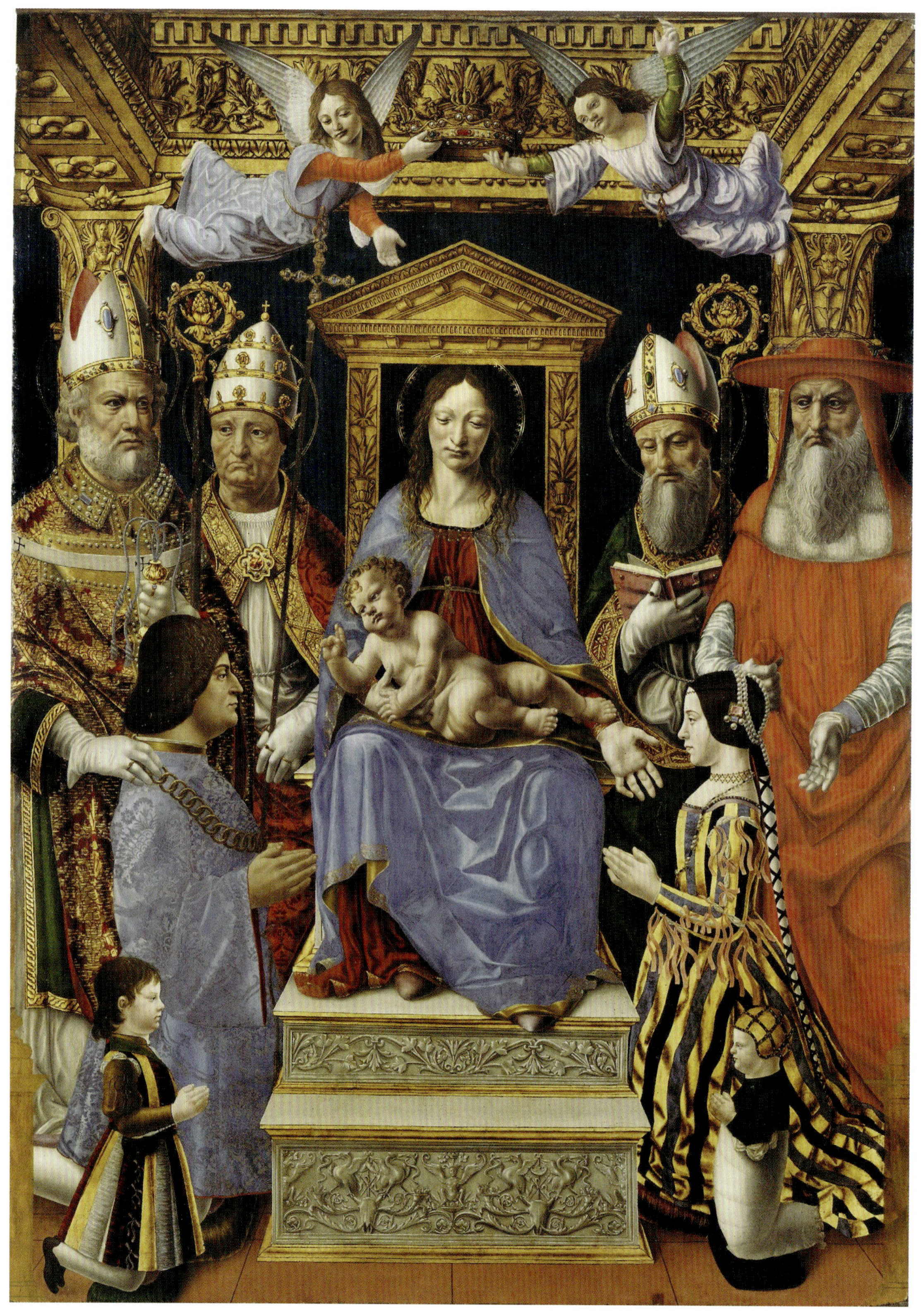

PALA SFORZESCA (c.1494) – OIL ON WOOD 230 × 165 cm – PINACOTECA DI BRERA

VIII

BLASPHEMY

ART AND PROPAGANDA UNDER IL MORO 1490–95

IN THE FIRST HALF of the 1490s Leonardo de Vinci was engaged on four projects commissioned and overseen by Il Moro, each bearing a political message: *The Lady with an Ermine*, the Sforza Horse, *The Last Supper* and a new version of *The Virgin of the Rocks* – which, like the *Pala Sforzesca* and the giant ducal frescoes in the Certosa di Pavia, subverted religious imagery to political propaganda.

LADY WITH AN ERMINE

In Summer 1490 it was announced that Isabel of Aragon was expecting Gian Galeazzo's child.[1] To Il Moro this came as surprising and unwelcome news, as his effete nephew had failed to consummate the marriage for over a year. Gian Galeazzo was now 21 and, in the eyes of many, old enough to rule by himself. Il Moro's claim that he was too immature to do so was now looking increasingly fatuous, and his status as Regent increasingly tenuous.

A couple of months later Il Moro learnt that he, too, was soon to become a father. The news prompted Leonardo's next Milanese portrait. The sitter was Il Moro's lover, Cecilia Gallerani.

Their affair had begun five years earlier, when Il Moro was 33 and Cecilia thirteen.[2] On 9 July 1485 Il Moro wrote to his brother Cardinal Ascanio in Rome, expressing the hope that his new girlfriend would soon fall pregnant, and asking Ascanio to help her ten year-old brother obtain the benefit of the wealthy Abbey of Casteggio.[3] In 1487, Cecilia Gallerani's[4] wedding to the aristocrat Giovanni Stefano dei Visconti di Crenna – arranged in 1483 – was annulled.

In 1490 Il Moro risked a diplomatic crisis with neighbouring Ferrara by repeatedly postponing his long-planned marriage to Duke Ercole's younger daughter Beatrice d'Este so that he could devote himself to Cecilia.[5]

The portrait he commissioned from Leonardo, now known as *The Lady with an Ermine*, anointed Cecilia as one of Il Moro's inner circle in much the same way as Leonardo's portrait of Galeazzo Sanseverino ('The Musician').

Multispectral analysis, carried out by Pascal Cotte of Lumière Technology in 2012, revealed that the portrait of Cecilia Gallerani existed in *two previous versions* before Leonardo da Vinci completed the painting as we now know it.[6] Significant alterations made to the original picture included the addition of a *sbernia* (one-sided shawl) over her left shoulder, and of the creature in her arms – which first took the form of a lifelike weasel before, in the final version, being beefed up into a creature that Cotte terms 'heraldic' but might be better described as an ermine on steroids.

Constant to all three versions is the position of Cecilia's shoulders, neck and head. Her head is turned sharply to the left and, like 'The Musician,' she gazes slightly upwards and out of the frame. It is presumed she is gazing in the direction of her lord and lover, Il Moro.

FIRST VERSION

It is not known exactly when Leonardo began the portrait – but the most likely time is Summer 1490. It is tempting to link the start of the portrait with the arrival of a new assistant in Leonardo's studio: the youthful (and engagingly pretty) Salai on 22 July 1490. With both a new portrait and the *Sforza Horse* on the go, Leonardo may have needed extra help.

Initially, according to Cotte's research, Cecilia was shown without any animal, in a dark red dress with gold interlace embroidery and black *nastri* (sleeve-ribbons), on a plain, dark blue ground. Her hands were crossed over her stomach, perhaps indicating pregnancy, and her hair tied in the *coazzone* (long ponytail) imported to Milan from Naples by Isabel of Aragon in 1489, swiftly becoming *de rigueur* at the Sforza court (the style had originated in northeast Spain in the 1470s).[7] The elaborate knot-pattern embroidery may also have been imported by Isabel, if her 'Saints & Devotees' wedding painting (*see p.35*) is anything to go by.

Este diplomat Giacomo Trotti reported to Ferrara that the nineteen-year-old Isabel of Aragon was so friendly towards Cecilia Gallerani – only a year or two her junior – that she served as her fashion advisor. 'The Duchess wants Cecilia to wear Catalan clothes; she has Cecilia eating out of her hand' he noted.[8] Isabel of Aragon had a vested interest in being on friendly terms with – and boosting the status of – Il Moro's mistress: the longer that relationship lasted, the longer the arrival in Milan of her ambitious younger cousin, Beatrice d'Este, would be delayed. Isabel and Beatrice had grown up together in Naples in the early 1480s, and there was little love lost between them.

In the initial version of her portrait Cecilia Gallerani wears a gown in the Aragonese colours of blood and gold. The portrait places her on a par with the reigning Duchess of Milan as a worthy partner of Il Moro, the Duke of Bari – an Aragonese fiefdom. The political statement was loud and clear: Cecilia, newly pregnant with Il Moro's child, was to be considered the main Sforza woman.

To court poet Bernardo Bellincioni (1452–92), in his sonnet *On the Portrait of Lady Cecilia by Leonardo*, Cecilia 'seems to listen not talk' (*la fa che par che ascolti e non favella*).[9] The fact that Bellincioni does not mention the ermine in this sonnet has led some commentators to suggest the creature was added after

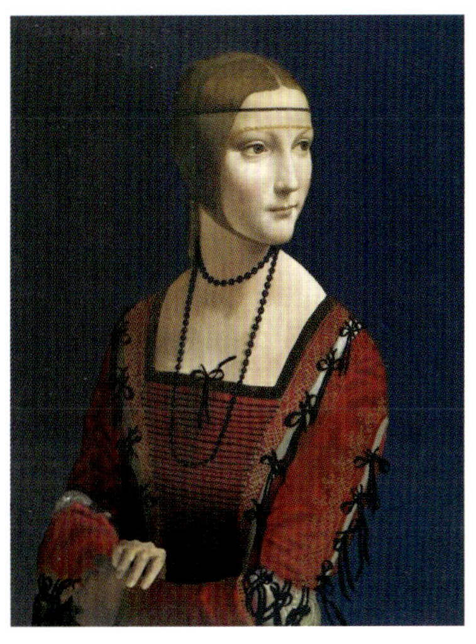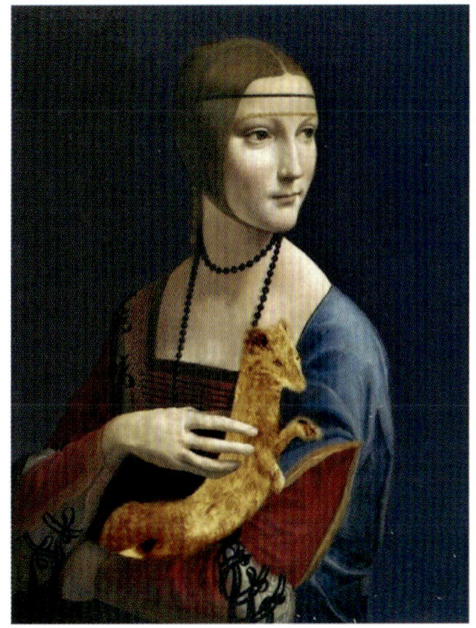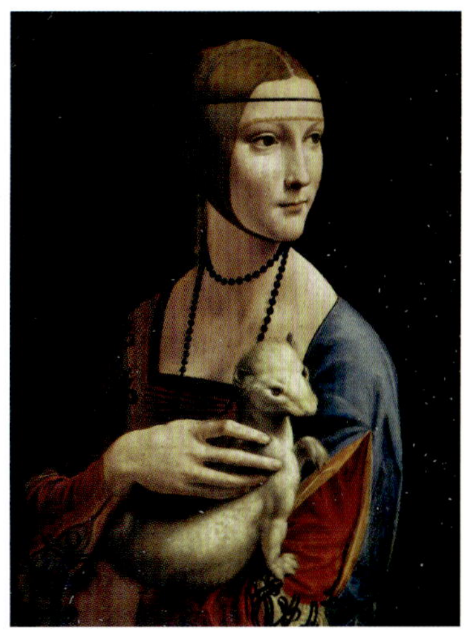

LEONARDO DA VINCI: *LADY WITH AN ERMINE* (1490/1)
SIMULATED 1st & 2nd VERSIONS – PASCAL COTTE/LUMIERE TECHNOLOGY   3rd VERSION – CZARTORYSKI MUSEUM, CRACOV

the poet's death in 1492. Cotte's discovery suggests, rather, that he may have been describing the initial, ermine-less version.

According to costume historian Elisabetta Gnignera, 'there is a clear affinity between the *Lady with an Ermine's* posture and the one traditionally assumed by the Holy Virgin when listening to the Angel of the Annunciation.'

SECOND VERSION

Multispectral analysis reveals that Leonardo extensively reworked his initial portrait – something he cannot have undertaken lightly or with pleasure, and which can only have been a directive from the work's commissioner: Il Moro. Cecilia was made to cradle a golden weasel in her arms, forcing her right elbow higher, and a *sbernia* – a one-sided cloak again introduced to northern Italy from Naples – added over her left shoulder.

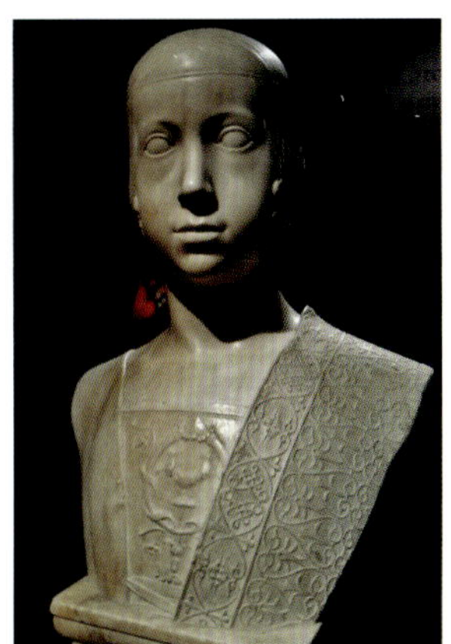

A *sbernia* is also worn in Cristoforo Romano's exquisite bust of Beatrice d'Este now in the Louvre (*left*). This clearly pre-dates her wedding to Il Moro in January 1491, as it shows Beatrice on a plinth that proclaims her the daughter of Duke Ercole of Ferrara; her chest is embroidered with her father's ring-and-flower emblem[10] combined with the Sforza sifting-cloth. Like Cecilia Gallerani, her hair is tied in a *coazzone* and her head is turned (though not as abruptly) to the left. Like Cecilia's red dress, Beatrice's *sbernia* is embroidered with *vinci* knot-patterning.

This bust almost certainly dates from 1490. Romano may well have accompanied Il Moro's personal envoy, Francesco da Casate, to Ferrara in August of that year.

Beatrice d'Este had spent her childhood in Naples, where her mother Eleonora was born. Fashion was her obsession.[11] One can well imagine her preparing for her future rôle as wife to Il Moro by staying abreast of the latest fashions in

Milan – and one can just as easily imagine the court of Milan being appraised of the latest fashions in Ferrara. The vestmental alterations to the portrait of Cecilia Gallerani, revealed by Pascal Cotte, may reflect fashion-based rivalry between Il Moro's lover and Il Moro's *fiancée.*

Romano, with what imagines to be uncompromising realism, shows Beatrice with snub nose, hamster cheeks and domed forehead – in evident contrast to the slender beauty of Leonardo's Cecilia. When he viewed Romano's bust back in Milan, probably in October 1490, Il Moro appears to have asked Leonardo to add a *sbernia* in Sforza colours of blue, white and red to Cecilia's portrait, and again postponed the wedding date, from November to January.

This marriage had been agreed in 1482, with the marriage contract signed in Ferrara on 10 May 1489 (just before Beatrice's fourteenth birthday) – when the wedding was slated for May 1490. In April, in the wake of the sudden death of Matthias Corvinus, Il Moro postponed it until the summer. In July 1490 he postponed it again, and in August sent his ambassador Francesco da Casate to Ferrara to propose an autumn wedding date, armed with a placatory ruby, pearl and emerald pendant.

Beatrice's father Duke Ercole was furious at these constant postponements, and hardly mollified to hear his own ambassador's explanation: that Il Moro was reluctant to abandon his bewitching mistress Cecilia because she was *bella come un fiore.*[12] Romano's bust will have made clear to Sforza courtiers that young Beatrice was no such beauty, and that Il Moro was marrying her out of a statesmanlike sense of duty.

On 26 November 1490 Il Moro's envoy Galeazzo Visconti was in Ferrara to fix the wedding for 16 January 1491. Midwinter marriages were not uncommon, if inconvenient; we have graphic accounts of the Arctic conditions facing the Ferrarese wedding party during their ten-day journey to Pavia across snow and frozen rivers.[13]

The overriding reason for this choice of date was surely Il Moro's desire to upstage the forthcoming birth of the child to Gian Galeazzo and Isabel of Aragon, due in the second half of January. Elaborate preparations for the Moro-Beatrice wedding were rushed ahead at breakneck speed, with Leonardo da Vinci in charge of pageantry.

Il Moro may well have intended Cecilia's portrait to be a talking-point among guests. As well as adding a *sbernia* in Sforza colours, Il Moro bade Leonardo reinforce the portrait's symbolism by adding a weasel – whose significance will have been readily grasped by a Renaissance audience weaned on the classics.

The weasel features in the Greek myth about the birth of Heracles, illegitimate son of Zeus, as related in the *Iliad* (Book XIX, 100–144) and Ovid's *Metamorphoses*[14] (Book IX, 273–323).

After deciding to procreate a hero to save mankind, Zeus selected Alcmene as mother due to her unrivalled beauty – then tricked her into sleeping with him by pretending to be her husband Amphitryon. When Alcmene was due to give birth – not just to Heracles but to his twin, Iphicles, sired by Amphitryon (the idea of unequal twins would be revisited in the frontispiece to the Uffizi *Sforziada*) – she was physically prevented from doing so by Eileithyia, the Goddess of Childbirth, acting under orders from Hera, Zeus's jealous wife. But Eileithyia was distracted by Alcemene's maid Galanthis (Γαλινθιάς), and Heracles safely delivered. Galanthis was turned into a weasel for her impertinent pains.[15]

Mythology also held that weasels conceived through the ear, and they consequently became associated with supernatural birth – specifically the Incarnation.[16]

Cotte's preliminary hypothesis showed the weasel with a grey coat. When I pointed out that Ovid used the word *flava* to refer to Galanthis as golden-haired, both as woman and weasel, Cotte sought – and found – proof in the underpaint that Leonardo's weasel originally had golden fur.

(The importance of the weasel in Renaissance literary symbolism finds an echo in the *Sforza Hours*, where Birago illustrates the Italian proverb 'if the Lion fails to defend itself, the Weasel will approach its ear and affect its mind.' Birago also used golden weasels in his decorative margins.)[17]

An erudite pun on Cecilia's surname was also involved: γαλέη (*galay*) is the Ancient Greek for weasel. The first to draw attention to this was Charles Holmes, Editor of the *Burlington Magazine*, in 1907 – in an article referring to the portrait as the *The Lady with a Weasel*.[18] The preference for weasel over ermine persisted for some time: Malaguzzi Valeri termed the work a *Ritratto di Donna con una Faina* in 1913 and *Lady with Weasel* was still in use in the 1952 edition of Bernard Berenson's *Italian Painters of the Renaissance*.

Although the Moro–Beatrice wedding ceremony took place in Pavia, the celebrations took place in Milan, and saw the Castello Sforzesco decked out with images of Francesco Sforza produced by an army of painters toiling night and day for a month. Francesco also appeared as a dummy on horseback beneath a triumphal arch.

The celebrations began with Leonardo's theatrical *Paradiso*. They included a *Festa per le Donne* on January 24, attended by 200 ladies of rank, with dancing peasant-girls clad in red, white and blue; and culminated, on January 26, with the start of a three-day *Giostra* (jousting tournament) at which the triumphant Galeazzo Sanseverino headed a troop sporting 'Scythian' costumes designed by Leonardo himself (evoked in the final illuminated *Sforziada* of 1496).

Isabel of Aragon, due to her impending confinement, was forced to miss the festivities. The birth of Il Duchetto passed almost unnoticed.

THIRD & FINAL VERSION

The final version of Leonardo's portrait no longer features a slender, feminine weasel but a muscular, virile ermine: given its pure white coat there can be scant doubt as to its intended identity, despite the absence of a black-tipped tail. (The whiteness also draws punning attention to the name of both Il Moro's mother and illegitimate daughter: *Bianca*.)

This final version of Leonardo's portrait surely celebrates, and must therefore post-date, the birth of Cecilia's son on 3 May 1491. The portrait has a political message that would be repeated in the Paris *Sforziada*: that the son of Il Moro and Cecilia was altogether sturdier than the baby born three months earlier to Isabel and the feeble Gian Galeazzo.

In the *Iliad*, Zeus declares that 'this day Eileithyia will bring into the world a human child born of stock with My blood in its veins ... he shall have dominion over all his neighbours.'

The Imperial/Caesarean reference, and Il Moro's ambition for his son, are evident. Cecilia's son was christened *Cesare*. A more imperious name, or a closer secular equivalent to *Zeus*, would be hard to find.

Underpinning Il Moro's dynastic ambitions were two apparently outrageous, Orwellian-sounding claims: *Younger is Better than Older* and *Illegitimate is Better than Legitimate*.

To justify these claims, Il Moro looked to no less a figure than Jesus Christ. His was the illegitimate birth *par excellence*, and he was younger than his cousin John the Baptist, together with whom he was portrayed by Leonardo da Vinci (himself illegitimate) in the *Virgin of the Rocks*.

Illegitimacy and the Divine lie at the heart of the mythological symbolism of *The Lady with an Ermine*, whose glorification of the illegitimate Cesare came only eighteen months after the legitimization of Il Moro's previous child, Bianca Sforza, prior to her betrothal to Galeazzo Sanseverino.

Ovid also talks of Eileithyia changing Galanthis's arms into forelegs – which may help explain the particularly sturdy front limbs of the creature in Cecilia's arms.

The symbolic interpretation of Cecilia's portrait has hitherto centred on Il Moro's membership of the Order of the Ermine, created in 1465 by King Ferrante of Naples. But this association is unlikely: Il Moro's membership lapsed in 1490 when relations with Naples became strained.[19]

Court poet Bellincioni, however, *did* link Il Moro to an ermine, describing him as *Italico Morel bianco Ermellino* – and as a true ermine despite his black name (*tutto ermellino è ben, se un nome ha nero*). Bellincioni went on to describe Phoebus (the Sun) as outshone by Il Moro's newborn son:

> *D'un Moro il seme cotal sol divenne ...*
> *Però che quando el vene*
> *Da lui fui vinto, si eh' e' fu l'ecclissi*

This *ecclissi* was the eclipse of the sun viewed in Milan (according to NASA calculations) on 8 March 1491, just eight weeks before Cesare's birth, and considered such a portentous event that Bellincioni referred to it in two other sonnets. In one, the sun is plunged into shadow by Cecilia's beautiful eyes (*Cecilia! sì bellissima oggi è quella/ Che a suoi begli occhi el sol par ombra oscura*); in the other, Phoebus hides his face (*Quel dì, che Febo il volto par coprissi*) on the day Cesare descends from Heaven as the son of Jupiter (*Da Giove el frutto a noi piove dal Cielo*).

Bellincioni's poems, like Birago's *Sforziada* frontispieces and Leonardo's works of art, aimed to peddle pro-Moro propaganda to the Milanese and diplomatic elite. The allegorical message contained within the portrait of Cecilia Gallerani will, by the inclusion of a weasel/ermine, have been made patently clear: The Lord (Zeus/Il Moro) has a son (Heracles/Cesare) by his beautiful mistress (Alecmene/Cecilia) despite the opposition of his legitimate spouse (Hera/Beatrice d'Este), and this son will 'have dominion over all.'

That Il Moro should vaunt his liaison may seem surprising but – until Emperor Maximilian promised him the Imperial investiture in 1493 – Il Moro could not base his claims to the ducal throne on dynastic legitimacy. Gian Galeazzo was indisputably the legitimate Duke of Milan and his son, Il Duchetto, indisputably his legitimate heir. Il Moro had to justify his claims by stressing his personal qualities – such as the prudence of the mulberry tree or the nobility/ integrity of the ermine (which, as Leonardo once noted, would sooner die than let its coat be sullied).

Il Moro was not a man to be trammelled by conventional morality. He portrayed himself as a superman or latterday Zeus, and his illegitimate son as a gift from God.

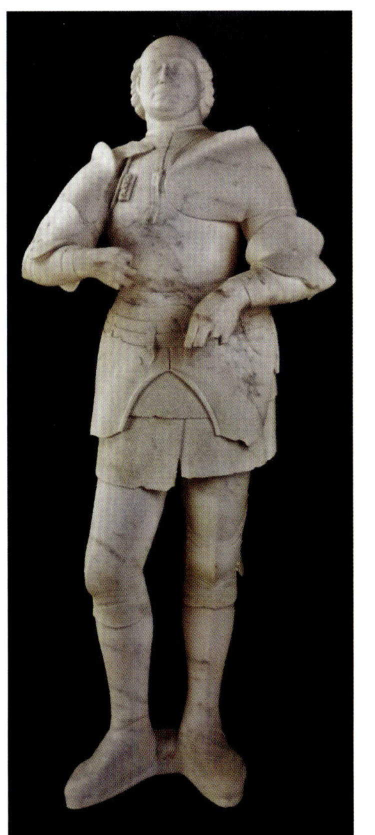

The *Lady with an Ermine* reflects the lengths to which Il Moro was prepared to go to exalt his illegitimate progeny. He took every opportunity to portray Gian Galeazzo as sick, vacuous and mentally/physically unfit to rule. Il Moro portrayed himself, in contrast, as robust and experienced. Il Moro's profiled portrayals make no effort to hide His Portliness, fat neck and double-chin. To our eyes, unflattering. But the message it sent out was: here is a man in full, sleek, resplendent health. He, not his sickly nephew, will be your Dear Leader for years to come.

FRANCESCO SFORZA MONUMENT

In the early 1490s a large sculpture of Francesco Sforza was finally produced – but not in Milan, and not on a horse.

On 4 June 1491 Alberto Maffioli, then working at the Certosa di Pavia, was commissioned to make two lifesize marble statues for the façade of the Duomo in Cremona, 50 miles east of Milan. They were to show Il Moro's father and mother, Beatrice Maria Visconti – who had married in Cremona in 1441, exactly fifty years earlier.

Il Moro's decision to commemorate his father in stone complemented the literary tribute paid him by the *Sforziada*, and was part of the same campaign to justify Il Moro's credentials as Francesco's rightful successor. The timing of the Cremona commission, just four months after Gian Galeazzo had fathered a son, reflected the need for that campaign to be stepped up.

Cremona was Bianca Maria's dower town – so it was natural the commission concern both parents rather than just Francesco. Il Moro was never keen to pay sculpted homage to Francesco alone – or in Milan, the Duchy's capital. In 1491 Leonardo's giant equestrian statue was still unfinished. It was much talked about – but most of the talk centred on Leonardo's mighty horse and Il Moro's munificent patronage, rather than on Francesco, who appears to have been absent from the giant clay model Leonardo completed in 1493. Leonardo's statue would never be cast.

Maffioli wanted Francesco placed in a portico niche near ground-level, and Bianca Maria higher up the façade. Il Moro disagreed: he had no wish for his father to have special status, and insisted both statues be placed side-by-side, twenty feet off the ground. Il Moro got his way, but Maffioli stubbornly sculpted Francesco in the sort of detail that stands up to close-quartered scrutiny, whereas his modelling of Bianca Maria – designed to be seen from some distance below – is correspondingly vague.

The statues were not, sadly, scrutinized in Cremona for long. They were carted off by the Venetians as war booty in 1499, and only 'recovered' (for a suitable sum) three centuries later by a citizen of Vicenza, where they remain (in the Musei Civici).[20]

VIRGIN OF THE ROCKS: SECOND VERSION

Leonardo's *Virgin of the Rocks* caused such a sensation in 1480s Milan that it was reproduced in embroidery on a lavish silk, linen and taffeta altar-cloth, 229 × 100cm, known as the *Paliotto Leonardesco* and now in the Museo Baroffio (*inv. S.A. 148*) in Sacro Monte sopra Varese, a hilltop pilgrimage site 35 miles northwest of Milan.

In 1493 the *Virgin of the Rocks* was back in the news. Il Moro was desperately seeking the Imperial investiture from Maximilian Habsburg. Along with bribes and his niece in marriage, what more prestigious gift could he offer than an imposing altarpiece by the man who was now, after a decade in Milan, acknowledged as the Great Leonardo? Il Moro even offered to send Leo's associate, Ambrogio de Predis, to Austria for a few months into the bargain.

But the altarpiece was in the city's foremost church, and not even Il Moro – not yet an all-powerful Duke – could confiscate it. An undated petition from Leonardo and Ambrogio[21] complained that they had not been paid properly for the altarpiece and wanted it back, and even had a client willing to pay its true value. This letter was curious: why would they have waited a decade before complaining of inadequate payment? The potential client appeared to be Il Moro himself.

Il Moro got his way – promising the church a replacement, upon which Leonardo set to work immediately. Yet with small but significant modifications: the hand of the Angel no longer pointed towards the baby on the left; and it seems that the altarpiece's two infant protagonists, John the Baptist and

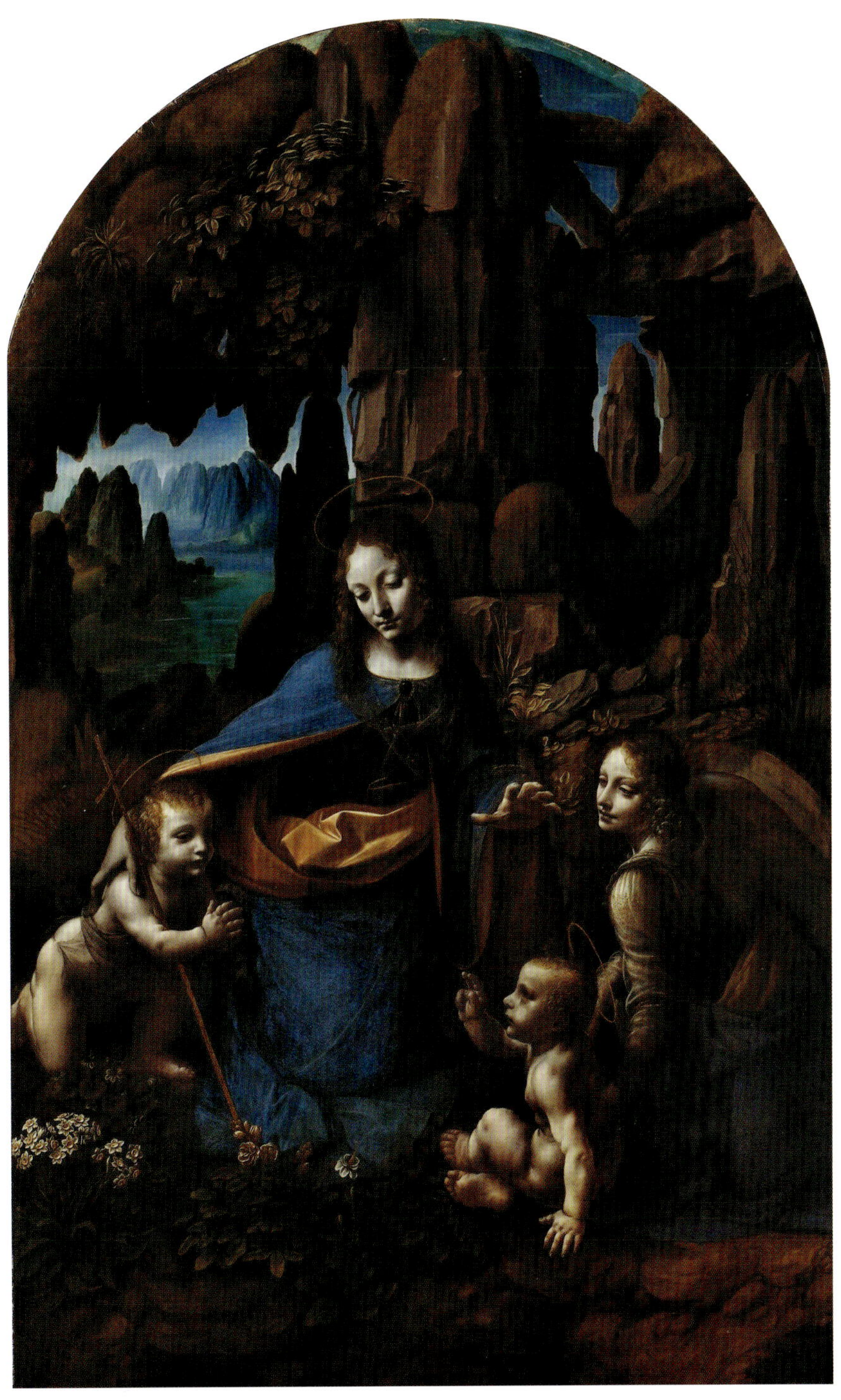

Jesus Christ, were now to be based on living models, whose likeness had to be beyond reproach.

The year 1493 marked an upswing in Il Moro's fortunes. On 25 January 1493 he received a legitimate male heir when Beatrice d'Este gave birth to Ercole.

On April 16 Beatrice wrote to her mother Eleonora, Duchess of Ferrara, from Villa Nova, near Vigevano, where she had brought her eleven-week old baby son to enjoy the country air. 'Every day I have been hoping the artist would bring me the portrait of Ercole, which my husband and I now send you' she reported. 'He is much bigger than this picture makes him appear, for it is already more than a week since it was done.'[22]

Duchess Eleonora subsequently forwarded the portrait to Beatrice's sister Isabella d'Este in Mantua. 'I enclose a drawing that has been sent to us from Milan, showing how well our grandson thrives' she gushed. 'It gives us a living witness to his beauty and well-being. And if you ask me whether the portrait is a good one, I need only tell you who has sent it and who is the master who has done this drawing, and I am sure you will be satisfied.'[23]

Who was this master in Milan whose reputation is beyond words, who fails to deliver on time, and whose name is sure to satisfy the demanding Isabella? Court portraitist Ambrogio de Predis – or Leonardo da Vinci, of whom Isabella d'Este was a zealous admirer?

There is every chance that the drawing mentioned by Beatrice is Leonardo's red-chalk portrait of baby boy in Sforza profile (*right*), now in the Queen's Collection in Windsor Castle. Its similarity with the figure of Jesus in the second (London) version of the *Virgin of the Rocks* is clear to see.

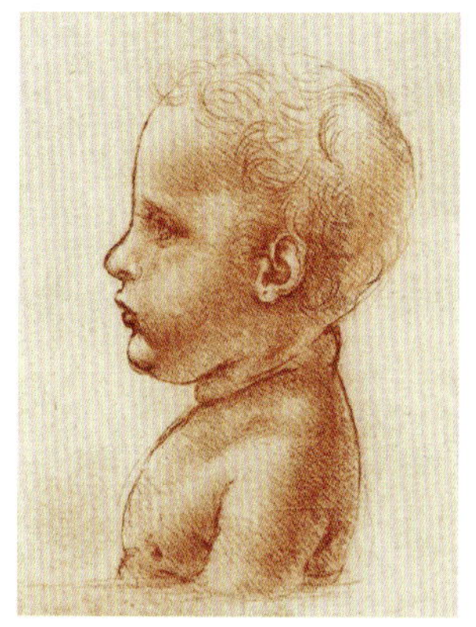

In other words, a second version of the *Virgin of the Rocks* was produced with Il Moro's new son portrayed as the Son of God; presumably John the Baptist was granted the features of Gian Galeazzo's son Francesco (Il Duchetto). Like John the Baptist preceding Jesus Christ, Francesco was slightly older (two years) than Ercole. The biblical age-gap may have been slightly different (six months), but their relationship was identical: their mothers (Mary/Elisabeth and Beatrice d'Este/Isabel of Aragon) were cousins (Luke I:36).

In the original *Virgin of the Rocks*, there was ambiguity as to the infants' identities: the infant by the waterside next to the Angel could logically be identified as John the Baptist, an impression reinforced by the Angel's pointing towards the other infant – why would an Angel point at John the Baptist rather than Christ? This ambiguity was removed from the second version: the Angel no longer points, and there is no water beneath the infant next to the Angel, only rocks.[24]

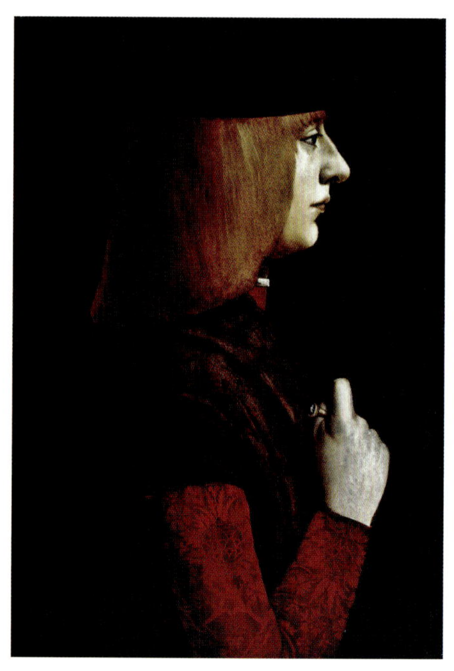

The allegorical message conveyed by this new version was Younger is Best. Just as Jesus came after John the Baptist yet was Lord of Lords, so Il Moro's son Ercole came after Il Duchetto, yet was the true heir to the Duchy of Milan. His father, Il Moro, was himself a younger brother.

Exactly the same message was peddled by Birago in the frontispiece cutting (now in the Uffizi) that shows a white baby on the left (doubtless representing Gian Galeazzo's second child) paying homage to a dark, Moorish baby on the right (symbolizing Ercole).

THE LADY IN THE AMBROSIANA

On 1 June 1493, just six weeks after Beatrice's letter to Ferrara about the portrait of her baby boy, a dispatch from the Ferrara Ambassador to Milan[25] referred to an unspecified agreement between Beatrice's sister-in-law Anna Sforza and Ambrogio de Predis. Malaguzzi Valeri, who discovered this document, plausibly argues such an agreement can only have concerned a portrait (*trattava certamente di un ritratto chi Predia le stava eseguendo*). The calendar backs him up.

Anna was in Milan on 24 February 1493 for the thanksgiving ceremony held in Santa Maria delle Grazie in honour of the babies newly born to Beatrice d'Este and Isabel of Aragon. Cartwright says Anna was wearing a 'camora of cloth-of-gold with crimson sleeves, lined with fur and edged with gold fringe' – and, two days later, a dress of 'black and gold, with a pearl-embroidered crimson hat.'[26] The lady in the Ambrosiana portrait is wearing a gold-fringed black gown over crimson sleeves, and pearls a plenty.

It is not improbable that Ambrogio painted Anna's portrait while she was in Milan in February, and that the ambassador's message concerned the delivery of the work in June, just before Anna returned from a joint Sforza/Este State visit to Venice.

Few female portraits are as attractive or mysterious as the one that ensures the international fame of the Ambrosiana. The name of the sitter is uncertain. Martin Kemp was the first authority to suggest that a 'highly credible candidate' would be Il Moro's niece Anna Sforza, younger sister of Empress Bianca Maria, who married Alfonso d'Este in January 1491.[27] The portrait is usually assigned to Ambrogio de Predis, whose links with the House of Este went back to at least 1482, when he painted the portrait (now lost) of Alfonso's mother,

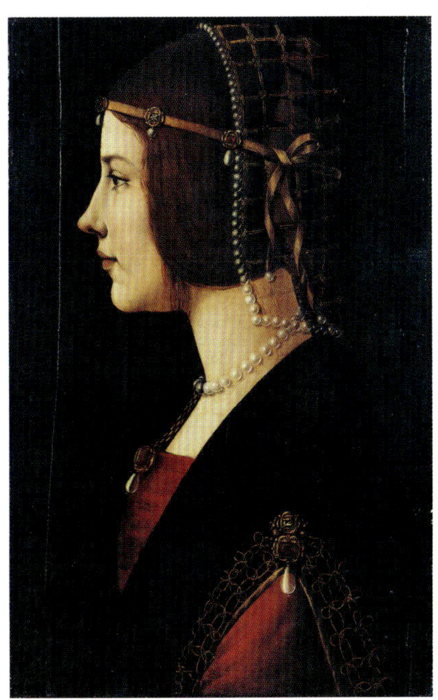

Duchess Eleonora. The interlocking circles or 'knot embroidery' around the shoulder of the Ambrosiana lady's dress are similar to the those on the Archangel's shoulder in the London version of the *Virgin of the Rocks*, on which Ambrogio is known to have collaborated, and on the collar of the accompanying Red Angel in the side-panel commonly attributed to him.

What Kemp modestly presents as a hunch is supported by physical and documentary evidence. The sitter's slightly bridged and upturned nose recalls that of Duchess Bona di Savoia – the mother of Bianca Maria and Anna. And the gleaming-eyed mood of the Ambrosiana belle is nearly matched by that of a male portrait in the Museum of Fine Arts in Houston. That the two may form some sort of pairing is suggested by their similar colours and near-identical dimensions (the male portrait is 54.3 × 38.8cm, the female 51 × 34cm). The proportionately larger head in the female portrait may be an example of Sforza one-upmanship and/or protocol: as in Leonardo's portrait of Bianca Sforza, the head occupies the top half of the picture.

The Houston subject appears unlike any identifiable Sforza, and is most probably Anna's husband Alfonso d'Este: he is wearing a ring with a cameo of Hercules, after whom his father Ercole was named; and he strikingly resembles the youth on Niccolò Fiorentino's 1492 medal of *Alfonsus Estiensis*, showing Alfonso aged around fifteen (*right*).

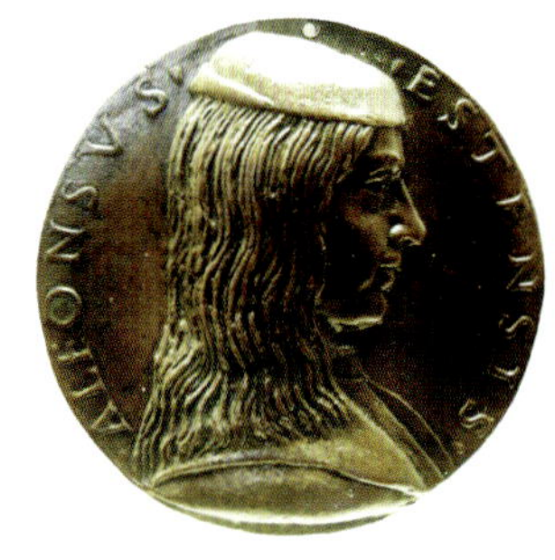

The female portrait has been in Milan since at least 1611, when it was recorded in the collection of Cardinal Borromeo. The male portrait was chronicled in Milan in 1706, as owned by the late Marchese Cesare Pagani. According to Malaguzzi Valeri it was still in Milan in 1913, as part of the Porro Collection, then sent to the USA on the steamship *Mississippi* in November 1914 and sold for $175 at the Duveen sale in New York on 29 April 1915, subsequently transiting via Knoedler & Co.

Another portrait should be cited in connection with the lady in the Ambrosiana. It was rediscovered by Elisabetta Gnignera and published in her book *Leonardo: La Bella Svelata* in 2016. It is known only from a black-and-white photograph (*right*) in the Fondazione Federico Zeri in Bologna, listing its owner (around 1940) as the American dealer Tudor Wilkinson (1879–1969) in Paris. Gnignera provides evidence suggesting it was sold at Wilkinson's estate sale in Paris in 1969; its current whereabouts are unknown.

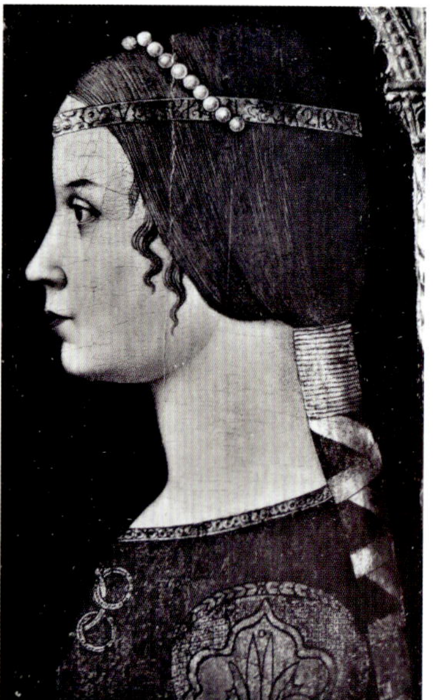

It shows a young woman with pearls in her hair, wearing a *coazzone* very similar in design to that worn by Bianca Sforza in her portrait by Leonardo. Gnignera identifies the sitter as Beatrice d'Este: both the kiss-curls and the *coazzone* are identical to those in Cristoforo Romano's 1490 bust of her in the Louvre.

The Zeri Foundation catalogued the portrait as 'anonymous.' Gnignera floats the name of Ferrarese artist Cosma Tura (*c.*1430–95). However, the similarities with the Ambrosiana portrait – notably to the treatment of the eye, eyebrow and nostril – are striking. There must be a strong possibility that Ambrogio de Predis is the author of both, and that the sitters are indeed Anna Sforza and Beatrice d'Este.

MUSICIANS

A group portrait now in London's National Gallery warrants attention in this context.

Painted on a poplar panel 95 × 76cm, titled *A Concert* and assigned to Ferrara artist Lorenzo Costa (1460–1535), it shows three musicians: a blond girl with her hand resting familiarly on the shoulder of a middle-aged lute player with straight, dark hair, clad in green and red and flanked on his other side, slightly in retreat, by a younger man with wavy blond locks.

Going on the different openings of the mouths, the musicians are engaged in polyphonic song. The score is placed on the ledge in front of them, alongside a fiddle, bow and recorder.

Sforza colours, order of precedence, the girl's sumptuous necklace ... this is clearly no trio of travelling troubadours, and you do not need a degree in

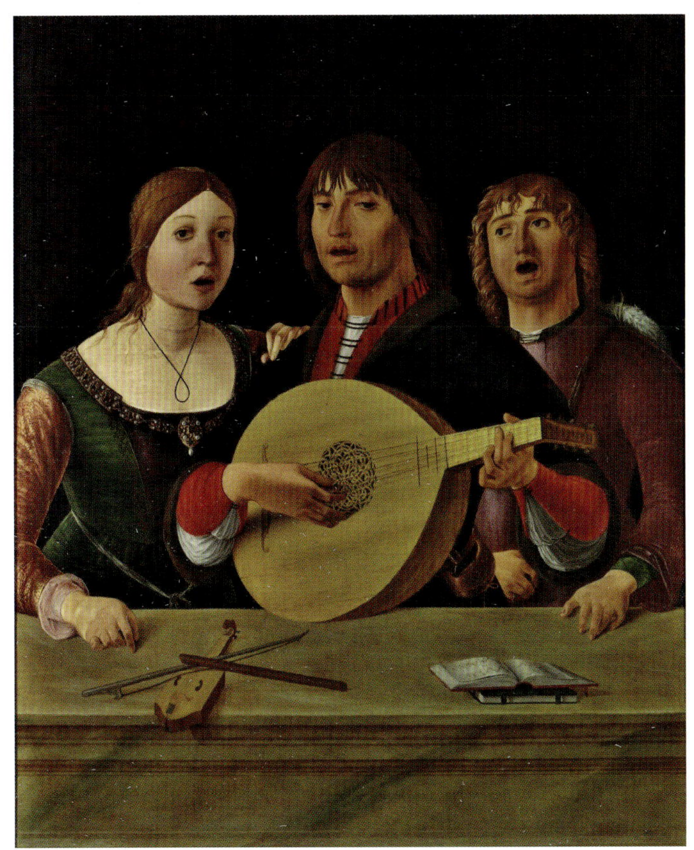

physiognomy to recognize Bianca Sforza, her father Il Moro and her fiancé Galeazzo Sanseverino.

The girl's green and *murray* (reddish-brown) colours are virtually identical to those worn by Bianca when she sat for Leonardo and, already, her hair is parted down the middle and tied in a ponytail.

The portrait can be dated to May 1493. On May 17 Il Moro arrived in Ferrara accompanied by his wife Beatrice, family and court. On May 25 Beatrice left Ferrara with her mother Eleonora, brother Alfonso and his wife Anna for Venice. Il Moro remained with his father-in-law, Duke Ercole, and was taken on a tour of the Este estates, returning to Milan on June 4.

Lorenzo Costa's painting may have been commissioned by Duke Ercole as a gift for his illustrious guest, perhaps in reply to the portraits of his son and daughter-in-law by Ambrogio de Predis.

THE TOMB OF ROBERTO SANSEVERINO

The Duke of Ferrara was not the only potentate to flatter Il Moro by alluding to his *Capitano Generale* and anointed son-in-law, Galeazzo Sanseverino.

On May 23 France and Austria signed the Treaty of Senlis, resolving their long-standing dispute over the Burgundian Succession. Il Moro could now court Maximilian Habsburg – King of the Romans and heir apparent to his ailing father Friedrich III as Holy Roman Emperor – without offending France. His aim: to secure the Imperial investiture.

Negotiations were brief and successful: on June 24 Maximilian wrote to Il Moro from Gmunden in Austria, accepting both to marry Il Moro's niece Bianca Maria and grant Il Moro the Imperial investiture in due course. 'Negotiations' is putting it politely. Il Moro resorted to epic bribery: 100,000 ducats for the investiture and 300,000 ducats for his niece's dowry.

It was during these lucrative negotiations that Maximilian Habsburg ordered a memorial to Roberto Sanseverino, Galeazzo's father.[28]

Roberto Sanseverino had died in 1487 fighting Archduke Sigmund – whom Maximilian had (forcefully) succeeded as Lord of Tyrol in 1490. In Summer 1493 Maximilian commissioned Bavarian stonemason Lucas Maurus von

Kempten to build a red marble monument to Roberto in the south transept of Trent Cathedral. It shows Roberto clad in his suit of Milanese armour, his left hand resting on his sword and his right brandishing a Venetian banner upside-down in sign of defeat. Roberto's armorial shield is propped up by his left foot.

The shield of the Bishop of Trent, Udalrico Frundsberg, is carved in white marble on the plinth above, accompanied by four other shields in red marble: those of Austria, Tyrol, Trent and St Wenceslas. The latter's presence may be because Wenceslas was the only previous Emperor to grant the Milanese investiture. The surrounding frame is inscribed:

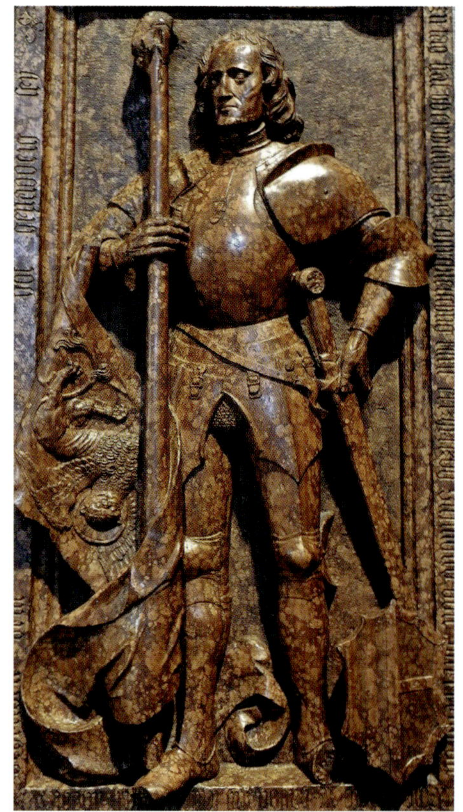

NACH CHRISTI GEPURD MCCCCLXXXVII JAR AN SAND LAURNTZII TAG HAT ÜBERWUND DER DURCHLEUCHTIG FURST ERTZHERZOG SIGMUND VON OSTERREICH DIE VENEDIGER UND JR HAUBTMANN SENIOR ROBERT LIGT HIE BEGRABEN DEM GOT GENADDEIG SEY

(On St Lawrence's Day 1487 the enlightened Count Sigmund of Austria overcame the Venetians and their leader Lord Roberto who here lies buried, God rest his soul)

Payment records indicate that Kempten received 70 Rhenish Gilders for his work: 10 gilders in mid-June, 10 at the start of August, and the remaining 50 on the Monday after Mary's Nativity (September 9).[29]

That Maximilian should commission a tomb for Roberto Sanseverino at precisely the moment he was wooing Sforza Milan indicates the tremendous prestige enjoyed by Roberto's sons – led by Galeazzo – at Il Moro's court. They may even have been involved in the tombstone's design, as its portrayal of their father is very similar in design to the marble statue of Francesco Sforza commissioned from Alberto Maffioli by Il Moro in 1491 (*see p.131*).

Roberto Sanseverino was effectively placed on an equal footing with the Sforza patriarch – which, genealogically, was fair enough: Francesco and Roberto were first cousins.

THE *PALA SFORZESCA*

On 19 August 1493 Friedrich III died in Linz. From this moment on, Il Moro felt secure that his longstanding aim to become Duke of Milan would soon be achieved. Il Moro no longer needed to hang on to his father's glorious coat-tails or belittle his hapless nephew. He could concentrate on self-glorification.

Bianca Maria's marriage to Maximilian took place on 30 November 1493. The Imperial deed of ducal investiture was issued on 5 September 1494.

Il Moro followed up on his renewed interest in the *Virgin of the Rocks* by commissioning an altarpiece (or *pala*) of his own. It again features the Virgin as the central figure, and is known as the *Pala Sforzesca* (*illustration p.124*).

It was destined for St Ambrogio ad Nemus – a small church (since completely rebuilt) outside the city walls, just over half-a-mile from the Castello Sforzesco. The church was closely associated with Milan's patron and founding saint, St Ambrose (*Ambrogio*) who, in the *Pala Sforzesca*, appears next to St Gregory, placing his arm on the shoulder of a kneeling Il Moro – blessed by an infant Christ squirming on his mother's lap.

Il Moro is sporting dark brown hair for the occasion (with swarthy complexion to match). On the other side of the Virgin are St Augustine, reading a book, and St Jerome, eyeing Il Moro sternly while gesturing to the kneeling figure of Beatrice d'Este, whose infant son Ercole (born 25 January 1493), half-clad in swaddling bands, kneels alongside her. Il Moro is flanked by his dark-haired, illegitimate son Cesare (born 3 May 1491).

The history of Renaissance Italy is littered with rulers born 'illegitimate.' No out-of-wedlock stigma was attached to a 'love child' – as Il Moro makes ceremoniously clear in the *Pala Sforzesca*. The child born to his mistress Cecilia Gallerani has equal billing with his legitimate son and heir by Beatrice d'Este. This glorifying of an 'illegitimate' child is also an issue in the Paris *Sforziada*, where Cesare is featured as a healthy sapling; and in the Polish *Sforziada*, originally containing a full-page portrait of Il Moro's illegitimate daughter.

The name Cesare was hardly chosen by chance for the son of a candidate to the investiture of the Holy Roman Empire; his presence in the *Pala*, next to his father, is no surprise. Young Ercole is shown next to his mother, and has her snub nose. He is clad from chest down in swaddling bands – echoing Andrea della Robbia's ceramic *putti* tondi, evoking the infant Christ, applied in 1487 to the façade of the Ospedale degli Innocenti next to the Basilica della Santissima Annunziata in Florence.[30] Ercole's swaddling in the *Pala Sforzesca* is surely intended to reinforce his status as The Chosen One – as already propounded by the choice of his features for the infant Christ in the second version of the *Virgin of the Rocks*. A similar message was conveyed by Birago in his frontispiece for the Uffizi *Sforziada*.

But there are more than birthrights at stake in Cesare's presence opposite Ercole in the *Pala Sforzesca*. Apart from enhancing the work's symmetrical solemnity, the presence of two of Il Moro's children also enables him to keep up with his nephew Gian Galeazzo who, by early 1494, also had two children: a son (Il Duchetto) and a daughter (Ippolita). Il Moro trumps Gian Galeazzo by having two boys.

Cesare is sumptuously clad in coloured stripes, some in the precious brownish-red colour known as *murray* produced from a *crimsyn-* or *grain*-based dye. His presence also underlines a theme at which Il Moro hammered away in the mid-1490s: the younger child takes precedence. This notion lies behind his obsession with the *Virgin of the Rocks*, as embodied by Jesus and John the Baptist. It is the central theme of his struggle for power – with his son and heir Ercole being not only more important than his elder half-brother Cesare, but above all more important than Il Duchetto, the son and heir of Gian Galeazzo and Isabel of Aragon, who was two years older than Ercole and the rightful heir to the Duchy of Milan.

The *Pala Sforzesca* is an important piece of political propaganda. This explains its ebullient if not garish colour scheme. Marooned today in a room at the Brera, underlit and surrounded by even bigger canvases, it is hard to assess its original impact. It needs to be imagined entrancing the faithful, glowing in candlelight above the high altar of a small but important church.

The altarpiece is mentioned in a letter from Ducal Secretary Marchesino Stanga to Il Moro dated 22 January 1494, referring to an unnamed artist and describing the work's content and appearance as *prefissata rigidamente* (rigidly prescribed). The letter implies that painting is about to start.

This dating precludes any possibility that both infants might be the children of Il Moro *and* Beatrice: their younger son, Francesco, was not born until 4 February 1495. The larger child in the *Pala* cannot be Ercole (later Massimiliano) in any case, for physical reasons. Ercole, as glowingly recorded by Birago, Ambrogio de Predis and others, was blond. Or are we to suppose he borrowed his father's *Grecian 2000* to pose for the *Pala*?

The solemnity of the *Pala* is reinforced by the unusual absence of Sforza emblems on Il Moro's sumptuous blue silk *turca*, coloured with the most expensive dye available (*alessandrino*).[31] The portrayal of Il Moro wearing the gold chain of ducal office may date the work's completion to after the death of Duke Gian Galeazzo on 21 October 1494 – or it may have been intended to crank up the psychological pressure on his nephew even further.

Identifying who painted the *Pala Sforzesca* has been befogged by the assumption that the same artist also painted the *Virgin with Saints and Devotees* in London's National Gallery (*see p.35*).[32] The two have evident compositional similarities (although the source for both is surely Vincenzo Foppa's *Pala Bottigella*, painted around 1485 and now in the Musei Civici di Pavia). With its ghostly skin, crudely defined garment folds, contorted faces and roughly outlined architectural detail, the smaller London *Virgin & Devotees* exudes none of the *Pala Sforzesca's* painterly accomplishment. The two works, although both on wood, are also physically different: the *Pala* is a massive 230 × 165cm and painted in oil, its smaller precedent a modest 56 × 49cm and painted in tempera.

Various names have been proposed for the artist of the Pala Sforzesca, none conclusively. His approach blends Bergognone and Leonardo; he has a luscious grasp of colour, a sophisticated ability to reproduce expensive cloth, and a taste for visual trickery.

The gold crown brandished by two angels above the Virgin's head blends so adroitly into the gilded architectural background as to be almost invisible.[33] The triangular outline of the Virgin's head, bust and arms echoes that of Christ in *The Last Supper*, and their left hands are virtually identical; but placed at

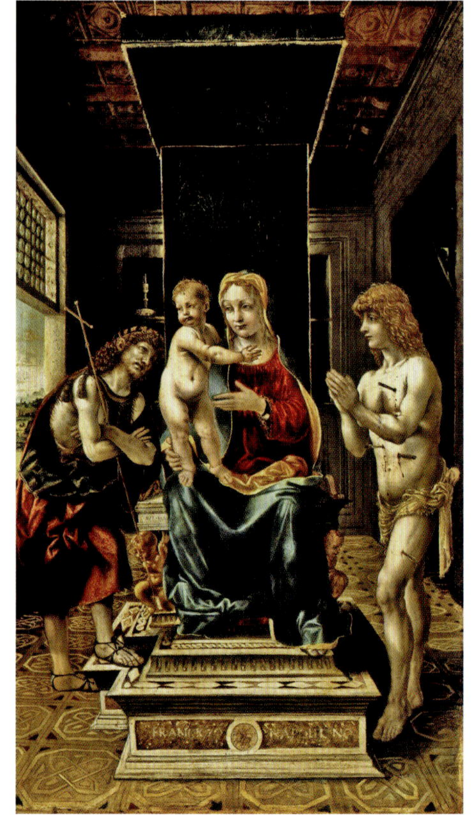

the end of her right arm is the gloved hand of St Gregory – who is averting his gaze in embarrassment at being made party to this irreverent joke.

If such acquaintance with *The Last Supper* means the *Pala* artist worked in the circle of Leonardo, then Francesco Napoletano might be a candidate. Another detail of the *Pala Sforzesca* is suggestive in this context. Most unusually, the Virgin's left foot protrudes over the platform of her throne. This also happens in the *Madonna and Child Enthroned with John the Baptist and St Sebastian* in the Zurich Kunsthaus, signed by Napoletano (*see opposite*). This protruding left foot may have been his humorous hallmark. Another example concerns the two side-panels from the London *Virgin of the Rocks*. The left foot of the green angel – generally attributed to Napoletano – protrudes over a stone ledge. The left leg of its red angel counterpart (attributed to Ambrogio de Predis) advances in exactly the same pose – yet stops just short of the ledge.[34]

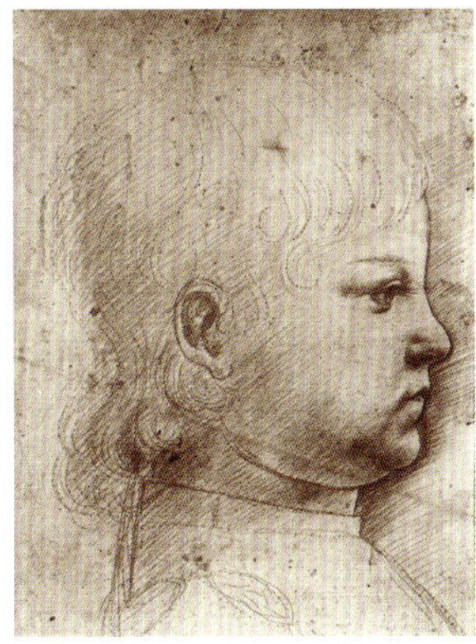

It is by no means certain that the *Pala Sforzesca* is the work of a single hand. The profiled heads of Il Moro, Beatrice d'Este and the two children smack – as one would expect – of Sforza family portraitist Ambrogio de Predis, who may well have produced the initial portraits as drawings, to be transferred to the panel using the *spolvero* technique, and completed in oils by another artist. A drawing of Cesare by Ambrogio survives in the Ambrosiana (*left*), pricked for transfer: it is not clear whether it dates from before December 1493, when Ambrogio travelled to Innsbruck with Bianca Maria, or from his return to Milan (he was back no later than July 1494, when he was mentioned in a solicitous letter from Il Moro to his court physician after being injured in a riding accident).[35]

The *Madonna & Devotees* celebrates a marriage. The *Pala Sforzesca* celebrates Il Moro's elevation to Duke of Milan, as the ducal chain and protective hand of St Ambrogio make clear. Pietro Marani contends that the work can only have been 'actuated' after Gian Galeazzo's death, as otherwise its 'endorsement of Ludovico's powers from the Virgin and Church Doctors' would have been 'interpreted as wrongful, or even blasphemous.'[36]

But Blasphemy held no fears for this One Moro Upon Earth. Rechannelling religious imagery as political propaganda underscored not only the second version of the *Virgin of the Rocks*, but also Birago's use of the Corvinus Calvary in the first *Sforziada* frontispiece, and much of Bergognone's work at the Certosa di Pavia. Bergognone would have been an obvious choice to paint the *Pala Sforzesca*, but was presumably too busy with frescoes at the Certosa di Pavia of equal dynastic importance.

THE CERTOSA DI PAVIA

The Certosa di Pavia was a major scene of construction and decoration during the early 1490s. Its importance to Moro-esque iconography, however, has tended to be overlooked in favour of Santa Maria delle Grazie – the site of Leonardo's *Last Supper* and Bramante's intended Sforza mausoleum and, being in central Milan, far more accessible. The Certosa – once at the far end of the Sforzas' 5-mile-long Pavia game park – stands to this day in isolated countryside.

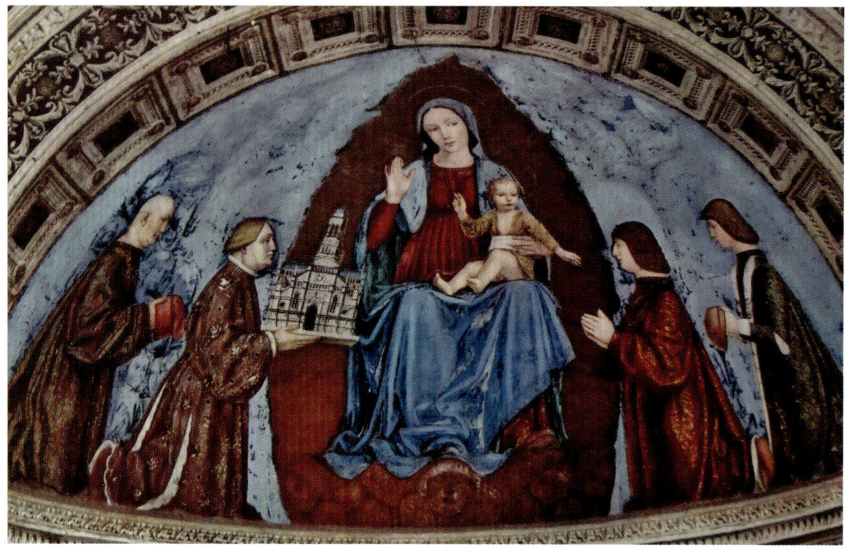

Its mighty church, towering above a vast monastery, contains the elaborate tomb of Gian Galeazzo Visconti (1351–1402): the only Duke of Milan, prior to Il Moro, to obtain the Imperial investiture. Gian Galeazzo laid the Certosa's foundation stone on 27 August 1396. His remains were re-interred in the church in 1474 by order of Duke Galeazzo Maria.

Building received fresh impetus under Il Moro from 1481. Like the *Sforziada*, the Certosa was a cultural project with propaganda potential that engaged his attention as soon as he had secured power as Regent. He appointed Giovanni Amadeo (*c.*1447–1522) as overseer,[37] supported for work on the façade by Antonio Mantegazza (died 1495) and Gian Giacomo Dolcebuono (*c.*1445–1504) and, for the interior sculpture, by Benedetto Briosco (*c.*1460–1517). Painted decoration was entrusted to Bergognone assisted by his younger brother Bernardino and Giacomo de Mottis.

FAÇADE

The church façade is fronted in various types of marble. The upper part dates from the mid-16th century, but the lower section was the subject of a vigorous sculpture campaign in the early 1490s, and is peppered throughout with gryphons, acanthus leaves, winged angel-heads, leaf-masks, winged sphinxes and frolicking cherubs culled from the same decorative repertoire as Birago's. One circular blind window portrays the youthful Duke Gian Galeazzo Sforza with ducal chain and long hair, either greeting worshippers or, like some Renaissance Rapunzel, seeking escape. The length of his hair brings to mind Birago's illustrations in the grammar-book commissioned for Il Moro's son Massimiliano (*see Chapter XII*). Another figure with beard and turban, emerging from a roundel, evokes the *haut-de-page* Moor in Birago's 'Uffizi' *Sforziada*.

TRANSEPT

Gian Galeazzo Visconti's double-decker tomb was commissioned by Il Moro and sculpted by Gian Cristoforo Romano and Benedetto Briosco between 1493

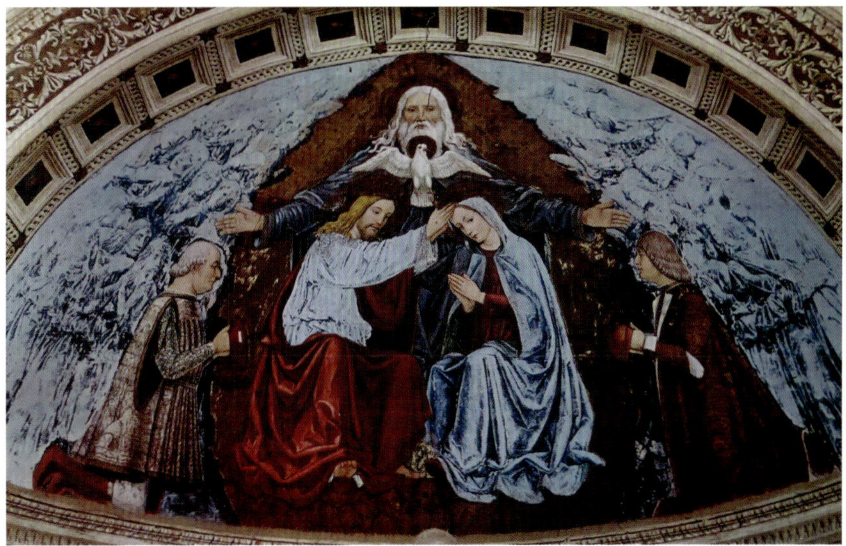

and 1497. It replaced a tomb from the early 1480s placed behind the altar (as Gian Galeazzo had stipulated in his will).[38] The new tomb was commissioned to emphasize that Il Moro, rather than his elder brother, was the true heir to Gian Galeazzo Visconti as the only other Duke of Milan worthy of Imperial investiture.

High at each end of the transept are Bergognone's most unequivocally political works at the Certosa: two giant semi-circular frescoes. Their precise dating is unknown, but 1493/4 seems likely. Both frescoes feature truncated golden mandorlas on a pale blue ground of swimming-pool intensity, originally peopled by heavenly hosts outlined in navy (now much faded). Both extol the Divine Right of Dukes.

The north transept fresco (*p.142*) shows *Gian Galeazzo Visconti Presenting a Model of the Certosa to the Virgin*. The Christ child on her lap, with his right hand raised in two-fingered blessing, is wearing a short gold shirt (with white sash) that leaves his midriff and bare legs exposed. Four dukes are kneeling before them: two Viscontis (Gian Galeazzo and his son Filippo Maria) to the left; and two Sforzas (Galeazzo Maria and his son Gian Galeazzo) to the right. The third Visconti duke, Filippo Maria's elder brother Giovanni Maria, murdered in 1412, is nowhere to be seen: aesthetic symmetry ranked higher than historical consistency on Il Moro's list of priorities.

Galeazzo Maria Sforza has his hands clasped in prayer. His son Gian Galeazzo, and Filippo Maria Visconti, are both holding a cap. Gian Galeazzo Visconti is proffering a model of the Certosa church, shown as it would have appeared in Il Moro's time. The Virgin and Child ignore him. All four dukes are clad in robes embroidered with dynastic emblems, although Galeazzo Maria is the only one wearing a ducal chain (in fact double-chain). Gian Galeazzo Visconti and Galeazzo Maria both wear reddish-brown *murray*; Gian Galeazzo's gown is embroidered with the sunbursts he used as his personal emblem, while Galeazzo Maria's features the *biscione* (viper) shield commonly used by both dynasties.

The symmetry is underlined by the similar gowns worn at each end of the composition – by Filippo Maria Visconti and Gian Galeazzo Sforza. Each is wearing a shimmering greenish gown embroidered with blue leaf-and-flower patterning (possibly evoking the sempervivium or quince). The implication is that Filippo Maria and Gian Galeazzo are to be considered in the same light: i.e. destined to have no direct successor – a reference to the fact that it was Il Moro, and his son, who would rule in Gian Galeazzo's wake, not his own son. Filippo Maria Visconti was also the man who refused to acknowledge Francesco Sforza, his son-in-law, as his successor. To be equated with him was, in Sforza dynastic terms, an insult. Yet again we see Il Moro playing mind games with his nephew.

The south transept fresco (*p.143*) officially depicts *The Coronation of the Virgin*. Its assertively triangular composition features God the Father at its apex, with full white beard and long white hair. He wears a dark blue gown that appears spangled with stars. His outstretched arms end in palms opened in benediction above the heads of Francesco and Il Moro. The Holy Spirit, in the form of a haloed dove, flutters just beneath God's chin, above Christ and Mary, both enthroned. Christ is apparently blessing – officially crowning – the Virgin with his outstretched hands. Her hands are clasped in prayer.

Francesco is holding his famously battered red campaign hat in his hands and looking humbly at the ground in front of him. He is wearing a white top with green floral embroidery, beneath a *murray*-lined tabard or *pellanda*, embroidered with his dog-and-pine emblem – the same colour combination as in his Ippolita grammar-book portrait. He is shod in high, dark red boots.

A grey-haired Il Moro is holding a ducal cap similar to that in the hands of Gian Galeazzo (and in his own hands in his sepulchral effigy); his golden, fur-trimmed gown has the white cuffs and elbow frills fashionable in 1490s Milan.

His gown is embroidered not with his favourite *scopetta*, but with the *moraglie* emblem of horse's reins and bit, accompanied by the motto *ICH VERGES NIT*. Whom or what Il Moro is vowing in God's presence not to forget remains a mystery.

Pietro Marani, who helped oversee the fresco's restoration in the 1990s, believes 'differences in style and handling' suggest the figures of Il Moro and Francesco may be the work of court portraitist Ambrogio de Predis (or one of his assistants).[39] This is highly plausible. De Predis was involved in the portraits in Birago's *Sforziada* frontispieces for precisely the same reason: to ensure the most accurate possible depiction of Il Moro and his father.

The two Certosa frescoes contain an unequivocal message as to Il Moro's Heaven-sanctioned superiority. One Duke of Milan is absent; four are deemed worthy 'only' of the company of the Virgin and Child (who ignore them); but Francesco Sforza and Il Moro kneel on high with the Holy Trinity – who have eyes for Il Moro alone.

A telling contrast can be made between the south transept fresco and that painted by Bergognone in 1508 in the Milan church of San Simpliciano

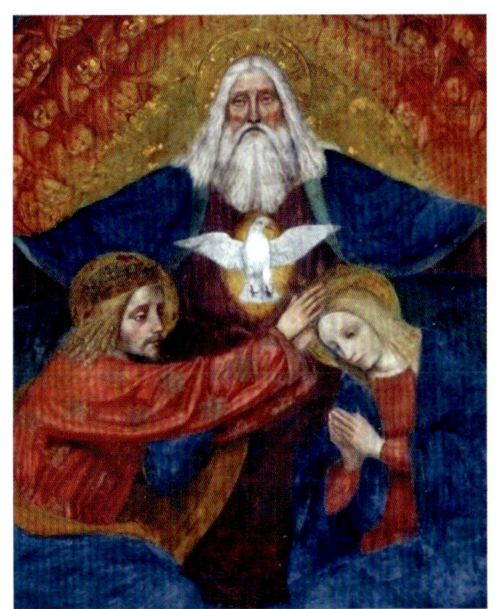

– where Christ looks attentively at the Virgin, who bows her head modestly as God the Father gazes straight ahead (*see left*). In the Certosa fresco, God the Father looks down to his left, towards Il Moro; the Virgin looks over her shoulder, towards Il Moro; and Christ, instead of looking at the Virgin, gazes down … towards Il Moro, suggesting that he, not Christ's mother, is the deserving recipient of divine benediction.

This is not just blasphemy: it is megalomania on a biblical scale.[40]

THE SFORZA HORSE

The Certosa Christ blesses Il Moro – but ignores Francesco. There was to be no figure equal, let alone superior, to Il Moro in his Sforza pantheon.

E un Dio in Cielo e Il Moro in Terra ('There is one God in Heaven and Il Moro upon Earth') as Pistoia, another *Sforziada* contributor, put it.

Il Moro's equine monument to Francesco Sforza, talked about and planned for over a decade, was ditched at the last moment.

Leonardo completed the clay model of his giant horse in time for Bianca Maria's proxy wedding to Emperor Maximilian in Milan Cathedral on 30 November 1493. There are conflicting accounts (Baldassare Taccone and Pietro Lazzarone) of where the horse was positioned, and whether it had a rider. On balance, it seems that a horse-and-rider 'in effigy' was erected under a canopy at the end of the nave, as if to suggest Francesco Sforza were physically present at the greatest day in his dynasty's history – his granddaughter's wedding to a Holy Roman Emperor; while Leonardo's giant model, which must have been enormously heavy and difficult to shift, remained (without a rider) in the Corte Vecchio, the old Visconti palace alongside the Cathedral where Leonardo lived and worked.

Taccone claimed that the ancient world had never seen the like of this 'great colossus':

> *Vedi che in corte fa far di metallo / Per memoria del Padre un gran colosso*
> *I'credo fermamente e senza fallo / Che Gretia e Roma mai vide il piu grosso,*
> *Guarda pur come e bello quel cavallo! Leonardo Vinci a farlo sol'e mosso.*

But this 'Wonder Horse' never made it from clay to bronze. The project was definitively abandoned in November 1494, when Il Moro dispatched the 70 tons of bronze, reputedly set aside for it, down river to Ferrara – ostensibly to help Duke Ercole d'Este make cannon.

In fact, by then, the *Sforza Horse* had served its purpose: now that Il Moro had the Imperial investiture sewn up, and with his nephew Gian Galeazzo conveniently dead, he no longer needed it to bolster his hereditary credentials.

Did Il Moro ever really intend to erect a monument to his father?

The *Sforza Horse* was the drawing-board project par excellence. It served a propaganda purpose for years and years, for next to no cost, and kept Leonardo in Milan into the bargain. It is surely no coincidence that, the moment his horse was consigned to the dustbin of history, Leonardo received another commission that would tie him to Milan for more years to come. After a giant horse, a giant fresco.

THE LAST SUPPER

The Last Supper is a natural subject for a painting in a monks' dining-hall, although betrayal is not a subject that would give most people an appetite.

Nor is execution – the opposite wall is given over to the Crucifixion – yet Il Moro, we are told, lunched in the refectory twice a week.

The Last Supper dates from 1494–97. It is a study in facial/manual expression, chromatic rhythm and mathematics – with Christ surrounded by four groups of three figures; beneath a ceiling with 36 coffers, arrayed six by six; with four tapestries hanging along each side wall, interspersed with three doors; and three background openings (door and two windows), echoed above by three semi-circular lunettes containing wreath-ringed shields featuring the coat of arms of: Ludovico & Beatrice, with the lettering *LV MA BE EST SF AN DU[X MLI]*; their elder son Massimiliano, Count of Pavia (*M MX SF AN CO PP*) to the left; and, to the right, their younger son Francesco, Duke of Bari (*SF AN DUX BAR*) – a title he assumed in 1497.

The background to each lunette appears a dull red today but was originally sky blue[41] – presaging the heavenly background to Il Moro's ducal shield in the Sala delle Asse (*see Chapter XIII*). Recent restoration of *The Last Supper* has revealed tree-and-flower patterning to the eight wall tapestries, with interlacing branches that again presage the decoration of the Sala delle Asse.

The opposite wall of the refectory is occupied in its entirety by a busy *Crucifixion* by Giovanni Donato da Montorfano (*c.*1460–1503), dated 1495. It incorporates faded devotional profiles at either end, showing Il Moro (*left*) and Beatrice d'Este (*right*), each flanked by a child.

These two pairs of figures are similarly positioned in the slightly earlier *Pala Sforzesca*, but here separated by 25 feet of wall rather than a yard of wood. The infants, this time, are their sons Ercole and Francesco. Following the birth of his second legitimate son (putting him 2-1 up on Gian Galeazzo), Il Moro no longer had any need to parade the illegitimate Cesare; it is Ercole who occupies Cesare's *Pala* place next to his father.

The appalling condition of these virtually illegible portraits is in striking contrast to the still vivid colours of the *Crucifixion*. A note in the archives suggests Il Moro was impatiently demanding that Leonardo get around to producing them.[42] Opinion as to whether he actually did so is divided. Perhaps he oversaw their production by his assistants: it is hard to credit the glorious Leonardo meekly adding to another man's handiwork.

INVESTITURE PORTRAIT

Equal mystery surrounds the name of the artist responsible for the most unusual portrait ever painted of the great *Il Moro* himself. This 53 × 36cm panel formerly belonged to the Trivulzio Collection, which it entered before 1800; it is now listed merely, on its occasional appearances at exhibitions, as being privately owned.

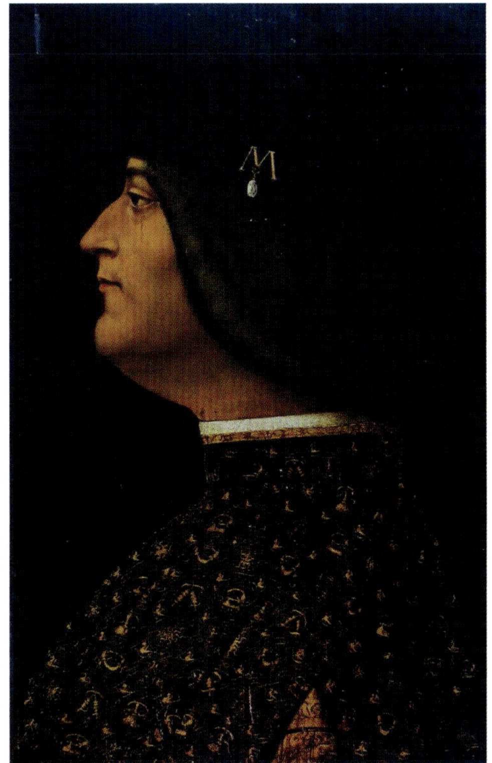

It shows Il Moro in a cloak of dark brown cloth and gold brocade, wearing a black felt cap with a single pearl dangling from a gold *M*. The picture's background is dark green (this may or may not be the original colour) but appears black in photographs. Evidence of *spolveri* (dusting) to the face suggests the portrait was originally drawn on paper before being transferred.

Pietro Marani claims the portrait must pre-date the award to Il Moro of the Golden Fleece by Henry VII in 1494, as 'otherwise the artist would not have failed to depict this.'[43] But there are stronger reasons to suppose the portrait dates from 1495, and was commissioned to mark Il Moro's investiture as Duke of Milan on May 26. He appears to be wearing it in the illuminated miniature depicting his investiture ceremony in the *Messale Arcimboldi* now in Milan's Biblioteca del Capitolo (*p.177*).

The cloak features five Sforza devices and two armorial shields within squares arrayed in a grid, alternating with narrower rows formed by the repetition of a sixth Sforza device: the dove and banner (no doubt bearing the motto *A BON DROIT*) within a diamond. Delicately entwined gold thread forms a background mesh of intricate knot patterning. The gold brocade revealed by the shoulder slash displays the top of the Sforza coat of arms with a crown, eagle and man-eating viper partly discernible. This is a garment in sharp stylistic contrast to the sober blue *robone* Il Moro donned for the *Pala Sforzesca* to play mock-modest second-fiddle to saints and spouse. Here he alone assumes the mantle of Sforza grandeur.

The two shields and the five other devices are spangled indiscriminately around the cloak rather than recurring in a set order. Chiara Buss, Curator of the exhibition *Seta Oro Cremisi* ('Silk Gold Crimson') held at Milan's Poldi Pezzoli Museum in 2009, reports that macrophotographic analysis reveals that the devices were not embroidered, but part of an enormous single pattern woven on a loom. As with the altar-cloth commissioned for Il Moro's 1495 investiture ceremony and now in Sacro Monte sopra Varese, we are in the presence of a piece of cloth whose cost, ambition and technical sophistication beggar belief.

The five devices are the *scopetta*, sifting-cloth, axe-and-log, horse's bit and sunburst. The two shields, both quartered, are the Sforza ducal coat of arms (imperial eagle/viper) and the Este arms (Imperial eagle/*fleurs-de-lys*). The *fleurs-de-lys* is not surrounded by its usual indented border, which would presumably have been impossible to convey on such a minute scale. More surprisingly, the normal positions of the eagle and *fleurs-de-lys* on the Este shield have been inverted.

The joint use of the Sforza and Este arms also recalls the Sacro Monte altar-cloth, and the repeated use of the dove with its *BY RIGHT* message chimes in with an investiture context (the dove was also a pet device of Il Moro's mother, Bianca Maria Visconti – and may have some Marian symbolism underscored by the gold *M* monogram on Il Moro's cap, ambiguously standing for both *Moro* and *Maria*).

The strongest indication that this cloak was made for Il Moro's Imperial investiture, however, lies in the choice of Sforza emblems for its decoration. Or rather, in what it is omitted: one of Il Moro's hallmark devices, constantly used from the first illuminated *Sforziada* in 1490 down to the end of his reign – the twin towers of Genoa.

Genoa being a French fiefdom, the towers' appearance in a garment prepared for a ceremony marking Milan's allegiance to a different foreign power, Austria, would have been *faux-pas* and *lèse-majesté* rolled into one.

For a similar reason, an English-bestowed Golden Fleece, upon which Marani appears to place such store, would have been given equally short shrift.

Marani claims the picture's 'handling appears rather flat and the volumes lack depth' – but these would be qualities, rather than defects, if the painting were conceived as some sort of icon (an interpretation that would tie in with the possible votive nature of the *M* for *Mary*). The artist surely deserves acclaim for the riveting detail of the pattern – painted in gold on red bole over a layer of brown, then scratched. Who can have been responsible for this *tour de force*?

The work was long held to be by Boltraffio (Malaguzzi Valeri) or Ambrogio de Predis (Berenson). Its intricacy may reflect the skill of a trained miniaturist – and certainly of someone used to working with a magnifying glass. De Predis, with his background in illumination and coin design, makes a feasible candidate – and one would expect such a prestigious work to be assigned to the court's Official Portrait specialist, although the softish treatment of the eye lacks his sharp-lashed clarity. Marani believes it the work of Bernardino de' Conti, who emerged in Ambrogio's ambit in the mid-1490s.

INVESTITURE ALTAR-CLOTH

The startling armorial altar-cloth in Sacro Monte's Museo Baroffio (*inv. 578*), 227 × 102cm, was donated to Santa Maria del Monte by Il Moro himself. It commemorates his investiture as Duke of Milan and appears to have been made for his investiture ceremony in May 1495. It is nothing less than 'one of the most complex and precious pieces of cloth ever woven … a hymn to the person who commissioned it, then at the peak of his social and political career.'[44]

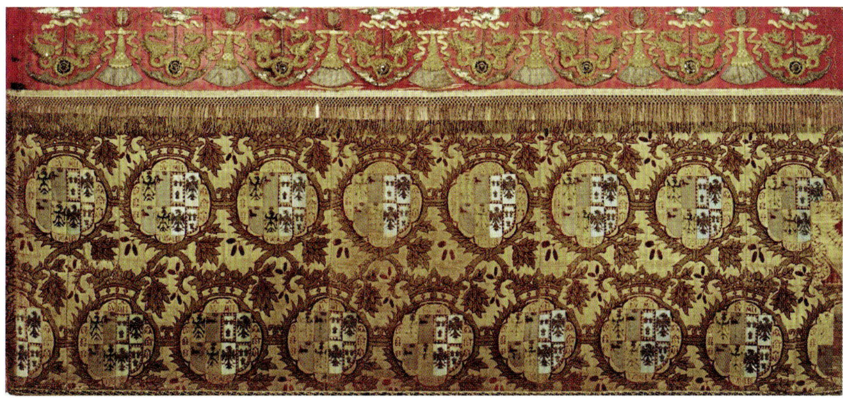

This altar-cloth (*above*) features a shield with the combined arms of the Houses of Sforza (quartered eagles and vipers) and Este (quartered eagles and *fleurs-de-lys*), surrounded by the letters ***DU MLI - LU MA - BE EST - SF AN - IUGALES*** (*Dux Mediolani - Ludovico Maria - Beatrix Estensis - Sforza Anglus*). *Iugales* translates roughly as *Conjugally Bound* or, to take a more cynical view, *Yoked Together*. The shield is topped by a crown held in place by a branch of date palm (to the left) and mulberry (to the right), each branch descending in a semi-circle to frame the shield before crossing at the bottom, where they are tied together. This motif is repeated sixteen times, in two staggered rows of eight, with each branch tied horizontally to the next.

Sforza arms had hitherto been topped by date palm and laurel (and, before the laurel, an olive-branch). The replacement of the laurel by the mulberry – of the *lauro* by the *moro* – is Il Moro's way of heralding Milan's rise to supremacy over Florence, and symbolically hailing his own glory as greater than that of Lorenzo de' Medici … a boast already broached by Birago's surrealist tree-and-sapling frontispiece to the Paris *Sforziada*.

The church of Santa Maria del Monte was revered by the Sforzas for several reasons, and not just because *Maria* was the middle name routinely bestowed on members of the family. It sits atop a hill so tall and steep that driving up it in a car is tough, let alone clambering up its *Via Matris* on foot (as hardy pilgrims do to this day). From 1476 it also hosted an Ambrosian convent with commanding views towards the Alps.

It is not far from the Castle of Angera (*Anglus* in Latin) on Lake Maggiore – a former Visconti stronghold that held mythical importance to the Sforzas and, abbreviated as *AN*, was systematically added to Il Moro's official title (as if his surname were *Sforza-Anglus*). After the end of the Visconti line in 1447, the Castle of Angera was acquired by the Borromeos – but confiscated by Il Moro in the 1480s.

The Sforzas' patronage of Santa Maria del Monte began in the reign of Galeazzo Maria (1466–76), when Sforza arms were added to paving and capitals in the church. A series of frescoes (destroyed in the 17th century) were painted in the church during Il Moro's reign; only a *Christ bearing the Cross between Nuns* remains. The names of the artists Il Moro hired to work at the church are not known, with the prestigious exception of Bernardino Butinone, who is chronicled at Santa Maria del Monte in 1488.

Butinone, who studied with Foppa and taught Bramantino, was a high-flying religious specialist who had frescoed the nave of Santa Maria delle Grazie in Milan earlier in the decade.

The Museo Boraffio contains another item of *Sforziada* relevance: a red priest's stole (*right*) repeatedly embroidered, in pale blue and gold thread, with a complex, sixteen-branch interlacing knot pattern (*inv. 656*).

Sixteen is also the number of framed shields on the altar-cloth … and even of the number of leaves on each mulberry branch. It is tempting to deduce that the stole embroidery and luxury altar-cloth were both made for Il Moro's investiture, and later donated to Santa Maria delle Monte.

The stole embroidery brings irresistibly to mind the six elaborate knot-patterns designed by Leonardo da Vinci and subsequently engraved. Although necessarily simplified for embroidery purposes, the stole's repeated motifs – all of them interlinked, and as identical to one another as could be expected from hand-stitching – come closest to the Leonardo pattern with Ambrosiana inventory number *9596b* (*see p.229*).

The criss-cross diamond motif, repeated around the middle ring of Leonardo's design, is also to be found, embroidered in gold, around the neck of the Madonna's gown in the second (London) version of the *Virgin of the Rocks*.

And it is found, embroidered in thicker gold, on the shoulder of Bianca Sforza's dress – in her *Sforziada* portrait drawn by Leonardo barely a year after Il Moro's investiture ceremony took place.

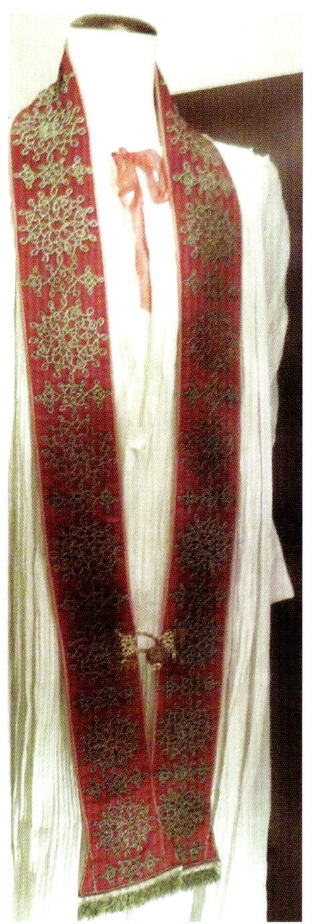

NOTES

1 It is not, perhaps, overly cynical to surmise that Il Moro may have held reasonable expectations that any offspring of this marriage between first cousins would be affected by the psychological problems often caused by interbreeding.

2 Nadia Covini, *Zanetta e Cecilia: Potere, Sangue e Passioni nella Milano di Ludovico il Moro in Viglevanum anno XXI* (2011), pp.42–51. Covini reports that Cecilia's elder sister Zanetta was the lover of Il Moro's secretary Aloisio da Terzago.

3 *Ibid.* The letter is in the Milan State Archives; Covini believes it was never sent, and drafted purely to show Cecilia. Her brother eventually received a (more modest) ecclesiastical benefit in 1491.

4 I am indebted to Elisabetta Gnignera for kindly permitting me to quote from her article *Cecilia o La Dama con l'Ermellino* and from her important contribution to Pascal Cotte's groundbreaking *Lumière on the Lady with an Ermine* (*op. cit.*).

5 The marriage between Il Moro and Beatrice d'Este was one of political convenience – effectively a mutual reinsurance policy between Milan and Ferrara against their neighbours Venice. Beatrice's father Duke Ercole had initially supported the regency of Bona di Savoia, but took a Realpolitik approach once Il Moro had consolidated his hold on power. To Il Moro, Beatrice had the additional cachet of her Neapolitan childhood: he wanted friendly relations with Naples for as long as possible. As with János and Bianca Maria, it was the betrothal – or *promessa di matrimonio* – that most interested Il Moro, because it sufficed to ensure the dynastic alliance; the wedding itself could wait.

6 Pascal Cotte, *Lumière on the Lady With An Ermine* (Vinci Editions, Paris 2014).

7 The *coazzone* was already established in Aragonese Spain in the 1470s, as shown in *Herod's Banquet* (*c*.1475) by Pedro García de Benabarre (died 1485), tempera & stucco on wood 198 × 126cm – the main panel from his *John the Baptist* altarpiece for the church of San Juan del Mercado in Lleida (halfway between Barcelona and Zaragoza). Salome is wearing a criss-cross *coazzone*, as is her lady-in-waiting on the far left. The panel is now in the Museu Nacional d'Art de Catalunya, Barcelona.

8 *cf* Daniela Pizzagalli: *La Dama con l'Ermellino: Vita e Passioni di Cecilia Gallerani nella Milano di Ludovico il Moro* (Rizzoli, Milan 2008), quoted by Elisabetta Gnignera in *Cecilia o la Dama con l'Ermellino* (*op. cit.*).

9 'The weasel became, in consequence, an allegory of the Virgin May conceiving through the Word of The Lord. There is a clear affinity between the posture of the *Lady with an Ermine* and the one traditionally assumed by the Virgin Mary when listening to the Angel of the Lord, although Cecilia's posture differs slightly in that she looks to the right, not left, of the viewer. This affinity seems to have been alluded to by court poet Bernardo Bellincioni in his sonnet *Sopra il Ritratto di Madonna Cecilia, qual fece Leonardo* (Elisabetta Gnignera: *Cecilia o la Dama con l'Ermellino*).

10 The flower is a carnation – often used in a marriage or betrothal context (*cf* the one tucked into the belt of Bianca Maria's dress in her wedding portrait by Ambrogio de Predis, now in Washington); here, however, the carnation was an emblem chosen by Alfonso for heraldic purposes, and remains in use in Ferrara today.

11 Apart from the circumstantial evidence, and Beatrice's physical appearance as a girl in her early teens, the bust can be dated with some confidence to the second half of 1490, given the words of Isabella d'Este in a letter to her younger sister dated 22 June 1491, asking to be sent 'for a few days this master Zohan Cristophoro, who made the marble portrait of Your Excellency' (cited in the catalogue to the exhibition *Une Renaissance Singulière* held in Brussels in 2003, which in turn quotes A. Venturi's *L'Arte Ferrarese* published in 1888). Isabella's urgent interest in acquiring Romano's services – reminiscent of her later attitude towards Leonardo and, indeed, to borrowing *The Lady with an Ermine* from Cecilia Gallerani – suggest the bust was a recent talking-point.

12 Despatches of Ambassador Trotti – Archivio di Stato di Modena.

13 As relayed by Julia Cartwright, *op. cit.*

14 Leonardo himself is recorded as owning a copy of the *Metamorphoses*, listed in the *Madrid II Codex* under *Ricordo de' libri ch'io lascio serrati nel cassone* (records of books I keep stored in a chest).

15 Alcmene and Amphitryon, Lord of Tiryns (and grandson of Perseus), were in exile in Thebes when Zeus slept with Alcmene. Zeus's wife Hera hurried from Olympus to Argos, where Nicippe, daughter of Pelops and wife of Sthenelus (son of Perseus), was seven months pregnant. Hera caused Nicippe to give birth to her baby prematurely and, at the same time, delayed Alcmena's labour pains. After driving Eileithyia, the Goddess of Childbirth, away from Alcmene, Hera told Zeus that the man who would be King of the Argives had indeed been born: Eurystheus, son of Sthenelus and Nicippe. Zeus and Hera agreed that Eurystheus should be Lord of Argolis, and that Heracles would be in his service until he had fulfilled his Twelve Labours, whereupon he would achieve immortality.

16 Leonardo was no stranger to the dogma of Immaculate Conception: it underpinned his first painting in Milan, the *Virgin of the Rocks*, in 1483. It was a dogma propounded by the Franciscans but not the Dominicans (who were guardians of the relics of Mary Magdalene, the leader of the virgin saints).

17 Elisabetta Gnignera (*op. cit.*), abetted by abundant documentation, points out the lingering importance of the weasel in Italian literary symbolism by citing a stanza from Tommaso Stigliani's poem *Mondo Nuovo* (1628): *Perché sì come mal può far difesa/ Co' piè il leone, e coll'armata bocca: Poiché segli è dentro l'orecchio appresa/ La donnola, che'l cerebro gli tocca* (rough meaning: *If the Lion fails to defend itself, the weasel will approach its ear and affect its mind*).

18 In a footnote to an article by A. Edith Hewett, *A Newly Discovered Portrait by Ambrogio de Predis*, published in the February 1907 issue of the *Burlington Magazine*. Holmes wrote: 'Is it not possible, since the Greek for weasel is γαλέη, that the animal was introduced into the picture as a humanistic pun upon Cecilia's surname?' Holmes was later director of the National Gallery of London.

19 Il Moro is thought to have been one of the 27 members of the Order of Ermine, founded by Ferrante I of Naples in 1465.

20 The statues were taken to the Doges' Palace when Venice conquered Cremona in 1499; they were later acquired by the Vicenza sculpture collector Girolamo Egidio di Velo (1792–1831).

21 Cited by Luca Beltrami in *Documenti e Memorie Riguardanti la Vita e le Opere di Leonardo da Vinci* (Milan, 1919).

22 Cited in Julia Cartwright, *Beatrice d'Este: Duchess of Milan* (J.M. Dent & Co Ltd, London 1899).

23 Cartwright, *ibid.*

24 Might the original 1483 version of the *Virgin of the Rocks* also have used another new-born child of Il Moro – Bianca – as model for the infant Christ?

25 Quoted by Malaguzzi Valeri (*op. cit.*) from *Lettere di Corrispondenti e di Corte di Milano* (State Archives, Modena).

26 In a report sent to Isabella d'Este in Mantua by her mother's maid of honour Teodora degli Angeli (cited by Cartwright, *op. cit.*).

27 Martin Kemp & Pascal Cotte, *La Bella Principessa* (Hodder & Stoughton, London 2010).

28 Restored by the Rotary Club di Trento in the late 1990s.

29 Information culled from the Innsbruck Landesarchiv (Raitbuch 1943, f.63) by D. Schönherr in 1883 and cited in Roberto Codroico: *Roberto di Sanseverino nel Duomo di Trento* (Trento Rotary Club, 1999).

30 Fiamma Domestici, *Della Robba* (Scala, Florence 2009).

31 For detailed discussion of dyes and fabrics in Renaissance Milan, see Chiara Buss (ed.), *Silk Gold Crimson – Secrets and Technology at the Visconti and Sforza Courts* (Silvana Editoriale, Milan 2009).

32 For further details of the atypical physical qualities of the National Gallery picture, including the use of mineral copper green and red lead/ vermilion/red lake for the draperies, see Marika Spring, Antonio Mazzotta, Ashok Roy, Rachel Billinge & David Peggie, *Painting Practice in Milan in the 1490s: The Influence of Leonardo* in the *National Gallery Technical Bulletin*, Volume 32.

33 In striking contrast to, say, the larger gold crown borne aloft by two angels in Filippino Lippi's earlier *Madonna and Child Enthroned*, now in the Uffizi.

34 Napoletano's possible authorship of the *Pala Sforzesca* was first proposed in 1910 by the German art historian Emil Jacobsen, in *Un Quadro e un Disegno del Maestro della Pala Sforzesca – Rassegna d'Arte X*.

35 Probably Il Moro's physician/astrologer, more usually referred to as Ambrogio Varese da Rosate (born 1437).

36 Pietro C. Marani, *Master of the Pala Sforzesca* in *The Legacy of Leonardo* (Skira, Milan 1998).

37 Amadeo later collaborated with Bramante at Santa Maria presso San Satiro in Milan and, in 1488, was commissioned by Ascanio Sforza to direct work at the new Pavia Cathedral, again in conjunction with Bramante.

38 In 1496 Il Moro attempted to locate and impound all extant copies of Gian Galeazzo Visconti's will and testament of 1397, wherein Gian Galeazzo Visconti decreed – in apparent violation of the conditions of his Imperial investiture in 1395 – that, should the male line of the Visconti succession become extinct, the Ducal title should fall to the descendants of his own first-born child, Valentina (1368–1408). This decree formed the basis of the claims to Milan of French King Louis XII, whose grandfather, Louis de Valois, Duc d'Orléans (1372–1407), married Valentina in 1387.

39 Pietro C. Marani (*op. cit.*). But Bergognone's own skill as a portraitist should not be under-estimated.

40 His Ducal Omnipotence declared himself able to 'turn the course of rivers and bring flowing streams into dry and barren land,' making the wilderness 'blossom like a rose' in an inscription added to the tower of the Castello in Vigevano in 1492.

41 Pietro C. Marani, *Leonardo – Il Cenacolo Svelato* (Skira, Milan 2011).

42 Edoardo Villata, *Leonardo da Vinci: I documenti e le Testimonianze Contemporanee* (Milan 1999).

43 Pietro C. Marani (catalogue entry) in *Silk Gold Crimson – Secrets and Technology at the Visconti and Sforza Courts* (Silvana Editoriale, Milan 2009).

44 Chiara Buss in *Silk Gold Crimson* (*ibid.*) describes the altarcloth as made of gold brocade (*broccato d'oro rizzo*), technically of triple-weave velvet (crimson, green and black) on a satin ground, covered with patten wefts of gold filé, with brocading wefts in gold and silver filé and pale blue silk outlined by thin threads of red pile. The use of three colours for the pile is the most ever woven, with precious crimsyn dye extending not only to the ground warp, which is rare enough, but also to the binding, which is unique. The weave is so complex that historic comparisons are impossible. Recent laboratory tests have established that it was woven in Milan by craftsmen from Florence or of the Florentine school. The main components were found to be luteolin and apigenin, pointing to the use of weld (*reseda luteola*) as yellow dye. Fisetin and sulfuretin were also found, indicating the use of young fustic (*rhus cotinus*). The altarcloth was also dyed with a mixture of Kermes and Armenian or Polish cochineal after treatment of the silk with tannins; and with a mixture of woad (*isatis tinctoria*) or indigo (*indigofera tinctoria*) – two species that cannot be distinguished from one another chemically (although woad is considered more likely). Weld (*reseda luteola*) and young fustic (*rhus cotinus*) were used for the yellow dye.

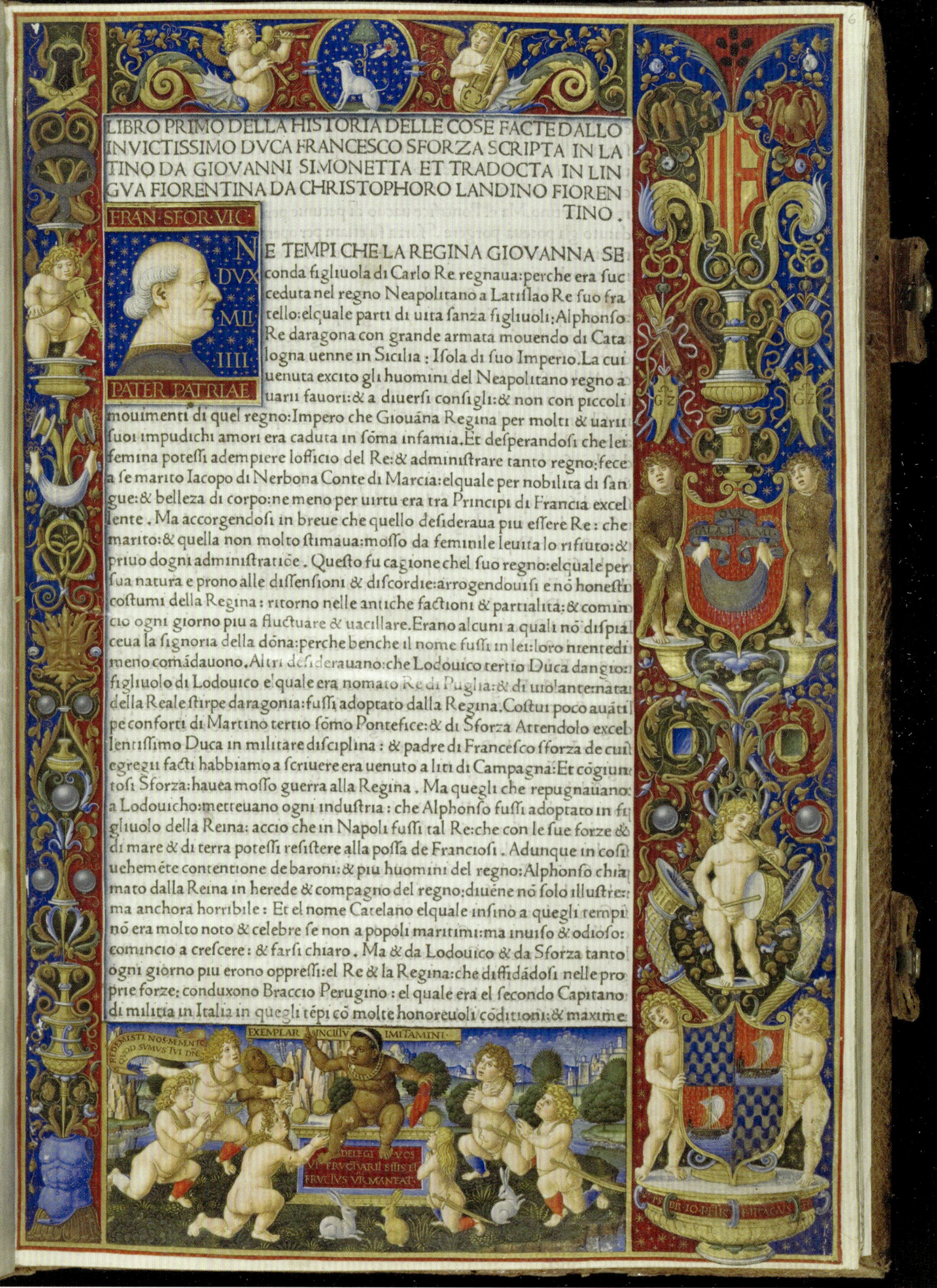

LIBRO PRIMO DELLA HISTORIA DELLE COSE FACTE DALLO
INVICTISSIMO DVCA FRANCESCO SFORZA SCRIPTA IN LA
TINO DA GIOVANNI SIMONETTA ET TRADOCTA IN LIN
GVA FIORENTINA DA CHRISTOPHORO LANDINO FIOREN
TINO .

NE TEMPI CHE LA REGINA GIOVANNA SE
conda figliuola di Carlo Re regnaua:perche era suc
ceduta nel regno Neapolitano a Latislao Re suo fra
tello:elquale parti di uita sanza figliuoli:Alphonso
Re daragona con grande armata mouendo di Cata
logna uenne in Sicilia : Isola di suo Imperio.La cui
uenuta excito gli huomini del Neapolitano regno a
uarii fauori:& a diuersi consigli:& non con piccoli
mouimenti di quel regno:Impero che Giouana Regina per molti & uarii
suoi impudichi amori era caduta in soma infamia.Et desperandosi che lei
femina potessi adempiere lofficio del Re:& administrare tanto regno:fece
a se marito Iacopo di Nerbona Conte di Marcia:elquale per nobilita di san
gue:& belleza di corpo:ne meno per uirtu era tra Principi di Francia excel
lente . Ma accorgendosi in breue che quello desideraua piu essere Re : che
marito:& quella non molto stimaua:mosso da feminile leuita lo rifiuto:&
priuo dogni administratioe . Questo fu cagione chel suo regno:elquale per
sua natura e prono alle dissensioni & discordie:arrogendouisi e nó honesti
costumi della Regina : ritorno nelle antiche factioni & partialita:& comin
cio ogni giorno piu a fluctuare & uacillare.Erano alcuni a quali nó dispial
ceua la signoria della dóna:perche benche il nome fussi in lei:loro nrentedi
meno comádauono.Altri desiderauano:che Lodouico tertio Duca dangioi
figliuolo di Lodouico elquale era nomato Re di Puglia:& di uiolantenata
della Reale stirpe daragonia:fussi adoptato dalla Regina.Costui poco auáti
pe conforti di Martino tertio sómo Pontefice:& di Sforza Attendolo exceb
lentissimo Duca in militare disciplina : & padre di Francesco sforza de cui
egregii facti habbiamo a scriuere era uenuto a liti di Campagna:Et cógiun
tosi Sforza:haua mosso guerra alla Regina . Ma quegli che repugnauano
a Lodouicho:metteuano ogni industria : che Alphonso fussi adoptato in fi
gliuolo della Reina: accio che in Napoli fussi tal Re:che con le sue forze &
di mare & di terra potessi resistere alla possa de Franciosi . Adunque in cosi
ueheméte contentione de baroni:& piu huomini del regno:Alphonso chia
mato dalla Reina in herede & compagno del regno:diuéne nó solo illustre:
ma anchora horribile : Et el nome Catelano elquale insino a quegli tempi
nó era molto noto & celebre se non a popoli maritimi:ma inuiso & odioso:
comincio a crescere : & farsi chiaro . Ma & da Lodouico & da Sforza tanto
ogni giorno piu erono oppressi:el Re & la Regina:che diffidádosi nelle pro
prie forze: conduxono Braccio Perugino : el quale era el secondo Capitano
di militia in Italia in quegli tépi có molte honoreuoli códitioni:& maxime

SFORZIADA (FRONTISPIECE) – BIBLIOTEKA NARODOWA, WARSAW (INC. F. 1347)

IX
DEATH AND BETRAYAL
THE ALTERED SFORZIADA

THE FIRST THREE illuminated *Sforziadas* saw Birago vaunt Il Moro's ducal credentials and lampoon his rival nephew. His fourth frontispiece, prepared three years later to mark the marriage of Il Moro's daughter, saw Leonardo da Vinci team up with Gianpietro Birago and Ambrogio de Predis to produce the ultimate Renaissance Superbook.

PROVENANCE

1496 Bianca Sforza/Galeazzo Sanseverino, Milan
1675 Zamość Academy, Zamość
1784 Zamoyski Estate, Zamość
1809 Zamoyski Library, Klemensow
1811 Blue Palace, Warsaw
1939 Monastery of Jasna Góra, Częstochowa
1948 Polish National Library, Warsaw

HISTORICAL BACKGROUND

The political landscape changed dramatically between the 'Uffizi' *Sforziada* of 1493 – when Il Moro was still Duke of Bari and Gian Galeazzo the father of two healthy young children – and the *Sforziada* of 1496, when Gian Galeazzo was dead and buried, and Il Moro undisputed Duke of Milan. The key to this turn-around was the French invasion of Italy in 1494, which Il Moro had exploited as the military solution to the biggest threat to his political existence: an invasion by Naples designed to wipe him off the map.

The death in January 1494 of Isabel of Aragon's grandfather King Ferrante, at the age of 72, made an attempted invasion by Naples inevitable. Ferrante had been a seasoned, and cautious, political operator with mixed emotional feelings regarding Milan. True, the rights of his granddaughter Isabel to reign as Duchess had been flouted by Il Moro. But Il Moro's wife, Beatrice d'Este, was also Ferrante's granddaughter, and had spent eight years in Naples under his guardianship.

There was no such tug of loyalties for his successor – his son Alfonso, Isabel's father and sworn enemy of Il Moro. Naples dominated the Tyrrhenian Sea. Milan did not have the naval means to resist invasion. This was why Il Moro had been cultivating French support since the start of the decade – as symbolized by the first illuminated *Sforziada.*

Alfonso began by sending a fleet to attack the coast south of Milan in July 1494. It was thwarted by bad weather and French ships and, after a brief landing at Porto Venere, 50 miles from Genoa, limped home with its sails between its legs.

Alfonso tried again in early September. This time his navy established a toehold at Rapallo, just fifteen miles from Genoa. But he was again repulsed by the French fleet, with the aid of mercenary Swiss ground forces.

These abortive naval strikes had been intended as part of a pincer movement whose second prong was an overland attack on Milan from the southeast.

In July Neapolitan troops, under Isabel of Aragon's brother Ferrandino and ex-Sforza General Gian Giacomo Trivulzio, moved up the peninsular to Cesena, with a view to attacking Milan along the Via Emilia, the Roman road that spears into Lombardy via Imola and Bologna.

Il Moro, who had received intelligence, was expecting them, and had already dispatched a troop of cavalry under Gaspare Sanseverino to Cotignola, the mythical cradle of the Sforza dynasty just off the Via Emilia, near Imola – the Sforza 'Stalingrad' that could not, for emotional reasons, be allowed to fall into enemy hands under any circumstances.

In August, in reply to the Neapolitans' arrival in Cesena, Il Moro poured in more troops under Count Caiazzo, the eldest and most military gifted of the Sanseverino brothers. The Neapolitans did not have the manpower to force their way through.

Over the next few weeks both sides were reinforced – the Milanese with support from the French, the Neapolitans with help from Florence. The stalemate persisted. The Neapolitans were hoping their navy would pave the way. News of its defeat at Rapallo in early September sapped morale.

On October 19 – a few days after Charles VIII had left Pavia, where he had seen with his own eyes that Gian Galeazzo, still technically Duke of Milan, was so poorly it would not be all that suspicious if he soon died – Sforza troops advanced from Cotignola towards Mordano, a neighbouring fortress town held by the Neapolitans, halfway between Cotignola and the Via Emilia.

On October 20, after calls for surrender had been ignored, the Milanese bombarded Mordano all morning, breached its walls, and put the town to the sword.

It was a decisive victory. Thwarted by sea and on land, the Neapolitans' threat to Milan was as good as over: Il Moro's decision to welcome the French into Italy seemed fully justified, and he could at last breathe freely.

Not so Gian Galeazzo. He was dead within 24 hours. A few hours later Il Moro – after fourteen years as Regent – was proclaimed Duke of Milan. The rights of Gian Galeazzo's infant son, Francesco, were ignored, as were those of his mother Isabel of Aragon to rule in his stead.

But Il Moro had opened a Gallic Pandora's box. The well-armed French blitzed down on Naples, smashing through Florence and Rome, and sent alarm bells ringing across Italy. An anti-French League was formed under Venetian sway. Il Moro had no choice but to sign up, or face invasion from Venice. The French were forced to withdraw. After marching all the way back up from Naples in the Spring of 1495, they were hounded out of Italy across the territory of the very State that had welcomed them in less than a year before: Il Moro's Milan.

By 1496, when Birago set to work on his fourth and final *Sforziada* frontispiece, his master was enjoying an uneasy triumph.

He had seen off one powerful enemy, Naples, but gained another (France) – even closer, even stronger.

Perhaps this is why Birago showed Il Moro bouncing around not on a throne but a tomb. Dancing on a volcano – and dicing with death.

FRANCESCO SFORZA MEDALLION

Francesco is shown on a blue ground heavily spangled with stars (21 six-armed asterisks, 50 four-armed crosses, 44 dots). ***FRAN SFOR VIC*** and ***PATER PATRIAE*** (no diphthong) appear in gold letters on rectangular red banners above and below; in *FRAN*, the bottom right of the letter *R* overlaps markedly with the bottom left of the letter *A*. His armour is grey (tarnished silver) with a gold collar; the breastplate appears to be plain, although only the very top part is visible. His expression is serene but grave. Several wisps of unruly hair emerge from the back of his head; none from his forehead. The initial *N* appears in gold in the top right-hand corner of the blue ground, above **DUX MLI IIII**, also in gold letters, right-justified over three rows: *DUX* at eyelid-level, *MLI* at chin-level, and *IIII* level with the top of the breastplate. This format is that of the Paris *Sforziada*, although the lettering of *DUX MLI IIII* is slightly larger, and *DUX* here is written in full.

ROUNDEL

After one portrait roundel in the London and Paris *Sforziadas*, and two in the 'Uffizi' *Sforziada*, none appear here. The right-hand border is dominated by armorial shields. Its portrait has emigrated to the previous folio and assumed full-page proportions.

HAUT-DE-PAGE

This features a small roundel with greyhound, hand and gold collar attached to a tree, on a star-spangled blue ground. The roundel is flattened at the top (by the red-and-gold frame of the page) and bottom (by the top of the text); both sides of the roundel are intersected by two blue clouds. The tree-and-greyhound was the favourite device of Francesco Sforza – although it derives from the Visconti (who used a leopard rather than a greyhound) – and is associated with faithfulness. Its message of 'do not provoke me' echoes the theme of the *bas-de-page*. Francesco Sforza was *Capitano Generale* (Commander-in-Chief) of the Duchy of Milan's armies under the Visconti; Galeazzo Sanseverino, co-hero of this frontispiece, held the same post under Il Moro. The roundel is flanked by musical putti with sharp, scaly tails reminiscent of the lavabo dolphins in the Certosa di Pavia, and the left-hand dolphin is almost identical to the one being 'sailed' by a young female in the Paris *Sforziada*. One of the musicians is playing the bagpipes, his counterpart strumming a lyre.

BAS-DE-PAGE

Eight naked cherubs are gathered on what appears to be an island in a river. Background trees in full leaf suggest it is summer. Five white cherubs kneel before a brown cherub holding a cardinal's hat. Another white cherub stands to the left, arm-in-arm with a small brown female cherub.

The dark-skinned central cherub, with chain and headband, clearly represents Il Moro. His pose and chubby folds are almost identical to those of the infant Christ in a polyptych painted by Macrino d'Alba for the Certosa di Pavia, dated 1496 (*below right*).[1] The infant Christ raises his right hand at a similar angle to Birago's Moor, but his left hand touches an orb rather than a cardinal's hat.

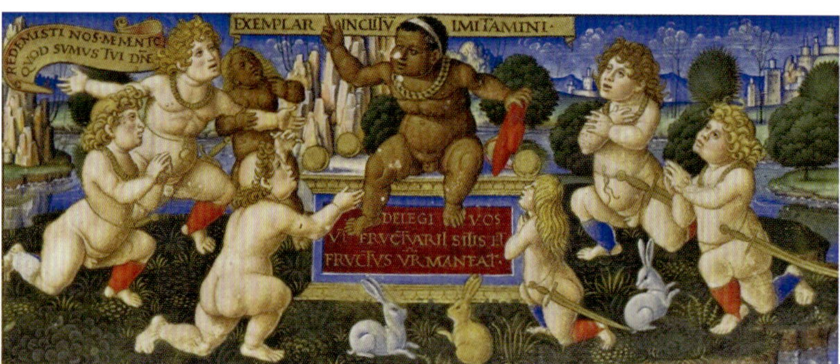

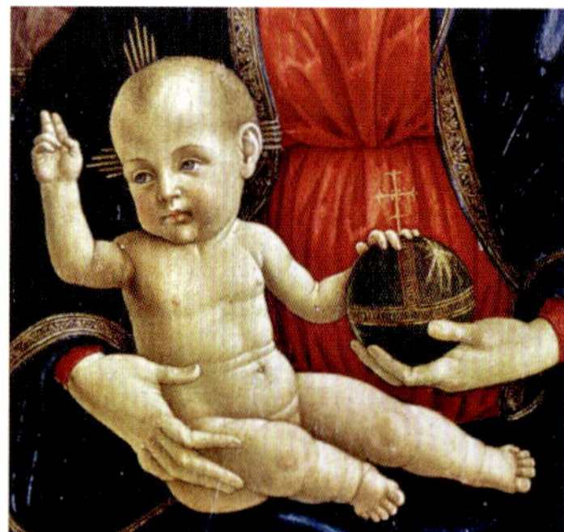

The second figure with dark skin is a blond-haired female – Il Moro's daughter Bianca, next to her husband-to-be, Galeazzo Sanseverino. The three larger kneeling figures with swords are Galeazzo's brothers; the figure with a tonsure is their half-brother, a cardinal. The Sanseverino brothers formed part of Il Moro's inner circle. Domineering and ambitious, they were collectively known, with a mixture of awe and scorn, as *I Gran Severini*.[2]

The gender of the smallest kneeling figure is ambiguous. If female, the likeliest candidate is the Sanseverinos' sister Eleonora – whose 1490 wedding to Giovanni Adorno[3] included a theatrical performance in which a wise and prudent Moor, *inbindato* (with headband), descended from Heaven flanked by four angels (as opposed to brother-soldiers) singing his praises[4] in a ceremony orchestrated by the court's special-effects maestro, Leonardo da Vinci.[5]

The figure's sexual ambiguity (which recalls that of the androgynous angel similarly positioned in Leonardo's *Virgin of the Rocks*) may well, as often with Birago, be intentional. He has portrayed the Moorish Bianca figure with nascent breasts, but there is no physical indication as to the gender of the small soldier. The long blond hair may merely indicate youth and, in what may be another of his homosexual jokes, Birago gives this figure the clumsiness of youth by having him poke the tip of his /her sword up a hare's bottom. The hare turns round, aghast.

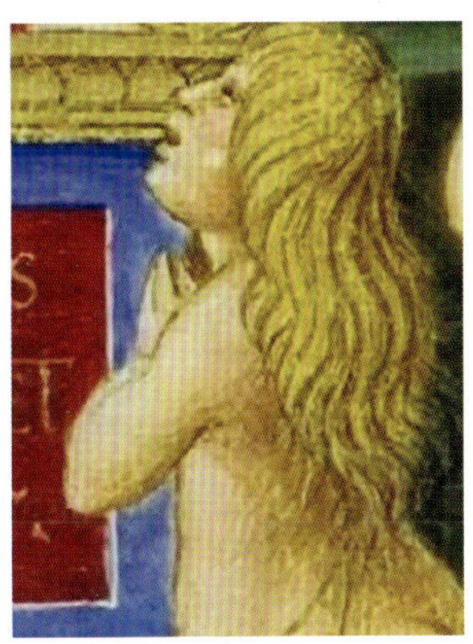 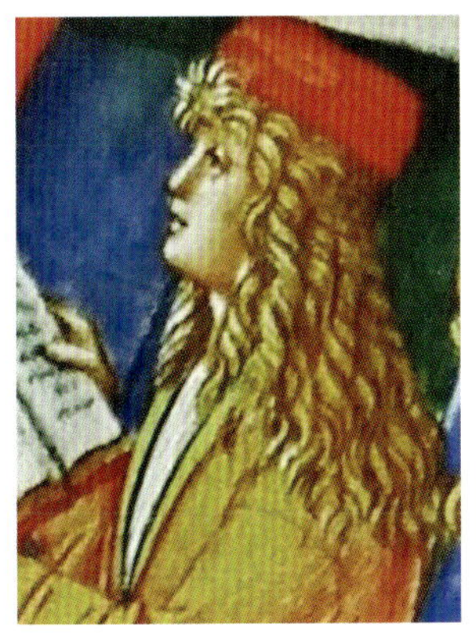

Il Moro's son and heir Massimiliano (born 1493) had long blond hair – as we know from Birago's illustrations for the *Donatus Grammatica* (*see p.218*). But what would Massimiliano be doing amidst all these Sanseverinos? Perhaps serving a symbolic double-purpose: to emphasize that the marriage is bringing the Sanseverinos into the House of Sforza; and to show that his half-sister Bianca was to be considered on an equal footing with Il Moro's legitimate children. A similar message had been trumpeted by the presence of the illegitimate Cesare in the *Pala Sforzesca* and the Paris *Sforziada*.

Il Moro is lolling on what resembles a sarcophagus, with gold balls in each corner (similar to the balls at the end of the generals' benches in the 'Uffizi' *Sforziada*). This may symbolize either the tomb of Il Moro's recently deceased nephew, Duke Gian Galeazzo; or that of Francesco Sforza, whose cumbersome paternal memory Il Moro has, with the Imperial investiture obtained, laid to rest. He is casually holding a cardinal's hat in his left hand and, with his right hand, pointing upwards in the general direction of Francesco. In the Paris *Sforziada*, too, Il Moro points heavenwards in the direction of Francesco's medallion; on that occasion his interlocutor was his hapless nephew, Gian Galeazzo.

Il Moro is also pointing at the name of *Braccio Perugino*[6] in the page's main body of text – originally a close ally, but later mortal rival, of Muzio Attendolo, the father of Francesco Sforza. The message to the Sanseverinos appears to be: *Stay Loyal.*

The sarcophagus doubles as an altar. The bridal couple are shown to the left. A dusky *Moorette* is accompanied by a larger white figure with wavy blond hair (Galeazzo Sanseverino). Portraying Miss White (Il Moro's daughter Bianca) as Mrs Black is another Birago joke. Her long blond hair is particularly incongruous against her dark skin. The half-obscured, background position in which Birago places Bianca hardly enshrines her status as bridal heroine – but perhaps reflects the fact that she was honoured elsewhere in this *Sforziada*.

Bianca's half-developed breasts – to be compared with the full-breasted sphinxes in the London *Sforziada* – reflect her age at the time of her marriage: almost, but not quite, a woman, i.e. yet to attain the age (fourteen) at which her marriage can be legally consummated. Birago draws attention to this deliberately. He could have avoided the matter by having Bianca appear clad, or by depicting her bridegroom with his arm discreetly raised a little higher.

The front of the altar/sarcophagus bears a gold-lettered inscription, on a red ground within a blue frame:

DELEGI VOS UT FRUCTUARII SITIS ET FRUCTUS V[ESTE]R MANEAT

'I have chosen you, that ye should go and bring forth fruit, and that your fruit should remain'

This passage from John 15:XVI sounds like a banal exhortation to found a family, but is quoted artfully out of context and addressed to the congregation, not just the bridal couple. Birago appears to take the words from the Latin Vulgate version of the Bible but, for some reason, slightly alters the first part of the phrase, which is usually given as *elegi vos [et posui vos] ut [eatis et] fructum adferatis*.

Birago omits the start of the verse, which begins *Ye have not chosen me* – a reminder to the assembled figures that Il Moro owes them nothing, and a warning to them not to get too big for their stockings – and ends *Whatsoever ye shall ask of the Father in my name, He may give it you* – portraying Il Moro as the guardian of the Sforza family heritage. The words in the verse are Christ's – reinforcing Birago's impious identification of Il Moro as Divine. Even more significantly, they are words spoken by Christ at the Last Supper – another reminder of the theme of betrayal that appears to have haunted Il Moro[7] once he achieved full ducal power.

Five of the figures have swords and identical stockings: red stocking on the left leg, blue-and-white stocking on the right. The colours (and elaborate halving) were standard Milan court livery, and depicted as such in illuminations dating back to the reigns of the Visconti – albeit as full-length tights rather than stockings, for which Birago had a fetish (he first assigns such stockings to the mocking putto in the London *Sforziada*).

The inference is that the Sanseverinos are swearing obeisance to the reigning Sforza, i.e. they are Moro Men. Three are praying to him. Another – the only figure with brown hair – has his arms folded reverentially. The tonsured figure has no sword or stockings. It has been suggested[8] that he is Guidantonio Arcimboldi, Archbishop of Milan from 1488–97. But what would his rôle be amidst this family group? He is more likely to be Cardinal Federigo Sanseverino, made a cardinal by Innocent VIII – at Sforza insistence – in 1489.

He is holding out his right hand plaintively, and shielding his eyes with his left hand, as if protecting himself from the glare of the sun – or rather, from the dazzling aura of Il Moro, who seems to be reminding him that he owes his cardinal's hat to Sforza backing and that, if he doesn't toe the Sforza line, he could lose it (Federigo would indeed lose his hat – but not until 1512, when he was briefly excommunicated by Pope Julius II for helping stage the rebellious Council of Pisa). In the meantime, Il Moro has 'borrowed' his hat in order, so to speak, to conduct his daughter's wedding.

The words assigned to the figures encircling Il Moro reinforce the impression that they form a coherent group:

REDEMISTI NOS - MEMENTO QUOD SUMUS TUI D[OMI]NE

'You have redeemed us – Remember thine handiwork are we, O Lord'

The first part of this quote is based on Psalm 31:V (*In manus tuas, Domine, commendo spiritum meum; redemisti me, Domine, Deus veritatis*) where the words are those of King David; they would be repeated by Christ on the Cross (*Into thine hand I commit my spirit: thou hast redeemed me, O Lord God of truth*).

The second part of the quote comes from *Ex More Docti Mystico*, an Ambrosian Chant traditionally sung at Catholic services during Lent, and written by St Gregory (Pope Gregory the Great, *c*.540–604) – who appears on the *Pala Sforzesca* as one of the Four Doctors of the Church.

The full verse is *Memento quod sumus tui/ Licet caduci, plasmatis/ Ne des honorem nominis/ Tui, precamur, alteri* ('Remember, though frail we be, That yet Thine handiwork are we; Nor let the honour of Thy name, Be by another put to shame'). Birago has added *D[omi]ne* as if to stress the Sanseverinos' obeisance towards Il Moro – their Lord in a religious as well as secular sense (the use of *Domine* here reinforces the idea that *Domino* is the semi-legible word on the plinth in the Uffizi *Sforziada*). Il Moro is again treated as God. As the poet Pistoia had recently proclaimed – there was 'One God In Heaven and One Moro Upon Earth.'[9]

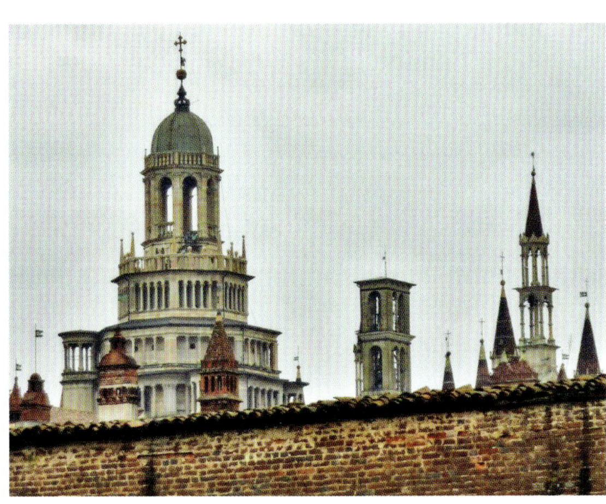

SETTING

The wedding is taking place on an island in a river, with a fortified town in the background. Distant buildings are visible to the right; towering rocks in the centre; and mountains by a river to the left.

We are looking towards the Alps. The town is Pavia. Its chunky hilltop castello can be seen on the far right, flanked by buildings of the town. A smaller, towered building some distance away, separated from the town by a mid-ground tree (and the head of the brown-haired Sanseverino), can be identified – thanks to its tall, tiered tower – as the Certosa di Pavia (*left*).

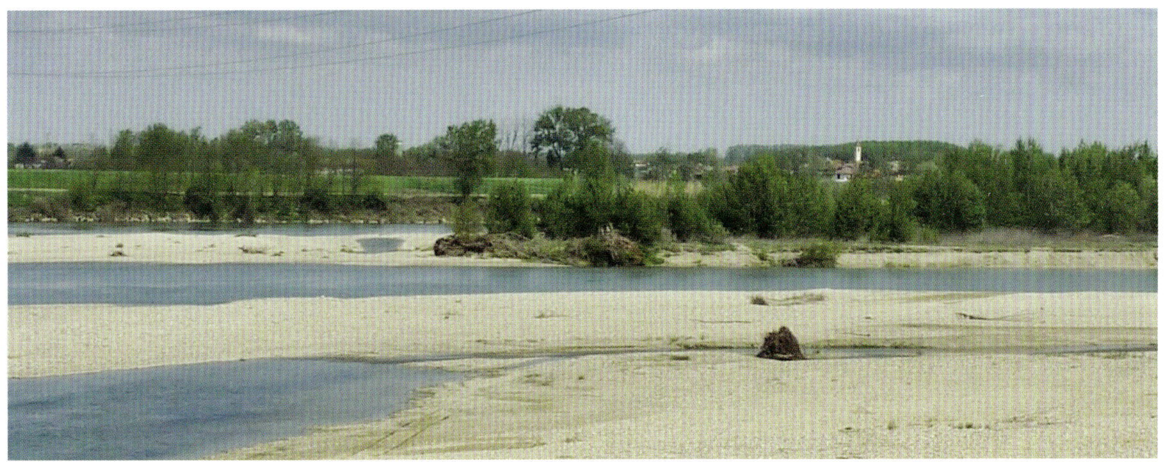

There is more to learn from this apparently random, but in fact carefully selected, setting. If we take the angles of view – rocks (Alps) centre, Pavia extreme right, Certosa in between – then draw the appropriate geometric conclusions on a map, we can deduce where the wedding scene is set: close to the confluence of the Rivers Po and Scrivia, just south of Sannazzaro de Burgondi, 25 miles southwest of Milan (*see bottom of previous page*). The river to the right, flowing past Pavia, is the Ticino.

The river to the left, flowing past more rocks to the left of Galeazzo (symbolizing the French Alps), is the Sesia. We are, in fact, at the spot where Il Moro (accompanied by Roberto Sanseverino) forded the broad, shallow Po – hereabouts peppered with sandbanks – on his way north from Tortona to Milan, and power, in 1479.[10] The viewer is facing north-northeast, with the central rocks placed exactly where Milan would be. Perhaps Birago is punningly referring to the *Rocchetta*, as Il Moro's domestic quarters in the Castello Sforzesco were known.

Behind the viewer lies the road from Milan to Genoa, which forks a few miles further on at Molino dei Torti: to the west lies Sanseverino's castle of Castelnuovo Scrivia, to the east Bianca's dower town of Voghera. Birago has a track record of including geographical settings in his work. The Paris *Sforziada* evokes the Tyrrhenian Sea between Genoa and Naples; the grammar book made for Il Moro's son Massimiliano shows the Castello Sforzesco in Milan visible through the classroom window, with the Sforza hunting-lodge of Mirabello in the middle distance – locating the classroom in the Castello at Pavia (of which Massimiliano was Count); in the *Sforza Hours*, Birago depicts the Castello Sant'Angelo in Rome, and the Certosa di Pavia on several occasions.

RIGHT BORDER

This is divided into red and blue halves, with green used down the middle inside the figures. It contains three shields but no profile medallion – the only illuminated *Sforziada* not to have one.

The border is topped by six pods and a brownish stalk flanked by two palm-sprigs, emerging from the top of a shield with the halved arms of Aragon and Sanseverino. This coat of arms belonged to Roberto Sanseverino,[11] and reflected his honorary induction into the House of Aragon by King Ferrante of Naples in 1461 (in reward for quelling a rebellion by Jean d'Anjou).

This coat of arms appears in the frontispiece (*right*) to the 1483 edition of Roberto Valturio's *De Re Militari*, translated *a nome et gloria del magnanimo capitanno*

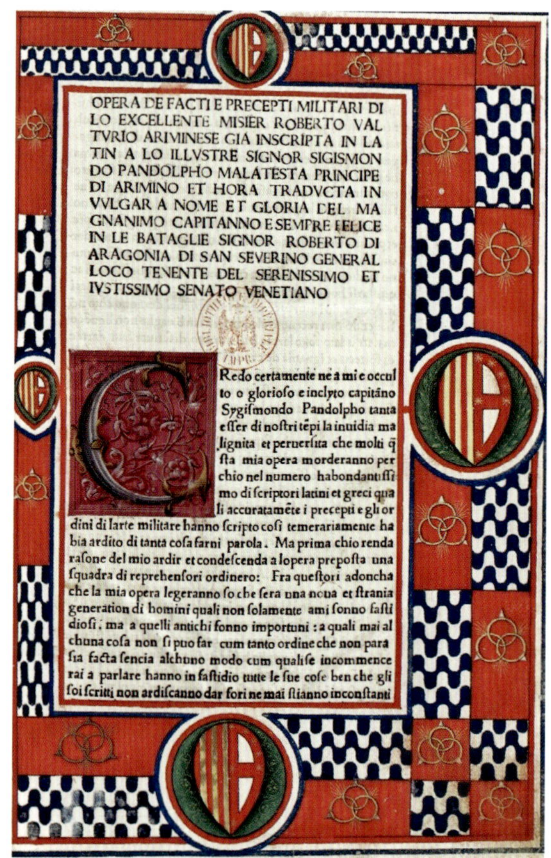

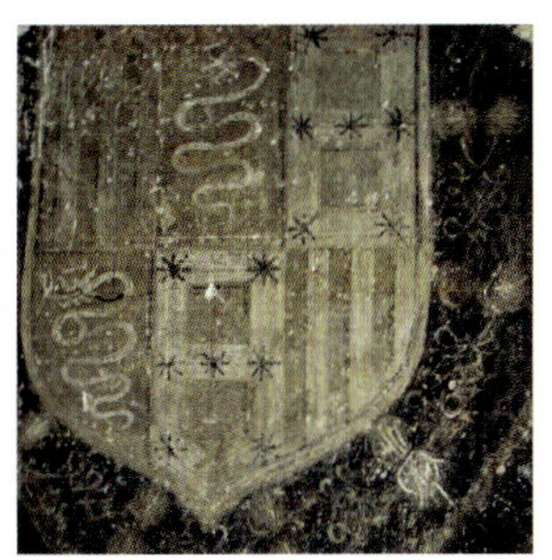

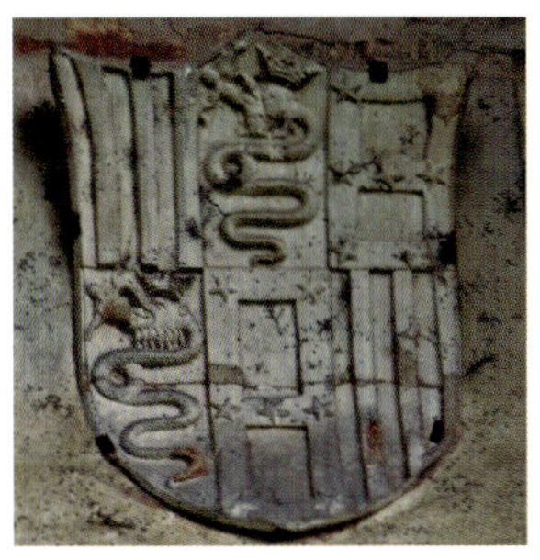

e sempre felice in le batiglie ('in the name and to the glory of the magnanimous and ever-successful Captain') *Signor Roberto di Aragonia di San Severino.*[12]

These arms were also used by Roberto's sons. They appear, in conjunction with a dedication to his son Gaspare ('Fracassa'), in an edition of Dante's *Divina Commedia* published in Venice in 1491,[13] and in two illuminated antiphonals[14] produced around 1493 for Cardinal Federigo Sanseverino in his capacity as Provost of Santa Maria Rossa in Crescenzago (the arms in these antiphonals are topped by the same cardinal's hat which Il Moro would dangle in the Polish *Sforziada*).

This family shield corresponds to the presence of five Sanseverino brothers in Birago's *bas-de-page*, although Birago has taken some aesthetic licence by painting the right (Sanseverino) half of the shield with a gold ground, rather than white or silver.

Galeazzo Sanseverino's personal arms were different. They incorporated the Sforza viper, and appear in his 1498 presentation copy of Luca Pacioli's *De Divina Proportione* (*below*) surrounded by the chain of the *Ordre de St-Michel* that he received from Charles VIII in 1494 – and flanked by the letters *GZ* that are repeated in both borders of Birago's Polish *Sforziada* frontispiece.

A second, tierced version of Galeazzo's arms, with the proportion of Aragon stripes downgraded from half to one-third, can be found at Villa Mirabello near Pavia: above the inside staircase, where the shield is ringed by the *Ordre de St-Michel*, and on the façade (*above left*). Sanseverino was granted Mirabello in the late 1490s and stayed there – with King François I and his brother-in-law the Duke of Alençon – before the Battle of Pavia in 1525, at which he was slain.[15]

The frontispiece to the 1483 edition of *De Re Militari* feature the arms of Roberto Sanseverino in all four borders – accompanied each time by blue-and-silver *vair* patterns and three interlocking diamond-rings.

The interlocking-ring device was also used by the Sforzas: Birago's re-quotes them in the Polish *Sforziada* to illustrate Sforza–Sanseverino dynastic union. The pointed-ring emblem appears in the left and right borders, while the *vair* pattern appears in the Sforza armorial shield lower right.

Arms quartered with red and blue-and-white *vair* recur in connection with the House of Sforza throughout the 15th century. They had a specifically family connotation – as opposed to the dynastic use of the viper emblem appropriated from the Viscontis.

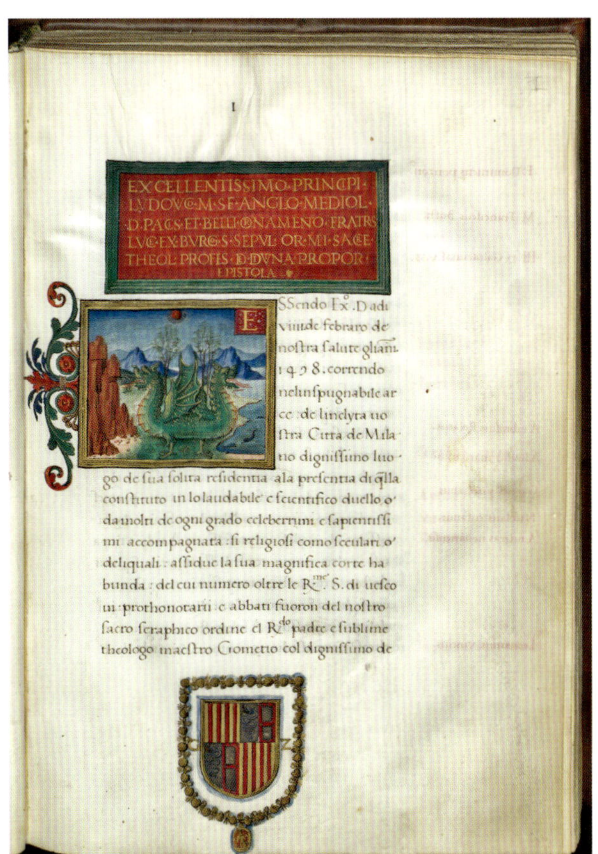

Having embellished the Sanseverino shield further up the right-hand border with extra gold, Birago transformed the Sforza shield even more drastically – inserting identical miniature scenes into its two red quarters. These show a Ship of State setting sail, beneath a red sky spangled with vertical streaks – a probable allusion to Baldassare Taccone's play *La Danae*, which sees Jupiter impregnate Danae by transforming himself into a shower of gold. This play was first performed on 31 January 1496, less than five months before the Bianca–Galeazzo wedding, at the house of Galeazzo's brother Gianfresco. The ship has a lone Moor at the helm, with a symbolic twelve oars along the side. It is modelled on the ship in the *bas-de-page* of the Paris *Sforziada* – where the Moor is solitary oarsman, but has a passenger: Duke Gian Galeazzo, since deceased.

Two naked putti flank the Sforza shield. They are standing on a gadrooned, covered font, ringed with the signature **PSBR IO PETR BIRAGUS FE** (*PRESBITER IOANNES PETRUS BIRAGUS FECIT*). Birago here signs his second successive *Sforziada* – perhaps a sign of fame.[16]

The font's design resembles that of the white marble fountain made in the 1480s in the workshop of Andrea del Verrocchio (where Leonardo apprenticed) for Matthias Corvinus, and placed in Buda Castle.[17] A font of similar gadrooned design also appears – used for baptism – in a Birago illumination for the *Sforza Hours* (*fol. 198v*).[18] It seems apposite that Presbyter Birago should place his signature on a font.

Between the Sforza and Sanseverino shields is a third shield of the same height, bearing a sifting-cloth – the classic Sforza matrimonial emblem – on a red ground with more gold rain, beneath the scrolled motto *TAL A TI QUAL A MI* (*To You As To Me*) entwined around the blue-sleeved arms that hold the cloth.

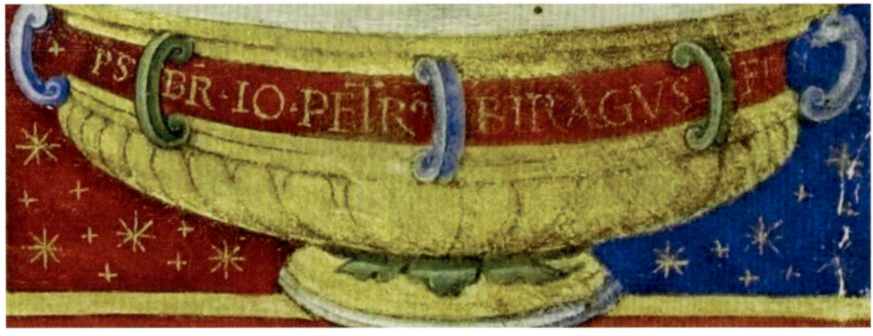

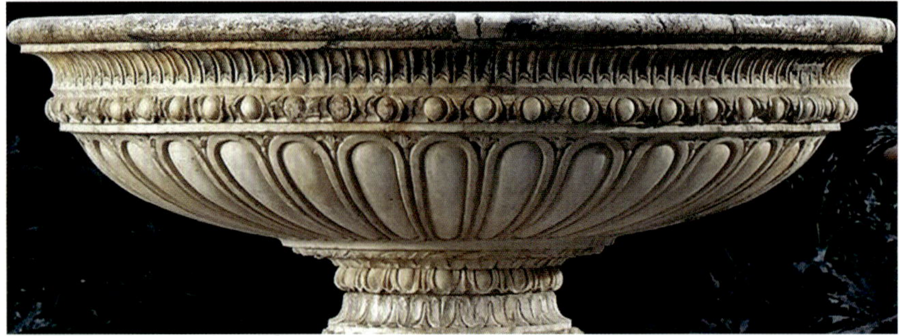

The shield is flanked by two 'Wild Men' clad from neck to ankle in animal-skin costumes with holes at the knee. The figure on the left has a long, rough, wooden club in his right hand; the figure on the right has a club in his left hand, but it is behind his legs and almost invisible to the naked eye. It is tempting to see here Birago mocking the knightly Sanseverino, whose favoured weapon was a slender lance rather than a ragged club.

Beneath the shield are a sapphire and emerald, ringed by scrolling foliage with pearl-drops, then a naked, winged-angel drummer-cum-piper on a green field strewn with acorns, flanked by two cornucopia. Like every figure in the right-hand border, this musician casts a shadow to the right, as if the sun were shining from the left – i.e. from the *bas-de-page* figure of Il Moro, the new Apollo. Above the shield is an urn flanked by golden military trophies: a quiver with four arrows, crossed by a bow; crossed swords below a circular shield; and crossed shields, one pair placed on crossed swords, the other on crossed clubs.

Impaled above both groups of trophies are two quinces – the emblem of Muzio Attendolo, Galeazzo's and Bianca's nearest common ancestor (Roberto Sanseverino was the son of Muzio's daughter Elisa). These trophies are similar to those in Muzio's full-page equestrian portrait in the de luxe manuscript of the *Vita di Muzio Attendolo Sforza* produced for Il Moro in 1491 (*see p.40*).

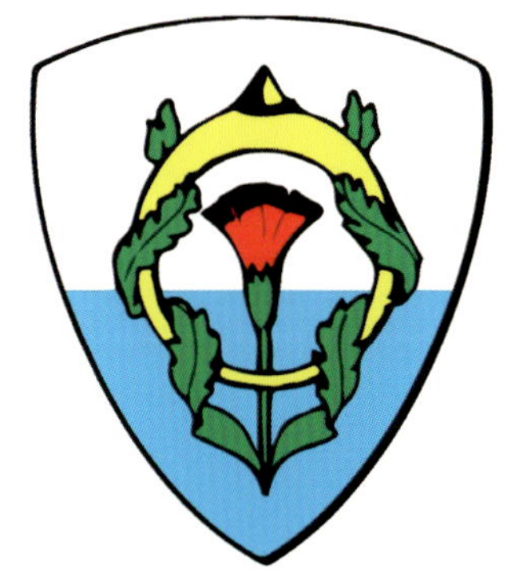

Above these trophies, dangling from crested dolphin-heads, are three interlocking rings, each with a sharply pointed, pyramidal diamond. Accounts vary as to how these rings came to be used by the Sforzas.[19] The most common explanation is that, as a reward for slaying troublesome mercenary Ottobuono Terzi in 1409, Muzio was given the right to use them by Niccolo III d'Este – who had himself been granted the right to use them by Pope Boniface IX after being made *Gonfaloniere* (Standard-Bearer) of the Church in 1403.[20] The Estes duly termed these rings 'episcopal' (*anelli episcopali*).

The right to use the rings was later bestowed by Francesco Sforza on Roberto Sanseverino – making it the most apposite symbol of the marriage between the two families, and explaining its presence in both the left and right borders of the *Sforziada* frontispiece.

The sifting-cloth used to separate flour from bran also appears in each border.[21] The combination of ring and sifting-cloth features on the bodice of Beatrice d'Este in her bust by Cristoforo Romano (*left*) – as a single integrated device, said to have been created by Beatrice's father Ercole I, that also incorporates a flower: originally a *margherita* (daisy or marguerite), later a *garofano* (carnation). This ring-and-flower emblem is carved in stone in the courtyard of Ferrara Castle, and is used to this day as the emblem of the Ferrara *Palio* (*above left*).

LEFT BORDER

The background is divided into blue (*left*) and red (*right*), with green used down the middle. A winged helmet at the top contains a curious black void, above a pair of crossed shields, with a *G* on one and a *Z* on the other, above a scrolling heart overlaid with a grey (originally silver) belt. The black void and silver belt represent alterations to Birago's original design. Their significance is discussed in *Chapter X*.

Further down comes a kneeling winged cherub, playing the fiddle on a round stand emerging from two flaming horns of plenty, just above two hands holding a white sifting-cloth whose contents are seeping on to three interlocking diamond rings.

Further down come a gold leaf-mask, pearls, scrolling, and a multi-tiered fountain supported on a narrow shaft that emerges from a headless, gold-spangled blue breastplate[22] above a bronze skirt.

The bottom section of the breastplate is curling upwards as if powerfully erect, in what appears to be Birago's now inevitable *Sforziada* homosexual allusion. Is he referring to Leonardo's involvement in this particular *Sforziada*, or lampooning Galeazzo Sanseverino?

DATE

Mid-1496. This *Sforziada*, with its full-page portrait of Bianca Sforza and frontispiece evoking her bridegroom's family, the Sanseverinos, was produced to commemorate their marriage on 20 June 1496. It would logically have been presented on that occasion, although there is no proof of that.

Background anecdote provides a possible clue about the volume's completion. On 8 June 1496 a court report cites an unnamed artist, painting the *camerini* next to the Sala delle Asse in the Castello Sforzesco, causing a scandal and storming out: *El pictore quale pinzeva li camerini nostri, ogi ha facto certo scandalo per el quale si è absentato … .*[23]

This unnamed artist is thought to have been Leonardo da Vinci, but the reason for such an outburst is unknown.

Could it have to do with a change in the date of Bianca's wedding, perhaps originally slated for her saint's day – July 9?

On May 25 news was sent from distant Ulm[24] that Emperor Maximilian was planning to cross the Alps with cavalry and a sizable retinue, to meet Il Moro in Bormio.

The news from Ulm will have taken nearly two weeks by horse-messenger to reach Milan, arriving around … June 7/8.

The date of Bianca's wedding may have been affected: Il Moro could not afford to keep his Imperial ally waiting. Suddenly the marriage would have been no longer a month but less than a fortnight away, and the new de luxe *Sforziada*, with its portrait and first quire, needed post-haste.

On the other hand, Il Moro may have settled on the June 20 date for some astrological reason.

Or to commemorate the birthday of his late nephew, Duke Gian Galeazzo – born in Abbiategrasso on 20 June 1469.

INTERPRETATION

The tone of Birago's frontispiece blends humour and menace. Like many despots, Il Moro was haunted by fear of treachery after achieving supreme power (perhaps partly from remorse about the unscrupulous means he had used *en route*): one of his first deeds as Duke was to commission Leonardo's *Last Supper*.

Il Moro's right index-finger jab towards the portrait of Francesco Sforza perhaps implies that Galeazzo Sanseverino is the 'new Francesco,' or that Il Moro is anointing Galeazzo his successor. This impression is underscored by the words pronounced by Il Moro: *EXEMPLAR INCLITU IMITAMINI* (*Imitate the Illustrious Example*).

Comparisons between Galeazzo Sanseverino and Francesco Sforza were inevitable: the Captain of Arms who marries the Duke's naturalized daughter, in each case called Bianca, and in each case twenty years his junior … .

Birago draws attention to these parallels by choosing, for the central image of the *haut-de-page*, the dog-and-pine emblem irrevocably associated with Francesco (*cf* his breastplate in the London *Sforziada* and his tabard in the Certosa di Pavia transept fresco).

No doubt Sanseverino's enemies also feared that he planned to pursue the Francesco parallel to its logical conclusion: by becoming Duke himself. Although Il Moro had stipulated that – should he die before their elder son Massimiliano reached his majority – his wife Beatrice should rule as Regent, recent history suggested any such precaution would have scant effect: Bona di Savoia's regency in the name of Gian Galeazzo lasted just three years; Isabel of Aragon was given no chance to rule in the name of Il Duchetto (in each case it was Il Moro himself who deprived the dowager duchesses of their rights).

Galeazzo Sanseverino had been Il Moro's effective Number Two since 1488. By marrying Bianca, and entering the Sforza family inner circle, he may well have considered himself a 'heartbeat from power.'

There is, significantly, no horse on the page, even though horses were Sanseverino's chief claim to fame; the implication is that Galeazzo is far more than a mere jouster or equerry.

By quoting the arms of Roberto Sanseverino top-right, Il Moro was paying off a moral debt: he owed his triumphant return to Milan, in 1479, in large part to Roberto – with whom he quarrelled irrevocably soon after.

It could be said that in 1496, in God-like fashion, he offered his only-begotten daughter to achieve redemption. Is she being brought to a tomb or an altar? Birago hardly portrays her as the epitome of a glamorous bride: she is blocked off unchivalrously by her husband-to-be, and the most minor figure in the *bas-de-page*. 'Best to keep at arm's length from this lot,' Birago seems to be saying.

BIRAGO QUOTES LEONARDO

Birago has Il Moro exhort his audience to 'imitate the illustrious example' (*EXEMPLAR INCLITU IMITAMINI*) – in apparent reference to Francesco Sforza. But these words could equally apply to Leonardo da Vinci, so numerous are Birago's *bas-de-page* references to his Florentine colleague:

'The Musician'

Same tilt of the head, same large eyes, same outline of the left cheek, same wavy blond hair, same fleshy nose ... the similarities between Birago's caricature of Galeazzo Sanseverino and Leonardo's 'Musician' are glaring.

To stress family kinship Birago grants all five, large white male figures the same bulging eyes – noticeably larger than those of Bianca and Il Moro.[25]

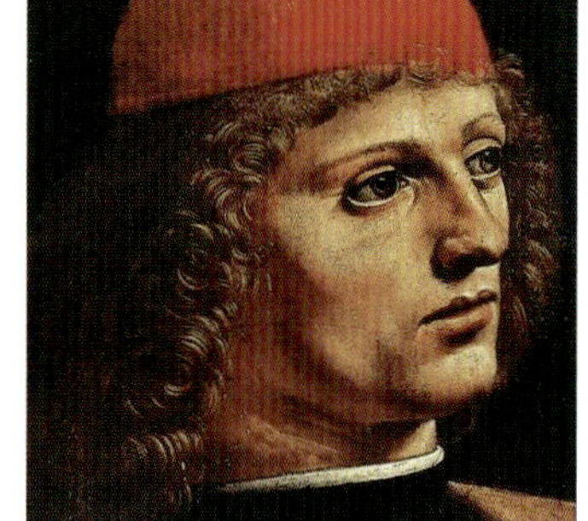

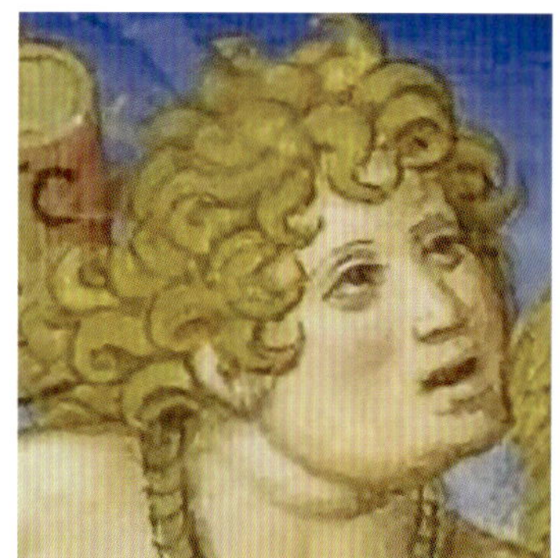

Vitruvian Man

Galeazzo's right arm is stretched out behind him; his left is not around his bride, nor even slightly bent to 'give her his arm' – but stretched out horizontally, as if blocking her off. It is a grotesquely unnatural pose. His right leg is sticking out at such a peculiar angle that we can hardly even see it, almost totally obscured by the kneeling figure in front

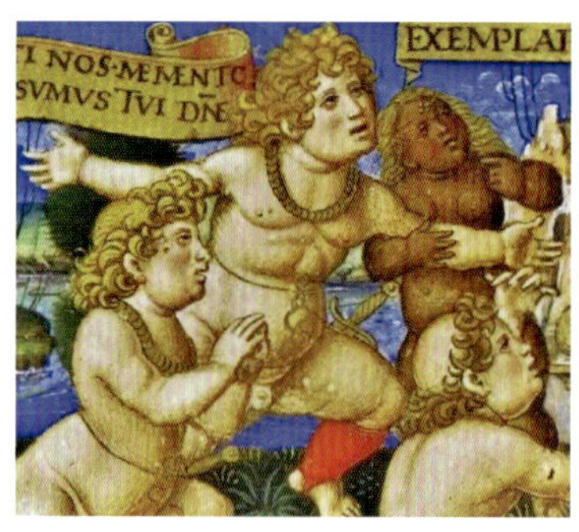

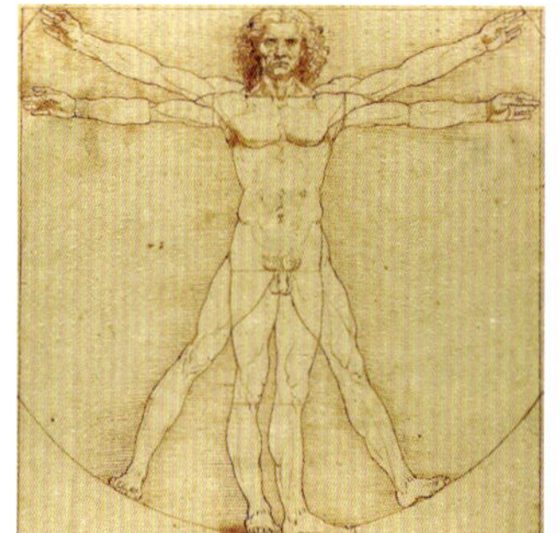

of him. The likely explanation of such physical contortion? Birago is quoting Leonardo's *Vitruvian Man*, and simultaneously sending up Sanseverino's pretensions to be the *uomo* (or *genero*) *ideale*.

The Last Supper

Birago has Il Moro quote Christ's words at the Last Supper. The reference to the giant mural in Santa Maria delle Grazie, upon which Leonardo was working at the time of this frontispiece, could not be clearer. Il Moro, like Christ, is shown addressing his 'disciples.'

La Belle Ferronnière

Bianca is naked except for a tiny *gioiello da testa* or *ferronnière* tied around her forehead, almost invisible to the naked eye. Perhaps it is added for a symbolic purpose: to quote Leonardo's *La Belle Ferronnière* – commonly supposed to depict Il Moro's mistress Lucrezia Crivelli.[26] Ticklishly topical: Crivelli became pregnant by Il Moro in 1496.

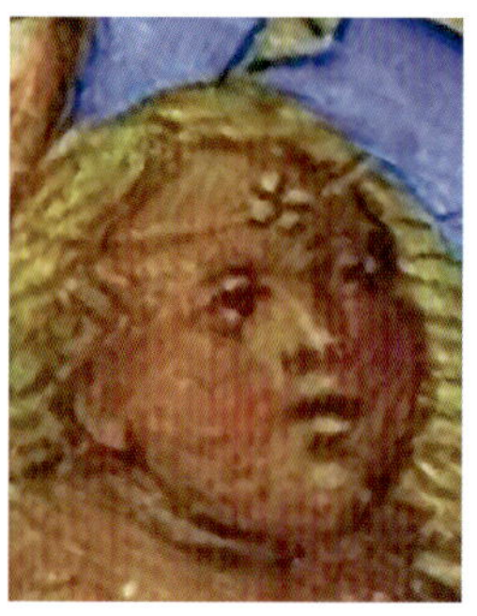

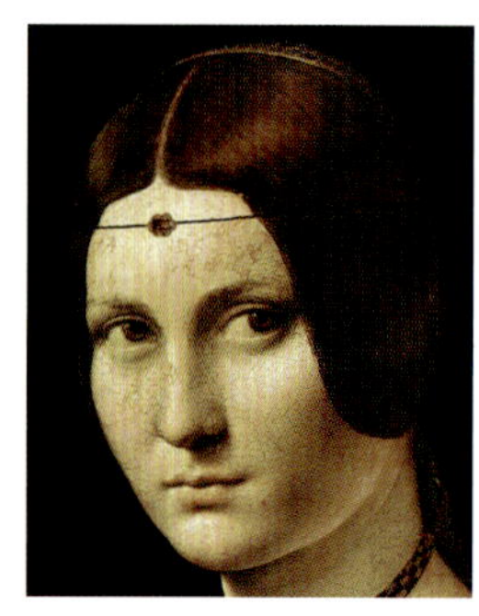

Virgin of the Rocks

The work that established Leonardo's Milanese reputation is the one Birago references most abundantly:

– his *bas-de-page* scene is located, like the *Virgin of the Rocks*, by the water's edge. Birago's stylized background rocks strongly recall those in the background of the *Virgin of the Rocks*.

– like Leonardo's angel in the first version of the *Virgin of the Rocks*, Bianca is pointing with her index finger at a blond-haired 'infant' on the far left of the picture (Galeazzo Sanseverino).

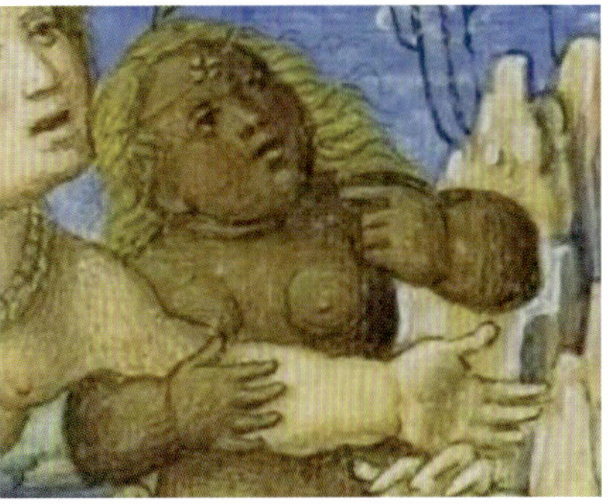
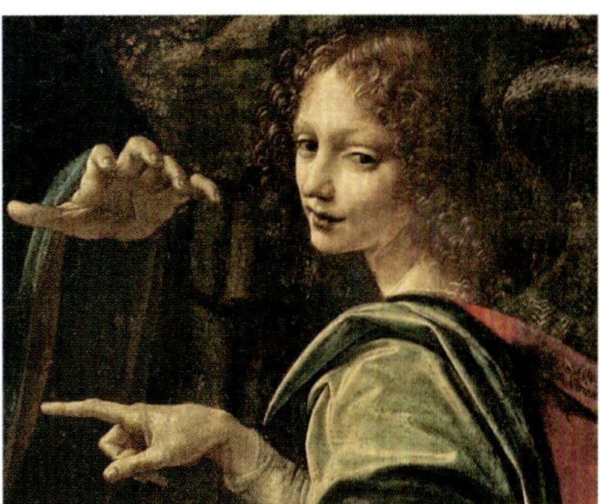

– the kneeling cherub to the left, hands clasped in prayer as he pays homage to Il Moro, seems to be modelled directly on the infant John the Baptist in the *Virgin of the Rocks*, who is similarly shown against the left edge of the picture with hands clasped in homage (to the infant Christ).

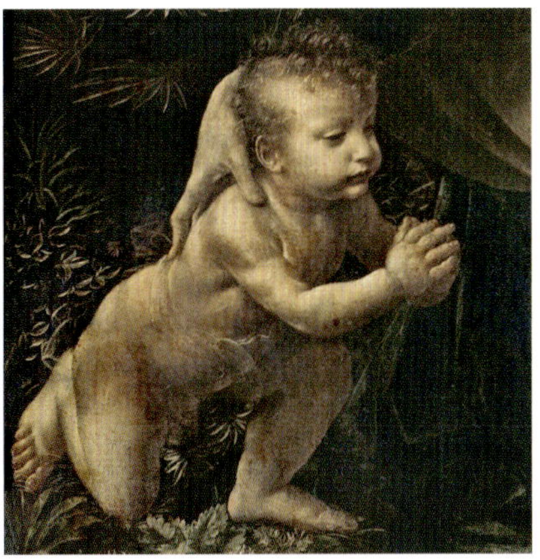
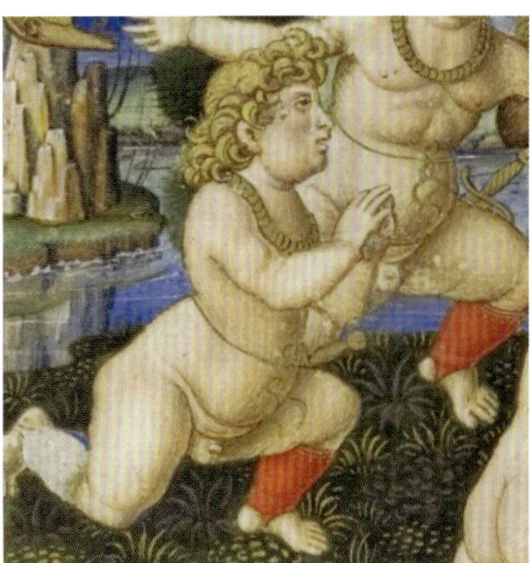

– the sexual ambiguity of the long-haired cherub to the right of Il Moro recalls that of the androgynous angel similarly positioned in the *Virgin of the Rocks*.

– the central position of the Virgin **Mary** is occupied in Birago's scene by her quasi-namesake Ludovico ***Maria*** Sforza.

– the *Virgin of the Rocks* is an altarpiece – and Il Moro is lolling on an altar, waiting for the bride and groom.

Ginevra de' Benci

Given this plethora of visual coincidences, one is entitled to wonder if the second cherub from the right in Birago's scene – the only one with brown hair and folded arms – is 'odd man out' for a reason. Is Birago quoting Leonardo's youthful portrait of *Ginevra de' Benci* who, it is believed, was originally (before her panel was shorn of its lower section) portrayed with arms crossed?[27]

Further References

There are further references to Leonardo around the borders of Birago's frontispiece:

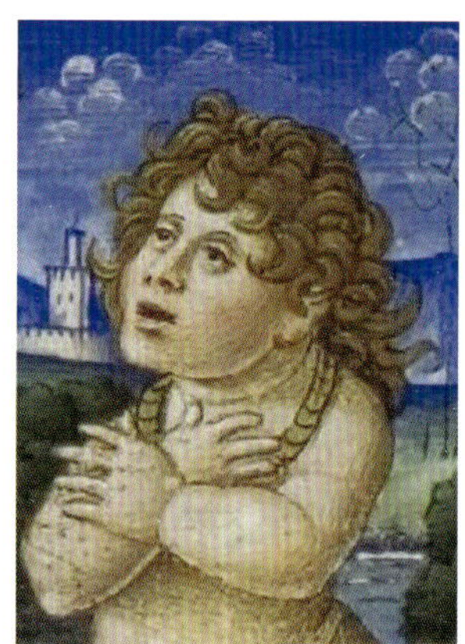

– the **Lyre-Player** at the top of the page evokes the instrument he reputedly played so well.

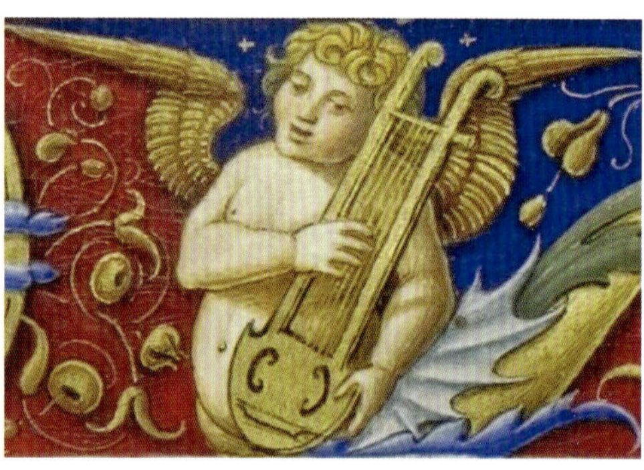

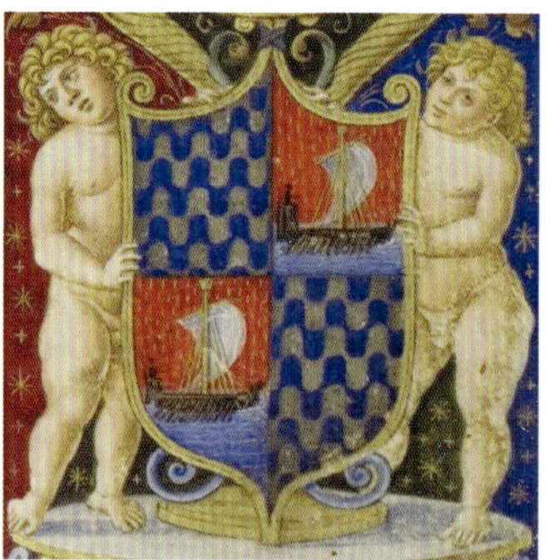

– the **Golden Rain** in the middle and lower armorial shields was a stage-effect for the 1496 production of *La Danae* master-minded by Leonardo.

– the **'Wild Men'** costumes recall those Leonardo designed for Galeazzo Sanseverino and his knights for a pageant celebrating Il Moro's wedding in 1491 (while the ragged staff recalls a Leonardo drawing in the Queen's Collection, *far right*).

Is the facetious Birago mocking Leonardo as a 'mere costume designer'?

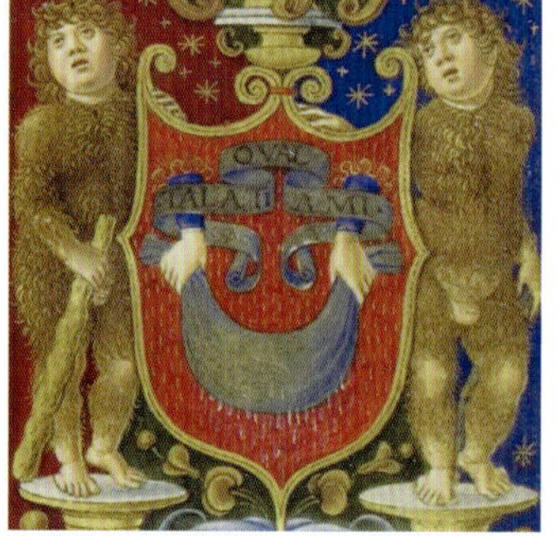

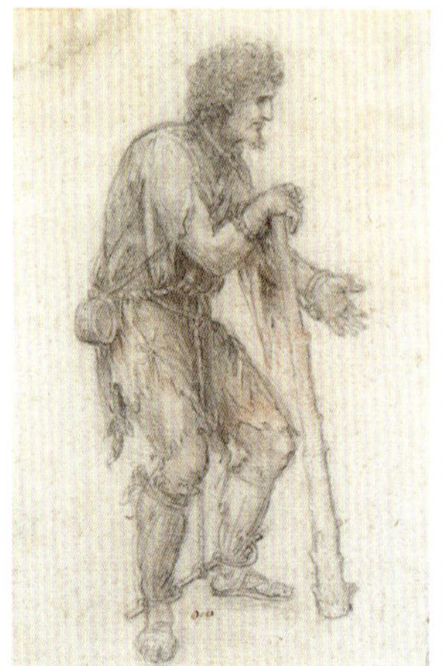

Or is Birago drawing attention to the artistic colleague with whom he collaborated on this final presentation copy of the *Sforziada*?

1 The Macrino d'Alba altarpiece is in the Certosa di Pavia's Chapel of Sant' Ugo, and features a *Virgin Enthroned*.

2 Gianfrancesco Sanseverino (c.1450–1502), the eldest of the Sanseverino brothers, was made a Milanese army captain in 1483, and became 2nd Count of Caiazzo after his father's death in 1487. **Antonio Maria Sanseverino** (c.1452–1509) is first mentioned in Milan in 1483. He was married to Margherita Pio de Savoia (died after 1524), daughter of Marco, Lord of Carpi. **Gaspare Sanseverino** (1455–1519), known as 'Fracassa' because of his turbulent temperament, is first mentioned in Florence in 1475. After Il Moro's split with his father Roberto he initially sided with the latter and, in January 1482, was besieged in Castelnuovo Scrivia by Gian Giacomo Trivulzio, captured, and taken to Milan – but escaped to France. He entered Milanese service in the late 1480s. **Cardinal Federigo Sanseverino** (c.1475–1516), much younger half-brother to the above, was named Bishop of Maillezais (in western France) in 1481. He was part of Isabel of Aragon's reception party in Genoa in January 1489 – a few weeks before he was secretly made an under-age cardinal, with Sforza backing, by Pope Innocent VIII. He became Provost of Crescenzago in Milan in 1492. He was arrested on 10 December 1494 by Pope Alexander VI, along with Cardinal Ascanio Sforza. Both priests were soon freed under pressure from Il Moro and Charles VIII. In February 1496, at Il Moro's request and with the support of Holy Roman Emperor Maximilian I, Federigo was appointed Bishop of Thérouanne, near St-Omer in northern France, a post he retained until November 1498.

3 Giovanni Adorno was a prominent Milanese courtier: along with Galeazzo and Antonio Maria Sanseverino, he was a witness to the swearing-in of Bernardino da Corte as the new Milan Castellan on 12 January 1495.

4 Elizabeth McGrath, *Ludovico Il Moro and His Moors* (2002).

5 Mariangela Mazzocchi Doglio, *Leonardo e gli Spettacoli del suo Tempo* (Milan, 1983).

6 More usually known as **Braccio da Montone** (1368–1424), born Andrea Fortebracci in Montone, 25 miles north of Perugia, and Muzio's exact contemporary and early companion. Later he fought for Giovanna II of Naples and Alfonso of Aragon in their power-struggle against Louis III of Anjou, whose troops were led by Muzio. The two most celebrated condottieri of their day clashed for the last time at Bazzano, near L'Aquila, on 2 June 1424. Muzio drowned in the River Pescara and Braccio was mortally wounded, dying in L'Aquila three days later.

7 And well it might. Ending in the suspected poisoning of his nephew in 1494, Il Moro's rise to power from the unlikely starting-point of Number 4 Son is littered with suspicious deaths – not forgetting his own betrayal of the man who helped engineer his rise, Roberto Sanseverino: Galeazzo's father. *The Last Supper* was commissioned by a man who knew the meaning of treachery.

8 Bogdan Horodyski, *Miniaturzysta Sforzów* (*Biuletyn Historii Stuki*, Warsaw 1954).

9 Cartwright, *op. cit.*

10 Source: *Associazione Famaleonis*.

11 This coat of arms was wrongly identified by Horodyski as a combination of the arms of Milan and Aragon, in line with his patriotic hypothesis that the Polish *Sforziada* was destined for Isabel of Aragon's daughter Bona Sforza, future Queen of Poland.

12 Roberto Valturio (1405–75). His book was first published in 1472 and dedicated to Sigismondo Pandolfo Malatesta (1417–68), the 'Wolf of Rimini.'

13 *Divina Commedia* by Dante, with commentary by Cristoforo Landino, illuminated by Antonio Grifo (?) and published by Pietro Cremonese, Venice 1491 (now in the Casa di Dante, Roma).

14 Now in the archives of Sant'Ambrogio in Milan.

15 Marco Galandra, *La Figura di Galeazzo Sanseverino e delle Consorte Banca Giovanna* (Agipapress, 14 May 2016).

16 Horodyski (*op. cit.*) was the first person to point out the identity of the *Sforziada* miniaturist, though mistook the font for a 'marble vase.'

17 Daniel Pocs, *White Marble Sculptures from Buda Castle, in Italy & Hungary: Humanism and Art in the Early Renaissance* – Villa I Tatti (Milan 2011).

18 The design of this fountain was probably based on the fountain attributed to Antonio Rossellino and Benedetto da Maiano, originally for Guglielmo de Pazzi's palazzo in Florence and now in the Metropolitan Museum, New York (Blumenthal Collection).

19 Another explanation of the interlocking rings has them down as originally an emblem of Cremona, and said to symbolize the triple alliance directed against Ladislas of Naples (brother of Giovanna II cited in the opening sentence of the *Sforziada*) concluded around 1412 between Cabrino Fondulo, who ruled Cremona 1406–20; Sigismund of Luxembourg, King of the Romans; and Antipope John XXIII (reigned 1410–15). Fondulo was beheaded in Pavia after Cremona was conquered in 1420 by the Duke of Milan, Filippo Maria Visconti, who 'recuperated' the ring-emblem as a symbol of the town (the emblem appears in a 15th century coat of arms on the ceiling of the arcade beneath Cremona's city hall, or Palazzo del Comune). When Filippo Maria's illegitimate daughter Bianca Maria (1423–68) was betrothed to Francesco Sforza in 1432, Cremona was provided as dowry. The marriage took place in 1441 at the church of San Sigismundo just outside Cremona. The rings were of special importance to Francesco Sforza as the emblem of the only territory to which he had legal title (as opposed to Milan, which he effectively conquered by force of arms). Coins were minted under his reign featuring the ring-emblem, and he granted its use, as a favour, to his leading allies – including the Borromeo, Cavazzi della Somaglia and Birago families, as well as the Sanseverinos.

20 This idiosyncratic ring appears in the 15th century Palazzo Borromeo in Milan, and in the 17th century Borromeo palace on Isola Bella in Lake Maggiore; the Borromeos claimed that the three rings represented the Visconti, Sforza and Borromeo families. The Medici used the same rings in combinations of either three or four – both appear on the dress of Pallas Athene in Botticelli's *Pallas and the Centaur* (c.1482) now in the Uffizi.

21 Horodyski (*op. cit.*) was bamboozled by the sifting-cloth, which he poetically likened to a 'bow filled with tears, which fall from the bow like rain.'

22 An identical gold-specked blue breastplate is to be found in Birago's image of *St George* in the *Sforza Hours* (fol. 195v).

23 Beltrami, *op. cit.*

24 In the event, due to domestic political squabbling (the German lords strongly opposed Maximilian embarking on another Italian venture) and money problems (anticipated tax income failed to arrive, so Maximilian had to beg loans from Milan and Venice), Maximilian's arrival was postponed until July.

25 The first art historian to identify 'The Musician' as Galeazzo Sanseverino was Paul Müller-Walde – albeit for two wrong reasons: he mistakenly supposed (a) that it was a companion portrait to the smiling female profile in the Ambrosiana, and (b) that the latter portrayed Galeazzo's bride Bianca.

26 This would suggest that *La Belle Ferronnière* was at least begun in 1496: *cf* the November 1496 report of the envoy of Ferrara: 'The latest news from Milan is that the Duke spends his whole time and finds all his pleasure in the company of a girl who is one of his wife's maidens. His conduct is ill-regarded.'

27 David Alan Brown, *Leonardo da Vinci – Origins of a Genius* (Yale University Press, 1998).

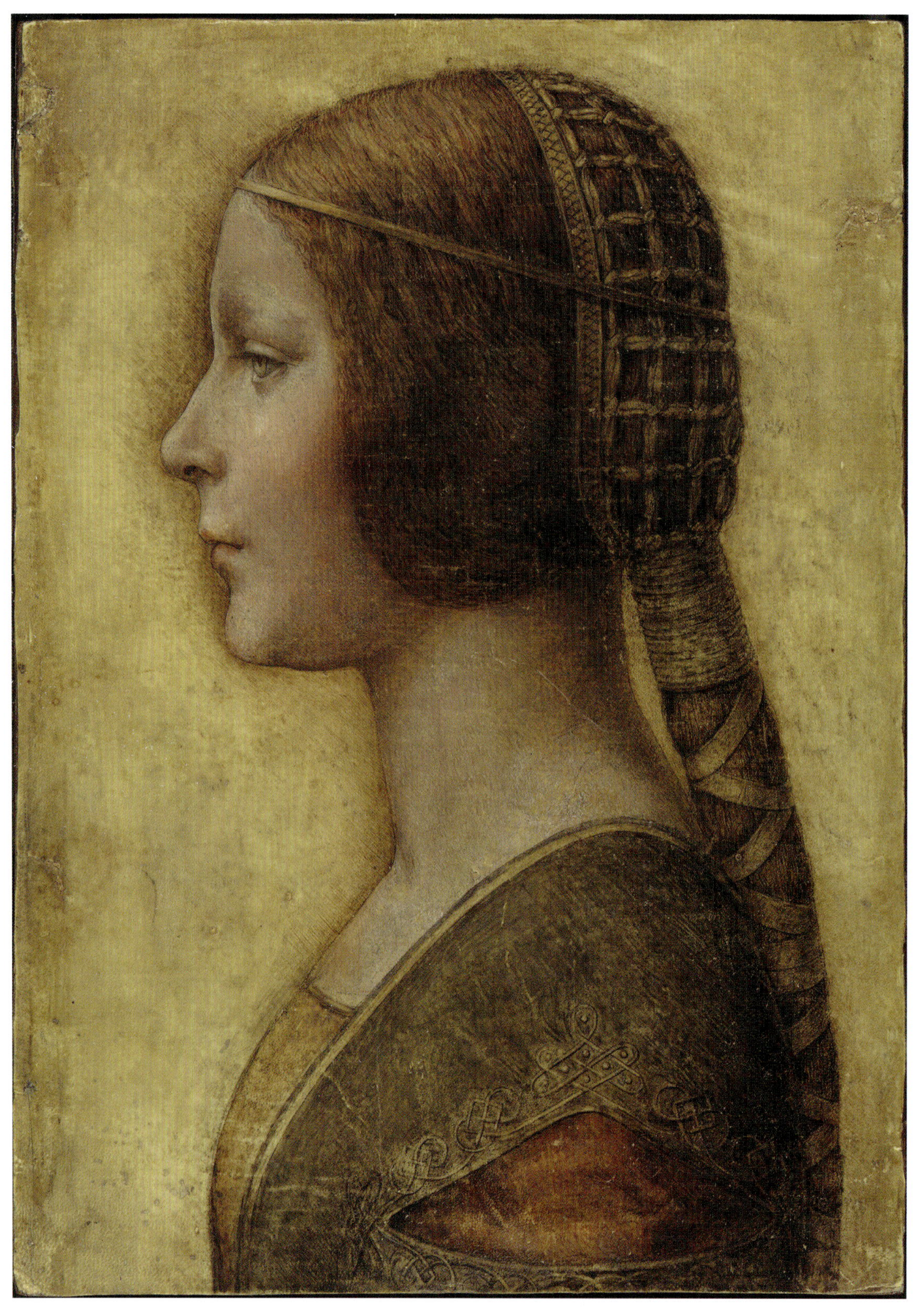

LEONARDO DA VINCI: *BIANCA SFORZA* (1496) – CHALK & INK ON VELLUM 33 × 24 cm

X

BIANCA SFORZA
THE LADY OF BOBBIO

LEONARDO DA VINCI'S innovative portrait of Bianca Sforza, teenage daughter of the Duke of Milan, was one of just four portraits he made during his sixteen-year stay at Il Moro's court. His other sitters are identified in this volume as Il Moro's mistresses, Cecilia Gallerani and Lucrezia Crivelli, and Bianca's husband, Galeazzo Sanseverino. Leonardo never painted Il Moro – or his wife Beatrice d'Este.

The *Sforziada* portrait of Bianca Sforza, originally placed on Folio *7r* (page 15) but later removed, shows Il Moro's daughter in profile,[1] facing left, probably aged thirteen.

Leonardo displayed little interest in the rigid convention of the Sforza portrait profile – but made an exception for the marriage of Il Moro's only daughter to his friend Galeazzo Sanseverino. Not even Ambrogio de Predis – portrayer of kings, emperors, Il Moro's sons and Il Moro himself – was deemed up to the task of capturing Il Moro's beloved daughter for eternity. Birago, on the next folio, counter-balanced the solemn protocol of Leonardo's portrait with a zanily irreverent *Sforziada* composition.

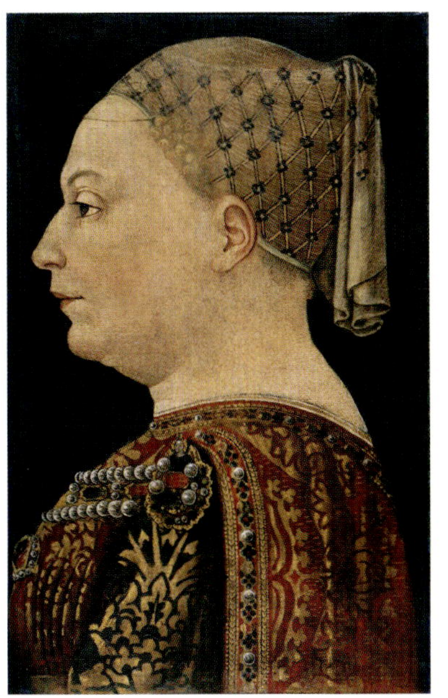

ANON.
BIANCA MARIA VISCONTI
49 × 31 cm
PINACOTECA DI BRERA

Leonardo's portrait of Bianca may also have been a reply to the profiled portraits of Ambrogio de Predis. The smiling twinkle in the eye of Ambrogio's sitters does not convey the psychological subtlety of Leonardo's *Musician*, *Lady with Ermine* or *Belle Ferronnière*. Is *La Belle Ferronnière* (on which Leonardo worked at roughly the same time as *Bianca*) looking at us with mistrust, hope or disdain? Is Bianca's gaze regal, serene or wistful? Is she gazing into the Future or the Past?

Leonardo shows Bianca with a fresh, rosy-cheeked complexion, a longish neck and a typical family nose – slightly bridged near the top – inherited from her paternal grandmother Bianca Maria Visconti, after whom she was named.

Her straw-blond hair is tied in a *coazzone* made of twine connected to an openwork grid-patterned net (comprising 96 squares in sixteen rows of six) lined with ribbon embroidered with an interlacing pattern.

Bianca, to employ the official fashion terminology, is wearing a *lionato* (tawny yellow) *camora* (dress) topped by a *sambugato* (elderberry green) *mongino* (surcoat) with a *cremexile* (dark red) shoulder aperture

171

ringed by gold embroidery.[2] Perhaps these are the same garments in which she attended Bianca Maria's proxy wedding to Maximilian in Milan Cathedral on 30 November 1493, when 'all the ladies of the Queen wore tan-coloured *camoras* and mantles of bright green satin' (as Beatrice d'Este informed her sister Isabella).[3]

Martin Kemp has explored the rules of proportion which Leonardo respected in his portrait of Bianca.[4] There is no reason to suppose that the portrait is idealized in any other way. Her head is somewhat small, the gap between nose and top lip unusually wide, she looks a tad thin; she is pleasant-looking, but this is no exercise in beauty propaganda.

Leonardo painted several attractive females, but that does not mean to say he embellished them. Bianca's clothes are sober. There is no sumptuous decoration to detract attention from the sitter's face and expression. Her lack of jewellery is par for the course among Leonardo's female sitters, mistresses excepted; neither Ginevra de' Benci, Mona Lisa nor the extravagant Isabella d'Este wear jewellery.

The relative plainness of Bianca's attire places maximum emphasis on the sitter, and on Leonardo's skill at capturing her likeness both physically and psychologically. This is his only known portrait on vellum – and his only large, coloured portrait in profile (his 1500 portrait of Isabella d'Este being virtually monochrome). Its exceptional subtlety is obtained through skilful use of the vellum support.

The simple, twine *coazzone* worn by Bianca has the same design as that worn by Beatrice d'Este in her 1490 bust by Romano (*right*), which features two devices on the bodice that recur in Birago's 1496 *Sforziada* frontispiece: the sifting-cloth and the pointed diamond ring.

Leonardo quotes two more decorative features from Beatrice's bust: the *coazzone*, and the knot-pattern embroidery on Beatrice's *shernia* – reproduced almost exactly on the top and sides of the triangular pattern around the shoulder aperture on Bianca's dress.

Were these similarities meant to show Il Moro's illegitimate daughter looking like a future duchess, on a social par with his wife, Beatrice d'Este?

Bianca's *vinci* pattern – of unparalleled design and remarkable complexity – is not just a Leonardo signature device but, as the work's only decorative feature, a focus of attention in the bottom-right of the picture that counterbalances Bianca's intent gaze upper left.

Certain motifs on the ceiling of the Sagrestia del Bramante (*see opposite*) at Santa Maria delle Grazie, completed just after the death of Bianca (who was buried under the

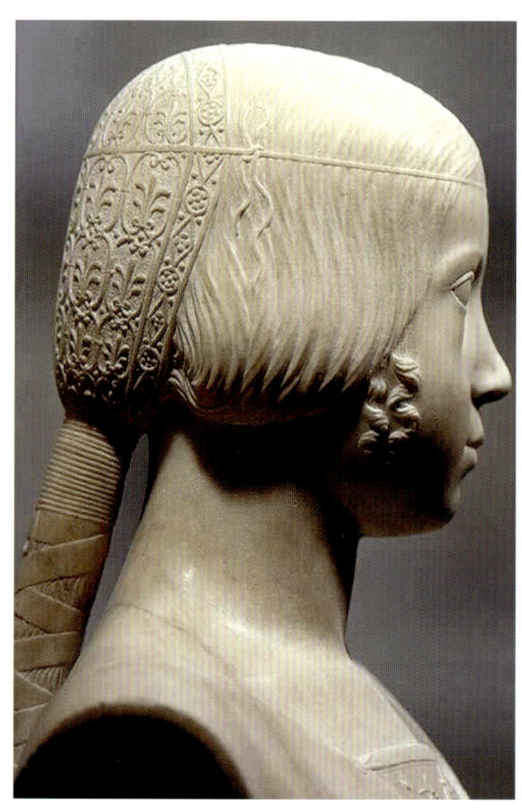

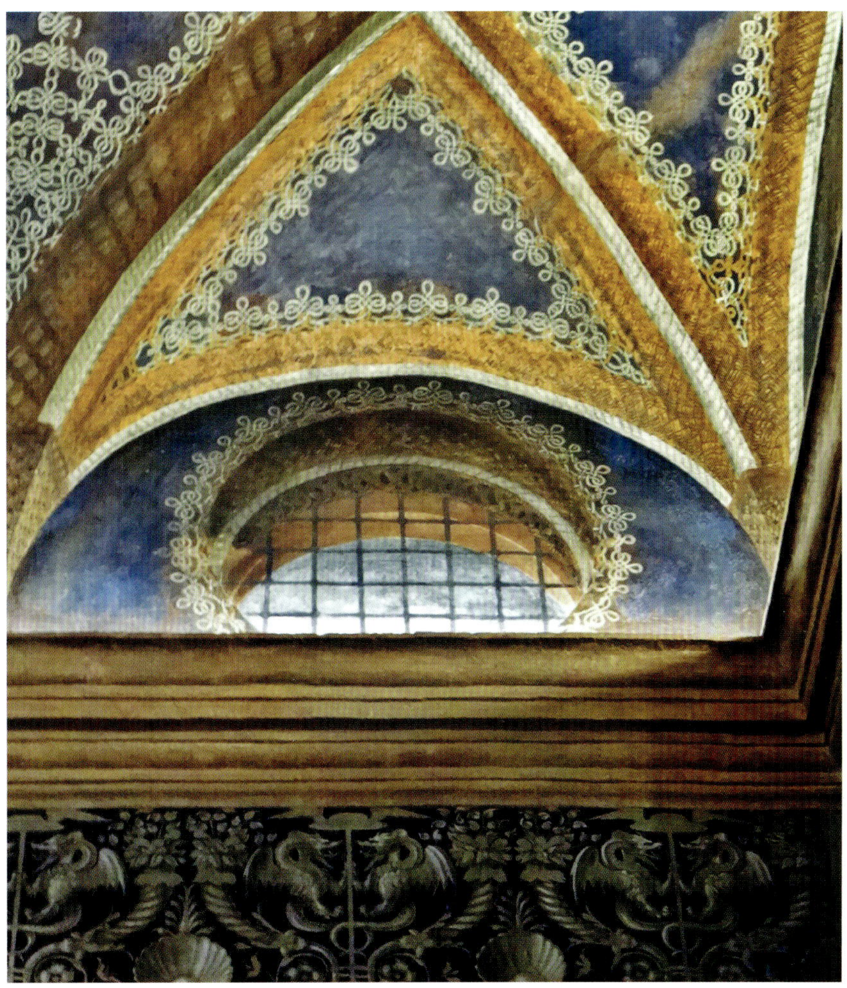

church cupola a hundred yards away), come close to the patterning along the sides of the triangular aperture in Bianca's *Sforziada* portrait.

The combination of square and circle in the pattern echoes the concept of Leonardo's *Vitruvian Man* (alluded to in the Birago frontispiece). Blending straight and curved lines within the same knot pattern is rare in Leonardo (although found in the gold trim around the collar of the Virgin's dress in the National Gallery version of the *Virgin of the Rocks*).

The main motif is repeated eight times, divided – at each corner of the triangle – by three larger motifs. This combination of three and eight echoes that of *The Last Supper* (eight tapestries, three windows, three arches above the picture). The recurrent use of eight is also prevalent in Leonardo's cupola designs and evokes the musical octave (cf 'The Musician').

Despite being one of the most technically innovative portraits in the history of art, creating the illusion of painting with red, white and black chalk, the influence of Leonardo's portrait of Bianca Sforza was virtually non-existent. It lay ignored and unknown for 500 years.

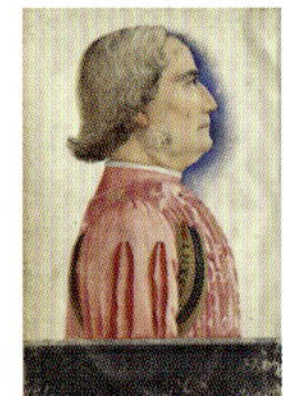
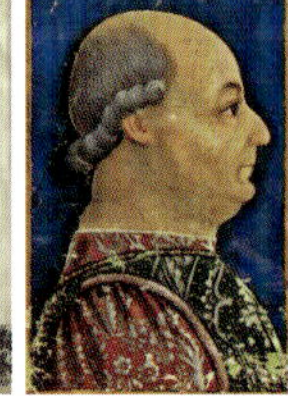
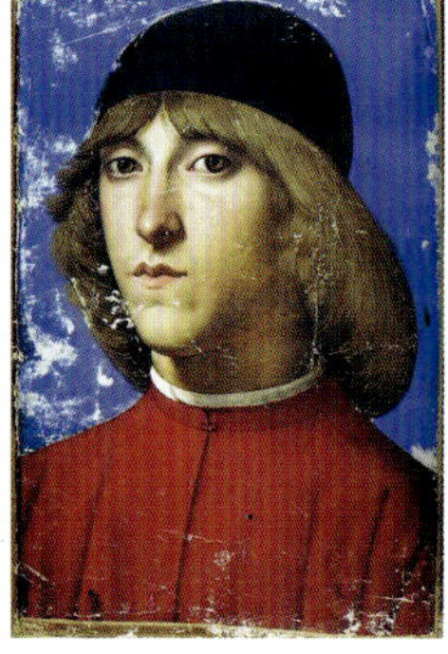
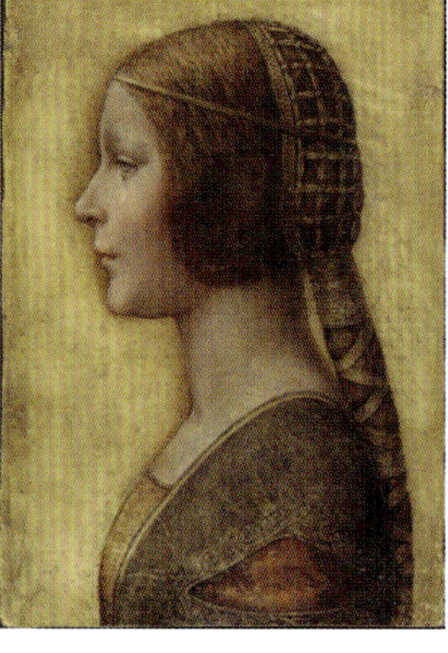
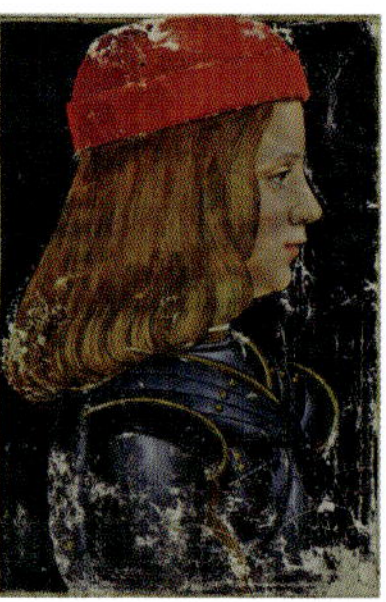
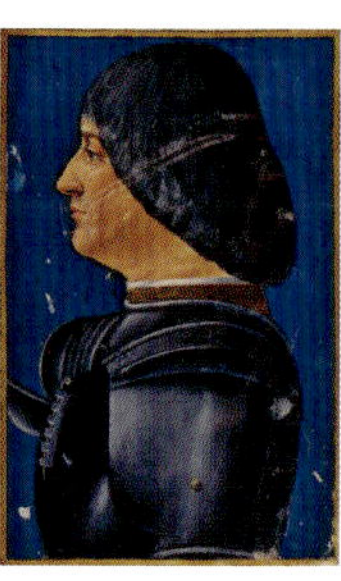

J. MARCELLO	FRAN. SFORZA	PIERO DE' MEDICI	BIANCA SFORZA	IL DUCHETTO	IL MORO
18.7 × 13 cm	19.2 × 14.5 cm	33 × 22.5 cm	35 × 24.5 cm	27.3 × 13.9 cm	25.1 × 12.8 cm

There were only five other full-page portraits in 15th century Italian books.

The first, attributed to the young Giovanni Bellini, is to be found in *De Situ Orbis*, a manuscript illuminated in Padua around 1453; the portrait shows the book's commissioner, Venetian general Jacopo Antonio Marcello (1398–1463) – who had helped Francesco Sforza conquer Milan in 1450. Francesco's own portrait, for his daughter's grammar-book (*see page 66*), dates from around 1460. Then came a lull until Gherardo's wedding portrait of Piero de' Medici (*see page 67*) in 1488/9. Leonardo's portrait of Bianca in 1496 was swiftly followed by the two Ambrogio de Predis portraits in the *Donatus Grammatica* commissioned by Il Moro for his son Massimiliano.

Two of the portraits were prompted by weddings. All six show the book's author, commissioner or destinatee – which suggests that the final illuminated *Sforziada* was intended for Bianca instead of (or as well as) Galeazzo Sanseverino. Bianca's portrait, originally around 35 × 24.5cm (it has been trimmed, and now measures 33.2 × 23.9cm), was the largest: six per cent bigger than the portrait of Piero de' Medici. Milanese one-upmanship: Il Moro saying his illegitimate daughter is worth just as much as Lorenzo's Nº1 son … in fact worth rather more, because he has Leonardo to do her portrait in regal profile.

Leonardo may well have relished the chance to outshine the Piero de' Medici portrait, which must have caused a stir in Renaissance art circles. But he had other reasons for being keen on the *Sforziada* commission. He may well have had a sentimental attachment to Bianca: like him, an illegitimate child, born at around the time he arrived in Milan. He had been friendly with Galeazzo Sanseverino for several years, designing costumes for him and visiting his stables to study equine physiology.

Then, any technical challenge excited Leonardo; he was always keen to explore new approaches – here by using coloured chalks on vellum rather than tempera. His love of experiment and innovation had just prompted (ultimately disastrous) attempts to find an alternative fresco technique for his *Last Supper*, begun a year or two before Bianca's portrait. In the *Sforziada*, however, he used innovation to stunning effect, notably in his treatment of Bianca's eye – created by a sophisticated combination of ink, coloured chalk and minute areas of the vellum surface being left untouched.

The commission was also a way for Il Moro to ensure Leonardo remained involved with the Francesco Sforza memorial project – after his phenomenal efforts to design and cast the bronze equine colossus had proved in vain.

And Leonardo may have been keen to respond to the late Il Puteolano, whose prefatory three-page *Sforziada* 'oration' to Il Moro lauded the written word as the only means of ensuring long-term glory – mocking Trajan, for instance, for all his long-gone 'expensive buildings' while claiming his reputation depended on the writings of Pliny the Younger. To Il Puteolano, the writings of Suetonius and Cornelius Tacitus perpetuated the memory of Julius Caesar (to whom Francesco Sforza is by implication likened) better than any building. 'Of ancient pictures and statues,' snorts Il Puteolano, 'none remain.'

This must have seemed provocative to Leonardo, whose *Sforziada* portrait of Bianca, placed a few pages after Il Puteolano's *Oratione*, offered him the chance to affirm art's superiority over the written word ... and assert its right to be considered one of the major art forms.

Leonardo made his own thoughts on the matter clear in his *Trattato della Pittura* – where he cites King Matthias Corvinus who, after receiving a portrait of his beloved, and a poem written in his honour, tells the poet his work is 'markedly inferior' to the picture, which 'serves a greater sense than yours, which is for the blind.'

Matthias then extols the 'divine proportions ... conjoined instantaneously' to create 'the divine beauty of this face before me,' before concluding that 'nothing made by man can rank higher' (*Codex Urbinas 14v-15r*).

BIANCA SFORZA (1483–96)

The first article on Bianca was written in 1912 by Alessandro Giulini.[5] It was based on the few archival documents that refer to her, and was necessarily short. Not a great deal of new information about her life has since emerged. Her place of birth is unknown. Her mother was Bernardina Corradi, who later married Antonio Gentili from Tortona, a former chamberlain at the Sforza court, and had other children; Il Moro gave her a liberal allowance and frequent access to Bianca.[6]

Bianca was also named *Giovanna*. Given the importance of the Milan–Naples alliance at the time of Bianca's birth, she may have been named after Queen Giovanna, the wife of the reigning King Ferrante, especially as Il Moro's elder sister Ippolita (1446–88) was married to their son, the future Alfonso II. Giovanna was also the name of the legendary Queen of Naples cited in the opening line of the *Sforziada*, while S. Giovanni (St John) assumes the features of Bianca's fiancé Galeazzo Sanseverino in Bergognone's 1490 *Crucifixion*.

Bianca's date of birth is unrecorded. She was alive by 29 April 1483, when Il Moro made a will settling 12,000 ducats in her favour. On 7 September 1489, in a document mentioning her imminent betrothal, she was described as aged six – i.e. she was born between 8 September 1482 and 29 April 1483.[7] A poem by Niccolò da Correggio pointedly described her age when she died, on 23 November 1496, as *due lustre e piu do mezzo il terzo un poco* ('two five-year spans and just over half of a third') – suggesting that she was thirteen. If she we were born in April 1483, she would have died at the age of 13 years 7 months.

Circumstantial evidence adds weight to this possibility. On 20 January 1483 Mantuan Ambassador Zaccaria Saggi informed Federico Gonzaga he had failed to obtain an audience with Il Moro because he was *in piacere con la Bernardina sua femina* ('in pleasure with his lady Bernardina').[8] Il Moro consorted with his ladies until well into pregnancy: in mid-February 1491 Ferrara Ambassador Trotti reported that Il Moro was still keen to make love to Cecilia Gallerani, even though she was over six months pregnant; however, by March 21, he 'no longer wanted to have relations with her' because she was 'now so big.' Cecilia gave birth six weeks later.

This suggests that, on 20 January 1483, Bianca's birth may still have been two or three months away. Another fact supports this eventuality: Il Moro's bastard son Leone,[9] born to a Roman mother in 1476, was legitimized on 29 April 1483 at the same time as Il Moro's will in Bianca's favour:[10] a significant recent event may have concentrated his mind.

Just four days earlier, on 25 April 1483, Leonardo is first mentioned in Milan (in the contract for the *Virgin of the Rocks*). Could it be that his arrival in the city coincided with Bianca's birth, and created a sentimental bond that led ultimately to Leonardo's portrait?

On 8 November 1489, from Vigevano, Duke Gian Galeazzo authorized Count Palatine Niccoló Gentili to legitimize Bianca (cited as *Johanna Blanca*) ahead of her betrothal to Galeazzo Sanseverino. On 14 December 1489, again in Vigevano, a deed was drawn up by notary Antonio Zunico entitling Il Moro to transmit property to Bianca or her husband – named as *Galeaz Sfortia Vicecomiti de Sancto Severino* – by gift, will or dowry. Il Moro's earlier will was officially revoked two days later. On 10 January 1490 Bianca and Galeazzo were officially betrothed in Milan's Castello Sforzesca.[11]

Bianca appeared on State occasions with the pomp due to her rank. When Beatrice d'Este entered Milan on 22 January 1491 as Il Moro's wife, Bianca rode in the State chariot, alongside Isabel of Aragon, to greet her at the church of San Eustorgio by the city walls. Bianca was also present at the tournament held on the Piazza del Castello a few days later, when Galeazzo Sanseverino appeared at the head of a troop of Scythians wearing Wild Men costumes designed by Leonardo da Vinci.

Bianca appears to have been a cheerful and popular girl. She was on intimate terms with Duke Gian Galeazzo and his wife Isabel of Aragon, and visited them in Pavia – as on 9 May 1493 when Bianca, aged ten, joined Isabella (22) and her ladies in a meadow near the villa of Mirabello in the castle park.[12]

Bianca attended the proxy wedding between her cousin Bianca Maria and Maximilian Habsburg in Milan Cathedral on 30 November 1493, and was among Beatrice d'Este's retinue when she received King Charles VIII of France at Asti in September 1494. Bianca was naturally present at the grandiose ceremony officially proclaiming her father Duke of Milan on 26 May 1495 – and is probably among the ladies in elaborate *coazzoni*, shown kneeling at the foot of the illumination recording the scene in the *Messale Arcimboldi* (*see left*).

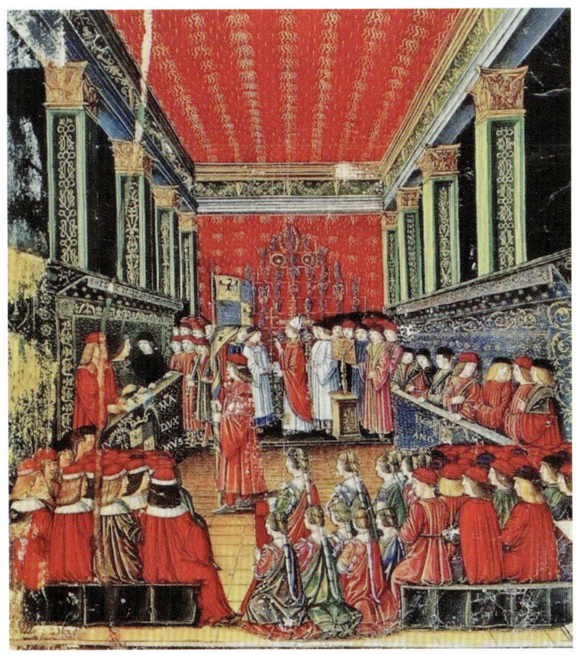

On 18 April 1495 Bianca had written her father an affectionate letter about how she had been helping her mother nurse her half-sister Margherita, who had fallen ill. She was equally attached to her young step-brothers Massimiliano and Francesco, and is named constantly in the daily reports about them sent to Il Moro whenever he was away. When her infant half-brother Francesco was poorly, Franceschino dal Maino informed Il Moro that Bianca had given him his bath, cuddled him and displayed *'gran gentiliza'*.

The Bianca-Galeazzo wedding ceremony, or *transductio ad maritum*, took place on 20 June 1496. Galeazzo Sanseverino was the number two figure at Il Moro's court. Some ranked him even higher: 'It seems to me', the Ferrara Ambassador Giacomo Trotti wrote waspishly on 7 August 1492, 'that Messer Galeazzo is Duke of Milan, as he can do whatever he wants, and has whatever he asks for or desires.'[13] The newly-weds were to live at Galeazzo's recently built palazzo just beyond the Porta Vercellina.

Bianca fell ill a few days after the wedding and was nursed by court doctors Ambrogio da Rosate and Niccolò da Cusano. Her step-brother Massimiliano, aged three, was also in attendance, passing on her medicine. Daily reports on her condition were sent to Il Moro after he left Milan on July 5 to meet Emperor Maximilian in the Tyolean Alps, in the company of Galeazzo Sanseverino and Beatrice d'Este.

Diplomatic dispatches[14] relate the background to this encounter – and reveal Maximilian's chaotic organization, dilatory progress and obsession with hunting. He had first announced, on May 24 from Ulm, that he intended to cross the Alps with 4,500 horsemen and 9,500 infantry, to meet Il Moro in Bormio. On June 14, still in Ulm, Maximilian announced he would be in Italy a little later than originally planned – by 'the end of June.' On June 20, in Kaufbeuren, Maximilian declared his meeting with Il Moro would be 'without pomp.' That same day, the Pisan ambassador asked for Maximilian's help against Florence.

On June 26, from Zirl, Maximilian set a new date for his encounter with Il Moro: July 7. He suggested they meet for a gala banquet in neutral territory: on top of Wormser Joch (Umbrail Pass). This was a ludicrous idea, as Brascha noted in his dispatch to Il Moro. The mountain summit had no buildings and might be covered in snow. On June 27 Maximilian backtracked – proposing to meet Il Moro in Bormio 'at the foot of the mountain.'

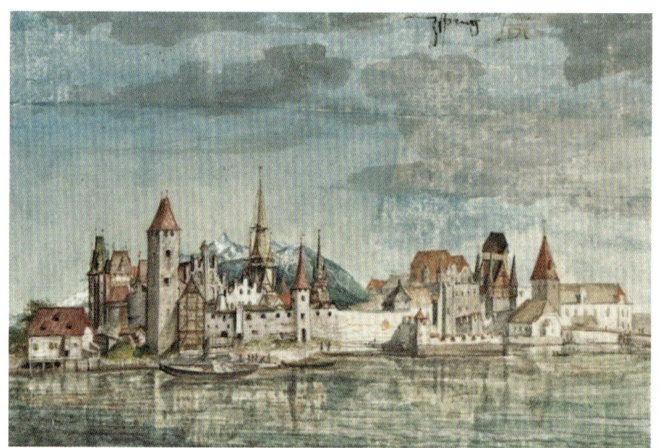

Maximilian lingered at his court in Innsbruck until July 5 – the same day that Il Moro left Milan (Maximilian was appraised twice-daily of Il Moro's progress by messengers on horseback). On July 7 Maximilian attended a memorial service in Stams for Archduke Sigmund, who had died there four months earlier, aged 68. On July 12 Maximilian reached Landeck and sent word to Il Moro to bring oats, wine, meat and grain. Next day, from Pfunds, Maximilian added melons and cherries to his wishlist. On July 14 he was in Nauders, where his retinue forcibly requisitioned grain and lodgings. On July 17 Maximilian arrived in Glorenza (Glurns) to await Il Moro. Their meeting was now to take place in Mals, on the Austrian side of the Alps, rather than in Bormio (or on top of a snowy mountain).

The 120-mile trip from Milan to Bormio is arduous enough, but crossing the Stelvio Pass (Stilfser Joch) and adjacent Umbrail Pass – at 9,000-feet, the second-highest passage over the Alps – was among the most challenging routes known to Renaissance horseman. There was no paved road here until the 1820s (and even today this is closed to traffic for eight months of the year). Why Il Moro should have wished to submit his pregnant wife to such a journey is a mystery. Did he consider her presence essential to his Imperial charm offensive? Did he hope the journey would be her undoing? Or did Beatrice insist on coming, unable to trust him out of her sight after hearing of his affair with Lucrezia Crivelli (who was already pregnant with Il Moro's son, to be born the following March)?

The Milanese cavalcade arrived at the monastery of Marienberg near Mals on July 19, a fortnight after setting out. That evening Maximilian entertained Il Moro and Beatrice in a marquee at nearby Glorenza, 3 miles down the Venosta Valley; we read of Beatrice being placed in the middle as Maximilian chivalrously cut the food; Sanseverino ate at

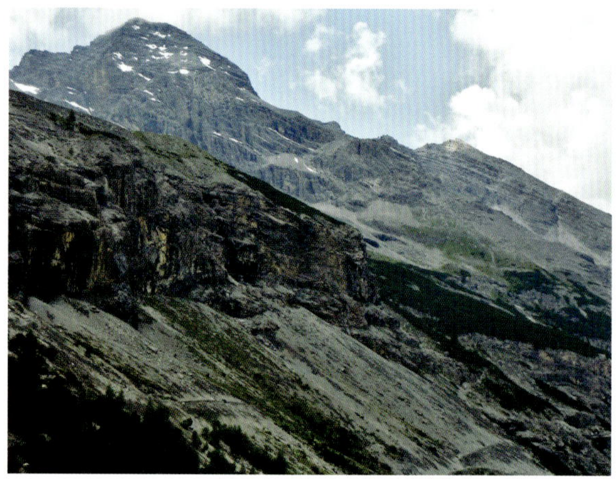

STELVIO PASS

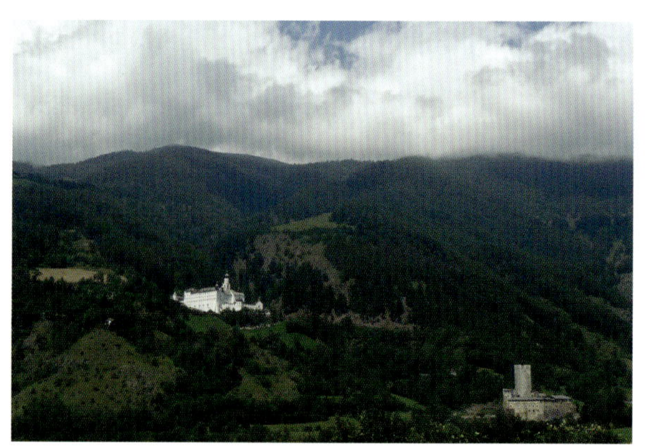

MARIENBERG

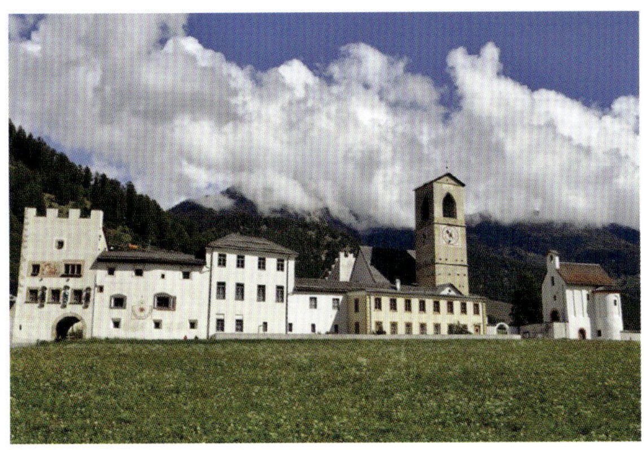

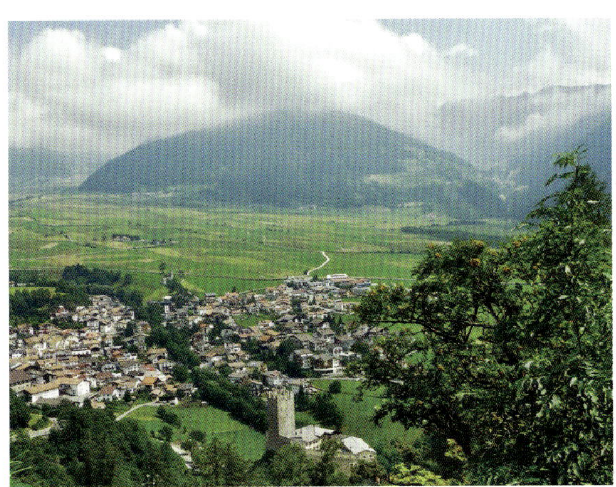

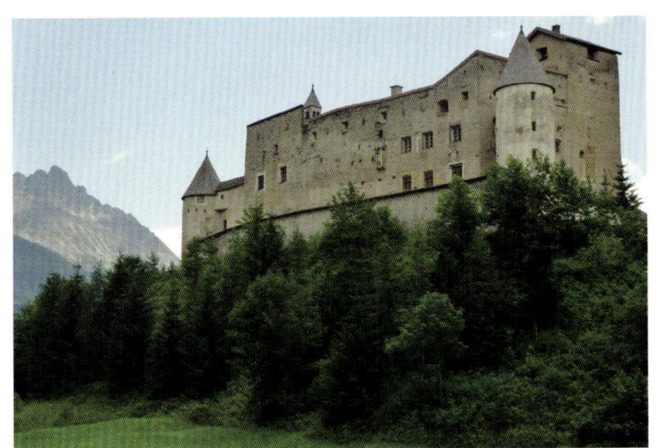

another table with Beatrice's ladies-in-waiting. Next day Maximilian and Il Moro went hunting and held private talks at the Benedictine abbey of Müstair, 6 miles southwest of Glorenza. On July 21 Maximilian announced he would come to Italy in three weeks' time (in the event, it would be six), and discussed the matter with Pisan envoys. On July 22 Maximilian accompanied the Milanese party back over the Alps to Bormio. On July 26 he returned to Nauders after promising to lead 10,000 men to Italy as soon as he had obtained the backing of the Diet of Lindau (*Nuove fantasie!* commented Il Moro to his aides, after asking the Emperor to receive the investitures of Pisa, Siena and Lucca).

On July 30, back in Milan, Bianca was declared better after a month-long illness. But she fell ill again on August 2 with a *passione de stomacho*. It sounds like the early stages of pregnancy, although it has been suggested the erratic symptoms and stomach pains recall those endured in his final months by Gian Galeazzo, who may have died of arsenic poisoning.[15]

Bianca again recovered. Il Moro and Beatrice returned to Milan in time for the feast of San Lorenzo on August 10. A few days later Bianca and Galeazzo Sanseverino accompanied them to Vigevano to prepare for the reception of Maximilian, who left Nauders on August 12. Next day, from Glorenza, he sent word to Il Moro vainly requesting Galeazzo Sanseverino be sent to him. By August 16 Maximilian was across the Alps in Bormio. On August 23 he was in Morbegno, fuming about the Venetians' failure to send him their loan – and saying he was staking his domestic reputation on the coming campaign, because the German princes were pro-French. On August 25 he crossed Lake Como to Bellagio, and continued via Torno (northeast of Como) to Cermenate, where he was greeted by Il Moro, Beatrice and their three year-old son.

Maximilian arrived in Vigevano on September 2 and stayed for three weeks. A meeting with foreign ambassadors took place on September 7, when a loquacious Il Moro asserted that he had no claim on Pisa; accused Savoy, Montferrat and Saluzzo of secretly supporting France; and called on Maximilian to send troops to protect Milan's frontier with France. Maximilian announced his ambition to

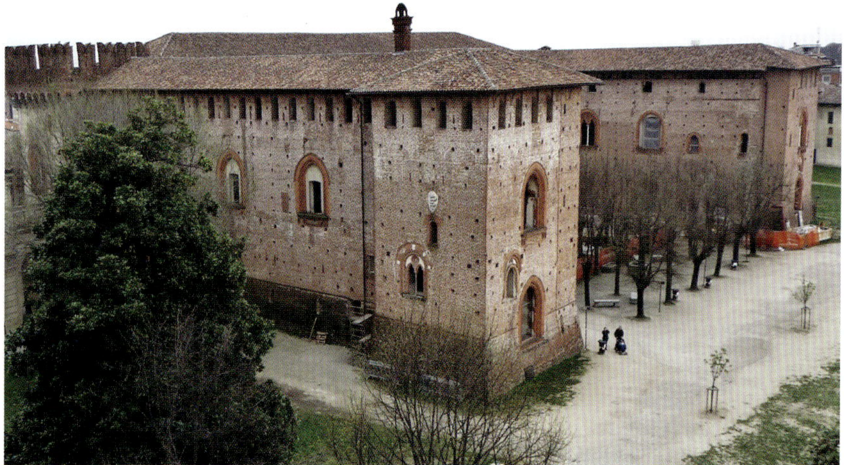

descend on Genoa, intercept the French fleet returning from Naples, affiliate Pisa to the Empire, and proceed to Leghorn to intimidate Florence. On September 14 the Venetian envoys reached Milan, staying in the former Palazzo del Verme (now owned by Cecilia Gallerani), before proceeding to Vigevano – where they were lodged in the new palazzo built for Galeazzo Sanseverino and Bianca, 300 yards from Il Moro's Castello. With Galeazzo bed-ridden from 'quartan ague' (probably a form of malaria), it was Bianca who welcomed the Venetian VIPs. Emperor Maximilian left Vigevano on September 23.

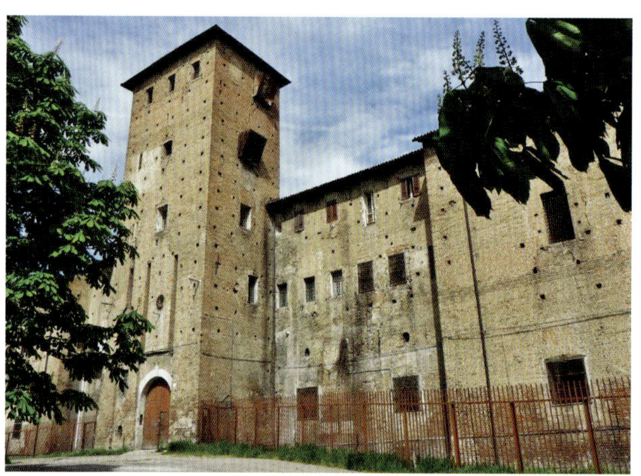

By October 1 Galeazzo had recovered, and accompanied Bianca to her dower-town of Voghera, where they were greeted with enthusiasm and stayed for several days. A report to Il Moro from court official Giacomo Seregno, dated October 4, described Bianca as *sana e bona voglia* ('healthy and in good spirits').

In early November the couple were in Milan. On November 8 they rode out to La Bicocca, the grand hunting-lodge owned by Guido Arcimboldi, Archbishop of Milan, 3 miles north of the city (still standing, but now within the city limits). After lunch they went hunting and killed a hare.

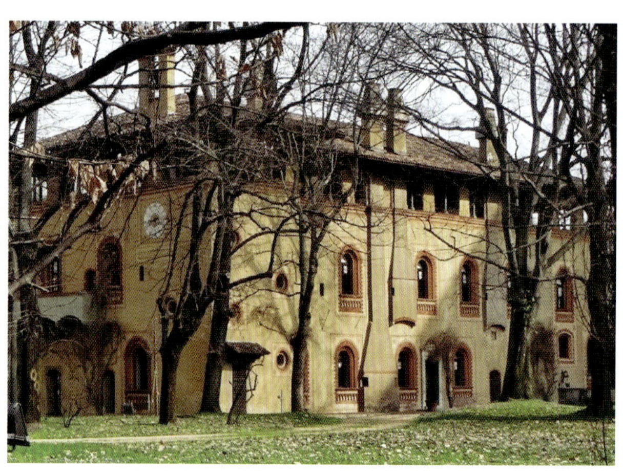

A few days later Galeazzo left Milan for the Visconti castle of Cusago, 8 miles to the west, before continuing to Abbiategrasso, then across the Ticino to Vigevano to join Il Moro for talks, prior to Emperor Maximilian's return from his Pisan campaign.

On November 22, the day he arrived in Vigevano, Galeazzo was summoned back to Milan by news of Bianca's sudden illness.[16]

Il Moro was so alarmed he put off his departure for Pavia, where he was due to meet Maximilian, and sent a courier to Milan for the latest news, writing to Galeazzo: 'I know that, since you are back in Milan, Bianca will have every possible care and attention. But as Maestro Ambrogio and the other doctors are with you, you might send Maestro Luigi … to bring me full details.'

Next evening a messenger galloped into Vigevano with news that Bianca had died. He was intercepted at the castle gates by Beatrice herself. Bianca had lost consciousness the previous morning, never recovered, and died that afternoon.[17]

Il Moro's reaction was extraordinarily stoic. He spent the night writing letters and giving orders for Bianca's funeral. His illegitimate son Leone, who had died earlier that year, had been buried in Santa Maria delle Grazie, where Leonardo was busy on *The Last Supper*. Now Il Moro wrote to both the Archbishop and Castellan of Milan, requesting Bianca be laid to rest in the same place:

> *'Since it has pleased God to take our Bianca to Himself, to our inexpressible sorrow, I wish her to be buried in the choir of Santa Maria delle Grazie. After sunset … let her be borne through the gardens of the castello to the church, and see that the gates of the castello are closed and guarded, so that no one shall know what is going on. In all other particulars let the same order be observed as in the funeral of our son Leone. Only, as I do not wish Bianca to be buried in a place where I can see her grave, take care that she is laid exactly behind the high altar of Le Grazie, so her tomb cannot be seen from the rest of the church.'*[18]

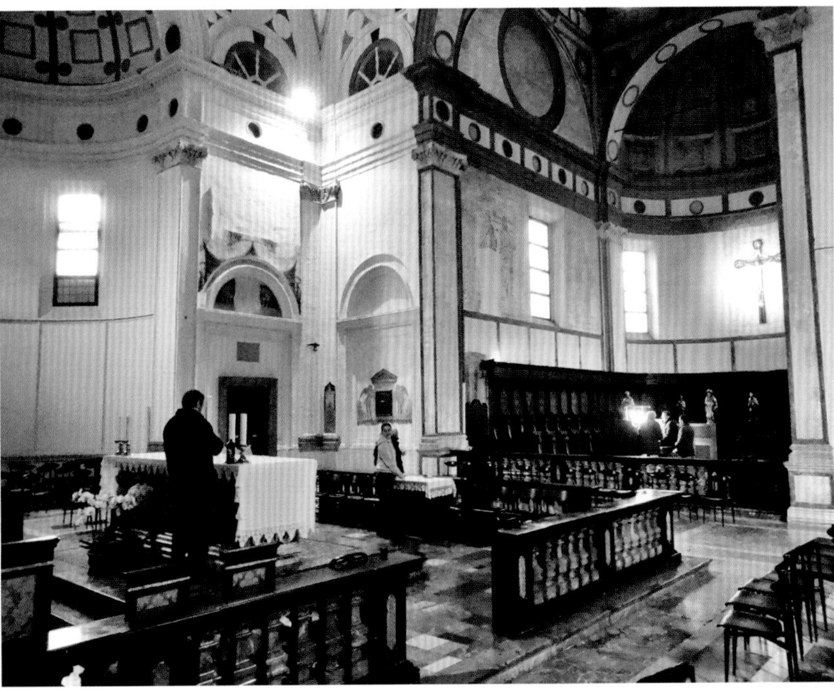

SANTA MARIA DELLE GRAZIE
(HIGH ALTAR)

ALTERED FRONTISPIECE

Birago's *Sforziada* frontispiece was altered, twice, to evoke Bianca's tragic death – by Birago himself. His alterations would remain undetected, in this Book of Doom, for over 500 years.

Birago's first modification involves an unusual black form (*right*) – the only time in any *Sforziada* frontispiece border that he uses a black ground. It has received no critical attention beyond Polish librarian Bogdan Horodyski's intuitive remark, in 1954, that it evoked 'an abyss.' The form is incongruously flanked by upstretched wings, and features the initials *GZ* in ghostly white, above a faintly outlined, asymmetrical form.

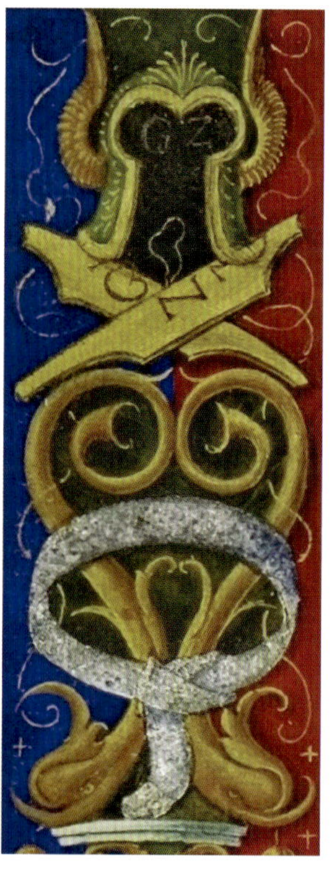

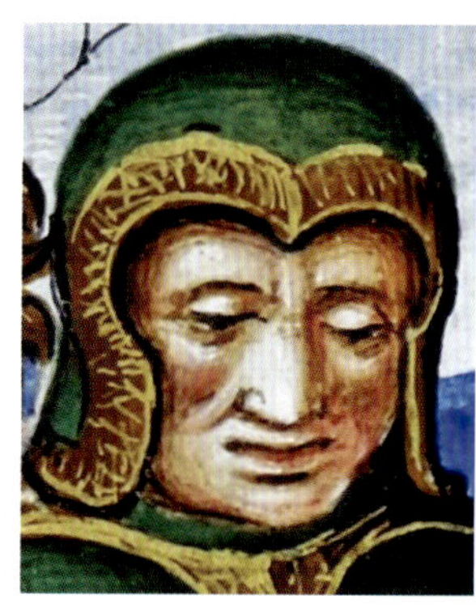

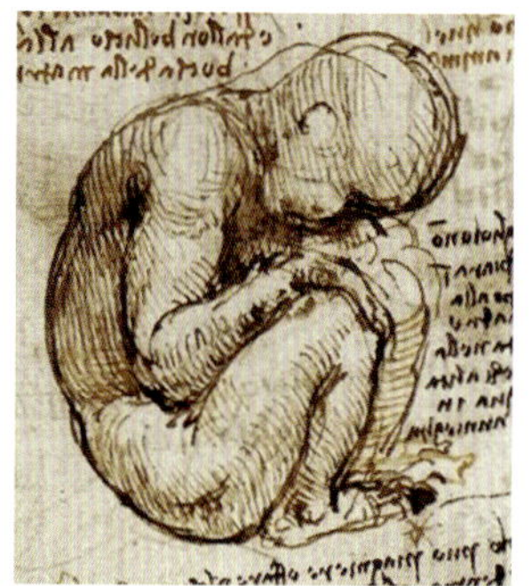

A little lower down, superimposed on a scrolling heart with a green interior, is a grey oval appearing to be part of a knotted belt whose tongue drops in a curve towards a white plinth (*right*).

Although not as rare as black, grey is not a common colour in Birago's border repertoire either. It may have originally been silver, which is equally rare. Close inspection, possible through the intense magnification produced by modern digital technology, reveals that the black 'form' and silver 'belt' were not part of the original frontispiece.

The headless helmet recalls the winged golden helmet used in the frontispiece for the 1491 biography of Muzio Attendolo prompted by Bianca's and Galeazzo's betrothal. This form of helmet was common at the time: contemporary examples are to be found in Birago's *Sforza Hours* (*see top right*) and elsewhere.

Probably, then, Birago's *Sforziada* helmet was originally a gold helmet like the one in the Muzio manuscript. The wings that flank it remain from the original frontispiece, but the interior of the helmet was reworked to mimic the outline of a female torso with a background of funereal black and the initials *GZ* (for *Galeazzo*) appearing in ghostly white, above a strange, curved, asymmetric form that peters out into the lower centre of the shield. The goal of this extraordinary modification appears to be to record that Bianca died while pregnant.

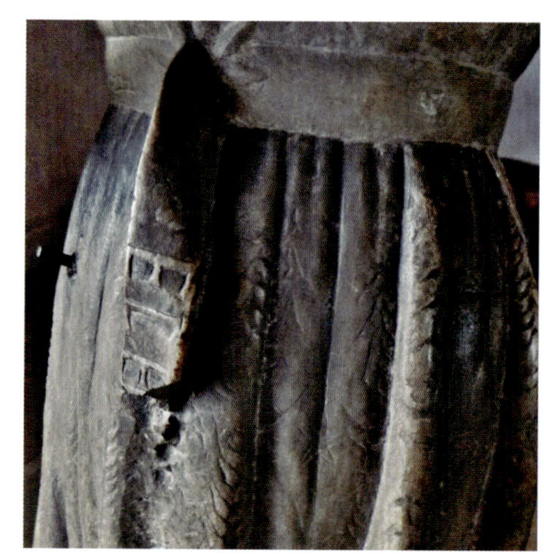

The strange, curved form – only clearly apparent using magnification – evokes the outline of a fœtus and umbilical chord, positioned roughly where – if the shape is interpreted as resembling a female torso – the womb would be. And who better to advise Birago about fœtus and womb than pioneering biologist Leonardo da Vinci?[19]

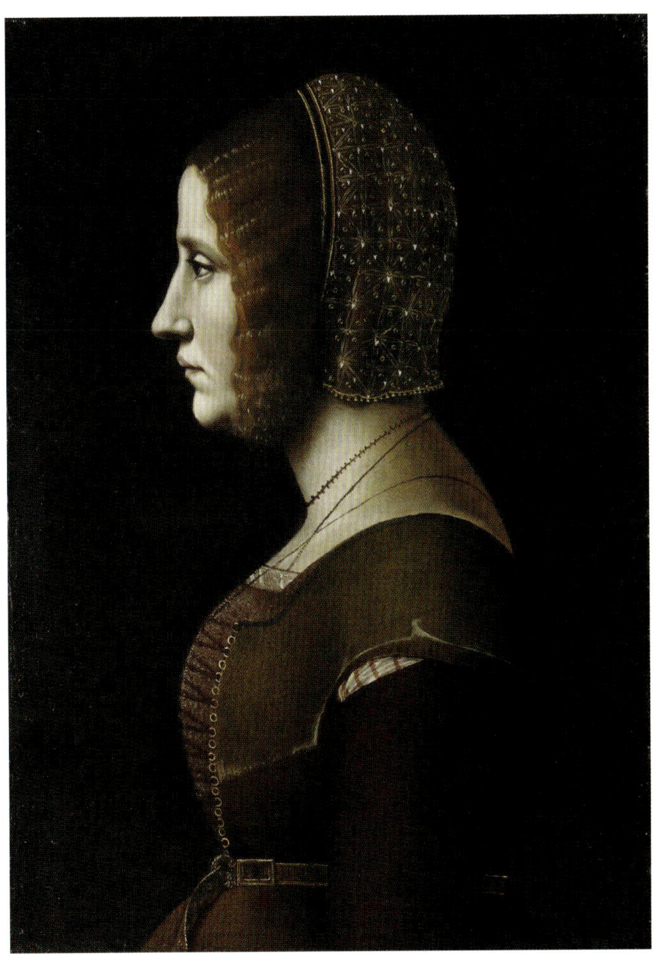

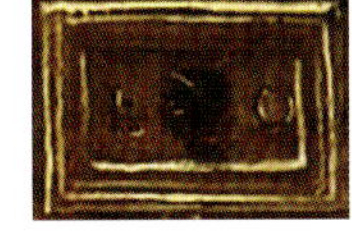

The 'belt' below represents the *cinxia* (woollen belt tied with the 'Knot of Hercules') worn in Ancient Rome by a bride to remind her husband he was 'belted and bound' (*cinctus vinctusque*). A similar belt is worn by the *Madonna del Coazzone* in the Castello Sforzesco (*see below opposite*), whose dress is adorned with ears of wheat as a symbol of fertility;[20] and by the *Woman in Profile* in London's National Gallery, attributed to Ambrogio de Predis and tentatively identified as Bianca's mother, Bernardina Corradi, by Martin Kemp. She sports a Moor's Head cameo in her belt, flanked by the initials ***L O*** (*see above right*).

There is a simple and ignoble reason why it was important that Bianca's pregnancy be a matter of record: because Galeazzo Sanseverino was only entitled to her 240,000-ducat dowry if the marriage had been consummated. By the time of her death he had yet to receive this dowry. Il Moro was in no position to pay it. His exchequer had been bled dry by the 400,000 ducats paid to Maximilian for the Imperial investiture and Bianca Maria's dowry (which he had to beg to pay in instalments). He couldn't even afford to pay Leonardo da Vinci, fobbing him off after *The Last Supper* with a vineyard outside the city walls.

The circumstances of Bianca's death strengthened Il Moro's moral hold on Sanseverino. While stressing that his fatherly-in-law affection for him remained undiminished (*amato et tenuto in locho de carissimo fiolo*), the 240,000-ducat dowry was kept dangling in front of Sanseverino from here on in. Sanseverino would never receive it.

Bianca was buried under Bramante's cupola. On December 4 a requiem for her soul was chanted in the Duomo in the presence of the court, and a funeral oration pronounced by Matteo Bossi.[21]

Il Moro felt the need to reassure Galeazzo Sanseverino that he would continue to regard him as a 'most beloved son,' and lost no time in sending a considerate, moving and dignified letter to Bianca's mother Bernardina, expressing his very deep pain (*nostro gravissimo dolore*) and acknowledging the incredible pain (*dolore incredibile*) news of Bianca's death must bring her:[22]

> *'We feel it would be a grave failure of duty on our part if we did not inform you with our own hand, as her mother, of this sad event, unlike any other loss that has befallen us. Yesterday morning, at 9 o'clock, having apparently been in perfect health until this hour, she fell into a sudden faint and, despite all the doctors could do for her, grew steadily worse until, at 5 o'clock this evening, her life on earth was ended. This event has caused us the most unutterable grief, both for the loss of such a daughter and because the blow was so sudden and unexpected. We know that it will be a great shock to your heart, but we must bear with patience the trials that are sent us here, and bow to the unalterable laws of nature. We entreat you, therefore, to bear this loss with patience and courage, and assure you that you will be no less beloved by us in future, than if Bianca were still alive.'*

Il Moro also fired off a message to his physician Ambrogio Rosate,[23] expressing disquiet about the treatment Bianca had received, and calling for an inquiry into her death. There is no trace of Ambrogio's conclusions. Either they were delivered verbally or, if written, lost or destroyed.

All the festivities planned in honour of Emperor Maximilian's return to Lombardy were scrapped. Il Moro sailed down the Ticino to Pavia in mourning to receive Maximilian on December 2. Instead of making a public entry through the town, Maximilian rode through the park to the private gate at the back of the Castello, and spent the evening alone with Il Moro and Beatrice. Two days later Maximilian attended the requiem mass for Bianca, then rode out to the Certosa di Pavia with Il Moro.

Not everyone reacted to Bianca's death with equal dignity. The marriage's under-age consummation was alluded to by Niccolò da Correggio (1450–1508) in what purported to be a commemorative ode:

> *Duo lustri i più do mezo il terzo un poco*
> *Bianca, del Duca figlia, avea perfecti*
> *A con Galeazzo i coniugali affecti*
> *Godeassi e pari era in lor te[n]de il foco*

There were two possible reasons for Niccolò da Correggio to suggest Bianca's death was caused by the 'ardour' (*foco*) of Galeazzo Sanseverino – i.e. sexually provoked – in this unpoetic outburst (*non è fra le sue rime migliori* – 'not his best rhymes' – sniffs Giulini).

Correggio abruptly departed from the Sforza court within months of Bianca's death. On 20 May 1497 news reached Venice that Correggio, 'in enmity with the Duke,' had left Milan – along with his mother Beatrice, a mainstay at court since her marriage to Il Moro's half-brother Tristan Sforza in 1455, and a staunch Moro loyalist (acting as his Milanese informant during his 1477–79 exile to Pisa).

Niccolò da Corregio was brought up at the Este court of his Uncle Borso. In 1472 he married Cassandra, daughter of Venetian military supremo Bartolomeo Colleoni. In 1475, after Colleoni's death, he entered Milanese service, siding with Il Moro during his clash with Bona da Savoia in 1480 – for which he was rewarded with the estate of Castellazzo nell'Alessandrino (now Castellazzo Bormida) in the western marches of the Duchy. Correggio also became a member of the Duke's Secret Council and was granted the signal privilege (shared by Galeazzo Sanseverino) of being able to add Visconti to his surname. So, for Correggio to be drummed out of town after two decades as a senior figure at the Sforza court, a bone of serious contention must have been a-gnawing. The official reason was Correggio's passive response to a French foray into Milanese territory in January 1497. Correggio was stripped of Castellazzo and, in the document announcing the fact, accused by Il Moro of serving him badly.

What can have caused Correggio's passivity? The surprising death of his cousin Beatrice d'Este, a few weeks after Bianca's? Was Correggio speaking for Beatrice when insinuating that Galeazzo Sanseverino had provoked his young wife's death? Correggio's ode to Bianca reaches a conclusion of sinister ambiguity, again stressing the fact that the marriage was consummated under-age:

> *Sol Galeazzo, a cui la messe in erba*
> *Fu tronca, i fructi sui vedendo persi*
> *Puo dir che contra lui Morte fu acerba*

> ('Only Galeazzo, for whom the harvest was reaped too soon, his fruits becoming lost, can say that Death was bitter for him')

Did these lost fruits include the dowry Sanseverino would never receive?

DOUBLE DEATH

The disturbing circumstances of Bianca's sudden death found an echo a biblical forty days later. On January 2, Beatrice d'Este reportedly spent the afternoon praying by Bianca's tomb in Santa Maria delle Grazie then, back at the Castello Sforzesca, enjoyed an evening of dancing before dying during premature childbirth.[24]

Did Beatrice really take ill after dancing the night away? When eight months pregnant? Did she really linger in a chilly church on a winter's day? If so, through piety or remorse? A different version of Beatrice's death was chronicled 220 years later by the Modena-based historian Ludovico Antonio Muratori.

On page 263 of Volume II of his *Antichità Estensi*, published in 1740, Muratori reports a rumour that Beatrice d'Este was 'poisoned by Francesca dal Verme at the behest of Galeazzo Sanseverino, as Francesca admitted some years later on her deathbed. Why was not said. It can be only observed that Bianca – Galeazzo's wife and bastard daughter of Duke Lodovico – had died a short time before.'[25]

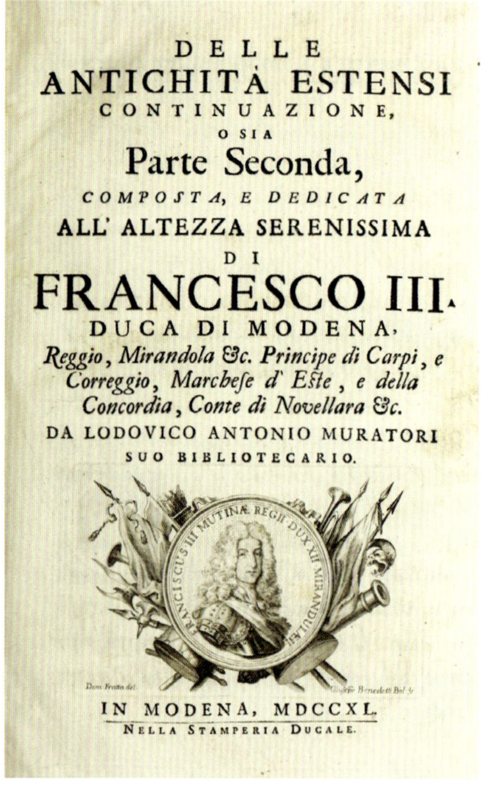

Muratori, an Este historian, dismisses the notion that dynasty heroine Beatrice was poisoned rather than died a natural death. But why mention the rumour of her murder in the first place? Why disquiet the slumber of this ferocious sleeping dog? And why does Muratori imply that, if Beatrice were murdered by order of Galeazzo Sanseverino, Bianca was murdered by order of Beatrice d'Este? Muratori must have had reason to think the two deaths inextricably intertwined.

The idea that Beatrice d'Este could have been involved in Bianca Sforza's death has never received serious consideration, given her apparent friendliness for Bianca and the absence of any obvious motive. Yet Beatrice had three.

The first motive was spite: retaliation against Il Moro for the humiliation of her own lady-in-waiting, Lucrezia Crivelli, becoming pregnant with Il Moro's child. Galeazzo Sanseverino was the go-between who had facilitated Il Moro's clandestine relationship with Lucrezia.

The second was jealousy: Leonardo da Vinci had never painted Beatrice's portrait, yet immortalized her husband's mistresses and her own step-daughter – the latter in ducal profile.

The third was power-politics. Birago's *Sforziada* frontispiece showed Il Moro warning the Sanseverinos not to get ideas above their station. Marriage to Bianca in 1496 consolidated Galeazzo's status within the Sforza inner family circle and made him a credible candidate to succeed Il Moro. True, Il Moro had named Beatrice as Regent in the event of his death – but that meant little. Bianca's illegitimate origins would have been no deterrent: the two elder half-brothers of Beatrice's father were bastards (Leonello and Borso), yet both had reigned over Ferrara. Beatrice had been raised by King Ferrante of Naples – also born illegitimate. *Sforziada* hero Francesco Sforza was illegitimate. So was his wife Bianca Maria.

At the time of Il Moro's investiture in May 1495, he had been granted the right to transmit his Ducal title to his own heirs – be they legitimate or *legitimized*. The previous two Dukes of Milan – Il Moro's brother and nephew – had been murdered, but their young wives (Bona di Savoia and Isabel of Aragon) had ruled either briefly or not at all. Any child of Bianca's was a potential rival to Beatrice's. Galeazzo Sanseverino's potential claims to the Regency, however, vanished if Bianca died before giving birth.

Galeazzo's reaction to Beatrice's death was suspiciously over-the-top. On 3 January 1497, within hours of her death, Ferrara Ambassador Antonius Costabilis was reporting to Duke Ercole d'Este that Galeazzo had 'above all others, by both word and deed, as well as his demonstrations of sorrow, given admirable expression to the affection he had for the Duchess, and taken care to make [her] virtues and goodness known to all.'[26]

Beatrice was plain, pushy and had served her dynastic purpose by bearing Il Moro two sons. Il Moro had little time for her, and 'after barely a year of marriage, forgot himself so far as to strike his wife.'[27] He preferred to consort with the wittiest and most beautiful women in Milan – and have them immortalized by Leonardo da Vinci. Beatrice had become a chubby matron by the age of twenty – as her sculpted effigy, now in the Certosa di Pavia, reveals.

Muratori's rumour-mongering was reported 195 years later, in 1912, by the Italian historian Alessandro Giulini – who claimed to have scoured the archives in vain for information about Francesca dal Verme, Beatrice d'Este's supposed poisoner. Her very existence was, he implied, open to doubt. Yet exist she did. The proof was brought to light another 99 years on, in 2011, by Carla Glori in *La Gioconda – In Memoria di Bianca*.

This esoteric volume, peppered with imaginatively labelled photographs and Surrealist poetry, and routinely mistranscribing the 15th century printed *s* as *f*, attempts to prove that Bianca Sforza was actually Mona Lisa. By the end of her 452-page tome, Glori appears to be tiring of this eccentric idea – not least because the Kemp-Cotte book on *La Bella Principessa* (which she generously references), published halfway through her research, suggests Bianca had blond hair. But Glori's archive research is extensive and, at times, groundbreaking – none more so than when it comes to the enigmatic Francesca dal Verme.

Glori reveals that Francesca was the illegitimate daughter of Pietro dal Verme, whose sister Antonia had married Il Moro's elder half-brother Sforza Secondo in 1451. Pietro cemented links between the Houses of Dal Verme and Sforza by marrying Il Moro's niece Chiara – illegitimate daughter of Duke Galeazzo Maria – on 24 April 1480.[28] Chiara was thirteen. She was Pietro's second wife.

In 1473, despite Sforza opposition, he had married Cecilia del Maino, who would die in suspicious circumstances.

The illustrious Dal Vermes, one of the most powerful families in the Duchy since the 14th century, had been created Earls of Bobbio and Voghera by Filippo Maria Visconti in 1436. Pietro dal Verme became Lord of Voghera in 1467 and Lord of Bobbio in 1484. He was naturally a supporter of Chiara's half-brother, Duke Gian Galeazzo, and said to have plotted with Roberto Sanseverino to overthrow Il Moro.

On 17 October 1485 Pietro was poisoned – rumour had it by his wife Chiara, at her uncle's behest. A month later Il Moro confiscated Pietro's titles and estates.[29] The castles of Zavattarello and Rocca d'Olgisio were awarded to Galeazzo Sanseverino; the Palazzo del Broletto in Milan later granted to Cecilia Gallerani; and the prosperous towns of Voghera and Bobbio, with its imposing Castello Malpesina, transferred to his daughter Bianca.

In June 1486 Chiara was sent 9,000 Imperial *lire*, officially to help raise her stepdaughter Francesca and stepson Francesco.[30] In 1489 Il Moro arranged her diplomatic remarriage to Fregosino – son of Paolo Fregoso, the ousted Doge of recently reconquered Genoa – and made sure she looked the part: Chiara's wedding inventory lists a dozen *mongini* (surcoats) in velvet and gold brocade, described as *molto ricchi*.[31]

One can imagine Il Moro's avuncular concern extending to Chiara's stepdaughter. Perhaps Francesca was one of Beatrice d'Este's ladies-in-waiting. She would have been in no position to refuse an indecent proposal from Il Moro's right-hand man, Galeazzo Sanseverino. And the art of poison ran in the family.

BOBBIO

Bobbio lies 70 miles south of Milan, and a challenging 25 miles southeast of Voghera over rough, hilly terrain. Today it is a picturesque backwater in the remote Trebbia Valley, lauded by Ernest Hemingway as one of the most beautiful in the world.

Back in the 15th century Bobbio was of strategic and commercial importance – straddling the *Via del Sale* (the Genoa Salt Route linking the Trebbia and

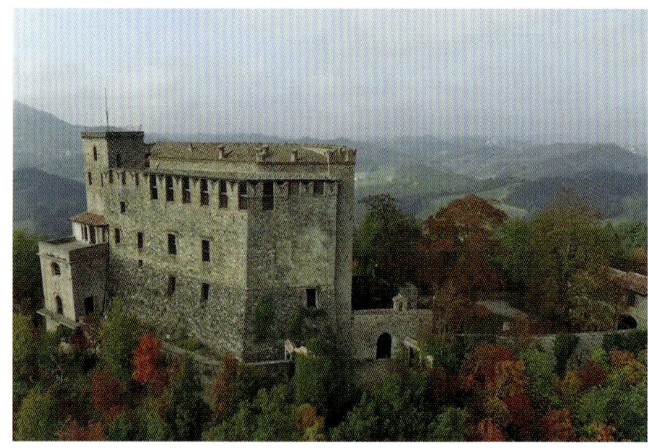

ZAVATTARELLO

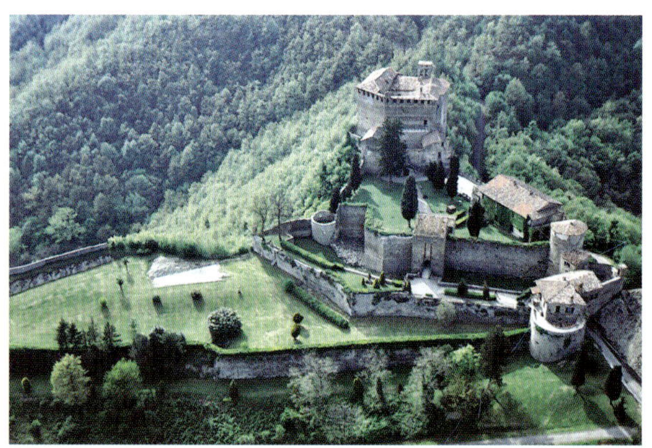

ROCCA D'OLGISIO

TREBBIA VALLEY

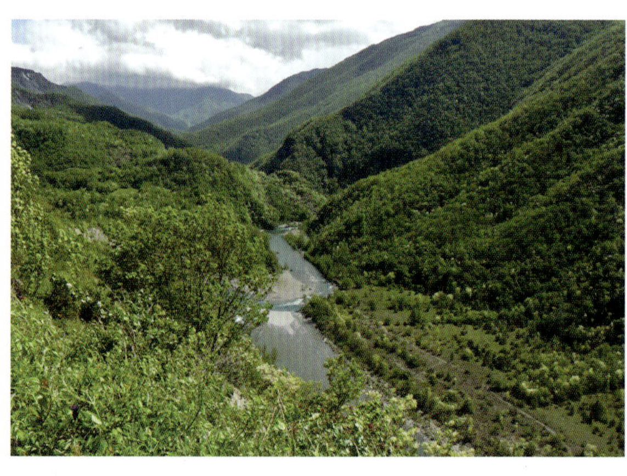

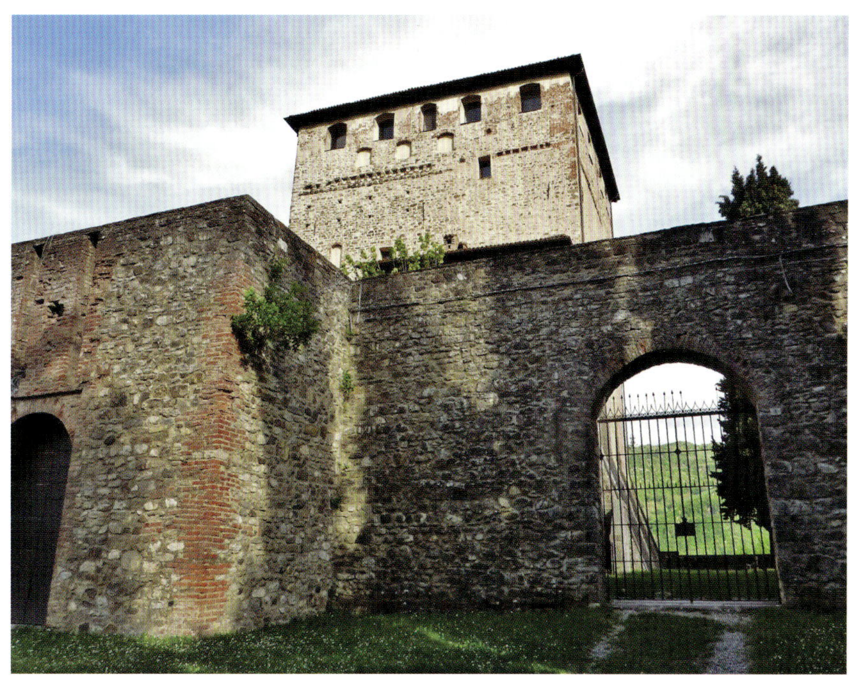

Taro Valleys) and the *Cammino di San Colombiano*, a Pilgrim's Way between Strasbourg and Rome.

Pilgrims stopped in Bobbio because of its abbey, founded in AD 614 by St Columbanus from Ireland, who sailed to France at the age of 42 and founded a monastery at Luxeuil in the Vosges. In 612, after journeying to Milan via Metz, Mainz, Lake Zurich and Lake Constance, he met Agilulf, King of the Lombards, and was granted a tract of secluded land in the Trebbia Valley.

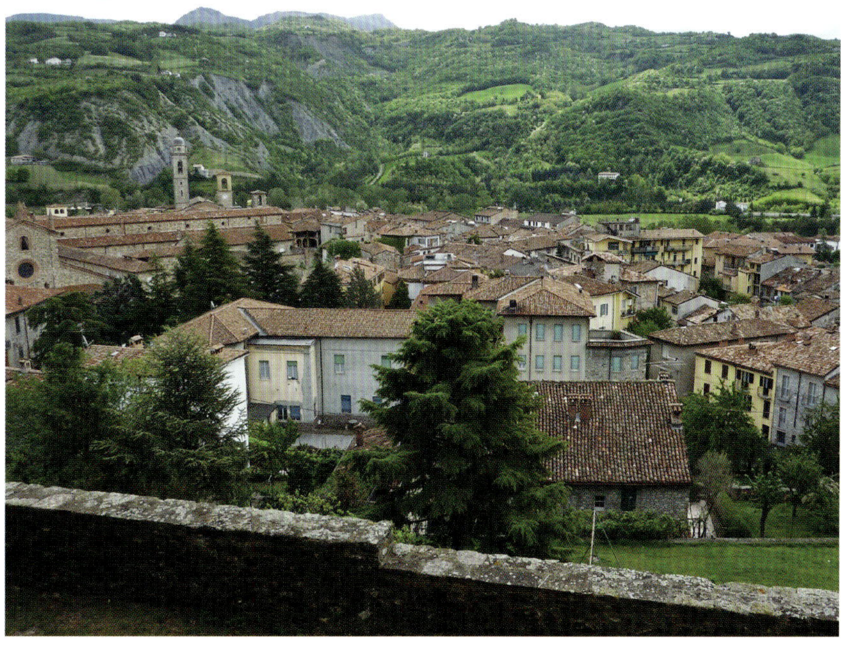

Columbanus founded his abbey then repaired to a cave in the chalky mountainside, where he died the next year; he was buried on a fateful November 23.

A *Vita Columbani* was written 25 years later by Brother Jonas of Bobbio. The Irish monks who followed St Columbanus to Bobbio included St Dungal, who died at Bobbio around 828 and bequeathed 27 volumes to the abbey library[32] which, by the start of the 10th century, had swollen to 600 volumes. Medieval Bobbio was renowned as one of the most famous manuscript centres in Christendom (and would be a source of inspiration for Umberto Eco's *The Name of the Rose*). Its school of illumination perpetuated an ornately Gaelic approach to manuscript decoration replete with interlacing patterns whose bewildering complexity (*example below right*) begs comparison with Leonardo's knots.

Bobbio Abbey was dissolved by Napoleon in 1803. Nothing remains of its original buildings – unlike the 15th century Basilica of San Colombano. The crypt houses St Columbanus's sarcophagus; the nave's frescoed decoration by Bergognone's pupil Bernardino Lanzani includes a frieze of alternating angel-heads, cornucopia and Leonardesque knots.

With his love of striking scenery – and his close ties to Bianca's husband Galeazzo Sanseverino – it would have been natural for Leonardo da Vinci to visit Bobbio. And Bobbio was in the news at Il Moro's court: in 1493 the scholar and historian Giorgio Merula removed some of the abbey's *codices* to Milan. Perhaps Leonardo (and Birago) inspected them. Many more volumes – now in Turin, the Vatican, Paris, Madrid, Berlin and above all the Ambrosiana – remained in Bobbio, including Bede's 9th century *Liber de Computo* (*Bobbio Computus*).[33]

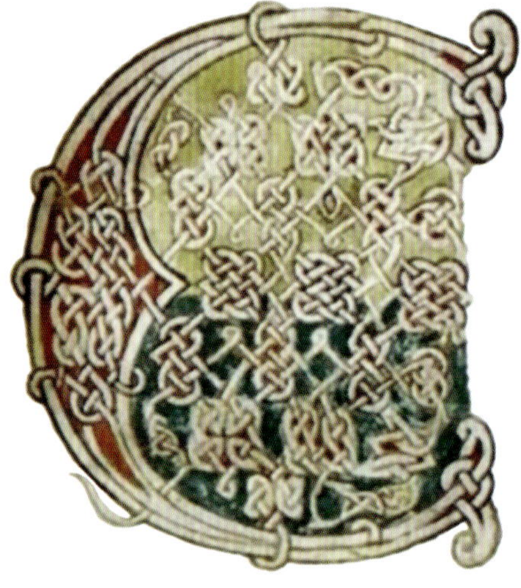

Nothing now remains in Bobbio to evoke its wondrous manuscript past, but some of the old abbey stonework and funeral monuments are preserved in the town museum (*see below*), swathed in intricate knotwork similar to that found in ancient Gaelic manuscripts ... and in Leonardo's *Portrait of Bianca Sforza*.

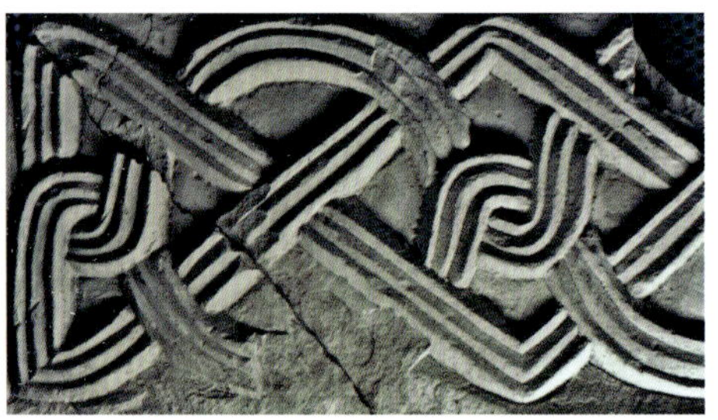

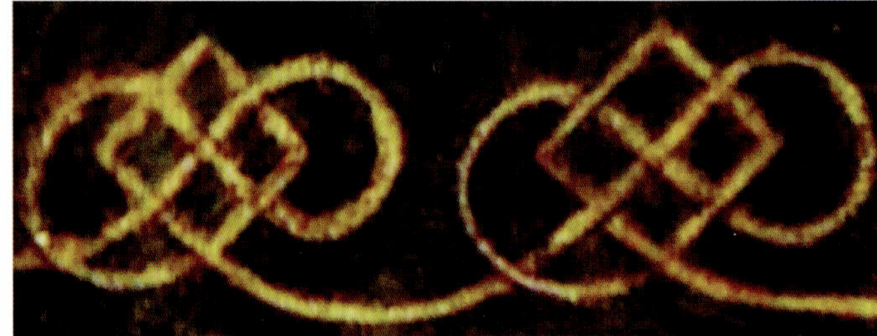

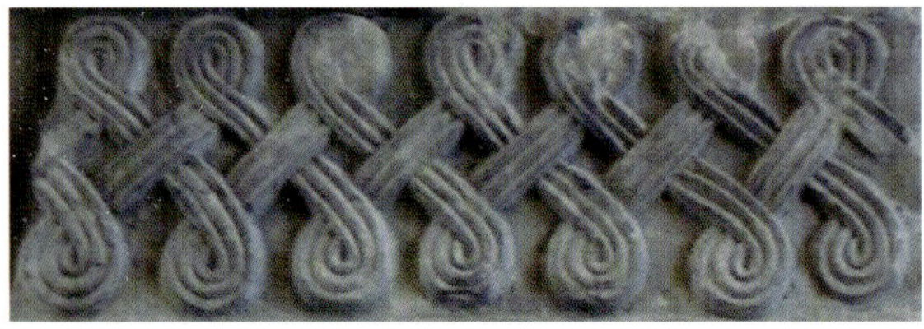

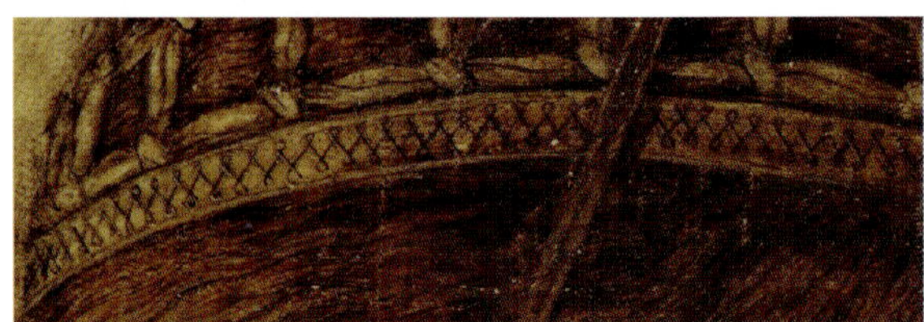

The most glorious reminder of Bobbio's past is the eleven-arched, 300-yard medieval bridge across the Trebbia, known as the Ponte Gobbo or *Ponte del Diavolo* (Devil's Bridge). With its gentle curves and eye-soothing proportions, this is a Taj Mahal among bridges (*see below*).

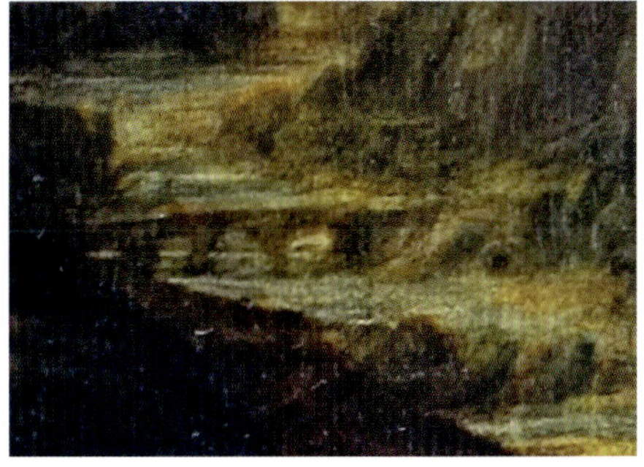

Some say this is the bridge Leonardo painted into the background of the *Mona Lisa* (the Ponte Buriano across the Arno, north of Arezzo, is also a candidate). It is even claimed that Mona Lisa's background landscape features twisting roads leading out of Bobbio along the Val Tidone, up towards Monte Penice, and northwest towards Voghera and Milan.[34]

Perhaps Leonardo created a synthesis – the best of both worlds. *Mona Lisa's* bridge has a flat top, like Ponte Buriano. *Mona Lisa's* bridge has unequal arches – like Bobbio.

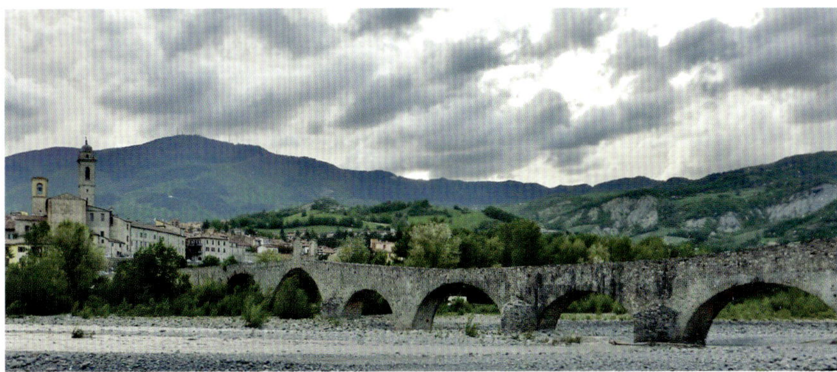

SIGNED LEONARDO

There is another reason to suppose Bobbio held memories for Leonardo. It concerns the triangular shoulder aperture in Bianca's portrait.

The shape and purpose of this aperture remain unexplained. The nearest equivalent belongs to the famous *Portrait of a Lady* in the Ambrosiana, attributed to Leonardo's colleague Ambrogio de Predis – whose knot-pattern, however, is far simpler.

Bianca's aperture serves partly to create perspective: it reveals a patch of slightly rumpled red cloth, subtly evoked by plays of shadow. This purpose is useful in that Leonardo eschews the jewellery that helps create perspective in other Sforza profiled portraits. Yet there must surely be some symbolic reason for the aperture and/or its surrounding knotwork: Sforza court portraits routinely feature jewellery or patterned embroidery which quote Sforza devices and help identify the sitter or indicate why the portrait was painted.

In Romano's bridal bust of Beatrice d'Este, the sifting-cloth and pointed-diamond ring reflect a Sforza-Este alliance. We may logically suppose that, somewhere in his portrait of Bianca Sforza, Leonardo evokes a Sforza–Sanseverino alliance.

The triangular aperture and knotwork embroidery are indeed the keys to interpreting this work – providing they are viewed as a whole, not separately, and providing you remember you are looking at a picture designed for a book – which can easily be turned upside-down.

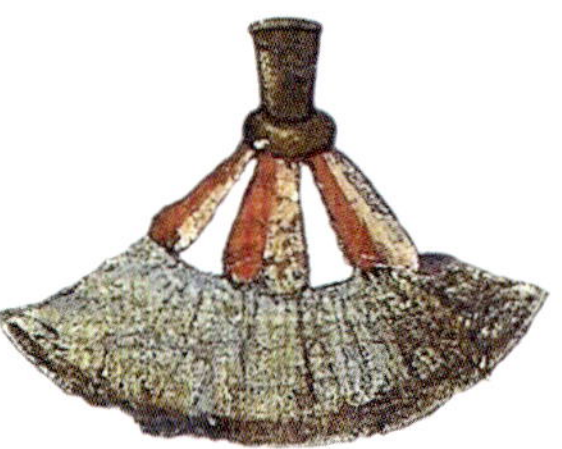

Viewed right-way up, they form the outline of a stylized *scopetta*: Il Moro's favoured personal device (*see top right*).

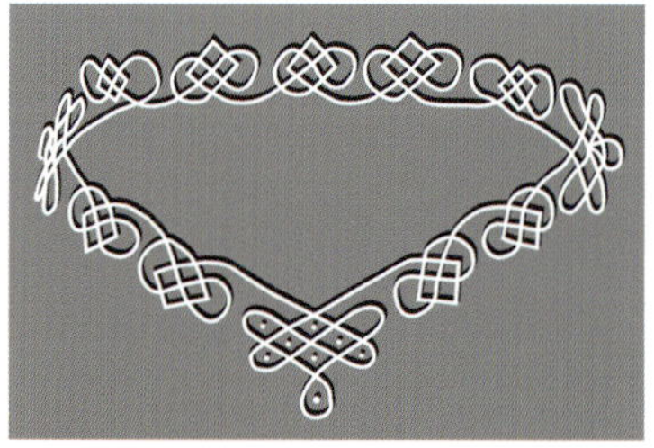

Upside-down, they form a stylized chain: that of the *Ordre de St-Michel*, which Sanseverino received from Charles VIII in Lyon in 1494, and which ends in an oval medallion (rather than a Golden Fleece). A comparison with the effigy of French grandee Gaston de Foix (*right*), who died in 1512, shows that such chains commonly featured interlacing *Vinci*-like knots.[35]

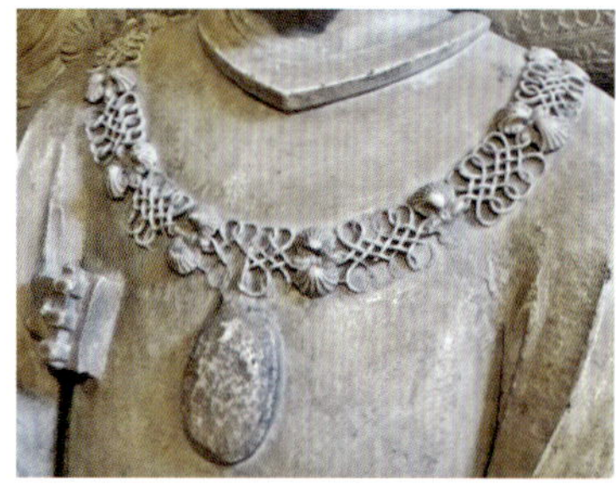

So Leonardo's portrait shows Bianca's dual allegiance to her husband and father – echoing the message of Birago's frontispiece.

But what about Bianca herself? Is her own status evoked by Leonardo's portrait?

Yes. Leonardo paid tribute to The Lady of Bobbio by citing one of the distinctive chalk cliffs above the town – where St Columbanus lived out his final days after unleashing Gaelic knots on Italy like some aesthetic plague.

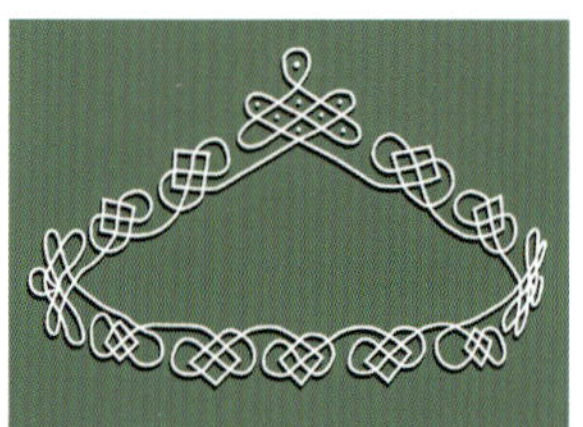

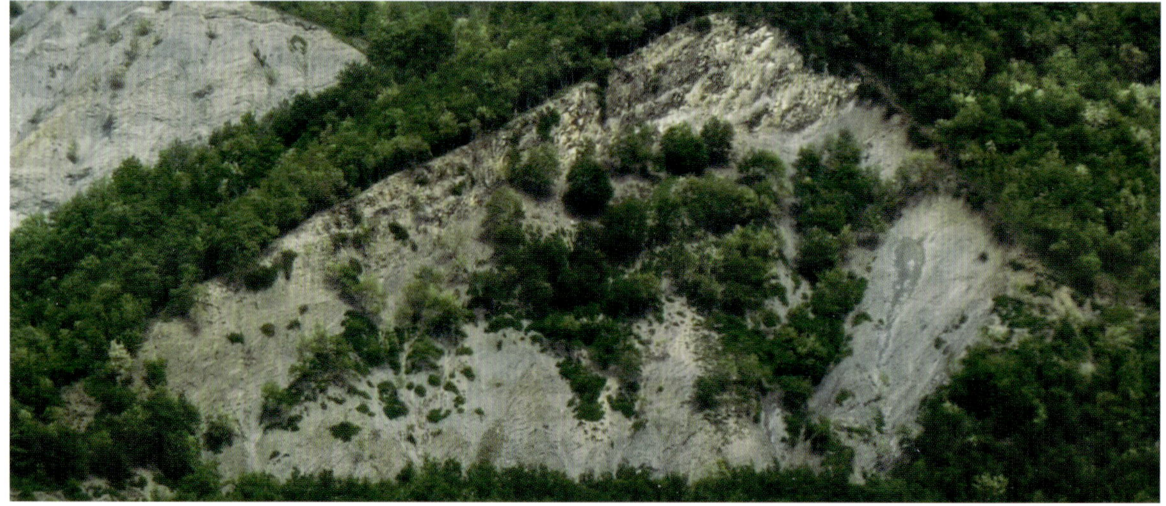

NOTES

1 The profiled portraits of the Sforza court originated from coins; they were initially intended more as hierarchical statements than essays in psychology. Ambrogio de Predis was the first Sforza artist to depict the character, as well as the physical features, of a profiled subject in his depiction of Matthias Corvinus for the Marliano *Epitalamion*, and he repeated this approach by subtly varying Francesco Sforza's mood in each of the four *Sforziada* medallions. De Predis retained this manner in some of his paintings, witness his wonderful female portrait in the Ambrosiana but, when it was merely a matter of rendering physical likeness, he did not bother evoking psychological subtleties – as is shown by the doltish expression in his two portraits of Bianca Maria, intended for people in faraway Austria who had never met her. The portrait of Anna Sforza was due to be seen by the courts of Ferrara and Milan, where everyone knew what she looked like; in this context, a successful portrait needed more than physical likeness.

2 Elisabetta Gnignera, *Leonardo – La Bella Svelata* (Scripta Maneant, Bologna 2016).

3 Cartwright, *op. cit.*

4 Martin Kemp & Pascal Cotte, *La Bella Principessa* (Hodder & Stoughton, London 2010).

5 Alessandro Giulini, *Bianca Sanseverino Sforza figlia di Lodovico il Moro* (Giornale della Societa Storica Lombarda, 1912), citing/ interpreting documents in the Milan State Archives.

6 Carla Glori, *La Gioconda – In Memoria di Bianca* (Edizioni Cappello, 2011).

7 Giulini, *op. cit.*

8 Quoted by Marzia de Luca in Volume XIII of *Carteggio degli Oratori Mantovani alla Corte Sforzesca*.

9 Il Moro's illegitimate son Leone (1476–96), named after Leone Sforza (1406–40), condottiero son of Muzio Attendolo, is first mentioned in May 1481, when Il Moro donated canals and land near Vigevano to him. He married Margherita Grassi (source: Nadia Covini, *Quasi-Città e la Corte di Ludovico il Moro*).

10 By procurator Giovan Tommaso Gentili, an elder relative of the Niccoló Gentili who legitimized Bianca in 1489.

11 Giulini, *op. cit.*

12 Cartwright, *op. cit.*

13 'Me pare che epso Messer Galeazzo sia Duca de Milano perché el po ciò ch'el vole et ha quello che sa dimandare et desiderare' – cited in Roberto Martinis, *Il Palazzo del Banco Mediceo: Edilizia e Arte della Diplomazia a Milano nel X Secolo* (*Annal di Archtettura* 2003).

14 For this and subsequent accounts of Maximilian's activity in Summer 1496, see *Österreichisches Staatsarchiv – Regesta Imperii* (www.regesta-imperii.de).

15 Carla Glori (*op. cit.*) advances, among other potential evidence as to Gian Galeazzo's death through long-term poisoning, that he was stricken with terrible stomach pains on 20 July 1494, but recovered thanks to a break in the Parma region, well away from the malevolent interference of Il Moro's henchmen.

16 It has been widely published that Bianca died in Vigevano but Alessandro Giulini, writing in 1912, claims this is not so – accusing Olga von Gertsfeldt's then-recently published *Pilgerfahrten in Italien* (Leipzig 1910) of mistakenly spreading this assumption. Von Gertsfeldt wrote that, to mark the marriage of Bianca and Galeazzo, *Glänzende Feste und Turniere wurden zu Ehren des jungen Paares veranstaltet und beide mit fürstlichen Geschenken überhäuft. Aber noch in demselben Jahre ereilte ein plötzlicher Tod die blühende junge Frau, die im November in Vigevano starb.* (Dazzling celebrations and tournaments were held in honour of the young couple, and both were showered with ducal gifts. But, that same year, the blooming young woman was suddenly struck down, dying in November in Vigevano.)

17 There is debate over the date of Bianca's death, with Giulini citing November 22. However, Il Moro's use of yesterday and today in his letter to Bianca's mother suggest that Glori is right to prefer November 23. One circumstantial argument in her favour is that it renders the gap between Bianca's death and that of Beatrice d'Este (on January 2) as precisely 40 days.

18 Archivio di Stato di Milano, Potenze Sovrane, Sforza, 1495.

19 The curious depiction of a two-part umbilical chord also chimes in with Leonardo's original conception of conception – with the male organ directly linked not only to the testicles, but also to the lungs and the spinal cord, and hence to the brain (Leonardo would later have doubts about these notions, but in sketches of the 1490s he portrayed the penis with two channels: one for the sperm from the testes; the other for spiritual powers transported from the brain along the spinal cord).

20 Elisabetta Gnignera, correspondence with the author.

21 This was not the first untimely death of a Bianca in the Sforza family in 1496. In August, Gian Galeazzo's posthumous daughter Bianca Maria, to whom Isabel of Aragon had given birth on 1 March 1495, died at the age of seventeen months; she was buried not in Santa Maria della Grazie, but in the church of Sant' Agostino (since rebuilt), close to the church of Sant' Ambrogio much frequented by Il Moro and Beatrice d'Este.

22 Carla Glori reproduces this letter, purportedly written in Il Moro's hand. The handwriting is shaky and it is unclear whether it addressed to Bernardina de CoNradis or CoRradis. Most commentators have opted for the former. Neither name exists in Italy today – unlike *Corradi*, proposed as the surname of Bianca's mother by Nadia Covini in her article *Zanette e Cicilia: Potere, Sangue e Passioni nella Milano di Ludovico Il Moro* (*Vigevanum* – Società Storica Vigevanese, May 2011). In support of this spelling, Covini cites the letter from the Mantuan Ambassador Zaccaria Saggi to Duke Federico Gonzaga, dated 20 January 1483 (*cf* footnote 8, above).

23 The letter is reproduced in Glori (*op. cit.*), p. 209. She accuses Giulini of misrepresenting the mood of Il Moro's letter to Rosate by adding three dots as if to imply uncertainty or hesitation, and insists Il Moro was definitely suspicious.

24 Cartwright, *op. cit.*

25 Muratori (*op.cit.*): *Beatrice avvelenata da Francesca dal Verme ad istanza di Galeazzo Sanseverino, per quanto essa Francesca dopo alcuni anni propalo morendo. Il perche non si dice, potendosi solamente osservare, che per attesato d'esso Corio era morta poco tempo prima Bianca bastarda d'esso Duca Lodovico, e moglie di Galeazzo suddetto.*

26 Cartwright, *op. cit.*

27 Eugène Müntz, *Leonardo da Vinci – Artist, Thinker and Man of Science* (William Heinemann, London 1898).

28 Carla Glori, *op. cit.*

29 On 18 November 1485 Il Moro confiscated lands from the Dal Vermes, ignoring the claims of Pietro's natural son Francesco dal Verme, Pietro's brothers Taddeo and Giovanni, and his sister Caterina. Bobbio was initially assigned to the Milanese Chancellery then, in 1489, to Bianca (*cf* Fabrizio Bernini, *I Conti Dal Verme*, Ed. Iuculano, 2006).

30 Carla Glori, *op. cit.*

31 Elisabetta Gnignera, *op. cit.*

32 Including the *Antiphonarium Benchorense*, which contains an *ymnum sancti Congilli abbatis nostri*, and evokes *nostri patroni Comgilli sancti* – placing Comgall atop a list of fifteen abbots that ends with Cronanus, who died in 691.

33 Dáibhí Ó Cróinín argues that the computus was compiled in southern Ireland in AD 658 before being used in Jarrow by The Venerable Bede – see *The Irish Provenance of Bede's Computus*, Peritia 2 (1983), pp.229–47.

34 Carla Glori, *op. cit.*

35 The heraldic proof that Galeazzo Sanseverino belonged to this Order is furnished by the presence of the Chain of St-Michel around his personal coat of arms on the front page of the copy of Pacioli's *Divina Proportione*, presented to him in 1498 (*see p.161*).

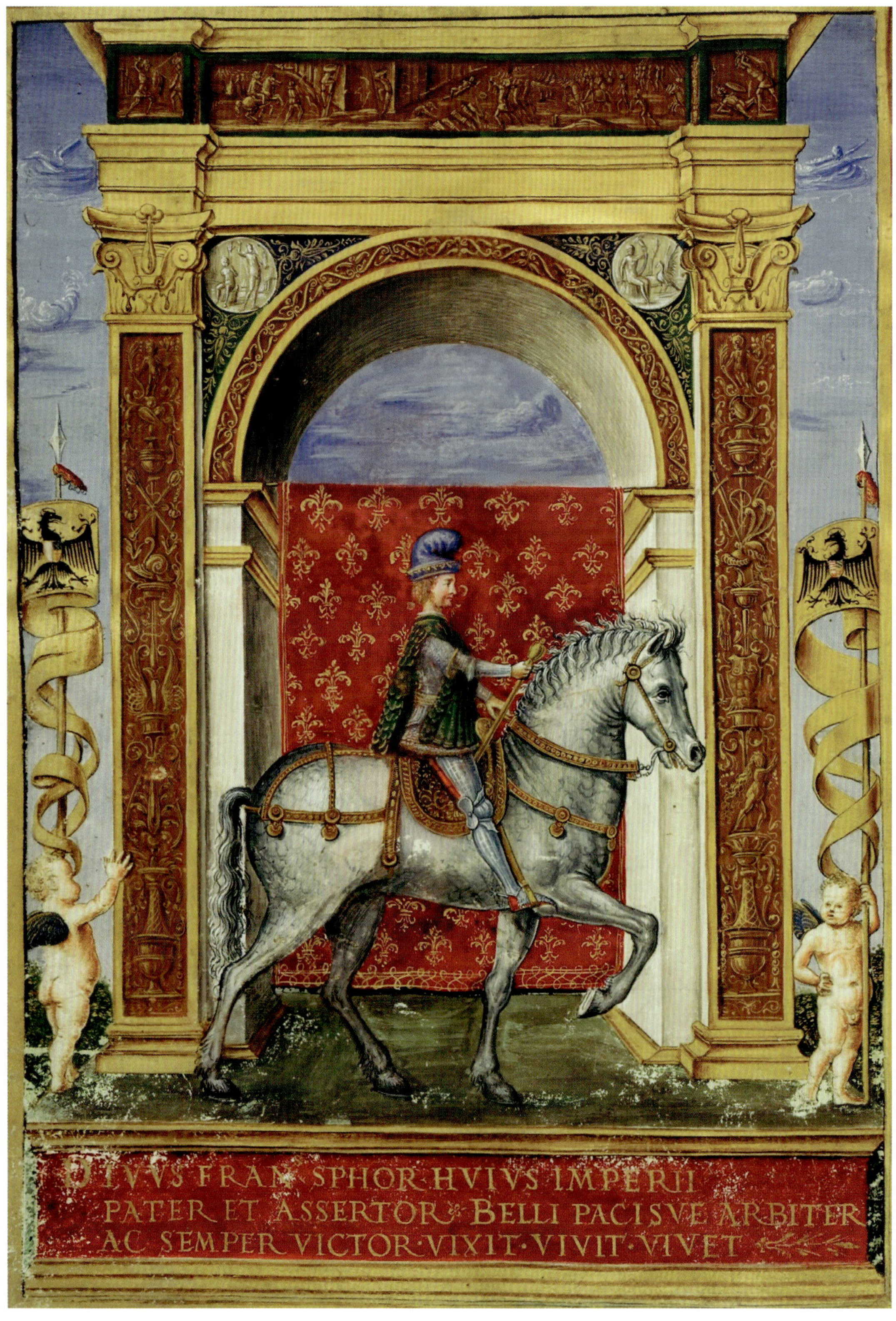

SFORZIADA 1486 EDITION (FRONTISPIECE) – BIBLIOTECA RICCARDIANA, FLORENCE (ED. RARE 428)

XI

FIT FOR AN EMPEROR?

THE UNCOMPLETED SFORZIADA

IN THE MID-1490s a copy of the 1486 Latin edition of the *Sforziada* was hauled out of a cupboard and transformed into a magnificent presentation volume by adding a full-page miniature of an equestrian knight beneath a triumphal arch. The volume was intended for Holy Roman Emperor Maximilian I. He never received it. The knight was not Maximilian. Nor was it Francesco Sforza, the book's hero.

PROVENANCE

Giovanni Battista Doni (1594–1647), Florence
Gabriello Riccardi (1606–75), Florence
Biblioteca Riccardiana, Florence

This 188*ff*, 27.5 × 20.3cm volume has two pages with mesmerizingly intricate illumination, and a 19th century brown leather binding by Gaetano Tartagli. How the book arrived in Florence – where it is recorded since the 17th century – is unknown. It is intriguing to note that the Riccardiana Library was greatly enlarged by a bequest from Vincenzio Capponi (1605–88), whose daughter Cassandra was married to Francesco Riccardi (1648–1719), and that the third illuminated *Sforziada* – whose cut-up frontispiece is also in Florence (at the Uffizi) – was once owned by the great bibliophile Alessandro Gregorio Capponi (1683–1746).

FULL-PAGE MINIATURE

The first illuminated page, inserted at the start of the volume, is set within thick borders of gold and dark green. It is one of just two textless, full-page miniatures among the six illuminated volumes devoted to Sforza history, and appears based on the knightly portrait of Muzio Attendoli in his manuscript biography of 1491.

ARCHITECTURE

The triumphal arch with brown Ionic pilasters whose military trophies include a golden helmet (*left*) and golden breastplate (*right*). The cornice features a frieze similar to that in the *Muzio* frontispiece. It depicts an attack on city walls: soldiers scale a ladder and archers are firing at the walls while knights line up behind them. This has been suggested as depicting Francesco Sforza's siege of Milan in 1450, prior to his seizure of power – but it shows an all-out

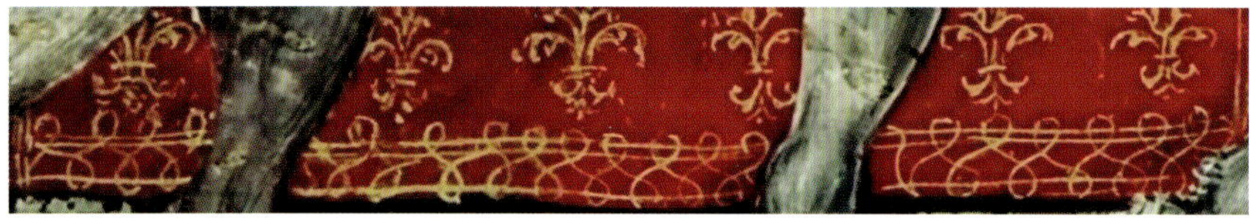

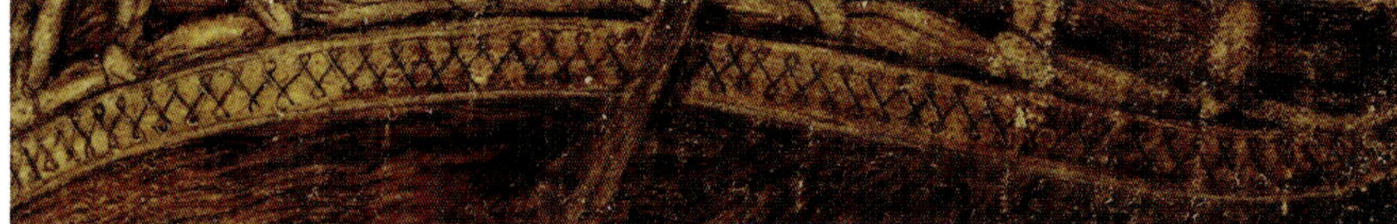

attack rather than a siege. On either side of the brown rim of the archway, with its decorative scrolling, are blue and green pendentives containing round medallions depicting *Apollo and Marsyas* (said to signify victory over barbarity) and *Prometheus* (signifying wisdom).

HANGING

The back of the arch is blocked off by a crimson hanging studded with gold floral motifs, whose form – if not colour – recall *fleurs-de-lys*. Yet they are not French lilies but Milanese mulberry branches, as used for Il Moro's investiture ceremony in May 1495.[1] The base of the hanging (*above top*) is lined with an interlacing motif of the type found in several works by Leonardo da Vinci, including the caul worn by Bianca Sforza in her portrait in the Polish *Sforziada*.

PUTTI

The arch is flanked by two naked, winged infant standard-bearers set against a blue sky with puffy light clouds; their spear-topped standards sport red pennants above trailing gold banners, each featuring a black Imperial eagle with the quartered arms of Emperor Maximilian on its chest. (Similar putti, with quince-adorned banners, flanked Muzio Attendolo in his manuscript biography.)

INSCRIPTION

The plinth at the foot of the monument has a gold-lettered inscription on a red ground across its entire width, reading:

DIVUS FRAN SPHOR HVIVS IMPERII
PATER ET ASSERTOR BELLI PACISVE ARBITER
AC SEMPER VICTOR VIXET VIVIT VIVET

Venerable Francesco Sforza: Of This Empire
Father & Protector – Arbiter of War & Peace
He Lived, Lives, Shall Live Forever Victorious

The *Clarissimus* reference of the Muzio Attendolo miniature is here upgraded to *Divus*, as befits a leader associated with a god-scale triple-lifesize horse. The alliterative play on words (*victor vixet vivet vivet*) recalls the *PRM ET PRM PATRIAE* inscription in the Paris *Sforziada*.

KNIGHT

A knight is shown, like Muzio, on a (dappled) grey steed in front of the arch, portrayed with gusto. Evans feels that the horse 'shares the vigour of Leonardo's equine studies' and that 'a similar quality animates Dürer's 1505 engraving of a Small Horse in the British Museum.'[2] The horse's pose is the same as in the illuminated Muzio portrait (*below left*), and stylistically more assured.

The only difference between the two illuminated horses is that the head of Muzio's steed is turned slightly to the right rather than gazing straight ahead – as in the equine monument to Marcus Aurelius in Rome (*below centre*), upon which both appear based; they may also be intended to evoke Leonardo da Vinci's doomed monument in honour of Francesco Sforza. Neither horse attains quite the expressive gusto of Birago's two steeds in his *October* miniature for the *Sforza Hours* (*see p.207*).

Although both knights are shown in armour brandishing the gold baton of an army general, the knight's pose here is slightly different from Muzio's: his legs are not bent at the knee but stretched out in front of him; his right arm is also stretched out in front of him, not hanging by his side.

The knight is wearing a dark green cape, tall blue hat and steel armour that allows glimpses of a red under-stocking. He sits on a florid-patterned brown saddle, but his legs appear short (descending no lower than the horse's under-carriage) – although a Milanese precedent exists in the monument to Bernabó Visconti now on the Castello Sforzesca (originally erected in San Giovanni in Conca, the Viscontis' private chapel).

As pointed out by Giovanna Lazzi, Head of the Biblioteca Riccardiana in Florence where this volume is kept, the knight is *not* Francesco Sforza – who is invariably portrayed in middle or old age, wearing his battered red campaigning hat, and with grey or dark brown hair. The rider here is a young man with blond, shoulder-length hair.

It has been suggested that the knight could be Emperor Maximilian, whose Imperial coat of arms appears on both illuminated pages. But the knight's profile does not resemble Maximilian's. We know from an abundance of

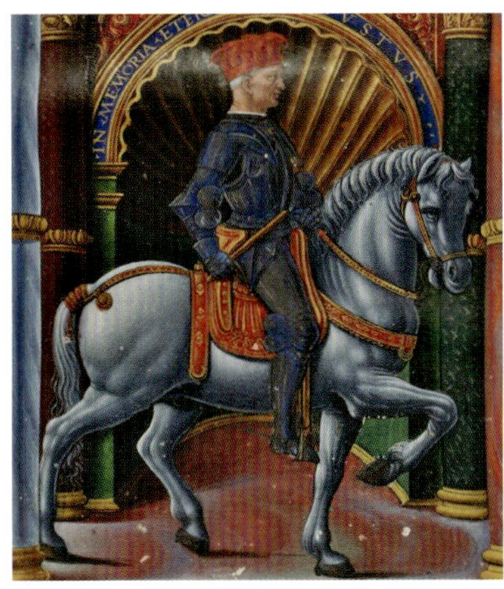

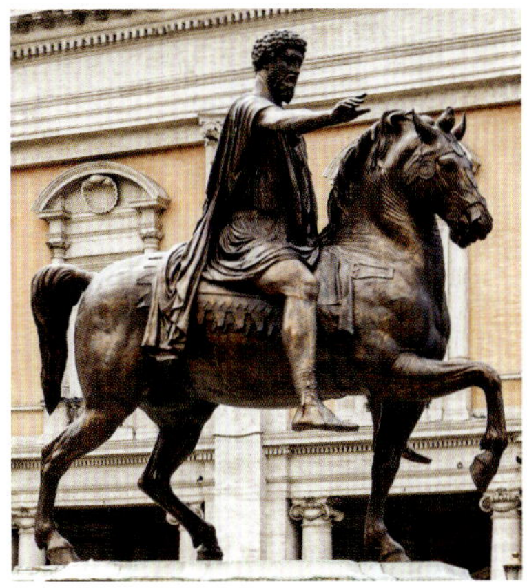

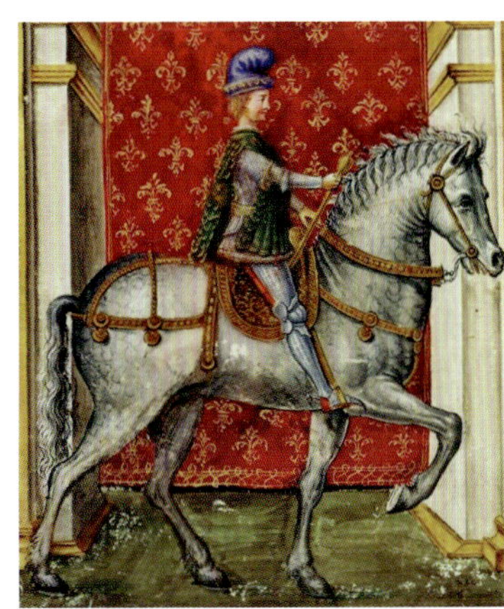

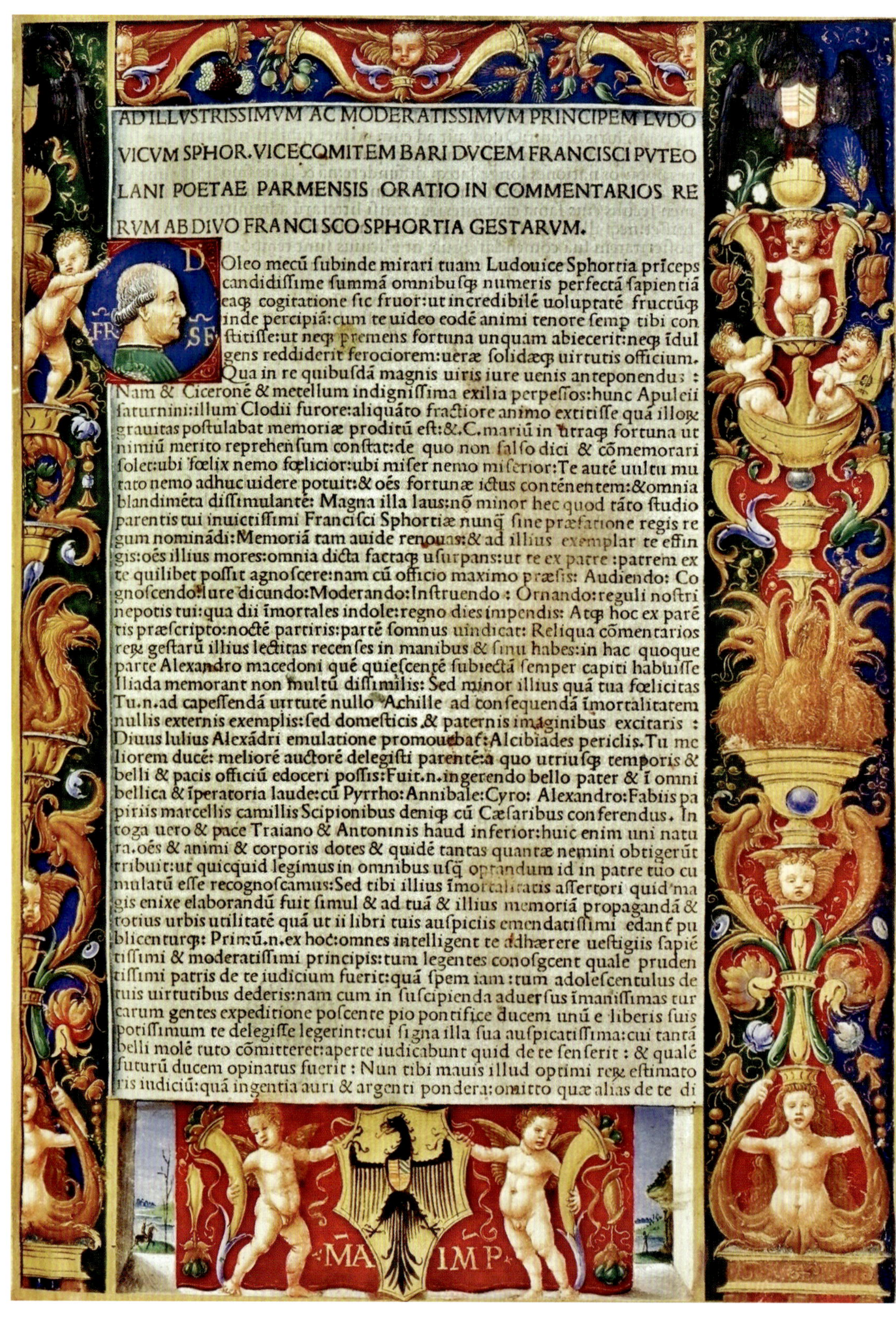

SFORZIADA 1486 EDITION (FOL. 1r) – BIBLIOTECA RICCARDIANA, FLORENCE

portraits, by Ambrogio de Predis and others, that Maximilian had brown hair and a grotesquely bridged nose.

It has also been suggested that the knight may represent an 'idealized' *condottiero* and is deliberately anonymous. As no insignia or emblems appear to help identify him, this is plausible – but why the need for such discretion? Does his blue hat offer a clue? Combined with the glimpses of red stocking, we have here the colours of Sforza livery. But why do no Sforza devices of the sort that pepper Birago's frontispieces appear here?

This 'ideal' knight may serve to evoke a previous Duke of Austria: Leopold III von Habsburg (1351–86), 'Der Gerechte' (*The Righteous*), who in 1365 married Viridis Visconti (1352–1414), daughter of Bernabó Visconti – known as the Habsburg *Stammmutter* (Matriarch), and a common ancestor of the Habsburgs and the Sforzas.

FRONTISPIECE

FRANCESCO SFORZA MEDALLION

A small, square, red medallion, with gold-embellished pendentives, features the bust of an aged Francesco in black-edged, right-facing profile, clad in green with steel armour visible at the shoulder. He is flanked at neck level by the gold lettering ***FR SF*** on a circular blue ground. The initial *D* of the text, top-right, straddles the blue ground/red pendentive. The left edge of the blue disc overlaps the left-hand border.

HAUT-DE-PAGE

This is divided into two horizontal grounds: top part red, lower blue. A central winged cherub-head is framed by two horns of plenty, one spilling forth quinces, the other barley. Two other end cherubs look inwards, each flanked by a single horn of plenty – one spilling forth grapes, the other red berries. The design of this *haut-de-page* appears directly inspired by that of the Muzio manuscript, but applies a far more sophisticated approach to perspective, with the more delicately shaded angel-heads shown at an angle rather than front-on.

BAS-DE-PAGE

As in the *Muzio* manuscript, this takes the form of a cherub-flanked shield with a riverscape background. Two winged cherubs stand on a window ledge, propping up a gold shield with the black eagle of Emperor Maximilian, its chest impaled with the quartered arms of (*clockwise from top left*) Hungary, Burgundy, Tyrol and Austria.

A halved Austria/Burgundy shield was the most common in Maximilian's heraldry. The combination here seems unprecedented. The nearest equivalent is the quartered shield positioned between Maximilian and Bianca Maria in the frescoed *Stammbaum* (family tree) in Schloss Tratzberg near Innsbruck – but this features a black Habsburg eagle rather than a red Tyrolean one.

The cherubs and shield are shown against a red banner with a horn of plenty towards each end, which the cherubs grasp with their other hand – a sleight of visual legerdemain suggesting the angels are simultaneously part of the banner, as well as standing on the ledge. The lower part of the gold shield is flanked by the lettering *MA* and *IMP* (*MAXIMILIAN IMPERATOR*). Gold ribbons flutter from the top of the shield; unusually, they are not symmetrical or of the same length. The left-hand ribbon ends in a tight curl, suggesting an *S*; the right-hand ribbon winds back on itself to end in a shape reminiscent of a *G*.

Golden leaves and green grapes issue from the horns of plenty. An elongated, blank gold shield flanks the left-hand horn of plenty. A golden vine-leaf and green grapes dangle from the base of the shield. An elongated gold helmet flanks the right-hand horn of plenty, again with a golden vine-leaf and green grapes dangling beneath. A landscape with green fields, a winding river and distant blue mountains – perhaps the Alps, leading to Austria – can be glimpsed through the window-frame to either side of the banner.[3] To the left is a rider beneath a tall, leafless tree; to the right, a figure standing beneath a building.

RIGHT BORDER

Like the right-hand border in the first Muzio frontispiece, the ground is halved green/blue, with a red ground for central motifs. At the bottom is a naked female figure with crown and long blond hair, her midriff transformed into two upwards scrolls that merge into stylized foliage supporting a winged angel-head beneath a gold bowl containing three gold gryphons. An urn flanked by horns of plenty leads up to a bowl containing two musical winged cherubs, one playing a tambourine, the other a lute; a stem in the middle is topped by another cherub flanked by horns of plenty, spilling forth white lilies (left horn) and ears of ripe and unripe barley (right). A gold helmet dangles from the left horn, a gold breastplate from the right – each is requoted in the *bas-de-page*. The cherub is topped by a golden globe, upon which perches a black eagle with outspread wings (*see right*), its chest impaled with the same quartered shield as elsewhere. The ornament virtually mirrors that of the left-hand border, except that here everything is portrayed full-on, not in semi-profile.

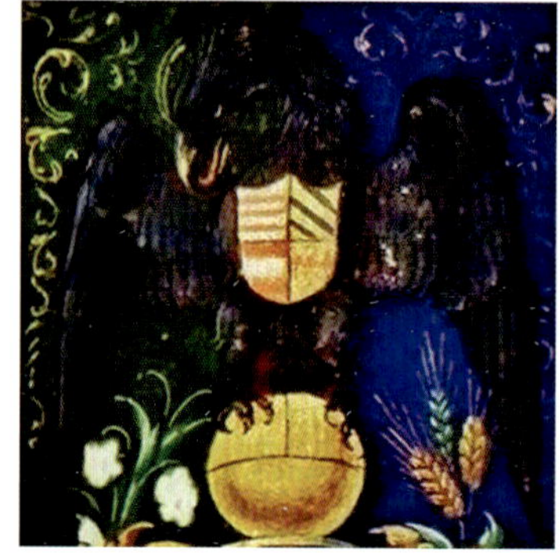

LEFT BORDER

The top part (eagle on globe) and bottom half of this border echo the left half of the right border, albeit it slanting slightly downwards. This is an extraordinary approach – the illuminated equivalent of italicization.

The background is dark green throughout; the ground of the central motifs (or what is visible thereof) is coloured blue. The two musical cherubs from the right border are omitted, while the cherub brandishing horns of plenty now has his arms around the roundel portrait of Francesco Sforza, as if rolling it into place. The text next to the left border is flanked by a thin line of blue shading, creating the illusionary effect that the border has been stuck down and is casting a shadow (this same *trompe-l'œil* effect is used by Birago in all four of his *Sforziada* frontispieces).

Both borders involve such liberal use of gold colouring that, allied to the engraving-like intricacy of the archway decoration, one wonders if a goldsmith were involved in the decoration of these two pages. The black eagles at the top of each border, however, are almost invisible against their dark green/navy blue backgrounds – a lack of colour clarity that, for Birago, would have been unthinkable. It suggests the finishing touches to these eagles – probably in the form of gold highlighting – was never applied.

ILLUMINATED INITIALS

The volume has 30 square illuminations containing the initial letter of every chapter bar one. The initials are in gold against a three-colour background of blue, red, and green with further, delicate gold patterning. The margins along-side the initials are embellished with scrolling foliage and flowers in a range of colours (*example below left*). The only chapter that does not start with an illuminated initial is *LIBER PRIMUS* – the very first chapter (*below right*) con-taining the start of the text proper, whose first sentence reads *Egnante Iohanna secuda Karuli Regis filia quae Ladislao fratri sine liberis e uita migrati i nea-politani regnu successerat Alphosus Taraconesiu rex magna classe e citeriore Hispania*. The square left for the initialled ***R*** of *Regnante* remains blank.

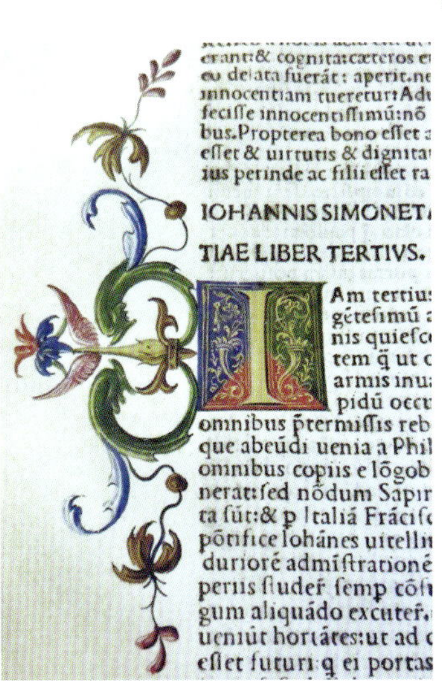

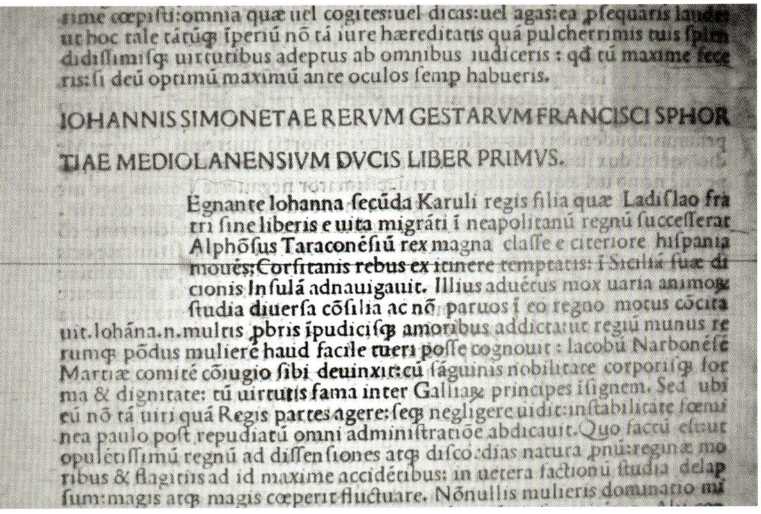

DATE

With Maximilian referred to as ***IMPerator*** at the base of the frontispiece, the illuminations cannot be earlier than August 1493 and the death of his father, Friedrich III. As the crimson hanging appears inspired by that used at Il Moro's investiture ceremony, they cannot be earlier than May 1495.

It may be relevant that three of the four inscriptions (*see pp.237/8*) on the ceiling of the Sala delle Asse in the Castello Sforzesco (and probably originally the fourth) refer to successive years of Maximilian's involvement with the House of Sforza, spanning the period 1493–96. Could these two pages of illumination date from as late as 1496?

INTERPRETATION

The illuminators of this Latin *Sforziada* appear to emanate from Birago's circle – but the frontispiece displays a freedom of handling Birago never attained, and the full-page miniature a mastery of detail that is exceptional even by Renaissance standards.

Suddenly, in the mid-1490s – when, for several years, the only *Sforziadas* to be illuminated were those from the recent 1490 *Florentine* edition – a copy of the second *Latin* edition from 1486 was granted an extra illuminated page opposite the frontispiece which, itself, was sumptuously illuminated for the occasion.

A Latin rather than 'Florentine' copy of the *Sforziada* was presumably chosen to honour the Holy *Roman* Emperor, whose arms are featured on both illuminated pages. So why is the book now in Florence, not in Austria? Why did it never get to Maximilian, if it were meant as a gift for him? There is no trace in the Austrian State Archives of its ever passing through Habsburg hands.

Why, if the horseman is not the book's titular hero Francesco Sforza, is he not Maximilian – the book's intended recipient?

The knight is no Sforza: uniquely among the six illuminated *Sforziadas*, there is no emblem, inscription or heraldic device to identify the involvement of Il Moro in the commissioning of this luxurious volume.

The knight has blond hair and a wispy beard. If, as suggested above, he is meant to evoke Duke Leopold III, on what is this depiction based? No portrait of Leopold (1351–86) is known to exist.

There is, though, a famous portrait of his blond-haired, wispy-bearded elder brother – Rudolf IV (1339–65), Duke of Austria and Count of Tyrol, who died in Milan five months after his brother's marriage to Viridis Visconti. This portrait (*see p.27*) is thought to be the first painted in three-quarter profile, and a likely influence on the pose of Leonardo's 'Musician' – Galeazzo Sanseverino.

Like Leopold III, Galeazzo Sanseverino was a fourth-born son marrying into the Milanese ruling family. Like Francesco Sforza, Galeazzo Sanseverino married the illegitimate daughter of the reigning Duke of Milan.

This Latin *Sforziada* quotes the golden shield, golden breastplate and golden helmet (*galea* in Latin) also featured in the illumination of the Muzio manuscript and the Polish *Sforziada* – two volumes celebrating the betrothal and marriage of Bianca Sforza and Galeazzo Sanseverino. After his elevation to the rank of the ducal Sforzas, does this de luxe Latin *Sforziada* see Sanseverino striving to ingratiate himself with a new 'equal': the most prestigious ruler in Europe – the Habsburg Emperor?

Is this the Sanseverino whom Birago and Il Moro warned in the Polish *Sforziada* not to get too big for his boots?

Sanseverino met Maximilian three times in 1496: in July in Tyrol (whose arms appear in this Latin *Sforziada's* unusual Imperial shield); in September in Vigevano; in December in Pavia. Twice that year Maximilian vainly requested Il Moro to send him Sanseverino for counsel and company: first in August, when Maximilian was preparing his military expedition to Italy; then in October, as he was preparing to attack Pisa.[4]

The volume's illumination is unlikely to have been put in hand before Maximilian and Sanseverino first met in August 1496 – with the aim of being presented to the 'forever victorious' Maximilian when he returned from the expected triumph of his Pisan campaign a few months later.

But, pounded by autumn storms and undermined by effete Milanese and Venetian support, the Pisan Campaign which Maximilian had grandly sketched out that summer, up in the Alps, proved a fiasco. His bedraggled forces would limp back to Austria in conditions presaging Napoleon's Retreat From Moscow, straggling over the Umbrail Pass knee-deep in snow. The illuminated Latin *Sforziada*, conceived as a gift fit for an emperor, did not go with them.

It was to prove another book of doom – completed but for one illuminated initial when Bianca's sudden death, nine days before Maximilian returned to Lombardy, rendered its purpose null and void … and cast Galeazzo Sanseverino into dynastic limbo.

NOTES

1 On 26 May 1495 (the feast of St Felicissimo), Il Moro was proclaimed Duke of Milan by Bishop Melchior of Brixen and Conrad Sturzl, Chancellor of the King of the Romans. A gallery hung with crimson satin embroidered with gold mulberry leaves and berries was erected for the occasion outside the Duomo.

2 Evans suggests that Dürer gained access to drawings by Leonardo through Pirckheimer's friendship with Sanseverino, who visited him in Nuremberg in 1502.

3 Giovanna Lazzi claims that this landscape evokes mirrors/pools of water, representing Genoa.

4 It has even been suggested, in various sources, that Maximilian awarded Sanseverino the Order of the Golden Fleece – but this assertion is based on an erroneous interpretation of the Order surrounding Galeazzo Sanseverino's coat of arms at the foot of folio 1 in the 130ff manuscript (285 × 250mm) of *De Divina Proportione* presented to Sanseverino by its author Luca Pacioli in 1498 (Biblioteca Ambrosiana S.P. 6). This Order is unquestionably the Ordre de St-Michel, bestowed upon Sanseverino by Charles VIII in 1494.

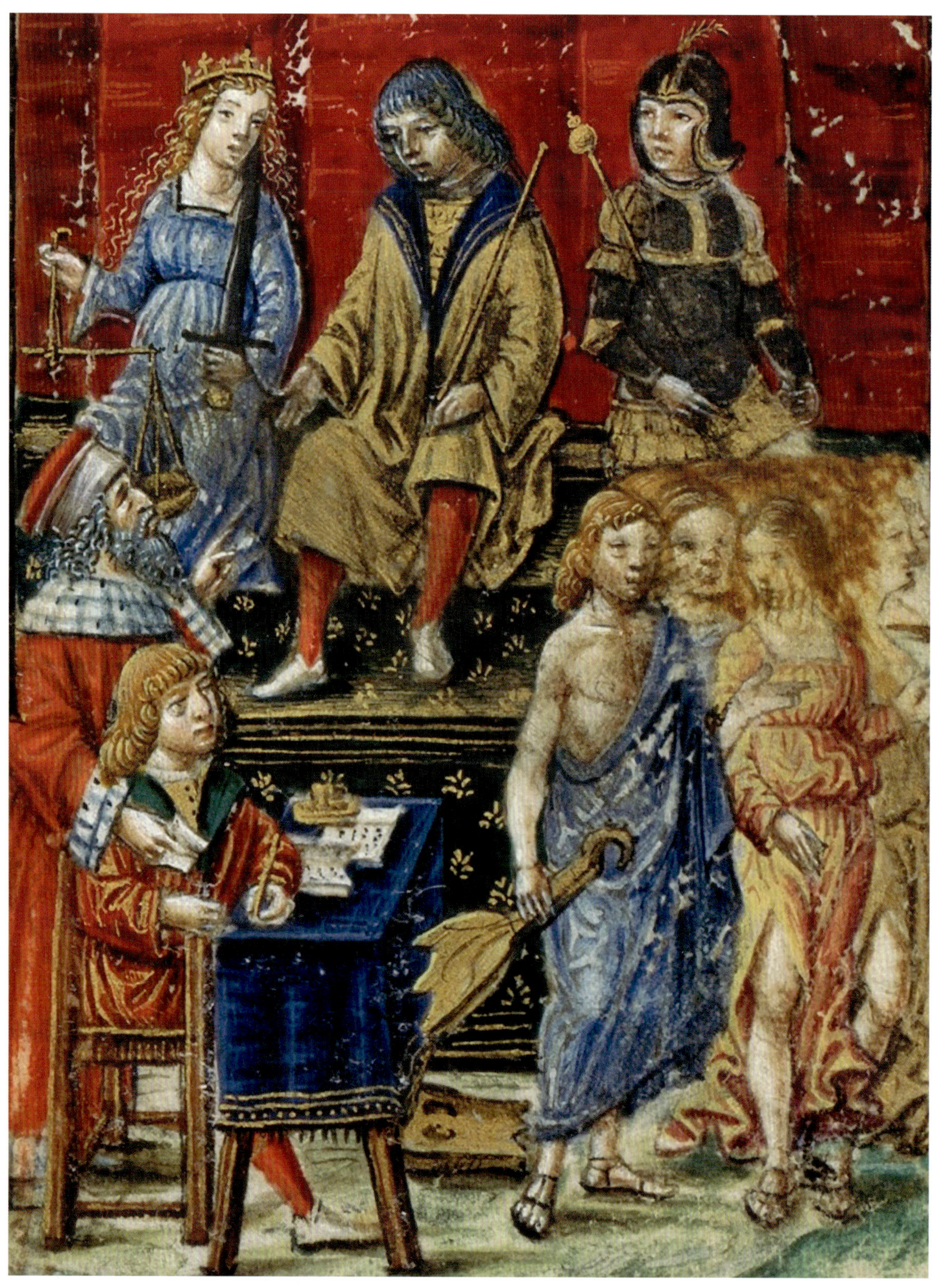

PAOLO E DARIA (ALLEGORY OF JUSTICE) – KUPFERSTICHKABINETT, BERLIN (MS 78 C27)

XII

OLD PALS' ACT

BIRAGO AND HIS MILANESE CIRCLE

AS WELL AS ILLUMINATING four *Sforziada* frontispieces, Gianpietro Birago was engaged on the greatest project of his career: a stupendous *Book of Hours* for Dowager Duchess Bona di Savoia. Meanwhile a host of fellow-illuminators were busy on the manifold books and official documents issuing forth in 1490s Milan. Most of Birago's fellow-miniaturists reflected his style – and were similarly inspired by Leonardo da Vinci.

THE *SFORZA HOURS*

The grandest project to engage Birago in the 1490s was a 348*ff* Book of Hours commissioned by Bona di Savoia, donated to the British Museum (*Add. MS 34294*) by Scottish connoisseur John Malcolm in 1893, and commonly referred to as the *Sforza Hours*.

Dowager Duchess Bona di Savoia had been a peripheral figure at the Milanese court since fleeing to France in October 1481, aged 32, to join her elder sister Charlotte, wife of King Louis XI. She returned in late 1483, after Louis and Charlotte – aged 42 – died within three months of each other. Bona remained an important patron of the arts (who once tried to hire Mantegna) from her base at Abbiategrasso, 25 miles west of Milan along the Naviglio Grande, where she ran what amounted to a miniature court-in-exile. Her palazzo now houses the town library. Much of its mural decoration – consisting essentially of the repetition *ad nauseam* of the motto *A BON DROIT* ('by right') – is still intact, as if to remind eternity that she was wronged by Il Moro.

The *Book of Hours* she commissioned from Birago is visually stunning. Its eye-battering colours would not be matched until 1960s Pop Art and its images of gore, bondage and transvestite freaks have the power to shock and awe even today.

The 348*ff* volume, on vellum, measures 13.1 × 9.3cm and includes 64 full-page miniatures – 48 original, 16 added later by the Flemish artist Gerard Horenbout – and 139 pages containing eleven lines of handwritten script and one or more historiated initials within lavishly illuminated borders (most, but not all, by Birago).

The *Book of Hours* resurfaced in Madrid in 1871 and was first discussed in print in 1894 by George F. Warner, Assistant Keeper of Manuscripts at the British Museum. In his 43-page introduction to the catalogue presenting the volume,

Warner remarked on the stylistic similarities between its illumination and that of the frontispiece of the London *Sforziada* and, in seeking to identify the artist, made a quizzical link with a letter unearthed by Girolamo d'Adda in the Milan State Archives nine years before.[1]

Sometime in the early 1490s *Johannes Petrus Biragus* complained to an *Illust. & Excell^mo Signor* about the theft[2] of 27 sheets from an unfinished *officiol* (Book of Hours) commissioned by Duchess Bona[3] – which he believed the Most Excellent Lord had recently received from the hands of Giovanni Maria Sforzino (1461–1520), a priest then based in Rome. Birago claimed to be owed 1220 *libre* for his work on the book, with the part 'now in your Excellency's possession' valued at over 500 ducats.

'The incomplete *Book of Hours* recently presented to Your Excellency was stolen from me by Brother Johanne Jacobo, a friar at the Abbey of San Marco in Milan' moaned Birago. 'The friar came to visit me several times and once, when I was out, furtively entered and stole the book.'[4] The missive may have been addressed to Birago's fellow-cleric Cardinal Ascanio, Vice-Chancellor to Pope Alexander VI.

The value Birago assigned to his work was five times what Leonardo had been offered for the *Virgin of the Rocks* in 1483 (together with Ambrogio and Evangelista de Predis). Birago may have been exaggerating but it seems that, in financial terms, he – not Leonardo – was the artistic superstar of Il Moro's Milan.

George F. Warner also commented on similarities between the *Sforza Hours* and illuminations in the *Donatus Grammatica* produced in the 1490s for Il Moro's son Massimiliano, citing Ambrogio de Predis as the author of its portraits and acutely remarking that, on stylistic grounds, he must also have been responsible for the medallion portraits in the *Sforziadas* – especially given the 'treatment of the eyes and strongly marked curve of the nostrils.'

Bona would remain on Milanese soil until December 1495, just after Il Moro's definitive break with France, whereupon she became a sporadic historical footnote – mentioned in Tours in April 1496 and Lyon in January 1499, before dying in November 1503 in the Castle of Fossano granted to her in April 1500 by her nephew Philibert of Savoy.

The missing pages of her decimated *officiol* would only be replaced in 1519 by Philibert's widow Margaret of Austria[5] – keen to complete the *Book of Hours* and present it to her nephew Charles V upon his election as Holy Roman Emperor.

THE BIRAGO STYLE

With its compositional verve, crisp outlines and magnificent colours, the *Sforza Hours* show Birago at the height of his powers. His highly individual style displays an extensive range of influences and characteristics. The quotations from, and stylistic similarities to, Leonardo's work suggest Birago had studied his work at close hindquarters. Evans suggests that Leonardo's monumental

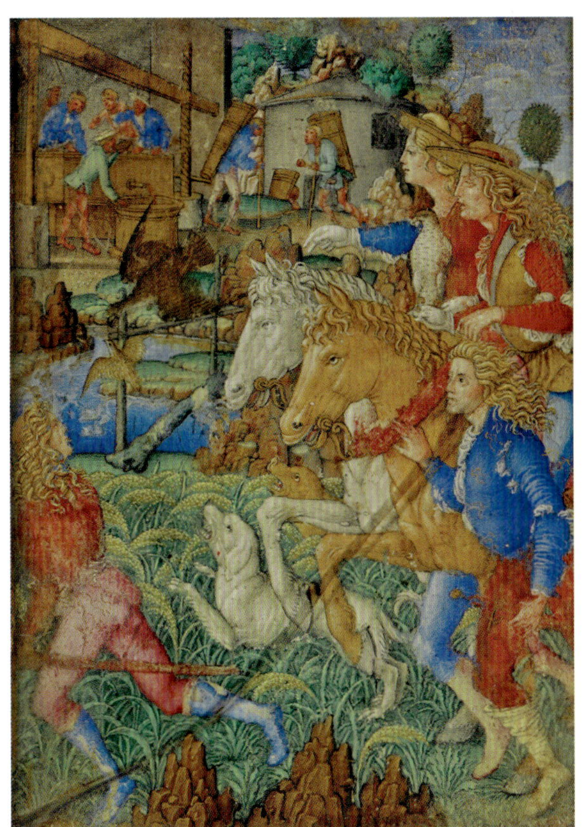

Sforza Horse was the 'probable source' of the magnificent Leonardesque horses in the *October* miniature for the *Sforza Hours*, 'with flowing manes and pricked-up ears, champing at the bit as their leg muscles swell with a purposeful stride (*see left*).'[6]

Birago had a passion for Leonardesque knots – habitually forming them with dragon-tails or writhing vipers – and also displayed a Leonardesque fetish for wavy/curly blond hair. Straight or dark hair is virtually non-existent in Birago's mature work. His occasional recourse to grotesque caricature recalls various Leonardo head-sketches.

But Birago had two weaknesses: he was hopeless at painting hands, and had no talent for portraiture. This is most evident in his depictions of Il Moro's son Massimiliano in the *Donatus Grammatica*, and in his half-hearted attempts to portray Bona's son Gian Galeazzo in the *Sforza Hours* – in his allegorical miniatures of *May* (where Gian Galeazzo is seated) and *October* (where he is on horseback alongside his wife Isabel of Aragon).

Birago readily quotes other artists in a variety of media – including goldwork (Caradosso), ceramics (Della Robbia), frescoes (Foppa), sculpted friezes (Amadeo) and architectural detail (Bramante). He frequently collaborated with other illuminators: sometimes on the same page, as in his *Sforza Hours Assumption* or in the *Sforziada* frontispieces; sometimes in the same book, as in a late 15th century vellum manuscript version of Jacobus de Voragine's *Golden Legend*, now in Warsaw (BOZ 11),[7] with an artist identified by the Polish National Library as Antonio Maria Sforza of Padua.

Birago's sharp, clear outlines also reflect an interest in the art of engraving – which he would pursue in his later career. His penchant for unsqueamish violence derives at least in part from the engravings of the German artist Martin Schongauer (1448–91), which he probably obtained in Venice. His interest in *trompe-l'œil* effects – *cf* the shaded upper and left edges around the text in the *Sforziada* frontispieces and earlier works, creating the appearance of a pasted-down sheet – was doubtless acquired in Venice as well.

Birago's rocky foregrounds are evocative of Mantegna, while his mountainous outcrops, often hollow, bring to mind Leonardo's *Virgin of the Rocks*.

His love of playful animals and mythical creatures, especially rabbits and/or hares (which Sforza dukes zealously hunted), was more typical of his era than his interest in topography, which he shared with Bergognone. The Certosa di Pavia, Castello Sforzesco, Rome's Castello Sant'Angelo and the Naples/Genoa waterfronts are among the sites and monuments Birago depicted.

His taste for allusion and ambiguity was shared by Il Moro. His wit, irony and barrack-room humour became increasingly prevalent in his *Sforziada* frontis-pieces.

CHARLES VIII'S PRAYER-BOOK

Along with Il Moro's Imperial Investiture diploma from 1495 (formerly in the Milan State Archives, now lost), the other project to busy Birago in the first half of the 1490s was a tiny Prayer Book presented by Il Moro to Charles VIII (*see p.92*), measuring just 6 × 3cm.

This technical *tour de force*, universally ascribed to Birago, is now in the Fondazione Giorgio Cini in Venice (*MS 4*).

Il Moro probably presented it to Charles VIII when he arrived in Italy in Spring 1494. It was recovered as a prize of war from the Fornovo battlefield after the French had fled in disarray on 6 July 1495.

OTHER COURT ARTISTS

Gianpietro Birago was the most illustrious of the many illuminators in Il Moro's Milan, whose number appears to have run into dozens. Two different illuminators seem to have worked on the de luxe Latin *Sforziada* intended for Emperor Maximilian, and three on the Muzio Attendolo biography produced concurrently with the first illuminated *Sforziada*. Two other artists collaborated with Birago and Ambrogio de Predis to produce the *Donatus Grammatica* for Il Moro's son Massimiliano, and another three to illustrate his *Liber Iesus*.

That would already make a dozen illuminators working on Milanese court projects during the 1490s. They must have been in regular contact with one another, maybe operating within the same workshop.

Other illuminators were employed to embellish official documents, such as the charter recording Il Moro's land grant to his wife Beatrice d'Este, dated 11 January 1494, now in British Library (*Add. MS 21413*) or the 1498 deed of transfer from Il Moro to Santa Maria delle Grazie, now in the Morgan Library & Museum, New York (*MS 434*). Both illuminators display great skill – although the profiled portraits within the grant's top-line medallions are awkwardly small.

Yet more illuminators were employed by private patrons such as Luca Pacioli – shown presenting his *De Divina Proportione* to Il Moro in a frontispiece illustration for the presentation copy of his book now in the Bibliothèque de Genève (*MS Langues Etrangères 210*) – or ecclesiastical patrons like the Archbishop of Milan, for his *Messale Arcimboldi* now in the city's Biblioteca del Capitol (*MS D1.13*), and Cardinal Federigo Sanseverino, whose handsome choirbooks for Santa Maria di Crescenzago are now in Milan's Biblioteca Capitolare di Sant'Ambrogio.

Birago was one of the few Renaissance illuminators to occasionally sign his works: the identity of most Milanese illuminators from Il Moro's time remains unknown. Such vague monikers as *Master B.F.*, represented by a John the Baptist formerly with the Chicago dealership Les Enluminures (current whereabouts unknown), or the *Douce Master* represented in Oxford's Bodleian Library, reflect the embryonic level of research in this field. The author of the exquisite portrayal of *Bianca Maria Sforza* now in the Österreichische Nationalbibliothek (*SN 2662, fol. 5v*) remains anonymous.

PAOLO E DARIA

One of the most sumptuously and allusively illustrated of all the manuscripts produced in Milan during the 1490s was a presentation copy of Gaspare Visconti's epic poem *Paolo e Daria*. It can be dated to 1494/5. Birago was not involved.

Bramante's 1480s landlord Gaspare Visconti became a major figure in Il Moro's Milan. He took part in the embassy to Naples to fetch Isabel of Aragon in 1488, succeeded Bellincioni as Court Poet in 1492, and was part of Bianca Maria's retinue travelling to Austria in December 1493. He was a member of the Ducal Council and, as an *Eques Auratus*, entitled to wear gilded armour.

In 1493 Visconti dedicated a set of poems, or *Rithimi*, to fellow-poet Niccolò da Correggio and, in 1495/6, dedicated a luxuriously bound album of 143 sonnets, handwritten in gold and silver lettering on vellum, to Beatrice d'Este. His dedication to the Duchess, apart from dropping the talismanic name of Galeazzo Sanseverino, suggests that Visconti remained uncertain about how he stood with Il Moro. He thanked 'the Most Illustrious Duchess' for 'graciously pleading' his cause with the Duke – as he had 'been told by many honourable persons, chief among whom is Messer Galeazzo Sanseverino.'

The printing of Gaspare Visconti's romantic epic *Li Due Amanti Paolo e Daria* was completed by Filippo Mantegazza in April 1495. It concerns two star-crossed lovers from 14th century Milan, whose remains were rediscovered in 1492 during excavations at the church of Sant'Ambrogio prior to the construction of a new Bramante cloister (that includes two bizarre pillars that look like tree trunks, in homage to the Vitruvian theory of architectural origins).

The text begins with a eulogy to Bramante and his architectural genius – and celebrates the Visconti line down to Il Moro, to whom the poem is dedicated. Il Moro is glorified as a patron of the arts, his reign as a 'golden age.'

A magnificent manuscript version of *Paolo e Daria* is now in the Kupferstichkabinett of the Staatliche Museen zu Berlin (*MS 78, C 27*). The style of its illumination, sometimes attributed to *Master B.F.*, is close to the Il Moro investiture scene in the *Messale Arcimboldi* and the deed recording Il Moro's gift of his Sforzesca estate to Santa Maria delle Grazie.

Each chapter in the *Paolo e Daria* manuscript begins with a full-page miniature featuring verses superimposed on a *trompe-l'œil* architectural background containing vignettes of episodes from the story, and/or scenes from contemporary Milan. Knotted gold ribbons flutter in abundance.

The final illumination (*see right*) occupies the bottom half of the last page (*fol. 110r*). The parchment appears to have been torn open to reveal a plant with tiny flower-buds and eleven star-shaped leaves. A fly, complete with shadow, completes the *trompe-l'œil* trickery further up the page. The blue sky behind the plant contains a sun whose rays cascade over the whole image. This sun is odd: it is black – as if we are witnessing a solar eclipse (perhaps the one viewed in Milan on 8 March 1491) – and not perfectly round, with a jagged right side. What seems like a white dove is flying in front of it. The Surrealist nature of the image suggests the lingering influence of Cristoforo de Predis.

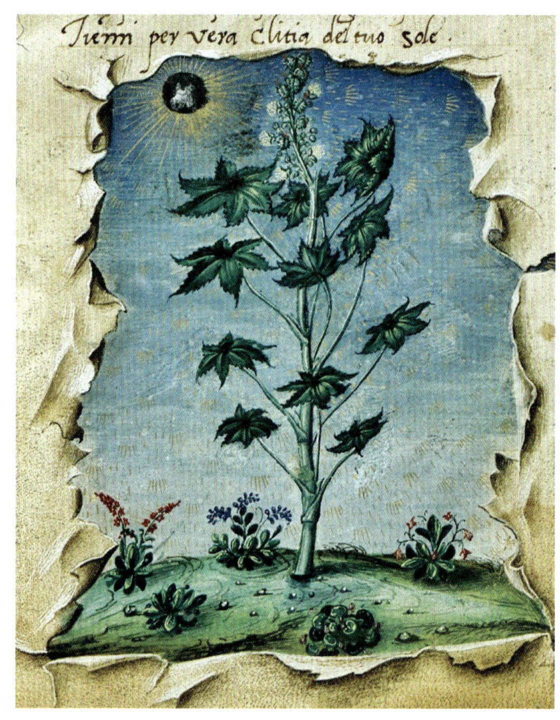

The page contains three types of script: to the left, two eight-line stanzas in black ink (the main text) over feint pencil lines to help the scribe write straight; notes in faded purple ink, in the same handwriting but smaller, in the margin opposite; and eight lines added in a vigorous, untidy hand, in black ink now slightly faded, that are squeezed awkwardly into the bottom right-hand corner.

Microscopic analysis has revealed that the 'dove' in front of the sun actually consists of paper fibres. The Kupferstichkabinett's Book & Paper Conservator Hanka Gerhold believes a tiny piece of paper must have once been glued over the sun, then scraped out. The eight lines added bottom right suggest the paper may have borne a face. They read:

> *Clitia dal sol non mai*
> *Torce il suo fior ma in lui*
> *Vuolge sempre ne' bei raggi suoi*
> *Così Leon.° gira*
> *Ad una il pensier sempre*
> *C'in amorosa sempre*
> *Per lei sol arde e sol per lei*
>   *sospira*

('Clytia never turns her flower away from the Sun, but always follows his beautiful rays; likewise Leo's thoughts always turn to the one he still loves, for whom the Sun burns and yearns')

The story of Clytia (the name comes from the Greek *klitos*, meaning 'tilt') is told in Ovid's *Metamorphoses* (*IV 214–276*). She was a nymph who loved the Sun (Helios). When Helios seduced her sister Leucothoë, Clytia jealously betrayed her to their father Orchamus, who promptly had Leucothoë buried alive. Helios never forgave Clytia, who faded away. Eventually Helios sprinkled nectar over her, transforming her into a plant with violet flowers – a heliotrope – that always followed the sun.

Author Gaspare Visconti appears to identify with Clytia as an erudite way of proclaiming his devotion to Il Moro. The *Leon* in the text may well refer to a sign of the Zodiac: that of the astrology-obsessed Il Moro, who was born on July 27 and therefore a Leo.[8] The image that once covered the sun may, then, have been a portrait of Il Moro – with the sun's jagged right side corresponding to the nose and chin of his illustrious Sforza profile (the blackened sun, of itself, could have been construed as referring to Il Moro).

This interpretation does not, however, consider the possibility that *Leon°* may not have been a Zodiac reference but an abbreviation of *Leonardo*. The heliotrope has a naturalist magnificence that Leonardo da Vinci might not have disowned. And Leonardo appears in the *Paolo e Daria* manuscript just a few pages earlier – in a tiny 'Allegory of Justice' framed by an archway, in the frontispiece of Chapter VIII (*fol. 97r, below*).

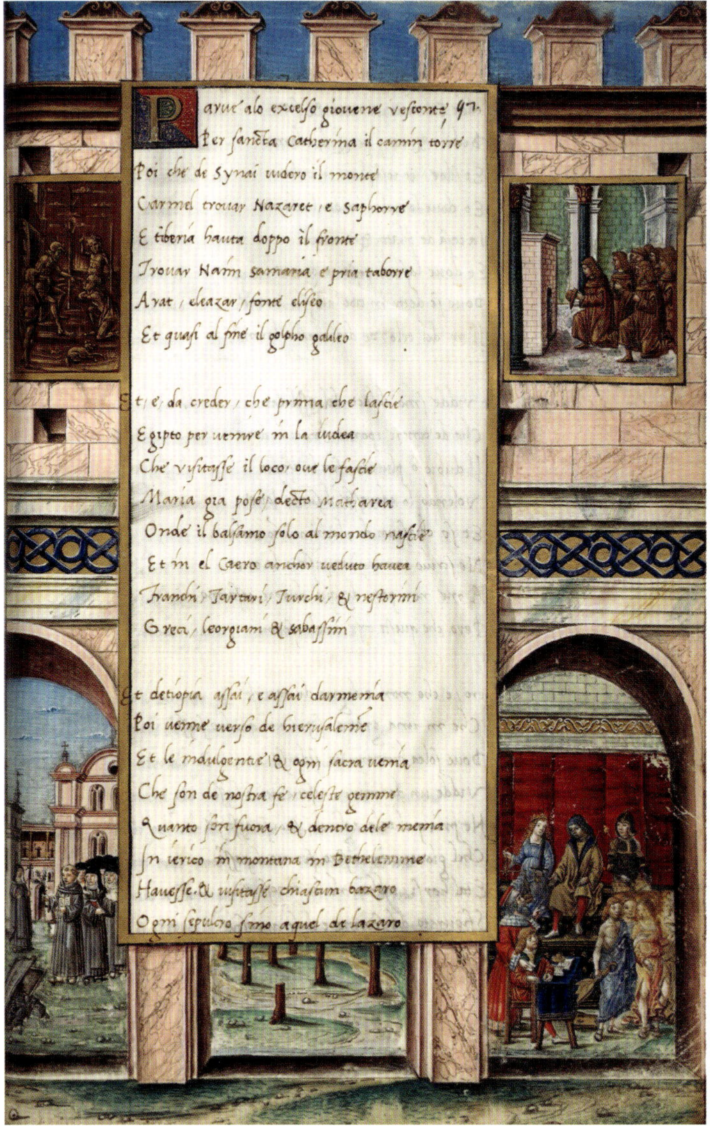

This 'Allegory' (*see p.204*) shows a dais surmounted by a gold-robed figure with dark grey hair – recognizable as Il Moro – flanked to his left by a broad-nosed, large-eyed soldier in gold-trimmed black helmet and gold-and-black armour – surely his Captain of Arms, Galeazzo Sanseverino. On his right is a long-haired blonde wearing Marian blue and a gold crown, brandishing the scales of justice in her right hand and a large sword in her left. She cannot be Il Moro's wife Beatrice d'Este or his mistress Lucrezia Crivelli – both brunettes. And *Justitia*, the Goddess of Justice, was a virgin (later transformed into the constellation Virgo).[9] There is every chance, then, that she represents Il Moro's blond-haired daughter Bianca: Sanseverino's betrothed. *Paolo e Daria* was published in 1495. The illuminated version probably dates from the same year. Bianca was still unmarried.

Beneath the dais is a venerable figure in ermine-trimmed scarlet robes, with long silver hair and an imposing silver beard. His right arm rests paternally on the shoulder of a ginger-haired, left-handed clerk, doodling away absent-mindedly with a wooden lyre at his feet: evidently a caricature of Leonardo da Vinci.

The lawyer figure behind him must be his father, Ser Piero – aged around 68 in 1495. He is brandishing a sheet of paper that surely represents the anonymous document denouncing Leonardo for sodomy, deposited in a Florence *tamburo* in April 1476.

The lawyer has the same beaky-nosed profile as Leonardo's pen-and-ink drawing of a *Seated Old Man* in the Royal Collection (*RCIN 912579*). One wonders if he were also the subject of the red chalk portrait of an old man in Turin's Biblioteca Reale often touted as a Leonardo self-portrait, despite showing a man who seems older than the 67 Leonardo was when he died (his father lived until eighty).

Further evidence of Leonardo's identity, and homosexual leanings, is provided by the group of eight strapping figures alongside. The clerk of court is gazing at them in such rapture that he fails to realise he is drawing on his desktop rather than in one of his two (full-looking) notebooks.

The group's most prominent figure is a handsome young man with long ginger hair, wearing a blue toga that exposes his hairy chest. He is clutching a bizarre contraption shaped like a miniature rocket, as if evoking one of Leonardo's scientific inventions.

The clerk's ginger hair – highly unusual in Renaissance (or indeed modern) Italy – echoes that of Heroclitus in Bramante's fresco (*see p.32*) for Gaspare Visconti. The scribe and Heroclitus also wear similar clothes – an orange *robone*[10] and golden *camicia* (shirt) – and are shown in the same three-quarter pose with their left elbows bent at precisely the same angle. The mimicry recalls Birago's imitation of the head of 'The Musician' when caricaturing Galeazzo Sanseverino in the *bas-de-page* of his final *Sforziada* frontispiece.

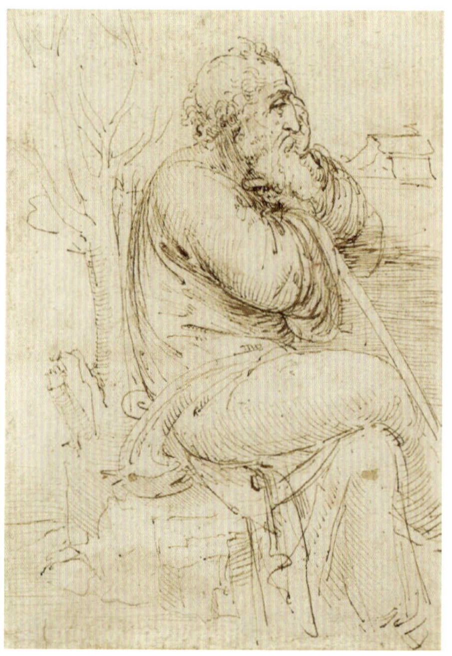

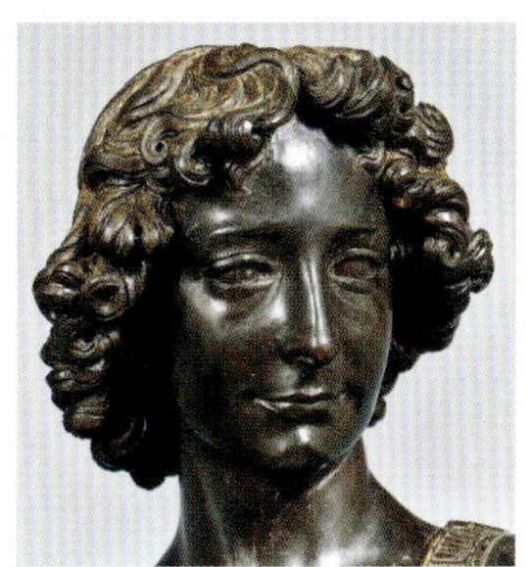 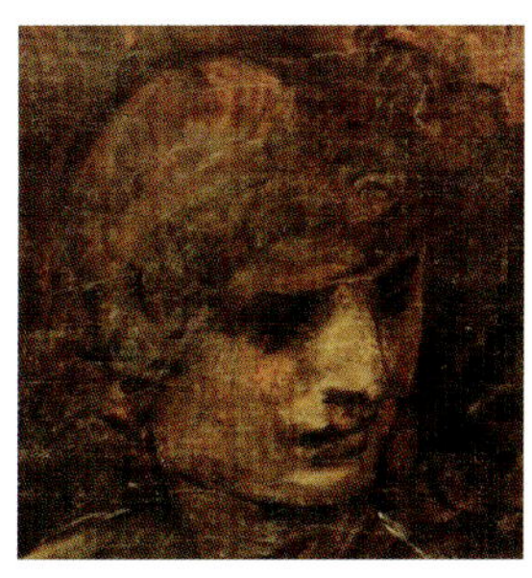 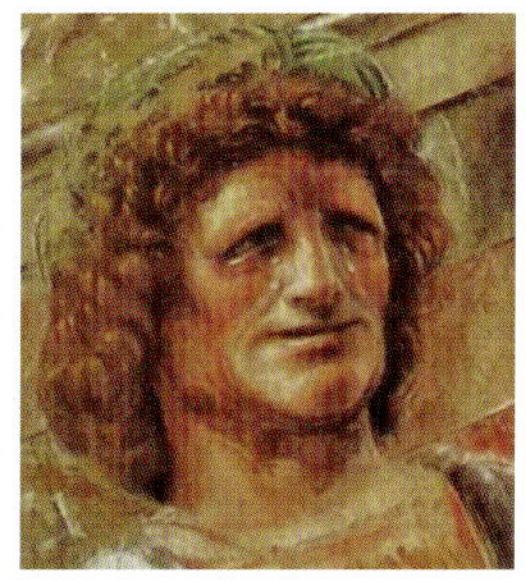 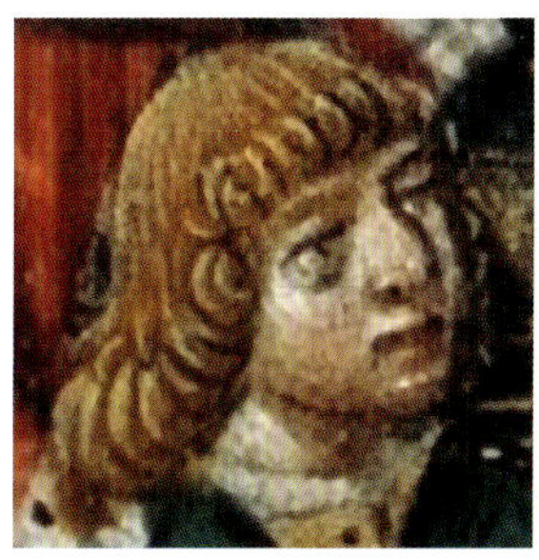

The clerk of court and Heroclitus tilt their heads in much the same fashion as the young man in Leonardo's unfinished *Adoration of the Magi* (*second from left*), commonly supposed to be a self-portrait, and Verrocchio's bronze *David* (*far left*), often considered to portray Leonardo.

The ginger-haired cherub in the London *Sforziada* frontispiece that appears to commit an act of sodomy is further evidence of the visual irreverence with which Leonardo was treated by Birago and his colleagues. It is the only cherub with straight, ginger hair in Birago's œuvre.

Yet to Birago and his circle, including the illuminator of *Paolo e Daria*, Leonardo was also a source of inspiration as well as mirth: the ginger-haired ruffian in the *Martydrom of St Catherine* (*below*) from the *Sforza Hours* appears based on a Leonardo drawing of a *Grotesque Head* now in Oxford's Christ Church Picture Gallery (*below left*).

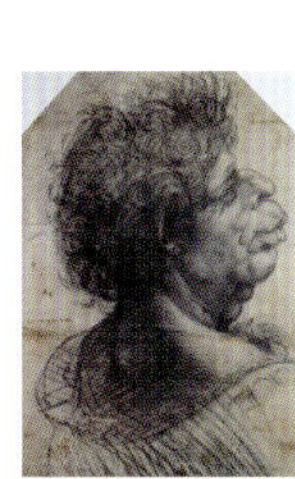

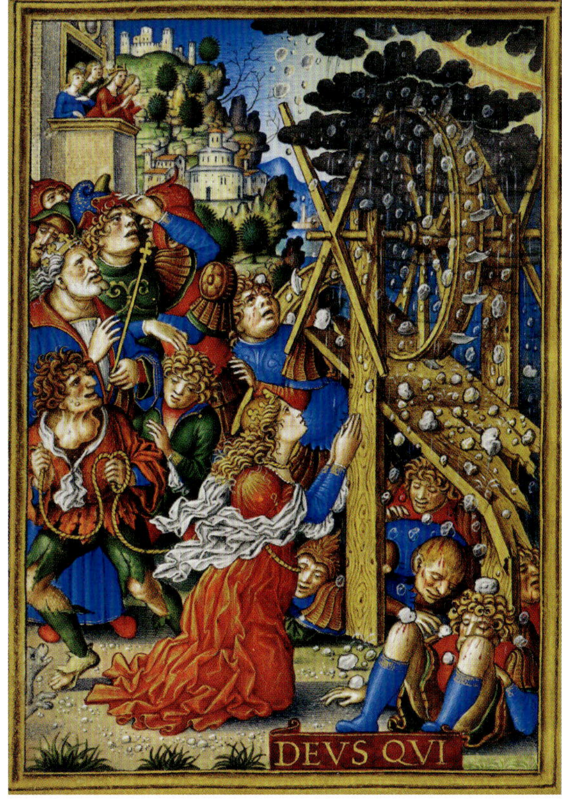

How on earth did this illustrious Renaissance Italian acquire ginger hair? Not from his Italian father. Ser Piero hailed from a long-established Tuscan family.

Recent anthropological research suggests that Leonardo was of partly Arab or Middle Eastern descent.[11] Alessandro Vezzosi, Director of the Museo Ideale in Leonardo's home town of Vinci, speaks of 'documented indications that his mother was Oriental – at least from the Mediterranean area, not a peasant of Vinci.' Vezzosi adds that 'a lot of prominent and well-to-do families bought women from eastern Europe and the Middle East. These young girls were then baptised, with the commonest names being Maria, Marta or Caterina.'

Their most likely origin was Constantinople, then home to a thriving slave trade with Genoa (Francesco el Giocondo – husband of the woman usually identified as the Mona Lisa – was a slave trader, according to Martin Kemp).[12] A chief source of these girls was Pera (now Beyoğlu), the Jewish district of Constantinople on the banks of the Golden Horn, and a Genoese possession from 1273–1453.[13]

Kemp's archival research suggests Leonardo's mother grew up about a mile from Vinci – so perhaps it was Leonardo's grandmother who hailed from the Orient. If so, red-haired Turks being about as common as red-haired Italians, we have to look beyond Pera and the Bosphorus for her family origins.

The northern shores of the Black Sea were once patrolled by a semi-nomadic Turkic people originating from the Asian steppe: the Khazars. Their empire stretched from Hungary to Kazakhstan, at the crossroads of China, Europe and the Middle East.[14] Their capital Atil ('Big River') stood near modern-day Astrakhan, where the Volga flows into the Caspian – still known to Muslims as the *Bahr ul-Khaza* (Khazar Sea).

The Khazars converted to Judaism in the early 9th century and formed an East European bulwark against Islam, whose fighters were startled by the Khazars' appearance: they had red hair. As the 13th century Arab historian Ibn Sa'id el-Maghribi put it: 'Their complexions are white, their eyes blue and their hair flowing and predominantly reddish.' The Mongol invasion scattered the Khazars across Eastern Europe and around the Black Sea. A sizeable Khazar community grew up in Pera.

BIRAGO'S HEADLINE PRINT

In his later career, Birago also produced engravings. One of the most successful reflects the close interest he took in Leonardo's work.

Birago's reproduction of *The Last Supper* was the first of thousands of mass-produced images that would enable Leonardo's fragile masterpiece to become one of the most familiar pictures in world art.

The impish Birago was not content to reproduce Leonardo's painting *tel quel*: he added Christ's words in Latin (*AMEN DICO VOBIS QVIA VNVS VESTRUM ME TRADITVRUS EST*) to the front of the tablecloth – recalling

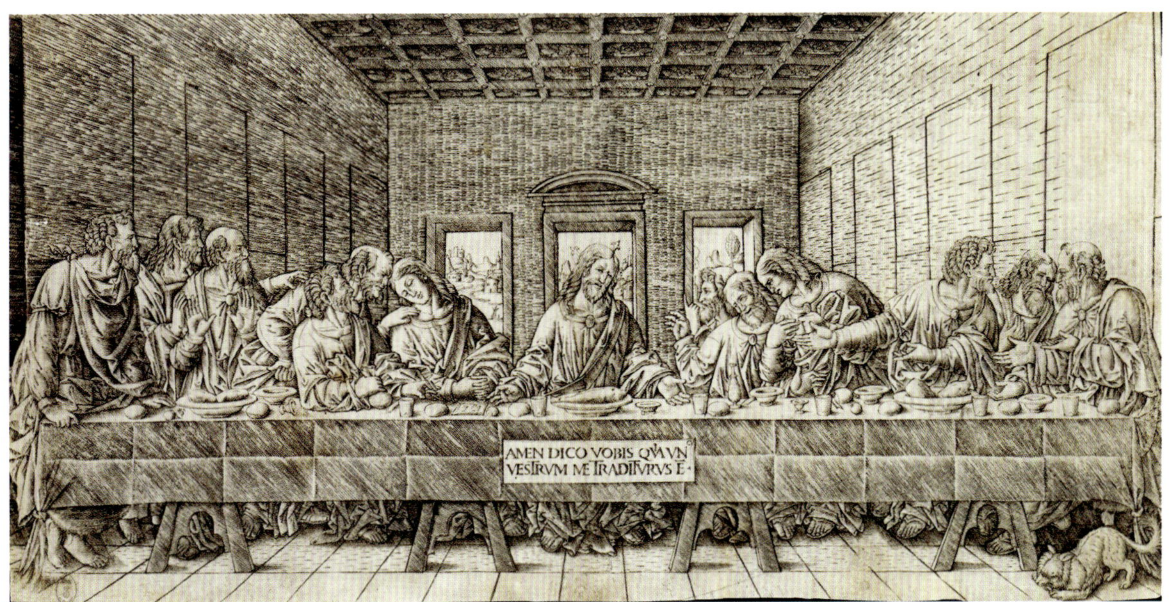

the similar warning of treachery delivered by Il Moro, quoting Christ, in the *bas-de-page* of the *Sforziada* now in Warsaw. Birago further emphasized the theme of treachery by impertinently adding a foreground cat – a symbol of infidelity.

So influential was Birago's print that it served as the basis for Rembrandt's red chalk drawing of *The Last Supper* (*c.*1635) now in New York's Metropolitan Museum. Rembrandt also included an animal bottom-right – but mistook Birago's cat for a dog.

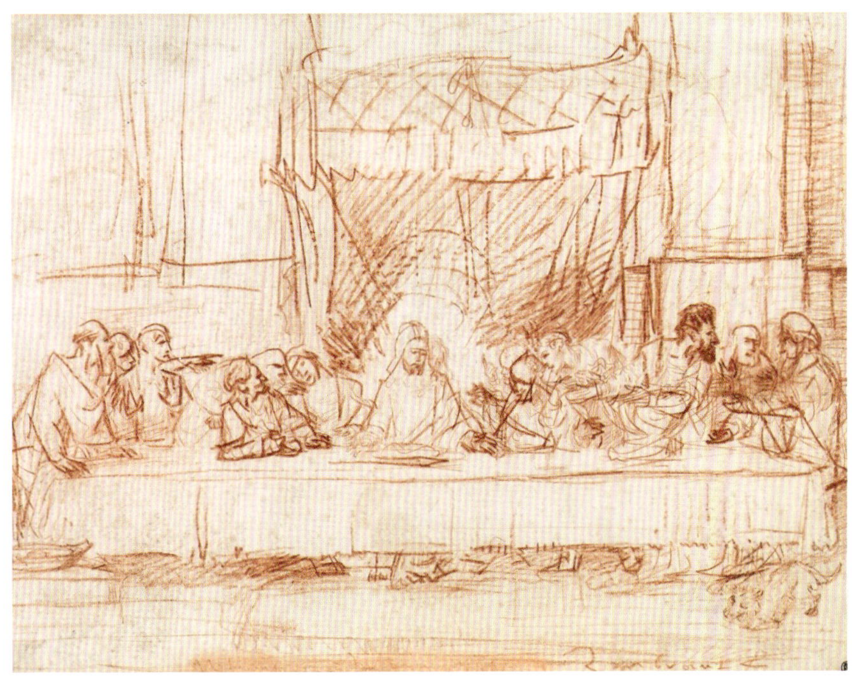

LIBER IESUS

Birago did not provide illuminations for the collection of prayers and grammar lessons – known as the **Liber Iesus** (Biblioteca Trivulziana, *cod. 2163*) – produced for Il Moro's eldest son Massimiliano in the mid-1490s. This 12*ff* volume contains four full-page miniatures by two anonymous illuminators evoking scenes from the young Duke's life, plus a decorative frontispiece with a blue breastplate bottom left and an historiated initial *P* featuring a *Salvator Mundi* with golden orb.

The most interesting illustration, usually attributed to Boccaccio Boccaccino, depicts the youthful Massimiliano shaking hands with Emperor Maximilian outside the castle of Carimate, ten miles south of Como (*below left*). Visible behind is a lake (Maggiore), town (Como) and distant mountains (Alps), whose misty blue tones evoke the background landscapes of Leonardo. Massimiliano, who was christened *Ercole* after his mother's father but renamed *Massimiliano* in the Emperor's honour, looks like a boy of six – yet we know that, when this meeting took place in late August 1496, he was three years and seven months old.

Another large miniature (*below right*) shows a vaulted hall with tableclothed dining-table; the same artist may have been responsible for the miniature at the start of Luca Pacioli's *De Divina Proportione* now in Geneva (*Bibliothèque de Genève, MS Langues Etrangères 210*). Massimiliano is seated opposite his *balia* (nanny) – Camilla of Aragon, Lady of Pesaro,[15] engaged in animated discussion with two men standing alongside. One of them is court physician/astrologer Ambrogio da Rosate (named in the text as *Maestro Ambroso*).

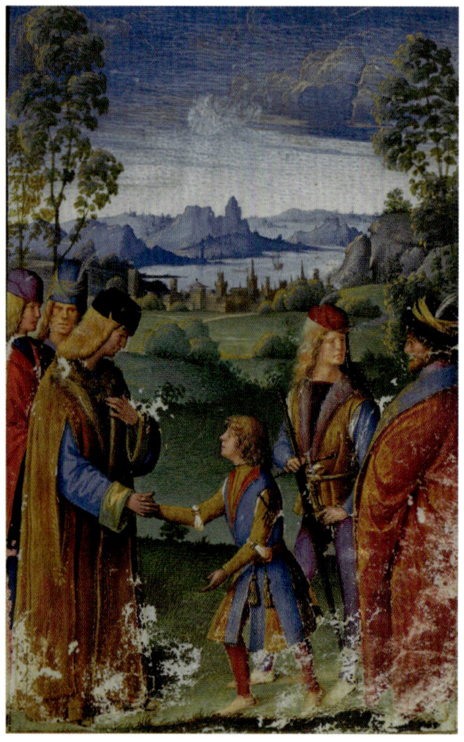

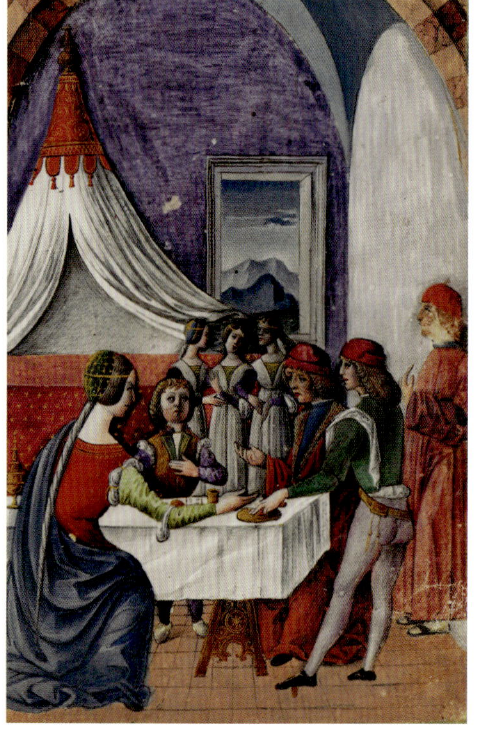

GRAMMATICA DEL DONATO

Birago and Ambrogio de Predis were both involved in the de luxe grammar book (commonly known as the *Donatus Grammatica*) that Il Moro commissioned for Massimiliano. This *54ff* recto verso manuscript, 27.5 × 18cm, contains nine full-page illuminations and is now in the Biblioteca Trivulziana (*cod. 2167*). The volume dates from between 1496 and 1498, as it refers in the present tense to Massimiliano's tutor Count Borella, who died that year.[16]

THE DE PREDIS PORTRAITS

The book contains two full-page tempera portraits by Ambrogio de Predis, of Massimiliano and his father Il Moro.

Massimiliano is shown facing right with straight, shoulder-length hair, looking about four years old. He wears a red cap and black armour, even though he is painted against a black ground that fills the entire folio.

Il Moro has straight, black hair streaked with grey, and is also wearing black armour. Arrogance, vulnerability, optimism, wistfulness: this is a despot in all his Shakespearian ambiguity – overladen with Ambrogio's gift to put a gleam in his sitter's eye. He also enjoys a little *trompe-l'œil* fun by having Il Moro's lance-holder protrude through the gold frame and on to the blank vellum border. Similarly, Massimiliano's red *berretto* slightly protrudes above his own gold frame.

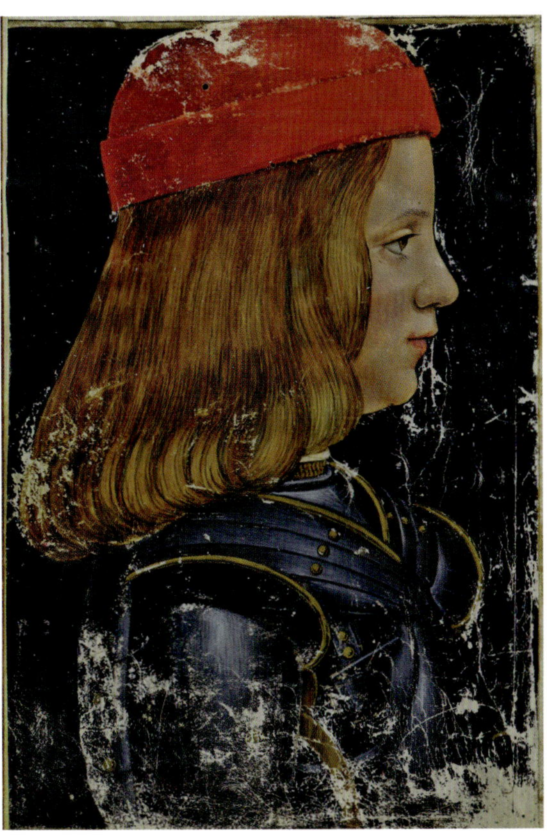

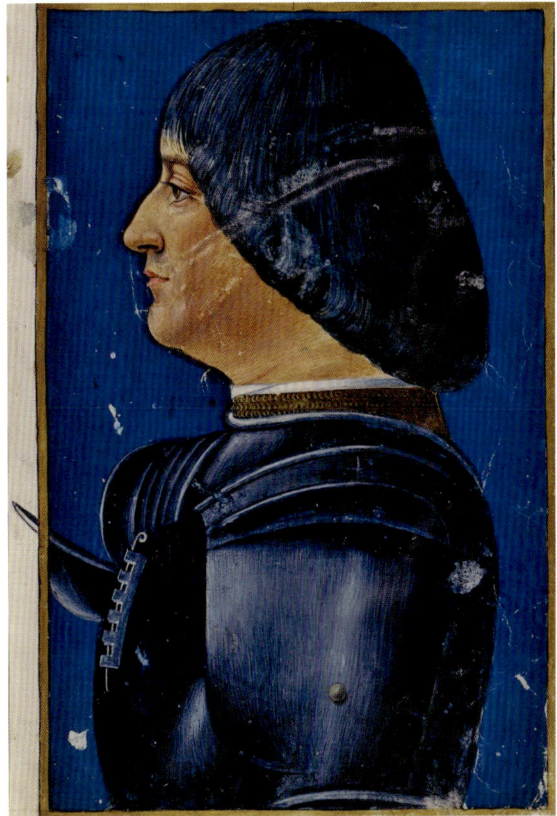

THE BIRAGO MINIATURES

The volume features four large miniatures by Birago, all featuring Massimiliano. *Folio 3v* has roughly the same layout as a *Sforziada* frontispiece, albeit with the left border wider than the right. The *bas-de-page* features Il Moro's coat of arms on a star-spangled ground. The *haut-de-page* incorporates a roundel portrait of Ludovico (*see right*). Even though Folio 3 disappeared during the 20th century (presumably stolen), it is clear from the Trivulziana's black-and-white reproduction that this Birago portrait is of vastly inferior quality to the medallion portraits in the *Sforziadas* produced by Ambrogio de Predis.

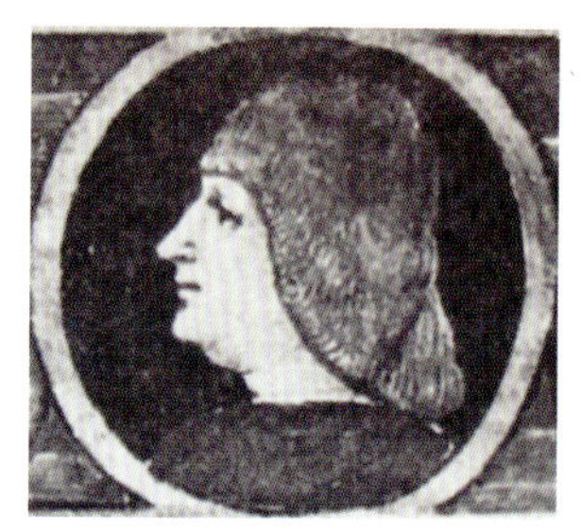

Folio 13v features a classroom scene in the Castle of Pavia (*below*). Massimiliano, fanned by a portly court dwarf, looks across his desk at his laurel-wreathed Preceptor, Count Borella. The dwarf has a dagger tucked into his belt; a similar dagger is tucked into the waist of one of Massimiliano's five less disciplined companions. The recourse to standardized group weaponry evokes the swords of the naked figures in the *bas-de-page* of Birago's Polish *Sforziada*.

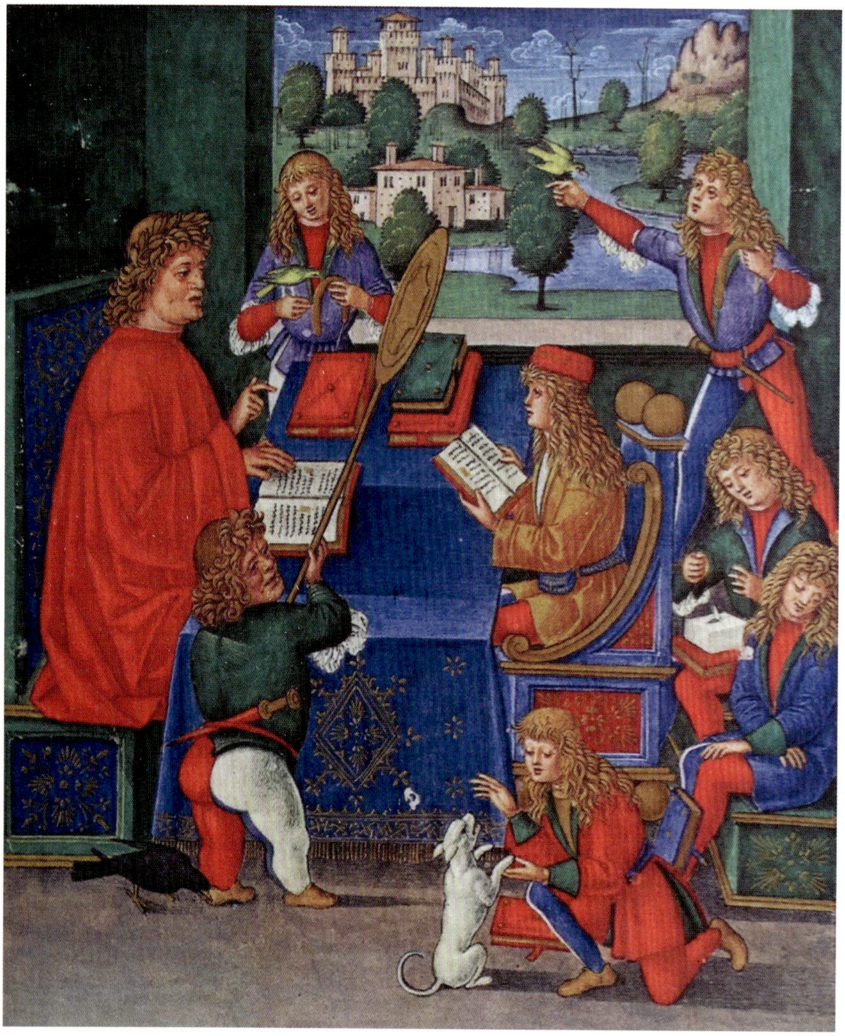

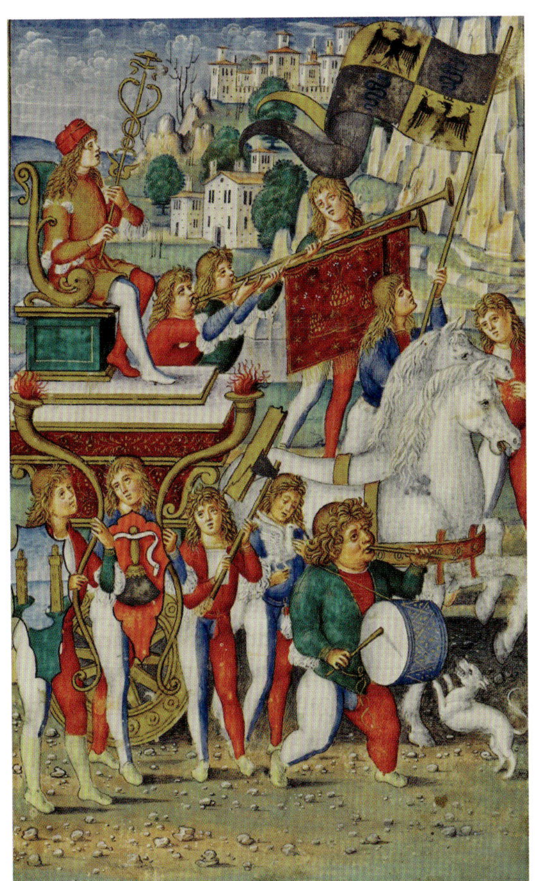

The classroom window gives on to a verdant landscape, with Milan's mighty Castello Sforzesco rising in the distance beyond the Villa Mirabello hunting lodge.

Folio 29r portrays Massimiliano enthroned on a horse-drawn chariot (*left*), whose two white horses recall, although with less finesse, those in Birago's *October* miniature for the *Sforza Hours*. The scene appears inspired by a miniature produced in Florence for King Matthias of Hungary in the late 1480s, showing his son János Corvinus on a chariot. Massimiliano holds a caduceus in both hands and is surrounded by trumpeters, youths bearing Sforza emblems and the portly court dwarf, who simultaneously plays a flute and beats a drum. The classroom's curly-tailed hound jumps about excitedly.

Folio 42v portrays Massimiliano flanked by two barefooted women with long blond hair and *lenzas* around their foreheads. The one on the left symbolizes *Virtue*, the one on the right symbolizes *Vice*. She stands close to a rocky abyss. The caption extols Massimiliano for wisely choosing between them.

OTHER MINIATURES

The *Donatus Grammatica* also boasts four miniatures by two unknown artists.

Folio 3r (now lost) showed a round-arched, pilastered gateway leading into a town with elegant buildings (Pavia) beneath a steep hill topped by a castle. Boys in the foreground street were involved in a scuffle that Massimiliano sought to quell. The same artist appears responsible for decorating *Folio 43r* with a large, square medallion featuring a giant, seated figure, crowned with a laurel-wreath, presumably Massimiliano's preceptor.

Folio 10v features Massimiliano on a white horse, flanked by three equerries in Sforza hose, riding through a town beneath the admiring gaze of a blond lady in an upstairs window. A white curly-haired terrier, reminiscent of the one added by Leonardo to Verrocchio's *Tobias and the Angel*, appears lower centre. *Folio 26r* contains a full-page *Picnic Scene*, apparently by the same artist. Its almost Surrealist feel includes a monkey chained to a ball; an African boy in bright yellow satin; three bodiless boys' heads emerging, Cheshire Cat-like, from a clump of trees; and a white tent topped by a preposterously heavy-looking bronze urn, and ringed by an unintelligible inscription reading *VPATMIDRPL*.

BINDING

The volume's painted and gold-embossed *recto-verso* brown leather binding involves a sophisticated interplay of geometric forms. Elaborate gold *vinci* knotwork encloses larger corner squares containing Sforza emblems as part of a continuous frame. The centre of each cover features two overlapping squares forming an eight-pointed star, each point of this star containing lettering that reads, clockwise from top, **LV.MA.SF.ANGL.DVX.MLI.** (*front*) and **MAX.SF.P.P.CO.** (*back*), respectively standing for *Ludovicus Maria Sfortia Anglus Dux Mediolani* and *Maximilianus Sfortia Papiae Comtes*. Further gold knot-patterning embellishes the areas above and beneath the coat of arms.

The binding (*right*) is almost identical to that of the 1488 *Epitalamion* containing the Ambrogio de Predis medallion portrait of Matthias Corvinus (*see p.70*) – of fundamental importance to the genesis of the illuminated *Sforziadas* – while the interlacing knot design recalls the illuminated borders of its frontispiece, and has similarities with: the ceiling of the Sagrestia del Bramante at Santa Maria delle Grazie; Leonardo's famous circular knot-pattern engravings; and the 1494 frontispiece of Luca Pacioli's *Summa*.

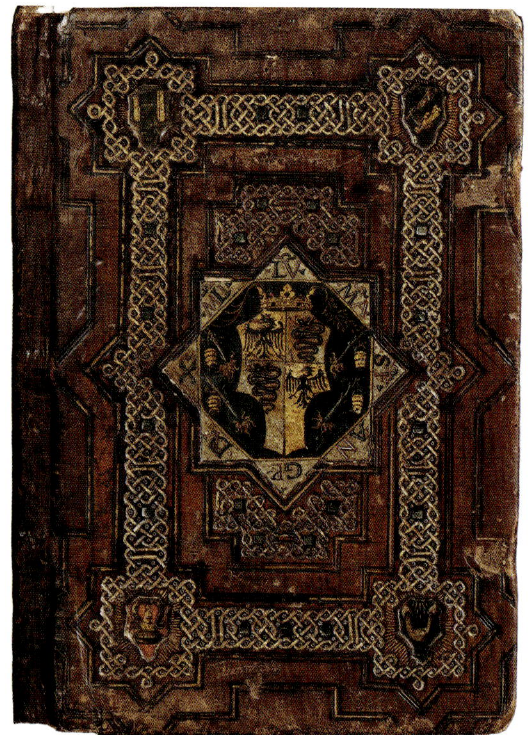

The inner octagon on the front cover contains quartered eagle/viper arms, flanked on either side by two firebrands and buckets, and topped by a crown with palm frond to the left and mulberry branch to the right. The use here of the ducal shield, rather than the combined arms of Il Moro and Beatrice d'Este, is repeated inside the book, suggesting – albeit not conclusively – that it post-dates Beatrice's death on 3 January 1497. The corners of the binding feature four emblems on shields, reading clockwise from top left: the twin towers of Genoa (on a blue ground); axe and branch (blue ground); sifting-cloth (blue ground); *scopetta* (red ground).

The inner octagon on the back cover contains the arms of the Count of Pavia: a halved shield with viper and three eagles, ringed by a leafy wreath with pine cones and fruit – not dissimilar to the wreathes used in the Santa Maria delle Grazie refectory above Leonardo's *Last Supper*. The corners of the binding again feature four emblems on shields, with only a slight difference in their order as compared to the front cover. Clockwise from top left: the twin towers of Genoa (on a blue ground); sifting-cloth (blue ground); axe and branch (blue ground); *scopetta* (red ground).

PRECEDENTS

In commissioning this book with portraits Il Moro was respecting family tradition. Alison Manges Nogueira suggests that the portraits in the *Codice Sforza*, which the teenage Il Moro used to study ancient history, were executed by Ambrogio's elder half-brother Cristoforo.[17] The slightly earlier book commissioned for Il Moro's elder sister Ippolita contains a full-page profiled portrait of Francesco Sforza sometimes attributed to Cristoforo de Predis (*see p.66*) that appears to have served as the prototype for Francesco's medallion portraits in the *Sforziadas*. Both the plain gold frame of Francesco's full-page portrait, and its dark blue background, are repeated in the portrait of Il Moro in the *Donatus Grammatica*.

But there is no Renaissance precedent for a full-page, plain ground, coloured portrait on vellum of a young child in profile. The nearest equivalent is Leonardo's 1496 portrait of Massimiliano's teenage half-sister, Bianca.

Hard on the heels of their *Sforziada* collaboration, the *Donatus Grammatica* saw Ambrogio de Predis and Gianpietro Birago team up again. Leonardo da Vinci may have had some input as regards the volume's stupendous knot-patterned binding: the same intricacy characterizes the bindings and frontispiece borders of the Marliano *Epithalamium* from 1488, suggesting this may have been another product of Leonardo's longstanding association with Ambrogio de Predis. Both men may, so to speak, had been involved in Il Moro's illuminated *Sforziada* project before it had even begun.

The *Donatus Grammatica* was its first sequel. The second would have Il Moro tied up in knots.

NOTES

1 George F. Warner, *Miniatures and Borders from the Book of Hours of Bona Sforza, Duchess of Milan, in the British Museum – introduction to the Museum's guide to the Book of Hours, containing 64 collotype plates, published by the Museum Trustees.* George Frederic Warner (1845–1936) was later knighted.

2 Only three of the illustrated pages stolen from Birago by Fra Gian Jacopo are known to have survived. All are now in the British Library: an *Adoration of the Magi*, presented to the Library in 1941; *May*, acquired in 1984; and *October*, acquired from the Chicago dealership Les Enluminures for £191,000 in 2004.

3 Evans thinks Bona's *Hours* may have been inspired by the *Très Riches Heures du Duc de Berry*, completed by Jean Colombe for her nephew Charles I de Savoie in the late 1480s. One of the grandest of the various French châteaux portrayed in this magnificent book is Mehun-sur-Yèvre, later owned by Il Moro's son-in-law Galeazzo Sanseverino.

4 *L'officiol imperfecto, qual novamente e sta presentato a V. Excell. e sta furato a mi da vostro fratre Johanne Jacobo, qual fu frate e covento de San Marco de Milano. Qual officiol e quello che fece fare la Illma Duchesse Bona ... dicto frate Johane Jacobo vene piu volte a visitarme ... et una volta essendo io fora de casa, furtivamente intrae et furome dicto officiol ... .*

5 Margaret almost certainly inherited the book from her husband Philibert II, who hosted Bona di Savoia at Fossano for the last three years of her life. A 1517 document records payment from Margaret to a scribe called Etienne de Lale for writing several leaves for a Book of Hours which came 'from the late Madame Bonne of Milan,' implying that Bona (Bonne) di Savoia had bequeathed the book to her nephew Philibert, before it passed to his widow Margaret after his death in 1504.

6 Mark Evans, *German Prints and Milanese Miniatures: Influences on – and from – Gianpietro Birago* (Apollo, 2001).

7 The Polish National Library claims that the volume entered the Library in 1946, at the same time as the *Sforziada* (both volumes previously having been in the Zamoyski Library) – but this date is unlikely: as late as 1954 Chief Librarian Bogdan Horodyski was lamenting the loss of the *Golden Legend* during World War II. Works of art recovered in Poland by the Soviet Army towards the end of the War were sent back to Poland from the USSR only gradually, the process continuing until 1957.

8 As proposed by Elisabetta Gnignera in her unpublished short essay *The Metamorphosis of Clitia* (e-mailed to the author 20 December 2013).

9 *Iustitia* or *Justitia* was the Roman personification of Justice: a virgin living among humans until mortal misdemeanours forced her to take flight and become the constellation Virgo.

10 According to Renaissance costume specialist Elisabetta Gnignera (correspondence with the author 17.2.2017), the *robone* was a loose-fitting garment worn by artists, poets and intellectuals.

11 Research carried out in 2005 by Luigi Capasso (Director of the Anthropology Research Institute at Chieti-Pescara University), based on around 200 fingerprints from some 50 sheets of paper known to have been handled by Leonardo during his life, concluded that there was a 60 per cent chance that his mother was of Middle Eastern origin. Capasso claimed the fingerprints included traces of saliva, blood and food Leonardo had recently eaten.

12 Martin Kemp & Giuseppe Pallanti, *Mona Lisa: The People and the Painting* (Oxford University Press, 2017).

13 Kevin Alan Brook, *The Jews of Khazaria* (Jason Aronson Publishers, Northvale, New Jersey 1999).

14 Kozár/Kazár remain common names in Hungary.

15 **Camilla of Aragon** was a grand-daughter of King Alfonso I of Naples. In 1475 she married Il Moro's cousin Costanzo Sforza (1447–83), becoming Lady of Pesaro; they had no children. She retired to Torricella in 1489 before entering Il Moro's household as nanny to his children.

16 **Giovanni Antonio Secco** was made tutor to Massimiliano in 1495, after a lifetime of distinguished Sforza service dating back to the reign of Galeazzo Maria, whom he served as Head of the Ducal Stables – a predecessor to Galeazzo Sanseverino in the post. He was made Count of Vimercate in 1475. He died in Milan in 1498 and was buried in Santa Maria delle Grazie – a stone's throw from the tombs of Bianca Sforza and Beatrice d'Este.

17 Alison Manges Nogueira, *Portraits of the Visconti & Sforza: Image & Propaganda in Milan c.1300–1500* (University of Michigan, 2008)

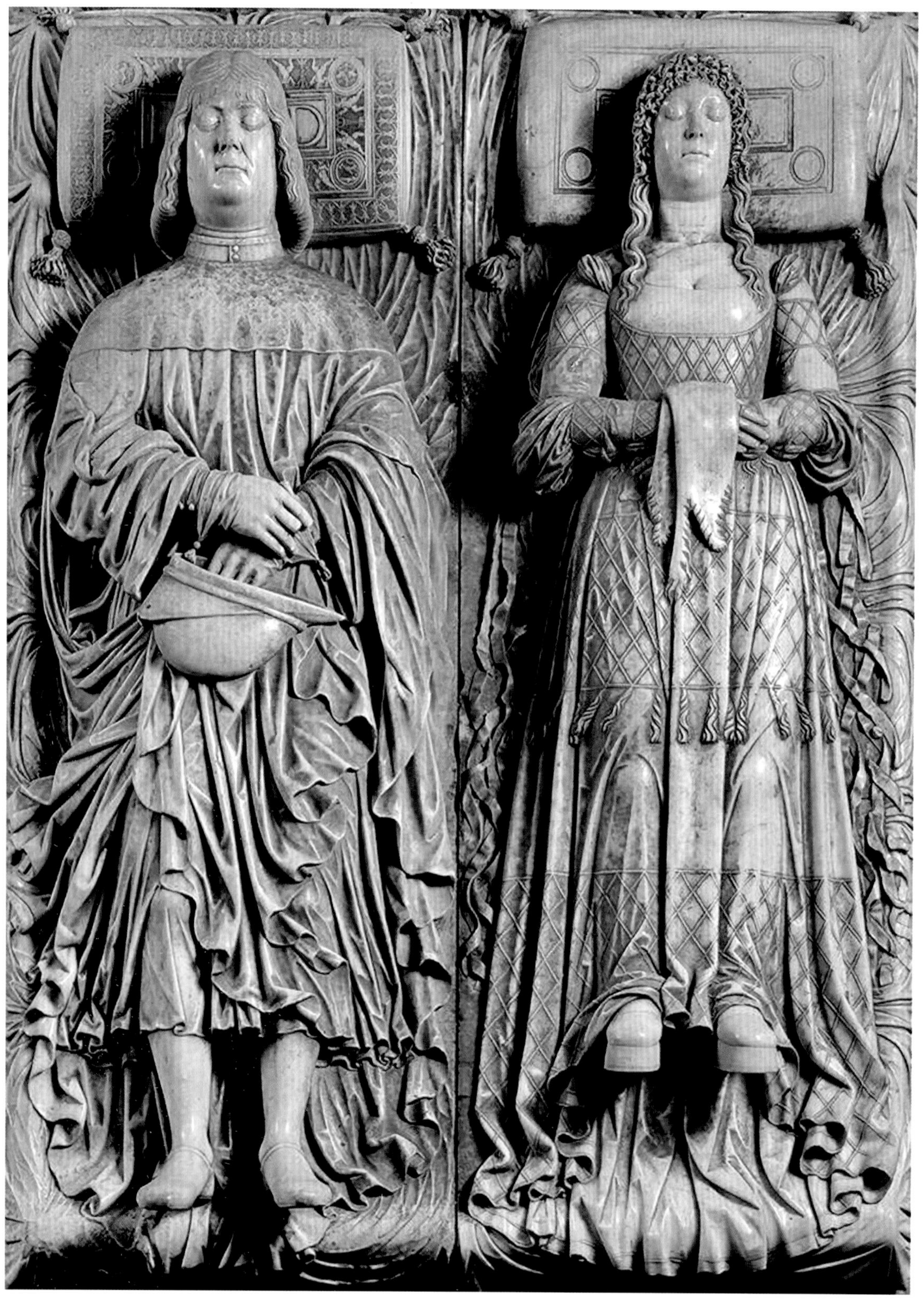

SOLARI: *LUDOVICO SFORZA & BEATRICE D'ESTE* (c.1498) – MARBLE 215 × 160 cm – CERTOSA DI PAVIA

XIII

APOTHEOSIS

ART AND PROPAGANDA UNDER IL MORO 1496–99

WHILE LEONARDO DA VINCI was immortalizing Il Moro's mistress Lucrezia Crivelli as *La Belle Ferronnière,* new stone busts of Milanese Dukes and Duchesses were artfully arranged at the Certosa di Pavia to cement the dynastic propaganda peddled by Bergognone's transept frescoes. Even the effigies Il Moro commissioned soon afterwards, of himself and his late wife, were conceived to make a posthumous political point. After helping design the vaults of the dome and sacristy at Santa Maria delle Grazie, Leonardo's final work for Il Moro was an epic stage-set: a *trompe-l'œil* revamp of a hall at the Castello Sforzesco into a ducal shrine.

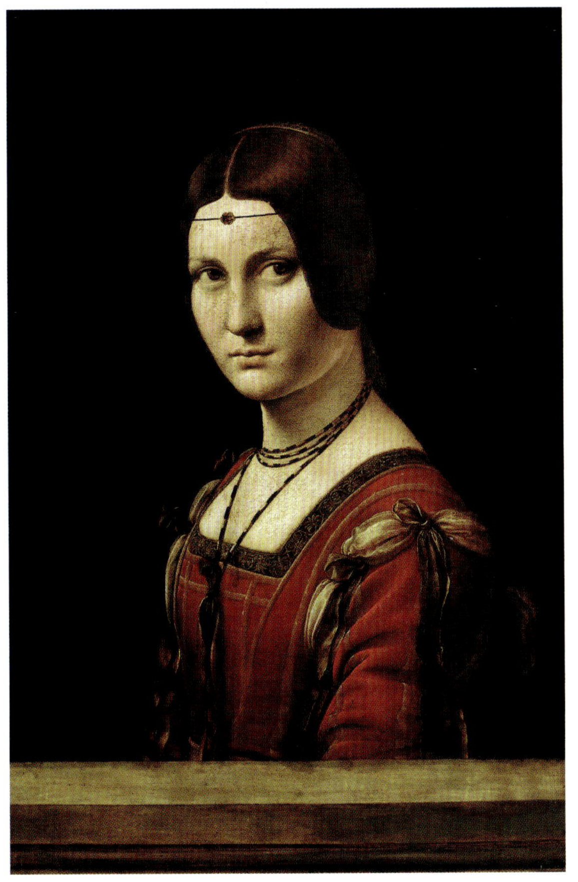

LEONARDO DA VINCI
LA BELLE FERRONNIERE
62 × 44 cm
LOUVRE, PARIS

COURT PORTRAITS

Leonardo's *Belle Ferronnière* is usually dated to around 1496, the year of Bianca's wedding and the final *Sforziada*. It is a portrait of almost photographic precision and rare psychological subtlety, simultaneously conveying defiance and vulnerability. It is commonly held to depict Lucrezia Crivelli, who is first mentioned as Il Moro's mistress in 1495 and bore him a son, Gianpaolo, in March 1497.

Perhaps, given Lucrezia's subdued expression, the portrait was not completed until after the death of Il Moro's wife, Beatrice d'Este, on 3 January 1497.

Of the four portraits Leonardo produced in Sforza Milan – 'The Musician' (here identified as Galeazzo Sanseverino), Cecilia Gallerani, Bianca Sforza and Lucrezia Crivelli – *La Belle Ferronnière* is the only one to lack an unusual feature (snatch of music, ermine, unprecedented knot pattern). Her hands and waist are blocked off from view. Was she, like Cecilia Gallerani, pregnant at the time Leonardo painted her? Was Leonardo loathe to paint her hands after all the complex alterations he had been compelled to make to the hands of his *Lady with an Ermine*?

The position of the bust in *La Belle Ferronnière*, turned slightly towards the viewer, is shared by another court portrait with which it must be virtually contemporary: that of *Francesco Sforza* (Il Duchetto), the elder son of the widowed Isabel of Aragon. This is in oil on panel, 65 × 42cm, and was completed on *15 June 1496* – as we learn from the unusually elaborate, signed inscription at the foot of the picture:

VERA IMAGO PRIMO GENITI LEGITIMI
ILLMI QUON DI JO GZI MARIAE SFORTIAE
MEDIOLANIS DUCIS DUM ESSET ETATIS
ANNORUM QUINTO MCCCCLXXXXVI DIE XV
JUNI. BERNARDINI DI COMITIBUS OPUS

'A true image of the first legitimate son of the most illustrious Gian Galeazzo Maria Sforza, Duke of Milan, aged five – 15 June 1496'

Drawing attention to such a precise date must have had a purpose. Was it a coincidence that the wedding between Bianca Sforza and Galeazzo Sanseverino took place just five days later? Perhaps Il Duchetto, shown here grasping the ducal seal, is clad in the finery he wore at the ceremony. Maybe De' Conti completed his portrait on the same day Leonardo finished his portrait of Bianca.

Bernardino de' Conti, the son of another artist, Baldassare, hailed from Castelseprio, 25 miles northwest of Milan. He is first documented on 16 February 1494 as *Magister Bernardinus de Comittibus de Castroseprio*, receiving payment from Ducal Secretary Jacopo Antiquario for a *Madonna and Child* altarpiece now in the church of San Pietro in Gessate.[1] Working in a style not dissimilar from that of Ambrogio de Predis, with whom he may have trained, he swiftly emerged as an important court portraitist – thought to be the author of Il Moro in his 1495 investiture cape (*see Chapter VIII*).[2]

De' Conti portraits often show sitters with their heads in sharp profile, but their chests and shoulders opened towards the viewer, presumably to showcase their jewellery and sartorial finery. It is an uncomfortable posture, one Leonardo da Vinci only toyed with (for his portrait sketch of Isabella d'Este in 1500). Isabella may have insisted upon it – it is worth noting that in February 1500, just before (or possibly during) Leonardo's own visit, Isabel of Aragon stayed with her in Mantua, presumably bringing the De' Conti portrait of her son with her.

Il Duchetto's posture is repeated, again in half-length format, in Bernardino de' Conti's small oil-on-panel *Portrait of a Lady Between Green Velvet Curtains,*

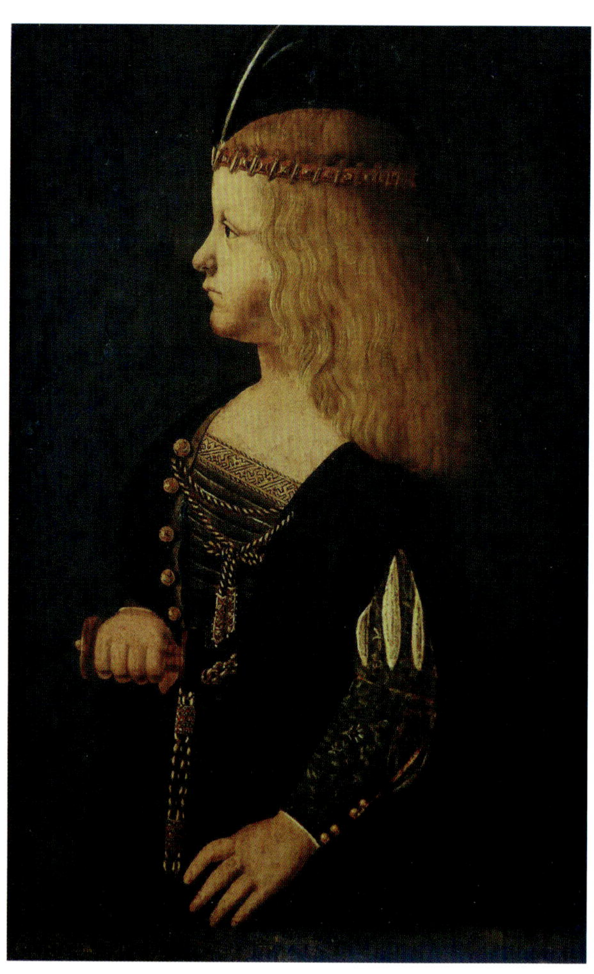

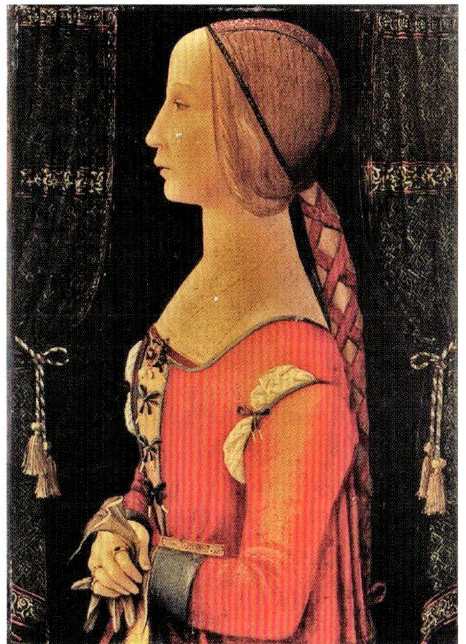

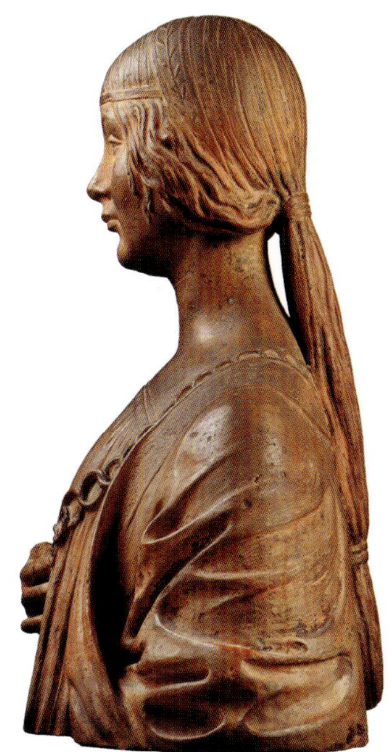

39 × 28.6cm, sold at Christie's New York on 15 May 1996 for $222,500. The lady is shown in Sforza profile holding her gloves of status. She has the same domed forehead, blond hair and criss-cross *coazzone* as the figure identified in *Chapter I* as Isabel of Aragon in the wedding-group with *Saints & Devotees* in London's National Gallery. De' Conti frames her between green curtains – *trompe-l'œil* versions, perhaps, of the curtains that theatrical Renaissance art patrons sometimes used to cover their paintings. Here the idea smacks of self-pity, bringing to mind the *unico nella disgrazia* epithet which Isabel applied to herself on account of her misfortunes.

Christie's indicated that the portrait was with Galerie Trotti in Paris in 1917 – a frontline gallery founded on Rue Royale in 1901 by the collector Count René Avogli Trotti in conjunction with dealer Marcel Nicolle. In 1906 the gallery moved to 8 Place Vendôme where, in premises now occupied by Christian Dior, it staged an exhibition of Italian Old Masters (*Tableaux Anciens de l'Ecole Italienne*) in January 1909.

In what may or may not be coincidence, Malaguzzi Valeri claims to have seen a portrait of Isabel of Aragon, dated *1497*, in the collection of Marchese Lodovico Trotti in Milan before World War I.[3] The Trotti family had a long and distinguished history. In 1490, Este Ambassador Giacomo Trotti reported back to Ferrara about the fashion tastes of the new Duchess, Isabel of Aragon.[4]

A work of some interest in this context is a terracotta bust, 64cm tall, offered for auction at the Vienna Dorotheum on 21 October 2015 and dated by thermoluminescence to 1470–1510. It was attributed to Benedetto Briosco, who worked in Milan and at the Certosa di Pavia. The sitter was proposed as Bianca Maria Sforza – a curious idea given the bust's lack of resemblance with Bianca Maria's bulging-eyed countenance, familiar from several contemporary portraits. The sitter bears a far closer resemblance to the subject of the Bernardino de' Conti portrait. Rather like Il Duchetto clutching the ducal seal, accompanied by an inscription emphasizing his rights, the subject of the bust is shown wearing a ducal chain, to which she ostentatiously draws attention with her right index figure.

Relatively few works of Renaissance art depict women wearing these heavy gold chains. One that does is the bust of Beatrice d'Este in the Certosa di Pavia. The corresponding Certosa bust of Isabel of Aragon does not.

CERTOSA BUSTS

These two busts are part of a group of seven that embellish the **Portale del Lavabo** (or Duchesses' Doorway) in the Certosa church, leading from the South Transept to the Lavabo with its marble washbasin and biblical panels sculpted by Alberto Maffioli of Carrara.

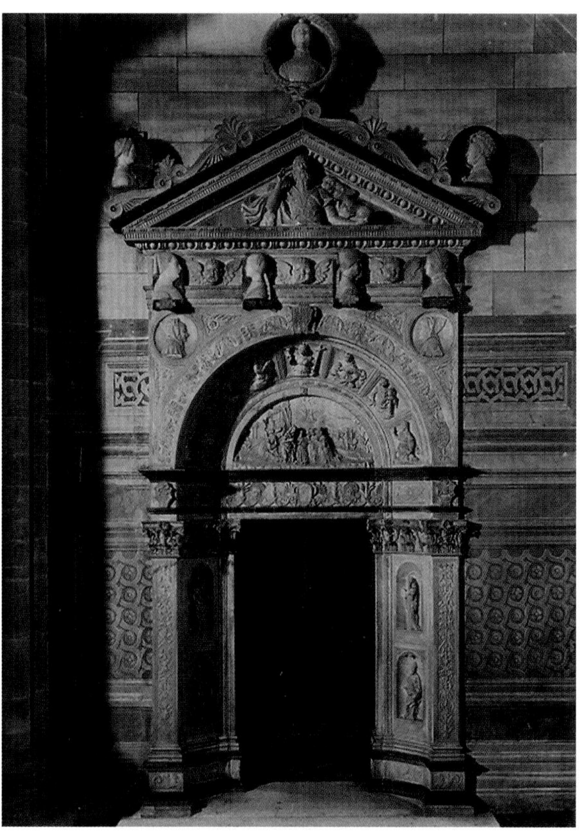

The doorway (*right*) is surmounted by a triangular pediment topped by a tondo containing a front-on bust of Caterina Visconti, and flanked by roundels with profiled busts of Antonia Malatesta and Beatrice di Tenda. Four more sculpted busts are arrayed beneath the pediment – Beatrice d'Este is left of centre, with her back to Isabel of Aragon. Beatrice faces Bianca Maria Visconti; Isabel faces Bona di Savoia.

Both Beatrice and Isabel are depicted wearing a *coazzone*, but Beatrice is the only duchess to wear a ducal chain.

The arrangement is broadly historical, starting at the top with the wife of Gian Galeazzo Visconti, the first duke to receive the Imperial investiture. Caterina Visconti (1361–1404) was Gian Galeazzo's first cousin as well as his wife; he deposed and murdered her father Bernabo. She bore two future Visconti dukes and was grandmother of Il Moro's mother Bianca Maria, the Sforza dynasty matriarch.

After her husband's death, Caterina was imprisoned, and possibly murdered, by her own son Giovanni Maria – whose wife Antonia Malatesta reigned as Duchess of Milan for just four years (1408–12) without providing an heir, then retired to provincial obscurity after her husband's own assassination. Her sister-in-law Beatrice di Tenda (*c.*1372–1418) was a rich widow when Filippo Maria married her in 1412, more for her money than the chance of an heir. He had her beheaded on a trumped-up adultery charge six years later (a tragedy immortalized by an eponymous Bellini opera in 1833).

The corresponding Portale della Sacrestia Vecchia (or Dukes' Doorway) leads from the north transept to the Old Sacristy. It is topped by Gian Galeazzo Visconti (Duke of Milan 1395–1402), wearing the ducal chain, above Filippo Maria (1412–47) to the left and Giovanni Maria Visconti (1402–12) to the right. Lower down, reading from left, Galeazzo Maria faces Gian Galeazzo while Il Moro faces his father Francesco.

The arrangement of the busts is not quite as historically accurate as first appears, but artfully contrived to serve propaganda. Il Moro is placed opposite Francesco, implying that he is his equal and worthy successor. Beatrice d'Este faces Francesco's wife Bianca Maria, leaving Isabel of Aragon to equate with the hapless Bona di Savoia. This selective approach mirrors that of the giant frescoes at the end of each transept, which place Il Moro and Francesco together in one, and crowd four other dukes into the other (Giovanni Maria Visconti is omitted altogether).

The transept doorways are believed to have been erected under Giovanni Antonio Amadeo, possibly in the late 1470s, but the busts are the work of later sculptors – tentatively identified as Maffioli (for the two tondi), Briosco (male busts) and Romano (female busts), and dated to around 1497.[5] No known records survive to advance these names and dates with total assurance. It is amusing to note that the number of portraits involved in the doorways – fourteen, split into two groups of seven – echoes the number and disposition of the putti in Birago's London *Sforziada bas-de-page*. And that, high up the walls, a long frieze of frolicking putti rings the entire transept.

SANTA MARIA DELLE GRAZIE

In January 1497, a few weeks after Bianca Sforza, Beatrice d'Este was buried in the Milanese church of Santa Maria della Grazie, beneath Bramante's vast cupola whose construction occupied much of the 1490s.

The original church had been completed in 1482. Guiniforte Solari's nave, with its quadripartite vaulting, remains; the decoration to its vaults and pillars, carried out between 1482 and 1485 by Bernardino Butinone, possibly assisted by Bernardino de' Rossi and Bernardino Zenale, has been restored. Lunettes above the West Door once portrayed the Virgin, St Dominic and Il Moro on one side; and St Peter and Beatrice d'Este on the other. These lunettes, which legend assigns to Leonardo, were replaced in 1594.

The east end of Solari's new church was destroyed within a few years of being built. The area was set aside for a Sforza mausoleum topped by a cupola, with an adjacent rectangular choir. The architect was Bramante.

Il Moro and his family were to be buried directly beneath Bramante's new, cupola. The burials, alas, began sooner than expected.

The first family member to be so honoured was Il Moro's eldest illegitimate son Leone, who died in 1496, aged twenty. Later the same year his sister Bianca was laid to rest close by, with Il Moro requesting her place of burial be out of the line of view of the ducal pew.[6] Shortly afterwards Il Moro's wife Beatrice joined her beneath the cupola inside a large coffin lined with black velvet.

The interior of Bramante's mighty crown of stone now bears little relationship to its original design. As old photos reveal, it was adorned with a pattern that replicates the inside of one of the six *Nodi Vinciani* conceived by Leonardo in the 1490s and preserved as copperplate engravings (the Ambrosiana owns a full set of these knot designs, on sheets measuring roughly 24 × 20cm).

The *raison-d'être* of these circular patterns has provoked much debate, but it is evident that they were conceived at least partly as cupola designs.[7] Each pattern is *reprised* in the corner of the sheet, evoking the pendentives to be found between the base of a cupola and its supporting arches (in Santa Maria delle Grazie these pendentives contain medallions featuring the Four Doctors of the Church).

The cupola of Santa Maria delle Grazie retains its sixteen original oculi (circular windows) and these, too, are reflected in a Leonardo knot design – by the intertwining motif repeated sixteen times around the inner rim of Ambrosiana engraving *Incs. 9596e.*

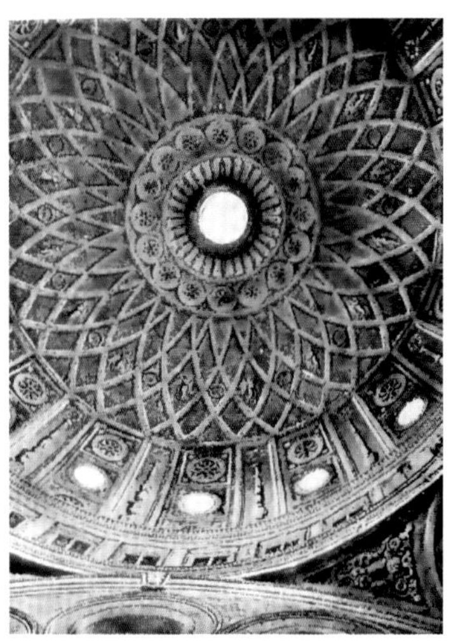

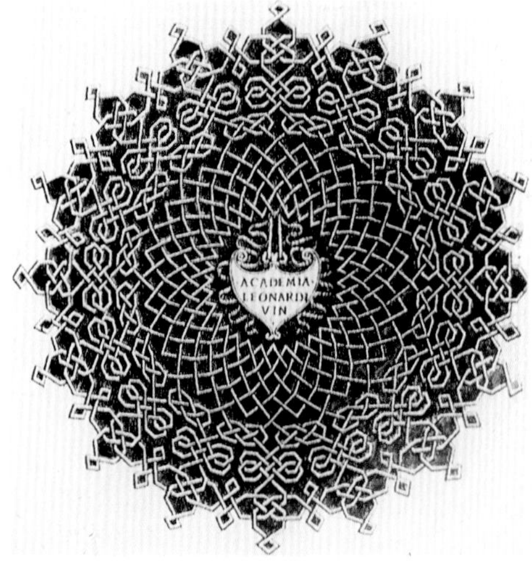

Each of the six Leonardo knot designs is uniquely complex and composed of a series of interwoven strands; the simplest consists of two, the most complex of thirty-eight.

But the patterns always appear as a continuous whole, without beginning or end – which may explain why the embroidery to Bianca Sforza's dress resolves itself into an enclosed triangle rather than bleeding off the page, in the manner of the Ambrosiana's female portrait by Ambrogio de Predis.[8]

The complexity of Leonardo's knot-patterns suggests they were conceived as more than cupola designs. They are essentially infinite – redolent of Alpha, Omega and the mysteries of the universe.

One source of possible inspiration are the intricate arabesques of the Muslim world, absorbed into the fashion of 15th century Spain and imported to Italy by the Aragon family – then brought from Naples to Milan by Isabel of Aragon in 1489. One of her ladies-in-waiting in the National Gallery's *Saints & Devotees* wedding-portrait, for instance, wears a dress embroidered with a complex knot pattern.

These knot designs are commonly referred to as *fantasia dei vinci* – a multiple pun on the words *vincere* (to triumph), *vinco* (wickerwork) and *vincio* ('I link' in Latin). Yet Signore da Vinci himself referred to them as *Gruppi di Bramante*.

Even though they are no longer to be found on Bramante's cupola, they can still be admired at Santa Maria delle Grazie – in the Old Sacristy, otherwise known as the *Sagrestia del Bramante* (*see p.173*).

This large, rectangular room, the size of a small church, is thought to date from the mid-1490s. With sad disregard for its artistic and historic importance, it now serves as a low-lit exhibition hall – making it hard to admire its pews' magnificent intarsia woodwork (mostly devoted to Sforza insignia) or the *grisaille* frieze consisting of Il Moro's dragon-flanked caduceus topped by Mercury's winged hat.

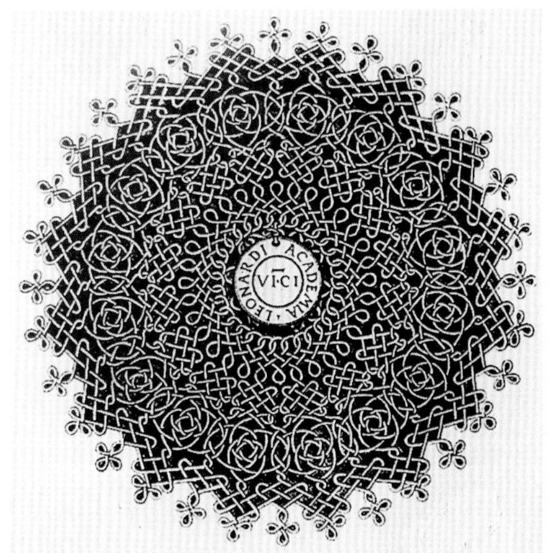

Above this frieze come circular windows and, above them, a ceiling supported by triangular vaults. The ceiling is painted throughout in midnight blue, and the vaults lined with white *fantasia dei vinci* – again reminiscent of a Leonardo knot design, and incorporating a distinctive interlacing motif, based on an inner core of four diamonds, to be found in one of the Ambrosiana engravings (*Incs. 9596b*). The same motif is to be found, in gold, on the shoulder of Bianca Sforza in her Leonardo portrait.

The *Sagrestia del Bramante* knot-patterning looks airy and lacy, viewed from below. Up close the lacework turns out to be rope: embroidery on an epic scale.

It is hard to imagine that Leonardo – at work on his *Last Supper* in the nearby refectory, while Bramante supervised his cupola – did not thread his way through their design.

LEONARDO'S 'ACADEMY'

Leonardo's knots are closely associated with his 'Academy.' Four of the six knot designs preserved in the Ambrosiana feature the word *Academia* accompanied by his name.

Many scholars are nevertheless sceptical that any such academy actually existed. A saleroom discovery suggests they could be wrong – and that such an academy was alive and chuntering, rather than just a pipedream curled up in the middle of Leonardo's spaghetti junctions.

In March 2003 an unpublished 92*ff* Italian manuscript by Henrico Boscano, entitled *Isola Beata* (*c.1513*), surfaced at Christie's London, selling to an undisclosed buyer for £175,490. The manuscript, which describes an imaginary shipwreck on a remote island, seems to have evaded the attention of most academics – with the noteworthy exception of Jill Pederson, who analysed it in her PhD dissertation *The Academia Leonardi Vinci: Visualizing Dialectic in Renaissance Milan 1480–99* (Johns Hopkins University, Baltimore, 2007).[9]

The *Isola Beata* manuscript measures 289 × 205mm, with 27 lines per page written in brown ink in what Boscano calls *lingua milanese* (and what Christie's bombastically upgraded to 'a partly Latinized form of Tuscan, with Northern Italian accents'). The volume lacks its clasps but retains its original Milanese olive/brown morocco binding – with gilt-tooled *vinci* knot patterning.

The volume was formerly in the collection of Count Oswald Seilern (1901–67), and had previously belonged to the Barnabite College in Vienna, where the Barnabites established themselves at the Michaelerkirche under Kaiser Ferdinand II in 1627. It may have been sent to Vienna by Gian Ambrogio Mazenta (1565–1635), whose brother Guido (died 1613) owned a number of Leonardo's manuscripts. Gian Ambrogio Mazenta was General of the Barnabite Order (founded in Milan in 1530) from 1612–17 – and, in his manuscript *Alcune Memorie de' Fatti di Leonardo da Vinci a Milano e de' suoi Libri* (Memories of Leonardo and His Books), penned in 1635, also talked of a Milanese academy.

Pederson contends that Boscano, writing under restored Sforza Duke Massimiliano, was looking back to a golden age of cultural patronage under his father Il Moro that had encompassed an *achademia* of artists, poets, humanists and musicians who met informally for rhetorical debate.

Boscano refers to this *achademia* as 'the forge and hearthstone of the wise' (*la fucina e la cimento delli savi*), and goes on to name such a heavenly host of members that it is hard to imagine he is making it all up. He starts with two *magnifici cavaglieri*: **Antonio Fregoso** from Genoa (died *c.*1530), more commonly known as Antoniotto, a poet who was raised by Cicco Simonetta, the Ducal Chancellor executed by Il Moro in 1480; and **Gaspare Visconti** (1461–99), author of *Paolo e Daria* and patron of Bramante, who hosted his own learned *soirées* at his Milan palazzo.[10]

There were three *pictori e ingegneri*: **Leonardo da Vinci** (well suited to a faraway island, in that he owned Mandeville's *Travels* and wrote some evocative accounts of the Orient); **Bramante**; and the goldsmith Cristoforo Foppa, better known as **Caradosso** (*c.*1452–1527), lauded by Bellincioni as one of Milan's four *stelle divine* or divine stars (along with Leonardo, the scholar and historian Giorgio Merula from Alessandria, and the Ferrara-based cannon-founder Giannino Bombadieri) to have 'blossomed in the shadow of Il Moro.'

Pederson suggests the academy may have been 'named' after its most famous member – citing the example of the *Accademia Bessarionea* in Rome, honouring Cardinal Bessarion (1402–72) rather than its *principe*, Theodore Gaza – and that it probably functioned along the lines of the slightly earlier Florentine 'academy' headed by Marsilio Ficino (1433–99), modelled on Plato's School of

Athens. This hosted such luminaries as Giovanni Pico della Mirandola, Angelo Poliziano and *Sforziada* translator Cristoforo Landino, and reputedly gathered at the Villa Careggi[11] and Ficino's palazzo on Via Sant' Egidio.

Not dissimilar academies were set up across the Alps by Konrad Celtis (1459–1508), an associate of Galeazzo Sanseverino's friend Willibald Pirckheimer. Celtis, engagingly styled the 'Arch-Humanist', was crowned Imperial Poet Laureate by Emperor Friedrich III in Nuremberg in 1487 and founded 'academies' (*Sofalitas Litterarum*) in four different cities (Cracov, Budapest, Vienna and Heidelberg).

Later evidence of a Milanese 'academy' can be found in Girolamo Borsieri's *Supplemento della Nobilità di Milano* published in 1619, which asserts that members of an *Academia Leonardi Vinci* included Bramante, Leonardo and 'excellent painters' like Leonardo's pupil Giovanni Antonio Boltraffio.

Among issues debated on the *Isola Beata* was the *Paragone* rivalry between the arts, with Boscano wondering whether writing or the visual arts were more likely to ensure enduring fame (the subject of Il Puteolano's *Sforziada* preface).

Boscano appears to come down on the side of Leonardo and his fellow-artists by concluding that it 'is not possible to express in writing what one can imagine painted or sculpted in marble' (*non si possano exprimere in scripto come per exemplo chi volesse scrivere duna formo sa imagine depinta o sculpita in marmo*). Pederson suggests that, by stressing the presence of artists alongside musicians, poets and literati, Boscano's *achademia* was embracing painters' attempts to raise their social and academic status in late Quattrocento Milan.

The Paragone issue was perhaps the most contentious and longest-running subject of debate in Sforza Milan – and keenly followed by Il Moro who, according to Lomazzo (in his 1584 *Trattato dell'Arte della Pittura, Scoltura et Architettura*), bade Leonardo compare the merits of painting and sculpture:[12]

> *Nel qual modo va discorrendo & argomentando Leonardo Vinci in un sua*
> *libro letto dà me questi anni passati ch'eglo scrisse di mano stanca à prieghi di*
> *Lodovico Sforza, Duca di Milano, in determinatione di questa questione se e piu*
> *nobile la pittura, ò la scultura.'*

> (As Leonardo discusses and argues in one of his books written in his left hand at
> the request of Lodovico Sforza, Duke of Milan, to determine whether painting
> or sculpture is nobler)

Leonardo's defence of the arts, specifically painting, received powerful backing from his fellow-Florentine Luca Pacioli (1445–1517), the Franciscan mathematician who moved to Milan in 1496 soon after completing his *Summa de Arithmetica, Geometria, Proportioni et Proportionalita*, calling on artists to strive for knowledge of geometry, arithmetic and perspective. That sounded like an identikit description of the approach espoused by Leonardo and Bramante, who also shared with Pacioli a keen interest in the art of perspective as pioneered by Piero della Francesca (*c*.1420–92). As well as hobnobbing with

Leonardo, Pacioli was a big Bramante man: the second part of his *De Divina Proportione*, entitled *Trattato dell'Archittetura*, discussed Bramante's architectural works in Milan.

The first chapter of *De Divina Proportione* sees Pacioli report on a 'praiseworthy academic duel' at the Castello Sforzesco on 9 February 1498, attended by 'many high-ranking, very famous and wise' figures including churchmen, scholars, theologians, councillors, architects, engineers and lawyers – notably Galeazzo Sanseverino; the Prior of Santa Maria delle Grazie; the doctors and astrologers Ambrogio da Rosate, Pirovano, Cusani and Marliano; and, of course, Leonardo da Vinci, glowingly described by Pacioli as *'compatriota nostro fiorentino, qual de sculptura getto e pictura con ciascuno el cognome verifica.'* Pacioli also termed Leonardo 'skilled in every mathematical discipline' and a Prince among Mortals.[13]

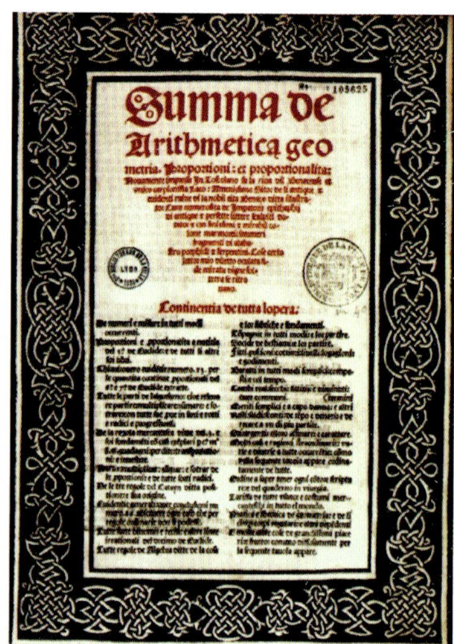

Leonardo provided sophisticated geometric illustrations – in coloured chalks on vellum, like his *Bianca Sforza* portrait – for Pacioli's *De Divina Proportione*, and may also have had some influence on the chapter initials with sophisticated interlacing designs[14] – stylistically similar to both the frontispiece of Pacioli's *Summa de Arithmetica, Geometria, Proportioni et Proportionalità*, published in Venice in 1494 (*right*), and the gold-embossed leather binding for the manuscript versions of *De Divine Proportione* produced in 1498.

Luca Pacioli is shown gazing at a rhombicuboctahedron, half-filled with water, in his portrait in Naples' Capodimonte Museum, where it is attributed to Jacopo de' Barberi. A figure with wavy blond hair lurks jarringly in the background, looking every inch an impertinent later addition, and diverting attention from Pacioli's steely scientific gaze. The lurker, according to Capodimonte, is Pacioli's one-time patron Guidobaldo da Montefeltro (1472–1508), Duke of Urbino. But he looks nothing like Guidobaldo's lank-haired portrait by Raphael in the Uffizi, and appears rather to be dressed in Milanese fashion.

In Milan Pacioli described Galeazzo Sanseverino as his 'own special patron,' and some feel that Sanseverino is the man depicted here[15] – presumably added by a different artist after Pacioli's move to Milan in 1496. There is enough physical resemblance with Leonardo's 'Musician' (whose black jerkin was originally dark red) for this identification to be plausible, if not conclusive.

Sanseverino was one of three recipients of manuscript copies of *De Divina Proportione*, Il Moro another.[16] The illuminated frontispieces to their respective volumes reflect no disparity of status. Both feature the recipient's coat of arms and a miniature: Il Moro is shown receiving his book from Pacioli; Sanseverino's miniature (*see p.161*) appears to feature the dragon Tarantasio emerging from the lake it haunted east of Milan where, according to legend, it was slain by Uberto Visconti when about to swallow a child. This fearsome image would be heraldically transformed into the viper or *biscione*, becoming the prime emblem of the Viscontis and their Sforza successors.[17]

SALA DELLE ASSE

Luca Pacioli does not say where in the Castello Sforzesco he, Leonardo, Sanseverino and others met for their 'academic duel' in early 1498. But Leonardo
da Vinci was soon at work on the perfect setting.

The Sala delle Asse (*below*) was one of Leonardo's most impressive achievements – and, after the *Sforza Horse* and *Last Supper*, the third epic commission he received from Il Moro to keep him in Milan.[18] It was also the ultimate
embodiment of one of Leonardo's principal rôles at the Sforza court: set-
designer. Transforming a vast chamber into an all-embracing glade of mulberry trees was interior design on an unprecedented scale. In its pristine,
freshly painted glory it must have dazzled and beguiled.

Yet for much of its existence it has been neglected. It was not even mentioned
by the omniscient Vasari – perhaps because, within a year of its completion,
the Castello had been overrun by the French and the Sala delle Asse reduced
to the status of just another room in a defensive fortress, rather than the showpiece hall of a prince's palace.

Its location on the ground floor of the north tower of the Corte Ducale made
it an obligatory transit point for anyone navigating the Castello's State Rooms.
It also became Il Moro's personal entrance hall, leading to and from the private

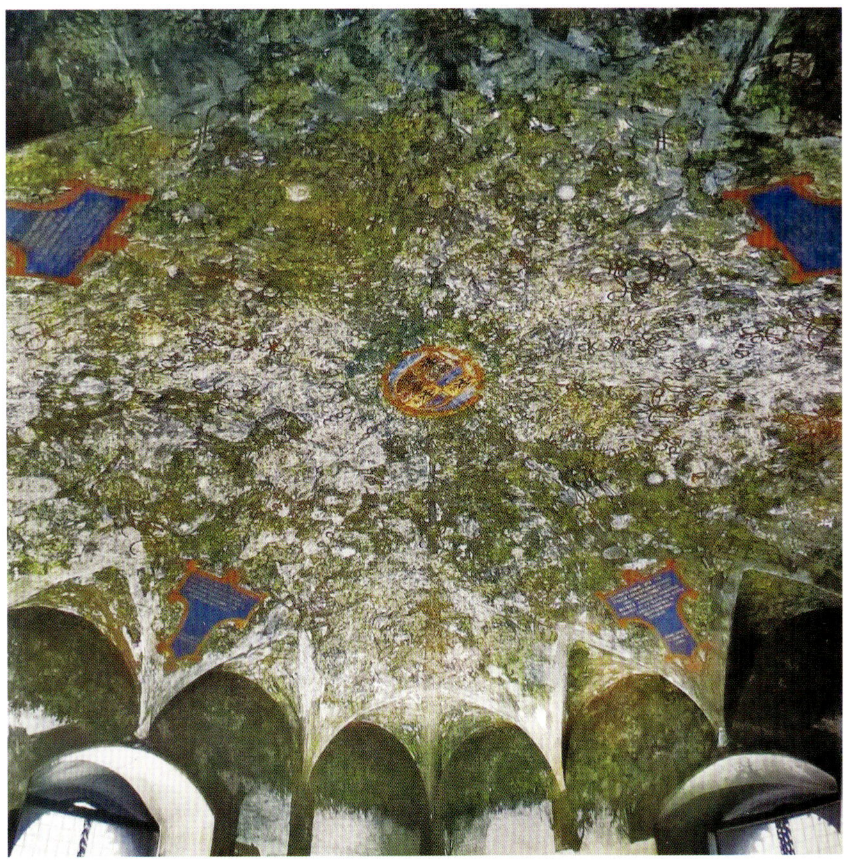

suite built for him in the 1490s by Bramante in the form of a *ponticella* (little bridge) over the castle moat. This *ponticella* also served as Il Moro's private exit to the castle's 300-hectare game park, and offered a short cut towards his mascot church of Sant'Ambrogio ad Nemus (where he was lording it over the altar in the *Pala Sforzesca*).

The Sala delle Asse also had symbolic and sentimental importance to Il Moro as the room used for the ceremony marking his appointment as Guardian to Gian Galeazzo in November 1480, confirming his status as Regent.

The State Rooms adjacent to the Sala delle Asse had been garishly decorated with giant, monotonously repeated Sforza emblems during the reign of Il Moro's brother, Galeazzo Maria, when the Sala delle Asse was referred as the *Camera deli Ducali* (Ducal Chamber) as it featured two large ducal devices – the *cimero del foco* (lion with fire-bucket) and the *colombine con i razi* (dove on sunburst) – painted on to the panelling after which the room was later named (*asse* meaning wooden boards)[19] and which lined the walls and ceiling from top to bottom to insulate the room from the cold. As the ground floor of the north tower, this was the chilliest place in the Castello.

Underneath this painted panelling lay a vast expanse of pristine wall. The chance to upstage his brother with a more sophisticated decorative scheme, create a showpiece for his personal sector of the castle, and tie his temperamental star artist down with another large-scale commission may all have been factors behind Il Moro's decision to tear off the panelling and have the room redecorated, in novel and grandiose fashion, as a showcase for his own emblem, the mulberry – reflecting his divine powers to turn a room of cold and frosty mornings into a leafy glade open to the summer skies.

The upper walls and ceiling of the Sala delle Asse are adorned with *trompe-l'œil* decoration of intertwining leafy branches, creating a verdant canopy that allows glimpses of the firmament, with a gold-rimmed oculus containing the combined coat of arms of the Duke of Milan and the House of Este (shown – as was originally the case for their arms above *The Last Supper* – against pale blue sky).

The canopy is formed by sixteen mulberry trees, two of which start life as separate trunks before merging at the top of the two windows.[20] A fluttering riot of entwined gold ribbons weaves its way through the treetops, creating abstract patterns derived from Leonardo's knot-designs.

Apart from nodding towards the Garden of Eden and the Hanging Gardens of Babylon, the new-look Sala delle Asse also paid tribute to one of Il Moro's childhood heroes, King Cyrus, whose horticultural vision and green-fingered genius were the stuff of Socratean legend.[21]

The mulberry idea behind this megalomaniac tribute to Il Moro's Milanese paradise derives from Ovid's *Metamorphoses* – specifically the tale of *Pyramus & Thisbe* (IV, 55–166) set in the mythical horticultural centre of Babylon: the story of two lovers from rival families, who arrange a tryst beneath a mulberry tree (*morus*).

Thisbe arrives first but, when a lioness prowls by fresh from a kill, she rushes off in a panic, dropping her shawl – which the lioness promptly stains with her bloody chops. Pyramus arrives to find the blood-soaked shawl, but no Thisbe; presuming her devoured, he falls upon his sword. His blood gushes forth at such a rate that it splatters the snow-white mulberry fruit in the branches above, staining them dark red. Thisbe returns, sees his prostrate body and commits suicide in turn.

With her dying words she exhorts the mulberry tree to yield blood-coloured fruit for ever more:

> *At tu quae ramis arbor miserabile corpus – nunc tegis unius, mox es tectura duorum –*
> *Signa tene caedis pullosque et luctibus aptos – semper habe fetus, gemini monimenta cruoris*

> (May thou, whose boughs shade now one wretched body, soon two, always bear fruit in pledge of our twin blood)

The gods are 'touched', and grant her prayer:

> *Vota tamen tetigere deos, tetigere parentes*
> *Nam color in pomo est, ubi permaturuit, ater, quodque rogis superest*

As well as serving as the inspiration for *Romeo and Juliet* (and the play-within-a-play in *A Midsummer Night's Dream*), this grim tale inspired an adaptation by one of the leading bards at Il Moro's court, Gaspare Visconti,[22] whose five-act drama *Pasitea* was completed just before the Sala delle Asse was transformed.

Visconti changed Thisbe's name to Pasitea, reflecting Il Moro's longstanding desire to upstage Florence: the new name derived from Politian's recent *Stanze per la Giostra*, where Venus sends *Pasitea, delle Grazie una sorella … quella che sovra a tutte e la piu bella* (a sister of the Graces … and most beautiful of them all) to Iulio in a dream. Politian had taken the name *Pasitea* from Homer.[23]

Visconti toned down the tragedy of Ovid's tale by adding a *deus ex machina* in the form of Apollo – another staple figure in Il Moro's Milan, invariably associated with Il Moro himself – to bring the lovers back to life.

Just before that admirable achievement, in the opening scene of Act V, Apollo reacts to seeing his beloved Daphne transformed into a laurel by declaring that the laurel will henceforth be 'the most glorious of trees – except only for the mulberry':

> *Fra gli arbori gloriosi serai prima*
> *Exceptuato solamente il Moro*

Visconti's 32-line *Prologue* is even more explicit in its homage to his ducal patron, with an envoy of Jupiter declaiming that Milan has attained glory and global fame 'under the shade of a mulberry tree' (*sotto un Moro a l'ombra*), thanks to Il Moro's 'rare and singular virtues':

Sì che per sue virtù nel mondo rare
D'ogni altro il Mor serà più singulare

This sort of fawning nonsense is echoed by Visconti's description of Il Moro elsewhere as a Sacred Prince, Duke of Dukes and King of Kings, no less (*Principe sagro, egregio trali egregi, Duca di duci e Re degli altri Regi*). It was mirrored in *La Danae*, the five-act drama by Baldassare Taccone whose 1496 première was stage-managed by Leonardo using a sophisticated array of shafts, pulleys and cage gears (as a sketch from the *Codex Atlanticus* makes clear), and which triumphantly concludes with the words *E viva el Moro triunfante e verde!*[24]

Visconti, meanwhile, has Apollo ask why the fruit of the mulberry is red, not white. A shepherd tells him about the stain of suicidal blood, whereupon Apollo declares that the fruit of the mulberry shall be forever red:

Onde, se'l moro e sempre inamorato
Haver non se ne die' gran maraviglia,
Che'l sangue de gli amanti non pur fuore
Ma tinto l'ha perfino in mezzo al cuore

The idea of Il Moro *sempre inamorato* may have raised wry eyebrows among Sforza courtiers, given his romantic track record – and the fact that his idyll with mistress Lucrezia Crivelli continued to blossom, and bear fruit, after the death of Beatrice d'Este.

The Sala delle Asse was intended as a meeting place for courtiers and a reception hall for visiting dignitaries. Whoever gathered here would be aware of Il Moro's all-seeing eye – and the protective embrace of what Pliny termed the 'wisest of trees' (*morus sapientissima arborum*).[25]

Birago had been the first artist to portray Il Moro as a sagacious mulberry back in 1492. The newlook Sala delle Asse would provide a giant, 3-D version of his Paris *Sforziada* frontispiece where Il Moro is represented as a giant, talking mulberry tree.

The politico-diplomatic side to the room's decoration has received only cursory attention from art historians, but reveals much about Il Moro's *fin-de-règne*.

While Leonardo da Vinci's vision of nature takes up 98 per cent of the decorated area, it is not the whole story. Along with the Sforza/Este shield in the middle of the ceiling, there are four blue shields spaced at regular intervals at the base of the ceiling: two above the room's windows, two directly opposite. This association of mulberries and military weaponry brings to mind the words of II Samuel 5 XXIV:

'When thou hearest the sound of a going in the tops of the mulberry trees, that
then thou shalt bestir thyself: for then shall the Lord go out before thee, to smite
the host of the Philistines.'

If there was anyone Il Moro was keen to smite in 1498 it was not, for all his cultural pretensions, Philistines – it was the French.

In 1495 the French army had conquered Naples but over-reached itself, limping back over the Alps decimated by syphilis. The likelihood of their return was always on the cards, and became a quasi-certainty when Charles VIII died, aged just 27, on 7 April 1498 – to be succeeded by his warmonger cousin Louis of Orléans. For Il Moro: the nightmare scenario.

The new Louis XII already had a toe-hold in Italy as Lord of Asti, on Lombardy's western frontier. For years he had been proclaiming himself the rightful Duke of Milan, as his paternal grandmother Valentina Visconti (1368–1408) was the daughter of Gian Galeazzo Visconti, the first Duke of Milan (and the only Duke, prior to Il Moro, to have obtained the Imperial investiture). With Louis XII in charge, a French attack on Milan was just a matter of time. It came, a year after he had been crowned in Rheims, in Summer 1499 – when Il Moro's chief military ally, Maximilian, was embroiled in a war in Switzerland.

Cause or coincidence, the calamitous news that Charles VIII had been succeeded by the Duke of Orléans reached Milan only days before Leonardo da Vinci began work on the Sala delle Asse. On 21 April 1498 Gualtiero Bescape reported to Il Moro that the room's boards were being taken down and 'Magistro Leonardo' had promised to finish the room *per tuto Septembre*; in the meantime, the scaffolding (*li ponti*) he had erected would enable the room to remain in use.[26]

The four shields added to Leonardo's mulberry glade – whose fussy borders recall those of Birago's signature plinth in the 'Uffizi' *Sforziada* (*see p.116*) – contained inscriptions (dated by year) evoking Il Moro's Imperial investiture, and implying his claim to the Duchy to be far stronger than anyone else's.

By stressing Il Moro's alliance with Emperor Maximilian, the shields metaphorically summoned the Holy Roman Empire to Il Moro's impecunious defence.

These gold-lettered inscriptions (*'certi epigrammi ... in lettere d'oro'*) were noted by the Venetian senator Marino Sanuto (1466–1535) when he visited the Sala delle Asse in September 1499.

Three of the four inscriptions cited Maximilian, and read as if they had been dictated by Il Moro.

The first shield referred to the wedding that linked the Houses of Sforza and Habsburg:

LVDOVICVS MEDIOL DVX DIVO
MAX RO REGI BLANCAM NEPOTEM IN
MATRIMONIVM LOCAVIT ET CVM EO
ARCTIOREM AFFINITATE IPSA
BENIVOLENTIAM INIVNXIT

AN SAL LXXXXIII
SVPRA MCCCC

Duke Ludovico of Milan offered his niece Bianca in marriage to Maximilian,
King of the Romans, entailing closer ties and goodwill – AD 1493

The second shield referred to Il Moro's investiture as Duke of Milan:

LVDOVICVS MEDIOL DVX
MEDIOL DUCATVS TITVLVM IVSQVE
QVOD MORTVO DVCE PHILIPPO AVO
IN GENTE SFORTIANA OBITINERE
NON POTVERAT AB DIVO MAX RO
REGE IMPERATOREQUE
MAGNIS CVMVLATVS
HONORIBVS ACCEPIT

AN SAL LXXXXV
SVPRA MCCCC

Duke Ludovico of Milan accepted with great honour from Maximilian, Emperor
& King of the Romans, his title to the Duchy of Milan, something the House of
Sforza had been unable to obtain since the death of his grandfather Duke Filippo
– AD 1495

The third shield referred to an anti-French summit staged by Il Moro and Maximilian, and invoked the dissuasive potential of Milan's alliance with the House of Habsburg:

LVDOVICVS MEDIOL DVX CVM
ITALIAM GALLORVM REGIS
ARMA SVSPECTA TENERENT
CVM BEATRICE CONIVGE IN GERMANIAM
TRAIECIT ET VT DIVVS MAX REX
CAROLI CONATIBVS IN
ITALIA SE OPPONERET
OBTINVIT

AN SAL LXXXXVI
SVPRA MCCCC

Duke Ludovico of Milan travelled with his wife Beatrice to Germany to persuade
Emperor Maximilian to counter the attempts of King Charles of France to
subjugate Italy by force of arms – AD 1496

Emperor Maximilian's support represented an insurance policy for Il Moro, who had no standing army to speak of, and relied heavily on mercenaries. Il Moro was under no illusions about Maximilian's dilatory character, but banked on the prestige of Imperial support as a deterrent to would-be aggressors.

The fourth shield in the Sala delle Asse no longer has its original inscription – nor did it even when Sanuto saw it in September 1499. The original inscription must surely have been dated *1494*, as part of a four-year Moro–Maximilian sequence spanning 1493–96; it probably referred to Il Moro's succeeding as Duke of Milan (on October 22) and stressed his legal right to the Duchy. Why the French mutilated this inscription, after capturing the Castello Sforzesco just before Sanuto's visit, is discussed in *Chapter XIV*.

The mention of Beatrice d'Este in the 1496 inscription ties in with the presence of the Este arms in the shield at the apex of the room, which has led some commentators to interpret Leonardo's design for the Sala delle Asse as a tribute to Il Moro's late wife. It was nothing of the sort, although this may have been a welcome (albeit hypocritical) propaganda side-effect. Like the quartered Sforza arms, the Este arms contain two Imperial eagles – making four Imperial eagles in all, matching the number of Maximilian shields. Like the Sforzas, the Estes were custodians of an Imperial fiefdom (Modena – to which Maximilian had renewed Duke Ercole's investiture in April 1494). This double dose of Imperial heraldry further served to reinforce the legitimacy of Il Moro's claims to Milan and his dynastic ties to the Habsburgs.

Il Moro was happy enough with his own Imperial arms in most circumstances, although he sometimes used the joint Milan–Este arms when Beatrice was alive – including on the wall above *The Last Supper*, and on the altar-cloth now in the Museo Baroffio in Sacro Monte sopra Varese, woven for Il Moro's investiture ceremony.

THE SFORZA EFFIGIES

In May 1498, as Leone, Bianca and Beatrice slumbered in unquiet earth beneath Bramante's dome, Il Moro funded the Milanese return of his great ally-turned-enemy: Roberto Sanseverino. To the fury of Trent's inhabitants, Emperor Maximilian permitted Roberto's body to be disinterred and removed to Milan – 'ransomed for a great sum,' in Corio's disapproving words,[27] and granted a 'funeral befitting an emperor' before being reburied in the family crypt in San Francesco Grande. The operation reflected the continuing clout of *I Gran Sanseverini* at Il Moro's court.

Meanwhile Il Moro had commissioned Cristoforo Solari (*c.*1460–1527) to sculpt effigies of Beatrice d'Este and himself for a majestic tomb in Santa Maria delle Grazie. These masterpieces of funereal statuary (*see p.222*) remained at Santa Maria until at least 1515, the date of the last known eye-witness account of their presence, then were removed either by the French (between 1515–21) or the Spanish (after 1535), and sold in 1564 to the Certosa di Pavia – where they have reclined in the north transept since 1891.

Il Moro and Beatrice are shown with their eyes closed on identical oblong pillows with similar but not identical corner-tassels. Beatrice's pillow has a plain geometric design but Il Moro's is a decorative riot. An outer frame of stylized leaves contains a middle border of chubby cherubs holding a torch in one hand and a bowl in the other, offered to serpents entwined around a narrow stand. The inner band features the large initials *L D* (*Ludovicus Dux*). Each corner circle contains a Sforza emblem: a lion rampant holding a quince; an axe-and-log; a *scopetta*; and a dragon-flanked caduceus topped by Mercury's winged hat.[28]

Il Moro is wearing the plain, flowing, knee-length *robone* in which he is generally portrayed, with a rounded (gold) collar fastened by two studs. He wears open shoes with slightly raised heels, and is holding his ducal cap in his left hand.

Beatrice is wearing a low-cut dress embroidered with lozenge-patterned thread (perhaps evoking the 'Diamond' nickname of the House of Este) – with tassels dangling from the waist, sleeves and upper arms, and ribbons gushing from the elbows to fall the length of her body. An animal pelt is draped over her hands, its eyes and snout just visible beneath her right hand. She has a plump face and well-developed bust: a matron at 21, and a far cry from the slip of a girl portrayed by Romano in 1490. Her hair is tightly curled above her forehead, then falls in waves over her shoulders and on to her bust. She is shod in high-soled clogs but, even so, ends a foot shorter than Il Moro.

True to the form of Birago's frontispieces, Leonardo's portraits and Bergognone's frescos and altarpieces, the effigies make a political statement: the Sforzas lie shins and ankles above other Italian dynasties.

Officially, Il Moro conceived these effigies to exalt his wife and their union. But they also, literally, belittle her. The modesty of his own attire is contrasted with Beatrice's frippery and vanity. The pelt draped over her arms is that of an ermine, a creature associated with childbirth – but also, at the court of Il Moro, irrevocably associated with Cecilia Gallerani, the mistress Il Moro had given up for Beatrice with obvious reluctance.

Beatrice's platform-soled feet descend only to the top of his calves. Rather than being concealed by the folds of her gown, or supported by a cushion, animal or heraldic device, they were left dangling mid-air.

Like Il Moro's Milan.

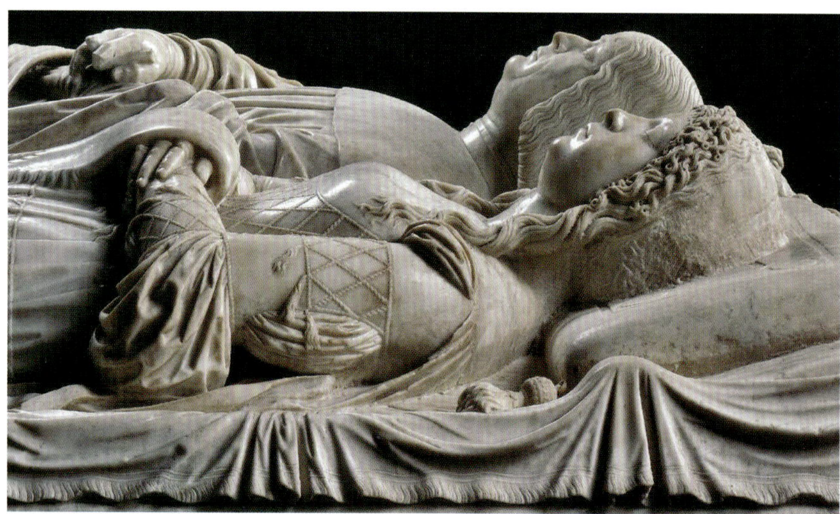

1 San Pietro in Gessate was built in the 1460s by Guiniforte Solari, who also directed construction at Santa Maria delle Grazie and at Milan's Ospedale Maggiore.

2 De' Conti's subsequent career, however, shows him adept at adapting to political circumstance. His profiles of Catellano Trivulzio (1505) and Charles d'Amboise, French Governor of Milan, suggest he leapt into the 'official portraitist' vacuum created by the departure to Innsbruck of Ambrogio de Predis. After 1506 he appears to have been in France. He is last heard of back in Italy in 1523.

3 Malaguzzi Valeri, *op. cit.*

4 Daniela Pizzagalli, *La Dama con l'Ermellino: Vita e Passioni di Cecilia Gallerani nella Milano di Ludovico il Moro* (Rizzoli, Milan 2008), quoted by Elisabetta Gnignera in *Cecilia o la Dama con l'Ermellino.*

5 *La Certosa di Pavia* (Cassa di Risparmio, Milan 1968).

6 Archivio di Stato di Milano, Vigevano, 23 November 1496.

7 A conclusion reached independently by Lamberto Donati in *Leonardo da Vinci ed il Libro Illustrato* (Amsterdam 1963).

8 As far as I have been able to ascertain – and an opinion shared by the Renaissance costume specialist Elisabetta Gnignera.

9 Another valuable source of ideas and information is Patrizia Costa's PhD thesis *The Sala delle Asse in the Sforza Castle* (University of Pittsburgh, 2006).

10 Niccolò da Correggio is cited in the same breath as these two knights by Beatrice d'Este's secretary Vincenzo Collo (1460–1508) in his reminiscences about the court. Correggio's absence from the Isola Beata line-up adds weight to the suggestion that he left Milan in a cloud in the wake of Beatrice's sudden death.

11 The Villa Medici at Careggi, just outside Florence, saw the deaths of both Lorenzo the Magnificent and Zofia Zamoyska, a future co-owner of the Polish *Sforziada*.

12 As cited by Carlo Pedretti in *Leonardo on Painting – A Lost Book* (University of California Press, 1964).

13 The *Platonic Solids* were applied by Plato (in *Timaeus*) to his cosmic scheme, and associated with the elements: cube/earth, fire/tetrahedron, air/octahedron, water/icosahedron. The fifth and final solid, the dodecahedron, symbolized the universe. They are discussed by Pacioli, along with the *Golden Ratio*, in his *Compendio de Divina Proportione*, illustrated by Leonardo da Vinci – the first of the three books comprising *De Divina Proportione.*

14 The original 28.5 × 20cm *De Divina Proportione* manuscript, dedicated to Galeazzo Sanseverino and dated 14 December 1498, is now in the Ambrosiana (SP 6 gia F 170 sup.).

15 Including Maike Vogt-Lüerssen and Katarzyna Pisarek (see *Epilogue*).

16 The manuscript version of *De Divina Proportione* dedicated to Il Moro is now in the Bibliothèque de Genève. A third manuscript copy, made for Pier Soderini (1450–1522), erstwhile Florentine Ambassador to France, is lost.

17 Other explanations for the Visconti *biscione* have the viper being forced to regurgitate the son of the Duke of Pavia during war with the Saracens, and cite the punning similarities between the name of the Viscontis' feudal seat (*Angara* – or *Anglus* in Latin) and the Latin for snake (*Anguis*) – *cf* Michel Pastoureau, *Une Histoire Symbolique du Moyen-Age Occidental* (Le Seuil, Paris 2004).

18 The Sala delle Asse's painted decor appears to have been forgotten about between the 17th and 19th centuries, but may have remained unaltered until at least 1661, when two Spanish surveyors referred to the room as *la [sala] quadra con volta a lunette (e) dipinte* in a report on the Castello Sforzesco (*Relatione Generale della visita et consegna della fabbrica castello di Milano*). The connection between Leonardo and the Sala delle Asse was first proposed by Italian historian Gerolamo Calvi in 1869, but Leonardo's decoration was not re-discovered until 1893, just after the army had vacated the castle, by German art historian Paul Müller-Walde (1858–1931).

19 A 1473 report signed Gadio suggests this panelling was carefully designed; its removal under Il Moro is unlikely to have resulted from shoddy workmanship or poor condition.

20 Prompting some commentators to claim the room has eighteen trees, disregarding the symbolic importance of the number 16 in Il Moro's Milan

(yet another example of this occurred later in 1498, when the cash-strapped duke paid off Leonardo's arrears by donating him a vineyard with an area precisely designated as 16 *pertiche*).

21 Socrates tells the story of the Spartan naval commander Lysander visiting Cyrus at his palace in Sardis in 407 BC and admiring his beautifully planned and tended gardens, exclaiming : 'O Cyrus, I am full of wonder at the beauty of everything, but much more do I admire the one who has measured out and ordered each kind of thing for you.'

22 Other works by Gaspare Visconti include *Rithimi* (1493), dedicated to Niccolò da Correggio; *Canzonieri* (Cod. Triv. n. 2153), dedicated to Beatrice d'Este and Bianca Maria Sforza; and *Di Paolo e Daria Amanti* (1495).

23 The phrase *Pasitea, delle Grazie* will have resonated at the Milanese court after Beatrice's burial in Santa Maria delle Grazie. And it is surely no coincidence that Politian, or *Poliziano* (1454–94), was a distinguished Florentine – tutor to Lorenzo de' Medici's children and member of the Platonic academy headed by Marsilio Ficino.

24 A 20 × 13cm pen and brown ink drawing in the New York Metropolitan Museum (*Rogers Fund* 1917 – 17.142.2) contains a sketch of the stage Leonardo envisaged, and lists the actors: Gian Cristofano (presumably the sculptor Gian Cristoforo Romano) as *Acrisius*, King of Argos and father of Danae; playwright Baldassare Taccone as the gardener *Sirus* (Cyrus); Francesco Romano as *Danae*; Gian Battista da Osimo as *Mercury*; and Gian Francesco Tantio as *Jupiter*, who transforms himself into a shower of gold to impregnate Danae.

25 Because the mulberry never buds until the cold weather is over, then brings forth its fruit at phenomenal speed.

26 Archivio di Stato, Milan, *Classe Belle Arti, Autografi 102, fasc. 34.*

27 Coria, *La Storia di Milano.*

28 Mercury, or Hermes in Greek mythology, is traditionally represented by a broad-rimmed hat (*petasos*) with a staff or caduceus entwined with two serpents (Il Moro transformed the Visconti/Sforza *biscione* into dragons). Mercury, the messenger of the gods, was the son of Jupiter/Zeus; a suitably modest figure for Il Moro to identify with – and a way to keep his religious options open, by adding a pagan deity to his association with Christ.

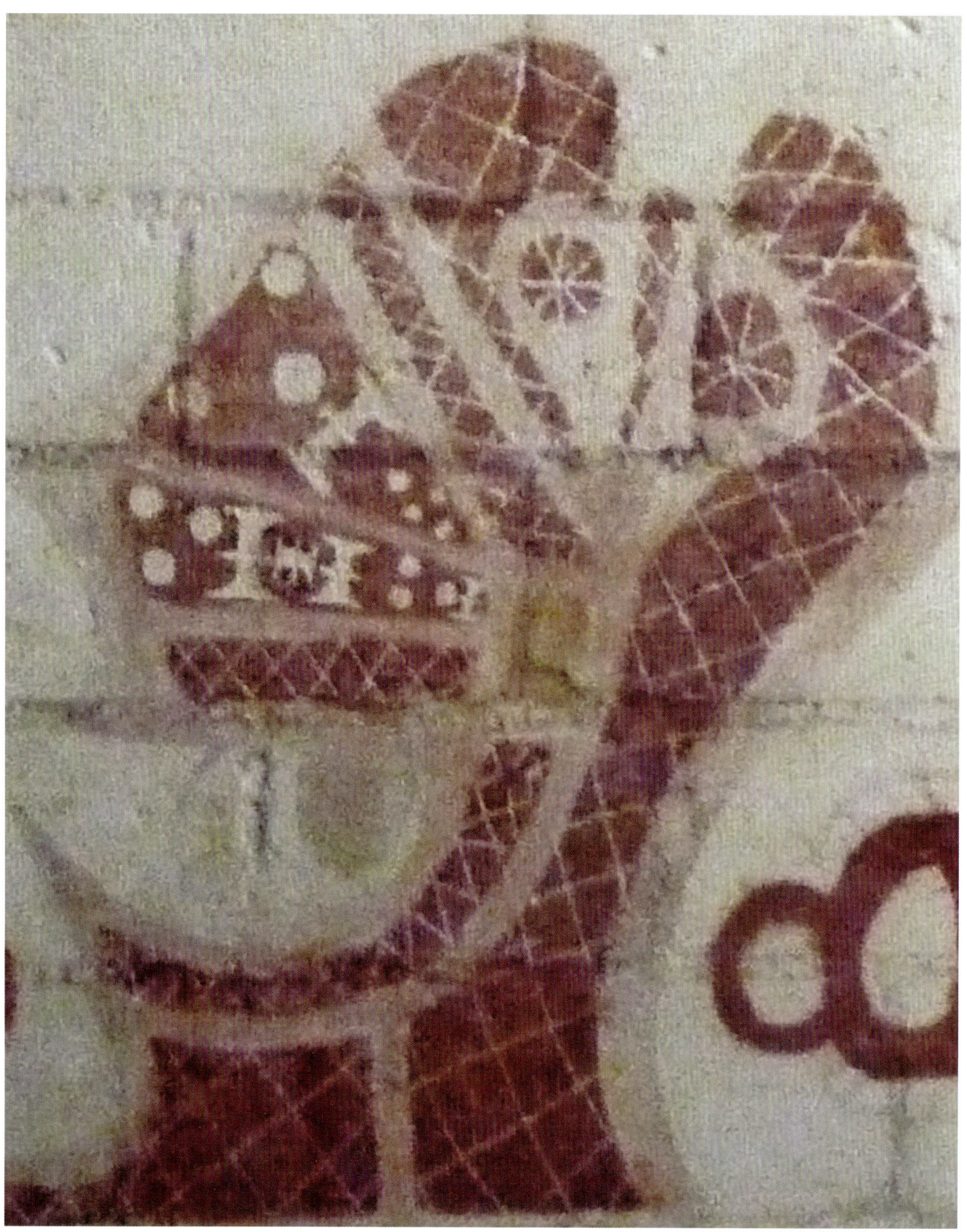

XIV

DUKE'S END

IL MORO'S BRUSH WITH ETERNITY

SOON AFTER BOUNCING AROUND on his father's tomb in Birago's final *Sforziada* frontispiece, pretending to be God, Il Moro was quoted by Venetian Senator Domenico Malipiero as claiming: 'The King of France is our courier, the Emperor our *condottiero*, Venice our chamberlain and the Pope our chaplain.' Before long the Divine Duke would be sounding less like Superman – and looking more like Humpty Dumpty.[1]

Florentine historian Francesco Guicciardini mocked Il Moro for vaunting himself as the 'Son of Fortune' while 'little remembering the inconstancy of human fame,' reporting that: 'Milan was full day and night of vain and glorious voices, celebrating with verses Latin and vulgar, and with public orations full of flattery, the wonderful wisdom of Lodovico Sforza, on which they said depended peace and war in Italy, exalting his name even to the third heaven.'[2]

Seventh Heaven was way out of sight. Pride begat the plunge into an abyss that began with Bianca's death in November 1496.

Not even an allusionist of Birago's panache could have imagined the irony of his fourth and final *bas-de-page* composition.

The Sanseverinos would indeed betray Il Moro, and both he and Galeazzo would, in very different circumstances, spend the last years of their lives in the country towards which Birago has Galeazzo Sanseverino symbolically gesturing: France.

BETRAYALS

On 17 January 1497 Il Moro publicly handed Galeazzo Sanseverino the baton of command and dispatched him to defend Alessandria against a French attack led by its recently recruited General, Gian Giacomo Trivulzio. It proved a mere shot across the bows. With Charles VIII ailing – possibly from syphilis contracted during his Naples campaign two years earlier – and his heir, the Duke of Orléans, reluctant to leave France at such a time, Trivulzio's foray was not followed up.

In April 1497 came the first sign of Sanseverino treachery: Galeazzo's brother Fracassa left Milan for his estate at Spineda, 25 miles east of Cremona, and made contact with the Venetians. Il Moro confiscated his other properties.

This was not the first sign of Il Moro's inner circle veering off the rails. Eminent courtier Niccolò da Correggio was accused by Il Moro of tacit complicity with Trivulzio in January 1497, and quit the Duchy in May.

Galeazzo Sanseverino was also in the firing line. In April 1497 Francesco Gonzaga, Duke of Mantua, accused him of intriguing to obtain his dismissal from his post of Captain-General of the Venetian Army.

The two would-be warlords would rub egos on several occasions over the next few years. They rubbed shoulders in September 1497 at a tournament in Brescia held in honour of Caterina Cornaro, Queen of Cyprus. Galeazzo appeared at the head of forty knights wearing black armour, with their hair dyed black. Next day he escorted the Queen back to her court at Asolo, near Treviso.

Charles VIII died on 7 April 1498 and was succeeded, as Louis XII, by the Duke of Orleans – whose hereditary claims to the Duchy of Milan were known and feared.

A new anti-French league was formed, involving Milan, Naples, the Pope and Emperor Maximilian. Francesco Gonzaga was offered overall command – and the title of *Captain of the King of the Romans*. Gonzaga also lobbied to be created *Captain General of Milan* – but Il Moro refused to replace Galeazzo Sanseverino.

In July 1499, with a French army mustering across the Alps, Sanseverino was again contested as head of the Sforza army – this time by his own brother, Gianfrancesco (Count Caiazzo). Il Moro again turned a deaf ear.

In early August a French army of 30,000 crossed the Alps to Louis XII's hereditary stronghold of Asti and continued their march eastwards along the Tanaro Valley, capturing Rocca d'Arazzo, 5 miles away, on August 13. The news sent shock-waves through the Duchy of Milan.

Despite the warning signs, Il Moro – much like Stalin in 1941 – was ill-prepared for a western invasion, either militarily or psychologically. He temporarily retreated to Santa Maria delle Grazie as if in need of spiritual sustenance. What he really needed were troops, and the wherewithal to hire them. As usual, he looked to Emperor Maximilian, and on August 14 received an exorbitant offer: 3,000 foot soldiers in return for 30,000 florins per month.

On August 18 Il Moro issued a Duchy-wide call to arms, introduced a string of tax-raising measures, and sought to shore up his domestic support by restoring the confiscated estates of various powerful Milanese families, notably the Borromeos. On August 19 he sent soldiers to Alessandria and assigned 3,000 troops for his own protection. On August 21 he appeared on the verge of abdicating, assigning the care of his sons and the Duchy to his brother Cardinal Ascanio.

The French advance continued – albeit with initial difficulties. Annone, just 2 miles along the Tanaro from Rocca d'Arazzo, withstood a four-day artillery pounding before surrendering on August 19 – and then largely because Galeazzo Sanseverino failed to respond to the distress beacons lit by the town's defending captain Alfonso Spagnuolo (who was captured by the French, dispatched to Asti and hanged).

Galeazzo Sanseverino, at this time, was in Alessandria (fifteen miles east of Annone) along with Il Moro's nephews Alessandro Sforza (*c.*1460–1523) and Count di Melzi (1474–1515) – illegitimate sons of Duke Galeazzo Maria. Ginevra, wife of town Governor Lucio Malvezzi (1462–1511), was Sanseverino's younger half-sister.

In the eyes of contemporaries, Galeazzo Sanseverino was less focused on saving the Duchy than having a good time. Venetian senator Marino Sanuto mocked him in his famous *Diarii* for spending more time whoring than warring (*Signor Galeazo sta in Alexandria atende a foze et dame, si dice mal di lui*). Milanese historian Bernardino Arluno, in his *Historia Mediolanensis*, also ridiculed the effeminate nature of Sanseverino's generalship (*deliciarum, munditiarum elegantiarum – que omnium artificem et magistrum aiebant amorumque levium imperatorem, amœnissimum ac suavissimum*). Arluno was writing thirty years later, under a subsequent Sforza ruler: Il Moro's son Francesco II. His attack on the closest ally of Francesco's father suggests a legacy of scorn and hatred.

Whether through cowardice or lucidity, Sanseverino advised Il Moro to order a strategic withdrawal from Alessandria to Pavia, adding that the state of the Duchy's defences inspired scant confidence (something which, as Captain General since 1488, he may have been in a position to do something about).

Il Moro was having none of it. First he dispatched Galeazzo's younger brother, Cardinal Federigo, to persuade him to hold Alessandria; then, on August 24, he recalled Galeazzo's eldest brother Gianfrancesco, Count Caiazzo, from the Adda region east of Milan (which he had been manning against Venetian advance) and redeployed him to Alessandria. Gianfrancesco, still sulking at his failure to land supreme command, dallied en route and never arrived.

Back in Milan the situation was growing volatile. On August 22, every household in the city was ordered to supply a soldier. On August 23 the merchant class were ordered to levy 25,000 men from the surrounding countryside and billet them in their homes. All able-bodied inhabitants of the city itself, aged between 20 and 45, were to be ready for conscription at a moment's notice. Two days later Il Moro sheepishly admitted to a gathering of leading citizens that he had failed to realize the French would invade so soon.

By August 24 the French had forded the River Tanaro at Felizzano, midway between Annone and Alessandria, and overthrown a 1,500-strong garrison, directed by Galeazzo's half-brother Ottaviano, at Valenza on the River Po. The French promptly wheeled south towards Alessandria, reaching the outskirts on August 25. A stalemate ensued until, to French astonishment, Galeazzo skedaddled from Alessandria on August 28 at the dead of night.

Galeazzo refused allegations of cowardice by claiming had received (bogus) orders to return to Milan from his brother Gianfrancesco.[3] Strategic withdrawal was the generous explanation. But Galeazzo was no Kutuzov.

He made for Pavia, halfway between Alessandria and Milan: a mighty walled stronghold with a colossal castle, defended on its exposed southwest flank by the 100 yard-wide Ticino.

But, in an act of civic insubordination that can have had few equals in history, civic leaders locked the gates on the head of their own army and berated him for cowardice. A soldier's place, they jeered, was out in the field – not behind city walls.

Pavia's reaction reflected both the widespread lack of respect for Galeazzo Sanseverino as a military commander, and the depths of unpopularity to which Il Moro's tax-grabbing regime had sunk.

Sanseverino galloped back to Milan. The game was up and most knew it. Milan was in uproar. On August 30 court treasurer Antonio Landriani was so brutally attacked in the street that he died the next day, when Galeazzo's palazzo and stables were sacked and torched by the mob.

The French pursued their inexorable advance across the Lomellina flatlands. The only obstacles now separating them from Milan were the Po and the Ticino. They avoided this dual hurdle by building a pontoon bridge across the Po east of Pavia, just after the confluence of the two rivers. On August 30 the French camped in Pavia's vast park and feasted on its bountiful game, then moved northwards to Binasco, a few miles from Milan. By September 4 they had been joined by a second French army arriving from the west, which encamped outside the Castello Sforzesco.

For many Milanese it was *sauve qui peut.* Many fled eastwards. Il Moro decided to flee north to Austria, announcing his decision to his entourage and the diplomatic corps on August 31 – insisting the withdrawal were temporary. That same day his two young sons, Massimiliano and Francesco, were siphoned on ahead with their uncle, Cardinal Ascanio, and their nanny, Camilla of Aragon.

Il Moro tarried forty-eight hours longer, winding up political business. His timetable included a meeting with Dowager Duchess Isabel of Aragon (*see p.273*).

Milan's impregnable Castello Sforzesco – one of the largest military complexes ever conceived – was entrusted to its castellan Bernardino da Corte, with enough supplies, weaponry and men to withstand a lengthy siege. Il Moro vowed to return within a month with 30,000 German soldiers. Galeazzo Sanseverino

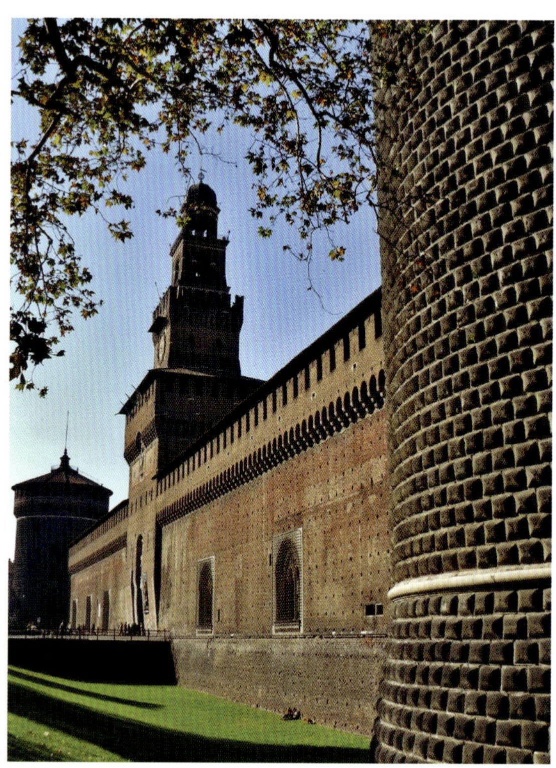

and Cardinal Ascanio Sforza expressed doubts about the castellan's trustworthiness, to no avail.

The theme of both Birago's final *Sforziada* frontispiece – and *The Last Supper* which Leonardo was painting at the same time – had proved prophetic.

Treachery.

First Gaspare 'Fracassa' Sanseverino abandoned Il Moro. Then Gianfrancesco Sanseverino failed to obey orders. Then Galeazzo Sanseverino fled Alessandria, opening the floodgates to the French. Soon Bernardino da Corte would surrender the Castello Sforzesco for thirty pieces of silver.

Yet the greatest act of betrayal lay ahead.

DUKE'S TRAVELS

When, at dawn on Monday 2 September 1499, Il Moro hoofed it out of town, little can he have imagined that he would be on horse- or mule-back for the next 33 days, covering 300 miles of inhospitable terrain, pursued initially by French cavalry, plagued throughout by sickness, targeted along the way by thieves and bandits and dogged latterly, amidst the throes of despair and exhaustion, by rows, desertion and incestuous backbiting.

Yet Il Moro – ultimately broke, physically broken and emotionally bereft after the capture of his mistress and baby boy, and the betrayal of his supposedly staunchest allies – survived in a mountainous, foreign, wintry wilderness to engineer one of the most improbable comebacks in military history: a Wild West epic played out to the beat of thundering hooves 400 years ahead of its time.[4]

Il Moro left Milan escorted by 300 *Stradioti* (Balkan mercenaries) and accompanied – initially at least – by a cavalcade of courtiers and civic dignitaries, including his mistress Lucrezia Crivelli[5] and their two year-old son; his nephews Alessandro Sforza, Count di Melzi and Hermes (Bianca Maria's elder brother); his own half-brother Giovanni Maria, Archbishop of Genoa; Galeazzo and Cardinal Federigo Sanseverino; Ippolito d'Este, the twenty year-old Archbishop of Milan; the Bishop of Lodi; ducal secretary Marchesino Stanga; and court astrologer Ambrogio Rosate.

The convoy was, initially, loaded with swag: a casket of jewellery; 250,000 ducats-worth of gold coin, packed up in narrow bags inside fifty padded boxes (pieces of eight were even stuffed inside soldiers' breastplates); and huge gold medallions of *Duke Galeazzo* (valued at 10,000 ducats) and an unspecified *Madonna Bianca* (worth 12,000 ducats). Other Sforza possessions – presumably bulkier and less suitable for turning into cash – were dispatched downriver for safe-keeping in Ferrara.

The booty Il Moro took with him was intended to pay his troops and hire reinforcements, as well as to cover the cost of the food and accommodation needed by his extensive retinue. The total amount would have comfortably sufficed had Il Moro been able to stick to his optimistic deadline. But, instead of one month, he did not return for five; and by then his finances had been further depleted by theft, and the bribes needed to force his way through to Austria unhindered.

Il Moro's band made swiftish going, covering the 25 miles north to Como on the first day, pausing in Barlassina *en route*. In Como Il Moro was hoping to meet up with 5,000 cavalry airily promised by Emperor Maximilian. There was no sign of them. The horsemen would only materialize in Morbegno, 40 miles and a couple of days away. Their numbers would barely exceed a couple of hundred.

When news of Il Moro's flight reached the French army commander Gian Giacomo Trivulzio near Pavia, probably that same afternoon, he dispatched a cavalry unit under his son, Count Mesocco, in frothing late-summer pursuit.

Il Moro met a diffident welcome in Como, whose inhabitants were hedging their political bets by flying the Imperial flag (i.e. wishing to appear neutral in Milan's conflict with France), and extorted money from Il Moro before allowing him to leave. The town stands at the southwest foot of Lake Como and, after sinking whatever craft remained to prevent their being used by their French pursuers, most of Il Moro's band continued their journey north by boat to Bellagio – at the tip of the peninsular separating Lake Como's southwest and southeast arms.

If, as seems likely, another part of the group continued from Como on horseback, they too will have needed ferrying across from Bellagio to the lake's eastern shore (the overland alternative entails a 35-mile detour).

The swiftest crossing from Bellagio to the east shore of Lake Como takes you to Varenna; a ferry service plies these waters to this day. Il Moro may have landed at Varenna – or 3 miles up the shore at Bellano, where he paused at the castle owned by Marchesino Stanga. Eight miles further north Il Moro wheeled right into the Adda Valley, heading east towards Tyrol. He had reached Morbegno – the valley's first town – by September 5.

We will never know whether Il Moro had a favourable breeze to speed him up the lake, or if there were enough moonlight on these early September nights to ride across rough country tracks after dusk. What we do know is that the

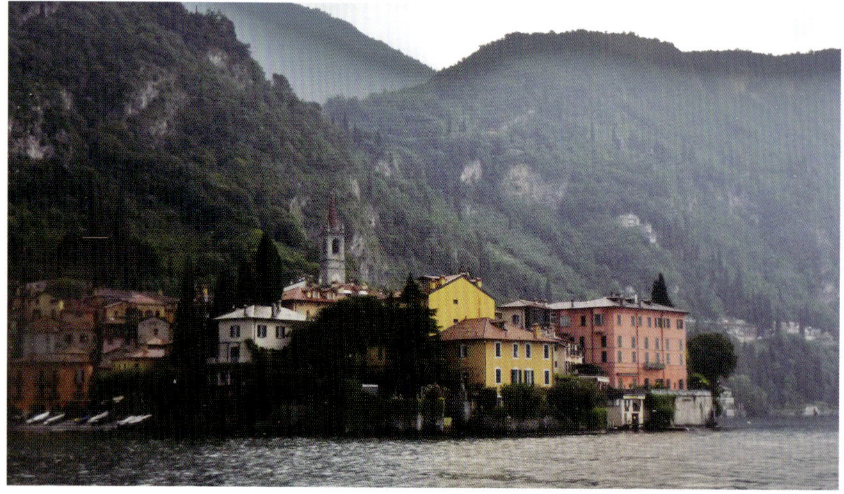

VARENNA

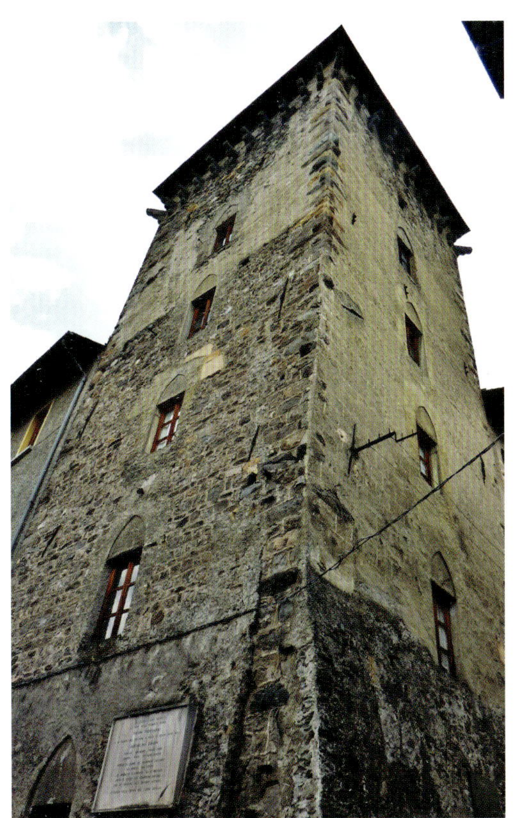

French horsemen went hell for leather in pursuit of the Sforza strongman and, despite giving him twelve hours' start, were soon closing in on him at such an alarming rate that Il Moro split his own group into two – with himself, his two elder sons and his leading aides (and most accomplished horsemen) speeding on ahead.

After an exhausting seventy-two hours, the French called off the chase just before Morbegno – having snared part of the second group ... including Astrologer Rosate and Lucrezia Crivelli with her baby son, along with 150,000 ducats of booty. Il Moro, with his German reinforcements, escaped, but not unscathed: he was ill with fever and spitting blood as he lurched along the valley to Sondrio, fifteen miles from Morbegno, where one of his treasure chests was stolen and part of his armed guard threw in the towel.

A further fifteen miles away lies Tirano, a fortress town at the juncture of two strategic roads: one leading over the Bernina Pass into Switzerland, the other over the Stelvio Pass into Tyrol. Il Moro had arrived here by September 9 and lingered for several days, reorganizing the town's defences under castellan Andreas von Lichtenstein, with a garrison 800-strong. He also dispatched Galeazzo Sanseverino to lay waste the Adda Valley back in the direction of Lake Como, to make life for the French invaders as tough as possible.

After leaving part of his baggage train in Tirano, Il Moro continued 25 miles east, over increasingly rough, hilly roads – to the Torre Alberti in Bormio, where he and Galeazzo Sanseverino had stayed (along with Beatrice d'Este) during their visit to Maximilian in Summer 1496.

The daunting Stelvio Pass over the Alps lay ahead. Several of Il Moro's leading acolytes, including Marchesino Stanga, now opted to return to Milan. Il Moro headed over the top. Unlike in 1496, when he veered north to Glorenza and Mals on the shortest route to Innsbruck, he continued eastwards in the direction of Bolzano, which stands midway along the road that rifles north from Verona to Innsbruck over the Brenner Pass.

His first major stopping-point en route to Bolzano was Merano, the former capital of Tyrol, which Il Moro's group – still numbering about 350 – reached on September 22. Emperor Maximilian invited him to stay permanently but Il Moro declined, considering Merano too close to the frontier. A violent dispute erupted here between Il Moro and Cardinal Federigo Sanseverino, apparently prompted by the preferential treatment extended to Galeazzo Sanseverino, who was considered by everyone apart from Il Moro as a coward and traitor for abandoning Alessandria, and universally branded a *puttana*.

Cardinal Federigo, who had earlier quarrelled so angrily with Cardinal Ascanio that their respective servants had scurried for cover, threatened to storm back to Milan, accompanied by the Archbishop of Genoa, the Bishop of Lodi and a number of other senior courtiers.

On September 25 Il Moro's band reached Bolzano, twenty miles east of Merano, where they were abandoned by Cardinal Ippolito d'Este – under severe pressure to return to Italy from his father, Duke Ercole d'Este of Ferrara, whose relationship with the invading French had been strained by his son's 'desertion' (which the Duke explained by his son's extreme youth ... and the pernicious influence of Galeazzo Sanseverino). Supplies in Bolzano were low, so Il Moro promptly moved north to Brixen, whose Prince-Bishop, Melchior von Meckau, had visited Milan to conduct Bianca Maria's proxy marriage to Maximilian in 1493 and Il Moro's investiture ceremony in 1495.

Il Moro left his sons in Brixen at the start of October and rode off north to Innsbruck, 50 miles away, to meet Maximilian. The peripatetic emperor kept him waiting several days, then suggested Il Moro's group repair to Trent, 55 miles south of Brixen. This they temporarily did, but local hostility forced them back to Brixen by the end of the month. By now Camilla, the forty-year-old governess of Il Moro's sons, had not surprisingly had enough. She returned to Italy in mid-November.

Exhausted by travel, racked by fever and gout, deserted by many and floored by the shock news that Milan's Castello Sforzesco had meekly surrendered to the enemy, Il Moro was at a low ebb. His morale was further sapped when his supposedly impregnable garrison at Tirano were booted out by the French and rolled up in Brixen in early November clamouring for pay. Then he had to pack his horses off to graze at the Bishop's estate in Bruneck, twenty miles to the east, as there was no fodder in Brixen; and send his bowmen to lodge in Trent as there was no room for them in Brixen. A triumphant return to Milan looked a million light years away.

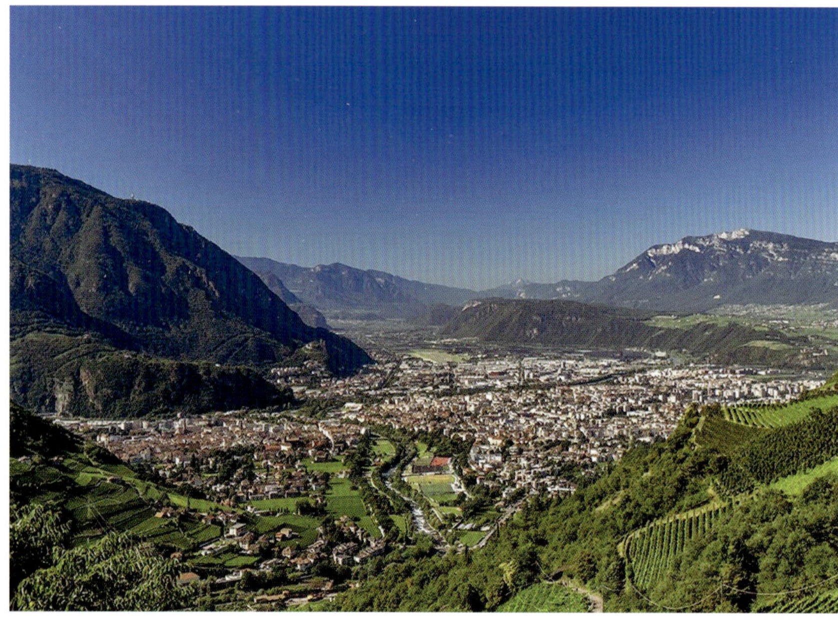

BOLZANO

MEANWHILE, BACK IN MILAN

Trivulzio entered Milan on September 7 after meeting a civic delegation led by Francesco Bernardino Visconti at Cascina, just south of the city. That evening Trivulzio dined with the Bishop of Como before retiring to the French camp at Binasco.

The French made their official entry into Milan on September 11 with 10,000 infantry. The city's surrender was signed next day in the Corte Vecchio near the Duomo, in what had until recently been the residence of Isabel of Aragon (she had just moved to the house vacated by court steward Ambrogio da Corte, who had fled Milan with Il Moro).

On September 13 capitulation terms were addressed to the Castello Sforzesco, involving a twelve-day armistice before the French took further action. Castellan Bernardino da Corte was offered a hefty bribe to surrender. After evacuating all the booty from the Castello he could (including tapestries and various goods and belongings owned by Il Moro and his late wife Beatrice d'Este), he quit the castle on September 18.

Bernardino da Corte would be compared, for baseness and treachery, to Galeazzo Sanseverino (*la vilta et perfidia de Bernardino Curcio* [*sic*] *non essere meno quella del Conte Galjeazo Sanseverino*) by the contemporary historian Giovanni Andrea del Prato in his *Storia di Milano 1499–1519*, which picked up where Bernardino Corio's history of the duchy (published 1503) left off. Del Prato (born 1488) was, like Bernardino Arluno, writing under a later Sforza Duke, Il Moro's son Francesco II. Like Arluno, he splattered Galeazzo Sanseverino with vitriol.

On September 18, the same day Bernardino da Corte moved out, Gian Giacomo Trivulzio moved in, occupying Il Moro's former apartment – presumably the rooms in the Ponticella leading off from the Sala delle Asse – and taking his meals in an adjacent room overlooking the castle park. Everything still left in the Castello was promptly removed, 'even the cheese' as one Italian observer put it. The main castle bell was lowered to the ground and packed off to France.

Soon afterwards the Sala delle Asse was strung up with scaffolding and an artist instructed to paint over one of the four shields on the ceiling with a wordy new inscription:

LVDOVICUS SFORTIA ALEXANDRIAM VRBEM

X MILIA SVORVM MILITVM PRÆSIDIO MVNITAM

TRIDVO A GALLIS EXPVGNATAM CAPTAMQUE CVM

RESCISSET ADHVC XL MILIA PASSVVM HOSTIVM CASTRIS

A SE DISTANTIBVS TERRITVS PER ALPINUM IVGA

CUM LIBERIS ET AMICIS PAUCISSIMIS IN NORICORVM

LATERBRAS AVFVGIT MEDIOL CETERÆQUE EIVS

DITIONIS VRBES LVDOVICO XII GALLORVM REGI

INVICTISSIMO AC DVCI EORVM LEGITTIMO SE DEDVNT

AN SAL LXXXXVIIII

SVPRA MCCCC

The new inscription portrayed Il Moro and the man in charge of defending Alessandria (Galeazzo Sanseverino) as cowards. *AMICIS PAUCISSIMIS* indeed. How bitchy can an inscription get?

We know from Venetian diarist Marino Sanuto that this inscription (since replaced), parodying the pompous self-regard of the other three shields, had been added to the ceiling of the Sala delle asse by September 28 – i.e. within ten days of the Castello falling to the French.

It was the first of several acts of revenge wrought upon Il Moro and Galeazzo Sanseverino by Trivulzio, the career general who had fled his native Milan, initially to Naples, after Sanseverino's sudden promotion in 1488. These acts, in all likelihood, included the obliteration of details in Birago's 'Uffizi' *Sforziada* frontispiece (using the same tone of blue as the shields in the Sala delle Asse).[6]

French King Louis XII had been watching events unfold from across the Alps in Lyon. He only set off for Italy on September 6, after learning of Il Moro's flight, making leisurely progress via Grenoble and Turin to Vigevano, home to Il Moro's favourite palazzo, where he arrived on September 26 and lingered for several days, mostly spent falcon-hunting. Then, instead of making for Milan, he detoured south to Pavia, arriving on October 2 in driving rain.

It was not until October 6, after a visit to the Certosa di Pavia, that Louis XII finally made his ceremonial entry into Milan. He was met at the Porta Ticinese by Trivulzio and presented with the keys to the city, a naked sword and two marshal's batons, which he bestowed upon Pierre de Rohan-Gié and Trivulzio himself. Louis XII then, as was traditional, stopped at the nearby church of Sant'Eustorgio to change into his ceremonial apparel of white damask and fur-lined cloak (crimson damask was obligatory for everybody else). The road to the Duomo had been carpeted with tapestries from Vigevano.

The King was preceded by Trivulzio, Comte de Ligny and Maréchal de Gié; 500 infantry; 300 riders; and every available French baron. Behind the King walked Cardinals Borgia and Della Rovere (future Pope Julius II); Cardinal Georges d'Amboise (Archbishop of Rouen) and Duc Philibert de Savoie; the Dukes of Ferrara and Valentinois; Marquesses of Mantua and Montferrat; and the Ambassadors of Florence, Genoa, Lucca, Pisa, Siena and Venice.

The Florentines squabbled over étiquette and precedence, refusing to be placed behind the Genoese. Everyone was jockeying for position. Two Genoese envoys died after falling off a platform in an apparently unrelated incident.

Louis XII spent six weeks in the Duchy, divided mostly between Milan and Pavia – where he met Isabel of Aragon. It was the Dowager Duchess's second excruciating audience in a matter of weeks. She was naïvely hoping that, with his evil uncle out of the way, the rights of her eight-year-old son (Il Duchetto) to inherit the Duchy might now be recognized.

Instead he was abducted by Louis XII as a prize of war and, on November 8, carted off back to France. Isabel would never see him again.

RE-TURN OF THE CENTURY

News of Louis XII's return to France, accompanied by the pesky Duchetto, seeped through to Il Moro in Brixen towards the end of November: his first glad tidings for months. His two main rivals for the title of Duke of Milan had left the coast physically clear.

Meanwhile Trivulzio's heavy-handed administration was arousing discontent. By December the murder of French soldiers had become an everyday occurrence in the streets of Milan. Popular support for Il Moro's return was starting to swell. On 1 January 1500 Trivulzio issued an extraordinary decree banning political gatherings in Milan – and banning talk in public of war, peace, Il Moro, King Louis or Emperor Maximilian. Soon after, alarmed by the city's rebellious mood and the discovery of an almost completed tunnel into the Castello Sforzesco built by Moro supporters, Trivulzio sent his own personal belongings off to his Alpine castle at Mesocco, near Bellinzona, for safe-keeping.

On January 10 Il Moro began military preparations, dispatching Galeazzo Visconti with saddlecloths of cash to hire an army among the Swiss. Il Moro boasted to supporters that he would soon have 30,000 men, and sent an advance force through Graubünden to Chiavenna, north of Lake Como. Four days later, in what a man as superstitious as Il Moro might have seen as an ill omen, fire destroyed the upper storey of the house in Brixen where he was staying. Next day however, accompanied by Cardinal Ascanio, he set off for Innsbruck to see the Emperor and negotiate his military support, kissing farewell to his two young sons for what would prove to be the final time.

On January 20 Maximilian entertained Il Moro with a jousting tourney, banquet and grand ball, and made his usual promises to back Il Moro's undertakings. Next day, after mass and lunch in a nearby abbey, Il Moro headed south to Merano and Cardinal Ascanio west towards Feldkirch, on the road that leads into Italy via Chur and Bellinzona (which had been recaptured by Il Moro supporters on January 25).

By January 28 Il Moro had crossed the Stelvio Pass to Bormio with 2,000 men. News of his advance reached Milan, where the flames of revolt were fanned by his Ghibelline supporters. Shops were closed and streets barricaded. On January 29 Comte de Ligny was sent to Como; his troops took control of the lake and forced Il Moro's supporters back to Chiavenna, beyond its northern shore. But next day Ligny was recalled to Milan by a panicky Trivulzio. Forces under Cardinal Ascanio captured the fortress at Musso, on the west bank of Lake Como, and commandeered eleven boats to sail down to Como itself.

On January 31 Il Moro's advance troops under Galeazzo Sanseverino reached Sondrio. Further west Galeazzo Visconti's forces, now several thousand strong, took Domodossola and swarmed down towards Lake Maggiore.

On February 1 Cardinal Ascanio spent the night at Barlassina south of Como, while Galeazzo Sanseverino left Bellagio for Como, with Il Moro not far behind. Milan was up in arms. Isabel of Aragon left the city with her two young daughters, Ippolita and Bona. Trivulzio withdrew into the Castello Sforzesco then, at dawn on February 3, led French troops west from the city towards Novara, just over twenty miles away. On February 4 Ascanio Sforza, Galeazzo Visconti, and Federigo and Galeazzo Sanseverino entered Milan and took up lodgings in the Archbishop's Palace – before Ascanio returned to meet Il Moro in Desio, ten miles away, to plan his ceremonial entry the next day.

Il Moro spent the night two miles north of Milan at the elegant Villa Mirabello (now well within the city limits, just beyond Mussolini's Stazione Centrale) formerly owned by Il Moro's recently murdered treasurer Antonio Landriani and, before him, by the Florentine Pigello Portinari, manager of the Milan branch of the Medici Bank (and commissioner of the superbly frescoed Portinari Chapel in the church of Sant'Eustorgio).

Next morning, February 5, flanked by Cardinal Ascanio Sforza and Cardinal Federigo Sanseverino and accompanied by an army that had grown to nearly 10,000, Il Moro trotted through the city's north gate, the Porta Nuova, and on to the Duomo. He was clad in crimson damask and a black velvet cap; Galeazzo Sanseverino, in flashy contrast, was sporting glittering white brocade with tall white plumes in his cap – 'better fitted' remarked one sarcastic chronicler 'for the service of Venus than of Mars.'

After addressing citizens that afternoon, Il Moro set up an interim cardinalate government under Ascanio Sforza, assisted by Federigo Sanseverino and Ippolito d'Este. They lost no time in instigating city-wide searches for goods owned by Il Moro that had been pillaged during his absence, and sent agents back to Austria to recover the treasure left with Il Moro's sons in Brixen.

Although the Castello Sforzesco remained stubbornly in enemy hands (and would do so for the next ten weeks – retroactively justifying Il Moro's earlier confidence in its ability to withstand prolonged siege), Il Moro's immediate military concern was to pursue the retreating French and hound them out of the Duchy. Buoyed by the euphoria of his triumphant return, and respecting the felicitous astral omens espied by his new astrologer Armodoro, Il Moro forgot the fatigue of a fortnight in the saddle.

Next day, February 6, Il Moro rode out of Milan on his last campaign.

THE LAST BATTLE

Il Moro headed twenty miles south to Pavia then ten miles west to Sannazzaro, where he reviewed his cosmopolitan troops. The French, meanwhile, fanned out southeast from Novara to occupy Vigevano and Mortara, both about fifteen miles away. By mid-February the two armies were ten miles apart, facing each other across the Lomellina flatlands. Both were awaiting the arrival of substantial numbers of mercenary Swiss troops.

Il Moro was on a roll. He made peace with the Sanseverino brothers Fracassa and Antonio Maria, ordered the levy of 10,000 Italians and, in the last week of February, made several important gains – capturing Valenza on the Po, west of Sannazzarro; Vigevano; and Vespolate, midway between Novara and Mortara.

The French were forced to retire to Mortara, leaving a purely defensive force in Novara. By the end of February Il Moro appeared to have gained the upper hand. Trivulzio supporters were leaving Milan in droves, mostly heading east towards Padua, Vicenza and Venetia. Il Moro received the support of Francesco Gonzaga, Marquess of Mantua, and urged Duke Ercole of Ferrara to get off the fence and provide military backing.

But Novara, perched on one of the few modest hilltops in Milan's western marches, provided stiffer resistance than Il Moro had anticipated. His assault began on March 5 but it was not until March 22, after heavy losses, that he was able to enter the town, two days after the arrival of extra artillery from Austria. Galliate, close by, fell the next day, but his over-wrought army – short of food and pay – were in no mood to celebrate. Cardinal Sanseverino was dispatched on (another) transalpine diplomatic mission to Maximilian, now in Freiburg – urging him to provide more troops and come to Italy himself. On March 24 Il Moro hurried back to Milan to seek the funds needed to put a halt to desertions. The cheers that greeted him in the streets were the last he would hear. His exchequer was almost bare.

Novara's resistance enabled the French to regroup within their Mortara stronghold. Their only aggressive military action in March was to capture Robbio, a few miles northwest on the road to Vercelli: a strategic move to smooth the arrival of new army from France under La Trémoille, followed by the Swiss troops recruited by the Bailiff of Dijon. By the start of April the French were significantly stronger than a month before. On April 5 they moved out of Mortara towards Novara, recaptured Vespolate, and sent troops to Trecate, 5 miles east of Novara, to cut off Il Moro's supply line from Milan – something they made sure of by destroying the nearby bridge across the River Ticino.

Il Moro had his own troops to worry about as well as the French. There was bitter hostility between the Italians, Swiss and Germans in his rag-tag army and that same day, April 5, some 300 men tried to desert – only to be forcibly returned to the Sforza camp after a lengthy cavalry pursuit.

On April 7 Il Moro sent forces under Galeazzo Sanseverino to resist the French advance. There was an indecisive clash a few miles outside Novara. Next day, April 8, the French kept on coming. Battle was joined beneath the town walls. By nightfall neither side could claim victory.

Fighting did not resume on April 9. This is often attributed to the refusal of the Swiss mercenaries engaged by either side to fight their compatriots.[7] The truth is more prosaic.

April 9 was spent parleying. Il Moro was playing for time, awaiting promised reinforcements from Milan: 10,000 men under Francesco Bernardo Visconti, Alessandro Sforza and Conte di Melzi.

Meanwhile large swathes of Il Moro's army deserted, or were threatening to desert, because they had not been paid. The Bailiff of Dijon exhorted Il Moro's Swiss troops to change sides and sign up for Louis XII. They refused. Instead, they asked Trivulzio for a safe passage to return home, threatening to resume battle if *he* refused. Trivulzo said he would think about it.

Il Moro withdrew, with his remaining troops, into Novara, unaware that his reinforcements had been delayed – it would prove crucially – by the lack of bridge over the Ticino.

That night his time ran out. First the Swiss told him he was sure to be taken prisoner unless he came back with them to Bellinzona. Il Moro accepted. Then Comte de Ligny sent two envoys to Il Moro, promising he would be well-treated if he surrendered. Il Moro accepted.

Then the Swiss, furious that the prospect of obtaining a ransom for Il Moro was about to slip through their fingers, told him they were engineering his escape whether he liked it or not. Il Moro had no choice but to accept. He was promptly dressed up as a pikeman to facilitate an incognito getaway.

Il Moro's word had seldom proved his bond, even in happier times, and the French were in no mood to accept his promised surrender at face value. They spent the night of April 9/10 surrounding the walls of Novara. When Il Moro's troops started to funnel out two hours before daybreak, hoping to catch the French napping, they faced a rude awakening.

The emerging troops were halted by torch-light and obliged to march, three at a time, through the serried ranks of the French army, being peered at intently – on the off chance that one of them looked like a Sforza duke. The process went on for hours. The sun was already high in the sky, and a reported 7,000 faces fruitlessly scrutinized, when French frustration boiled over and La Trémoille insisted Il Moro be handed over without further ado, lest battle be resumed.

The outward march of Il Moro's men continued, one at a time. Il Moro was betrayed by his chubby figure and clumsy pikemanship. His identity was con-firmed by one of his own reward-seeking Swiss troops.

In one final act of bravura, the dumpy duke refused to surrender to anyone other than Comte de Ligny, his 'kinsman' (Il Moro's sister-in-law Bona di Savoia was Ligny's aunt). Il Moro coolly announced that he was surrendering as per the terms agreed overnight – so he expected civil treatment, *merci*.

The French snorted that the deal was off as he had tried to escape, then paraded him along the lines to show the war was over, then locked him up in Novara Castle.

Trivulzio had a medallion minted – complete with Sforza and Trivulzio shields – to celebrate Il Moro's demise. It reads:

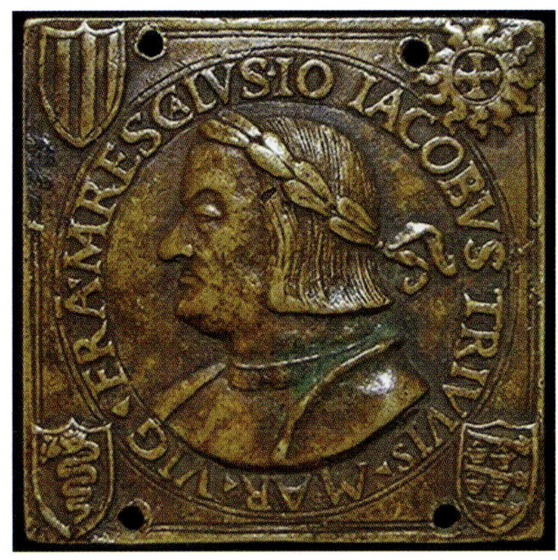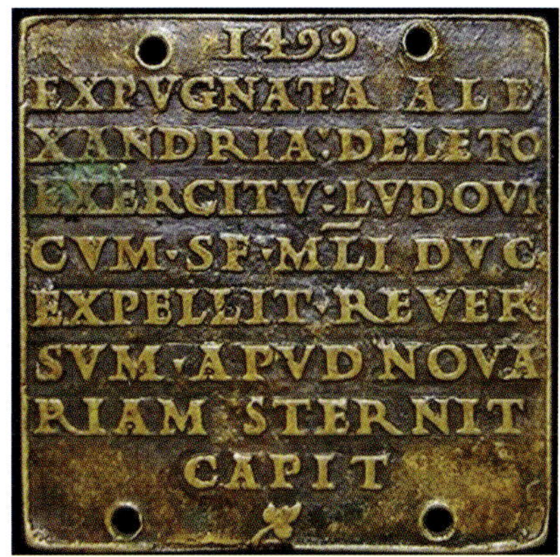

EXPVGNATA ALEXANDRIA : DELETO EXERCITV : LVDOVICVM SF.
MLI DVC EXPELLIT REVERSVM APVD NOVARIAM STERNIT CAPIT

*Expelled from Alessandria, with his army destroyed, Ludovico Sforza, Duke of Milan,
was driven away, then defeated and captured at Novara upon his return*

News of Il Moro's capture prompted the French troops in the Castello
Sforzesca to pour forth and take control of the city. Its erstwhile Governor,
Il Moro's brother Cardinal Ascanio, fled but was captured at Rivolta d'Adda,
fifteen miles east of Milan, then delivered to the Venetians and taken to Crema
(April 13), then on to Brescia, Verona and Venice itself where, on April 28, the
Venetians accepted French demands for his extradition. He left on May 6 and
was bundled off to Bourges and stuck up a tower.

Il Moro was held captive in Novara for a week. On April 17 he departed for
France under heavy guard, travelling initially on horseback, then in a litter. He
was in poor health, again spitting blood, and could hardly stand. He was carted
over the Alps, reaching Grenoble on April 29, then Lyon on May 2 where, clad
in black from head to foot, he was paraded through the streets in humiliating
fashion under the surreptitious gaze of Louis XII before being locked up in the
(now-destroyed) fortress of Pierre-Encise, high above the Rhône.

His pleas for an audience with the King were ignored. He was held in Lyon
for a fortnight, pending the completion of a wood and iron cage that was to
serve as his bedroom during his journey to the moated, beefy-walled castle
of Lys-Saint-Georges, 25 miles southwest of Bourges in the heart of *La France
Profonde*: his place of imprisonment for the next four years.

The Sanseverino brothers met differing fates. Fracassa was also imprisoned in
Novara. Antonio Maria was removed to Vercelli but soon released. Gianfrancesco (Count Caiazzo) remained in French service. Cardinal Federigo was in
Austria, and would remain there until August. In May, along with Emperor
Maximilian, he was named godfather to the son (a namesake Federico)
recently born to Isabella d'Este. On July 20 both Federigo and Antonio Maria
were entertained by Emperor Maximilian in Augsburg.

Galeazzo Sanseverino was taken by the Swiss to Cerano, a few miles southeast
of Novara, and offered to Louis XII for 100,000 ducats. The King showed no

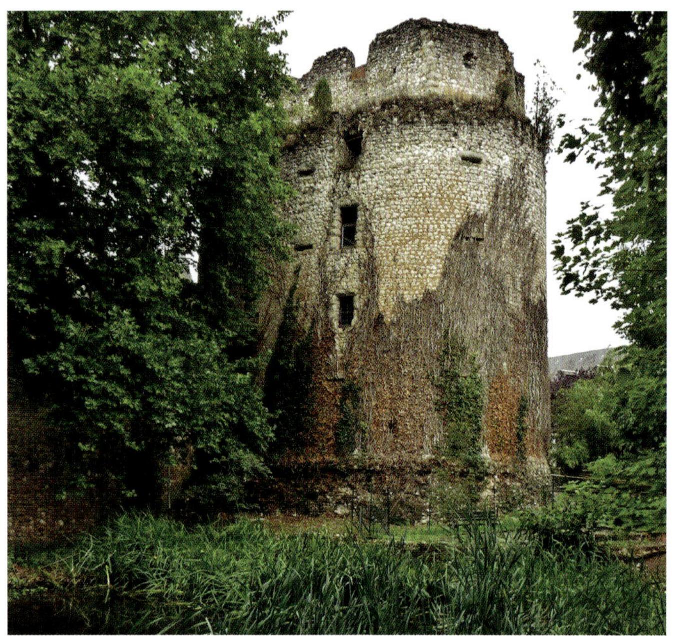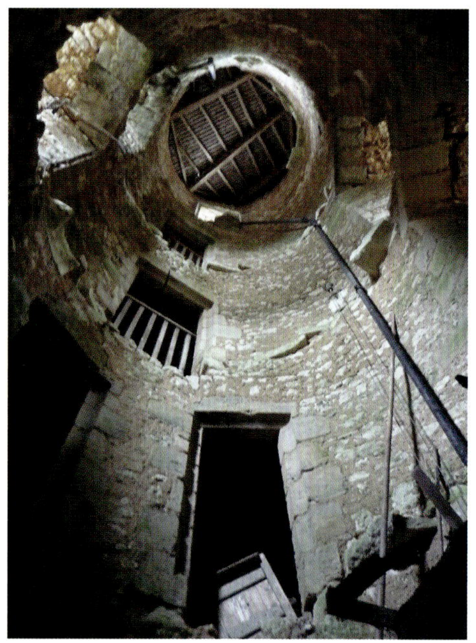

interest. The Swiss sold him for a cut-price 1,000 ducats to the Bailiff of Dijon, who took him to Milan and offered to release him for 5,000 ducats. Much haggling later – on June 9 – Galeazzo was freed by family and relatives for 3,000 ducats. He demanded the Venetians a right of safe passage and headed east.

On July 13, in Mantua, he received a message from Emperor Maximilian in Augsburg, expressing sorrow over his capture, delight at his release, and offering him the same post he had held under Il Moro: *Captain General*. A week later, under pressure from Francesco Gonzaga (Maximilian's Captain General in Italy), Maximilian back-tracked, downgrading Galeazzo's new title from Captain General to *Captain of Arms*.

By August Galeazzo was back in Innsbruck after a tortuous journey via Lake Garda and Trent. There was talk of Maximilian returning to attack Milan but, despite the advance presence of 400 Habsburg knights in Mantua, nothing came of it.

Cardinal Georges d'Amboise temporarily replaced Trivulzio as Louis XII's Regent in Milan before returning to France with Trivulzio and La Trémoille on 8 June 1500. Pierre de Sacierges, Bishop of Luçon, assumed control until Louis XII appointed a new Governor of Milan, Georges d'Amboise's nephew Charles d'Amboise, who arrived in mid-July. Trivulzio's governorship of Milan came in for severe criticism, especially from Comte de Ligny, and he was not allowed to return to Italy until October, and then only in a semi-private capacity – although Louis XII compensated for his demotion by granting him Galeazzo Sanseverino's former fiefdom of Castelnuovo Scrivia.

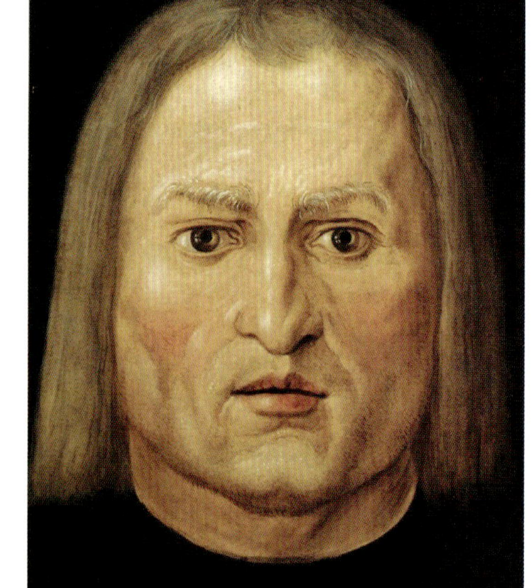

In October 1501 Galeazzo Sanseverino was back in Trent with Maximilian to talk peace terms with the French Governor of Milan. Sanuto described him as pale, clad in mourning, with empty pockets and a sorrowful mien, adding: 'The Germans hold him of little account, but he is always with His Imperial Majesty, who seems very fond of him' (*Diarii IV – 129*). The 'Germans' were fed up with all the Italian exiles – up to 250 of them were reportedly still in Innsbruck.

In February 1502 Galeazzo accompanied Maximilian to Nuremberg, staying several weeks with his old pal Willi Pirckheimer, and – still clad in mourning black – meeting up with Albrecht Dürer, who painted his portrait.[8]

In September 1502 Galeazzo became Conte di Caiazzo after his elder brother Gianfrancesco died in French service near Naples. In 1503 Galeazzo was in Augsburg and Constance, where Maximilian ordered that he receive payment for an outstanding debt of 900 guilders.

Galeazzo had no luck in securing an important and/or lucrative post at the Habsburg court; and any hopes he may have held of becoming Regent of Milan, on the back of a successful Habsburg invasion, were scuppered in September 1504 when Maximilian made *Realpolitik* peace with the French by signing the Treaty of Blois.

During negotiations Maximilian politely requested, without much hope, that Il Moro be released. The erstwhile Italian potentate was, however, moved from isolated Lys to more prestigious Loches, and granted comfortable living quarters in the guard-house. One day he tried to escape – some sources say disguised as a washerwoman, others hidden under a cartload of hay. He was no more convincing in drag than dressed as a pikeman. He got lost in the woods and was sniffed out by the hounds.

From Il Principio to Mr Toad. The proudest Prince of the Renaissance was banished from the guard-house and hurled in the slammer.

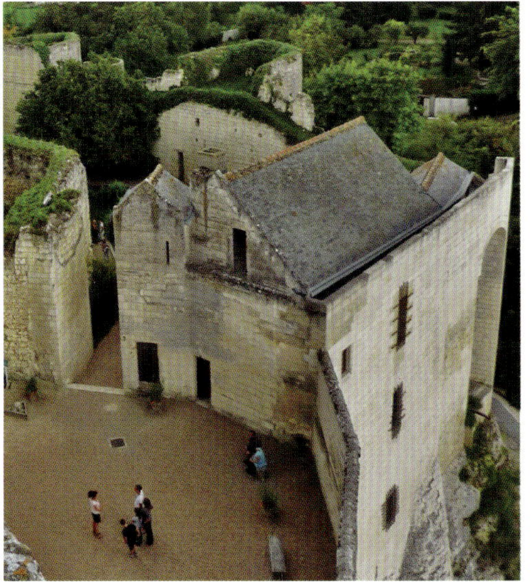

CASTLE OF LOCHES
ENTRANCE TO DUNGEONS
IL MORO'S CELL

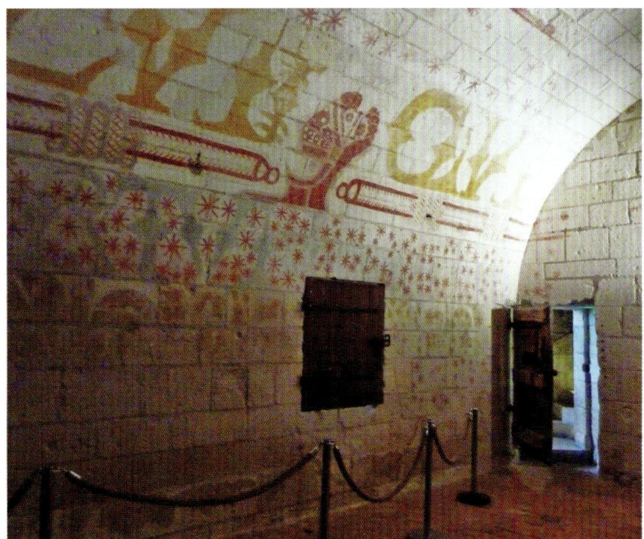

ABOUT-TURN

The Treaty of Blois, by ending hostilities between Austria and France, meant Il Moro's former in-law was no longer outlawed.[9] Leaving Il Moro's sons Massimiliano (aged eleven) and Francesco (aged nine) in Innsbruck, Galeazzo Sanseverino accepted the mediation of his brothers Federigo and Antonio Maria, and hurried to a meeting with Charles d'Amboise in Milan. Galeazzo needed a job but, while he was about it, petitioned Louis XII to restore his various homes and estates, and pay him Bianca's 240,000-ducat dowry. His list of demands – more those of a victor dictating peace terms than a defeated enemy seeking redemption – were penned (in Latin) on an unsigned document now in France's Archives Nationales (*MS Fr. 3087, fol. 103*).[10]

Louis XII refused to return to Galeazzo the estates he had given to Trivulzio in 1499, but Sanseverino was allowed to recover Bianca's dower town of Voghera – following the death of Comte de Ligny, who had seized it in 1500 after a battle with the Dal Vermes.

Louis XII also invited Galeazzo to France and gave him a job. On 21 September 1505, in an astonishing promotion for a former N°2 Enemy, Louis XII made Galeazzo Sanseverino *Grand Ecuyer* (Master of the Horse) – the only foreigner in French history ever to hold the post. He joined Louis XII's inner circle, appearing at his side at official events, and sporting the French sword of state on ceremonial occasions.

Il Moro learnt of this ultimate act of betrayal while eyeing his Rudolf Hess of a future from behind bars, and pondered it in his heart.

Il Moro never forgot the man some held responsible for the death of his daughter and, as his Captain of Arms, most blamed for his defeat by the French.

Bosom friend one minute, traitor the next.

The image of a headless black helmet, added to the final *Sforziada* that symbolically commemorated the watershed in Il Moro's fortunes, hammered away inside his brain.

One of the last things Il Moro did, before he died a prisoner in the Castle of Loches on 27 May 1508, aged 55, was to go from *auctor* to *pinctor*, request a brush and paint, and decorate the walls of his cell.

He wanted black paint but they only had blue, yellow and blood red.

He painted a giant, headless helmet. Criss-crossed with Este diamonds. Not front-on but in left-facing profile.

The same profile as Leonardo's portrait of his daughter Bianca. The same headless helmet as in his daughter's *Sforziada*. The same criss-cross pattern as on his wife's effigy.

The helmet is flanked by two lances circled with victor's rings. The lances extend the whole length of the wall, pointing in at the helmet, aiming to smash it to smithereens.

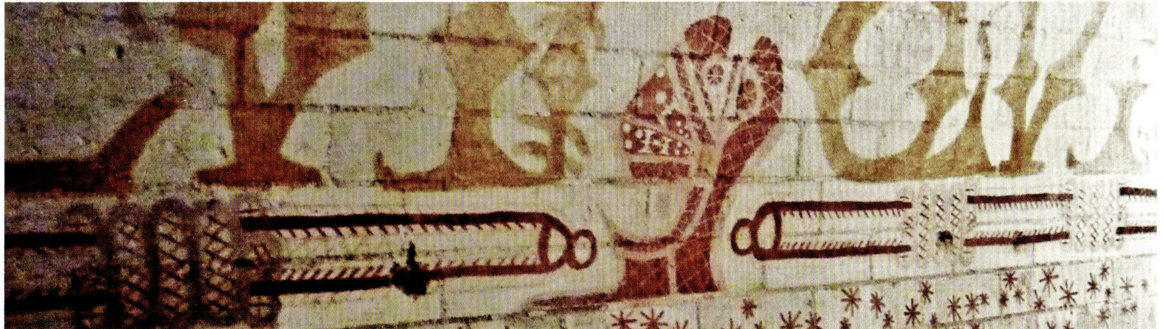

NOTES

1 Domenico Malipiero, *Annali Veneti dall'Anno 1457 al 1500*.

2 Francesco Guicciardini, *La Historia d'Italia* (Florence 1561).

3 Galeazzo Sanseverino may have received intelligence from his friend Willibald Pirckheimer – commander of Nuremberg troops during the Swabian War between the Holy Roman Empire/ Swabian League (founded in 1488) and the Swiss – to the effect that Imperial troops would be in no position to reinforce Il Moro's defence against the French any time soon (the Swabian War broke out in February 1499, with the Swiss earning a decisive victory at the Battle of Dornach, just south of Basel, in July: Il Moro helped broker peace talks, but the Peace of Basel – finally freeing up whatever troops Maximilian might care to send Il Moro's way – was not signed until September 22).

4 The story of the French invasion, Il Moro's flight and subsequent return are based primarily on archive material quoted in Léon-Gabriel Pélissier, *Louis XII et Ludovic Sforza* (Charles Boehm, Montpellier 1896).

5 Lucrezia was courteously treated in Milan, and later settled in the small town of Caneto sull'Oglio, twenty miles west of Mantua, at the invitation of Isabella d'Este.

6 This suggests the Uffizi *Sforziada* was kept in the Castello Sforzesco. Another act of artistic vandalism that can be imputed with some confidence to Trivulzio is the defacement of Leonardo's 'Musician' portrait of Galeazzo Sanseverino. Until restored to its original appearance in 1905, this portrait contained no hand or musical score and its doublet, originally red, had been overpainted black (an act of vandalism that remains uncorrected). The most feasible explanation for these radical modifications: Trivulzio found the portrait in Sanseverino's palazzo in Vigevano and sought to obscure the identity of the sitter by obliterating the snatch of musical score; presumably – as per Cecilia Gallerani's weasel/ermine – this contained an allusion to the sitter's identity. That Trivulzio did not purely and simply destroy the portrait of

his bitterest enemy surely reflects his esteem for Leonardo, whom he later commissioned to design his own memorial.

7 The Swiss Confederation had allied itself to Charles VIII in November 1495 following the Diet of Worms earlier in the year, which heralded an administrative and fiscal rationalization of the Empire, and saw Maximilian claim exclusive recruitment rights among the Swiss cantons. Some Swiss mercenaries had unofficially signed up for Charles VIII's Naples campaign in 1494.

8 Mark Evans has suggested that Dürer may have gained access to drawings by Leonardo through Pirckheimer's friendship with Sanseverino.

9 The Treaty of Blois, signed on 22 September 1504, concerned the proposed marriage between the future Emperor Charles V and Louis XII's daughter Claude. It stipulated that, if Louis XII died without male issue, Charles would receive as dowry the Duchy of Milan, Genoa and its dependencies, and the Duchies of Brittany and Burgundy. The engagement was soon called off. In 1506 Claude was betrothed to the future François I.

10 Memoriale eorum que pectuntur pro Dᶰᵒ Galeazio San Severino

Point 3 of this 'Memorandum' begins: *Petit dotem que uxoris sue, que est ducentorum quadraginta milium*, and charts Sanseverino's 'petition for his wife's dowry of 240,000 [ducats], as it can be most clearly demonstrated that Ludovico never settled it and, although there were no children, the dowry ought by rights to have been given; it is clear and widely known that, according to the laws and statutes observed in Milan, a wife's dowry is due once the marriage has been consummated.'

The rest of the document translates from the original Latin as follows:

1. May he be absolved of all things undertaken against the most Christian Lord the King of France

2. That the following formal ducal properties – given to him by Duke Ludovico, and which he inhabited before his capture – be restored to him:

– **Castelnuovo** [**Scrivia**]; now held by the Count of Mesocco [i.e. Gian Giacomo Trivulzio, who in the early 1480s was granted authority over the town of Mesocco and the surrounding

Val Mesolcina, between Bellinzona and the San Bernardino Pass in what is now southern Switzerland]

– The castle and town of **Voghera**; now held by Comte de Ligny

– Cassina possessions near Voghera; not known if now owned by Comte de Ligny or someone else

– Castle of **Algesio** [**Olgisio**] with its domains; now held by Bernardino Curcio

– Theoretical possessions in **Ticino**; not known who now inhabits them

– Lodging in **Pizzale** [near Voghera]; not known who owns it

– House at Porta Vercellina, **Milan**

– Stable and house in park near **Milan** Castle

– House in the town of **Pavia** near church of San Francesco

– Divers properties belonging to Galeazzo

– Fort and town of **Zavattarello** [near Bobbio] with possessions; not known who owns it

– Castle and town of **Silvano Pietra** [near Voghera] with possessions; not known who owns it

4. Petitions for the return of properties of which he has been unduly deprived, as acknowledged by the Lord Cardinal of Rouen, who restored them to D. Galeaz when he was in Milan but, due to the opposition of their current inhabitants, without effect. The Count of Mesocco [Trivulzio] has most of them. D. G. does not know who owns the others.

5. Because, prior to Ludovico's expulsion from Milan, D.G. had not annulled debts contracted that year for himself and his family, as he did every year by the end of the year … before the aforementioned expulsion he had ordained that the said debts be paid from that year's income. The Most Christian King, upon accepting the good faith of D.G. in wishing to pay off his debts, is petitioned that, if satisfaction be not obtained, it is only fair that creditors be satisfied with the profits from the aforesaid properties, and therefore responsible for the said debts, which are worth much less than the said profits. As a result D.G. is not to be troubled by this matter.

6. Should Galeazzo have other debtors, his Most Christian Majesty to show favour and help in obtaining their just resolution.

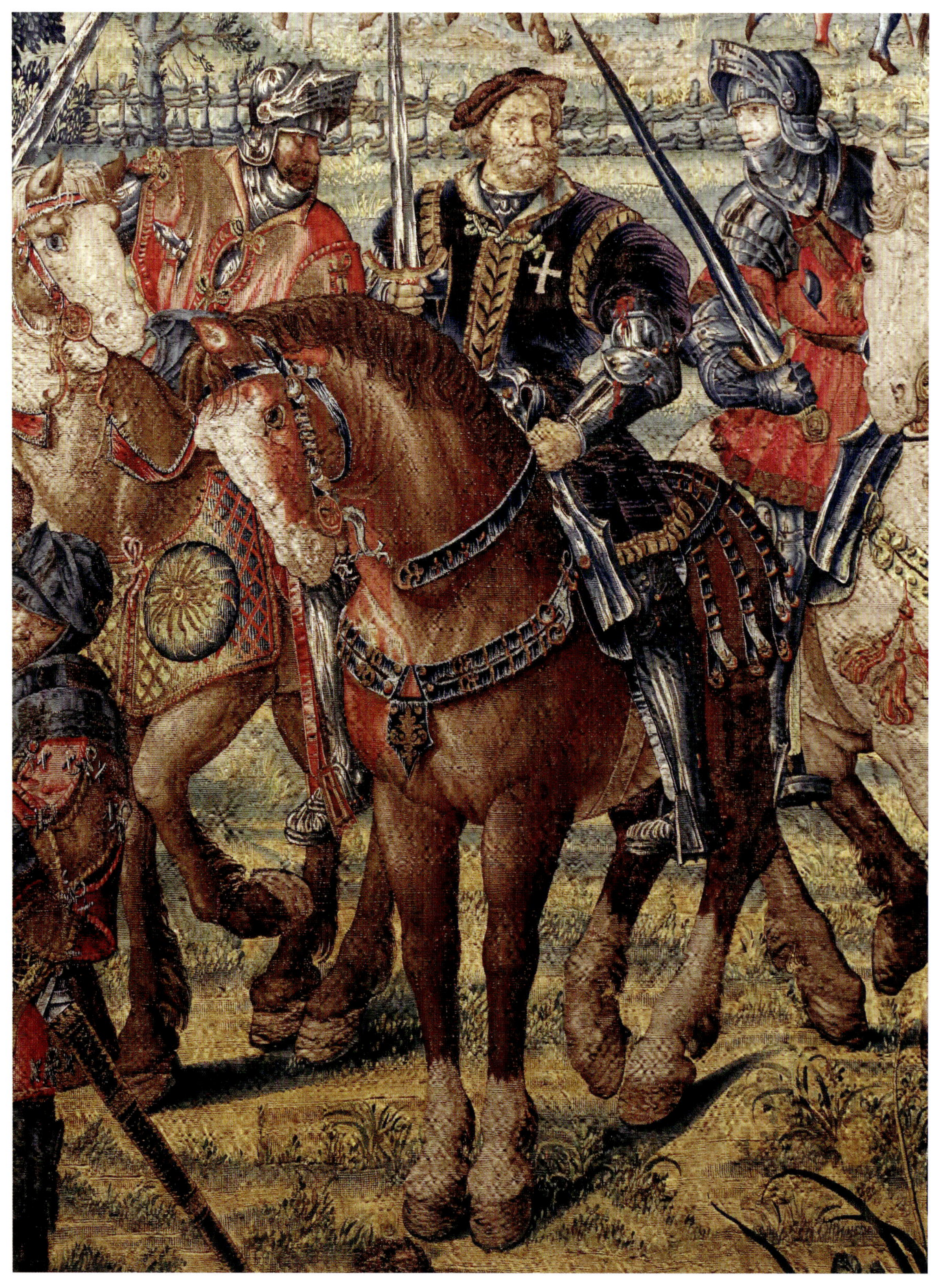

BERNARD VAN ORLEY: *BATTLE OF PAVIA* (*c.*1530) – TAPESTRY – MUSEO DI CAPODIMONTE (INV. IGMN 144489)

XV

BEYOND A BOUNDARY

LEONARDO, DE PREDIS, BIRAGO – AND DÜRER

LEONARDO DA VINCI ENDED his days in France but, like Gianpietro Birago, never crossed the Alps in the other direction – to Austria and Germany. Largely thanks to Galeazzo Sanseverino their work would, however, come to the attention of the greatest artist of the Germanic world: Albrecht Dürer, who also admired their colleague Ambrogio de Predis.

Leonardo da Vinci is last recorded in Milan on 14 December 1499 – transferring his savings to Florence – before leaving for Venice. Perhaps he lingered in the hope of new patrons. He would later work for both Louis XII and his successor François I, and on the design of a funerary monument for France's mercenary general Gian Giacomo Trivulzio.

The main reason, however, why Leonardo showed no inclination to flee the French lay elsewhere: in his ties with Louis de Luxembourg, Comte de Ligny (1467–1503), Grand Chamberlain and Marshal of France. These ties were cited in hush-hush fashion in a Leonardo manuscript, known as the *Ligny Memorandum* (part of the *Codice Atlantico* in the Ambrosiana), in connection with a meeting in Rome and onward journey to Naples.[1]

The *Memorandum* is commonly supposed to date from 1499, but Martin Kemp suggests it may date from Ligny's trip to Italy in 1494.[2] He bases this interpretation on the *Memorandum*'s reference to the French artist Jean Perréal, in connection with 'dry colouring' (*colorire a secco*) – which Kemp feels could refer to Leonardo's use of coloured chalks in his portrait of *Bianca Sforza*.

A 1499 dating, however, is more likely. In Autumn 1499 Ligny was planning to descend on southern Italy and establish a regional power-base around Altamura,[3] 30 miles inland from Bari; he had, at the instigation of Charles VIII, married the Princess of Altamura in 1495. By mid-September 1499 – almost as soon as the conquest of Milan had been completed – Ligny was in secret contact with the Venetians, who regarded the southern Adriatic and heel of Italy as their sphere of influence. Ligny was keen to obtain their backing, or at least benevolent neutrality, and offered to cede 'whatever suited them' from areas adjacent to his estates.

Venice's response was non-committal. Undeterred, Ligny tried again at the end of September, sending a personal envoy to Venice to argue that the time was ripe to carry out his plans, as 'with Venetian support the campaign would be easy.' As bait Ligny threw in a promise to act as an advocate of Venice's regional claims to Louis XII.

Events in Lombardy scuppered Ligny's project. His presence was required during Louis XII's six-week visit in October/November; to help establish French rule in the recalcitrant Alpine borderlands; and to deal with the Return Of Il Moro in early 1500. When the French finally re-descended on Naples in 1501, it was under Louis XII in alliance with Spain.

King Federico was ousted (and, like Il Duchetto, removed to the Loire Valley) and replaced as King of Naples by Louis XII. The carve-up proved short-lived. The House of Aragon returned to rule Naples under Fernando the Catholic after the Battle of Garigliano in December 1503.

Unless new documents come to light, we will never know why Leonardo envisaged joining Comte de Ligny's prospective Mezzogiorno campaign. Taste for adventure? Appointment as official war artist or military engineer? Promise of a share in the spoils? Or, simply, the need for a new patron/employer?

A 1499 dating for the *Ligny Memorandum* would suggest its talk of *colorire a seccho* cannot be linked to Leonardo's portrait of Bianca Sforza – but possibly to his portrait of Isabella d'Este, now in the Louvre. This portrait was executed in early 1500 in Mantua – a midway stop on the 200-mile journey from Milan to Venice. Perhaps Leonardo's decision to go to Venice had something to do with its importance in the eyes of his putative patron, the Comte de Ligny.

Or perhaps he had heard good things about it from Gianpietro Birago, who had trodden the same path nearly thirty years before. And who better to have introduced Leonardo to Ligny than the artist who once counted Ligny's aunt as his chief patron?

Ligny was the son of Marie de Savoie, the slightly elder sister of Bona di Savoia.[4]

Another work may also have been on Leonardo's mind when he left Milan: his *Salvator Mundi*, returned to public view in 2011 after being lost for many years. It appears to derive from the Christ in Rogier van der Weyden's *Braque Family Triptych* (*c*.1452), now in the Louvre – perhaps familiar in northern Italy through Martin Schongauer's ink drawing of the late 1460s (now in the Uffizi).

Doubts exist about the year Leonardo began his *Salvator Mundi*. The 2011 *Leonardo* exhibition at London's National Gallery advanced 1499. Martin Kemp has proposed 1504. It may have been in-between.

Amidst all the subtle body movements that dominate Leonardo's portraits and œuvre as a whole, two works stand out for the sitter's uncompromising rigidity: his 1496 portrait of *Bianca Sforza*, shown in austere profile; and his *Salvator Mundi*, shown head-on.

It would not be illogical for the *Salvator Mundi* to have been Leonardo's next painting after the Bianca portrait especially as, in the interim, Leonardo had been working on sophisticated geometric illustrations for Luca Pacioli's *De Divina Proportione.*

And, between 1496 and 1501, we reach a centennial Holy Year. **1500 AD**. As painted upper left on a very similar picture to the *Salvator Mundi*, by another of the world's greatest artists: Albrecht Dürer.

DÜRER AND ITALY

Leonardo da Vinci's *Salvator Mundi* and Dürer's *Self-Portrait* reflect the dichotomy between God and Mammon – and between the Catholic mysticism of Latin Europe and the militant Protestantism unleashed north of the Alps by Martin Luther, whom Dürer revered.

Perhaps neither artist was aware of the other's painting when working on his own. But Dürer would soon show great curiosity about Leonardo's art. Abetted by Galeazzo Sanseverino and the humanist Willibald Pirckheimer (1470–1530), he would help spread appreciation of Leonardo – and of his Milanese colleagues Ambrogio de Predis and Gianpietro Birago – across the Alps.

Leonardo da Vinci never set foot on German or Austrian soil, but Albrecht Dürer (1471–1528) is twice recorded as visiting Italy.

The first time was in 1494 when he was 23. That autumn Dürer left his plague-stricken home city of Nuremberg for Venice. The following summer, in a series of watercolour landscapes, he charted his return journey to Innsbruck via Padua, Lake Garda, Arco, Trent, Segonzano, Bolzen, Chiusa and the Brenner Pass.

In Trent, Roberto Sanseverino's grand new tomb in the Duomo had been completed barely two years before Dürer's visit, as a symbol of Tyrolean victory over Venetian aggression. Dürer would hear the Sanseverino name again before long – from his Nuremberg patron Willibald Pirckheimer. They were the same age, and friends since childhood. Dürer was born in a house rented from the Pirckheimer family. Willibald left Nuremberg in 1488 to study in Italy, first in Padua, then (from 1491) in Pavia, where he met Galeazzo Sanseverino. He remained in Pavia until his marriage to Crescentia Rieter in October 1495.

THE CELTIS CHEST

At some stage between his time in Pavia and 1501, Willibald Pirckheimer acquired a volume of Italian songs and sonnets, written in gold and silver script on leaves tinted green and purple. He may have received it from Sanseverino as a wedding present: it contains two magnificent full-page illuminations by Gianpietro Birago.

These depict *Apollo and the Muses* (*see p. 75*) and *Daphne and Apollo* (*see p. 266*), and were used as the basis for woodcuts produced by an unknown German artist (sometimes identified as Dürer's student Hans von Kulmbach) in 1501.[5]

The woodcut version of *Daphne and Apollo* (*see following page*) was topped by the arms of the Pirckheimer and Rieter families, strongly implying the original to be in Pirckheimer's possession.

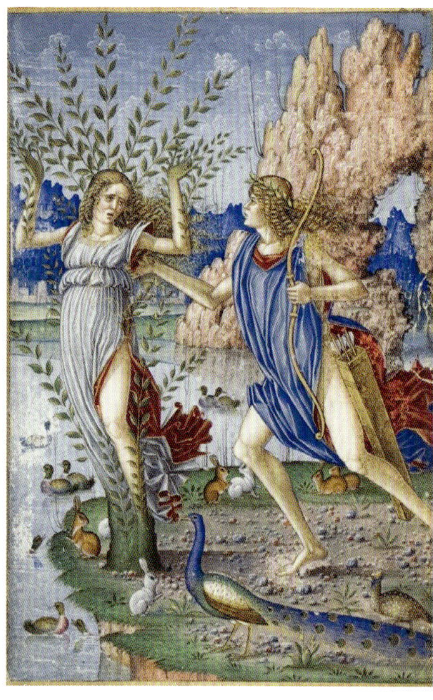 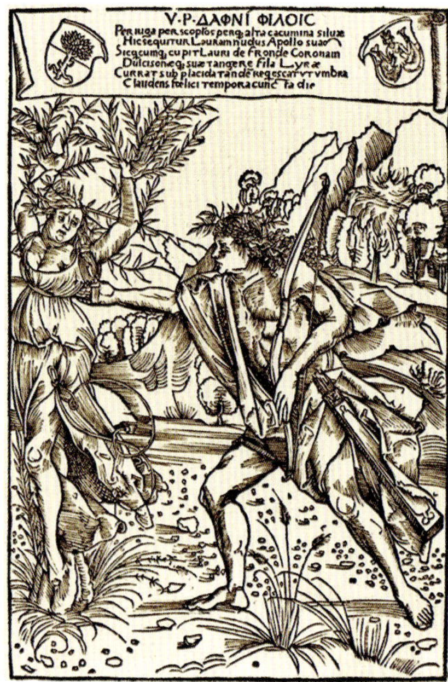

The woodcuts were published in Nuremberg in 1502, in the *Quatuor Libri Amorum* compiled by Konrad Celtis and dedicated to Emperor Maximilian, who the previous year had granted Celtis a charter to found a *Collegium Poetarum et Mathematicorum* at Vienna University.

Apollo and the Muses would again be published in 1507, by Erhard Öglin of Augsburg, in two separate books edited by Celtis: *De Gestis Imperatoris Friderici* by Guntherus Ligurius and *Melopiae* by Petrus Tritonius.

Konrad Celtis rose to prominence during the reign of Maximilian's father Friedrich III who, as Holy Roman Emperor, crowned Celtis Imperial Poet Laureate – literally, with a silver laurel crown – in Nuremberg in 1487.

After the death of Celtis on 4 February 1508, the Poet Laureate's coronation regalia (seal, ring, royal certificate and silver crown) were inherited by Vienna University, along with a special wooden box designed to keep them in. This 31 × 31 × 31cm casket, known as the *Celtis-Kiste* (Celtis Chest), survives. It is still the property of Vienna University. It sees Birago and Dürer go head-to-head – or rather back-to-back.

One side of the box features Birago's figure of Apollo from his *Apollo and the Muses*, based on the German woodcut version of his original miniature (*see opposite*).

The other side features a copy of Dürer's *Philosophia* – which, like Birago's *Apollo*, had also been used to illustrate the *Quatuor Libri Amorum*.

Dürer may have had an even earlier link to Birago: Mark Evans suggests that the archer Apollo in the woodcut resembles the figure of Hercules in Dürer's painting *Hercules Slaying the Stymphalian Birds* (1500).

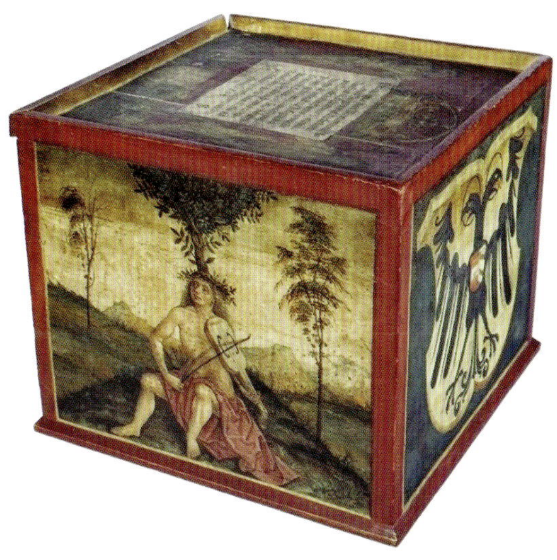

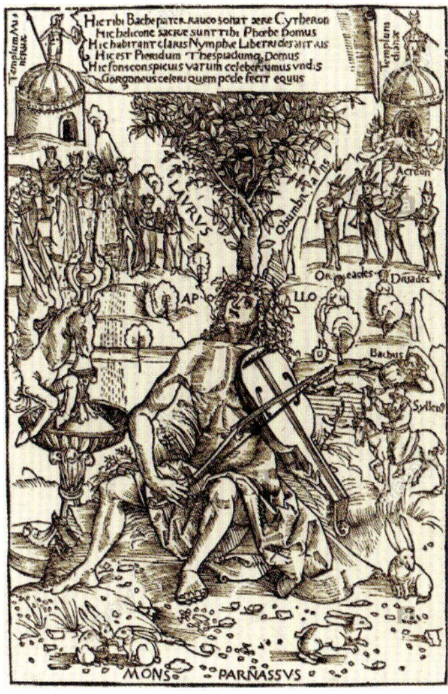

DÜRER AND DE PREDIS

Like Birago, Ambrogio de Predis also made an impact north of the Alps. He had accompanied Bianca Maria to Innsbruck after her proxy marriage to Maximilian in 1493, and returned to Austria after the fall of Il Moro. In August 1501 he is mentioned in the Habsburg Archives as owed money by the Imperial exchequer for providing a 'cloth of black velvet and some silver vessels.' In 1502 he painted Maximilian's portrait, now in the Kunsthistorisches Museum (*below left*). Its influence on Dürer can be seen in the latter's *Feast of the Rosary*

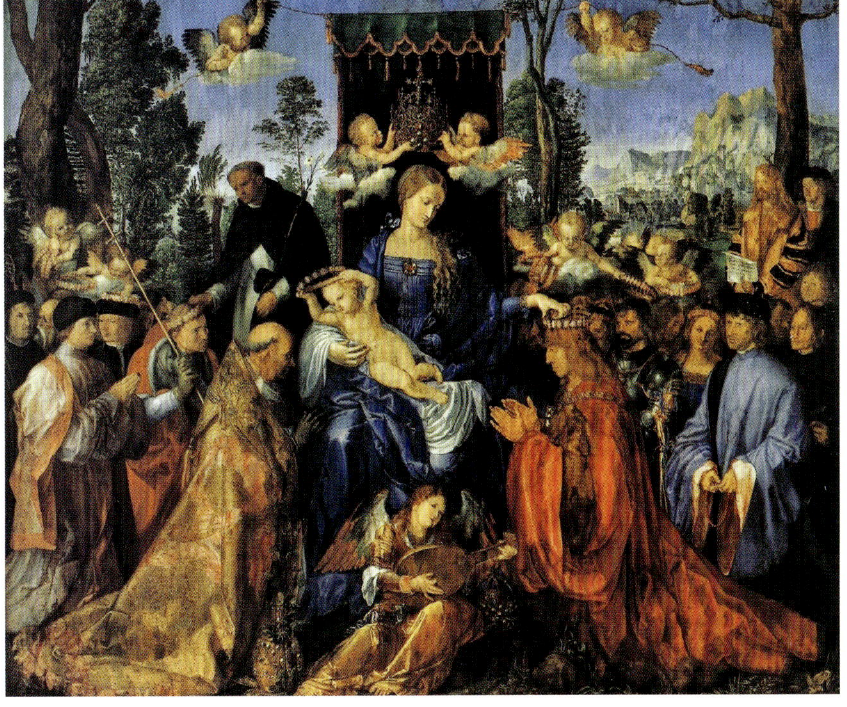

(1506), now in the Národni Galerie, Prague. This large, 162 × 192cm painting is something of a Teutonic *Pala Sforzesca*, featuring not Il Moro and Beatrice but the two supreme authorities of the Catholic world: Pope Julius II, being crowned by the Infant Christ; and Holy Roman Emperor Maximilian I, being crowned by the Virgin Mary. The pair are flanked not by Doctors of the Church but by a gaggle of clerics and, behind the Emperor, pretty much every Tom, Dick and available Heinrich. The dark furrow dividing Maximilian's backswept locks is identical to that in his 1502 portrait by Ambrogio de Predis.

DÜRER AND LEONARDO

Dürer's artistic Milanese affinities extended beyond Birago and Ambrogio de Predis to Leonardo da Vinci.[6] Dürer religiously copied Leonardo's six famous *vinci* knot patterns (though failed to understand their architectural significance, treating the corner pendentives as leafy offshoots), while his horse studies strike many commentators as closely influenced by Leonardo's. As eloquently demonstrated by Mark Evans[7] and Franz Winzinger,[8] the likely source of Dürer's Leonardesque knowledge was Galeazzo Sanseverino, keeper of the Sforza Stables.

Leonardo's strongest influence on Dürer, however, came through his earliest Milanese painting: 'The Musician'. This seems to have served as a reverse-image template for Dürer's 1521 portrait of *Bernhard von Reesen* now in the Dresden Gemäldegalerie (*below second left*). Dürer's reverence for 'The Musician' is also apparent in the sideways gaze, with rear eye half-obscured by the nose, that typify several of his portraits, notably of Emperor Maximilian (*below second right*) and Willibald Pirckheimer (*below far right*) – the two men of greatest importance to Sanseverino on German soil (one as patron, the other as friend).

Further, hitherto unremarked evidence of Dürer's acquaintance with 'The Musician' is to be found in his 1508 painting *Die Marter der Zehntausend Christen* (Martyrdom of the Ten Thousand) – commissioned by Friedrich III, Elector of Saxony, for his new Schlosskirche in Wittenberg.

This illustrates the 3rd century slaying of 10,000 Christian soldiers on Mount Ararat by order of Persian King Shapur the Great.

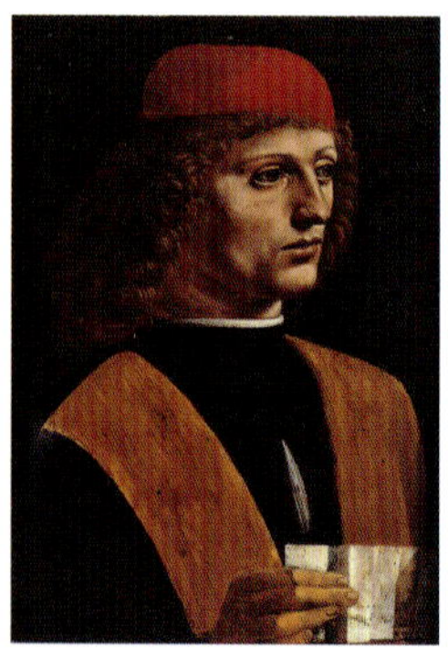
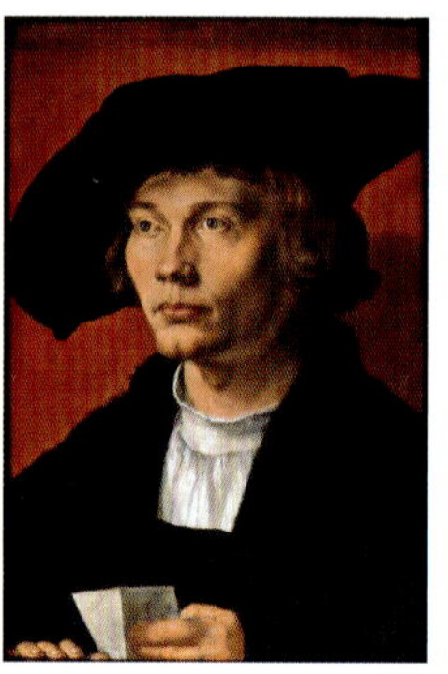
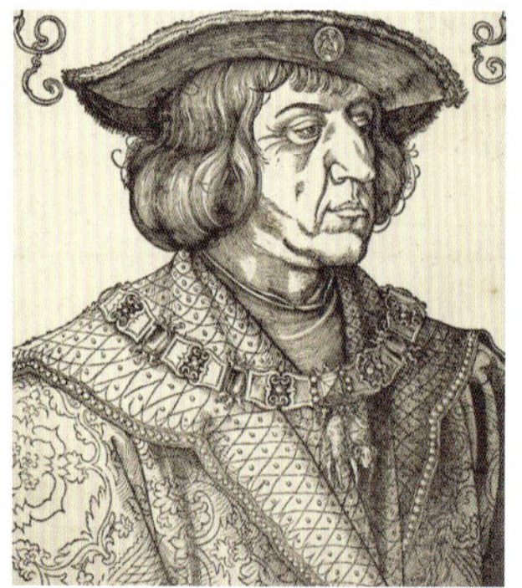
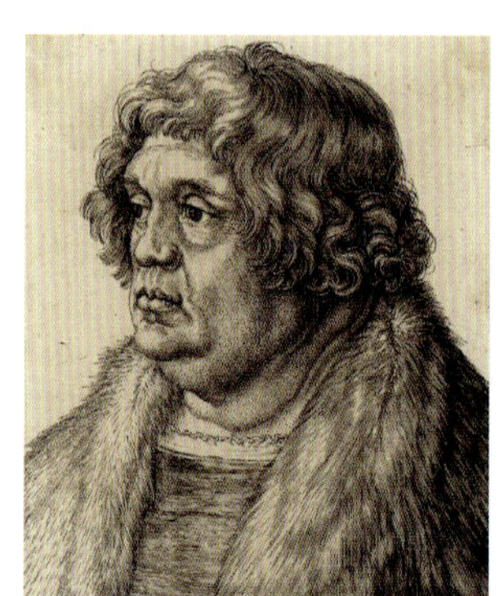

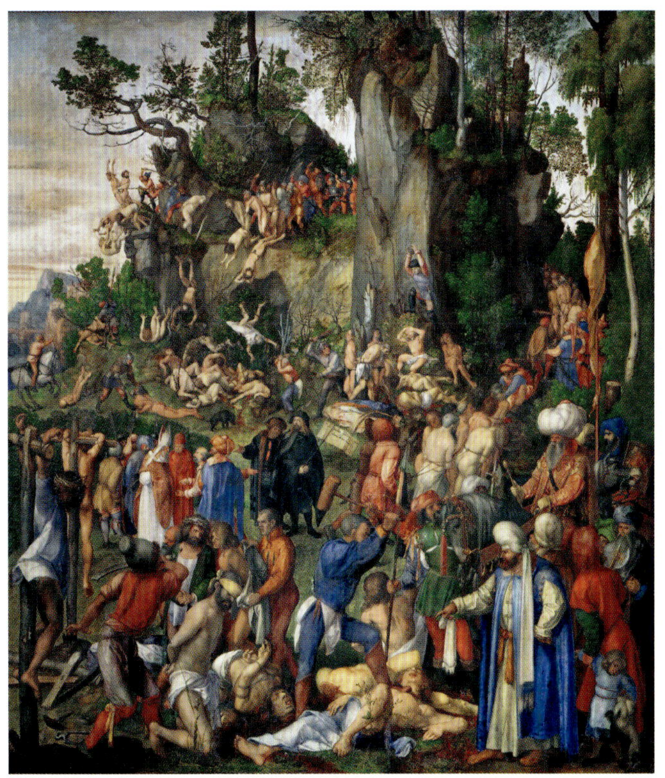

At the heart of *The Martyrdom* are two recognizable figures: the late Konrad Celtis, who died while the work was being painted, and Albrecht Dürer himself. Dürer is brandishing a banner that reads *Iste fatiebat Ano Domini 1508 – Albertus Dürer Aleman*. This banner (*see below left*) is no smooth piece of cloth or vellum, but is folded into nine, in precisely the same way as the snatch of score clutched by 'The Musician' (*below centre*): same shadow two-thirds of the way along, same dark band towards the left, same falling away at the end....

Unless we are to believe in the powers of telepathy, the uncanny physical similarities between this banner and the snatch of score held by 'The Musician' mean Dürer must have had first-hand knowledge of Leonardo's portrait. Who else but Galeazzo Sanseverino could have shown it to him? And how else could Sanseverino have shown it to him unless he had the portrait – or a copy of it – with him during his Austrian exile, when he met Dürer during his stay with Pirckheimer in Nuremberg in Summer 1502? And why would Sanseverino have this portrait with him unless he were the sitter?

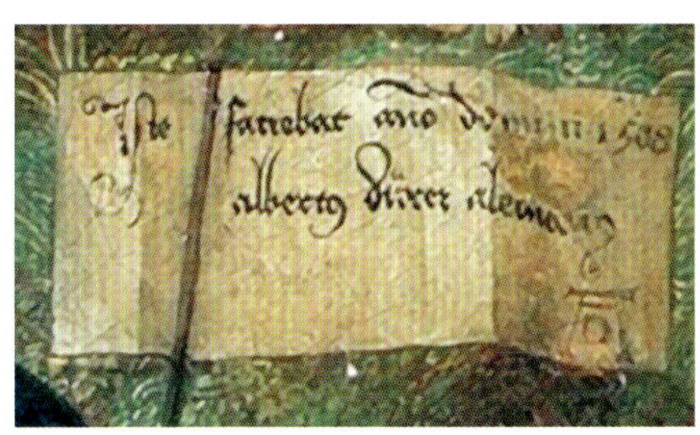

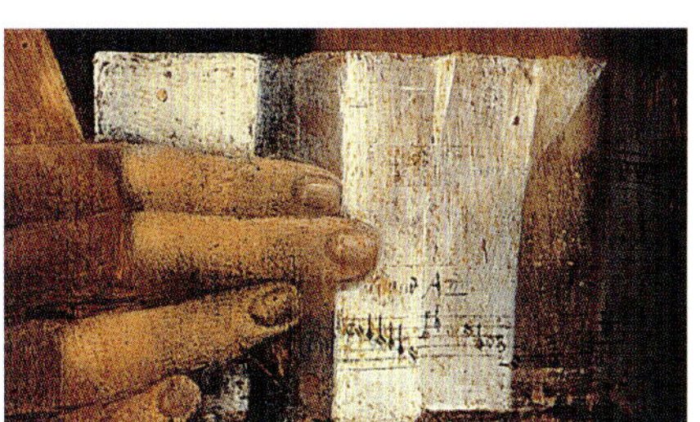

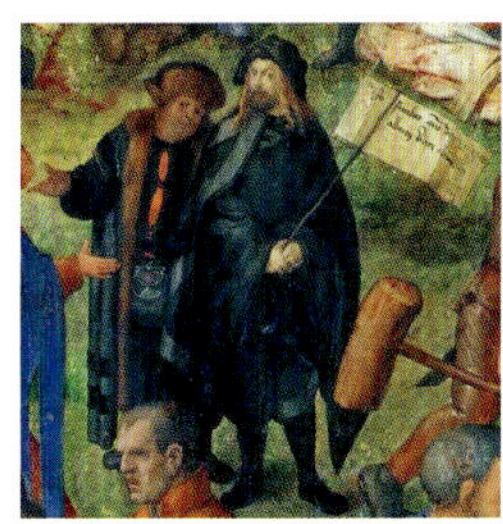

LAST YEARS OF GALEAZZO SANSEVERINO

Galeazzo Sanseverino returned to Milan in 1504 after the Treaty of Blois, to a polite reception from the French but, we may suppose, a torrent of fruity verbiage from the Milanese. A few months later he crossed the Alps as a French employee: hired by Louis XII as his Master Of The Horse. In April 1507 Sanseverino returned to Milan with the French after their reconquest of Genoa. Perhaps he met up with Isabella d'Este and Leonardo da Vinci – who had been hired by Louis XII to erect temporary triumphal arches and choreograph victory pageants.

Galeazzo Sanseverino would find himself involved in some of the most famous events in European history. He took part in the Battle of the Spurs at Enguine-gatte, near Calais, in August 1513. In October 1514, aged 56, clad in natty blue satin, he represented France in a jousting tournament in Abbeville[9] to mark the marriage of Louis XII to Mary Tudor, the sister of King Henry VIII. In June 1520 he crossed lances with the Duke of Bedford and glances with Henry VIII on the Field of the Cloth of Gold.

Like Leonardo da Vinci, Galeazzo Sanseverino enjoyed even greater favour under François I than under Louis XII. In October 1515 he accompanied the new king on his triumphant entry into Milan – while his former charge, the newly deposed Duke Massimiliano Sforza, quit Italy for France. In 1516 Galeazzo was awarded the fairy-tale château of Mehun-sur-Yèvre, near Bourges (*right, as it is today*).[10] That same year Leonardo was invited by François I to settle as his guest in Amboise on the Loire – around twenty miles from both Loches, where Il Moro had died in 1508, and Blois, where Galeazzo Sanseverino oversaw the Royal Stables.

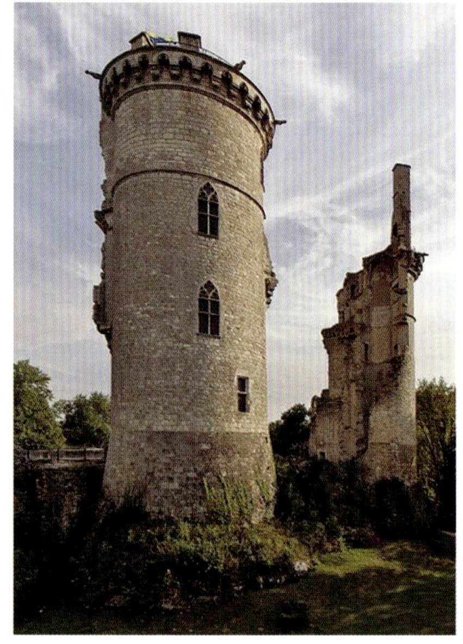

In 1517 Sanseverino was granted French citizenship. Soon after-wards, as a widower of almost sixty, he remarried – again to a teenage bride. Costanza del Carretto,[11] aged fourteen, was born in Chiavari, a coastal town 25 miles east of Genoa. Her well-connected family hailed from Finale, 40 miles the other side of Genoa, and had long enjoyed Sforza and Imperial protection. Her father Alfonso I del Carretto (1457–1516) had been invested with the title of Marchese di Finale & Noli by Emperor Maximilian in December 1496.[12]

In April 1519 Galeazzo Sanseverino was awarded a royal annual pension of 20,000 crowns and, upon the death of his brother Gaspare (Fracassa), acquired his Lombardy estates of Calvatore and Spineda. He would spend many of his remaining days in Italy. In April 1522 he was among the French forces defeated by Emperor Charles V at the Battle of Bicocca – close to where he and Bianca went hare-hunting in Autumn 1496. He took part in the Siege of Milan of 1523. In October 1524 he was in Vigevano. Four months later, on 24 February 1525, he was one of the 12,000 to die at Mirabello during the Battle of Pavia, when Charles V again overcame the French and captured François I.

There is even an image (*see p.262*) of the grey-haired, full-bearded Galeazzo at his last battle,[13] perched on a chestnut steed in black armour with white

Maltese Cross: he had doubtless been inducted to the Knights of St John by his wife's uncle Fabrizio del Caretto, Grand Master of the Order from 1512–21.

Sword erect, stoic and immobile, splendidly indifferent as the King of France is hauled away before his eyes and the enemy closes in: Van Orley's famous tapestry shows Sanseverino seconds from death.[14]

His body, it is said, was taken to the Certosa di Pavia, and laid to rest in the very chapel containing the Bergognone altarpiece wherein he and Bianca weep beneath the Cross.[15]

Birago's Book of Doom frontispiece, showing the walls of Pavia and the tower of the Certosa, had proved prophetic.[16]

NOTES

1 That Leonardo should have hobnobbed with Jean Perréal, in and before 1499, is hardly surprising. They were kindred spirits: artists, architects, theatre designers and more besides – like Bramante, *uomi universali* par excellence. The links between Leonardo, Ligny and Perréal (who drew a silverpoint portrait of Ligny, now in Chantilly) are intriguing – with a common thread provided by Ligny's aunt, Bona da Savoia, who eked out her last years in Fossano as a guest of her nephew Philibert of Savoy, who died in 1504 and was buried in Brou, near Bourg-en-Bresse, in a magnificent church, partly designed by ... Jean Perréal, at the behest of Philibert's widow Margaret of Austria (daughter of Emperor Maximilian). When the French invaders were dividing up the Milanese spoils after chasing out Il Moro in 1500, Ligny obtained the Castle of Voghera, previously owned by ... Il Moro's daughter Bianca, and one of the last places she visited before her death. Ligny embellished the Castle with frescoes by Bramantino, the star pupil of Leonardo's friend Bramante.

2 Martin Kemp & Pascal Cotte, *op. cit.*

3 The future King Federico of Naples offered Ligny the hand of his daughter Carlotta (who had been raised in France); she would marry Comte Guy de Laval (in Lyon) in July 1500.

4 Bona di Savoia's eldest sister Charlotte (1441–83) was Queen of France, married to Louis XI; their daughter Anne de Beaujeu – Bona's niece – was Regent 1483–91. Il Moro's cultivating of Charles VIII, including the possible gift of an illuminated Sforziada, had anti-Bona connotations.

5 Mark Evans, *German Prints and Milanese Miniatures: Influences on – and from – Gianpietro Birago* (Apollo, 2001).

6 Mark Evans, *Dürer and Italy Revisited: the German Connection* (British Museum, 2004).

7 Franz Winzinger, *Dürer und Leonardo* (Pantheon Vol. XXIX, 1971).

8 It is claimed that Dürer portrayed Leonardo da Vinci and Galeazzo Sanseverino in his final work: the *Four Apostles* he presented to his native Nuremberg in October 1526 (now in Munich's Alte Pinakothek), and whose composition is based on a 1488 triptych by Giovanni Bellini in Santa Maria dei Frari in Venice. Dürer's St Mark is unquestionably modelled on **Friedrich der Weise** (1463–1525), his patron from 1496, while his St John portrays **Philipp Melanchthon** (1497–1560), professor at Wittenberg University founded by Friedrich in 1502, and a bastion of the Reformation. St Peter is said to be embodied by **Galeazzo Sanseverino**, who has the same broad face and bushy beard as in Bernard van Orley's *Battle of Pavia* tapestry. St Paul is claimed as Dürer's final tribute to **Leonardo da Vinci** (although his appearance must derive from secondary sources, as Dürer never met him).

9 Galeazzo retained lifelong prowess as a jousting knight, and was cited by Baldassare Castiglione in *Il Cortigiano* for his 'physical grace and agility' – achieved under the guidance of Pietro Monte, a Spanish master-of-arms who moved to northern Italy in the 1470s.

10 The Château of Mehun was the grandest residence of Jean, Duc de Berry (1340–1416) – and where he kept his library. Joan of Arc visited in 1429 and King Charles VII died here in 1461.

11 Details of Galeazzo's second marriage are flimsy; it was long held in some quarters that he had remarried as early as 1498. That was always unlikely: in 1498 Il Moro informed his niece Caterina Sforza that his widowed son-in-law had no intention of re-marrying; and Galeazzo's 1504 attempts to reclaim (from the French) the unpaid dowry he felt due from 1496 would have had scant justification if he had remarried in the meantime. New evidence about his second wife was brought to light by Carla Glori (*op. cit.*) in 2011.

12 Costanza's mother Peretta Usodimare (*c.*1478–1550) was an illegitimate grand-daughter of Pope Innocent VIII. Peretta was Alfonso's second wife; they married in Rome in November 1488, a year after the death of his first wife Bianca Simonetta (daughter of ducal secretary Angelo Simonetta, and widow of Duke Galeazzo Maria's illegitimate son Carlo, Conte di Magenta). In 1499 Alfonso joined Il Moro's supporters – including Galeazzo Sanseverino – in Innsbruck and accompanied Il Moro's briefly triumphant return to Milan. He was captured at Novara but released soon after, deprived of his Finale/Noli estates, and forced to re-settle in Chiavari – only regaining his title, and returning to Finale, in 1514.

13 Sanseverino appears in the monumental series of seven Flemish tapestries, each around 14 × 30ft, designed by Bernard van Orley, woven in the Brussels workshop of Willem and Jan Dermoyen, and presented to Emperor Charles V in 1531. The tapestries have been in the Museo Nazionale di Capodimonte, Naples, since 1862.

14 Galeazzo's widow Costanza remained known as Madame La Grande (the honorary title bestowed on the wife of Le Grand Ecuyer), was granted an annual pension of 2,000 livres and, from 1531, took up residence at the Castello di Zena near Piacenza. She died in 1564 – the same year that the effigies of Il Moro and Beatrice d'Este, originally installed in Santa Maria delle Grazie, were removed to the Certosa di Pavia ... close to the bones of Galeazzo Sanseverino.

15 Pierangelo Laurora (*op. cit.*) asserts this chapel to be Sanseverino's final resting place – although without establishing any link with the figures of Bianca and Sanseverino in Bergognone's *Crucifixion* (see Chapter I).

16 Like Leonardo, Ambrogio de Predis and Galeazzo Sanseverino, Birago enjoyed a professional second wind under the French invaders who had seen off Il Moro. On 15 April 1506 he was granted a copyright privilege in the name of Louis XII. One of the artworld's great political survivors, who spent his life manoeuvering between ducal Milan, republican Venice and papal Rome, Birago is last mentioned after the Sforzas' return, under Il Moro's son Massimiliano – as author of a letter dated 7 July 1513 wherein he signs off as capellanis et pictore – 'chaplain and artist' (Archivio di Stato di Milano); cf Malaguzzi Valeri III, p.225.

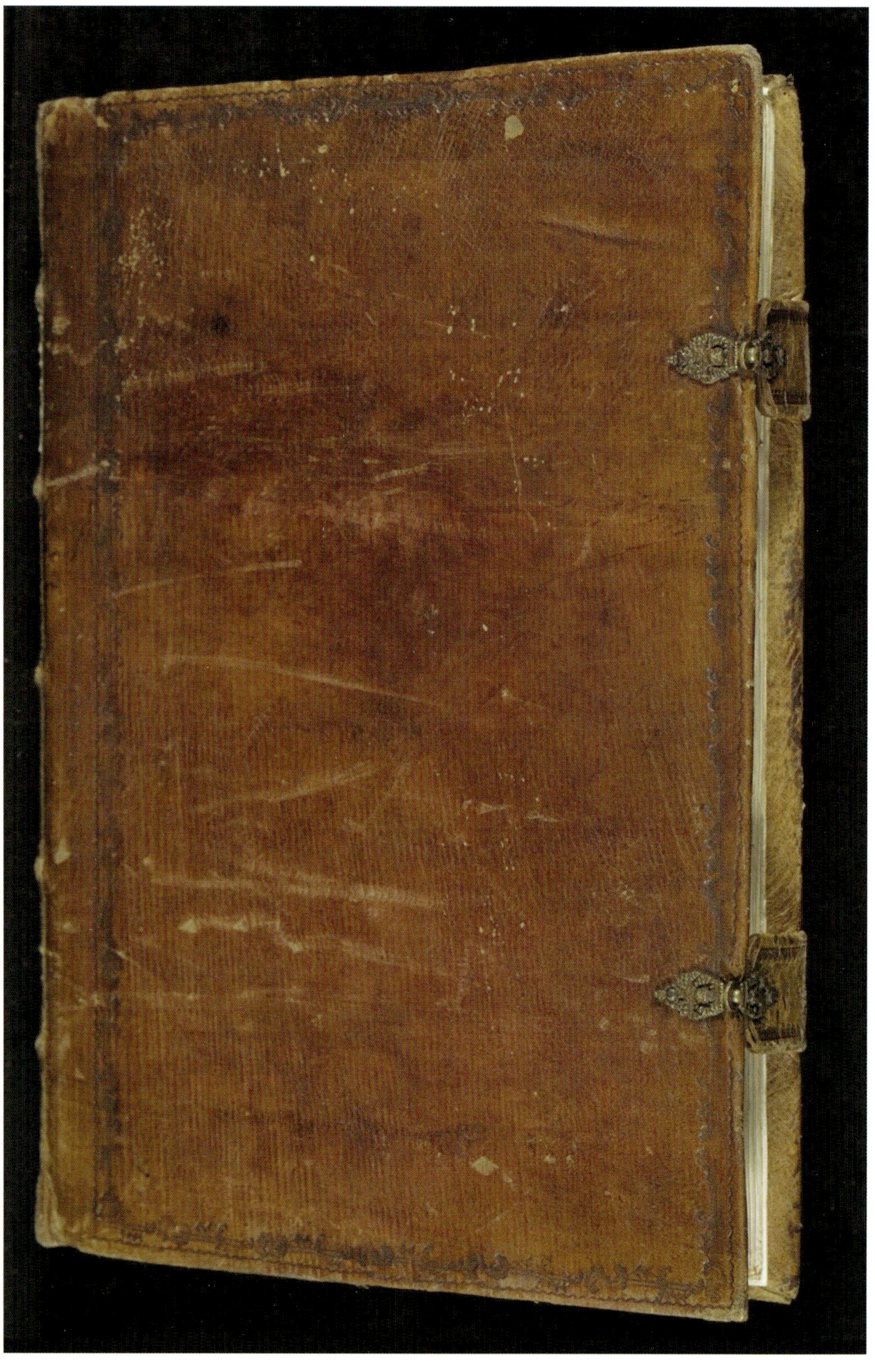

XVI

DOOMSDAY BOOK
THE FATE OF THE FINAL SFORZIADA

THE FINAL ILLUMINATED *SFORZIADA* is first documented in south-west Poland in 1675. By then it had twice been rebound. Where had it been for the previous 175 years – and how did it wind up in Warsaw?

On 31 August 1499, two days before his flight from Milan to Austria, Il Moro met Isabel of Aragon and suggested she allow her son, Il Duchetto, to come with him. Isabel refused. Il Moro then suggested she come too. He was rebuffed.

Il Moro could have ignored Isabel and taken Il Duchetto anyway. But the effect on public opinion would have been disastrous.

Instead, Il Moro had a deed drawn up[1] transferring his rights to the Duchy of Bari[2] to Isabel of Aragon, and assigning her an annual income of 6,000 ducats.[3]

Il Moro's deed was motivated by the fear that Louis XII would install Il Duchetto as his puppet Duke, scuppering Il Moro's justification for a future return to Milan from Austria to restore Sforza rule. Il Moro wanted Isabel, and her son, out of the way.

The exchange between the humiliated Il Moro, and the woman he had spent a decade humiliating, but whose co-operation he now desperately needed, must have been excruciating. Did he offer her anything else?

Regaining 'her' Milanese Duchy, on behalf of her children, would remain Isabel of Aragon's *raison d'être* for many years to come, and she was determined they would be brought up as Sforzas. So successful was she that her daughter Bona, and Bona's daughter Anna would, halfway across Europe, continue using the Sforza viper[4] until almost the end of the next century. They will have been made fully *au fait* with the story of their great-grandfather Francesco, the family patriarch.

Isabel may have asked for a de luxe *Sforziada* to aid her in this task. And she had sentimental and family reasons for wanting the one with Bianca's portrait, and not just because it quotes the blood-and-gold arms of Aragon in the shield top-right.

Isabel was on friendly terms with Leonardo. Birago's frontispiece, with its portrayal of Il Moro as a bumptious megalomaniac and the Sanseverinos as simpering sycophants, may have amused her; Birago had also produced the stupendous *Sforza Hours* for Isabel's mother-in-law Bona di Savoia, after whom Isabel's daughter was named. Isabel had been close to Bianca since she was a young child – just six years old when Isabel arrived in Milan in 1489. They were cousins: Isabel's mother was Il Moro's sister.[5] With Galeazzo Sanseverino, Il Moro, his two young sons and brother Cardinal Ascanio *en route* for Austrian exile, Isabel of Aragon was Bianca's closest living relative. It is easier to imagine Isabel wishing to possess the *Sforziada* containing Leonardo's portrait of Bianca, rather than the earlier (Paris) volume portraying her husband as a dependent weakling.

Some commentators believe Galeazzo Sanseverino was the book's original recipient because it features his family arms. But it is doubtful that Isabel would have wished to own a volume conceived solely as a gift for the man she held complicit in her husband's death. The *Sforziada* also features Bianca's family arms – and her portrait. It may have been a gift to Bianca herself, or presented jointly to the newly-wedded couple.

There is another reason why possessing this *Sforziada* would have been significant to Isabel – or to anybody else. It was arguably the most prestigious incunabulum in existence: one of the largest books produced by the nascent printing industry; one of the tiny percentage to be printed on vellum; with a superb frontispiece by one of the finest illuminators of the age; and among only a handful of 15th century books to include a full-page portrait – by the greatest artist alive.

This biography of the founder of the Sforza dynasty was the *nec plus ultra* of family heirlooms, to rank with – if not above – any piece of regalia that Il Moro may have given Isabel.[6]

Isabel initially accepted Il Moro's offer and made plans to leave Milan at the start of September. Four galleys were prepared for her and her entourage in Genoa, and Count Caiazzo (Gianfrancesco Sanseverino) – whose brother-in-law Giovanni Adorno lived in Genoa – was assigned to escort her there.[7] Isabel moved out of her lodgings in the Corte Vecchia ... but was prevented from leaving Milan by the French.

On 5 September 1499 an edict was issued in the name of Louis XII stipulating that – pending an assessment of her situation – Isabel, her son and her daughters were free to go as they pleased, as long as they remained on Milanese soil (*che la illustrissima duchessa Isabella, fiolo et fiole possino star in Milan et andar dove li parerà, senza che li siano netadi altramente, et da questo particulare soa majestà concederà li termini oportuni*).[8]

This was a cagey move from the French – keen, at this early stage of their conquest, to appear magnanimous towards the popular Dowager Duchess and her son; but above all desperate to prevent Il Duchetto vanishing into thin air, to form a future rallying-point for Sforza Legitimists and/or anyone else (e.g. Venice or the Pope) keen to chase the French out of Italy. It was implied that any decision on the future of Isabel and her family would depend on Louis XII, who was about to set off for Milan from Lyon. To Isabel the edict offered a glimmer of hope that Louis XII might be prepared to give sympathetic consideration to her son's ducal rights.

At the same time, news reached Milan that various Il Moro supporters had been captured on their flight towards Austria, including one of Isabel's bitterest enemies: Ambrogio da Rosate, Il Moro's court physician (and astrologer), whom she believed responsible – in conjunction with Galeazzo Sanseverino – for the death of her husband in October 1494.

If Rosate were now to admit his guilt, implicating Il Moro in her husband's death, Isabel would have fresh grounds to press the rights of her son to Louis XII – and to appeal to Emperor Maximilian to withdraw support from Il Moro.

An inquiry into Gian Galeazzo's death was promptly launched under Pierantonio dal Verme[9] and Giovanni Borromeo (not perhaps the most impartial of assessors, given their families' hostility towards Il Moro). Rosate is said to have admitted poisoning Gian Galeazzo at Il Moro's behest, using a syrup.[10]

But the meeting between Isabel, her son and the French King proved a disaster. Louis XII had Il Duchetto detained and, in November, taken to France. In 1505, aged fourteen, he was made Abbot of Marmoutier, just across the Loire from Tours. He died there – officially of 'apoplexy' – on 29 December 1511, aged twenty.[11]

Isabel remained in Milan until the eve of Il Moro's return in February 1500 – then, like Leonardo da Vinci, decamped to Mantua. She and Leonardo were acquaintances of many years' standing.

The first theatrical *festa* which Leonardo is known to have organized in Sforza employ, *Il Paradiso*, was staged in Isabel's honour on 13 January 1490 – three days after Bianca had been betrothed to Galeazzo Sanseverino. (Astonishingly, *Il Paradiso* would be reprised at the Clos Lucé in Amboise, Leonardo's final home, in honour of François I on 19 June 1518 – Leonardo's 'last identifiable work.'[12])

Leonardo and Isabel must have met at court throughout the 1490s. In April 1497, shortly after the death of his wife Beatrice, Il Moro separated Isabel from her son by insisting she leave the Castello Sforzesco and move to the Corte Vecchia near the Duomo – to rooms located across the courtyard from Leonardo's own. A sheet in the *Codex Atlanticus* – dated 'first day of August 1499' – features sketches and notes 'for the bath-house of the Duchess,' which can only refer to Isabel of Aragon and a request to Leonardo for neighbourly help.

Leonardo was in Mantua between 14 December 1499, when he is last mentioned in Milan, and 13 March 1500, when he is mentioned in Venice.[13] Isabel left Milan on 1 February 1500 with her daughters Ippolita and Bona. She rode (or sailed down the River Lambro) to Piacenza with a retinue of thirty, but was refused entry to nearby Cremona for fear that her arrival would provoke an outbreak of popular fervour. She boated twelve miles along the Po to Torricella del Pizzo, writing to the Marquess of Mantua on February 3 to advise him of her impending arrival. First she planned to visit Antonia Gonzaga at Dosolo, a further thirty-five miles along the Po, before mooring at Borgoforte, ten miles south of Mantua, and completing the journey by land – requesting the Marquess send carriages for her suite and baggage.

Isabel probably arrived in Mantua on February 5, leaving on February 8. She may have met Leonardo there; the *Sforziada*, with its full-page profiled portrait by Leonardo, may have been with her.

Isabella d'Este – then 25, and six months pregnant with her first son[14] – was a vociferous admirer of Leonardo da Vinci, and pestered him for years afterwards to provide her with a painted version of the portrait he made during his visit. Although this portrait – in pencil and red, ochre and white chalk – was pricked for transfer, Leonardo shrugged her off.

In fact, Leonardo drew two portraits of Isabella – leaving one with his hostess (her husband later gave it away) and keeping one for himself, presumably the one that has been in the Louvre since 1860 (*right*). This portrait, at 61.0 × 46.5cm, is nearly twice as big as Bianca Sforza's – although Isabella's head takes up only one-third of the sheet compared to Bianca's one-half.

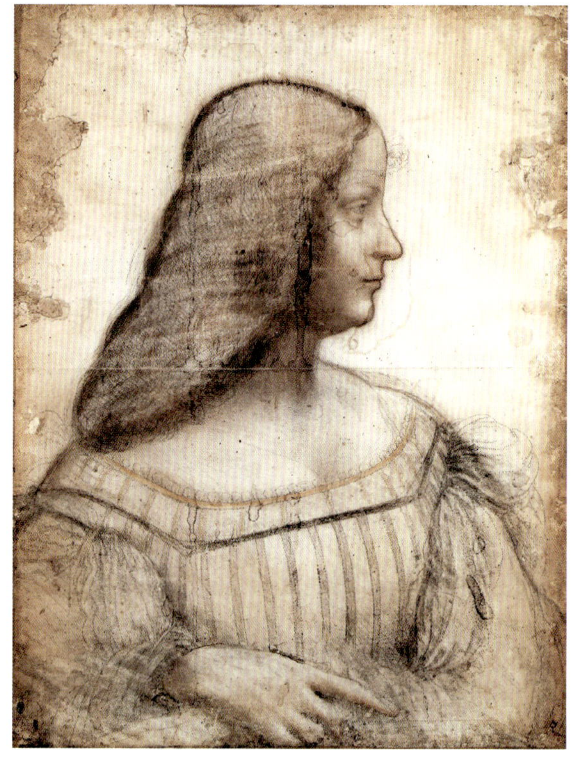

Like Bianca (and in contrast to other portraits of Isabella), she is wearing no jewellery. Isabella's head, like Bianca's, is in crisply outlined profile. But, unlike Bianca, Isabella's bust is shown four-fifths front-on – a combination that appears to have been pioneered in Sforza Milan by Bernardino de' Conti in his portrait of Il Duchetto dated 15 June 1496 (*see p.224*).

Isabel of Aragon left Mantua for Naples, travelling first to Bologna, 75 miles to the south, arriving on February 11. She was met by its strongman ruler Giovanni Bentivoglio and a large welcoming committee, and stayed several days. She must have reached Naples in March 1500, probably completing her journey by sea from Leghorn.[15]

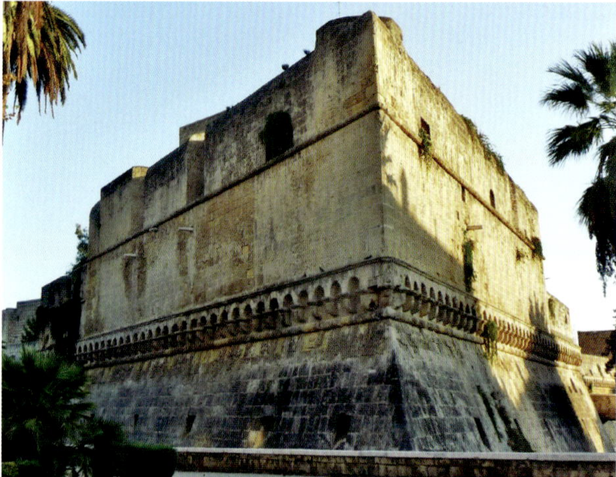

Isabel split her time between Naples and the nearby island of Ischia, where her daughter Ippolita died in January 1501. A few months later her uncle and host, King Federico, was ousted by a Franco-Spanish regional carve-up. Isabel, along with her seven-year-old daughter Bona and a number of once-prominent Milanese families (Lampugnani, Cusani, Meravigli), withdrew across the peninsular to the banks of the Adriatic, 180 miles away. To Il Moro's promised duchy: Bari.[16]

AUSTRIA

After being kissed goodbye by their father Il Moro in Brixen on 15 January 1500, and effectively orphaned, Massimilano and Francesco endured a turbulent youth.

On 25 April 1500, when news of Il Moro's capture reached Brixen, the boys were moved to Innsbruck along with what remained of their ducal treasure: around 60,000 ducats. That sum would have happily covered their living expenses for the next few years – had not Emperor Maximilian promptly confiscated it. Massimiliano and Francesco were to grow up in straitened circumstances, fobbed off for most of the time on Emperor Maximilian's estranged wife Bianca Maria, their much older cousin.

The boys left Brixen for Innsbruck with all their belongings. Could the final illuminated *Sforziada* have been among them?[17] It is possible that Il Moro or Galeazzo Sanseverino brought the volume with them from Milan in September 1499. But improbable. Their fight relied on speed, which meant travelling light. Baggage will have been confined to essentials – and anything that could be converted into cash. A family history book, even one adorned with a portrait by Leonardo da Vinci, was hardly a lucrative asset.

Massimiliano and Francesco were joined in Innsbruck in May 1501 by Bianca Maria's elder brother Ermes Sforza, Margrave of Tortona, who had been freed by the French in December 1500. He died in September 1503, probably of syphilis, and was buried in the Premonstratensian Abbey of Wilten to the south of the city.

To Emperor Maximilian the boys remained political assets. From time to time he wheeled them out to impress his German barons. In January 1502 the Governor of Regensburg, Reichshauptmann Sigismund von Rorbach, described them as *liebe hertzine kind, zuchtig und wolgezogen* ('dear, sweet children, shy and well brought-up').[18] They are variously recorded in Wels, Linz, Steiermark and Constance.

In 1508, after the death of Il Moro, the brothers were split up. Massimiliano, aged fifteen, was sent to Mechlin, to the court of Maximilian's daughter Margaret, Regent of the Habsburg Netherlands; in October 1511 he joined her Privy Council, a post which came with welcome remuneration.

Francesco, as a younger brother, was initially destined for the cloth – there was talk of his becoming a canon of Cologne Cathedral. He enrolled at the University of Vienna, to which the Sforzas claimed historic ties,[19] and where he was styled *Princeps Franciscus Sforzia Anglus* in university records. After the death of Empress Bianca Maria, in Innsbruck on 31 December 1510, only Francesco attended her funeral.

In July 1512 the Swiss, inspired by Cardinal Matthäus Schinner, Bishop of Sion (1465–1522), conquered Milan. Bianca Maria's half-brother Ottaviano Sforza (1477–c.1541), Bishop of Lodi, was installed as Governor, and Massimiliano summoned back to Innsbruck from Mechlin. He was described by the Venetian ambassador, who met him in Ulm on August 9, as of medium height with brown hair, dark eyes and an aquiline nose. Massimiliano reached Innsbruck on August 14 and was besieged by Milanese noblemen urging him to return to Lombardy as Duke. On September 15 he was in Trent, awaiting Cardinal Matthäus Lang (1469–1540), Bishop of Gürk and Emperor Maximilian's Italian representative. Their progress was slow, with Massimiliano suffering from bouts of malaria. On October 28 they were in Verona; on November 10 in Mantua, visiting Isabella d'Este, Massimiliano's aunt, who complained he had become thoroughly German. On November 16 he was in Cremona. It was not until December 29 that Massimiliano entered Milan and was hailed as Duke.

He cut an uninspiring figure. He had inherited his mother's taste for fine clothes and extravagance, and acquired a reputation for indolence that contrasted with his soberly attired, well-educated brother. He and Francesco met at the Certosa di Pavia on 27 July 1513 for the first time in five years. Massimiliano was jealous of his brainy sibling, accusing him of wanting to become Duke himself, and dispatched him to Rome a few months later as his envoy to the Vatican.

Pope Leo X suggested that Massimiliano marry Isabel of Aragon's daughter, Bona Sforza. To Isabel this seemed a perfect opportunity for her family to reassert its rights to the Duchy of Milan. That she should entertain the idea of her daughter marrying Il Moro's son suggests that she and Il Moro did not part in 1499 on such venomous terms as one might suppose. Isabel canvassed her cousin Isabella d'Este to support the marriage when they met in Naples in November 1514. It is not impossible that, as a token of cousinly goodwill, Massimiliano sent Bona the final illuminated *Sforziada*.

But the proposed wedding came to nothing. The death of Louis XII, on 1 January 1515, changed the political landscape. The French, under new king François I, returned to Italy, arriving unexpectedly over the southerly, undefended Maddelena Pass then spearing east at Milan. Their victory at the Battle of Marignano on September 14 compelled Massimiliano to abdicate. Like Il Duchetto, he was removed to France, where he pursued a life of relative ease, attached to the court, until his sudden death in 1530. Brother Francesco escaped to Trent with a band of Sforza die-hards to fight another day.[20]

POLAND

Bona Sforza, Isabel of Aragon's sole surviving daughter and, after 1511, only child, grew up in Bari and Naples, the vehicle of her mother's remaining ambition. She was already twenty when mooted as a possible bride to Duke Massimiliano Sforza. When that union fell through, her marital future acquired fresh urgency.

The solution came in the unlikely shape of a fifty-year-old Pole.

Zygmunt Jagiellon, unflatteringly known as Sigismund the Old, had succeeded as King of Poland and Grand Duke of Lithuania in 1506 – and ruled one of the largest realms in Europe. His twenty-year-old wife Barbara Zapolya died on 2 October 1515 without providing a male heir. Finding a new, fertile young bride was, for Sigismund, a dynastic priority. Bona's family background suggested she could fit the bill.

Their wedding by proxy was conducted by Jan Konarski, the seventy-year-old Bishop of Cracov, on 6 December 1517, at Castel Capuano in Naples. Then it was back across the peninsular to Manfredonia on the Adriatic, 70 miles up the coast from Bari. Bona departed on 3 February 1518 accompanied by a 350-strong retinue[21] under veteran *condottiero* Prospero Colonna[22] – Isabel of Aragon's rumoured lover[23] – and, possibly, by the final illuminated *Sforziada* containing Leonardo's portrait of her mother's cousin.

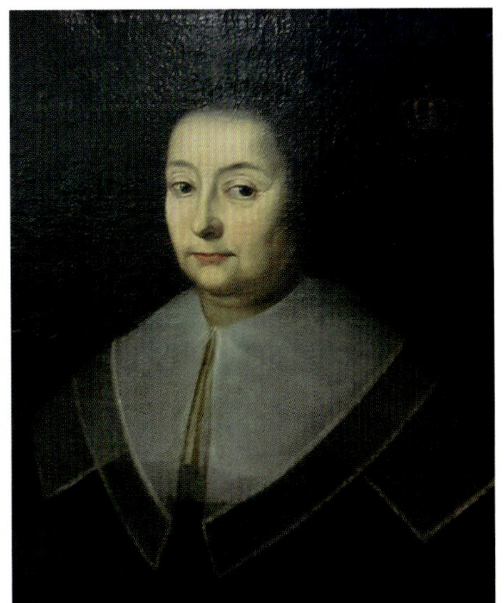

Bona's fleet landed at the Habsburg port of Rijeka (now Fiume in Croatia). Her journey northeast to Cracov progressed via Ljubljana, Maribor, Graz, Vienna (March 19), Olomouc (March 29) and Auschwitz (April 11).

She was joined *en route* by the Archbishop of Milan, Ippolito d'Este, appointed to the post by his brother-in-law Il Moro back in 1497 when just eighteen, and also in charge of the wealthy archbishopric of Esztergom in Hungary. It cannot be ruled out that Cardinal d'Este brought the final illuminated *Sforziada* with him as a wedding gift:[24] in 1499, just before Il Moro's flight to Tyrol, various precious Sforza belongings had been dispatched to Ferrara for safekeeping under Duke Ercole d'Este, Ippolito's father.

Bona arrived in Cracov on 15 April 1518 and was crowned Queen of Poland three days later, wearing a blue satin dress embroidered with gold. The celebrations lasted for over a week, whereupon Prospero Colonna departed for Naples – this time travelling via Hungary, probably at Cardinal d'Este's invitation.

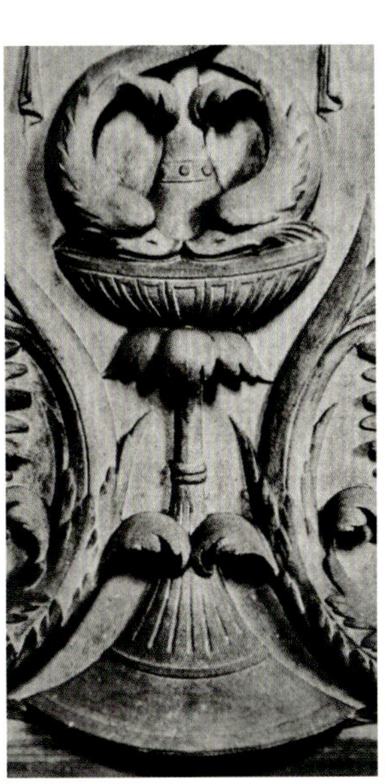

Over the next nine years Bona (*above left*) bore Sigismund six children: Izabela (1519), Zygmunt August (1520), Zofia (1522), Anna (1523), Katarzyna (1526) and Olbracht (1527). Four became monarchs.

This spate of births coincided with one of the finest Renaissance constructions north of the Alps: the Sigismund Chapel (*Zygmuntowska*) in Cracov's Wawel Cathedral, commissioned by Sigismund the Old as a family mausoleum.

Renaissance taste had been brought to Poland by Italian craftsmen around 1500, and the decorative motifs they employed on Sigismund's new, golden-domed chapel would not have looked out of place in Rome, Florence or Milan.

Several of these sculpted motifs – consciously or not – echo Birago's illuminations in the Polish *Sforziada*. One bowl (*see left*) has gadrooned sides and a leafy support that recall the font in Birago's frontispiece, and stands on a stylized triangular base whose form uncannily resembles Il Moro's *scopetta*.

Bona quoted her family viper relentlessly – on coins,[25] tiles and picture-frames, and in books. So did the two children who succeeded her on the Polish throne: Zygmunt August,[26] who reigned as Sigismund II from 1548–72; and Anna, who dutifully remained by her mother's side until a late political marriage propelled her to the throne in 1575.

BONA SFORZA'S SON: ZYGMUNT AUGUST

Zygmunt August became Grand Duke of Lithuania in 1544, and succeeded Sigismund the Old as King of Poland in 1548. His relationship with his Italian mother was so tempestuous that some commentators think it inconceivable that she could have bequeathed him the *Sforziada*, were it in her possession.[27] Bona quit Cracov for Warsaw immediately after Zygmunt August succeeded her husband to the Polish throne: she deplored his pro-Calvinist leanings and violently disapproved of his second marriage, to Barbara Radziwiłł, in 1551. In 1556 Bona left Poland and – after tortuous negotiations with the *Sejm* (parliament) about what she was entitled to take – returned to Bari, where she died in November 1557, reportedly poisoned at the behest of King Philip II of Spain.[28]

Zygmunt August's Library would eventually surpass 4,000 volumes, becoming one of the most extensive in Europe. His books were bound in brown calf and impressed (on the front) with the title and royal arms and (on the back) the mention *SIGISMUND AUGUSTI REGIS POLONIAE MONUMENTUM*. In 1565 Zygmunt August transferred his library for safekeeping to the Castle of Tykocin, halfway between Warsaw and Vilnius and 8 miles southwest of Knyszyn, the country retreat where Zygmunt August established Europe's first Arabian stud, stabled 3,000 horses and went hunting for weeks on end.

1565 also saw Zygmunt August hire a new Chancellery Secretary armed with a letter of commendation from the Venetian Senate: a Law graduate from the University of Padua named Jan Zamoyski (1542–1605), who hailed from a family of minor nobility in southeast Poland, and had studied in Paris and Strasbourg before enrolling at Padua, where he acquired his first book – Guillaume Budé's *Annotationes* (1508) – on 20 June 1561, sixty-five years to the day after Bianca Sforza wed Galeazzo Sanseverino.

In 1569 – the year the Union of Lublin created the Poland-Lithuania Commonwealth – Zygmunt August commissioned Zamoyski to reorganize the Royal Archives. In 1571 Zamoyski cemented his political emergence by marrying Anna Ossolińską, niece of the Castellan of Sandomierz, one of the largest provinces of southern Poland.

Zygmunt August died in Knyszyn in 1572, last male ruler of the Jagiellonian Dynasty. To this day the Zamoyski Library (now part of the Polish National Library in Warsaw) contains 95 volumes once owned by Zygmunt August, with no indication as to whether they were appropriated by Jan Zamoyski or presented to him by the King. Was the *Sforziada* among them?

Jan Zamoyski appears to have enjoyed particularly close ties with King Zygmunt August. He commissioned a sarcophagus for the King's entrails, which remained in Knyszyn until 1824, and was made Lord of Knyszyn in 1574 by Zygmunt August's successor, the Frenchman Henri de Valois – whose election by the *Sejm* had been facilitated by Zamoyski's eloquent advocacy.

When Henri suddenly abandoned Poland in 1575 to become King Henri III of France, the Polish throne again fell vacant – with the successful candidate expected to marry Bona Sforza's 52-year-old daughter Anna. Zamoyski successfully championed the cause of Stefan Batory, Prince of Transylvania (and a fellow Padua *alumnus*). On 1 May 1576, in Cracov, Batory was crowned King of Poland, married Anna and made Jan Zamoyski Vice-Chancellor.

BONA SFORZA'S DAUGHTER: ANNA

Anna's 1576 coronation portrait[29] by Marcin Kober (*below right*) offers a major piece of evidence along the *Sforziada* mystery trail. She is depicted with long blond hair framing a high-domed forehead topped by an enormous crown, holding an orb and sceptre. Her gold-embroidered white robe trails to the floor.

Dangling from a chain, at the level of her right ankle, is a silver *scopetta* (*below left*) – referred to as a *scapula* in the Latin inscription beneath the portrait.

This *scapula* recalls the *scopetta* made of pearls and precious stones, worn as a hair brooch by Il Moro's niece Bianca Maria in her 1493 wedding portrait by Ambrogio de Predis (*left*). It also resembles the silver *scopetta* on Il Moro's chest (alongside his ducal chain) in his Giovio portrait in the Uffizi (*below*).

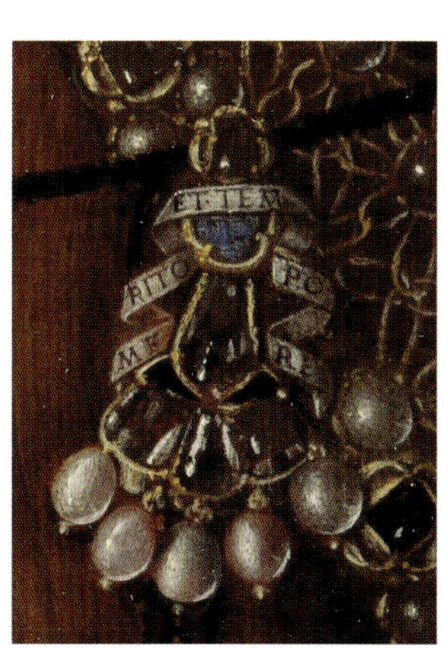

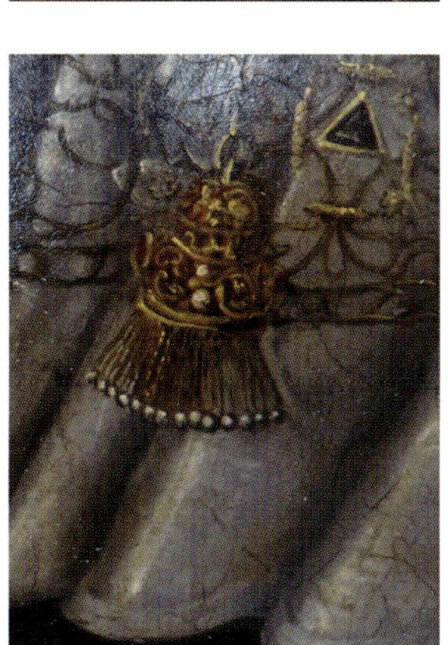

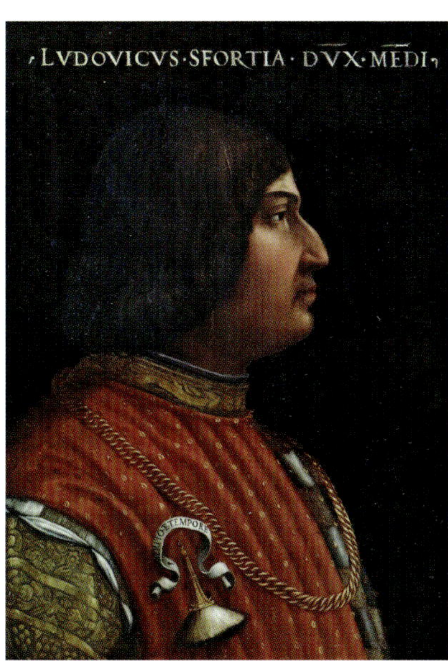

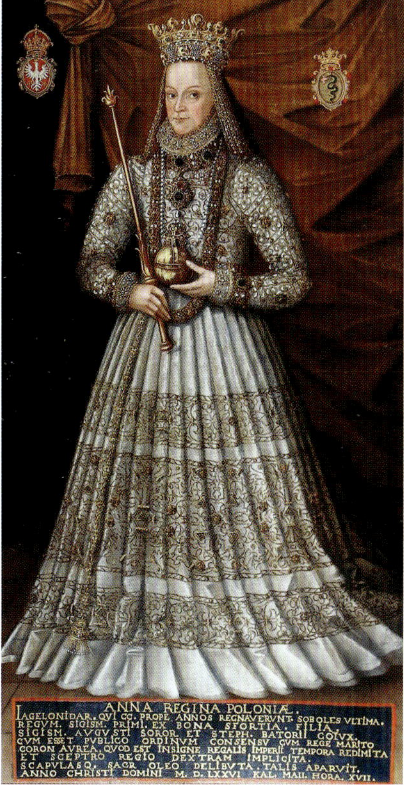

The presence in Poland of Il Moro's personal emblem suggests it may have been a gift from Il Moro to his niece, Isabel of Aragon. Given to her at their parting meeting? When he also gave her the Duchy of Bari? And the *Sforziada*?[30]

The career of Jan Zamoyski thrived under Stefan and Anna. On 1 March 1578 he was made Crown Chancellor. On 11 August 1581 he was created *Hetman Wielki* (Commander-in-Chief) after a successful military campaign against Ivan the Terrible.

On 29 December 1577 Zamoyski had married for a second time, to Krystyna Radziwiłłona – whose late father had been Hetman and Chancellor of Lithuania, and cousin to Zygmunt August's ill-fated bride Barbara. Like Zamyoski's first wife Anna, Krystyna died tragically young – on 28 February 1580, aged nineteen.

On 12 June 1583 Zamoyski married for a third time, to King Stefan's fourteen-year-old niece Gryzelda. Some speculate he may have received the *Sforziada* from Queen Anna on this occasion.[31] An Army Commander marrying into the family of the Head of State: there was something of the Galeazzo Sanseverino (or Francesco Sforza) about Jan Zamoyski. Did the ageing, childless Queen offer the *Sforziada* to him as a trusted political supporter whose humanist, Renaissance and Italophile leanings qualified him as a worthy recipient of a precious family heirloom?

There was little love lost, or ever present, between Anna and Stefan Batory, who declined to sleep with her and, keen to ensure an heir, eventually mooted the politically unacceptable idea of divorce. Stefan no doubt expected to outlive his wife, who was ten years older, then re-marry and found a family. But he died first – ten years before she did.

His succession was disputed by Habsburg Archduke Maximilian III and Queen Anna's nephew, Sigismund Vasa of Sweden. In January 1588 Jan Zamoyski defeated Maximilian at the Battle of Byczyna, in southwest Poland, and hauled him back to Zamość as prisoner. In 1589 Zamoyski was rewarded with the title of hereditary count.

Also in 1589 Dowager Queen Anna commissioned a monumental tomb (*opposite*), in honour of her mother Bona Sforza, for Bari's great pilgrim Basilica di San Nicola – having successfully petitioned Pope Sixtus V to allow her mother's remains to be transferred there from Bari Cathedral.

The displacement was carried out in solemn pomp on 15 May 1589, and Bona's corpse laid to rest behind the altar (echoes here of the position of Bianca's tomb in Santa Maria delle Grazie). The monument, by Andrea Sarti da Carrara, and his assistants Francesco Zaccarelli and Ciccardo Bernucci,[32] comprises five imposing marble figures: a kneeling Bona flanked by two alcoved bishops (St Casimir of Lithuania and St Stanislas of Poland) above two reclining maidens holding armorial shields. It was completed in 1593, the year that marked the one-hundredth anniversary of the high-point of the Sforza dynasty: the elevation of Bona Sforza's aunt, Bianca Maria, to the status of Holy Roman Empress.

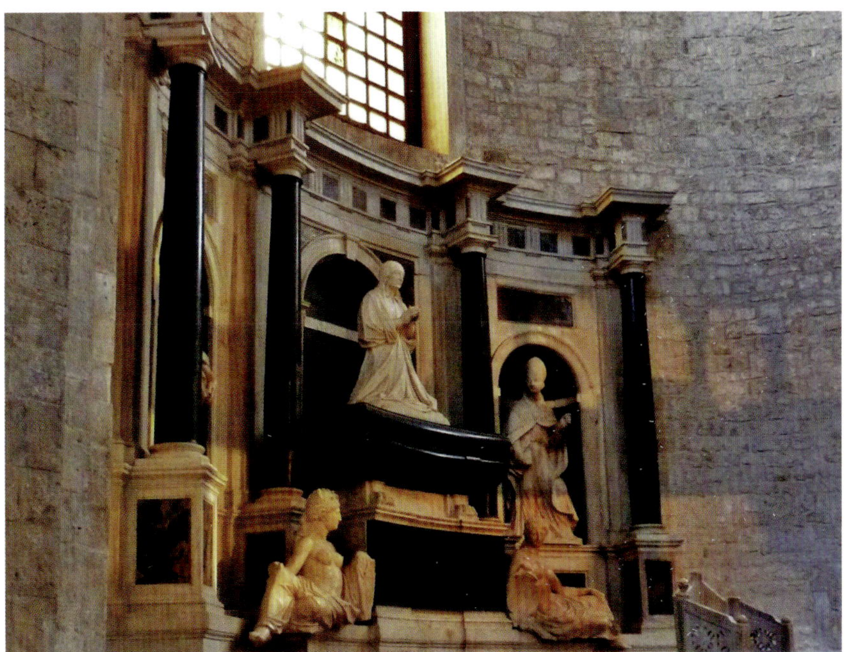

On 5 May 1594 Anna commissioned the Florentine Santi Gucci – who had earlier sculpted monuments to herself and her brother Zygmunt August in the adjacent Sigismund Chapel – to carve the tomb of King Stefan in the Vasa Chapel of Cracov's Wawel Cathedral. Work was completed in Summer 1595.

Anna died on 9 September 1596, known to Poles as *Last Of The Jagiellonians*. She was also, effectively, the Last Of The Sforzas.

ZAMOŚĆ

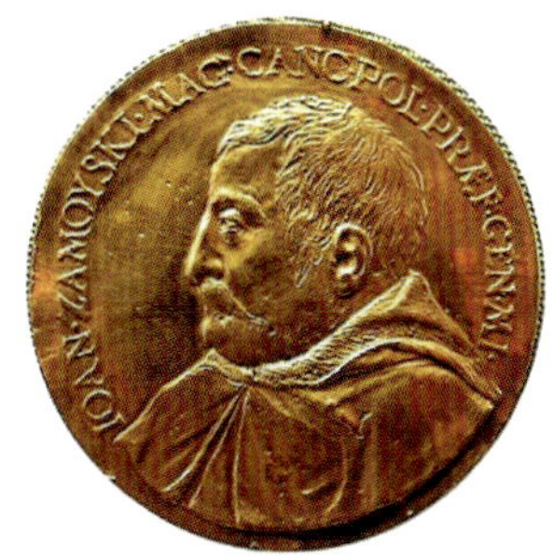

It was not until 1589, six years after her marriage to Jan Zamoyski, that Anna's niece Gryzelda Batory fell pregnant. The daughter was still-born. In March 1590 Gryzelda gave birth to another daughter, prematurely. She died soon afterwards, aged twenty. The daughter, named *Anna*, died two weeks later.

By 1590 Jan Zamoyski (*left*) was thrice married without an heir. He ruled over a fiefdom 17,000 km^2 in size: almost as big as modern-day Wales (or as the Duchy of Milan in the time of Il Moro). In the words of 20th century Polish historian Zdzisław Spieralski, 'no one after him in Poland – kings included – ever wielded so much power.'[33]

A decade earlier, in 1580, Jan Zamoyski had drawn up plans with Bernardo Morando, an architect from Padua, to erect a town from scratch in his hereditary heartland of southeast Poland, located on the vibrant commercial route from Lvov to Lublin – ultimately linking the Black Sea to the Baltic. With its grid-patterned streets and arcaded main square, enclosed behind colossal brick walls, Zamość (*see p.284*) constitutes one of the best-preserved examples of the Renaissance *città ideale* and is now a UNESCO World Heritage site.

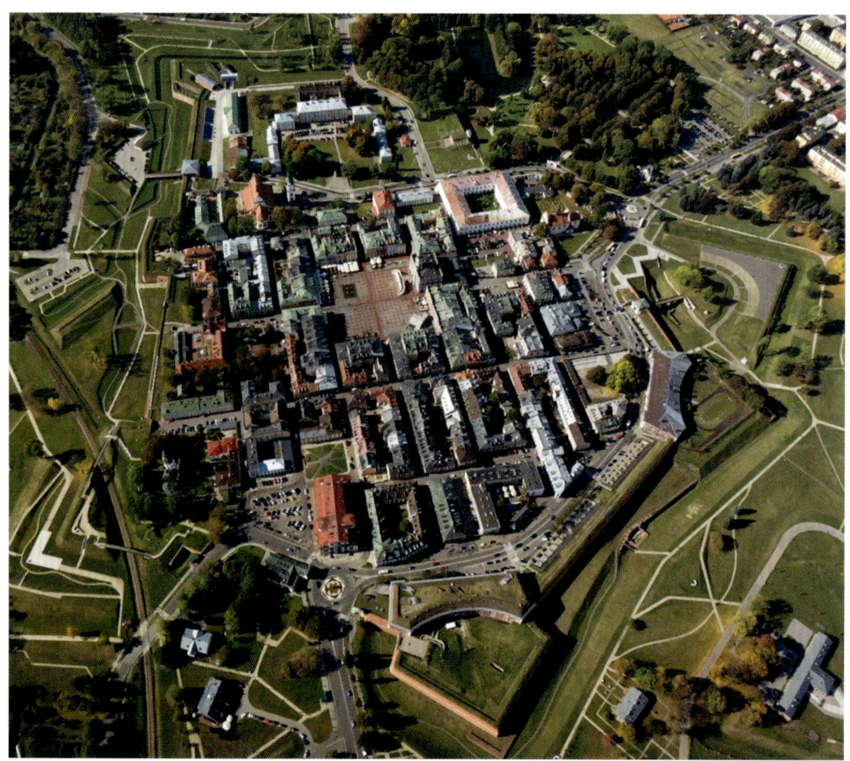

In 1592 Jan Zamoyski married for a fourth time, to Barbara Tarnowska, daughter of the Castellan of Sandomierz. On 1 April 1594 he at last received a son and heir, named Tomasz. That same year, armed with a papal bull of approval from Clement VII dated October 29, he founded an *Akademia* in Zamość (*see below*) – inspired by the academy created in Strasbourg by Johannes Sturm in 1538, where Zamoyski had studied around 1560. Zamoyski was intent on making his own town one of the most powerful seats of learning in Central Europe: his Academy was only the third (and first private) institution of higher education in Poland, after Cracov (1364) and Poznan (1519). It initially had three departments – Law, Medicine and the Liberal Arts – and seven professors. The number of students would climb from around 70 in 1600 to 120 in 1640.

As well as a successful warlord and astute political operator, Zamoyski was a scholar – in the words of Stanisław Łępicki, 'one of those rare men whom the fates allow to spend their lives with a sword in one hand and a book in the other.'[34] There are similarities with fellow-dynasty founder Francesco Sforza – perhaps a Zamoyski rôle model; a luxury edition of Francesco's biography may well have been a prized Zamoyski possession. A 1617 copperplate engraving in honour of the ILLUSTRISSIMUM ET EXCELLENTISSIMUM DOMINUM shows Zamyoski advancing on horseback through a triumphal arch in

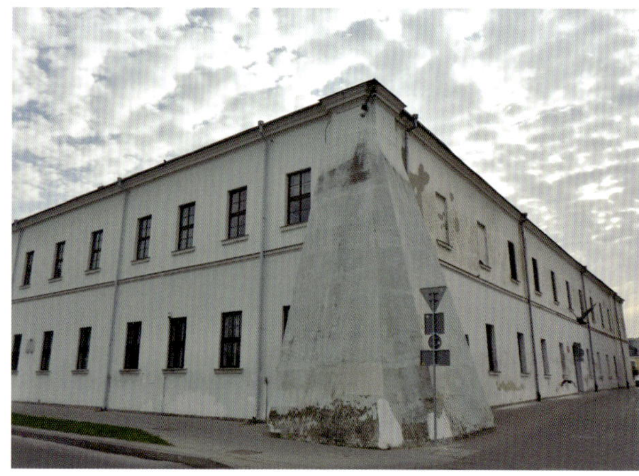

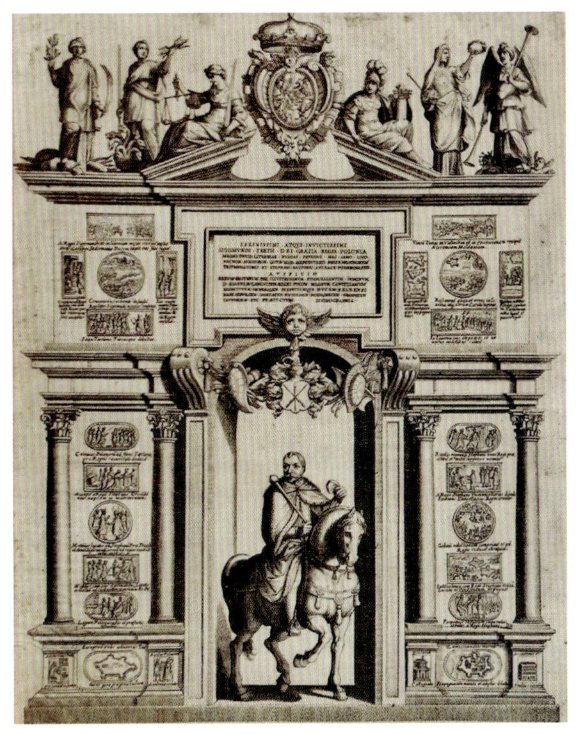

a manner that brings to mind Leonardo's aborted monument to Francesco Sforza.

Zamoyski's books were not kept in his Academy but in his muscular, large-towered château at one end of Zamość, in chests in a room that also housed his archives and served as his treasury. It was only after Zamoyski's death that eight cabinets were made to display his books in more traditional fashion.[35]

Zamoyski pursued his bibliophile interests even more actively after retiring to Zamość in 1602. In 1603 he became the first foreign statesman to write to Thomas James, Keeper of the newly-opened Bodleian Library in Oxford (requesting copies of the title-pages of works by Cicero).

Zamoyski also hired agents in Italy to acquire Renaissance artworks. Prominent among these was the Capponi family[36] who, in Venice in 1604, secured two paintings by Domenico Tintoretto (son of the great Jacopo) for Zamość's grand new Catholic church. The *Capponi* name has been conjured with before: in conjunction with the Uffizi *Sforziada* and its likely ownership by Cardinal Luigi Capponi and Marchese Alessandro Gregorio Capponi in the 17th and 18th centuries. It is a strange coincidence to come across the Capponi name in an earlier Polish context. It cannot be discounted that they or other agents acquired the *Sforziada* for Zamoyski in Italy.[37]

Jan Zamoyski died on 8 June 1605. His black tombstone in Zamość Cathedral is framed with military trophies that would not look out of place in a *Sforziada* frontispiece.

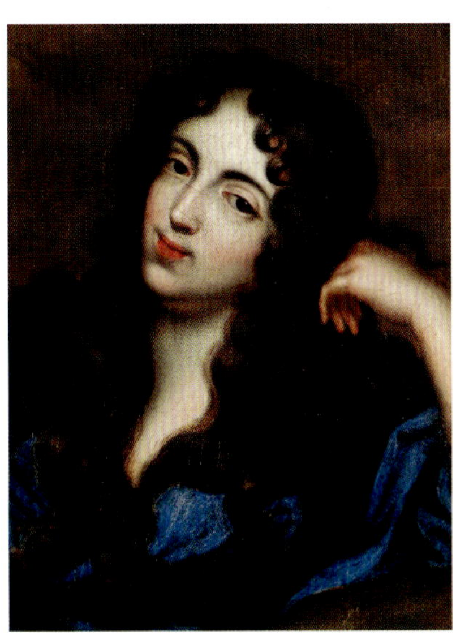

ANON.
MARIA KAZIMIERA (DETAIL)
WAWEL CASTLE, CRACOV

He was succeeded as Count by his eleven-year-old son Tomasz, who grew up to become Polish Chancellor in turn, under Bona Sforza's great-grandson Władysław IV. Tomasz occupied the post for just three years before his death in 1638, at the age of 43. He was succeeded as Count by his ten-year-old son, another Jan – later known as *Sobiepan* ('the Self-Minded') to distinguish him from his namesake grandfather.

In 1658 Jan Sobiepan married Marie-Casimire Louise da La Grange d'Arquien (1641–1716), whose life was baroque even by 17th century standards. She was born in Paris, the second daughter of impoverished Burgundian aristocrats. Her mother had been governess to Marie-Louise Gonzaga (1611–67) – great-great-granddaughter of Bianca Sforza's Leonardo-loving step-aunt, Isabella d'Este.

Marie-Louise adopted little Marie-Casimire as her own and took her to Poland with her when she married Władysław IV in Warsaw on 10 March 1646, becoming Queen Ludwika Maria.[38] Władysław IV died in 1648, but Queen Ludwika Maria kept her throne by remarrying a year later – to Władysław's younger half-brother, Jan Kazimierz.

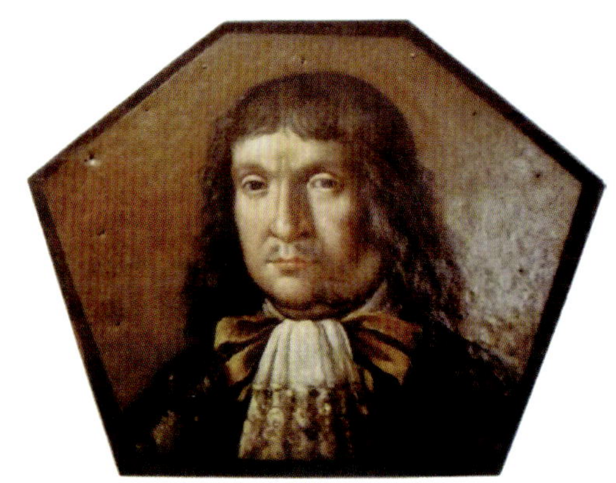

Young Marie-Casimire learnt Polish and served as a lady-in-waiting at the court of Warsaw before her social-climbing marriage to Jan Sobiepan (*right*). She was sixteen. Between 1659 and 1664 she bore him three daughters and a son. None survived infancy. When Jan Sobiepan died in 1665 without a direct heir, the senior Zamoyski line became extinct. The title of Count fell into abeyance, prompting a family feud that dragged on for years.

Jan Sobiepan's eldest sister Gryzelda, who also lived in Zamość, was keen to prevent his estate and possessions from falling into the hands of Marie-Casimire – and fought to advance the claims of her son Michał Korybut (born 1540) to succeed as Count. Michał Korybut attended university in Prague then spent time at the courts of Dresden and Vienna before following in the footsteps of his late father, Jeremi Wiśniowiecki, by becoming a soldier and taking part in the Ukrainian Campaign of 1663.

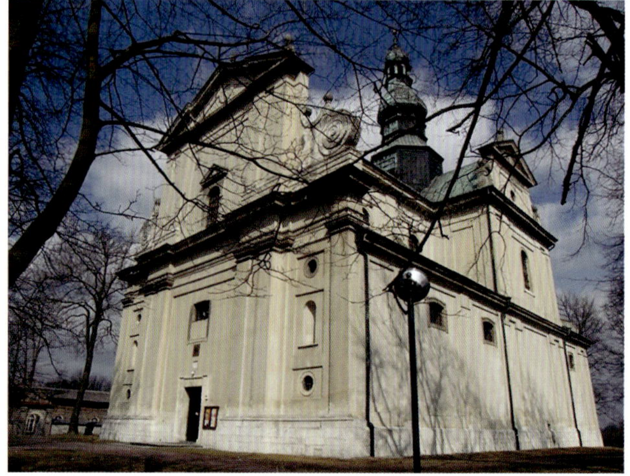

Sobiepan's second sister, Joanna Barbara, had died in 1553 but her son Stanisław Koniecpolski (*c.*1643–82) also clamoured for a share of the spoils. In fact, Koniecpolski did more than clamour: he made off with some of Jan Sobiepan's books and the family archives. The latter were only rediscovered in 1837 in the town of Koniecpol, home to Koniecpolski's family seat, 150 miles west of Zamość – stashed away in the tower of its magnificent baroque church (*right*), built in the 1630s by Stanisław's namesake grandfather, Grand Hetman from 1618–46 and one of Jan Sobiepan's predecessors as Palatine of Sandomierz.

Rather than linger in Zamość to fight for her inheritance, Marie-Casimire lost no time in remarrying. Sobiepan's reputation for booze and domestic violence may explain why he was not six feet under[39] before his widow wedded the dashing military commander Jan Sobieski (whose father Jakub, Castellan of Cracov, had studied at Zamość Academy). Their passionate correspondence (published in 1859) has helped their marriage become the stuff of romantic legend, with Marie-Casimire immortalized for generations of Polish schoolchildren as *Marysieńka* (Sobieski's pet name for her).

Things were just as chaotic in Poland as a whole as they were in Zamość. Poland had been decimated by the Swedish invasion of 1655–60, known as The Deluge. The reign of King Jan Kazimierz had proved a disaster. He abdicated on 16 September 1668, a year after the death of his Queen Ludwika Maria, and promptly departed for Paris, where he became Abbot of St Germain-des-Prés.[40]

A new king was not elected until June 1669: Sobiepan's young nephew Michał Korybut – a compromise anti-French candidate whom the nobility expected to manipulate. Her ambition sated, Michał's mother Gryzelda patched up her quarrel with Marie-Casimire. The dispute over Sobiepan's inheritance, however, would only be resolved after the early deaths of both Gryzelda and her son.

Gryzelda died in Zamość on 17 April 1672, aged 48.[41] King Michał Korybut died on 10 November 1673, aged just 33, reportedly choking to death on a cucumber. He was succeeded, on 19 May 1674, by Jan Sobieski. Marie-Casimire became Queen of Poland.[42]

The *Sejm* ordered Stanisław Koniecpolski to return the Zamoyski books he had 'borrowed.' Jan Sobieski ended Zamoyski shenanigans by appointing a new Count: 37-year-old Marcin, head of the 'junior line' of the House of Zamoyski. A microscopic look at the Zamoyski family tree reveals just how junior: the great-great-grandfathers of Marcin and Jan Sobiepan were cousins. Marcin and Jan Sobiepan's common ancestor, Tomasz Łazin, lived in the Quattrocento.

Marcin would amply justify his call from obscurity. Seven generations – and a dozen descendants – would succeed him as Counts Zamoyski until the Communists extinguished the title in 1946.

The decade-long interregnum that followed the death of Jan Sobiepan was not without consequence for the final illuminated *Sforziada*.

In 1669–70 Academy Chancellor Bazyli Rudomicz reorganized the Zamoyski library into eight sections: *Theology, Law, Medicine, Philosophy, History, Rhetoric, Mathematics* and *Poetry* (*with Grammar*). In 1674 the library was transferred from the Château and merged with that of the Academy – in delayed accordance with Jan Sobiepan's will and testament.

Marcin Zamoyski (born 1637) was a confirmed bachelor when inducted as new Count in 1676. He swiftly remedied that by marrying Anna Franciszka Gnińska and siring five children over the next ten years. But, when he died in 1689, the new Count of Zamość was again a ten-year-old boy: his eldest son Tomasz, who fathered only girls. He was succeeded by his younger brother Michał Zdzisław, who had first three daughters, then three sons. All three became Count.

THE ZAMOYSKI–CZARTORYSKI ALLIANCE

Michał's eldest son, Tomasz Antoni, was Count from 1735–51. He was succeeded by his teenage son Klemens, who married Konstancja Czartoryska in 1763. The history of the book-loving Zamoyskis and art-loving Czartoryskis would henceforth be enduringly intertwined.

Klemens died without issue in 1767, aged just 29. In 1768 his widow Konstancja married his 52-year-old *uncle*, Andrzej – recent Polish Chancellor (1764–67) and future author of a blueprint for political reform known as the *Zamoyski Code* (not the runaway success it sounds – it was never implemented). The title of Count, meanwhile, reverted to Andrzej's elder brother Jan Jakub. During the First Partition of Poland, in 1772, Zamość and its Academy were assigned to Austrian control; the *Sforziada* was mentioned in a new inventory of the Academy Library drawn up in 1776.

After drinking and gambling his way through the family fortune Jan Jakub was forced to resign as Count – replaced in 1780 by his brother Andrzej, who died in 1792 and was succeeded by his two sons – Alexander August, who died in 1800, then Stanisław Kostka.

On 20 May 1798 Stanisław Kostka had married Zofia Czartoryska at Puławy, the Czartoryski country-seat 75 miles northwest of Zamość. That same day Zofia's mother, Izabela Fleming, laid the foundation-stone of a colonnaded 'Temple of Sybil' (*below*) aping Rome's Temple of Vesta: the first home of the celebrated Czartoryski Museum, which survives (in Cracov) to this day.

In 1799 Stanisław Kostka and Zofia met her eldest brother, Adam Jerzy Czartoryski, in Vienna before he departed for Italy as Russian Envoy to the courts of Savoy and Naples.

Adam Jerzy enjoyed, and sketched, the sights of Italy during his unhectic assignment before being urgently summoned back to St Petersburg at the end of March 1801 after the assassination of Tsar Paul I. He was fêted *en route* at the Pitti Palace in Florence by Napoleon's brother-in-law Joachim Murat – who probably presented him with the two paintings he gifted to his mother's new museum when he stopped off in Puławy on his way back to Russia: Raphael's *Portrait of a Young Man* (now lost) and Leonardo da Vinci's *Lady with an Ermine*.[43]

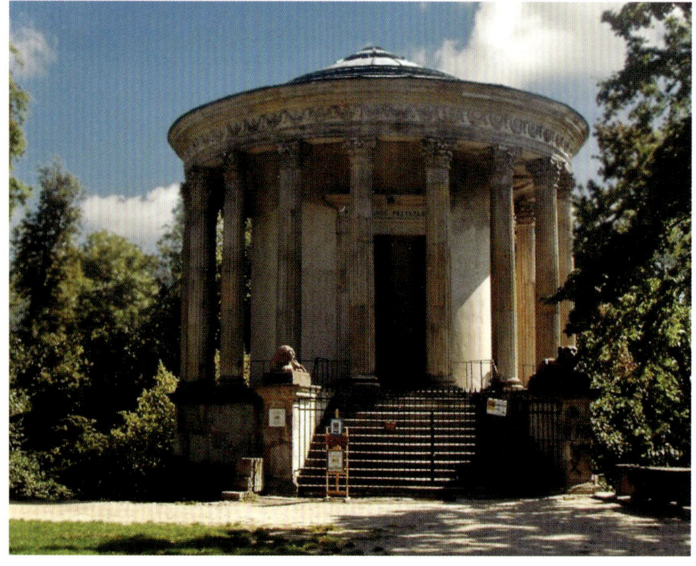

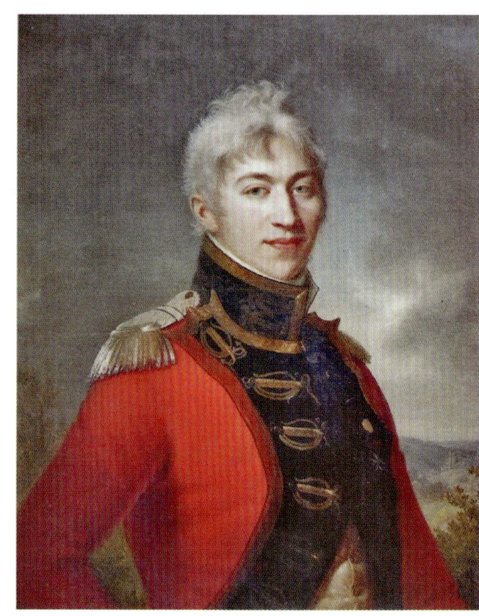

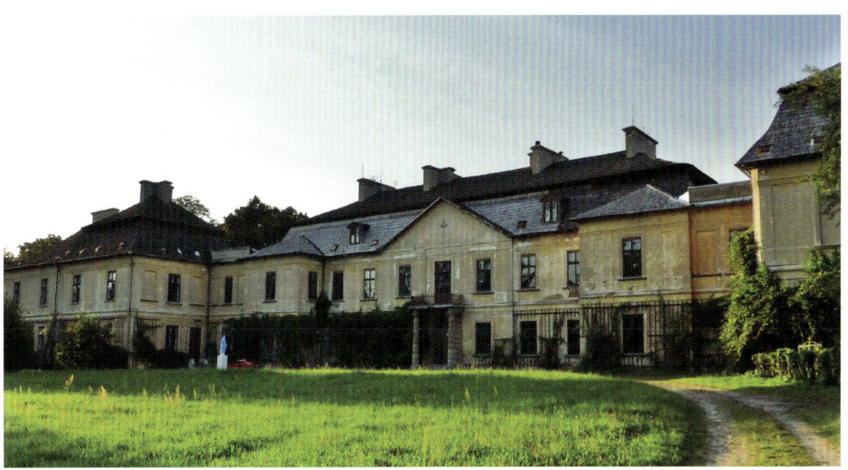

In 1800, soon after becoming Count, Stanisław Kostka set about recouping the family library from the Academy and putting it in order. An inventory listed 4,533 books and 456 manuscripts. He also dreamed of transforming the family château in Zamość into a mini-Versailles, commissioning Napoleon's favourite architects, Charles Percier and Pierre Fontaine, to draw up plans.[44] These were scuppered by lack of money and the turbulent political situation, with Austrian troops billeted permanently in the town; in 1809 Zamość was stormed by Prince Józef Poniatowski and integrated into the Duchy of Warsaw. Stanisław Kostka relocated the family seat to Klemensów (*above*),[45] twelve miles to the west: a country-house built in the mid-18th century (and named after his mother's first husband) in the heart of a hilly, wooded park landscaped in English Romantic style.

In 1811 Stanisław Kostka and Zofia acquired a residence in Warsaw: the Blue Palace, formerly owned by Zofia's parents. The Zamoyski Library was moved here, and many books – though not the *Sforziada* – sumptuously rebound for the occasion.

On 25 September 1817 Stanisław Kostka's niece, Anna Zofia Sapieha, married the 47-year-old Adam Jerzy Czartoryski at the Potocki Palace in Radzyń (40 miles northeast of Puławy). A few months later Adam Jerzy acquired the library of the late Tadeusz Czacki (1765–1813) – author, book-lover, art collector and prominent figure of the Polish Enlightenment. The library was housed in Poryck (now Pavlivka in Ukraine, 60 miles east of Zamość). Its highlight was a 15th century 354*ff* manuscript of the *Golden Legend* (*Legenda Aurea*) by Jacobus de Voragine, with illuminations by ... Gianpietro Birago.[46]

Czacki had been made regional Inspector of Schools by Adam Jerzy's father, Adam Kazimierz Czartoryski, and visited Zamość at least twice. In December 1784, after the Academy had been closed down, Czacki noted in dismay that its books had been deposited in the basement and were not properly secured. In 1798 he recorded borrowing some volumes from the Academy. As an erudite bibliophile clearly *au fait* with the Zamoyski book collection, Czacki will have been well placed to remark upon the similarities between the *Sforziada* frontispiece and the illustrations in his own *Golden Legend* – and may have mentioned them to Adam Jerzy Czartoryski.

What was a second Birago book doing in Poland? The *ex-libris* (printed by one Hieronim Wietor) in this *Golden Legend* reveals that it was owned by Krzysztof Szydłowiecki (1467–1532),[47] Polish Chancellor under Sigismund the Old and part of the delegation dispatched to usher Bona Sforza on to Polish soil at Olomouc in March 1518.

This *Golden Legend* is now, like the *Sforziada,* in the Polish National Library[48] – but, in a dramatic twist, it was bequeathed not by the Czartoryskis … but by the Zamoyskis. Maybe Adam Jerzy Czartoryski gifted it to his brother-in-law. Maybe Stanisław Kostka bought it from him. Perhaps they swapped: one Golden Legend for one Golden Girl. Given that Birago books are as rare as Leonardo pictures, to find two in the same Polish collection is an almighty coincidence. If the Zamoyskis had two Biragos, maybe the Czartoryskis had two Leonardos. First Cecilia Gallerani, then Bianca Sforza?

A new Zamyoski Library building was erected next to the Blue Palace in 1820. It was doomed almost from the start. Its roof collapsed in 1846, with no funds available to undertake repairs; the Library stayed closed till 1868. Many of its books and artworks disappeared in the disorderly interim.

THE *EMIGRACIJA*

The careers of the two brothers-in-law, Adam Jerzy Czartoryski and Stanisław Kostka Zamoyski, evolved in dramatic contrast after Poland's 1830 Uprising against Russian rule.

Despite his earlier years in Russian service, Adam Jerzy played a leading anti-Tsarist rôle during the Uprising – initially as President of the Provisional Government, then as Head of the Supreme Council and moving light behind an independent confederation of Poland's southern provinces. When the Uprising was crushed he was sentenced to death and fled to London. He never set foot on Polish soil again.

Stanisław Kostka, after serving as President of the Senate of the Kingdom of Poland, was held hostage in St Petersburg after the Uprising and only allowed to leave Russia in 1832. He was compelled to abandon his title and estates to his eldest son Konstanty and forced into permanent exile, spent mainly in Vienna (in the Palais Pálffy opposite the Hofburg).

In Autumn 1833 his wife Zofia settled in Florence and rented the prestigious 15th century Villa Careggi just outside the city: the house where Cosimo and Lorenzo de' Medici lived and died, and the seat of Ficino's Platonic Academy. Zofia was renowned for her charity work and musicianship (she composed a celebrated song about the life of Jan Zamoyski), swiftly becoming an eminent figure in the city's Polish community. In May 1835 she was diagnosed with uterine cancer and died at Villa Careggi on 27 February 1837. Her funeral was held on March 4 in the high-society church of Santissima Annunziata – in

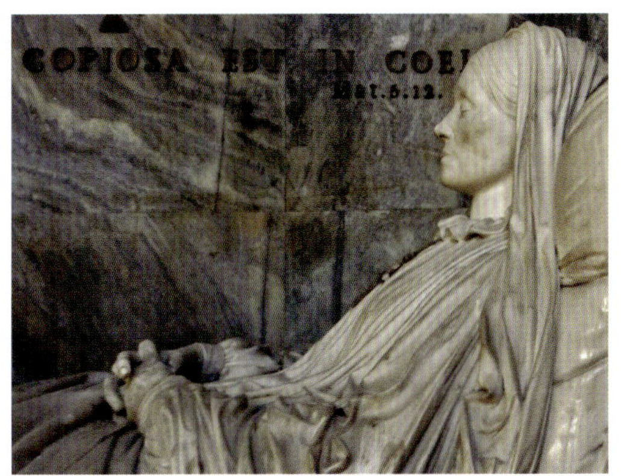

whose cloisters Leonardo da Vinci had lived in 1500 – and she was buried in Santa Croce, the Florentine pantheon, across the nave from Michelangelo, in an exquisite tomb (*left*) carved by Lorenzo Bartolini (1777–1850).

Did Zofia bring the portrait of Bianca Sforza with her from Poland? There is no trace of her will and testament in the Florence municipal archives. Coincidentally or not, it was in Florence that the portrait would resurface a century later.

Adam Jerzy Czartoryski, meanwhile, was one of many thousands of Poles who took part in the *Wielka Emigracja* (Great Emigration) to France. He spent the last 27 years of his life in and around Paris, arriving in 1834.

Initially he lived close to the Champs-Elysées, moving in 1843 to the stylish 17th century Hôtel Lambert[49] on the Ile St-Louis. This became the political headquarters of Poland-In-Exile, and a meeting-point for compatriots like Chopin and national poet Adam Mickiewicz, and for such French cultural giants as Hector Berlioz, Eugène Delacroix and George Sand. It was also home to the exiled Czartoryski art collection. Could Bianca's portrait have been part of it?

Adam Jerzy's right-hand man was his nephew Władysław Zamoyski – son of Zofia and Stanisław Kostka, and recorded in Florence in the 1830s.[50] Did he convey Bianca's portrait from Florence to Paris?

Adam Jerzy himself died at the Château of Montfermeil, his palatial country residence just northeast of Paris, on 15 July 1861. He was succeeded as head of the Hôtel Lambert by his son Władysław (1828–94) and by Władysław Zamoyski – joined in Paris from 1862 until his death in 1868 by his elder brother Andrzej Artur. The Czartoryski Collection provided many of the artworks for the *Salle Polonaise* at the 1865 Exposition des Beaux-Arts held at the Palais de l'Industrie on the Champs-Elysées.

The Franco-Prussian War of 1870 heralded the demise of the Hôtel Lambert. Władysław Czartoryski packed up and hid the museum's collections as best he could before escaping to London; some items vanished in the process. He also donated works of art to the Polish Museum founded in Rapperswil (near Zurich) by Count Władysław Broel-Plater in 1870 as a 'refuge for historic memorabilia dishonoured and plundered in the homeland.'[51]

Władysław Czartoryski returned to France after the fall of the Commune in 1871. He was a scion of the French Establishment: his first marriage, in 1855, had taken place amidst the Napoleonic grandeur of La Malmaison; his second, in 1872, was to a grand-daughter of King Louis-Philippe. In 1876 he oversaw the return the Czartoryski Collection to Polish soil – to Cracov (then capital of Austrian-controlled Galicia), where he was offered use of the old arsenal building. The new Czartoryski Museum opened in 1878.

Soon afterwards another new art museum was created in northwest Poland – by Adam Jerzy's daughter Izabela, who had reinforced the Czartoryski/Zamoyski dynastic alliance by marrying Jan Działyński, grandson of Stanisław Kostka and Zofia. Izabela created her own museum at Gołuchów (between Poznan and Łódź) in a ruined castle she transformed into a Loire Valley château (*see below*). Her own, left-facing, profiled portrait adorns the château to this day.

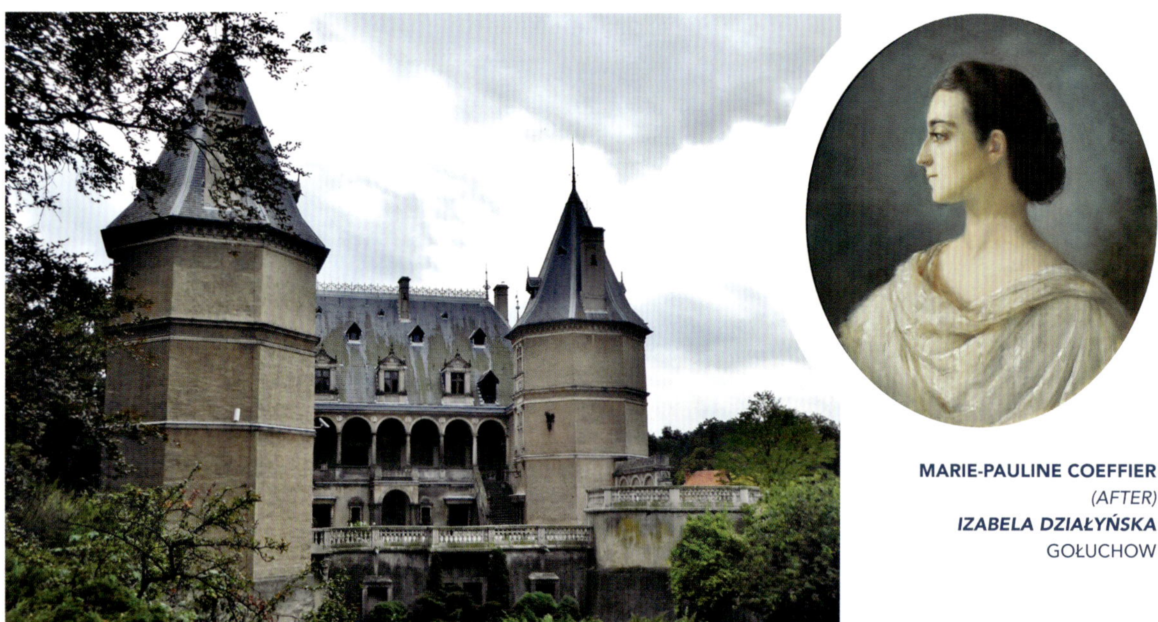

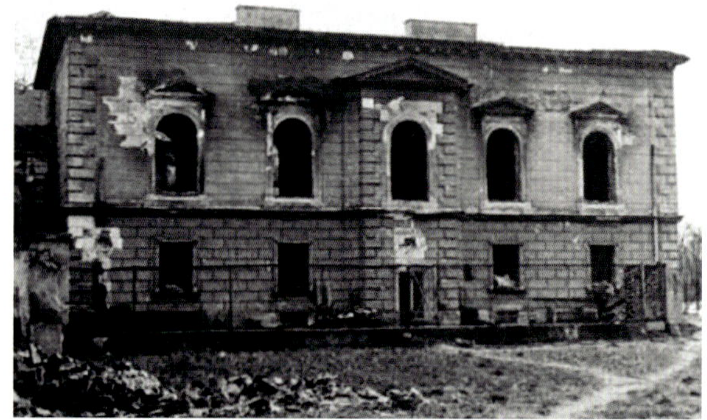
MARIE-PAULINE COEFFIER
(AFTER)
IZABELA DZIAŁYŃSKA
GOŁUCHOW

Izabela died in Menton, on the Côte d'Azur, on 18 March 1899. Zamoyskis were on almost permanent parade in France during the Belle Epoque. The 14th Count Tomasz Franciszek Zamoyski (1832–89) died just along the coast from Menton, in San Remo on the Italian Riviera. His wife, Countess Maria Zamoyska (1851–1945), was a noted Paris society beauty.[52] In Paris in 1894 Stanisław Kostka's grandson Andrzej Zamoyski presented one of the world's most famous violins, the 1713 *Gibson Stradivarius*, to the Polish prodigy violinist Bronisław Huberman.[53]

Maurycy Klemens, 15th Count Zamoyski, was Polish Ambassador in Paris from 1919–24. A few months after his death on 5 May 1939 the *Sforziada* was spirited away from the Blue Palace by his son Jan, 16th Count Zamoyski, and – according to Jan's son Marcin – deposited in the monastery of Jasna Góra in Częstochowa for safekeeping during World War II.[54] On 7 September 1939 a bomb destroyed part of the Blue Palace manuscript store. On 25 September 1939 the Library entrance was gutted by fire. On 8 August 1944 the main hall of the Library was set ablaze by the Nazis and burnt to a shell, with 120,000 books going up in flames.

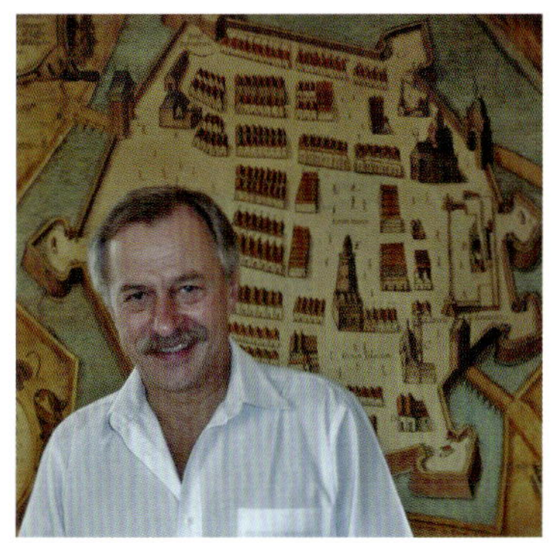

In 1948, after the Communist take-over, the final Count Zamoyski diplomatically deposited the *Sforziada* in the new Polish National Library, where it has remained to this day.

There is no trace of the portrait it once contained in Poland, or of its ever passing through any of the châteaux and palaces which the Zamoyskis or Czartoryskis inhabited. It is not among the 800 items from the Czatoryski Museum lost during World War II, nor is it recorded as missing from Gołuchów (whose museum still lacks about 40 per cent of its pre-war holdings).[55]

The portrait resurfaced in 1998, in an auction held at Christie's New York on January 30. It was described as the 'Property of a Lady' and catalogued as an early 19th century German *Head of a Young Girl in Profile to the left in Renaissance Dress*.

It sold for $21,850 to American dealer Kate Ganz.

She re-sold it, at a slight loss, in January 2007.

Then all hell broke loose.

NOTES

1 Various sources, inc. Cartwright (*op. cit.*), who describes the document as 'duly signed and witnessed.'

2 Although Il Moro had been stripped of his title as Duke of Bari by Alfonso II of Naples in 1494, he was re-invested with Bari in September 1496 after Alfonso's abdication by his son Ferrandino, who subsequently decreed that the title could be transmitted to Il Moro's second son Francesco. This decree was eventually promulgated by King Federico, Ferrandino's uncle and successor, on 20 June 1497 – one year to the day after Bianca Sforza's marriage to Galeazzo Sanseverino. Does this curious coincidence imply there was some connection between Bianca and Bari, and explain why Il Moro might have bestowed Bianca's *Sforziada* on Isabel of Aragon at the same time as the Duchy of Bari?

3 Constance J. Moffat (*op. cit.*) claims Il Moro renounced the Duchy of **Milan** in favour of Isabel of Aragon at this meeting, citing Caterina Santoro, *Gli Offici del Comune di Milano e del Dominio Visconteo-Sforzesco 1216–1515* (Giuffrè, Milan, 1968, p.359). With the French at the city gates, this would have been a hollow gift if not poisoned chalice – but what more could Isabel have asked for?

4 Bona used the Sforza viper on coinage and in illuminated books; tiles with the Sforza viper were applied to stoves in the Royal Palace in Cracov; a 16th century Flemish tapestry (now in the Palace of the Grand Dukes of Lithuania, Vilnius), said to have belonged to Bona's son Zygmunt August, features the Sforza viper impaled on the arms of Lithuania. Bona was still describing herself as a Sforza (*BONA SFORTIA ARAGONIA*) in the large-lettered inscription she had chiselled into the cornice around two sides of the courtyard in Bari Castle in 1548.

5 We read of Bianca visiting Isabel and her husband Gian Galeazzo at Pavia in May 1493, and playing with them in the grounds of Mirabello hunting lodge in the castle park – Malaguzzi-Valeri (*op. cit.*), p.53.

6 There are two other ways in which Isabel of Aragon could have received the *Sforziada* in Milan in late 1499: it may have been looted when Galeazzo Sanseverino's palazzo was sacked by the mob on August 31, then conveyed to her by a supporter; or it may have been presented to her by King Louis XII after being confiscated by French troops.

7 Sanuto II, 1210.

8 Sanuto II, 1303/04.

9 Pierantonio dal Verme was a nephew of the Pietro dal Verme assassinated at Il Moro's behest in 1485. His attempts to regain possession of Voghera and Bobbio after Il Moro's demise were thwarted by the French, who awarded these properties to Comte de Ligny. There was even a pitched battle between the French and the Dal Vermes in Bobbio in 1501, during which 200 people are said to have died.

10 L. Collison-Morley, *The Story of the Sforzas* (George Routledge & Sons Ltd, London 1933).

11 Letter from Jehan le Veau (Blois) to Margaret of Austria, dated 29.12.1511. Later scribes claimed Il Duchetto met his death in Summer 1512 while hunting, one source says crushed by his horse. Such confusion only adds weight to the suspicion that Il Duchetto was murdered shortly after coming of age, when France's hold on Lombardy was under threat. Massimiliano also benefited from Il Duchetto's death by becoming the undisputed focal point of Sforza supporters.

12 Nicholl (*op. cit.*), p. 497.

13 In a letter from the musician Lorenzo Guznago to Isabella d'Este.

14 The future Duke Federico II was born on 17 May 1500 and reigned 1533–40. in 1549 Federico's son Francesco III married Katharina of Austria (1533–72), great-granddaughter of Emperor Maximilian. After Francesco's death in 1550 at the age of sixteen, Katharina remarried – in 1553, to the book-loving King Zygmunt August of Poland (who had earlier been married to her elder sister Elisabeth).

15 Isabel of Aragon was accompanied to Naples by her daughters Ippolita and Bona. Her fourth and final child, Bianca Maria, born in early 1495 (posthumously to Gian Galeazzo), died in 1496. Isabel self-pityingly signed herself *unica della disgrazia* from the time of her husband's suspect death in Autumn 1494 until her eldest daughter became Queen of Poland 24 years later.

16 Isabel's uncle Federico, as King of Naples, officially created her Duchess of Bari on 10 April 1500; but Federico was deposed on 25 June 1501, when Naples fell to the French. Her title to Bari was only confirmed on 25 July 1501 by Fernando II. Isabel left Naples for Bari in September 1501. After the Aragonese regained Naples in 1504, Isabel and Bona spent much time in the city – Naples was larger, richer and more cosmopolitan.

17 The possibility that the final *Sforziada* was taken by Il Moro to Austria in 1499, left for safekeeping with Maximilian, never recovered and ultimately despatched to Poland in 1543, to mark the marriage between Maximilian's great-granddaughter Elisabeth and Bona Sforza's son Zygmunt August, is no more unlikely than the *Sforziada* reaching Poland via France.

18 Sabine Weiss, *Die Vergessene Kaiserin: Bianca Maria Sforza – Kaiser Maximilans Zweite Gemahlin* (Tyrolia, Innsbruck 2010).

19 Vienna University, sometimes known as *Alma Mater Rudolphina*, was founded in March 1365 by Rudolf IV of Austria (1339–65), *Der Stifter* (The Founder), who died in Milan on 27 July 1365. His visit to Milan followed the marriage (on 23 February 1365) of his younger brother, Duke Leopold III of Austria and Count of Tyrol (1351–86), to Viridis Visconti (1352–1414), daughter of Bernabò Visconti. Viridis would become known as the Habsburg *Stammmutter* (Matriarch), and a common ancestor of the Habsburgs and the Sforzas – something not lost on Galeazzo Sanseverino.

20 In 1517 the diarist Antonio de Beatis met Francesco Sforza in Trent during his European travels with Cardinal Luigi of Aragon, describing him as 'well-read, energetic and prudent.' After a Papal/Imperial army under Prospero Colonna conquered Milan in November 1521, Francesco returned to the city in early April 1522 as Duke; his penchant for signing himself *Dux Mediolani et Barii* did not endear him to Isabel of Aragon or Bona Sforza (Francesco renounced his claims to Bari under pressure from Charles V in 1525). The Sforza restoration was confirmed by the defeat of the French at the Battle of Bicocca on 27 April 1522. When the French returned in October 1524, Francesco retreated to Soncino, just over 30 miles east of Milan. The four-month French occupation of Milan was ended by their ignominious defeat outside Pavia (at which Galeazzo Sanseverino was slain) in February 1525. In 1526, when Francesco was seriously ill (possibly as the result of a failed assassination attempt with a poisoned dagger in August 1523), there was talk of the Venetians engineering the return of his brother Massimiliano as their puppet duke – prompting two letters from Massimiliano (signed *Maximiliano*) to his

brother disclaiming all involvement in any such scheme: the first (August 26) from Amboise, the second (September 28) from Blois, citing their half-brother Gianpaolo (*il signore Joanne Paulo nostro commune fratello*) as go-between. Gianpaolo Sforza (1497–1535), Marquess of Caravaggio, was Il Moro's son by Lucrezia Crivelli. Francesco was officially invested by Charles V as Duke of Milan (at the hefty cost of 400,000 ducats) in January 1530, as part of a deal whereby Pope Clement VII agreed to invest Charles V with Naples and crown him Holy Roman Emperor. On 25 May 1530 Francesco's brother Massimiliano died in Paris (his remains were repatriated to Milan and interred in the Duomo). In March 1533 Charles V visited Milan to discuss Francesco's marital status and, in September 1533, by proxy in Lille, Francesco married Charles V's eleven-year-old niece Christina of Denmark. Just over two years later, on 2 November 1535, Francesco died. He had been ill for years and was a virtual cripple. Milan passed into Habsburg hands for almost 325 years.

21 Bari taxes were raised to unprecedented levels to finance Bona's ten-day wedding celebrations in Naples and exorbitant 500,000-ducat dowry. Isabel never saw her daughter again. Her plans to travel to Poland after the birth of Bona's first child (Izabela, born 18 January 1519) were scuppered by the outbreak of the Polish-Teutonic War.

22 Prospero Colonna, like Il Moro and Leonardo da Vinci (and King Richard III of England), was born in 1452 and, coincidentally, married a (Covella) Sanseverino.

23 Studies of Isabel's skull have revealed traces of mercury – a common early 16th century treatment for syphilis.

24 After Ippolito's sudden death in 1520, Bona Sforza kept in touch with his nephew and successor as Archbishop of Milan, Ippolito II d'Este – sending him, for instance, some family medals in 1532 (Mieczysław Morka, *The Beginnings of Medallic Art in Poland during the Times of Zygmunt I and Bona Sforza* – Artibus et Historiæ Vol. 29, N° 58, 2008).

25 A 1546 coin features a shield with the Sforza viper flanked by two naked figures, in whom D.R. Edward Wright sees a reference to the woodwose flanking one of the shields in Birago's final *Sforziada* frontispiece (Morka, *op. cit.*).

26 It may also be significant that Zygmunt August's father Sigismund the Old took to styling himself *PATER PATRIAE*, abbreviated on coins to *PP*, after his marriage to Bona – the same title attributed to Francesco Sforza in the *Sforziada* frontispieces (Morka, *op. cit.*).

27 D.R. Edward Wright, *Ludovico Il Moro and the Sforziada by Giovanni Simonetta in Warsaw* (2011).

28 Angela Campanella, *Bona Sforza – Regina di Polonia, Duchessa di Bari* (Giuseppe Leterza, Bari 2008).

29 Portrait at Wawel Cathedral, Cracov.

30 Even if it were Louis XII, not Il Moro, who gave Isabel the *Sforziada*, the same logic holds good: Louis XII had just as strong a reason for wishing Isabel away from Milan (and just as much guilt to

assuage – after kidnapping her son – by seeing her off with a parting gift).

31 D.R. Edward Wright, *op. cit.*

32 *Bona Sforza Regina di Polonia e Duchessa di Bari* (Edizione Levante, Bari 1984).

33 Zdzisław Spieralski, *Jan Zamoyski* (Wiedza Powszechna, Warsaw 1989).

34 Stanisław Łempicki, *Hetman Jan Zamoyski Współpracownikiem Heidensteina* (Pamiętnik Literacki, Lvov 1917).

35 Tomasz Makowski, *The History of the Zamyoski Library in Biblioteka Ordynacji Zamojskiej – Od Jana do Jana* (Polish National Library, Warsaw 2005).

36 According to his Italian-born, Poland-based descendant Tessa Capponi-Borowska.

37 The works were moved to the new Transfiguration Church in nearby Tarnogród in 1783, and still hang there above the altar.

38 They left Paris in December 1644 on a three-month overland journey to Danzig via Cambrai and Brussels. For further information about Marysieńka, see Kazimierz Waliszewski, Marysieńka (E. Plon, Nourrit & Cie, Paris 1898).

39 Jan Sobiepan died suddenly on 7 April 1665, but was not buried until early June; Marysieńka and Jan Sobieski were secretly married in Warsaw in the middle of May by the Bishop of Béziers, with the Queen of Poland's connivance; their marriage was officially celebrated on July 6. They had been secretly courting for some time; Sobieski was almost a neighbour of Sobiepan's, with imposing residences (both now in Ukraine) at Yavorov (50 miles south of Zamość) and Żółkiew (60 miles southeast, on the road to Lvov).

40 After the death of Jan Kazimierz in 1672 his belongings and works of art were inherited by his sister-in-law Anne-Marie de Gonzague, a prominent society hostess, who died in Paris in 1684.

41 In her will Gryzelda appeared to express remorse about the fate of her brother's library, beseeching 'the honourable executors of this my own will and testament that the said library be handed over to Zamość Academy in its entirety immediately after my burial.'

42 Marysieńka's Warsaw residence (as recorded in 1669) was – like Bona Sforza's – in Ujazdów.

43 Adam Jerzy had been exiled to St Petersburg with his younger brother Konstanty in 1795 as part of a deal whereby the Czartoryskis, who had taken an active part in the 1794 Kosciuszko Uprising against Russian rule (following the Third Partition which wiped Poland off the map), were allowed to keep their family estates. In June 1799 Adam Jerzy was appointed Russian Ambassador to the House of Sardinia (Savoy) by Tsar Paul I. Contemporary observers considered the appointment a banishment, due to suspicions that the dark-haired Czartoryski had sired the baby girl (Maria) born on 29 May 1799 to Louise of Baden (1779–1826), wife of Paul's eldest son Alexander (future Tsar Alexander I): the baby had dark hair, whereas both Louise and Alexander were blond.
Adam Jerzy proceeded overland from St Petersburg via Międzyrzec (in Austrian Poland), where he met

his eldest sister Maria, to Vienna, where he stayed several months. His paternal aunt Princess Izabela Lubomirska (1736–1816), who had quit Poland in 1785, was in the city (where she 'received all the most distinguished figures of Viennese society') – as were his sisters Maria and Zofia Zamyoska ('then at the peak of her beauty'). Adam Jerzy visited Venice, Verona and Mantua before arriving in Florence in late 1799 ('it was a melancholy time of year, and the roads were almost impracticable'). The Court of Savoy had been expelled from Turin by the French in December 1798 and was now based at the Villa di Poggio Imperiale on the outskirts of Florence. Czartoryski had monthly meetings with the wise-cracking King Carlo Emanuele IV di Savoia (1751–1819), and 'profited from my leisure time to visit the masterpieces of art in the galleries.' He journeyed south to Rome with the court in the wake of Napoleon's success at the Battle of Marengo (14 June 1800). After several months in Rome, partly spent sketching monuments and scenery, Czartoryski was appointed Russian Envoy to the Court of Naples. He had time to visit nearby Pompei and Vesuvius (nearly falling into the volcano crater) before receiving a letter from new Tsar Alexander I dated 17 March 1801 (i.e. 29 March 1801, Western-style), summoning him back to St Petersburg following the assassination of Tsar Paul I six days earlier (i.e. March 11/23).

Czartoryski travelled back to Russia via Rome and Florence, where he was entertained to an official dinner in the Pitti Palace by the swaggering Napoleonic general Joachim Murat, who had entered the city in triumph two months earlier. Czartoryski continued to Vienna and Puławy – where 'I found my whole family but, much as they wished me to stay, they felt I had to go on at once.' The *Lady with an Ermine* and Raphael's *Portrait of a Young Man*, which he had acquired in Italy, were destined for his mother's new museum. Czartoryski continued to St Petersburg via Riga, travelling 'day and night.'

44 A first-hand account of the Zamoyski family by Englishman George Burnett was published in 1807 after his return from ten months in Poland, during which he visited Zamoyski's estates (and his wife's family at Puławy). Burnett records that Stanislas Kostka's planned new château would have been of a scale 'far surpassing in magnificence and elegance anything to be found in Poland – in completeness, perhaps anything in Europe' and would contain a theatre, tennis-court, and 'an extensive library.' But Burnett also noted, presciently, that 'the plan is perhaps too extensive to be carried into execution. His Excellency talks of expending £100,000, perhaps £200,000. But his architect (an Italian) declared to me that it would cost £1m. His Excellency may have half the money.'

45 The château was named after Klemens Jerzy (1738–67), 8th Count Zamoyski – the first Zamoyski to marry a Czartoryski. In 1768 his widow Konstancja (1742–97) remarried to Klementy's uncle [sic] Andrzej (1717–92), who became 10th Count in 1780; their children included the future Counts Stanisław Kostka and his elder brother Alexander August (1770–1800).

46 'Un Homme de Rien' in *Galerie des Contemporains Illustres – Tome VI* (A. René & Ce, Paris 1843).

47 *Cf* catalogue entry n°21 of exhibition *More Precious Than Gold – Treasures of the Polish National Library* (2003).

48 The *Golden Legend* was one of many books deposited by the Nazis in the 18th century château in Garbicz, a Polish village just east of the Oder (then known as Görbitsch and part of Germany). The château was owned by Ellhard von Risselmann, a friend of Hans Frank, the Nazi boss of occupied Poland. It was assigned as a secret depository for Nazi loot In March 1944; from November 1944 to January 1945 Frank had an estimated 165,000 volumes transported there. They were removed to Russia at the end of World War II, then fraternally returned to the Polish National Library in the late 1950s.

49 Czartoryski paid 175,000 francs to buy the Hôtel Lambert, and a further 130,000 francs on a five-month renovation programme, before moving in in mid-November 1843.

50 Evidence of Władysław Zamoyski's presence in 1830s Florence is provided by his signature in the register of the *Gabinetto Scientifico Letteraro G.P. Viesseux.*

51 Most of its collection – 3,000 artworks, 2,000 items of memorabilia, 20,000 engravings, 9,000 coins/medals, 92,000 books and 27,000 manuscripts – was transported back to Poland in 1927, in fourteen rail carriages. Most of this material was destroyed by the Nazis.

52 In *Society Recollections in Paris and Vienna 1879–1904*, an 'English Officer' notes that 'a Christchurch man and private secretary of Comte Zamoyski once related to me how he went with Comtesse Zamoyska to consult the famous palm-reader Adolphe Desbarolles; after examining her hand, Desbarolles informed her that she had three children, which she told him was not the case, as she only had two. Desbarolles assured her that she must have made a mistake, which rather annoyed the Comtesse.'

53 Whereby hangs another tale, possibly two: Huberman (who later founded the Palestine Philharmonic, forerunner of the Israel Philharmonic) had the Gibson stolen from his New York dressing room in the 1936.

54 As reported to the author by Marcin Zamoyski in Zamość on 3 September 2011. It appears that a variety of hiding-places were used: two of the most treasured Zamoyski manuscripts – the *Tyniec Sacramentary* and *Zamoyski Codex* – were hidden in the church at Łowicz, 40 miles west of Warsaw. Ironically, the Poles managed to hide some of the leading works from the Warsaw art museum, including Jan Matejko's *Battle of Grunwald* and Skarga's *Sermon*, in a railway marshalling shed in … Zamość. Which, during World War II, was briefly renamed, would you believe, *Himmlerstadt*.

55 Some items looted from Gołuchów were sold by Paris dealer Georges Wildenstein (*cf* Peter Harclerode & Brendan Pittaway, *The Lost Masters – The Looting of Europe's Treasurehouses*, Orion, London 1999). Giannino Marchig worked for the Wildensteins as a restorer.

THE SILVERMAN LEONARDO

THE LATTERDAY FATE OF BIANCA SFORZA

ON 16 JANUARY 2008 I emerged from the press preview of the Brussels Art & Antiques Fair into a rainy Belgian afternoon and joined the lengthy queue for a taxi.

'Mind if I join you!?' boomed a plummy American voice when my turn came at last.

A large, wide-eyed, friendly-faced man bundled in beside me.[1] A talker, an art-lover, a collector perhaps … some sort of market insider, or he wouldn't have been at the Fair before it opened to the public.

He learnt I was a journalist. 'May have a story for you one day!' he grinned, when the taxi reached my hotel. 'I'll let you know!'

I thanked him and glanced down at the name on his card.

PETER SILVERMAN

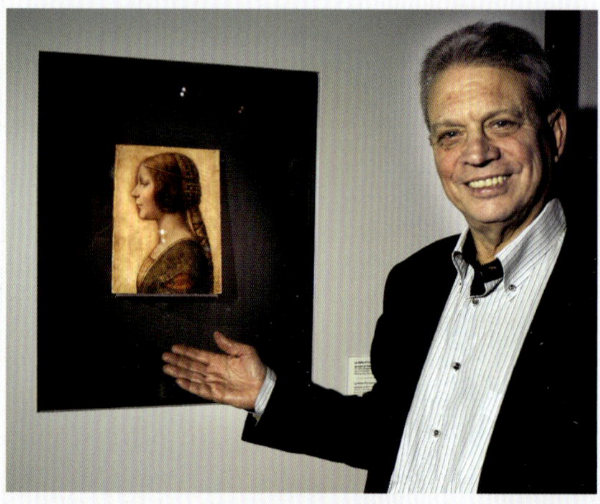

Silverman grew up in the 'tough streets' of post-war Brooklyn – a 'fiercely competitive environment' that turned him into 'a hard fighter – someone who always wanted to win and be the best.' His Jewish grandparents had fled Tsarist pogroms in Białystok for New York's Lower East Side, where his bootlegging grandfather was gunned down in 1932. Silverman's mother danced on Broadway for Busby Berkeley.

Silverman quit New York for Paris in the early 1960s – inspired by Hemingway's *Moveable Feast,* and the prospect of free enrolment at the Sorbonne.

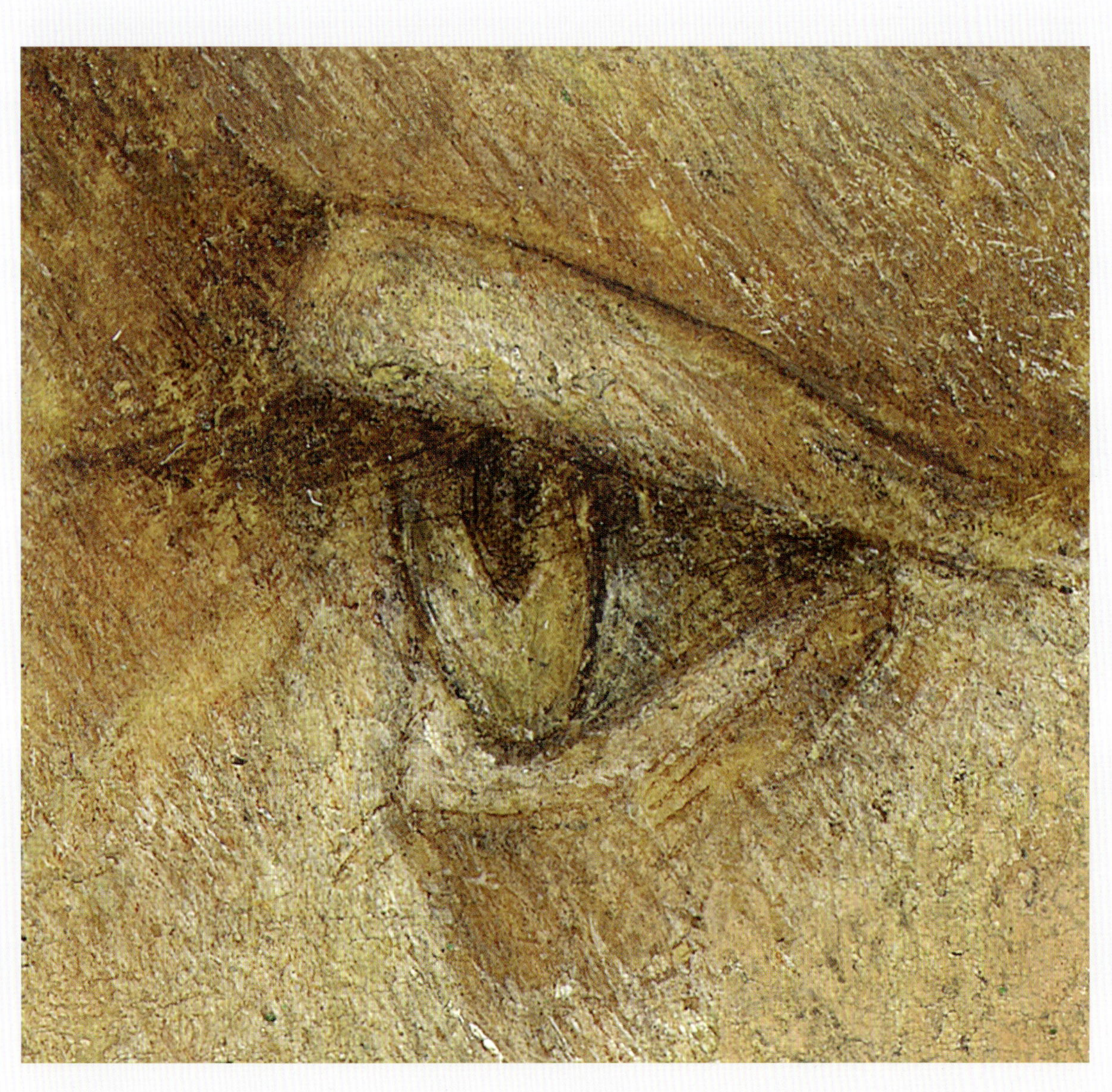

Three years later he met Irene Dürking, a German PhD student. They married, moved to Munich and ran language courses, whose success enabled Silverman to start collecting (Himalayan art, initially). When Irene was struck down by leukemia, aged 33, Silverman sold the business and returned to Paris, where he collected works of art with his new partner Kathleen Onorato, an Italo-American who had just completed her Masters at the Sorbonne. Their flat, less than a mile from the Arc de Triomphe, would become a repository for exquisite pictures and sculpture bought for a song – then later recognized as by Boucher, Van Dyck, Raphael, Donatello and Michelangelo, among others.

When Peter Silverman sauntered into Kate Ganz's New York gallery on Wednesday 24 January 2007, Ganz had known him for years. 'He was always around' as she put it.

Petite and stylish with magnetic eyes, **Kate Ganz** was one of four children born into a family with German Jewish roots. Her parents Victor and Sally built up an exceptional picture collection, concentrating first on Picasso, then on four emerging American artists of the 1960s: Robert Rauschenberg, Jasper Johns, Frank Stella and Eva Hesse.

Victor Ganz died in 1987. Twelve pictures from the family art collection were sold at Sotheby's in 1988, bringing $48.5m. Ten years later, after his widow's death, a further 58 works amassed $206.5m – then an auction record for a private collection. The sale took place at Christie's New York premises at 502 Park Avenue on 10 November 1997 – a month or so before Kate Ganz Dorment (as she then was) signed the lease of her new Manhattan gallery, and just eleven weeks before she paid $21,850 for a *Young Girl in Profile in Renaissance Dress* at … Christie's New York.

Silverman had underbid on the portrait, but did not know who bought it, and feared that his 'lovely lady' was 'gone for ever.' When he found her gazing out from a stand on a table by the entrance to Ganz's gallery in 2007, he 'froze.' Ganz wanted $21,000, but accepted Silverman's offer of $19,000. He returned to collect the work the following day.

Christie's had declared the work to be in 'ink and bodycolor,' Ganz in 'gouache over graphite.' Neither were accurate. Ganz also labelled the portrait 'a carefully rendered study based on a number of paintings by Leonardo da Vinci' that 'may have been made by a German artist studying in Italy.' Silverman thought otherwise.

'I struggled to see on which Leonardo work it could possibly have been based' he declared. 'Any 19th century German artist keen to study Leonardo's female portraits would have been better off going to the Louvre.' He would later believe that 'it was perhaps fortunate – at least for art history – that the portrait fell into my hands and did not wind up on some rich guy's wall in Texas or Alabama as a "nice 19th century German thing"!'

Silverman felt it was by 'somebody in the Leonardo circle' and submitted the portrait to Paris art restorer **Caroline Corrigan** for microscopic analysis.

Her August 2007 report described the work as an 'early 16th century drawing on vellum in very good condition.' Around one-fifth of the surface had been restored, she added, but so skilfully it 'should not be treated in any way.' She also warned against removing the vellum from its oak panel. The work was 'too rare and precious to risk anything.'

In January 2008 Silverman happened across **Nicholas Turner** at a Louvre exhibition of drawings by Polidoro da Caravaggio (1492–1543). Turner had been Deputy Keeper of Drawings at the British Museum and Curator of Drawings at the Getty Museum in Los Angeles. Silverman showed him an image of his Ganz gallery purchase on his mobile phone. Turner had already seen it courtesy of Simon Dickinson, a prominent Old Master dealer in London. 'Do not rule out Leonardo!' he instructed.

On 5 March 2008 **Mina Gregori** – 83-year-old *doyenne* of Italian art historians – visited Silverman's flat to inspect the portrait, accompanied by **Catherine Goguel** of the Louvre's Graphic Art Department. Both remarked on the work's left-handedness, with Gregori extolling its 'extraordinary quality' and suggesting Silverman seek the artist in the circle of Leonardo.

Days later flamboyant Franco-Italian art consultant **Giammarco Cappuzzo** advised Silverman to take the portrait to Lumière Technology, whose pioneering multispectral camera could penetrate artworks in unprecedented detail. The two men made the 2½-mile journey from Silverman's flat to Lumière's premises on Boulevard St-Germain astride Cappuzzo's scooter, Silverman clutching the portrait in his arms. Lumière's optical engineer **Pascal Cotte** scanned the portrait, ran the scan through his digital database and, two hours later, announced it was in all probability a Leonardo.

Cotte was not conjuring rabbits out of a hat. He had already conducted exhaustive multispectral analysis of Leonardo's *Mona Lisa* and *Lady with an Ermine* (and would later digitize *La Belle Ferronnière*).

Cotte produced ultra-violet, infra-red, false colour and X-ray images of Silverman's portrait, as well as raking light reflectographs – generating 20 gigabytes of data that would take many weeks to probe in full. *Pentimenti* (artist's corrections) to the facial profile and top of the sitter's head were a solid indication that the work was no copy.

On March 19 Silverman e-mailed Oxford University's **Martin Kemp**, Britain's leading Leonardo expert, attaching a digital image of the portrait. 'I would love to know your thoughts' he wrote. Kemp was 'suspicious of the colour' but thought the portrait 'pretty, delicate and sophisticated' and felt there was 'a fair chance' it could be a Leonardo. He never accepted money or expenses for inspecting works, so did not know when he could examine the portrait in person.

On April 16 Nicholas Turner sent Silverman his 'main thoughts' about the portrait, dating it to the 'mid-1480s to 1490s.' The hair's 'extraordinary sense of texture' recalled Leonardo's drawings of 'waves, tornadoes and other natural phenomena: Instead of using the vellum's smoother side, like scribes and illuminators, the artist had preferred its rougher side, whose grainy texture 'slightly abrades as the artist draws.'

Silverman also sent an image to Milanese art historian **Cristina Geddo** – an authority on the Circle of Leonardo. The portrait's 'tremendous quality' immediately convinced her it was by Leonardo himself. After inspecting the work at Silverman's flat on May 28, then viewing the multispectral images at Lumière Technology, she confirmed the portrait was 'executed in an experimental technique dating from the origins of pastel – a neglected area of Leonardo studies.'

On 11 June 2008 Geddo formally attributed the portrait to Leonardo da Vinci in the first scholarly monograph on the work, *Il 'Pastello' Ritrovato: Un Nuovo Ritratto di Leonardo?*[2] She remarked that the work had been laid down on its oak panel using 'copious amounts of glue' and that 'the poor adherence of the vellum to the wooden backing has resulted in considerable lifting in the upper centre, increasing the losses of pigment in the face and neck.' She suggested the rougher, outer side of the animal skin had been used it as was more porous and better suited to absorbing colour.

To Geddo, the portrait offered unique evidence of the 'dry colour' technique Leonardo is known to have pioneered before 1500, while the ink hatching detached the head from the background and gave it 'the moulding force of a bas-relief.' The portrait conformed to Leonardo's theories about how light falling from above creates the most charming facial shadows. The eye's 'forceful magnetism' and 'perfect anatomical structure' saw Leonardo use the 'natural colour of the vellum to capture the transparency of the yellow/green iris reflecting the daylight.' Leonardo, added Geddo, was 'one of the few painters of the Italian Renaissance to portray light-coloured eyes.'

She was less impressed by the portrait's restoration than Catherine Corrigan. 'It is essential to take account of the changes that have occurred as a result of old restoration, which is both invasive and, more seriously, deceptive' wrote Geddo. 'Without compromising the general effect of the work, it impairs its overall legibility.' Watercolour retouching had brought 'a covering of lavish cosmetics to the purity of a Renaissance face' whose 'initial, diaphanous tonality' had been undermined by a 'mawkish rose tint.' There was 'heavy brushwork' to the cheek, forehead and areas of the neck. The knot patterning was 'poorly retouched with the point of the brush in black ink.'

Geddo concluded that 'the degradation of the media and interventions of the restorer, which not even the cleverest faker would have known how to achieve, ought to be considered decisive arguments in favour of the work's authenticity.'

Those later critical of the Leonardo attribution – often confusing restoration with original colouring – would have been well advised to consult Geddo's incisive analysis of the work's condition before rushing into judgment. She declared the portrait to be a 'unique, definitive and autonomous work, fluctuating between drawing, painting and miniature' with a 'rare mix of materials and techniques.' Such an experimental procedure provided, of itself, 'indisputable proof of Leonardo's hand.'

In June the portrait was subjected to Raman spectroscopy at Swiss Federal Laboratories then, in September, to Carbon-14 testing at the Federal Institute of Technology in Zurich. This dated the vellum to 1440–1650.

Meanwhile Mina Gregori, after re-examining the portrait, had penned a declaration formally endorsing Leonardo's authorship due to the 'inimitable delicacy' of the 'almost imperceptible' tonal degradations in the unrestored areas of the cheek, and the 'brightness and transparency of the girl's eye … only to be found in other drawings by Leonardo.'

Alessandro Vezzosi, founder and director of the Museo Ideale in Leonardo's home town of Vinci, made the portrait a last-minute addition to his luxurious volume *Leonardo Infinito* – presenting it unequivocally as a Leonardo and, in all probability, a *ritratto nuziale* ('marriage portrait'). Another Italian art historian prominent in the Leonardo field, **Pietro Marani**, was keen to publish the work as a Leonardo too, reported Silverman – but changed his mind when Vezzosi got in ahead of him.

Vezzosi waxed lyrical about the work's 'refined intensity and aura of mystery, dynamic interplay of light and shadow, and suffused softness of the light, rose-tinted flesh.' He felt its left-handed handling was 'impressive in its fluidity, certainty and precision.' The use of parchment filled a 'previously incomprehensible gap, given the frequency of its use among Leonardo's Milanese collaborators (in particular Ambrogio de Predis).'

Carlo Pedretti (1928–2018), head of Leonardo Studies at the University of California, penned the Introduction to Vezzosi's book. He termed the portrait an 'extraordinary work of art' and drew attention to its 'impeccable, typical Lombard hairstyle … drawn without a single perspectival error.'

The first media mention of the portrait came in Germany, where Silverman had family connections. On 7 July 2008, under the headline *Schöne im Schubfach* ('Beauty in the Drawer'), *Der Spiegel* reported that the portrait had been owned by a Swiss art enthusiast for ten years before being discovered by Peter Silverman and re-attributed to Leonardo. This *Hochzeitsporträt* (Marriage Portrait) was now valued at 'up to €200m.'

Un Nouveau Léonard de Vinci! screamed *Paris Match* two days later, with Julien Pfyffer reporting that the work's owner was maintaining anonymity for insurance reasons. Silverman was described here, and often subsequently, as a 'Canadian collector.'

Vezzosi's weighty tome caught the eye of the *Sunday Times* Vatican correspondent John Follain, whose 750-word article *Picture Kept In A Drawer 'Is £100m Da Vinci,'* published on 27 July 2008, called Pedretti 'the world's leading expert on Leonardo' and cited his belief that the portrait could be 'the most important discovery since the early 20th century re-establishment of the *Lady with an Ermine* as a genuine work by Leonardo.'

Follain also quoted Silverman's reaction to discovering the portrait: 'My heart started to beat a million times a minute. I immediately thought this could be a Florentine artist. The idea of Leonardo came to me in a flash.' The portrait's owner, continued Follain trustingly, 'was originally going to give it to his daughter as a wedding present, though now he has changed his mind.'

Julien Pfyffer returned in *Paris Match* on August 6 with a profile of Lumière Technology. Pascal Cotte revealed that, when examining the portrait, he had found a striking parallel with Leonardo's *Lady with an Ermine*, 'a very rare touch: the artist drew the eyelashes both above and under the eye.'

One man raising a languid eyelash and supercilious eyebrow at these revelations was **Nicholas Penny**, boss of London's National Gallery. On August 18 Silverman confronted him about his 'silence, indifference and lack of support on this Leonardo thing.' Penny replied blithely that he was 'very suspicious of the portrait on vellum that you are claiming as a work by Leonardo,' explaining:

> 'It is both obviously old and worn, and yet highly appealing and legible – there is something about the balance between damage and survival that I find hard to believe; it seems designed to tell you immediately that it is by a left-handed artist; every bit of it can be conveniently compared with other portraits of that date; and provenance is very important for Leonardo's drawings – you bought this from a very well-known and very well-informed dealer, Kate Ganz, as a 19th century work.'

Two of Penny's reasons were *non sequiturs*: that because the work was by a left-handed artist, and showed similarities with other works from the 1490s, it couldn't be either. Even more disturbing was his intimation that a 'well-known dealer' was more to be trusted about Leonardo attributions than specialist academics like Turner and Gregori.

Follain's story was spotted by the *New York Times*'s Italian correspondent Elisabetta Povoledo, who penned a 1,230-word article once back from vacation on August 23. Entitled *A Portrait by Leonardo? Scholars and Skeptics Differ*, it offered a foretaste of what would become remorseless American efforts to cast doubt on the portrait's authenticity.

The Leonardo attribution 'has not gone unchallenged' stated Povoledo. Having failed to find anyone willing to dismiss Leonardo's authorship outright, she resorted to innuendo. **Carmen C. Bambach**, the Chilean Curator of Drawings at New York's Metropolitan Museum and a noted Leonardo specialist, admitted that she (like Nicholas Penny) had only seen a photograph of the work [courtesy of Martin Kemp, who had 'personally shown her a series of digital files' when he had been in New York earlier that year]. Choosing her words with the diplomacy of a papal nuncio, Bambach told Povoledo the portrait 'does not seem to resemble the drawings and paintings by the great master.'

After noting that the work 'did not cause a furore when it went on sale at Christie's in New York,' Povoledo cited **Hugo Chapman** – Turner's successor as Assistant Keeper of Prints & Drawings at the British Museum, and a former Christie's employee – as saying: 'The market is a fairly efficient place. This would be an amazing miss.'

Carbon-14 testing was tendentiously juxtaposed with a quote from Simon Dickinson's London rival Jean-Luc Baroni – to the effect that such tests 'can be very useful, but they can't guarantee an attribution.' Baroni went to give the portrait a casual kiss of commercial death: 'If one expert says yes and the other says no, it makes it unsellable.'

By now Silverman's 'first encounter' with the portrait had become even more melodramatic: when he first saw it, he told Povoledo, 'I didn't dare speak the *L*-word.' Offers to buy the work had 'already started pouring in' – with a top bid of 'more than $50 million, by an intermediary acting on behalf of a Russian.'

Povoledo was back on August 30 with a 630-word article headlined *Dealer Who Sold Portrait Joins Leonardo Debate*. Kate Ganz had rung in from Los Angeles to correct Silverman's cock-and-bull story about the portrait's purchase.

Silverman assured Povoledo he had been 'trying to save Ganz the embarrassment of having let a Leonardo slip through her fingers.'

Povoledo gave Ganz free rein to denigrate the portrait. 'At the end of the day, when you talk about connoisseurship' she pontificated 'it comes down to whether something is beautiful enough to be a Leonardo, whether it resonates with all of the qualities that define his handwriting – sublime modeling, exquisite delicacy, an unparalleled understanding of anatomy – and to me this drawing has none of those things.'

Ganz's remarks were purely subjective. To scholars like Turner, Gregori, Geddo and Vezzosi, the drawing possessed every one of the qualities she enumerated.

Povoledo's article was picked up on September 2 by the American on-line platform *ArtInfo*, which ran it under the more abrasive headline *Seller of Disputed Leonardo Says It's Just a Copy*.

Nicholas Turner released an in-depth survey of the portrait a few days later. 'This remarkable drawing by Leonardo fits stylistically into his œuvre' he declared. 'The drawing is handled with such finesse that it is quite simply beyond the competence of a later retoucher. The obsessive quest to record the appearance of everything within the artist's view, seemingly down to the last particle, is characteristic of Leonardo.'

In early October Martin Kemp travelled to see the portrait – not in Silverman's Paris flat but at the Zurich Freeport. He, Peter Silverman and Giammarco Cappuzzo were ushered into a 'starkly functional and unwelcoming room.' A 'small strongbox' was brought in and its 'aged wooden panel' plonked on a 'sponged wedge' on the table in front of them.

'The physical presence of a work of art is always very different from even the best photographic images' wrote Kemp afterwards (perhaps with Nicholas Penny and Carmen Bambach in mind). 'The first moments are always edgy.

If a certain *zing* does not occur, the encounter is going to be hard going. The portrait *zinged* decisively.'[3]

Kemp's follow-up report on October 19 described the portrait's facial profile as 'subtle to an inexpressible degree.' He was so enthralled that he embarked on a book about the portrait with Pascal Cotte. But when Kemp heard that Silverman was angling for Simon Dickinson to show the portrait in March 2009 at TEFAF Maastricht, the world's ritziest art fair, he blew a gasket – pleading that its first public outing be 'in a wholly non-commercial venue' and not until 'all the research data and analyses have been published in full.'

Dickinson believed 'an asking price in the region of €100 million could be considered reasonable,' but the TEFAF idea was swiftly abandoned. 'I must stress' he wrote to Silverman 'that I would not advise you to be in a hurry with the marketing, as an item of this importance and value will inevitably take time to position.'

The Vienna Albertina – with its fabled collection of Old Master Drawings – was mooted as an alternative venue to 'out' the portrait by Silverman's pal Eckart Lingenauber, who knew the museum's Director Klaus Schröder. The portrait was dispatched to Vienna for inspection in early 2009. But the stars were ill-aligned. Lingenauber was an expert on the Tsarist-era painters Franz Roubaud and Alexei Harlamoff. Schröder was an authority on American Pop Artist Mel Ramos, and had published on nothing earlier than 19th century railways. He had once been wrapped over the knuckles by the Austrian Culture Ministry for packing off 57 Dürers to the Prado without an export license.

The Albertina never released the results of its inspection – if, indeed, one ever took place – and Schröder hardly gave the portrait a second glance. 'It is a very special and exciting drawing' he commented suavely. 'We could not share your enthusiasm completely.'

LUMIERE TECHNOLOGY

On 3 January 2009 I heard back from Peter Silverman. 'I once mentioned I had an amazing scoop' he wrote. 'It is even more amazing than I first imagined.'

I visited his Paris flat on February 6. Drawings and paintings lined the walls. Busts and sculptures sprouted from tables and consoles. He handed me a reproduction of a profiled portrait of a young girl in a ponytail and green dress. 'What do you reckon?' he asked.

Poised but intense. Spatially assured. It brought to my mind the Nazarenes – a group of early 19th century German artists working in Italy who advocated a return to medieval and early Renaissance art. They were forerunners of England's Pre-Raphaelites, who emerged thirty years later.

The portrait was Pre-Raphaelite all right, said Silverman – he had cause to think it dated from the 1490s, when Raphael was barely into his teens.

The yellowish ground of the 33 × 23.9cm reproduction in my lap ('real life size' as Silverman put it) accentuated the work's decorative impact over its psychological subtlety. Being a reproduction made it look like a painting. It was, in fact, a drawing – made in ink and three types of chalk (black, white and red).

No one could have guessed that this flaxen-haired girl in her green dress had been brought to life in red, white and black. It was an astonishing *tour de force*.

'We think it's a Leonardo' chuckled Silverman. 'Bought it from a New York dealer a year or two ago. She got it from Christie's but didn't recognize it.'

'What did Christie's say it was?'

'19th century German' replied Silverman. 'But we know it isn't. It's been carbon-tested to between 1440 and 1650. Christie's mucked up. Big Time.'

Three days later I visited Lumière Technology, to be greeted by their dapper CEO Jean Penicaut, who sped through the technical details of Lumière's patented, 13-channel multispectral camera. By revealing a picture's successive colour layers, its pigments could be identified without taking physical samples. The camera had already been used by some top museums (Kröller-Müller, Van Gogh, Cleveland) and the Art Institute of Chicago, with Lumière keen to build up a comparative database of pictures from around the world.

But, complained Penicaut, 'no one wants to collaborate with a private body' and their camera was perceived as 'extremely dangerous for a number of people with entrenched interests, including auction houses and people doing *catalogues raisonnés*. They'll suddenly have to face the fact that they're not the only ones who can say *Yea* or *Nay*.'

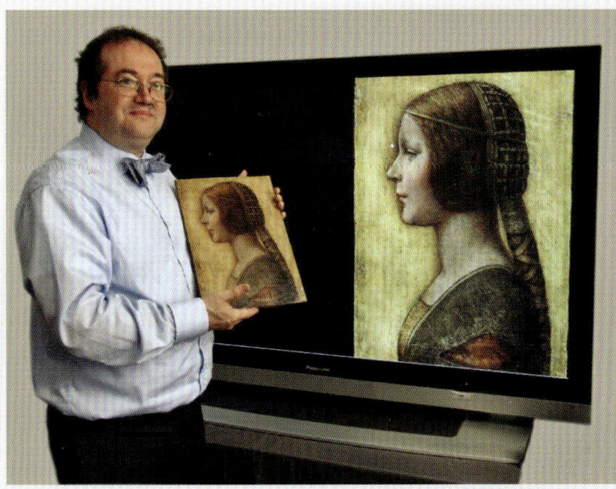

PASCAL COTTE

We ventured downstairs into Pascal Cotte's lair, where the bow-tied boffin was spinning on a swivel-chair and surveying a beckoning bank of computer monitors. 'Look at this' he quipped.

Up popped a female nose in no-nostril overdrive. 'Bit big' burbled Cotte. He zoomed out, slightly, so that the eye in Silverman's portrait occupied the entire 4ft-wide screen. The detail was sensational.

Cotte's analysis would occupy 70 pages of the book about the portrait he was soon to co-author with Martin Kemp – who, on May 15, informed Silverman that *La Bella Milanese* (as he was now calling the portrait) contained a fingerprint that had been likened to those in Leonardo's *St Jerome* by Peter Paul Biro, who sounded like a Rubens doodle but was actually a burly Canadian fingerprint specialist. This, declared Kemp, was 'one more component in what is as consistent a body of evidence as I have ever seen. I do not have the slightest flicker of doubt that we are dealing with a work of great beauty and originality that contributes something special to Leonardo's *œuvre*. It deserves to be in the public domain.'

Silverman agreed. First he sounded out Bill Griswold, Director of the Morgan Library in New York – but was told that Library statutes did not allow works in private hands to be shown unless promised as gifts. Then came negotiations to display the portrait at Christ Church Picture Gallery, home to Oxford University's premier art collection. When these collapsed Simon Dickinson contacted Johann Kräftner, head of the stylish Liechtenstein Museum in Vienna, with a view to the portrait being shown there in late September. But the Prince of Liechtenstein had no intention of footing the bill, and a cost-projection of €250,000 prompted Silverman to seek financial help – from, of all people, Christie's.

He fired off an e-mail to Noël Annesley, Christie's Senior Consultant for Old Master Drawings – and Deputy Chairman of Christie's International when the portrait was sold in 1998. Silverman had known him for thirty years. Annesley had joined what was then *Christie's, Manson & Wood* in 1964. Christie's was his life.

'I think it natural to inform you that I have now concluded the footwork on what Martin Kemp, Carlo Pedretti and Nick Turner are calling the most important art historical discovery in perhaps the past 50 years' boasted Silverman. 'If Christie's do not wish to lose out on this I suggest you contact me as soon as possible.'

Annesley contacted Nick Turner instead. Christie's Head of Drawings Benjamin Perronnet (who had only joined the firm in 2006) was told to get back to Silverman.

'I WILL NOT DEAL WITH ANY LOWER ECHELON PEOPLE from your company' stormed Silverman to Annesley. The Liechtenstein Museum wished to show his Leonardo – its first public outing. He wanted to make it a major event. This would require considerable funding. Silverman suggested that Christie's work with him to devise a common strategy. 'I promise you first go if you can assure me that you are more than mildly involved.'

Christie's had zero interest in underwriting an event advertising how they had 'mucked up big time' on a Leonardo. Silverman's portrait would never be shown at the Liechtenstein Museum (which closed its doors to the public two years later).

On 2 September 2009 Silverman informed me that the '*L* launch' would now be mid-September, at the Blenheim Literary Festival in Woodstock – just around the corner from Martin Kemp's home. Forty years after the original Woodstock Festival, it sounded a good omen – if hardly likely to attract Leonardo groupies in their hundreds of thousands.

In an interview with *The Independent* ahead of the Festival – where he would be speaking in Blenheim Palace on September 18 (tickets £12, including glass of wine) – Martin Kemp piled further pressure on Christie's. Under the headline *Face of a Dead Princess* he suggested that the sitter was Bianca, illegitimate daughter of Duke Ludovico Sforza, and announced he was renaming her *La*

Bella Principessa. It was a metaphorical title. Bianca Sforza was no *Principessa*, but *Signora* of Voghera and Bobbio. She was no *Bella,* but a wistful teenager.

Silverman was now keen for me to file a story, promising 'an exclusive on the fingerprint evidence and the forensic report.' I proposed an article to *Art+Auction* but never received a No (three months later the portrait would make the cover of *ARTnews,* their bitter rivals). *Art+Auction* was in crisis. The editor had resigned, not been replaced, and writers were not getting paid. No publication likes to get wrong side of a potential advertiser as big as Christie's, but I would soon have reason to interpret *Art+Auction*'s indifference in more sinister light.

Meanwhile I offered the story to London art trade weekly *Antiques Trade Gazette.* The editor replied the same day. 'Sounds good. We could use 400 words and a pic.'

On October 9 I sent 1,380. ATG gave it the whole of page 3 beneath the head-line *Is this the greatest art market discovery of the century?* It was certainly the biggest story in ATG's 40-year history – whooshing the paper's name, via the internet, worldwide. Within minutes of the article going on-line on October 12 it was being googled from New York to Nagasaki. Search-engines would continue to throw up *Leonardo* and *ATG* in the same computerized breath for years to come.

The title ATG assigned my article – *Fingerprint points to $19,000 portrait being revalued as £100m work by Leonardo da Vinci* – was misleading: I had written that the bedrock of Kemp's Leonardo attribution was 'scientific evidence obtained by the revolutionary multispectral camera pioneered by Lumière Technology.'

Pascal Cotte found the title 'far too sensationalistic' and Jean Penicaut asked me to change it. Yet Lumière Technology were soon revelling in the publicity – counting 1,500 press articles and TV reports on 'every channel on earth' as their website zoomed from 150 to 3,000 hits a day.

CNN picked up on my story on October 13, followed by ABC News, who quoted Christie's as saying the Leonardo attribution was 'based on unproven scientific techniques which were not available to us at the time.' The word 'unproven' was gratuitous and dishonest: a foretaste of the sort of damage-limitation tactics Christie's were prepared to employ.

Next day *The Times* ran an opinion piece by Sir Timothy Clifford, formerly Dir-ector of Scotland's National Galleries, entitled *How I Know The New Portrait Is By Leonardo.* 'As soon as I saw this portrait I was well on the way to being persuaded that here was not just a Leonardo drawing, but a masterpiece' he wrote. 'It is an iconic image of haunting beauty.'

Other media coverage was less *à propos.* Take two articles by Ulli Tückmantel in Düsseldorf's *Rheinische Post.*

On October 15 'Tookie' subjected his readers to the musings of Maike Vogt-Lüerssen, a former biology student from Seaford Meadows, Australia, who had convinced herself that *La Bella Principessa* was not Bianca Sforza but 'Lucrezia Borgia's pretty cousin and lady-in-waiting Angela Borgia Lanzol, a real It-Girl of her time.'

Tückmantel's second article, on October 20, was less frivolous. It was headlined *Millionenstreit um Leonardo Da Vinci* ('Million-Dollar Wrangle over Leonardo') and devoted to Frank Zöllner, professor in art history at Leipzig University. Zöllner dismissed the fingerprint evidence as a 'PR stunt' and damned the portrait as 'wooden, pedantic and undynamic, the reddened cheeks more indicative of a 19th century dating' (which, being the fruit of 19th century restoration, they were).

Silverman, who had invited Zöllner to inspect the portrait eighteen months earlier, accused him of 'bad-will, jealousy and envy' and hit the roof at Zöllner's insinuation that the portrait had been smuggled into Switzerland without paying tax. Zöllner scoffed that, if it really were a \$100m Leonardo, Silverman would have had to pay \$7.6m in duty to export it from France.

'Sehr Geehrter Customs Inspecteur!' snarled Silverman punningly (*Zöllner* meaning 'customs officer'). 'I am not particularly sensitive to calumny and jealousy, but a denunciation of a Jew coming from a German goes beyond my patience!'

GANGS OF NEW YORK

On October 16 Kemp informed Silverman and Turner that Noël Annesley bore overall responsibility for the misidentification of the portrait and that 'going back to him was a bad idea.' Kemp also believed that Ganz had 'almost certainly' sought the opinion of the Metropolitan Museum's Drawings & Prints Curator, George Goldner, with whom she was 'very friendly.' What Kemp dubbed 'the New York gang' were 'almost bound to be hostile in an act of closing their ranks, since they all missed it.'

Kemp had also gleaned from *ARTnews* editor Milton Esterow – preparing a 'big spread' – that Keith Christiansen (the Met's European Paintings Curator) had received an advanced copy of his book, so 'they now have the advantage of being able to work on my text negatively before its publication.'

'These guys are only interested in covering their very red asses!' Silverman declared to me. Silverman promptly e-mailed Christiansen admitting he had sent him the draft of Kemp's book without permission, and piously hoping he would adhere to 'absolute confidentiality – even within the Met.'

Esterow's six-page article came out in the January 2010 issue of *ARTnews*, with the portrait on the front cover beneath the headline *Is She or Isn't She A Leonardo?*

In what may be some sort of journalistic record, Esterow's article quoted a staggering ten anonymous sources. The only opponent of the Leonardo attribution willing to be named was the Albertina's Klaus Schröder. 'No one thinks it's a Leonardo' he burbled. Esterow re-cited Carmen Bambach's non-committal quote to the *New York Times* sixteen months earlier – noting ruefully that she 'declined to make any further comment' – and mentioned Vezzosi's and Gregori's support for the attribution (but not Nicholas Turner's).[4]

Although Martin Kemp was quoted extensively, Esterow also devoted a quarter of his article to the fingerprint evidence – damning Biro's previous work on Jackson Pollock as 'controversial.'

Christie's were quoted as saying 'discussions surrounding the possible re-attribution rely heavily on cutting-edge scientific techniques which were not available to us at the time … until scholars are all in agreement we cannot comment on this particular work.' Esterow's strenuous efforts to evoke such scholarly disagreement will have had Christie's purring.

Peter Silverman told Esterow that, although not the drawing's owner, he would 'reap all benefits of any Hollywood movie contact that may come along.'

The portrait's public debut came along eleven weeks later in the Swedish port of Gothenburg. It was unveiled at a press conference with white-gloved pomp, then solemnly showcased against a black ground, unframed. The exhibition, quirkily entitled *…And There Was Light*, took place in a converted dockside factory. Swedish Culture Minister Lena Adelsohn Liljeroth cut the ribbon at the March 19 opening bash attended by Cotte, Penicaut, Biro, Vezzosi and Silverman, fresh from brandishing *La Bella* at a former Miss Nigeria on a Norwegian TV chat-show under the bemused gaze of the country's ex-Prime Minister, Gro Harlem Brundtland.

The Gothenburg exhibition – accompanied by a sumptuously illustrated 260-page catalogue – had been put together by Vezzosi and Francesco Buranelli, Director General of the Vatican Museums, with Silvio Berlusconi as President of the Committee of Honour. It was fun and informative, if not for the purist, evoking the superstars of the Renaissance via tactile video screens, Raphael's earliest known painting, a lifesize resin reproduction of Michelangelo's *David*, and models of Leonardo inventions. The show cost Excellent Exhibitions from Malmö €2.5 million to stage, and they needed 200,000 visitors to break even. Although crowds snaked around the building on the first weekend, only 120,000 bought tickets during the five-month run.

The Gothenburg opening coincided with the release of the new Kemp/Cotte book (including a chapter on the fingerprint evidence by Peter Paul Biro). On April 11 London's *Daily Telegraph* ran a positive 700-word review by Martin Gayford, who declared: 'My own hunch, without having seen the original, is that Kemp is right.'

Next day came a vicious 1,940-word article in the same newspaper by Richard Dorment, Kate Ganz's husband at the time she acquired the work.

'*La Bella Principessa* has been touted as Leonardo's missing masterpiece, but the experts beg to differ' wrote Dorment beneath the banner headline *La Bella Principessa: a £100m Leonardo, or a copy?*

Dorment had marshalled an army of unidentified 'scholars' to reject the attribution 'utterly.' The portrait was derided as 'a screaming 20th century fake' by one particularly courageous 'museum director' who 'asked not to be named' – but was described as a 'well-known connoisseur of Italian painting and sculpture' (and widely assumed to be Nicholas Penny).

Dorment re-used Esterow's Klaus Schröder quote in full but, like Esterow, was unable to get anything out of Carmen Bambach – surmising instead that she was 'among those who vehemently reject Kemp's attribution' (along with Everett Fahy, the Met's Head of European Paintings).

Sententiously declaring that 'sometimes silence is more damning than words,' Dorment revealed that Martin Clayton, Keeper of the Queen's Drawings, had 'not endorsed' Kemp's attribution. Clayton was furious, later stating that his position prevented him 'from getting involved in public controversies about the authorship of a work in a private collection' – adding (perhaps with Carmen Bambach and Nicholas Penny in mind) that 'I could not in any case make a statement about the authorship of a drawing until I have seen it in the flesh.'

Dorment took swipes at Silverman ('a fantasist') and the Gothenburg show ('a circus'). Pascal Cotte's scientific analysis was mocked as 'barely intelligible' and based on 'claims to have used technology.' Martin Kemp was belittled as an 'expert on Leonardo's scientific work' and accused of 'steamrolling' the public into accepting his attribution in a book 'purporting' to be a work of scholarship. His book was 'not art history – it is advocacy.'

'Kemp's opponents point out that of the 4,000 or so surviving drawings by Leonardo, not a single one is on vellum' reported Dorment, either ignorantly or dishonestly. Just after completing Bianca's portrait, Leonardo provided ink and wash illustrations for three de luxe vellum editions of *De Divina Proportione* by his Sforza court colleague Luca Pacioli: one (now in the Ambrosiana) was dedicated to Bianca's father Il Moro; another (now in Geneva) to her husband Galeazzo Sanseverino.

Kemp deplored the 'aggressive tone' of Dorment's article. Biro called the article 'mean-spirited and uninformed.' Silverman, convinced that Ganz was behind it, termed it a 'not-too-subtle exercise in disinformation.' The *Daily Telegraph* waited a week before publishing Silverman's eight-point response – not as a *Letter to the Editor*, as he had every right to expect, but on their website, early one Sunday morning. It disappeared a few hours later.

Silverman tackled Nicholas Penny on April 13. 'Knowing your scrupulousness, I find it hard to believe you would pronounce on something you have never seen. So I do not believe you have been correctly cited. Right or wrong?'

'You ask whether I have been misrepresented by Richard Dorment' retorted Penny on April 15. 'I have not. I do not endorse the attribution to Leonardo.'

'The fact that NP is calling a work a *screaming fake* when he has refused even to see it in the original seems very arrogant to me' commented Nicholas Turner.

Christie's had described the portrait as 'The Property of a Lady'. The lady's identity had remained confidential, and could easily have never been known: when news of the Leonardo attribution broke she was 85. Three weeks after Dorment's article she took Christie's to court.

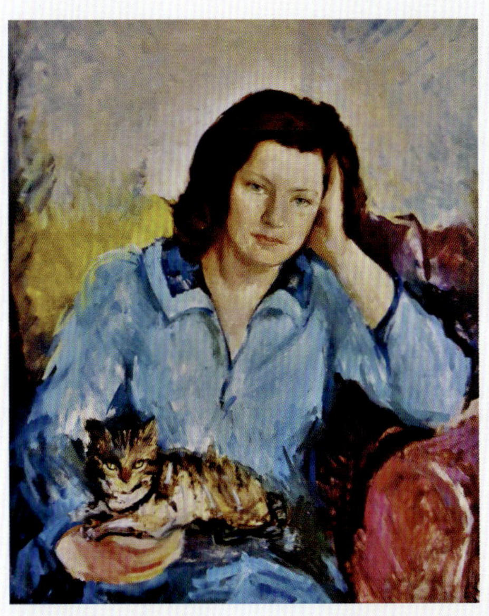

GIANNINO MARCHIG
PORTRAIT OF JEANNE (1969)

Jeanne Marchig, *née* Janina Paszkowska, was born in Warsaw in 1924 into a family of doctors and lawyers. She was an only child. Her father died before she was born; her mother, Elzbieta Chrostowska, fled 1930s Poland for Sweden, where Janina later married, becoming Janina Hama. The marriage did not last. She met the Italian picture restorer Giannino Marchig in 1949 – the year he moved from Italy to Switzerland. In 1955 they married, settling in Lausanne. She changed her name to *Jeanne* but retained Swedish citizenship for the rest of her life.

Giannino Marchig was born in 1897 in Trieste, then part of the Habsburg Empire. In 1915 his family moved to Florence. He was an artist of precocious talent, becoming Professor of Drawing at the Florence Accademia at the age of 23. His paintings were shown at every Venice Biennale from 1920 until 1936, and in thirty international exhibitions before 1939.

Although Marchig lived until he was fifty under the same roof as his mother, on the banks of the Arno, his piercing blue eye for the fairer sex extended beyond a youthful penchant for racy nudes. One of his lady friends was an Italian aristocrat, who reportedly gifted him the portrait later known as *La Bella Principessa*.[5]

Marchig was Secretary of the Florence branch of the *Sindacato Nazionale Fascista di Belle Arti* (Fascist National Art Union) from 1931. In 1943, after the fall of Mussolini, he was tasked with the safekeeping of paintings owned by his friend Bernard Berenson during the Nazi Occupation.[6]

After the war Marchig stopped painting, worked briefly as an exhibition curator and art magazine editor, then devoted himself to restoration. His interest in restoration had been prompted by Augusto Vermehren (1888–1978), who had succeeded his father Otto (1861–1917) as Chief Restorer at the Uffizi in Florence (the museum in Otto's native Güstrow, in northern Germany, contains his winsome copies of Renaissance works – one of them, by Titian, entitled *La Bella*).

Marchig would establish an avant-garde reputation as a restorer through recourse to X-rays and pigment analysis. He also wrote about technique, complaining that easy-to-use tubes of paint had 'reduced this most virile of artistic disciplines to a Sunday pastime' with painting 'no longer a matter of the mind (*cosa mentale*, as Leonardo would have said), but more and more about visual reality'.

One of the last works Marchig restored, in 1976, was the 'Landsdowne' version of Leonardo's *Madonna of the Yarnwinder* – for the celebrated dealer Daniel Wildenstein, who called him 'a restorer *sans pareil*'.[7]

When Jeanne married Giannino she was 31, he 58. The Bianca Sforza portrait had been in his possession 'for some time' – not hung on the wall but, she said, kept it in a 'special folder' as he considered it might fade in strong daylight.[8]

In 1960 the Marchigs moved to a villa in the swish Geneva suburb of Cologny, where Jeanne would enjoy an intimate relationship with Prince Sadruddin Aga Khan[9] (who owned the nearby Château de Bellerive, and twice ran unsuccessfully for Secretary-General of the United Nations). Giannino died in 1983, three years after being granted a major retrospective in his native Trieste. Jeanne donated the bulk of his archives to the Getty Research Institute in Los Angeles. Posthumous exhibitions of his work were held in Geneva in 1985 and the Uffizi in 1994, and a lavish 240-page monograph published in 2000.[10]

In 1989 Jeanne founded the Marchig Animal Welfare Trust 'because of her deep concern for nature, and in memory of her husband.' She moved to a new house in Cologny, where she lived with a soft-spoken, twinkle-eyed Queenslander, Bryan Deschamp – a Carmelite priest who worked for Australian Intelligence in Latin America before moving to Geneva as Senior Policy Advisor to the UN Commission for Refugees.

On 5 July 2007 Christie's sold Piero di Cosimo's *Jason and Queen Hypsipyle* (1499) for £240,000. On 7 July 2009 they sold Giulano Bugiardini's *Portrait of a Young Gentleman* (*c.*1505) for £825,000. Both works – painted within a decade of Madame Marchig's Bianca Sforza portrait – came from the collection of Giannino Marchig. Jeanne Marchig had been anonymously consigning works to Christie's, initially with her husband, since 1969. She was a major client. When news of the Leonardo attribution broke it was Noël Annesley, no less, who gave her a call.

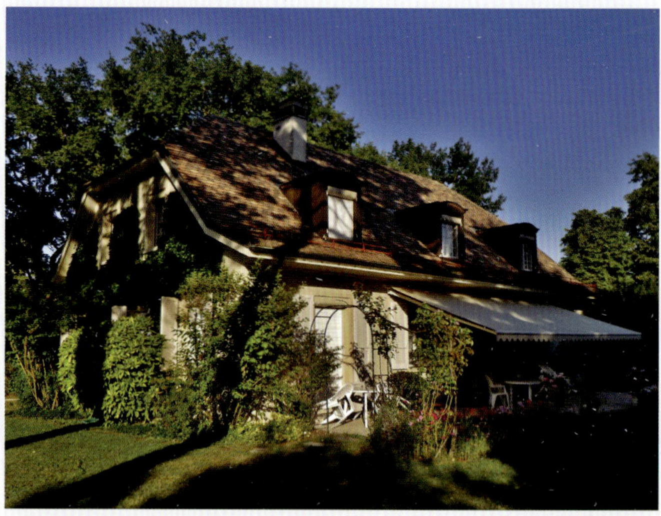

JEANNE MARCHIG'S HOME
COLOGNY NEAR GENEVA

His placatory efforts were given short shrift. Jeanne Marchig told him she found the arguments for a Leonardo attribution 'most convincing, and supported by scientific evidence' and expressed her 'devastation' at Christie's incompetence. In 1997, when consigning the portrait, she had told their expert François Borne that her husband believed it was by Ghirlandaio (1449–94) – Leonardo's fellow-apprentice in Verrocchio's Florence studio.

Richard Dorment's article in the *Daily Telegraph* was a godsend (or Ganzsend) to Christie's, and they gleefully forwarded it to Madame Marchig. By now Annesley had handed her over to Christie's Head of Dispute Resolution, Sandra Cobden. Her first letter to Madame Marchig saw her 'wanting to resolve this amicably' and opining, with the subtlety of a sledgehammer, that 'one of the things I find most interesting is how many experts have decided to stand on the sidelines.' She also informed Madame Marchig that the Cobden family were 'the lucky caretakers of four beloved rescue cats [so] I looked at the website for your foundation with interest. You do remarkable, needed and good work.'

If Christie's thought the feline-fancying octogenarian susceptible to that sort of tummy-tickling they had another think coming. 'Such language!' sniffed Madame Marchig incredulously. 'Talking about cats!'

She was convinced that Christie's were 'playing for time, hoping I'll die.'

On 3 May 2010 she lodged a complaint in the Federal Court of Manhattan seeking damages 'for the misattribution of a drawing sold far below its actual value, solely because of the defendant's willful refusal and failure to investigate the plaintiff's believed attribution' and for 'making of false statements in connection with the auction and sale.' The Marchig Animal Welfare Trust was named as co-plaintiff.

Although Jeanne Marchig had presented the work to Christie's 'as a work of the Italian Renaissance,' this attribution was 'summarily rejected' by Christie's expert François Borne 'after about fifteen minutes of examination.' Christie's were accused of failing to 'undertake any investigation whatsoever as to the viability of plaintiff's belief that the drawing dated from the Italian Renaissance' and their 'insistence and conclusion that the drawing was of German origin from the 19th century was contrary to the evidence and expertise readily available at the time' and 'based solely upon Borne's arbitrary and unsupported opinion.'

After referring to my article in *Antiques Trade Gazette*, the complaint cited 'overwhelming expert, esthetic, forensic and scientific evidence, as well as scholarly opinion' in favour of the Leonardo attribution, claiming the work was worth over $150m.

Christie's sued for selling £100m 'Da Vinci' for £11,400 headlined the *Guardian* on May 5, reporting that Madame Marchig was seeking unspecified but 'substantial' damages and asserting there was 'ample evidence' the portrait was by Leonardo. 'Other experts,' reported Dalya Alberge, were unconvinced. She cited only one: Jacques Franck, 'Da Vinci consultant at UCLA' (University of California).

'It's not Leonardo's hand' Franck told her. 'The drawing presents anatomical mistakes, notably the link between the neck and the bust.' Franck's biological qualifications were not apparent in the name-dropping autobiography on his personal website, where he bragged about copying Leonardos from the age of eight.

Lawyers for Jeanne Marchig and Christie's winged wordy memoranda at each other throughout the summer of 2010, with Madame Marchig adding a request that Christie's return the work's original frame – as, without her 'knowledge or consent, Borne, or someone at Christie's, changed the frame and it was sold with the changed frame.' She said the frame 'looked very precious – a sort of small Cassetta frame with an ivory-coloured background with a typically patterned Florentine design. I am not sure whether the motif was in silver, painted, or otherwise.'[11]

Christie's replied that they would 'get back' to Madame Marchig about the frame, but didn't. However, on June 7, Sarah Cobden informed her that Christie's had taken 'the opportunity to … inspect the painting [*sic*] again. To be blunt … the painting [re-*sic*] simply does not appear to our eyes to be a work by Leonardo da Vinci. This is due, in part, to the heavy layer of what appears to be shellac on the surface which obscures many of the painting's details.'

Lumière's Pascal Cotte disputed Cobden's assertion. The work had a 'covering of gum arabic to protect the fragile drawing. *Heavy* is not correct. I would say *usual*.' Some details might 'be obscure to the human eye, but NOT to the camera.'

Cobden also opined slyly that 'most of the proponents of the new attribution have a significant financial stake … Luminere [*sic*] Technology is struggling to get a firm financial footing for its company and its product; Silverman is seeking to increase his investment in the painting as well as to publish his book on the topic; one of the experts on whom Silverman relies … are [*sic*] connected to the book publication project or other publicity projects.'

Cobden concluded that 'the new attribution to Leonardo da Vinci is based on the Luminere [re-*sic*] Technology and the new fingerprint analysis. Such tools weren't available when Christie's sold your painting. An auction house is not legally liable for any change in attribution that is based on new technology that was not available at the time the original attribution was made.'

New technology like carbon-dating – and not so new technology like microscopes – had been readily available to Christie's in 1998, but ignored.

THE PORTRAIT'S BOOKISH ORIGINS

On May 7 Kemp and Cotte had addressed the Leonardo da Vinci Society at London's Courtauld Institute on *The Bella Principessa, a new Da Vinci – How do we know? The Scientific Proof.*

Cotte's video presentation showed, amongst other things, that palmprints had been deliberately applied to the neck to create a nuanced texture, whereas the fingerprint top-left appeared to have been created by accident when the vellum sheet was picked up – suggesting the sheet had already been folded in two before the artist set to work on it. He also demonstrated that, had Bianca Sforza's eyes been blue, Leonardo would have been unable to use the three-chalk technique – whose spectral range extended only from red to green.

'Pascal's scientific evidence contributes significantly towards strengthening Martin's case' wrote Society Vice-President Francis Ames-Lewis. 'It is technically such a profoundly unusual work as to suggest Leonardo as the only artist of the time who had the inventiveness and readiness to experiment that the drawing shows.'

Mina Gregori also broadcast her latest thoughts on the portrait in the May 2010 issue of high-brow Italian art review *Paragoni*. 'My examination,' she specified, 'was exclusively visual, carried out by carefully scrutinizing the work's surface following the traditional approach of the connoisseur – an approach that is today too readily disregarded.'

Gregori found that 'the brightness and transparency of the girl's eye are only to be found in other drawings by Leonardo' and noted 'the subtle colouring in the un-retouched areas of the cheek, where the tonal gradations are almost imperceptible. This inimitable delicacy made me think of this same famous characteristic found in the face of the *Mona Lisa*.'

Further backing for the Leonardo attribution came from Italian fashion historian Elisabetta Gnignera, who was adamant that *La Bella* was wearing a 'beautiful example of a late 15th century/early 16th century *coazzone*: the so-called *acconciatura alla Spagnuola* especially loved by Beatrice d'Este during the years she lived in Milan.'

Gnignera's research would grow into a 244-page volume, *La Bella Svelata* ('La Bella Revealed'), assessing the portrait's hairstyle and costume with the help of numerous late Quattrocento works of art.[12] When she advised Pascal Cotte to use his digital megacamera to look for the pins needed to keep the ribbons of Bianca's *coazzone* in place, Cotte found them in giant close-up: they were too minute to be detected by the naked eye.

Silverman was now entertaining hopes of showing the portrait in Rome – the dynamic Marina Mattei sounded keen to exhibit it at the Capitoline Museums, where she was Director. But Silverman was beginning to feel the strain. On May 9, a few days after imploring Kate Ganz to 'stop your unwarranted, nasty crusade,' Silverman accused Gina Thomas, London correspondent of the *Frankfurter Allgemeine Zeitung*, of being part of a conspiracy. She had written that the Leonardo attribution had 'met great scepticism in professional circles' (none of the sceptics were named) and that Madame Marchig's arguments were based 'largely on technical findings' whereas Christie's 'relied on connoisseurship' – all beneath the scandalmonger headline *Die Falsche Prinzessin* (The Fake Princess).

'Are you friends with Richard Dorment?' snapped Silverman.

On July 1 Peter Paul Biro alerted Kemp and Cotte that the next edition of *The New Yorker* would be running a 'potentially prejudiced and cherry-picked article about me, my work and the drawing.' *The New Yorker*, he pointed out, was 'owned by Condé Nast, which in turn is owned by Si Newhouse – a major client of Christie's.'

'Christie's and their friends are getting us much as they can in the public domain rubbishing the portrait and those who have worked on it' replied Kemp – who had assured *The New Yorker* that Biro's work on the portrait was 'exemplary.'

David Grann's 16,000-word article on July 12 implied Biro was sleazy and incompetent. When Biro sued *The New Yorker* for libel, a Federal judge paid implicit tribute to Grann's verbal craftiness – declaring that his article did 'not make express accusations against Biro, or suggest concrete conclusions about whether or not he is a fraud.'

Silverman, Kemp and Cotte would soon, however, receive a crucial boost – originating from Tampa and refocusing discussion of the Leonardo attribution, equally improbably, on Warsaw.

In September 2010 David Wright, Emeritus Professor of Art History at South Florida University, wrote to Martin Kemp out of the blue – referring him to a Sforza history book (the 'Sforziada') in Poland's National Library. He advised Kemp that the book's dimensions closely corresponded to those of the portrait, and that it contained illuminations pertaining to Bianca Sforza's marriage.

On December 17 Silverman braved the freezing Warsaw winter to visit the Library. The *Sforziada* was magicked out of a 'metal-armoured case' beneath the stone-cold gaze of Anna Zawisza, white-gloved Head of Manuscripts. Silverman thumbed through its 200 pages, finally spotting a 'protruding remnant' between pages 161 and 162: cast-iron (or at least metal-armoured) evidence of a 'cut and extracted page of vellum.'

'Wow!' ejaculated Silverman.

He promptly e-mailed the news to Kemp and Turner, declaring his intention to call a press conference to announce his discovery.

'Please do not produce premature ejaculations' growled Kemp. 'There is a great deal to do before the theory is nailed down. We saw what happened previously with fragmentary media announcements and antagonising important people.'

On December 20 Silverman protested that 'no decision has been made as to the dates of going public' – then promptly outlined a series of projected press articles starting January 4.

'The unconsidered and unilateral decision to go public undermines any sense that I can trust you to operate in a collegial manner!' fumed Kemp. 'Your actions constitute the most profoundly misguided thing I have seen in 40 years in the art world.'

Cristina Funghini, the Italian curator who was liaising between Silverman and the Capitoline Museums about a possible show in Rome, echoed Kemp's sentiments.

'Turner, Strinati and Buranelli all give the same advice: keep silence and secret till the very end' she admonished Silverman. 'The way to proceed is not like the Indiana Jones of art history!'

On December 22 Silverman agreed to delay releasing the Warsaw news.

Meanwhile Kemp advised Tomasz Ososiński, the Library's Keeper of Early Printed Books, that he wished to see the *Sforziada* himself, proposing a 'programme of collaborative research.' That was fine by Ososiński, although he felt any portrait likely to have been placed before the Birago frontispiece rather than on page 162.

On 31 January 2011 Cotte and Kemp spent 'three hours plus' in the Polish National Library (*see below left*) with 'encouraging results.' Page 162 was a red herring, but three folios from the first quire were missing. Cotte obtained spectral data of the remaining half of the excised sheet that once contained the portrait – which must, he surmised, have been extracted 'when the book was rebound and trimmed in the 17th or early 18th century,' as its three stitch holes were intact. Macrophotography showed that the portrait's dimensions and stitch-holes matched the *Sforziada* perfectly, as did the thickness of the vellum (0.14/0.15mm).

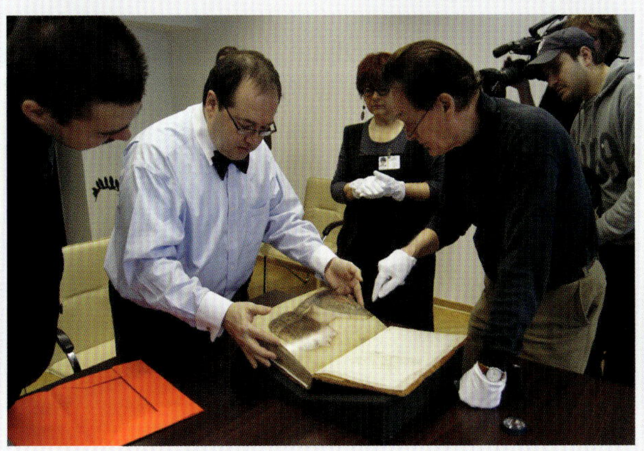

Kemp and Cotte's illustrated 21-page technical report on *La Bella Principessa and the Warsaw Sforziad* took nearly eight months to complete. It concluded that the portrait of *Bianca Sforza* was 'now one of the works by Leonardo about which we know most in terms of its patronage, subject, date, original location, function and innovatory technique.' On September 19 Kemp sent advance copies to Pietro Marani, who declared it 'of high interest,' and Carmen Bambach, who did not bother to download it.

The report was released to the media a week later. Kemp had insisted on a September 28 deadline – then gave an advance exclusive to Dalya Alberge of the *Guardian*, whose 800-word article on September 27, headlined *Is this portrait a lost Leonardo?*, presented Kemp as the hero of a 'needle-in-a-haystack' search for a 15th century volume that he managed to track down 'against the odds.' Pascal Cotte was downgraded to an anonymous 'specialist,' David Wright not even mentioned. Alberge rehashed Jacques Franck's anatomical objection from her May 5 article before lazily concluding 'the debate will no doubt continue.'

Eric Biétry-Rivierre of *Le Figaro*, however, beneath the headline *Mystery of Leonardo's Thirteenth Portrait Elucidated*, declared the portrait's 'long-contested provenance' had been 'established after a lengthy investigation. Leonardo da Vinci is indeed the author.'

Biétry-Rivierre was one of the few journalists willing or able to understand the work of Lumière Technology, calling Pascal Cotte 'a serious version of Dan Brown' who had 'pierced Leonardo's secrets' not through 'esoterism or the supernatural but through science and technology.'

The Warsaw Report came too late to bolster the portrait's chances of inclusion in the blockbuster exhibition *Leonardo da Vinci: Painter at the Court of Milan* slated for London's National Gallery that November (and which, despite its title, would include more drawings than paintings).

The show opened on November 9, with another recently discovered Leonardo the focus of attention: his heavily restored *Salvator Mundi*. Its owners, reported Kemp, had 'acted very shrewdly' – securing the opinions of Leonardo scholars 'in a very systematic and quiet way ... in marked contrast to what happened to the *Bella Principessa*, which got a lot of premature publicity before the work was really done.'

One reason advanced for not showing *La Bella Principessa* at the National Gallery was its private ownership. No such qualms applied to the *Salvator Mundi* – rumoured to be available for around \$200m:[13] a double show of hypocrisy given that the *Salvator Mundi* was also painted outside the *Leonardo In Milan* timeline.

On September 8 Silverman's U.K. lawyer Brinsley Dresden had written to National Gallery supremo Nicholas Penny asking that *La Bella Principessa* be treated in the same manner as the *Salvator Mundi*, and offering to submit it for examination by a panel of 'suitably qualified and experienced experts' – providing that, if they agreed the portrait were by Leonardo, it would be included in the exhibition. Silverman also declared that *La Bella Principessa* was not for sale, nor would be for the next twelve months.

Penny replied on September 19 that there could be 'no question of setting in motion some kind of process of the type your client proposes' – reinforcing Silverman's suspicions that the portrait's exclusion was due to behind-the-scenes pressure from New York. His lawyer then requested access to Nicholas Penny's correspondence with the Metropolitan Museum under the U.K.'s Freedom of Information Act. The request was ultimately declined.

When Silverman subsequently learned that exhibition curator Luke Syson had lined up a new job at the Metropolitan Museum for after the show, his frustration reached melting-point.

On December 10, in the weekend edition of the French newspaper *Libération*, Vincent Noce trotted out the Dorment line about the Kemp/Cotte book being 'advocacy' and accused Lumière of 'spectacularizing science, with the risk of fuelling fiction' – while declining to reference their Warsaw report. In an article outrageously headlined *False Airs of a Princess*, Noce happily cited Hugo Chapman's ex-Christie's nonsense about Leonardo never using vellum and asserted that the Leonardo attribution had been greeted with 'scepticism in all the top museums' – starting, of course, with Klaus Schröder's Albertina.

'At least, on Saturday, only left-wing loonies read the damn thing' commented Lumière's Jean Penicaut.

Lumière had recently digitized *La Belle Ferronnière*, ascertaining that it had been painted on the same panel as *Lady with an Ermine*. But, when Penicaut asked Penny if they could digitize the *Salvator Mundi*, he was cold-shouldered. Lumière were initially blackballed from the National Gallery's *Leonardo* symposium on 13/14 January 2012, but Pascal Cotte was eventually invited at Martin Kemp's insistence.

On January 25 a *National Geographic* video documentary about *La Bella* was aired in the United States, entitled *Mystery of a Masterpiece*. It was relayed in the February print issue of *National Geographic*, as *Lady with a Secret*, with a snazzy lead photo of the portrait being handled with white kid gloves. Silverman's book about his discovery, *Leonardo's Lost Princess*, was published soon afterwards. Its bashful subtitle, *One Man's Quest to Authenticate an Unknown Portrait by Leonardo da Vinci*, made short shrift of the contributions of Kemp and Cotte.

MEETING MADAME MARCHIG

Despite her feisty confrontation with Christie's, Madame Marchig had told Peter Silverman 'I don't want to be bothered by journalists.' Luckily she would make an exception.

I was vetted by her partner Bryan Deschamp at the *Montbrillant* restaurant next to Geneva rail station on 25 October 2010, then invited for lunch in suburban Cologny on November 18. Her spacious villa stood behind tall hedges at the end of a leafy drive flanked on one side by open fields. The hall and stairwell were lined with drawings by her late husband. Double-doors led into the main room. A settee and marble coffee-table, topped by a copy of the Christie's 1998 catalogue, were to the right. The dining-table was to the left. French windows opposite led out to a large garden and the patio where Madame Marchig dined in summer. 'Campari?' murmured Bryan.

Ten minutes later the hall doors opened and, small but stately, Jeanne Marchig made her entrance. 'At last, Simon' she said, proffering her hand like a latterday Catherine the Great. 'Pleased to meet you.'

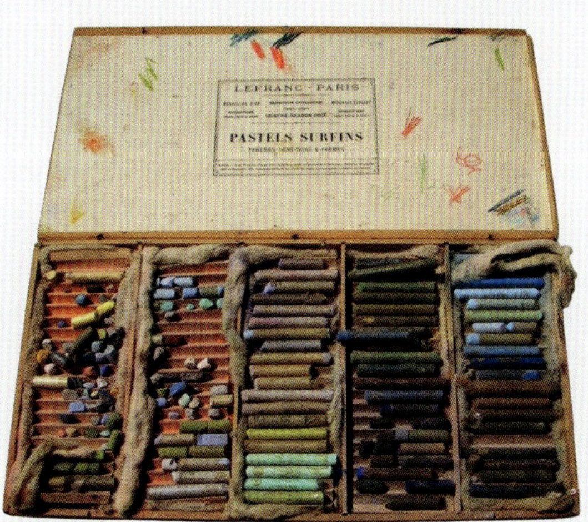

Lunch was served by Maria, her Portuguese maid. Afterwards Madame Marchig showed me the box of *Pastels Surfins* made by Lefranc of Paris in the 1930s (*left*) which her husband used to restore the portrait (as pigment analysis by Lumière Technology confirmed). The box bore the stamp of *Alle Belle Arti* – an artists' store at 3 Piazza San Marco in Florence, just around the corner from the Accademia where Giannino Marchig taught.

Jeanne Marchig told me she was confident that her case against Christie's would lead to a substantial pay-out to her Animal Welfare Fund Trust, but would soon be disillusioned. Ten weeks later, on 31 January 2011, District Judge John G. Koeltl ruled that Christie's had no case to answer as New York's six-year Statute of Limitations had expired before Jeanne Marchig brought the case.

She vowed to appeal 'immediately. My lawyer strongly recommends it. The Judge's decision is based on a technicality, not taking into account that ten years have to be deducted from the Statute of Limitations as the drawing was locked away and unknown to the external world. The events started to unfold only in 2008. I only learnt about the Leonardo attribution in 2009. How could I have exceeded the statutes of limitation?'

She felt 'very bitter,' and sarcastically wondered 'whether damages for Holocaust victims are also time-barred?'

On February 21 I conducted a phone interview from Christie's Chairman Ed Dolman. He was joined in his office by COO Lisa King, which showed how seriously Christie's were taking things.

I had first met Dolman at a Belgian house-sale in 1995. After working his way up from auction porter to head of Christie's Amsterdam he was a surprise choice (ahead of Noël Annesley, among others) as global CEO in the wake of the Christie's/Sotheby's price-fixing collusion scandal in 1999. In his younger days Dolman drove a white Rolls Royce and cultivated a wideboy image. Although we shared a taste for beer and cricket, I did not expect our interview to yield any insider knowledge.

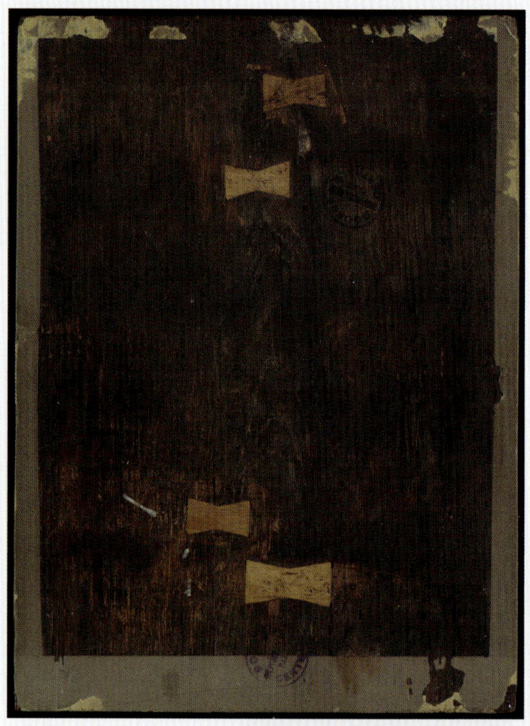

'We don't believe this is a Leonardo' declared Dolman and King. 'There is no case to answer unless we see new evidence in the Appeal.'

But I was surprised to learn how much effort Christie's claimed to have put into assessing the final item of a 402-lot Part II auction.

'When it was first offered we employed some of the most renowned experts in the field' asserted King, as if a whole battalion had been flown in specially. 'François Borne has an incredibly high reputation' added Dolman. 'Noël Annesley is probably the greatest Old Master Drawings specialist.'[14]

Lisa King resigned from Christie's three weeks after our interview. Ed Dolman left soon after, in June, to work for the Qatar Museums Authority. Pushed, shoved or head-hunted, Dolman's departure doubtless had nothing to do with *La Bella Principessa*. Or did it? I had a double-think when I tried to track down François Borne – only to discover that his London gallery, Salamander Fine Arts, had closed suddenly in late 2010. (Early in 2019 the normally bluff Dolman, now head of Christie's auction rivals Phillips, remained chary about discussing the Marchig case – but remembered François Borne as 'a bit strange.')

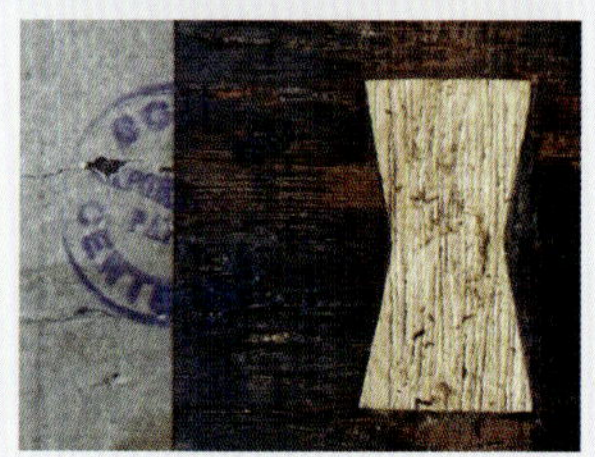

On March 15, three weeks after speaking to Dolman, I was able to handle the portrait (with kid gloves) in the Zurich Freeport. I had last seen it in Sweden two years before, behind glass. I was intrigued by its wooden support: an ancient plank of dark brown oak (*above right*). It had a crack at one end and was thicker at the top than at the bottom – and thicker to the right than to the left.

Jeanne Marchig lodged her Appeal on March 29. It was heard by the US Court of Appeals on June 24, with Bryan Deschamp in attendance. On July 12 Circuit Judges Richard C. Wesley, Debra Ann Livingston and Gerard E. Lynch issued a Summary Order upholding Judge Koeltl's interpretation of the statute of limitations in every respect bar the frame, as it 'may not have been clear to her [Madame Marchig] until 2009 that the painting [sic] was sold in a different frame than the one she provided.'

Silverman thought the judges had 'left Altman and Jeanne a big foot in the door.' His American lawyer, Eric Kaufman, felt she had 'lost the multi-million dollar claim and is left with a claim for just the frame.'

Altman thought he at least had an opening to call witnesses such as Borne, ask troubling questions that Borne and Christie's would be forced to answer, and possibly get a twelve-man jury to rule on the case.

'Not a chance' opined Kaufman.

On July 20 Jeanne Marchig wrote to Silverman that Christie's had brazenly declared they had no record of the frame – even though she had a letter, signed by Borne on a Christie's letterhead, advising her to 'change the frame' so her 'superb German drawing' would look more 19th century German and less 'Italian pastiche.' (She had earlier informed me she had 'no photograph of the *Bella* in her original frame, nor am I aware of one.')[15]

She should, she admitted balefully, have foreseen Christie's would 'find a way around it with all the lawyers they employ. I never expected such a lack of fairness. When I was sending other paintings for sale, they were all framed – but it was never mentioned in the consignment agreement!'

On July 26 Altman petitioned for a re-hearing about the frame. On August 10 Madame Marchig 'nearly had a stroke' when she read the letter Christie's had sent him. 'They deny having ever received the frame, and advise Altman to drop the case. The tone of the letter is quite shocking!'

Altman's pursuit of the frame enabled him to grill Kate Ganz for two and a half hours on Broadway on November 2, in the presence of her lawyer husband Daniel Belin and Christie's attorney Joseph A. Patella. The official goal was to ascertain whether the portrait had appeared at the auction viewing in the Marchig frame. Ganz was clear it hadn't – but had plenty else to say about the portrait.

'When I walked into the room and saw it, it had a quality about it that made me think of Leonardo da Vinci!' she exclaimed. 'I thought – this looks like it might be something older and better, more important than what it's been catalogued as. I thought this object has the chance – across a crowded room, you understand – of being something. I thought it might be something to do – I wasn't quite sure – with Leonardo da Vinci.'

'Your initial reaction when you saw it was the vague possibility that it could be a Leonardo?' queried Altman.

'More than a vague possibility!' effused Ganz. 'I mean, I spent $22,000 on it! I think I'm very knowledgeable about Leonardo's work – I've seen many of his works – I go out of my way to see them. During the first few weeks I felt that I had not really made a mistake, because I think the object was and still is a beautiful small object.'

Ganz said she had taken this 'small object' to the 'Chief Conservator at the Metropolitan Museum' who 'determined that it was too dangerous to try to remove it from the support.' She also showed it, 'within a month of purchasing it,' to Leo Steinberg – whom she labelled 'the most distinguished art historian in New York, and really worldwide, for Leonardo da Vinci at that time' (Steinberg had published on Leonardo's *Last Supper*, a work as far removed in scale and technique from a book-sized vellum portrait as it is possible to imagine). Steinberg 'looked at it for a moment' and declared it 'about a hundred years old.'

Steinberg was unable to confirm making such a lightning appraisal. He had died a few months earlier.

Ganz claimed she then lost interest in the portrait and stuck it in a drawer. This hardly squared with her handwriting on notepaper pilfered from the *Four Columns Inn* in Newfane, Vermont, just after her wedding with Daniel Belin in May 2001: '*Strangely lifeless, no independent vitality, shading forward, Leonardesque imitation, Colin Eisler.*' Ganz claimed these were 'notes that I took in a subsequent conversation with Leo Steinberg' rather than with Mr Eisler – a professor at New York University specializing in Flemish and German paintings. Either way, it was clear that Ganz was continuing to probe the portrait more than three years after buying it.

During the nine years the portrait was in her possession it had been seen by 'a lot of people. My gallery is always visited by the chief Old Master Drawings curator at every major museum in America and other places.' At her 2007 exhibition she had shown and talked about the drawing 'with the Curator of Italian Drawings at the National Gallery in Washington, the Curator of Italian Drawings at the Getty Museum, and with the Curator of Italian Drawings at the Art Institute of Chicago.'

Ganz dismissed Kemp's research on the portrait as 'just as absurd and far-fetched as all of the other research that he's come up with' and claimed that David Wright first contacted Peter Silverman with his hunch about the *Sforziada* because he was after 'some remuneration' – a gratuitous slur. Wright first contacted Martin Kemp, not Silverman, and never sought payment. In fact, Wright complained to me that he had done Silverman 'an immense favor as to the origin of the Leonardo drawing, from which he stands to earn a huge sum. I have conducted various investigations peripheral to the Leonardo attribution to the benefit my own academic reputation but with no financial support from anyone. Indeed, I have personally spent nearly $1500 on costly publications and mailings to Martin [Kemp].'[16]

Parts of Ganz's testimony were cited in Jeanne Marchig's sworn *Declaration* about the frame on November 28, when she attested to personally packing the portrait – in its frame – before shipping it from Geneva to New York with eight other drawings. (She also produced the letter she had faxed Christie's after the sale, complaining about the 'exaggerated amount' they were charging her for transport.)

On 2 January 2012 Jeanne Marchig e-mailed me from Fuerteventura in the Canary Islands, where she routinely wintered: a familiar figure by her hotel pool, brandishing not a cocktail but a lap-top – religiously scanning the latest share-prices and keeping a twice-daily eye on her portfolio.

She did not sound full of New Year cheer, having suffered 'many vicissitudes, and bad luck plaguing me. I can't understand how a judge could be so one-sided. *Everything* was in Christie's favour. I spare you the details. Can it be possible that this is the way American justice works?'

She and Christie's reached an out-of-court settlement regarding the frame on April 19, with Christie's agreeing to transfer $40,000 – twice the price of the portrait – to the Marchig Animal Welfare Trust 'within seven business days.' On May 14 Madame Marchig was fuming that they still hadn't.

'Her anger at being screwed by Christie's lasted until her death' was the blunt assessment of Richard Altman, who felt 'the real bad guys in this case were the three judges on the Court of Appeals. New York law was absolutely clear that the statute of limitations does not run when there is a continuing relation between the client and the fiduciary, and only begins when the client termin-ates the relation. Jeanne and Christie's did other deals before and after the one with the drawing, and had a relation that extended over 40 years. The court's analysis was outcome-driven – i.e. poor Christie's should not have to pay Jeanne despite their colossal fuck-up.'[17]

Altman also harboured regrets: 'Had they allowed the case to go forward, I would have destroyed Christie's!'

Jeanne Marchig died on 2 May 2013. After a funeral conducted by a Franciscan friar at the Evangelical Church in Cologny, the 'cat-caring philanthropist who consigned Christie's to the dog-house'[18] was buried next to her husband Giannino in the gently sloping cemetery in neighbouring Vandœuvres.

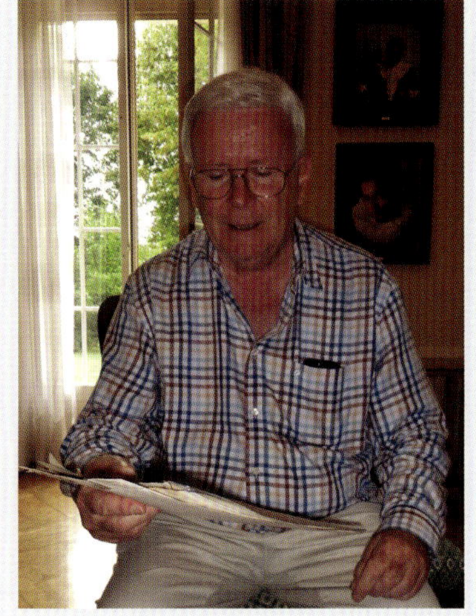

BRYAN DESCHAMP

On August 16 I lunched with Bryan Deschamp in Geneva. He arrived clutching a sheet of paper containing a photograph of the portrait in its lost frame, which he had found among Jeanne Marchig's papers (*see p.324*). She had either forgotten about its existence, or lied, when claim-ing that she knew of 'no photograph of the *Bella* in her original frame.' Beneath the photograph she had written *attributed to William Morris (?) the caligrapher* [sic]. Above the portrait, also in pencil but in a dif-ferent hand, were the names *Martin Beisly*, *Alex Meddowes* and *Margie Christian* – bracketed together (in Jeanne Marchig's handwriting) as *Christie's English … .*

Beisly was Christie's Director of Victorian & 19th Century Pictures, Meddowes Deputy Chairman of Christie's Scotland; Margie Christian was the sister of art historian John Christian. The inscriptions implied that Christie's associated the frame with the renowned English designer William Morris (1834–96), guru of the Arts and Crafts movement. Small wonder it disappeared.

Five days later, after dinner at the nearby tennis club, Deschamp invited me to explore the dimly-lit basement of Jeanne Marchig's villa. Amidst much loose paperwork (including some of Giannino's correspondence from the 1940s) we found two intriguing folders. One (*below left*) had a white plastified cover and was fastened by a strap. It featured the handwritten words top-left, in faded ink, *restauro dopo guerra per B. Berenson* ('restored after the war for B. Berenson'). At 36 × 24.5cm it was just large enough to have contained the 33 × 24cm portrait of Bianca Sforza.

The second, slightly larger folder (*below right*), in brown leather embossed with stylized rose motifs, was fronted by the handwritten inscription *Libro del cassierato di ms Gio. Battista Gucci del'año: 1599* ('Accounts Register of MS Gio. Battista Gucci, 1599'). The Gucci in question was probably a notary – hence the honorific *MS* (for *Messere*).

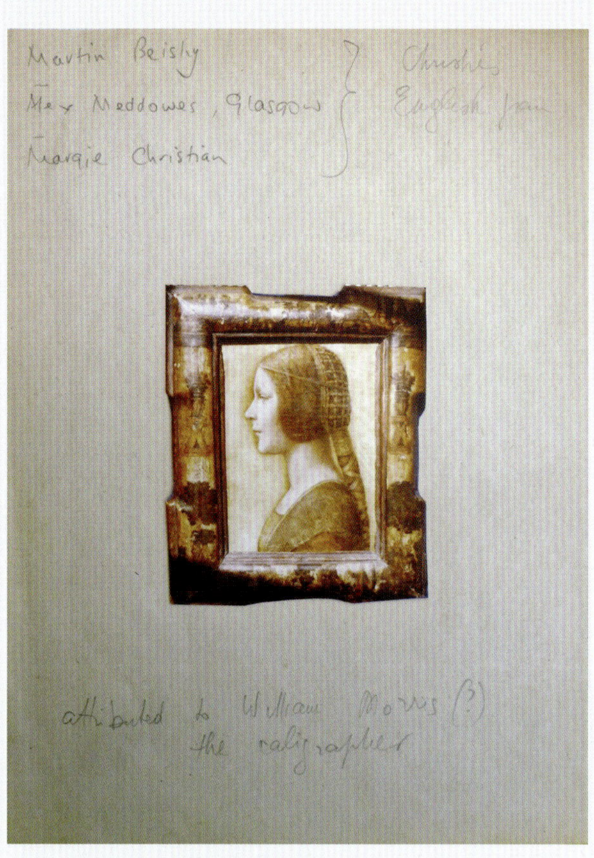

A family of Gucci notaries is first mentioned in Florence in 1529. City archives mention a *Giovan Battista Gucci* in the Santo Spirito district in 1634. The rose was and remains the Gucci family emblem.[19]

Giannino Marchig may have acquired this folder from an antiques dealer to protect Bianca's portrait because of its convenient size (41 × 30cm). But there is another possibility. During the 16th century three Guccis worked as architects and sculptors in Poland: Matteo Gucci, and his relatives Santi and Pietro

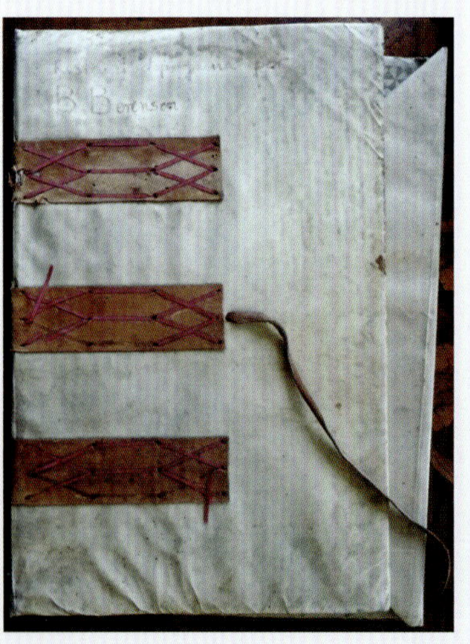

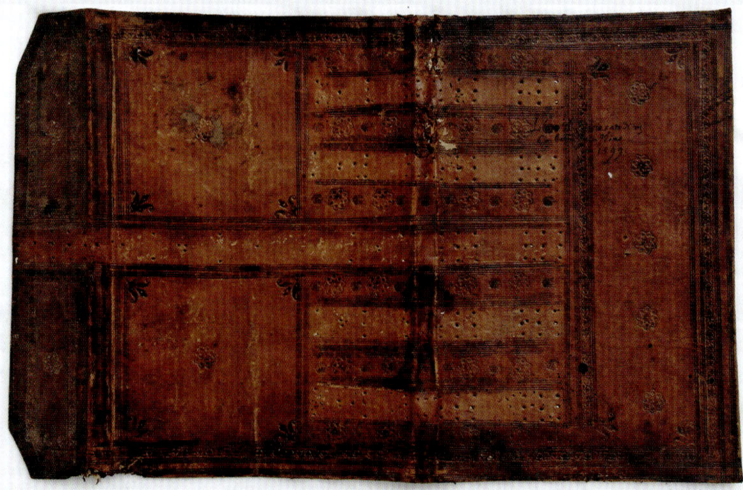

(who were brothers). Santi Gucci (*c.*1530–1600) is first cited in 1558 as being granted *serwitoriat* status – exempting him from municipal taxes – by Bona Sforza's son King Zygmunt August. Over the next four decades Santi acquired a prestige in the cultural sphere comparable to that of Jan Zamoyski (for whom he worked in 1591) in the political field, sculpting monuments to Zygmunt August, his sister Queen Anna and her husband King Stefan Batory. Did Santi Gucci acquire or receive Leonardo's portrait in Poland, and send it back to his family in Italy?

The two folders were among the effects bequeathed to the Museo Revoltella in Giannino Marchig's native Trieste, already home to several of his paintings. The 285-lot auction of Jeanne Marchig's estate, featuring sixty works by Giannino, took place at her Cologny home on 8/9 October 2013. It received scant publicity. Only a dozen or so turned up. Prices were derisory.

By then Bryan Deschamp had moved to Rome. He lived initially at the Carmelite College of Sant'Alberto on (appropriately enough) *Via Sforza Pallavicini*, just outside the Vatican. Then he lodged with friends in Ostia, a few miles away towards the coast. He had declined steadily since Jeanne's death, afflicted by Parkinson's disease, and died on 28 February 2017, aged 73.

WHEN IN ROME

A month after the Marchig auction in Switzerland, Peter Silverman pulled off one of the greatest one-twos in art history: having rescued a Leonardo from oblivion, he repeated the trick with a Michelangelo. On 7 November 2013 a limewood Crucifix he had bought from a Bavarian dealer as '17th century German' for DM 5,000 in 1985 entered the Louvre, valued for insurance purposes at €25 million. The label read *Florence, Late 15th Century, Michelangelo?*

Owning such works, declaimed Silverman, was 'both a joy and a heavy responsibility. You never really get used to being a custodian of a work of true genius.'

On 26 May 2014 the Crucifix went on show at the Capitoline Museums in Rome – as part of the blockbuster exhibition *Michelangelo 1564–2014*.

Silverman's attempts to show his Leonardo at the Capitoline had collapsed outside the Temple of Doom. But now he found an *alter ego* with the clout to bring *La Bella* back to Italy: Vittorio Sgarbi, onetime Italian Culture Minister and longtime irascible host of a TV culture show that enjoyed prime-time viewing. Vulgar yet erudite, narcissistic on a Lagerfeldian scale, the provocative Sgarbi was box-office wherever he went.

The portrait's quality and commercial potential caught Sgarbi's eye and, just after the Michelangelo opening, he and Silverman talked turkey over rooftop drinks at Sgarbi's fortified penthouse 200 yards from the Capitoline Hill. The upshot: after authentication by the State-appointed *Venaria Reale* Conservation & Restoration Centre in Turin, Bianca's portrait – now with a green and gold frame designed by Martin Kemp (based on that of Andrea Solari's 1507 portrait of *Charles d'Amboise* in the Louvre) – went on show on December 5

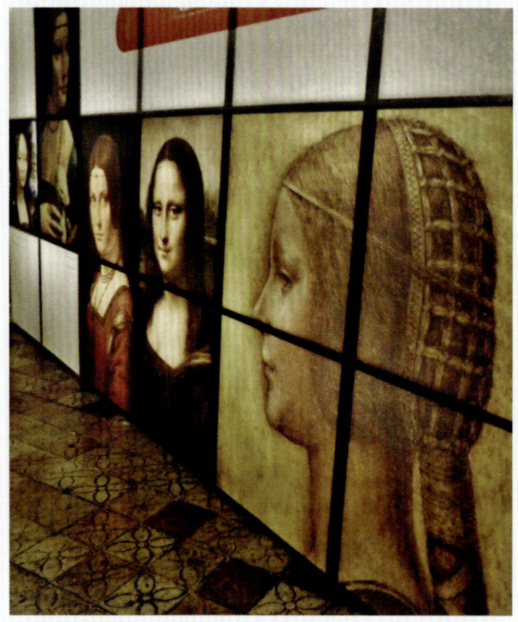
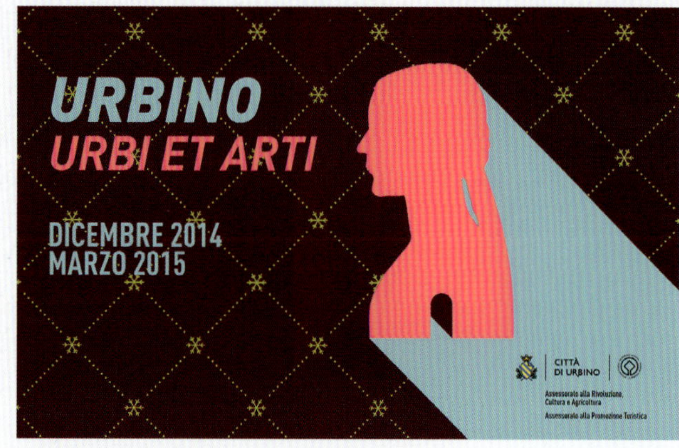

URBINO
EXHIBITION INSTALLATION
& POSTER

in the Palazzo Ducale in hilltop Urbino, one of the most magical settings of the Renaissance.

Sgarbi was Urbino's official Cultural Advisor, which helped. But, although quaint and historic, Urbino is tiny (population 15,000). Could Sgarbo bounce Bianca into the bigtime?

Rome's Palazzo Braschi, Milan's Palazzo Bagatti Valsecchi and Turin's Palazzo Madama were touted as prospective venues – in vain. Bianca's next outing, in March 2015, was in Lugano (population 64,000) in Italian-speaking Switzer-land. The opening was hijacked by an aggressive local official trying to score political points. Silverman wrote to the Mayor expressing 'regret and annoy-ance.'

Next up was Monza of Formula One fame (population 120,000) on May 20. Sgarbi's catalogue preface slammed those opposed to the Leonardo attribution as 'careless liars spreading tall tales like blind black cats on a moonless night.' Martin Kemp was beamed in by tele-link for the theatrical opening. Monza's palatial Villa Reale – home to the Italian royal family in the 19th century – made a majestic setting.[20]

POLES APART

Soon after Leonardo's portrait of Bianca Sforza had gone on show in Monza, Katarzyna Pisarek published a 17,000-word article in *Artibus & Historiae* – a twice-yearly journal edited by her Polish compatriot Józef Grabski, whose Advisory Committee included the Metropolitan Museum's Everett Fahy (cited by Richard Dorment as a 'vehement opponent' of the Leonardo attribution).

In *La Bella Principessa: Arguments Against the Attribution to Leonardo*, Pisarek – a self-styled 'independent art historian specializing in attribution'

– insisted Galeazzo Sanseverino was not, as generally supposed, the intended recipient of what she referred to as 'the manuscript,' and suggested the *Sforziada* was illuminated not in 1496 but 1490. Her aim was to show there was 'no reason to insert a picture of Bianca.'

Pisarek was aping her Communist-era compatriot Bogdan Horodyski, former Director of the Polish National Library – whose patriotic 1954 analysis of the frontispiece claimed that Birago was a closet supporter of Duke Gian Galeazzo, the hapless father of Poland's future Queen Bona Sforza.[21]

Pisarek harped on about Peter Paul Biro's 'dubious' fingerprint evidence, omitting to mention that this had been removed as inconclusive from the second edition of the Kemp/Cotte book. Their macrophotographic proof that three folios were missing from the *Sforziada*'s first quire was ignored, Pisarek preferring the opinion of a Polish National Library employee called Jolanta Sokołowska (status unspecified) that just one folio was missing.

Pisarek's arguments were deprecated as 'cherry-picking' and 'manipulative science of the worst kind' by the Dutch forum *Authentication In Art*.

Why was Pisarek suddenly 'so concerned to address this portrait, when she had no record as a Leonardo scholar?' wondered Martin Kemp. He presumed it 'resulted from a kind of Polish solidarity.' He submitted an official Reply to her article, deploring Pisarek's 'weak grasp of Renaissance drawing techniques' among other failings. *Artibus & Historiae* – echoing the *Daily Telegraph*'s treatment of Peter Silverman's reply to Richard Dorment – refused to publish it.

On November 29 Waldemar Januszczak – born in England to Polish parents – unleashed a scurrilous article in the *Sunday Times* headlined *Is this a £100m Leonardo or Sally from the Bolton Co-op?*[22] Januszczak's purported goal was to plug the rambling 'memoirs' of forger Shaun Greenhalgh, a serial con-man fresh from 56 months in jail. These memoirs would not be published until 2017, but 400 copies were declared 'available' privately through Januszczak's company ZCZ Films, which had sprouted a publishing arm for the occasion.

In a last-minute postscript to his 'memoirs,' added for no reason that Januszczak could adequately explain, Greenhalgh jokily claimed to have fabricated the Leonardo portrait in 1978, when he was seventeen, taking a supermarket check-out girl called Alison (Sally) as his subject. Alison had since vanished without trace, even though she (or any of her friends or acquaintances) could have earned a tabloid fortune by coming forward to corroborate Greenhalgh's story.

'The story of how Greenhalgh claims he made the drawing is hilarious' noted Januszczak. 'From the outside, the art world looks like a world of beauty, inspiration, civilisation and culture. It is not. It is a cesspit.'

Peter Silverman's offer to pay Greenhalgh £10,000 if he could reproduce the portrait on vellum was not taken up. Martin Kemp laughed off Greenhalgh's 'silliness' but deplored his slur on the late Jeanne Marchig – who had asserted under oath that her husband already owned the work when they married in 1955. Next day the *Guardian*'s Jonathan Jones dovetailed with Januszczak by smearing the Leonardo as an olden rather than modern forgery, floating the exotic idea that it was 'created as a fake Leonardo in about 1650.'

Flat, dead, dull, ugly, pastiche, cold, miserable, clumsy, crude, lifeless ... Jones flailed at the portrait with the plodding repetitiveness of an apprentice bass guitarist in a student heavy-metal band. His 2008 *Guardian* profile of Nicholas Penny had struck similarly repetitive chords, albeit in a major key (*high-brow ... down-to-earth ... strikingly learned ... outstanding ... oozes learning ...*).

The Jones/Januszczak assaults preceded a seminar held in London on December 1 by conservationist talkshop ArtWatch UK, offering a fresh platform for its members Katarzyna Pisarek and Jacques Franck to attack the Leonardo portrait. Pisarek 'aligned herself' with conference host Michael Daley in suggesting it was a forgery – with Giannino Marchig the most likely culprit.

Her views, along with those of Januszczak and Greenhalgh, were complaisantly relayed on December 4 in the *New York Times*. 'Adding characters like Shaun Greenhalgh and Alison from the supermarket into the mix will liven up the debate' giggled journalist Scott Reyburn – making it 'ever more difficult to discern what the scientifically minded Leonardo would have recognized as the truth.' The latter phrase could have been written by Christie's PR department.

'It is deeply regrettable for the sake of Leonardo, the History of Art and the patrimony of mankind that so much demonstrable nonsense has been mindlessly regurgitated in certain sectors of the press' observed the habitually mild-mannered Pascal Cotte, who picked twenty holes in Greenhalgh's 'outlandish' forgery claims – among them the fact that the portrait had first been restored 200 years ago; contained white lead pigment over 250 years old; and was mounted on a panel of varying thickness, unlike any school desk previously known.

Having already, as Martin Kemp noted, undertaken 'a series of sustained assaults on the Leonardo attribution,' ArtWatch returned on 24 February 2016 with an article on their website: *Problems with La Bella Principessa*. Its author Michael Daley dismissed Jeanne Marchig's sworn testimony as 'the widow's hearsay claims' and ridiculed Kemp and Silverman for 'vainly trawling' Bernard Berenson's archives at I Tatti in search of the portrait's pre-Marchig provenance.

Codswallop. Silverman had merely asked the I Tatti archivist to check out any Berenson references to Ghirlandaio – the most likely author of the portrait in Marchig's eyes. The search was fruitless. There are also eleven short letters from Marchig to Berenson in the I Tatti archives which I 'trawled through' myself for twenty minutes in October 2011. They contain no mention of the portrait either, which proved nothing.

Four-fifths of the way through his disjointed text Daley gave vent to his hatred of Martin Kemp, whom he accused of 'slanting arguments, manipulating quotations and rigging visual evidence … two decades earlier we had experienced Kemp's invective and sneering distaste for traditional connoisseurs' (a term Daley apparently applied to himself).

'To include the figurally impoverished and stylistically anachronistic *La Bella Principessa* in Leonardo's oeuvre would disjunct his revolutionary arc of insights' frothed Daley, accusing Kemp of 'weasel words' and of co-authoring a 'book of advocacy' (Daley availing himself here of the weasel words of Richard Dorment).

Daley was indebted to Kate Ganz in dubbing the portrait 'composed from features drawn from a number of bona fide Leonardos' (Ganz had declared it 'based on a number of paintings by Leonardo da Vinci,' without being able to name any). At the same time, in a Dada-esque attempt to prove the portrait's 20th century origins, Daley likened Bianca's eye to an 'almost Cubist construction.'

The nonsense kept on coming. On May 15 *The Art Newspaper* ran an article by Vincent Noce approvingly citing Greenhalgh and Pisarek, and rehashing the story of the portrait's acquisition in terms virtually copy-pasted from Richard Dorment's article of 2010. 'Silverman's discovery made a thrilling story, but it was a complete fabrication' wrote Dorment. 'It's a seductive tale, but a fictitious one' parroted Noce. Peter Silverman, he wrote, had spared no expense in attempting to authenticate his Leonardo, citing the 'positive opinions' of Martin Kemp, Mina Gregori, Alessandro Vezzosi and Nicholas Turner as if they had been bought.

To find such an unbalanced piece in *The Art Newspaper* came as no surprise. A couple of years earlier I had mentioned the portrait to its Founder-Editor Anna Somers Cocks – to be greeted with a regally peremptory 'We don't believe in it.'

On May 24 Pisarek returned to the ArtWatch website with arcane analysis of the *Sforziada* stitch-holes which, given that the portrait had been removed before the book was re-stitched, was of mystifying relevance. She also lavished nearly 700 words on an esoteric interpretation of the Warsaw *Sforziada* frontispiece by amateur historian Carla Glori – not once mentioning that Glori's bizarre theories sprang from her recent book attempting to prove that Bianca Sforza was the Mona Lisa.[23]

Pisarek's approach was disarming. She admitted she had not read Elisabetta Gnignera's study of 1490s Milanese fashion because it was in Italian, preferring to consult her Polish compatriot Zdzisław Żygulski (1921–2015) – a renowned expert on ancient weaponry. Giannino Marchig 'would have been able to make such a drawing if he had wanted to' because he was a 'Leonardesque painter' (Pisarek cannot have seen any of Marchig's paintings). She cited Julia Cartwright's romanticized account of Bianca Sforza's life as it was 'the only one I could find in the English language.' Her assertion that Galeazzo Sanseverino was 'married' to Bianca in 1489 rather than 'betrothed' was, she admitted, based on his Wikipedia entry. When caught out confusing paper with vellum in her analysis of the *Sforziada*, she sighed: 'They look so similar.'

The eventual publication of Greenhalgh's book, in 2017, offered the *Guardian* a fresh opportunity to claim the portrait was a fake. On May 27 it ran a sycophantic review – purportedly written by Simon Parkin, their Video Games Critic [sic] – extolling Greenhalgh as a 'softly-spoken artist' who had 'created several hundred exquisite forgeries' and been described by the authoritative Waldemar Januszczak as a 'one-man Renaissance.'

Ten days later Tokyo's Mitsubishi Ichigokan Museum declared it was no longer prepared to show *La Bella Principessa* as a work by Leonardo, merely as 'attributed.' A furious Silverman immediately withdrew the loan. The portrait was next seen in Peking in Summer 2018, at a Riverside Museum exhibition evoking *Da Vinci & Lu Ban* (a mythical Chinese engineer of the 5th century B.C.); then in Tianjin (Autumn 2018) and Nanjing (Winter 2018/19) as part of an exhibition styled *Renaissance Masters – The Art of Leonardo da Vinci, Michelangelo and Raffaello*.

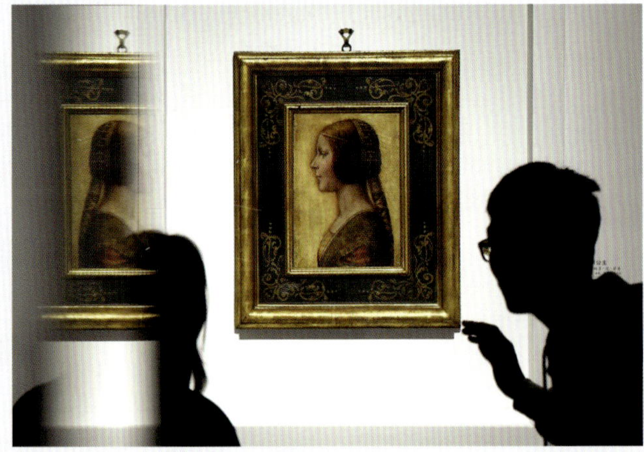

In February 2011 Silverman had turned down an offer from a 'Luxembourg-based investment fund' to buy the portrait for €60 million because he felt that the 'vital new info' unearthed by Kemp and Cotte in Warsaw would enhance its value. Soon afterwards a potential buyer had proposed 'a certain sum and a good lifetime annuity' for the portrait. He had also been promised $350,000 to show it in Japan (Shizuoka, Fukuoka and Tokyo) between November 2011 and June 2012. Then a tsunami ploughed into Japan's northeast coast, killing 16,000 people and flattening 120,000 buildings. The deal was off.

Silverman's eccentric promotional strategy suggested that he enjoyed the kudos of owning a Leonardo more than the financial rewards of selling one. Broad-minded and gregarious, he exudes a noisy self-assurance that is not to all tastes. Blessed with a formidable 'eye,' he has made a string of impressive artistic discoveries – and gleefully let dealers and curators know all about them, ensuring their inevitable jealousy is laced with personal animosity. Perhaps this explains the hostility to the Leonardo attribution. Maybe there have been other incentives.

'I imagined the world would enthusiastically greet the discovery of a new work by the most famous artist ever to walk the earth' says Silverman. 'I was stupidly naïve.'

A campaign is under way trumpeted Richard Dorment in April 2010. It was indeed, from California to Cracov: a campaign to defend the reputations of Kate Ganz and Christie's at all costs, by cynically and unscrupulously lambasting the reputations of others – and by subjecting one of the most accomplished portraits ever drawn to persistent derision and denigration. The attacks fell at regular intervals, timed to undermine the Leonardo attribution at strategic moments – the release of the Kemp-Cotte book, the launch of Jeanne Marchig's court case, the portrait's display in Italian palaces … .

'Why has Leonardo's authorship of this masterpiece not received universal acceptance?' wonders Nicholas Turner. 'There is such a watertight case for the period of the portrait, and Leonardo's responsibility for it, that no more needs to be said. Art historians who do not believe it is his cannot be blind. Does their reputation take precedence over doing justice to one of the great geniuses in the history of mankind? The opinion that it is a "screaming fake" is just absurd.'

'You shouldn't be so foolish as to think even the greatest art will just carry on on its own' Nicholas Penny warned *Guardian* readers in 2008. 'One can't underestimate the amount of junk which is clogging up the minds of people who should be receiving it.'

NOTES

1 In his book *Leonardo's Lost Princess*, Silverman inexplicably dates our encounter to Summer 2007 – even though BRAFA has always been held in January.

2 Later published in *Artes*, the review of the University of Pavia.

3 Martin Kemp, *Living with Leonardo* (Thames & Hudson, London 2018).

4 Nicholas Turner had succeeded George Goldner as Drawings Curator at the Getty – and accused Goldner of spending around $1 million on six fake drawings.

5 Information provided by Jeanne Marchig's partner Bryan Deschamp to her lawyer Richard Altman.

6 Ernest Samuels, *Bernard Berenson: The Making of a Legend* (Belknap Press, 1979).

7 Jeanne Marchig & Susanna Ragionieri, *Giannino Marchig* (Skira, Milan 2000).

8 E-mail from Jeanne Marchig to the author, 17 January 2011.

9 Information provided to the author by Jeanne Marchig's partner Bryan Deschamp.

10 Marchig & Ragionieri, *op. cit.*

11 E-mail from Jeanne Marchig to the author, 20 December 2010.

12 Published by Scripta Maneant of Bologna in 2016, in a limited edition of 1,999 copies priced at €2,000 – a volume almost as luxurious as the Sforziada itself!

13 The *Salvator Mundi* was owned at the time by a consortium, who sold it for around $80m to Geneva businessman Yves Bouvier – who re-sold it privately to Monaco-based Russian oligarch Dmitry Rybolovlev for $127.5m in May 2013. It was reportedly sold to the Louvre Abu Dhabi by Christie's New York for $450.3m on 15 November 2017.

14 According to Silverman, Nicolas Schwed, Christie's Head of Old Master Drawings in Paris, was also consulted – later telling Silverman that Christie's catalogue attribution reflected the fact that they 'did not want to take any chances.'

15 E-mail from Jeanne Marchig to the author, 20 December 2010.

16 E-mail from David Wright to the author, 19 September 2011.

17 E-mail from Richard Altman to the author, 18 February 2019.

18 As per my obituary for *The Huffington Post*.

19 Elisabetta Gnignera, correspondence with the author, 11 October 2013.

20 So did Milan's Palazzo Reale, ten miles down the road, which hosted a *Leonardo da Vinci* show that Summer. Plans to show the portrait in Riga, as a highlight of the city's tenure as European 2014 Culture Capital, fell through.

21 Horodyski's twenty-page article in *Biuletyn Historii Sztuki* has received scant adequate attention from Western art historians – who have contented themselves with a five-page summary in French (by library employee Maria Wierzbicka) that omits many salient points. An English translation of Horodyski's original Polish text was commissioned from the eminent Warsaw-based historian Konrad Ajewski during research for the present book.

22 It is tempting to think that the name Sally was chosen in honour of Kate Ganz's mother.

23 Carla Glori, *op.cit.*

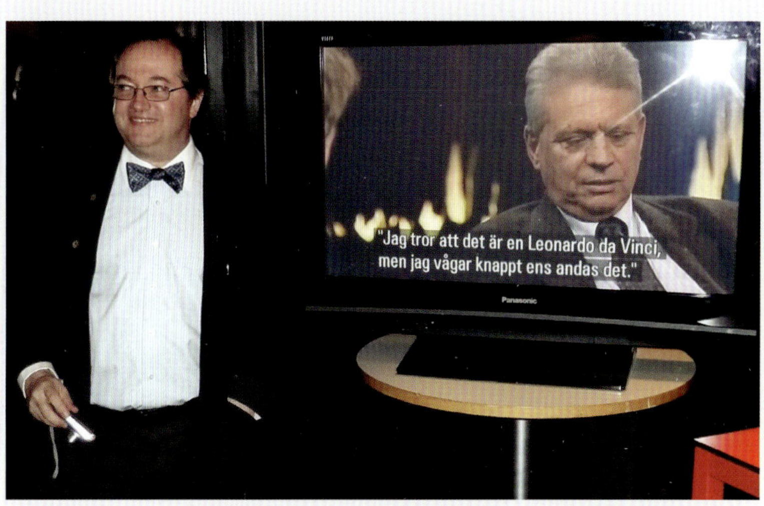

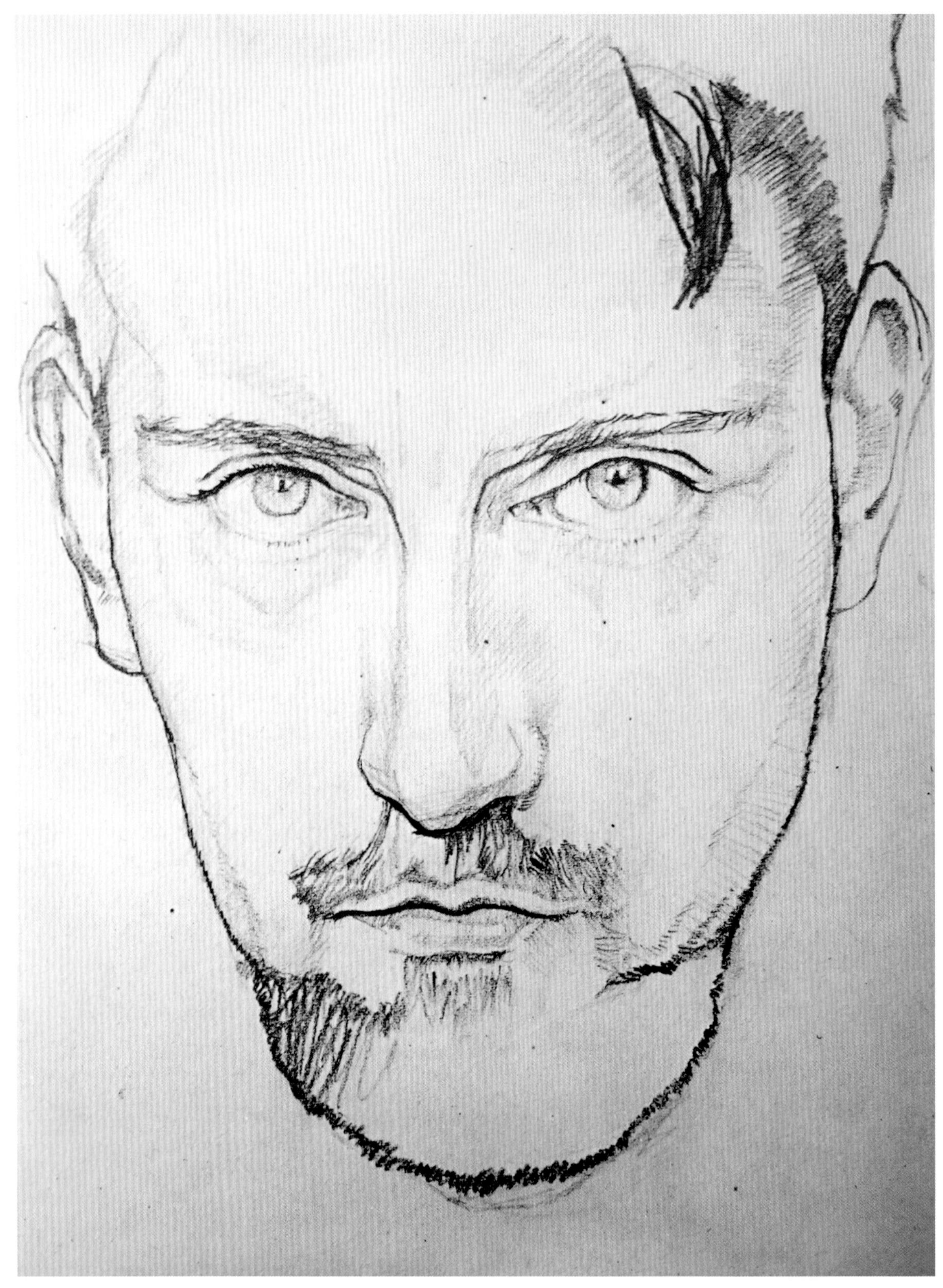

GIANNINO MARCHIG: *SELF-PORTRAIT* (*c.*1920) – GRAPHITE 23 × 19 cm

KEEP IT DARK

GIANNINO MARCHIG'S BELLA PRINCIPESSA

BIANCA SFORZA, THE HEROINE of this *Sforziada*, died within months of its completion. Just four years later her husband and her father were forced into exile. The Book of Doom was exiled, too – from Italy to Poland, where it spent 200 years in a provincial backwater before being transferred to a private library in Warsaw.

Discreetly re-bound, mundanely classified as a history book and miscatalogued as a manuscript, it long escaped attention. Bianca's portrait was removed along the way. By the time it went on show at Christie's New York, in January 1998, the portrait cannot have been seen by more than a few hundred people – perhaps only ever by a few dozen.

Few artistic masterpieces can have endured or merited such long-term oblivion. Leonardo da Vinci conveyed the hopes, fears and uncertainties of adolescence with mesmerizing subtlety – using the flattened timelessness of an icon and the stilted pose of a Sforza Duchess. His portrait of *Bianca Sforza* consecrated her emergence from childhood obscurity on to the competitive political stage. It consigned her to belated eternity and may unwittingly have signed her death warrant.

Martin Kemp and Pascal Cotte have shown, by comparing the *Sforziada* now in Warsaw with those in London and Paris, that its thick vellum pages had been trimmed – a laborious process involving the removal of all 52 original sheets of vellum from their binding.[1] As the portrait of Bianca Sforza is the same size as all the other folios, it must have been trimmed at the same time and retained in the *Sforziada* when it received its second binding – doubtless reflecting a change of ownership.

The example of the London *Sforziada* – the only illuminated *Sforziada* to retain its original binding with Sforza insignia – suggests the original binding of the Polish *Sforziada* would have reflected its commissioner or recipient. Whether these insignia belonged to Il Moro, his daughter Bianca and/or Galeazzo Sanseverino, they will have been unsuited to a new owner.

Given the Sforziada's presence in Poland, the event most likely to have prompted this rebinding is the marriage of Bianca's second cousin, Bona Sforza, to Sigismund Jagiellon, and her coronation as Queen of Poland in 1518. A new binding would probably have been embellished with insignia representing her Sforza/Aragon family background or the new Sforza-Jagiellon union.

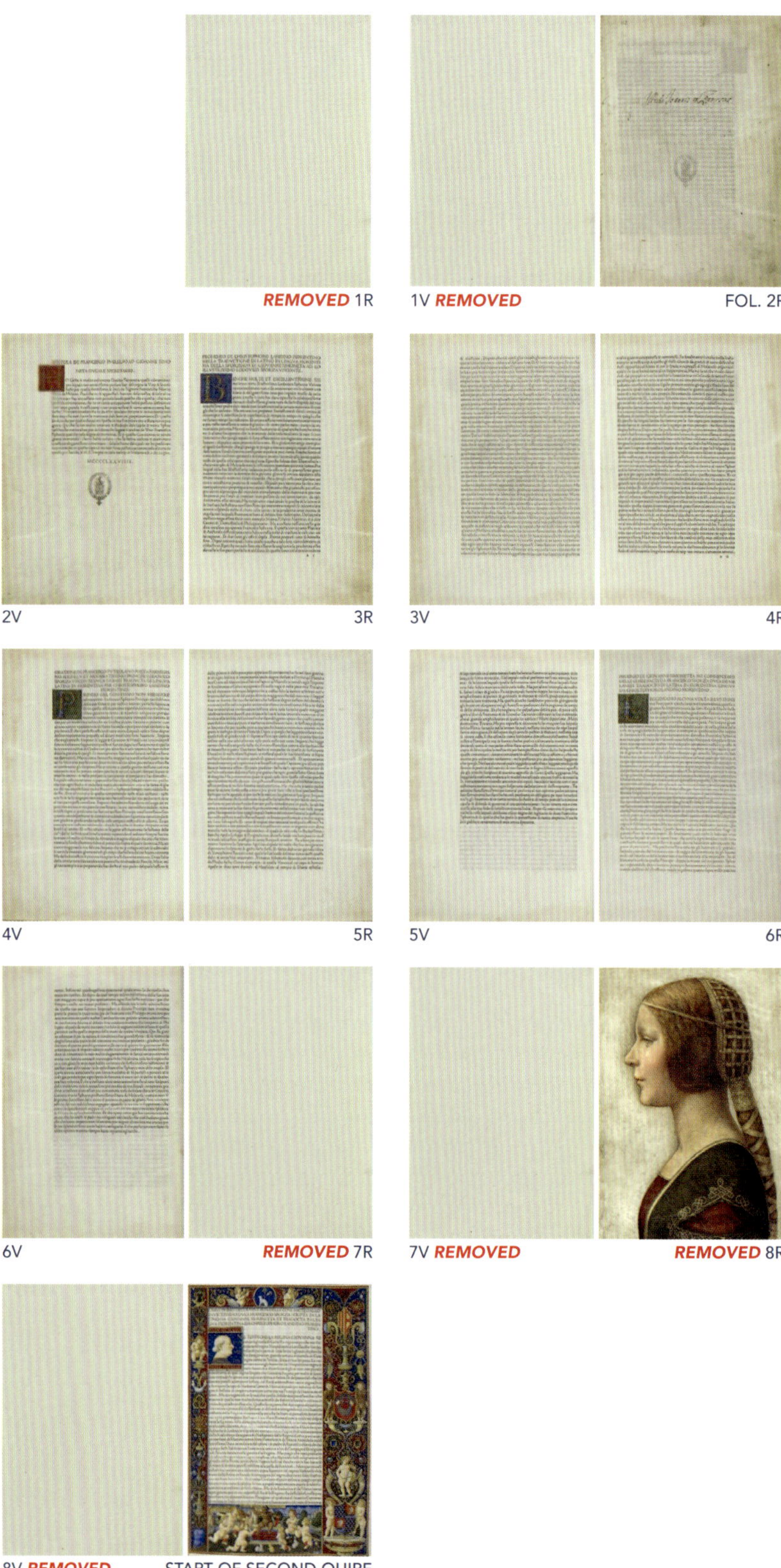

REMOVED 1R
1V *REMOVED*
FOL. 2R
2V
3R
3V
4R
4V
5R
5V
6R
6V
REMOVED 7R
7V *REMOVED*
REMOVED 8R
8V *REMOVED*
START OF SECOND QUIRE

Within the next 150 years, after entering the possession of the Zamoyski family, the *Sforziada* was re-bound again. The prime reason for this re-binding appears to have been the removal of the portrait.

The *Portrait of Bianca Sforza* is scarred by two knife-marks a few millimetres from its left edge. One is 2cm long, the other about 6cm. These marks appear to represent unsuccessful attempts to remove the portrait while it was still in the book. When these attempts failed, it was resolved to remove the binding and isolate the sheet of vellum containing the portrait.

This is confirmed by the current composition of the *Sforziada*'s first quire. The entire sheet of vellum bearing Leonardo's portrait, and one additional half-sheet, were removed: i.e. three of the eight folios (or six of its sixteen pages) that originally formed the quire.

Bianca's portrait was on the outer sheet of the first quire, on the recto of Folio 8. The other half of this sheet (Folio 1), whose two sides were entirely blank, was removed at the same time.

Curiously, however, the quire's second sheet of vellum was cut in half. One half of this sheet (Folio 2) contains Filelfo's opening *Epistola*. The other half (Folio 7) was left blank, to ensure that the portrait did not face a page of text. This blank folio was discarded. As a result, the now-severed Folio 2 could not be stitched into the new binding as part of a full sheet of vellum, but had to be stuck on to Folio 3 with glue. Such a messy and apparently unnecessary operation is only likely to have been undertaken if Folio 7 contained something embarrassing.

Traces of colour may have transferred from Folio 8r (bearing Leonardo's portrait) to the *verso* of Folio 7 opposite. Removing Folio 7 would have avoided any such smudge marks on the page which, after the removal of the folio containing Bianca's portrait, would have found itself opposite Birago's frontispiece. Instead of facing a blank page, the frontispiece now faces a page of text (from Simonetta's *Proemio*).

It looks as if the volume were rebound to remove any trace of evidence that it once contained a work of art. Whoever removed the portrait was not keen to advertise the fact.

Similar discretion affected the *Sforziada*'s new binding. This is a darker brown than the tan-shaded leather commonly used for the books possessed by King Zygmunt August in the mid-16th century, many of which were later owned by Jan Zamoyski. It has none of the decorative fancy found on other books owned by Zamoyski, nor does it feature the gilt-embossed Zamoyski livery used by Count Stanisław Kostka Zamoyski in the early 19th century. The floral patterning to the *Sforziada*'s spine and edges is innocuous. Five tiny holes at the foot of the back cover suggest the former presence of a chain for keeping the volume attached to a shelf – reinforcing the belief of Polish National Library staff that the binding dates back to 'the 17th century if not earlier'.[2]

The book is mentioned halfway down the Zamoyski Library inventories of 1675 and 1776. The (admittedly slipshod) inventory of 1800 does not mention it at all. The grotty yellow label affixed to its spine, flagging up the name of *Simonetta* above a smudgy reference to *Duc F. Sforza*, seems designed to deter rather than attract attention.

The inventory of 1675, drawn up by Professor Adrian Krobski, saw the 4,000 volumes in the Zamość Academy Library listed under the title *Regestrum Omnium Librorum Qui Existant In Bibliotheca Academiae Zamośćensis*. The *Sforziada* was cited as *Storia dell' duca Sforsa* ('History of the Sforza Duke') under *Libri Historici* (History Books).

During this inventory the following inscription was added to all books:

> *Testamento Illu'mi Joannis in Zamosac Palatani Sandomiriensis legatus Bibliothecae Academiae Zamośćensis*

> (Bequeathed to the Library of the Zamość Academy according to the will of the Most Illustrious Jan of Zamość, Palatine of Sandomierz)

These words were written on the very first page of every book,[3] even if this were the title page – as shown, for instance, by the 1602 edition of *De Collectione Verborum* by Dionysus of Halicarnassus now in the Polish National Library (*below left*). The handwriting of the inscription is hasty – to be expected when the same phrase is written out many hundreds of times – and Krobski appears to have been abetted by at least one assistant, as the handwriting at the front of the *Sforziada* and on the title-page of the Dionysus is clearly different. The entries in the inventory itself (*below right*), which is also preserved in the Polish National Library (*BN BOZ1544*), are far neater.

But only four of the eleven words from the 1675 inscription – *Illu'mi Joannis in Zamosac* – remain in the *Sforziada*. They were written on what was originally Folio 2r, with the text of the book beginning overleaf with Filelfo's *Epistola*. In other words, by 1675, Folio 2 was the first folio in the *Sforziada*: the outer

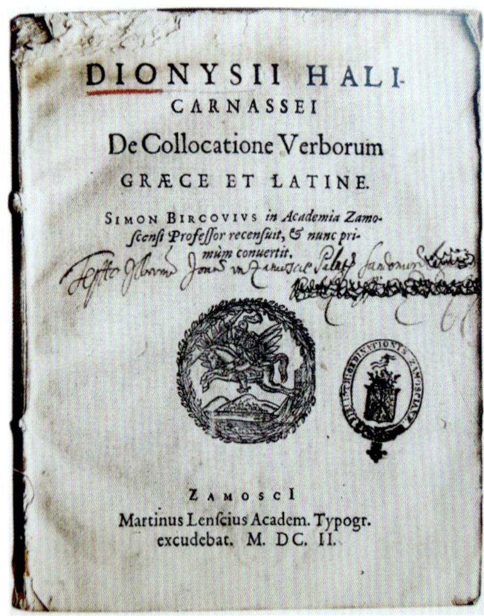
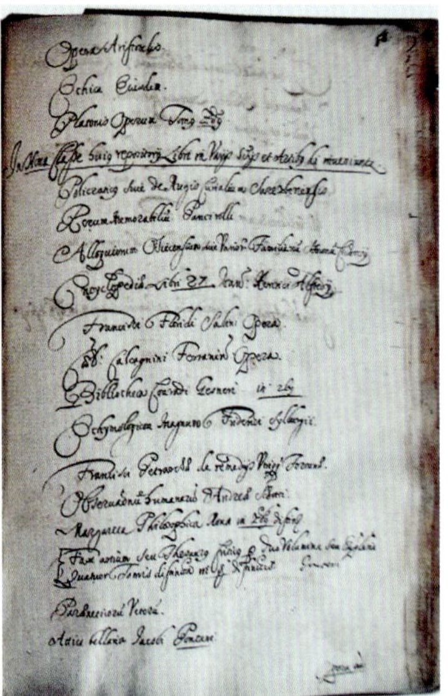

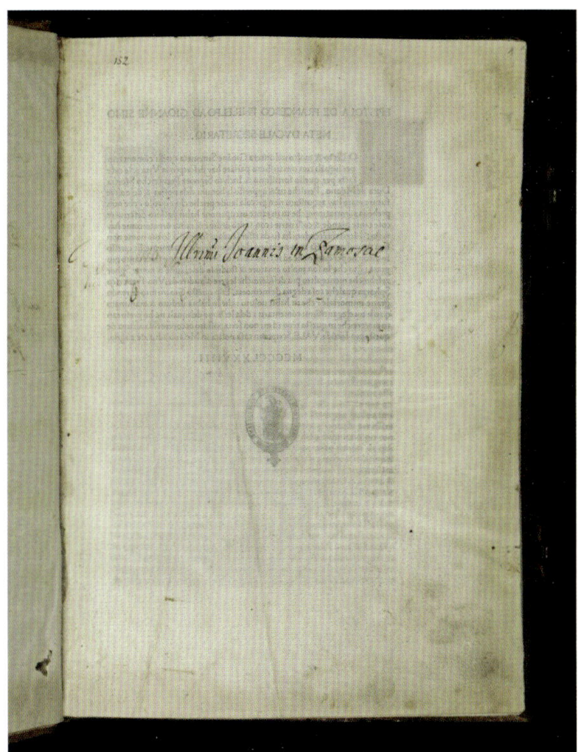

sheet of the first quire, containing Folios 1 and 8, had already been removed. **By 1675 Leonardo da Vinci's _Portrait of Bianca Sforza_ was no longer inside the book.**

Some time later seven words were erased from the inscription (their outline remains faintly discernible) in order to remove all reference to the _Academy Library_ and _Palatine of Sandomierz_. The four remaining words now refer solely to _Most Illustrious Jan_, giving the impression that the Jan in question is dynasty founder Jan Zamoyski (who never held the office of Palatine of Sandomierz) rather than his reprobate grandson Jan Sobiepan, who became Palatine of Sandomierz in 1659.

This alteration must have been carried out after 1784 – when Zamość Academy was closed down by order of Habsburg Emperor Joseph II – and was most probably ordered by Count Stanisław Kostka, who recuperated the Academy's volumes in 1800 before transferring them to Warsaw in 1811.

Something else suggests the portrait's removal may have been a hurried affair: the oak board on which it is mounted is not flat.

This plank of dark brown oak (_see p.320_) is clearly of considerable age. It has a crack at one end and its back has been reinforced on two separate occasions with butterfly-joints (the two lighter ones inserted by Giannino Marchig) – a complicated operation to prevent the panel from splitting, and one that no restorer would undertake unless they believed the panel of great significance.

Close examination of the panel suggests what that significance might be. It is thicker towards the top, and thicker towards the right: 5.5mm thick bottom left, 7mm thick bottom right, and 9mm thick at the top. In other words, it has been carefully sawn and planed to ensure a slight incline from bottom left to top right.[4] It is, in fact, shaped like the back cover of a book intended to be read on a lectern. This suggests that, when Bianca's portrait was removed and the book re-bound, one of the boards that had helped form the cover was re-used to mount the portrait.

If the portrait were removed during the disorderly interregnum between Jan Sobiepan's death in 1665 and the appointment of his successor in 1676, two candidates stand out: his widow **Marie-Casimire** and his nephew **Stanisław Koniecpolski**, who removed some of his uncle's books and archives before being obliged to return them by the Polish parliament in 1674. Marie-Casimire was Queen Consort of Poland from 1674–96, then lived in Rome from 1699–1714 before returning to her native France, where she died on 1 January 1716 at the Château of Blois (home two centuries before to a Master Of The Horse called Galeazzo Sanseverino).

The portrait could also have been owned by any member of
the extensive and much-travelled Zamoyski dynasty – allied
from the 1760s to Poland's leading family of art collectors,
the Czartoryskis. It may or may not be significant that in
1793 **Zofia Zamoyska** – whose mother Izabela founded
the Czartoryski Museum and whose brother Adam Jerzy
brought Leonardo's *Lady with an Ermine* back from Italy –
was the fifteen year-old subject of an anonymous portrait
(*right*, now in Kozłówka Palace) that is of similar size and left-
facing profile to Leonardo's Bianca; profiled portraits,
especially of adolescents, were almost unheard of in late
18th century Poland. Zofia died in Florence, while her son
Władysław moved to Paris as assistant to her bother Adam
Jerzy at the Hôtel Lambert, the cultural and political centre
of Poles in exile.

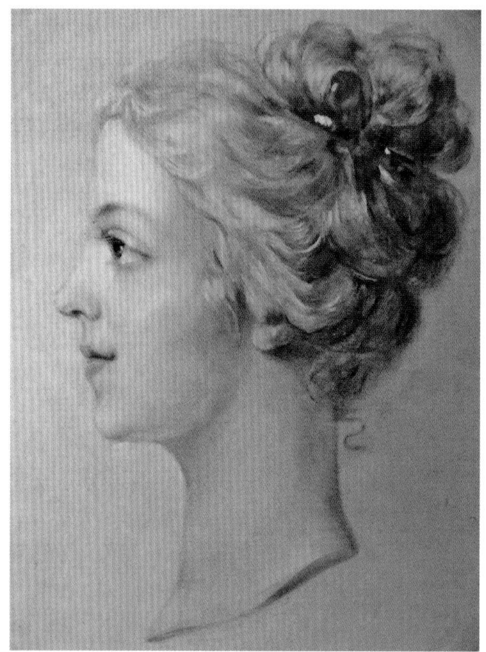

Mention of France is significant because the portrait's oak
panel features two circular, identical stamps in purple ink
reading **DOUANE CENTRALE - EXPORTATION PARIS**
(*see p.320*). French customs officials are unable to say precisely when this model was in use: it can merely be dated to the first decades of
the Third Republic (roughly 1870–1920). The stamps suggest the portrait was
sent out of France from Paris by train – either to a new owner following a commercial transaction[5] or as part of a collection in the throes of relocation. It was
presumably sent to neighbouring Italy where, by 1949, it was in the possession
of Giannino Marchig.

GIANNINO MARCHIG'S BELLA PRINCIPESSA

According to his widow Jeanne, Giannino Marchig did not hang the portrait
on the wall but stored it in a folder, because he 'considered strong daylight may
fade out a drawing.'[6] That may be true of pencil drawings – but not of drawings in coloured chalks protected by gum arabic. What was the real reason
Giannino Marchig kept the portrait in the dark, out of sight – and mind?

On 25 September 2011 Jeanne Marchig's lawyer, Richard Altman, wrote to
Jean Penicaut of Lumière Technology about Giannino Marchig's links with
Berenson:

> *They were indeed friends, but I do not believe that he received the drawing from
> Berenson. Jeanne has always told me that she did not know how he obtained it. I
> have my suspicions … .*

On 23 February 2019, with Jeanne Marchig and her partner Bryan Deschamp
both deceased, Altman revealed to me what those suspicions were.

'Bryan told me that Giannino had had an affair with an Italian princess before
he met Jeanne, and she gave him the drawing during the Fascist era. He must
have learned that from Jeanne, but I never asked her about it. Quite a romantic
story!'[7]

It is eminently understandable that Richard Altman had no wish to quiz his client about her husband's former mistress, and that Jeanne Marchig should have had no wish to divulge this information to anyone other than her partner Bryan Deschamp.

This 'principessa' was actually a marchioness.

Marchesa Pellegrina Paulucci de Calboli (1891–1944), *née* Rosselli del Turco Sassatello, came from an august Florentine family with an artistic tradition dating back to Leonardo's time: Cosimo Rosselli (1439–1507) worked in the Sistine Chapel, his half-brother Francesco (1445–1513) served Matthias Corvinus, and their cousin Bernardino di Stefano (1450–1526) helped decorate Florence's Palazzo Vecchio. Pellegrina's great-grandfather, Luigi Rosselli del Turco was, from 1811–16, Director of the Florence Accademia – where Giannino Marchig would teach just over a century later.

From 1851 until 1922 Pellegrina's family lived in the Palazzo Rosselli del Turco in Via dei Serragli – on the south bank of the Arno just 300 yards from Marchig's home on Piazza degli Scarlatti. They also owned a country house at Caldine just north of Florence, not far from Bernard Berenson's residence I Tatti.

Pellegrina was married to the 'highly-strung' Marchese Gian Raniero Paulucci de Calboli Ginnasi (1892–1944).[8] Berenson dined at their '100-room' palace in the centre of Forlì (70 miles northeast of Florence) in November 1928.[9] Berenson's long-term assistant, Nicky Mariano, described Pellegrina as 'a charming creature, graceful, gay, quick-witted with a natural gift for appreciating art and poetry.'[10]

It was Pellegrina who introduced Giannino Marchig – 'a man of exquisite taste and sensibility' in Mariano's words – to Bernard Berenson in the early 1930s. The liaison between Pellegrina and Giannino Marchig may have dated from a decade earlier, when she was single and living in Florence.[11]

The Paulucci de Calboli family also owned a villa in Ladino, a village four miles southwest of Forlì, that had belonged to Cardinal Luigi Capponi (1582–1659) when he was Archbishop of nearby Ravenna. Capponi hailed from an illustrious Florentine family, later became Head of the Vatican Library, and – another of those coincidences in which this story abounds – was a likely owner of the Uffizi *Sforziada*.

Pellegrina and Gian Raniero allowed their Ladino villa to be used by Partisans during the last months of Mussolini's régime and the ensuing Nazi occupation. The SS caught up with them. On 14 August 1944 Gian Raniero received a bullet outside Castrocaro cemetery, 1½ miles from Ladino. His farewell note to Pellegrina enjoined their teenage son Cosimo to 'have faith and forgive, everything and everyone' (*abbiate fede e sappiate perdonare, tutto e tutti*).

Three weeks later, at dusk on September 5, Pellegrina was driven to Forlì Aerodrome, on the southern outskirts of town, and shot.

Giannino Marchig's portrait was associated with unspeakable tragedy. He had good reason to keep it dark.

NOTES

1 Martin Kemp & Pascal Cotte, *op. cit.*

2 Information ascertained on the author's behalf by Konrad Ajewski (November 2011).

3 Krobski's inscription does not, however, appear at the front of the *Sforziada* today – because an additional sheet of paper (not vellum) was subsequently added, containing an elegantly penned nine-line summary of the book (albeit mistaking the number of chapters as 30 not 31). This sheet was presumably added to compensate for the book's absence of title page.

4 Author's observations based on examination of the panel in Zurich on 15 March 2012.

5 Drawings auctioned in Paris as by Leonardo (listed in Mireur's *Dictionnaire des Ventes d'Art en France et à l'Etranger pendant les XVIIIe & XIXe siècles*, published 1911) – include:
  – a *Portrait d'une Jeune Dame de profil* from the collection of the late *Chevalier A.D.* of Turin that fetched 4,200 francs in December 1860, then 5,000 francs when re-offered in 1869; 'A.D.' was the nephew of Milan drawings dealer Giuseppe Vallardi (1784–1863), an advisor to the Ambrosiana who sold the *Pisanello Album* to Louvre in 1856
  – an ink on vellum *Portrait de Jeune Femme, Figure de Profil* from the collection of the artist Jean Gigoux, sold for 65 francs in 1882
  – an ink on vellum *Portrait de Femme en Buste, la Tête de Profil* from the Lefèvre Collection, sold for 150 francs in 1895
An anonymous *Tête de Jeune Fille* described as a *dessin aux trois crayons* fetched 2,000 francs in 1894 at the estate sale of porcelain connoisseur Octave Fremin du Sartel (1823–94), whose father Jean-Philippe was bodyguard to Louis XVIII.

6 E-mail from Jeanne Marchig to the author, 17 January 2011.

7 E-mail from Richard Altman to the author, 23 February 2019.

8 Nicky Mariano, *Forty Years with Berenson* (Alfred A. Knopf, New York 1967). Mariano described Pellegrina as 'very dear' and 'very close' to Berenson.

9 Ernest Samuels, *op. cit.*

10 Nicky Mariano, *op. cit.*

11 No images of Pellegrina Paulucci de Calboli, *née* Rosselli del Turco, are to be found on internet or in the regional archives (Archivio di Stato di Forlì-Cesena). I am most grateful to Pellegrina's grandson *Avvocato* Gian Raniero Paulucci de Calboli Ginnasi and his wife Laura, who maintain the family presence in Forlì, for their kindness in providing a rare (and poignant) photograph of Pellegrina for this book – 'our best official family photo'.

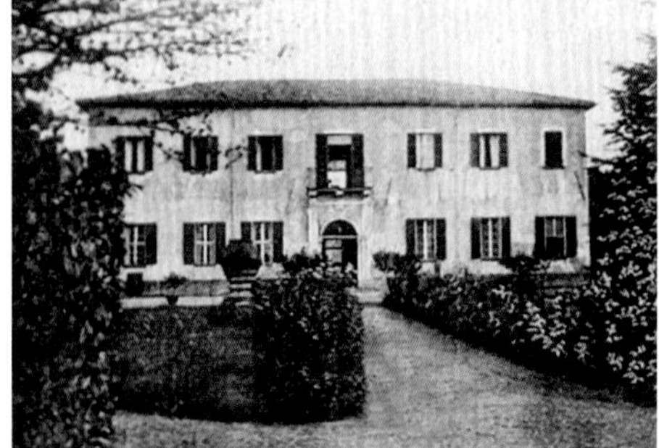

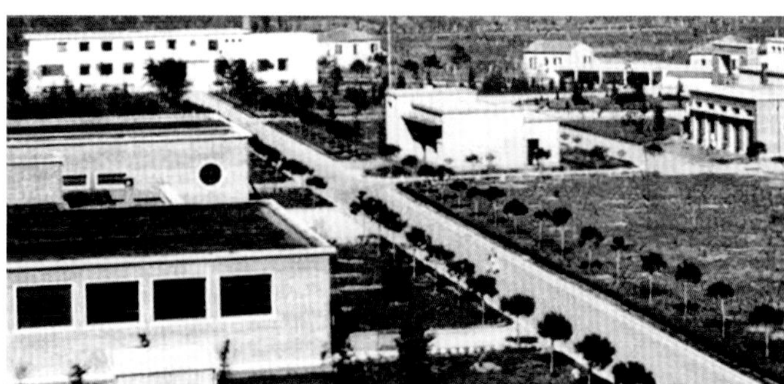

VILLA LADINO & FORLÌ AERODROME (c.1940)

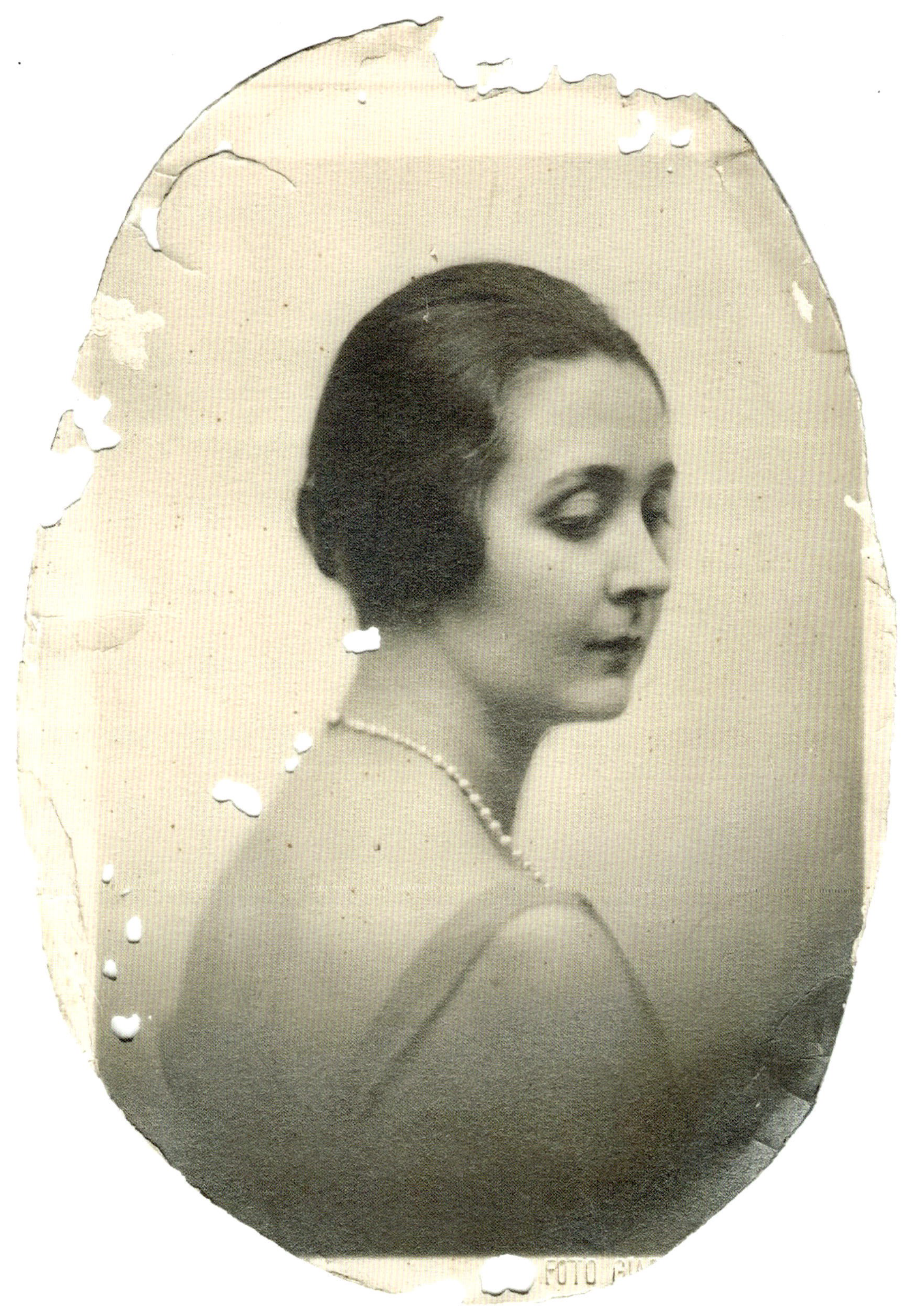

PELLEGRINA ROSSELLI DEL TURCO (*c.*1920)

SELECT BIBLIOGRAPHY

Konrad Ajewski, *Zbiory Artystyczne i Galeria Muzealna Ordynacji Zamojskiej w Warszawie* (Muzeum Zamoyskich, Kozłówka 1997); *Stanisława Kostki Zamoyskiego Zycie i Działalność 1775–1856* (Tow. Naukowe Warszawskie, Warsaw 2010)

Francis Ames-Lewis, *Isabella & Leonardo* (Yale University Press, 2012)

Luca Beltrami, *Documenti e Memorie riguardanti la vita e le opere di Leonardo da Vinci* (Milan, 1919)

Ilona Berkovits, *Illuminated Manuscripts in Hungary* (Corvina Press, Budapest 1969)

Luca Bernardini, *Polish Travellers and Residents in Florence* (Nardini Editore, Florence 2005)

Flaminia Bradati, *Gaillon tra Flamboyant e Rinascimento* (Campisano Editore, Rome 2009)

Kevin Alan Brook, *The Jews of Khazaria* (Rowman & Littlefield, Lanham 2010)

David Alan Brown, *Leonardo da Vinci – Origins of a Genius* (Yale University Press, 1998)

George Burnett, *View of the Present State of Poland* (Longman, Hurst, Rees & Orme, London 1807)

Chiara Buss (ed.), *Silk Gold Crimson – Secrets and Technology at the Visconti and Sforza Courts* (Silvana Editoriale, Milan 2009)

Felice Calvi, *Bianca Maria Sforza-Visconti* (Antonio Vallardi, Milan 1888)

Julia Cartwright, *Beatrice d'Este: Duchess of Milan* (J.M. Dent & Co, London 1899); *A History of Milan under the Sforza* (Methuen & Co, London 1907); *Italian Gardens of the Renaissance* (Charles Scribner's Sons, New York 1914)

André Chastel, *Renaissance Italienne 1460–1500* (Gallimard, Paris 1965)

Kenneth Clark, *Leonardo da Vinci* (Cambridge University Press, 1939)

Gustave Clausse, *Les Sforza et les Arts en Milanais* (Ernest Leroux, Paris 1909)

Roberto Codroico, *Roberto di Sanseverino nel Duomo di Trento* (Edizioni Osiride, Rovereto 1999)

Luisa Cogliati Arano, *Miniatori Lombardi al Tempo di Leonardo – I De Predis* (FIMantiquari n°7, 1995)

Bernardino Corio, *Patria Historia* (A. Minuziano, Milan 1503)

Patrizia Costa, *The Sala della Asse in the Sforza Castle* (University of Pittsburgh, 2006)

Pascal Cotte, *Lumière on The Lady with an Ermine* (Vinci Editions, Paris 2014)

Nadia Covini, *Zanette e Cicilia: Potere, Sangue e Passioni nella Milano di Ludovico Il Moro* (Viglevanum Anno XXI, May 2011)

Csaba Csapodi & Klára Csapodiné Gárdonyi, *Bibliotheca Corviniana* (Magyar Helikon Corvina, Budapest 1976)

Lamberto Donati, *Leonardo da Vinci ed il Libro Illustrato* (Erasmus, Amsterdam 1963)

Mark Evans, *New Light on the* Sforziada *Frontispieces of Giovan Pietro Birago* (The British Library Journal Vol. 13 n°2, 1987); *The Sforza Hours* (British Library, London 1992); *German Prints and Milanese Miniatures: Influences on – and from – Giovan Pietro Birago* (Apollo, 2001); *Dürer and Italy Revisited: the German Connection* (British Museum, 2004)

Péter Farbaky & Louis A. Waldman (eds), *Italy & Hungary: Humanism and Art in the Early Renaissance* (Villa I Tatti, 2011)

Rinaldo Fulin (ed.), *I Diarii di Marino Sanuto* (F. Visentini, Venice 1879–1903)

Adam Gielgud, *Memoirs of Prince Adam Czartoryski* (Remingon & Co, London 1888)

Paolo Giovio, *Dialogo dell'Imprese Militari et Amorose* (Antonio Barre, Rome 1555)

Alessandro Giulini, *Bianca Sanseverino Sforza figlia di Lodovico il Moro* (Giornale della Societa Storica Lombarda, 1912)

Carla Glori, *La Gioconda – In Memoria di Bianca* (Edizioni Cappello, Savona 2011)

Laura Paola Gnaccolini, *Giovan Pietro Birago: Miniatore per Re Mattia Corvino* (Arte Lombarda, 2003)

Elisabetta Gnignera, *I Soperchi Ornamenti – Copricapi e Acconciature Femminili nell'Italia del Quattrocento* (Protagon Editori Toscan, Siena 2010); *Leonardo – La Bella Svelata* (Scripta Maneant, Bologna 2016)

Shaun Greenhalgh, *A Forger's Tale* (Allen & Unwin, London 2017)

John Hale (ed.), *The Travel Journal of Antonio de Beatis 1517–18* (Hakluyt Society, London 1979)

Peter Harclerode & Brendan Pittaway, *The Lost Masters – The Looting of Europe's Treasurehouses* (Orion, London 1999)

Ludwig Heinrich Heydenreich, *Leonardo da Vinci* (Holbein-Verlag, Basel 1953)

Bogdan Horodyski, *Miniaturzysta Sforzów* (Biuletyn Historii Stuki, Warsaw 1954)

Gary Ianziti, *Humanistic Historiography under the Sforzas* (Clarendon Press, Oxford 1988)

Martin Kemp, *Leonardo* (Oxford University Press, 2004); *Leonardo da Vinci – The Marvellous Works of Nature and Man* (Oxford University Press, 2006); *Living with Leonardo* (Thames & Hudson, London 2018)

Martin Kemp & Pascal Cotte, *La Bella Principessa – The Story of the New Masterpiece by Leonardo da Vinci* (Hodder & Stoughton, London 2010); *La Bella Principessa di Leonardo da Vinci – Ritratto di Bianca Sforza* (Mandragora, Florence 2012)

Ross King, *Leonardo and The Last Supper* (Bloomsbury, London 2012)

Giovanna Lazzi, *La Biblioteca Riccardiana di Firenze* (Edizioni Polistampa, Florence 2009)

Elizabeth McGrath, *Ludovico Il Moro and His Moors* (2002)

Tomasz Makowski, *The History of the Zamoyski Library in Biblioteka Ordynacji Zamojskiej – Od Jana do Jana* (Polish National Library, Warsaw 2005)

Francesco Malaguzzi Valeri, *La Corte di Lodovico Il Moro* (Ulrico Hoepli, Milan 1913–23)

Alison Manges Nogueira, *Portraits of the Visconti & Sforza: Image & Propaganda in Milan c.1300–1500* (University of Michigan, 2008)

Pietro C. Marani, *Leonardo da Vinci – The Complete Paintings* (Harry N. Abrams, New York 2003); *Leonardo: Il Cenacolo Svelato* (Skira, Milan 2011)

Pietro C. Marani *et al.*, *The Legacy of Leonardo – Painters in Lombardy 1490–1530* (Skira, Milan 1998)

Jeanne Marchig & Susanna Ragionieri, *Giannino Marchig* (Skira, Milan 2000)

Nicky Mariano, *Forty Years with Berenson* (Alfred A. Knopf, New York 1967)

Gian Ambrogio Mazenta, *Alcune Memorie de' Fatti di Leonardo da Vinci a Milano e de' suoi Libri* (manuscript, 1635)

Constance J. Moffat, *Heraldic Imagery at the Sforza Court in the 1490s* (University of California, 1986)

Eugène Müntz, *Leonardo da Vinci – Artist, Thinker and Man of Science* (William Heinemann, London 1898)

Lodovico Antonio Muratori, *Delle Antichita Estensi* (Stamperia Ducale, Modena 1740)

Charles Nicholl, *Leonardo da Vinci* (Penguin Books, London 2007)

Jill Pederson, *The Academia Leonardi Vinci: Visualizing Dialectic in Renaissance Milan 1480–99* (John Hopkins University, Baltimore 2007)

Carlo Pedretti, *Leonardo da Vinci On Painting: A Lost Book (Libro A)* (University of California, 1964)

Léon-Gabriel Pélissier, *Documents pour l'Histoire de la Domination Française dans le Milanais 1499–1513* (Edouard Privat, Toulouse 1891); *Louis XII et Ludovic Sforza* (Charles Boehm, Montpellier 1896)

Elisabeth Pellegrin, *La Bibliothèque des Visconti et des Sforza* (Institut de Recherche et d'Histoire des Textes, Paris 1955)

G.A. Prato, *Cronaca Milanese 1499–1519* (Archivio Storico Italiano, 1842)

Gary M. Radke, *Leonardo da Vinci and the Art of Sculpture* (Yale University Press, 2009)

Ernest Renan, *Ma Sœur Henriette* (Calmann Lévy, Paris 1895)

Ernest Samuels, *Bernard Berenson: The Making of a Legend* (Belknap Press, 1979)

Peter Silverman, *Leonardo's Lost Princess* (John Wiley & Sons, Hoboken 2012)

Zdzisław Spieralski, *Jan Zamoyski* (Wiedza Powszechna, Warsaw 1989)

Halina Tchórzewska-Kabata, *More Precious Than Gold: Treasures of the Polish National Library* (Biblioteka Narodowa, Warsaw 2000)

Pompilio Totti, *Ritratti et Elogi di Capitani Illustri* (Rome, 1635)

Joseph Van Praet, *Catalogue des Livres Imprimés sur Vélin de la Bibliothèque du Roi – Volume V* (Paris, 1822)

Giorgio Vasari, *Le Vite dei Più Eccellenti Pittori, Scultori e Architetti* (Newton Compton, Rome 2010)

Alessandro Vezzosi, *Profilo Nuziale da Giovane Dama* (2009)

Tullio Vidona, *The Journal of Roberto da Sanseverino (1417–87) – A Study on Navigation & Seafaring in the 15th Century* (University of British Columbia, 1993)

Gaspare Visconti, *I Canzonieri per Beatrice d'Este e per Bianca Maria Sforza* (Edizioni Il Saggiatore, Milan 1979)

Kazimierz Waliszewski, *Marysieńka* (E. Plon, Nourrit & Cie, Paris 1898)

George F. Warner, *Miniatures & Borders from the Book of Hours of Bona Sforza, Duchess of Milan, in the British Museum* (London 1894)

Sabine Weiss, *Die Vergessene Kaiserin: Bianca Maria Sforza – Kaiser Maximilans Zweite Gemahlin* (Tyrolia, Innsbruck 2010)

D.R. Edward Wright, *Ludovico Il Moro and the Sforziada by Giovanni Simonetta in Warsaw* (2011)

PICTURE CREDITS

A.H. BALDWIN & SONS, LONDON: 29

ALBERTINA, VIENNA: 113, 178

ALTE PINAKOTHEK, MUNICH: 89

ALTOMANI & SONS, MILAN: 53

ARCHIV DER UNIVERSITÄT WIEN: 267

ARCHIVIO STORICO CIVICO, MILAN: 91

ARCHIVIO DI STATO DI MILANO: 184

BASILICA DI SAN SIMPLICIANO, MILAN: 145

BAYERISCHES NATIONALMUSEUM, MUNICH: 50

BENVENUTI MARTINEZ COLLECTION, MILAN: 34

BIBLIOTECA DEL CAPITOLO, MILAN: 177

BIBLIOTECA GUARNACCI, VOLTERRA: 70

BIBLIOTECA NAZIONALE VITTORIO EMANUELE III, NAPLES: 67, 174

BIBLIOTECA REALE, TURIN: 21, 56

BIBLIOTECA RICCARDIANA, FLORENCE (SU CONCESSIONE DEL MINISTERO PER I BENI E LE ATTIVITA CULTURALI): 194, 196, 197, 198, 200, 201

BIBLIOTEKA NARODOWA, WARSAW: 76, 152, 156, 157, 162, 166, 167, 168, 182, 272, 336, 337

BIBLIOTHEQUE NATIONALE DE FRANCE: 14, 22, 40, 45, 46, 48, 96, 98, 100, 102, 103, 160, 174, 197

BPK / KUPFERSTICHKABINETT, STAATLICHE MUSEEN ZU BERLIN: 81; 204, 211, 213 (VOLKER H. SCHNEIDER); 210 (JÖRG P. ANDERS)

CHRIST CHURCH, OXFORD: 14, 213

CHRISTIE'S: 225

COMUNE DI MILANO (ALL RIGHTS RESERVED): 13, 42, 52, 66, 157, 174, 216, 217, 218, 219, 220

COTTE, PASCAL / LUMIERE TECHNOLOGY: 2, 106, 127, 297, 317

DE AGOSTINI PICTURE LIBRARY / BRIDGEMAN IMAGES: 18, 36 (G. CIGOLINI), 192

DOMMUSEUM, VIENNA: 27

DOROTHEUM, VIENNA: 225

DR JÖRN GÜNTHER RARE BOOKS AG, STALDEN: 69

FONDAZIONE GIORGIO CINI, VENICE: 92

FONDAZIONE ZERI, UNIVERSITA DI BOLOGNA: 136

FÖSZEKESEGYHÁZI KINCSTÁR, ESZTERGOM: 83

GABINETTO FOTOGRAFICO DELLE GALLERIE DEGLI UFFIZI: 14, 27, 109, 111, 112, 113, 116, 117, 213, 281

GALLERIE DELL'ACCADEMIA, VENICE: 166

GEMÄLDEGALERIE, DRESDEN: 268

G. SARTI, PARIS: 101

HERZOG AUGUST BIBLIOTHEK, WOLFENBÜTTEL: 75, 266

JEANNE MARCHIG ESTATE: 311, 324, 332

KUNSTHISTORISCHES MUSEUM, VIENNA: 15, 267, 269

KUNSTHAUS ZÜRICH: 140

LOUVRE, PARIS – BRIDGEMAN IMAGES: 24, 98, 166, 167, 223

MAGYAR NEMZETI MUZEUM, BUDAPEST: 15

MALAGUZZI VALERI, 'LA CORTE DI LODOVICO IL MORO': 228

METROPOLITAN MUSEUM, NEW YORK (GIFT OF DR & MRS GOODWIN M. BREININ): 215

MONDADORI PORTFOLIO / VENERANDA BIBLIOTECA AMBROSIANA: 58, 59, 60, 161

MORGAN LIBRARY & MUSEUM, NEW YORK: 14

MUSEI CIVICI, MANTUA: 15

MUSEE CONDE, CHANTILLY: 16

MUSEO BAROFFIO, SACRO MONTE DI VARESE: 149, 150

MUSEO DEI MOBILI DEL CASTELLO SFORZESCO, MILAN: 19

MUSEO DEL BARGELLO, FLORENCE: 213

MUSEO DELLA CERTOSA DI PAVIA – POLO MUSEALE DELLA LOMBARDIA: 37, 156

MUSEO DI CAPODIMONTE, NAPLES: 16, 262

MUSEO NAZIONALE DI SAN MARTINO, NAPLES: 99

MUSEUM OF FINE ARTS, HOUSTON (ROBERT LEE BLAFFER MEMORIAL COLLECTION / GIFT OF SARAH CAMPBELL BLAFFER): 134

MUZEUM KSIAZAT CZARTORYSKICH, CRACOV: 127

MUZEUM LUBELSKIE, LUBLIN: 279

MUZEUM PALACU KROLA JAN III, WILANOW: 285, 288

MUZEUM SAKRALNE KATEDRY, ZAMOSC: 286

MUZEUM ZAMEK, GOLUCHOW: 292

MUZEUM ZAMOYSKICH, KOZLOWKA: 338

NÁRODNI GALERIE, PRAGUE: 267

NATIONAL GALLERY, LONDON: 35 (PRESENTED BY LADY MARGARET WATNEY IN MEMORY OF VERNON J. WATNEY), 133, 137 (SALTING BEQUEST), 183 (PRESENTED BY MRS GUTEKUNST IN MEMORY OF OTTO GUTEKUNST)

NATIONAL GALLERY, WASHINGTON (KREISS COLLECTION): 80, 136

PAULUCCI DE CALBOLI GINNASI, GIAN RANIERO: 341

PINACOTECA DI BRERA: 13, 32, 124, 171, 213, 224

PINACOTECA CIVICA, VICENZA: 131

PINACOTECA DEL CASTELLO SFORZESCO, MILAN: 14, 36

PRIVATE COLLECTION, ITALY: 147

RMN-GRAND PALAIS (RENE-GABRIEL OJEDA): 88

ROYAL COLLECTION TRUST / HER MAJESTY QUEEN ELIZABETH II (2019): 16, 134, 182, 212

SILVERMAN, PETER & ONORATO, KATHLEEN: 13, 170, 174, 190, 196

STAIFF, KYM: 192, 193

THE BRITISH LIBRARY BOARD: 22, 72, 78, 82, 83, 84, 85, 90, 109, 182, 207, 213

VENERANDA BIBLIOTECA AMBROSIANA (PAOLO MANUSARDI) / MONDADORI PORTFOLIO / BRIDGEMAN IMAGES: 13, 26, 135, 141, 166, 268, 269

WAWEL CATHEDRAL, CRACOV: 279, 281

THE AUTHOR: 5, 43, 82, 83 (2), 104, 138, 159 (2), 161, 173, 178, 179 (2), 180 (3), 181, 182, 188, 189 (2), 190 (2), 191, 192 (2), 201, 242, 246, 248, 249, 258 (2), 259 (2), 261, 276, 283, 284, 289, 291, 292, 293, 296, 305, 312, 319, 320, 323, 324 (2), 326 (2), 331

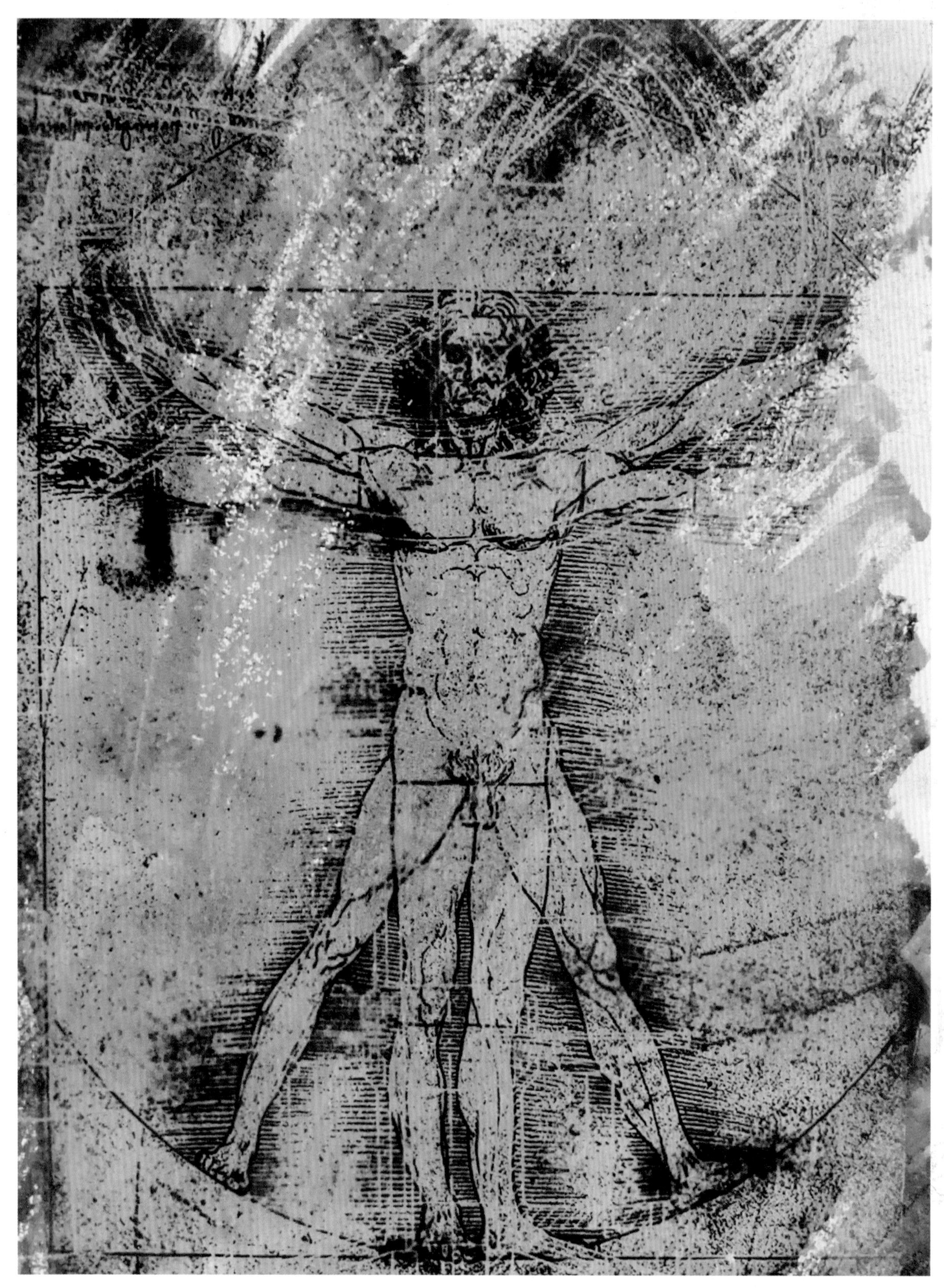

DIMA GORYACHKIN: *HOMAGE TO LEONARDO* (2016)